Sports Law
Cases & Materials

Fourth Edition

VERSTEEG, RUSS, & SAHL, JACK P.
Sports Law: Cases & Materials
4th Edition

Published by:

 **Vandeplas Publishing, LLC — November 2019**

801 International Parkway, 5th Floor
Lake Mary, FL. 32746
USA

www.vandeplaspublishing.com

ISBN-13: 978-1-60042-505-9

SPORTS LAW
CASES & MATERIALS
Fourth Edition

BY

RUSS VERSTEEG *&* JACK P. SAHL

Table of Contents

Principal cases are in bold

A

B

C

D

J

K

N

O

P

R

T

U

V

A great deal has happened in the world of Sports Law since the publication of the third edition of this book in 2014. Both the high-stakes and passionate emotions relating to companies and individuals involved at multiple levels in sports probably explain, in part, the frantic pace of Sports Law-related litigation, legislation, and controversy. Deflategate, complex gender-related issues, the expanded use of instant replay in officiating, the blockbuster development of online media, online sports betting, and e-sports are just some of the things that have captured public attention. In this fourth edition, we have not tried to include everything new that has occurred. Nor have we undertaken a wholesale revision of the text; the stable of primary cases and articles remains virtually unchanged (although we have aggressively re-edited most of the primary cases and articles in an effort to delete material that we considered distracting and/or surplusage). And we have attempted to bring the book up-to-date by referencing matters (*i.e.*, mostly case law) that have either reinforced or changed the legal doctrines illustrated by the book's primary cases and articles. Most of that type of updated material appears in the notes and questions that follow the cases and articles.

A book often reflects more about its authors than about the book's content. That is probably true about this book. We have over 50 years combined experience teaching Sports Law at several law schools. During that time, we have developed a certain perspective about what constitutes "Sports Law." In our experience, many students sign up for our Sports Law classes wanting to become sports agents, and they assume that a class on Sports Law will prepare them for that. Although we always want to encourage students to dream and to pursue those dreams, in our opinion sports agency comprises only a small part of Sports Law. When all is said and done, we typically counsel students to think in very broad terms about the multiple possibilities for a variety of sports-related careers. To that end, we encourage students to consider the multifaceted possibilities of how they might merge their passion for sports with their interest and training in law.

Thus, this book is designed to introduce students to a variety of topics that relate to Sports Law, not just sports agency. Given that goal, the text includes cases and excerpts of articles that concern very diverse topics. The first chapter is something of an "immersion chapter," throwing students into cases and materials intended to catch their attention and strike a nerve about a number of the most sensitive and volatile Sports Law topics today – drugs, the Olympic Games, and the relationships among individuals, the government, and various private organizations. The subsequent chapters tackle Torts, Contracts, Antitrust and Labor Law, Constitutional Law,

Title IX (the statutory prohibition of sex-based discrimination in educational programs) and the Rehabilitation and American with Disabilities Acts, the legal and business aspects of the NCAA, Agency, and Intellectual Property. The principal goal is to provide a broad-brush introduction to most of the topics that are likely to confront a modern Sports Lawyer. Probably the most notable omission is Tax Law. In our opinion, the tax laws are so specialized and subject to change that even a cursory treatment would run the risk of misleading the reader.

The book is intended to be used by undergraduate, graduate, or law students. We have intentionally limited the number of cases that deal with each topic. Many law school case books today are simply too long. They contain so much material that they are impractical. For the benefit of undergraduates and graduate students, we have tried to define legal terms and explain legal doctrines in a clear, concise manner. For law students, we have tried to avoid "talking down" to them when presenting those definitions and explanations. It is a difficult balance, and we hope that the law students will consider those definitions and explanations as refreshers.

Most of the questions are meant to be either thought-provoking or are intended to encourage students to restate and clarify major points. We hope that the questions encourage students not to settle for simplistic legal thinking. We believe that in an expanding field such as Sports Law we need to challenge traditional legal thinking and analysis, and constantly explore new paradigms if we are going to protect the interests of those people involved in sports and further the values that sports encourage.

We think that students may read the chapters in almost any order. So a professor should not feel "chained" to the textbook's sequence. This is the order that we have found works best for us, but others should feel free to arrange his or her syllabus differently, depending upon individual preference. The only glaring exception to that general statement is that Chapters 2-4 are probably best read in sequence. Also, Chapters 8 (Title IX, The Rehabilitation Act, and The Americans with Disabilities Act) and 9 (NCAA) will probably make more sense to students if they have first read Chapter 7 (Constitutional Law).

We have liberally edited the cases and articles included in this text. We sometimes use *** to indicate that we have omitted a sentence or more from the original. But in many instances, we have cut sentences, paragraphs, and/or entire sections from cases and articles without making any notation. Occasionally we've expanded a case citation (*i.e.*, given a more complete case name than was provided by a court) to help students who might wish to look it up more easily. Our goal in editing the materials has been to focus students' attention on only one, two, or occasionally three issues in each case or article; and to remove those issues that we considered esoteric, overly-complex, and/or tangential to the main point of the case or article. We have cut most footnotes from the cases and articles. When we have retained footnotes, we have simply renumbered them, beginning sequentially with each case or article in the text (*i.e.*, so the footnote numbers in this text do not match the footnote numbers in the original case or article).

There is a long list of people whom we would like to thank. Each of us has taken the liberty of writing Acknowledgements and a Dedication separately.

Russ VerSteeg. First, I owe a debt of thanks to John O'Brien, Dean of New England Law, | Boston who first asked me if I'd be interested in teaching Sports Law. Similarly, I'd like to thank both Dean O'Brien and the Board of Trustees of New England Law | Boston who funded my work on the first edition with an Honorable James R. Lawton Summer Research Stipend in the summer of 2005, and with a sabbatical during the Spring Semester 2010 for the second edition. I would also like to thank the authors who have granted permission to use articles and/or portions of articles as part of the text. A number of people have also allowed me to use their photographs. Professors Elizabeth Spahn (second cousin, once-removed, yes indeed, of Warren Spahn… "Spahn & Sain and pray for rain") and Sonya Garza (a rabid Texas Longhorn fan/alumna) helped me with some of the finer points of Constitutional Law, and I'm indebted to them for their assistance. Professor James Bemiller at the University of Tennessee (and one of the most accomplished pole vault coaches of the modern era) contributed many thoughts and ideas in conversations about how to best teach and write about Sports Law. My friend, Jan Johnson, National Safety Chairman for the Pole Vault, was instrumental in encouraging me to combine my interests in Sports Law and the sport of pole vaulting, and I'm eternally indebted to him for that.

I had three research assistants whose help on the first edition was invaluable. Amy Peterson, who recently resigned as Associate Counsel for the Detroit Tigers, Jayme Yarow, and Melissa Gill, currently Director of Academic success at Loyola University Chicago School of Law, were responsible for a great deal of the research, notes, and details in the first edition. Melissa Gill was the driving force in the macroscopic planning and organization, obtaining permissions, keeping track of organizational details, and formatting the text. On the third edition my research assistant, Kim Maruncic, a mathematician and ice hockey enthusiast, was exceptional. Kim's attention to detail, judgment, insight, and willingness to go the extra mile contributed immeasurably to the final product. Kim worked as Legal Intern for the Boston Red Sox in the summer 2014, and is currently an associate at Goodwin Procter LLP in Boston. Lastly, I want to thank Cassandra Inacio, an alumna of Rutgers University's women's soccer team, who served as my research assistant for the fourth edition. In addition, hundreds of students who took my Sports Law classes at New England Law | Boston during the past 20-plus years have contributed by raising insightful questions, making perceptive comments, and catching mistakes in the cases, materials, and text.

Russ VerSteeg
Boston, July 2019

Jack P. Sahl. My contributions to this edition have benefited from numerous discussions over the past 30 years with faculty colleagues, sports law practitioners, franchise owners, athletic administrators, coaches, athletes, and former and current students. Their insights and support have provided a unique opportunity for me to examine the ever-evolving intersection of sports, law and society. In particular, Professor Stanton Wheeler who taught me Sports Law at Yale deserves special mention for inspiring me to teach and write about the subject and to develop my own course materials. There are too many other deserving persons to specifically identify here, but my thanks to them all for taking my calls for help, visiting my classes, joining me on panels, and simply offering their opinions. This edition would be a very different product without their input.

I also wish to thank in particular my primary research assistant, Joseph L. Manno, for his superb research, thoughtful suggestions, and engaging enthusiasm for this project. Research assistants, Allyson G. Murray, Elizabeth Emmanuel, and University of Akron Law School librarians, Kyle S. Passmore, Lynn M. Lenart, Annette A. Souare and Amy S. McCoy, provided additional research and assistance. I am sure I have overlooked some persons deserving of recognition and to you I offer my sincere gratitude for your assistance.

Jack P. Sahl
Akron, 2014

Russ VerSteeg

I'm dedicating my contribution to the fourth edition to the memory of our daughter, Whitney VerSteeg. Whitney played multiple youth team sports while she was growing up: baseball, soccer, field hockey, and basketball. She was an excellent swimmer and ice skater. She fell in love with horseback riding and skiing at an early age, and it was those two sports that shaped much of her adult life. During high school, Whitney competed seriously in equestrian sports and continued that passion for the rest of her days. She loved to travel. Somehow she managed to visit an incredible list of places: Greece, France, England, Turkey, Holland, China, Italy, Spain, Malta, Mexico, Peru, Thiland, Myanmar, Vietnam, Japan, and Argentina. After earning her undergraduate degree in Classical Archaeology at UNC-Greensboro, she earned her paralegal degree at Duke University. The siren song of ski slopes – first in Utah and later in Montana – lured her to those mountain venues (taking her beloved horse, Ricochette, aka Ricky with her!). She worked at Deer Valley, Park City Mountain Resort, Brighton, and the Yellostone Club. She also donated her time and skills to the non-profits, Women in Action and She Jumps. Ski Patrolling and Avalanche Rescue – occupations focused on helping others – dominated her career. And although she relocated west, she remained true to her roots – an ardent Boston Red Sox fan.

Whitney Barclay VerSteeg
05-29-1986 – 02-25-2019

Fortunately, on many occasions, Whitney took the time to educate me about nuances involved in legal and safety aspects of skiing and equestrian sports. She set me straight on matters such as helmet safety and concussion protocol. I'm eternally grateful for the humor and enthusiasm she brought to the world in general, and for love and support she gave to me. I miss her every day.

Jack P. Sahl

I dedicate this book to my wife, Professor Joann M. Sahl, and our two children, Mandakani and Anish, who patiently supported my work on this edition. Projects of this sort inevitably take time away from loved ones. Their love, kindness, and zest for life are inspiring. I also dedicate this book to the memory of "my Judge," the Honorable William J. Holloway, Jr. of the United States Court of Appeals for the Tenth Circuit, who taught me much about the law and the importance of public service, and to the memory of Quintin Johnstone, the Justus S. Hotchkiss Professor of Law at Yale, who changed my life by helping me to become a law teacher, author, and active bar member. In working on this book, as in my career generally, I have benefitted immensely from their generosity, their practical wisdom, and their enduring goodness.

A Note For Undergraduates & Graduate Students on the American Legal System, Courts, and Appellate Decisions

I. CIVIL VS. CRIMINAL CASES

In the American legal system today there are a number of important distinctions that are useful to understand. First, there are basically two types of cases: Criminal and Civil. For example, if a police officer stops you and gives you a ticket (requiring that you pay a fine) for speeding in your car or for drunk driving, the officer charges you with a criminal violation, because the state legislature has passed written laws (statutes) that prohibit speeding and drunk driving. If you refuse to pay your fine, the district attorney could charge you and have your case tried in state court as a criminal matter. When the state government, usually represented by the district attorney, prosecutes a defendant/accused, that case is a criminal case.

On the other hand, a civil case is a case brought not by the government but typically by one individual (for example, a private citizen) against another individual. For example, let's suppose that when you were speeding or driving drunk, you also lost control of your car and hit another car, causing property damage to the car that you hit and personal injury to the other driver. The driver of the other car may sue you in state court as a civil matter, using various legal theories – such as negligence – in an effort to recover from you the money needed to repair or replace the car and for medical expenses, or as compensation for pain, suffering, or permanent injuries/loss caused by the fact that you caused the accident.

II. ROLES OF JUDGE & JURY

Without going into exceptional circumstances, in both criminal and civil cases, the people involved typically have an opportunity to have a jury decide the case. A judge presides, and the judge is responsible for deciding abstract legal questions and explaining the law to the jurors. The jurors are responsible for deciding questions about facts. Ordinarily, that means that the jurors get to decide which witnesses they believe are telling the truth and when and how events occurred. So the judge will explain to the jury that it is illegal to have a certain amount of blood-alcohol when driving (that's the law) but the jurors will decide whether they believe the accuracy of the breathalyzer test and/or the witness's testimony regarding how many glasses of wine he or she drank.

III. APPEALS

After the jury reaches a verdict (criminal cases) or decides whether a defendant is liable (civil cases) and therefore owes the plaintiff money (and if so how much), in some circumstances the party who lost at trial has the right to appeal the decision of the trial court. In most states, there is an intermediate appellate court (such as the Massachusetts Appeals Court) to which a person may appeal a trial court decision. As a rule, when appealing to an intermediate state appeals court, three appellate judges will read the lawyers' briefs about the case, and will listen to oral arguments and ask the lawyers questions before making an appellate decision. Ordinarily, an appeals court does not review the jury's decisions regarding the facts (there are some limited exceptions to that statement) but rather the appellate judges must decide whether the trial judge made a mistake about "the law." For example, if the trial judge mistakenly told the jurors the wrong blood-alcohol limit, or if the judge mistakenly gave an incorrect legal definition of "negligence" to the jury, those are the types of legal errors that could be grounds for reversal on appeal.

After the appellate court has rendered its written decision, in some circumstances a person may appeal *that decision* to the state's highest court (typically called the "supreme court"... except in New York where they call their trial courts supreme courts), such as the Massachusetts Supreme Judicial Court (SJC). The appeals process at the supreme court level is similar to the process at the intermediate appeals court, but ordinarily all justices (typically nine in number) read the lawyers' briefs and participate in the oral arguments with the lawyers. Again, the supreme court typically only reviews issues of law, not fact.

IV. FEDERAL COURTS

This summary so far has focused on the state court systems. But an analogous group of courts exists to consider cases involving federal criminal and civil laws. The federal courts also consider cases involving questions of U.S. Constitutional Law as well as certain cases where the parties are from different states (diversity jurisdiction). The U.S. District Courts are the federal trial courts where there may be juries. The Federal Appellate Courts (there are many different federal courts of appeals which consider cases, depending upon which region of the country the District Court case came from) are the intermediate courts of appeal in the federal system. And the U.S. Supreme Court is the highest court in the country.

V. WRITTEN OPINIONS

Most of the cases in this text are civil cases, but see if you can spot the criminal exceptions. Many of the decisions are written by appellate judges, either from intermediate appellate state or federal courts, or from state supreme courts or the U.S. Supreme Court. Thus, what you will be reading will be judges' explanations regarding questions of law. So you will have the opportunity to read what a group of judges thinks the correct ruling on the law should be. Therefore, by the time that these judges get around to writing the opinion that you will read, the people involved (typically the plaintiff and the defendant) have already presented their arguments, witnesses, and documentary and forensic evidence at trial to a judge and a jury in a courtroom. In addition, the lawyers representing the parties have then, after the trial, researched statutes, constitutions, law review articles, and other prior appellate decisions relating to the same or similar legal questions, and have written appellate briefs, explaining their legal analysis for the appellate judges. The appellate judges, in turn, have read those briefs, and the lawyers have met with the appellate judges at oral argument, where each side has had a certain amount of time to verbally explain their analysis of the law and the judges have had an opportunity to ask the lawyers questions. After oral arguments, the judges have had an opportunity to discuss the legal questions and collaborate to write the decision/case that you read in this text. One judge usually writes the "majority opinion," usually what you read in the text, but occasionally other judges disagree with the majority and write their own "dissenting opinion" to explain why they disagree with the majority. Every now and then, a judge will also write a "concurring opinion" if he or she basically agrees with the majority's result, but wishes to add his or her own reasons or spin on why.

VI. SUMMARY JUDGMENT

There is one other way that judges frequently resolve cases: summary judgment. After the plaintiff's lawyer has filed his/her complaint and after the defendant's lawyer has filed his/her answer, it is possible that both parties essentially agree on the facts that really matter to a case (*i.e.*, who did what to whom, when, how, and why). In those instances, we say that there are "no genuine issues of material fact." If there are no genuine issues of material fact, then there is no reason to have a jury, since, as you may recall, that's what the jury is for, to decide what the facts are.

If there are no genuine material facts in dispute (and therefore no need for a jury), one or both parties may then file a motion for summary judgment. If the trial judge agrees that there are no genuine questions regarding material facts, then the judge simply must decide questions about "the law." In other words, the judge is free to determine whether the plaintiff or defendant wins by applying the abstract legal rules that are applicable to the facts as agreed upon by the parties. Decisions based on summary judgment are very efficient because they save everybody the time and expense of a trial.

Decisions based on summary judgment, like a court's decision based on the outcome of a jury trial, may be appealed to higher courts. Many of the cases in this text are appeals from a trial judge's decision on a motion for summary judgment.

CHAPTER 1
OLYMPICS, PRIVATE ASSOCIATIONS, PERFORMANCE ENHANCING DRUGS

This chapter serves as a broad introduction to a variety of sports law topics. Here you will meet a number of contemporary and emotionally-charged issues and questions regarding the different levels of power and influence that affect decisions relating to the Olympic Games, problems regarding the use of performance-enhancing substances and drugs, and issues relating to the scope of power that private associations possess to control their own members.

Every two years, for several weeks, the sports world's attention focuses on the Olympic Games (alternating Summer Games and Winter Games since 1994). The business and political concerns associated with the Games are immense. These materials present background information regarding the structure and organization of the Olympics. Pay particular attention to the roles played by the various organizations involved (*e.g.*, IOC, USOC, and NGB's). In some ways, the issues that relate to these Olympic organizations will continue to be relevant in later chapters where we meet other sports organizations such as the National Collegiate Athletic Association (NCAA) and the various professional sports organizations such as Major League Baseball (MLB), the National Football League (NFL), the National Hockey League (NHL), and the National Basketball Association (NBA). As is true with most aspects of law and society, as the financial stakes associated with the Olympics have risen, the legal issues have multiplied correspondingly. The Court of Arbitration for Sport, for example, is just one additional layer of complexity that has become part of the judging and officiating process of the Olympic Games.

During the past several years, legal issues relating to performance enhancing drugs have dominated the sports pages. The BALCO scandal, Major League Baseball, and Congress have harnessed our attention on anabolic steroids in particular. The issues surrounding steroid use and other performance-enhancing drugs provide fertile ground for thinking about and examining the values associated with the legal aspects of sports.

The first case, *Defrantz*, has a lot of information. You may wish to think about it on distinct levels. *First*, try to understand the facts and events that led up to this controversy. What are the roles of the IOC, USOC, and various government officials (including President Carter). What are the athletes asking for? *Second*, the athletes are relying on a federal statute (written law) and arguing that the USOC has violated that statute in a manner that will injure them. The court discusses at length its analysis of the statute and why it (the court) does not think that the USOC has violated it. When taking notes, isolate that discussion and see if you can explain in your own words why the court thinks that there has been no statutory violation. *Third*, the court discusses whether the USOC has violated the constitutional rights of the athletes. Pay attention to the court's discussion of "state action" and note the court's determination as to why it believes that none of the athletes' constitutional rights were violated. You will have an opportunity to explore constitutional issues in greater depth in Chapter 7.

DEFRANTZ V. UNITED STATES OLYMPIC COMMITTEE
492 F.SUPP. 1181 (1980)
UNITED STATES DISTRICT COURT, DISTRICT OF COLUMBIA

JOHN H. PRATT, DISTRICT JUDGE.

MEMORANDUM OPINION

Plaintiffs, 25 athletes and one member of the Executive Board of defendant United States Olympic Committee (USOC), have moved for an injunction barring defendant USOC from carrying out a resolution, adopted by the USOC House of Delegates on April 12, 1980, not to send an American team to participate in the Games of the XXIInd Olympiad to be held in Moscow in the summer of 1980. Plaintiffs allege that in preventing American athletes from competing in the Summer Olympics, defendant has exceeded its statutory powers and has abridged plaintiffs' constitutional rights.

For the reasons discussed below, we find that plaintiffs have failed to state a claim upon which relief can be granted. Accordingly, we deny plaintiffs' claim for injunctive and declaratory relief and dismiss the action.

THE FACTS

In essence, the action before us involves a dispute between athletes who wish to compete in the Olympic Games to be held in Moscow this summer, and the United States Olympic Committee, which has denied them that opportunity in the wake of the invasion and continued occupation of Afghanistan by Soviet military forces. Because this dispute confronts us with questions concerning the statutory authority of the USOC, its place and appropriate role in the international Olympic movement, and its relationship to the United States Government and with certain United States officials, we begin with a brief discussion of the organizational structure of the Olympic Games and the facts which have brought this action before us. These facts are not in dispute.

According to its Rules and By-laws, the International Olympic Committee (IOC) governs the Olympic movement and owns the rights of the Olympic games. IOC Rules provide that National Olympic Committees (NOC) may be established "as the sole authorities responsible for the representation of the respective countries at the Olympic Games," so long as the NOC's rules and regulations are approved by the IOC. The USOC is one such National Olympic Committee.

The USOC is a corporation created and granted a federal charter by Congress in 1950. Pub.L. No. 81-805, 64 Stat. 899. This charter was revised by the Amateur Sports Act of 1978, Pub.L. No.

95-606, 92 Stat. 3045, 36 U.S.C. ss 371 et seq. Under this statute, defendant USOC has "exclusive jurisdiction" and authority over participation and representation of the United States in the Olympic Games.

The routine procedure initiating the participation of a national team in Olympic competition is the acceptance by the NOC of an invitation from the Olympic Organizing Committee for the particular games. In accordance with this routine procedure under IOC Rules, the Moscow Olympic Organizing Committee extended an invitation to the USOC to participate in the summer games. Recent international and domestic events, however, have made acceptance of this invitation, which must come on or before May 24, 1980, anything but routine.

On December 27, 1979, the Soviet Union launched an invasion of its neighbor, Afghanistan. That country's ruler was deposed and killed and a new government was installed. Fighting has been at times intense, casualties have been high, and hundreds of thousands of Afghan citizens have fled their homeland. At present, an estimated 100,000 Soviet troops remain in Afghanistan, and fighting continues.

President Carter termed the invasion a threat to the security of the Persian Gulf area as well as a threat to world peace and stability and he moved to take direct sanctions against the Soviet Union. These sanctions included a curtailment of agricultural and high technology exports to the Soviet Union, and restrictions on commerce with the Soviets. The Administration also turned its attention to a boycott of the summer Olympic Games as a further sanction against the Soviet Union.

As the affidavit of then Acting Secretary of State Warren Christopher makes clear, the Administration was concerned that "(t)he presence of American competitors would be taken by the Soviets as evidence that their invasion had faded from memory or was not a matter of great consequence or concern to this nation." The Administration's concern was sharpened because "(t)he Soviet Union has made clear that it intends the Games to serve important national political ends. For the U.S.S.R., international sports competition is an instrument of government policy and a means to advance foreign policy goals."

With these concerns in mind, the Administration strenuously urged a boycott of the Moscow games. On January 20, 1980, President Carter wrote the President of the United States Olympic Committee to urge that the USOC propose to the IOC that the 1980 summer games be transferred from Moscow, postponed, or cancelled if the Soviet forces were not withdrawn within a month. On January 23, 1980 the President delivered his State of the Union Message, in which he said that he would not support sending American athletes to Moscow while Soviet military forces remained in Afghanistan.

Following these statements, the United States House of Representatives passed, by a vote of 386 to 12, a Concurrent Resolution opposing participation by United States athletes in the Moscow Games unless Soviet troops were withdrawn from Afghanistan by February 20th. The Senate passed a similar resolution by a vote of 88 to 4.

As this was unfolding, the USOC's 86 member Executive Board held a meeting in Colorado Springs on January 26, 1980, inviting White House counsel Lloyd Cutler to address them "because no officer or any member of the Board was knowledgeable about the far-reaching implications of the Soviet invasion." According to USOC President [Robert] Kane, in early January some USOC officers became concerned that sending American athletes to Moscow could expose them to danger if hostility erupted at the games, and that acceptance of the invitation could be seen as tacit approval of or at least acceptance of the Soviet invasion. Mr. Culter also met with USOC officers at least twice in February to discuss the matter further. On each occasion, according to the Kane affidavit, Mr. Cutler urged Mr. Kane to convene an emergency meeting of the USOC Executive Board to act on the Moscow problem. However, legal counsel for the USOC advised Mr. Kane that only the House of Delegates and not the USOC Executive Board could decide whether or not to send a team to Moscow.

On March 21, 1980, President Carter told members of the Athletes Advisory Council, an official body of the USOC, that American athletes will not participate in the Moscow summer games. On April 8, 1980, the President sent a telegram to the president and officers of the USOC and to its House of Delegates, urging the USOC vote against sending an American team to Moscow. In an April 10th speech, the President said that "if legal actions are necessary to enforce (my) decision not to send a team to Moscow, then I will take those legal actions." Among the legal measures the President apparently contemplated was invoking the sanctions of the International Emergency Economic Powers Act, 50 U.S.C. ss 1701 et seq. On April 10 and 11, 1980, the 13 member Administrative Committee of the USOC met in Colorado Springs and voted to support a resolution against sending a team to Moscow. Only Anita DeFrantz, a plaintiff in this action, dissented.

At the President's request and over initial objections by the USOC, Vice President Mondale addressed the assembled House of Delegates prior to their vote on April 12, 1980. The Vice President strongly and vigorously urged the House of Delegates to support a resolution rejecting American participation in the summer games in Moscow.

After what USOC President Kane describes in his affidavit as "full, open, complete and orderly debate by advocates of each motion," the House of Delegates, on a secret ballot, passed by a vote of 1,604 to 798, a resolution, which provided in pertinent part:

> RESOLVED that since the President of the United States has advised the United States Olympic Committee that in light of international events the national security of the country is threatened, the USOC has decided not send a team to the 1980 Summer Games in Moscow . . .
> FURTHER RESOLVED, that if the President of the United States advises the United States Olympic Committee, on or before May 20, 1980, that international events have become compatible with the national interest and the national security is no longer threatened, the USOC will enter its athletes in the 1980 Summer Games.

Plaintiffs describe these attempts by the Administration to persuade the USOC to vote not to send an American team to Moscow as "a campaign to coerce defendant USOC into compliance with the President's demand for a boycott of the Olympic Games." In addition, plaintiffs' complaint alleges that the President and other Executive Branch officials threatened to terminate federal funding of the USOC and that they raised the possibility of revoking the federal income tax exemption of the USOC if the USOC did not support the President's decision to boycott the 1980 Games. The complaint also alleges that these officials state that the Federal government would provide increased funding to the USOC if the USOC supported a boycott.

* * *

Plaintiffs allege that ...[the inability to compete in the Games] will result in great and irreparable injury to the athletes. "Many would lose a once-in-a-lifetime opportunity to participate in the Olympic Games, and the honor and prestige that such participation affords. Most of the class members are at or near their physical peaks at the present time and will not physically be capable of reaching the same or higher levels at a later period of their lives."

In summary, plaintiffs ask this court to declare the April 12, 1980 resolution of the USOC House of Delegates null and void because it violated statutory authority and constitutional provisions and to permanently enjoin the USOC from carrying out that resolution.

* * *

Because of the time constraints involved in this action, this court granted plaintiffs' motion that a trial of the action on the merits be advanced and consolidated with the hearing of the application for a preliminary and permanent injunction.

* * *

ANALYSIS

This action presents us with several issues for decision, falling into two distinct categories; one is statutory and the other is constitutional. We turn first to the statutory issues.

1. The Amateur Sports Act of 1978

Plaintiffs allege in their complaint that by its decision not to send an American team to compete in the summer Olympic Games in Moscow, defendant USOC has violated the Amateur Sports Act of 1978, supra, (The Act).... We deal with two of the alleged violations here. Reduced to their essentials, these allegations are that the Act does not give, and that Congress intended to deny, the USOC the authority to decide not to enter an American team in the Olympics, except perhaps for sports-related reasons, and that the Act guarantees to certain athletes a right to compete in the Olympic Games which defendant denied them. We consider each allegation in turn.

(a) The USOC's Authority Not to Send a Team to Moscow

The United States Olympic Committee was first incorporated and granted a federal charter in 1950. Pub.L. No. 81-805, supra. However, predecessors to the now federally-chartered USOC have existed since 1896, and since that time, they have exercised the authority granted by the International Olympic Committee to represent the United States as its National Olympic Committee in matters pertaining to participation in Olympic games. It is unquestioned by plaintiffs that under the International Olympic Committees Rules and By-laws, the National Olympic Committees have the right to determine their nation's participation in the Olympics. IOC Rule 24B provides that "NOC's shall be the sole authorities responsible for the representation of the respective countries at the Olympic Games . . ." and Chapter 5, paragraph 7 of the By-laws to Rule 24 provides that "(r)epresentation covers the decision to participate . . . .". Nothing in the IOC Charter, Rules or By-laws requires a NOC, such as the USOC, to accept an invitation to participate in any particular Olympic contest and the President of the IOC has said that participation in the Olympic games is entirely voluntary. As defendant has argued, an invitation to participate is just that, an invitation, which may be accepted or declined.

Because defendant USOC clearly has the power under IOC Rules to decide not to enter an American team in Olympic competition, the question then becomes whether the Amateur Sports Act of 1978, which rewrote the USOC's charter, denies the USOC that power. Plaintiffs emphatically argue that it does, and defendant and the Government just as emphatically argue that it does not.

Plaintiffs' argument is simple and straightforward: The Act by its terms does not expressly confer on the USOC the power to decline to participate in the Olympic Games, and if any such power can be inferred from the statute, the power must be exercised for sports-related reasons. Defendant and the Government respond that the Act gives the USOC broad powers, including the authority to decide not to accept an invitation to send an American team to the Olympics.

* * *

[W]e would expect that if Congress intended to limit or deny to the USOC powers it already enjoyed as a National Olympic Committee, such limitation or denial would be clear and explicit. No such language appears in the statute. Indeed, far from precluding this authority, the language of the statute appears to embrace it. *** We accordingly conclude that the USOC has the authority to decide not to send an American team to the Olympics.

Plaintiffs next argue that if the USOC does have the authority to decide not to accept an invitation to send an American team to the Moscow Olympics, that decision must be based on "sports-related considerations." In support of their argument, plaintiffs point to ss 392(a)(5) and (b) of the Act, which plaintiffs acknowledge "are not in terms applicable to the USOC," but rather concern situations in which national governing bodies of various sports,[1] which are subordinate to the USOC, are asked to sanction the holding of international competitions below the level

---

1 A national governing body is a non-profit amateur sports organization, which acts as this country's representative in the corresponding international sports federation for that particular sport. It sets goals and directs policy in the sport it governs and has the power to sanction internal competitions held in the United States in their sport.

of the Olympic or Pan American Games in the United States or the participation of the United States athletes in such competition abroad. These sections provide that a national governing body may withhold its sanctions only upon clear and convincing evidence that holding or participating in the competition "would be detrimental to the best interests of the sport." Plaintiffs argue by analogy that a similar "sports-related" limitation must attach to any authority the USOC might have to decide not to participate in an Olympic competition. We cannot agree.

The provision on which plaintiffs place reliance by analogy is specifically concerned with eliminating the feuding between various amateur athletic organizations and national governing bodies, which for so long characterized amateur athletics. As all parties recognize, this friction, such as the well-publicized power struggles between the NCAA and the AAU, was a major reason for passage of the Act, and the provisions plaintiffs cite, among others, are aimed at eliminating this senseless strife, which the Senate and House Committee reports indicate had dramatically harmed the ability of the United States to compete effectively in international competition. In order to eliminate this internecine squabbling, the Act elevated the USOC to a supervisory role over the various amateur athletic organizations, and provided that the USOC establish procedures for the swift and equitable settlement of these disputes. *** [I]t also directed that the national governing bodies of the various sports could only withhold their approvals of international competition for sports-related reasons. Previously, many of these bodies had withheld their sanction of certain athletic competitions in order to further their own interests at the expense of other groups and to the detriment of athletes wishing to participate.

In brief, this sports-related limitation is intimately tied to the specific purpose of curbing the arbitrary and unrestrained power of various athletic organizations subordinate to the USOC not to allow athletes to compete in international competition below the level of the Olympic Games and the Pan American Games. This purpose has nothing to do with a decision by the USOC to exercise authority granted by the IOC to decide not to participate in an Olympic competition.

* * *

We therefore conclude that the USOC not only had the authority to decide not to send an American team to the summer Olympics, but also that it could do so for reasons not directly related to sports considerations.

* * *

2. Constitutional Claims

Plaintiffs have alleged that the decision of the USOC not to enter an American team in the summer Olympics has violated certain rights guaranteed to plaintiffs under the First, Fifth and Ninth Amendments to the United States Constitution. This presents us with two questions: (1) whether the USOC's decision was "governmental action" (state action), and, assuming state action is found, (2) whether the USOC's decision abridged any constitutionally protected rights.

(a) State Action

Although federally chartered, defendant is a private organization. Because the Due Process Clause of the Fifth Amendment, on which plaintiffs place great reliance, applies only to actions by the federal government, plaintiffs must show that the USOC vote is a "governmental act," i.e., state action. ***

Here...there is no factual justification for finding that the federal government and the USOC enjoyed the "symbiotic relationship" which courts have required to find state action. The USOC has received no federal funding and it exists and operates independently of the federal government. Its chartering statute gives it "exclusive jurisdiction" over "all matters pertaining to the participation of the United States in the Olympic Games . . . ." 36 U.S.C. s 374(3).

* * *

Plaintiffs...argue that by the actions of certain federal officials, the federal government initiated, encouraged, and approved of the result reached (i.e., the vote of the USOC not to send an American team to the summer Olympics). Plaintiffs advance a novel theory. Essentially, their argument is that the campaign of governmental persuasion, personally led by President Carter, crossed the line from "governmental recommendation," which plaintiffs find acceptable and presumably necessary to the operation of our form of government, into the area of "affirmative pressure that effectively places the government's prestige behind the challenged action," and thus, results in state action. We cannot agree.

Plaintiff can point to no case outside the area of discrimination law, which in any way supports their theory, and we can find none. ***

The USOC is an independent body, and nothing in its chartering statute gives the federal government the right to control that body or its officers. Furthermore, the facts here do not indicate that the federal government was able to exercise any type of "de facto" control over the USOC. ***

We accordingly find that the decision of the USOC not to send an American team to the summer Olympics was not state action, and therefore, [it] does not give rise to an actionable claim for the infringements of the constitutional rights alleged.

(b) Constitutionally Protected Rights

Assuming arguendo that the vote of the USOC constituted state action, we turn briefly to plaintiffs' contention that by this action they have been deprived of their constitutional rights to liberty, to self-expression, to travel, and to pursue their chosen occupation of athletic endeavor. Were we to find state action in this case, we would conclude that defendant USOC has violated no constitutionally protected right of plaintiffs.

We note that other courts have considered the right to compete in amateur athletics and have found no deprivation of constitutionally protected rights. [I]n Parish v. National *Collegiate*

Athletic Association, 506 F.2d 1028 (5th Cir. 1975), [basketball players sought an injunction to prevent the NCAA from enforcing its ruling declaring certain athletes ineligible to compete in tournaments and televised games] the court, quoting *Mitchell v. Louisiana High School Athletics Association*, 430 F.2d 1155, 1158 (5th Cir. 1970), stated that:

> . . . the privilege of participation in interscholastic activities must be deemed to fall . . . outside the protection of due process.

Plaintiffs have been unable to draw our attention to any court decision, which finds that the rights allegedly violated here enjoy constitutional protection, and we can find none. *** Defendant has not denied plaintiffs the right to engage in every amateur athletic competition. Defendant has not denied plaintiffs the right to engage in their chosen occupation. Defendant has not even denied plaintiffs the right to travel, only the right to travel for one specific purpose. We can find no justification and no authority for the expansive reading of the Constitution which plaintiffs urge. To find as plaintiffs recommend would be to open the floodgates to a torrent of lawsuits. The courts have correctly recognized that many of life's disappointments, even major ones, do not enjoy constitutional protection. This is one such instance.

At this point, we find it appropriate to note that we have respect and admiration for the discipline, sacrifice, and perseverance, which earns young men and women the opportunity to compete in the Olympic Games. Ordinarily, talent alone has determined whether an American would have the privilege of participating in the Olympics. This year, unexpectedly, things are different. We express no view on the merits of the decision made. We do express our understanding of the deep disappointment and frustrations felt by thousands of American athletes. In doing so, we also recognize that the responsibilities of citizenship often fall more heavily on some than on others. Some are called to military duty. Others never serve. Some return from military service unscathed. Others never return. These are the simple, although harsh, facts of life, and they are immutable.

NOTES & QUESTIONS

1. The United States Government seemed to be saying that there was something wrong or tainted by the Soviet Union's plans to make a political statement with the Games: "(t)he Soviet Union has made it clear that it intends the Games to serve important national political ends. For the U.S.S.R., international sports competition is an instrument of government policy and a means to advance foreign policy goals." Clearly this was nothing new. Isn't this precisely what occurred at the 1936 Berlin Olympics when Aldolf Hitler used the Games as a stage to promote his ideology? Isn't this just the sort of thing that the United States did when it hosted the Games in Los Angeles in 1984 four years after the Moscow Games, promoting U.S. democratic ideals? Isn't the politicization of the Games something that we've simply come to expect as part of the modern Games? Should the host country's politics be grounds for deciding whether to participate?

2. What do you think about the U.S. Government's threats to alter the USOC's tax exempt status and its funding as a means to persuade the USOC not to send a team to Moscow?

3. Explain in your own words the chain of command structure among the IOC, USOC, and the NGB's?

4. Based on the discussion in this case, can you formulate a scenario in which "state action" would be present?

5. DeFrantz became the fifth woman ever named to hold a seat on the 93-member IOC, and is both the first African-American and the first American woman to serve on the committee. She became the first female vice-president of the IOC executive committee in 1997. She was instrumental in convincing 43 African nations not to boycott the 1984 Los Angeles Games when South African runner Zola Budd was allowed to compete for Great Britain. Only Ethiopia, an ally of the boycotting Soviet Union, refused. In 1992, Defrantz became chair of the IOC's Committee on Women and Sports and played a key role in adding women's soccer and softball to the Atlanta Games as medal sports in 1996.

WALTON-FLOYD V. THE UNITED STATES OLYMPIC COMMITTEE
965 SW2D 35 (1998)
COURT OF APPEALS OF TEXAS, HOUSTON (1ST DIST.)

ANDELL, JUSTICE.

* * *

BACKGROUND

The USOC coordinates the United States's participation in international amateur athletic competitions. It resolves disputes among athletes and sports organizations or between competing sports organizations, and provides uniformity in the area of amateur athletics, thereby protecting the rights of amateur athletes to compete. The USOC has the power to sue and be sued. 36 U.S.C.A. § 375(a)(1), (5), (6) (West 1988).

The USOC selects the United States's governing bodies for every sport in the Olympics and Pan-American games. 36 U.S.C.A. § 375(a)(4) (West 1988). In track and field, the USOC recognizes The Athletic Congress (TAC) as the national governing body.[1] TAC coordinates and conducts track and field competitions to ensure competitions comply with the rules and regulations of the International Amateur Athletic Federation (IAAF). The IAAF rules provide for punishment

---

1 Editor's note: Today TAC has changed its name to USA Track & Field.

or suspension of athletes who use certain performance enhancing drugs. The IAAF publishes a list of the banned substances.

The USOC issued the appellant [Delisa Walton-Floyd] a card listing many of the more common substances on the banned list. The card warns:

This list is not complete. It is the athlete's responsibility to check the status of all medications. CALL THE USOC HOTLINE 1-800-233-0393.

The appellant's husband, who was also her trainer, obtained a box of Sydnocarb. He testified the box appeared to be labeled in Russian, he could not read the writing, and he did not have it translated. The box had no instructions and did not list ingredients.

The appellant's husband testified that he called the USOC hotline to inquire about Sydnocarb's status and that the USOC operator told him Sydnocarb was a carbohydrate supplement not on the banned list. He admitted, however, that the hotline operator did not specifically tell him that Sydnocarb was safe to use, nor did she give any other assurances. The appellant called the hotline, with similar results, then began using Sydnocarb. She and her husband testified they called the hotline on subsequent occasions to inquire about the status of Sydnocarb, and that each time, the USOC's operator told them it was not on the banned list.

After the appellant's semi-final heat at the IAAF World Championships, she provided meet officials with a urine sample, which they divided into two samples. The first sample tested positive for amphetamines, a prohibited substance. IAAF officials told her the test results and invited her to attend a testing of the second sample, which also tested positive for amphetamines. The IAAF relayed the results to TAC, which suspended her from further competition. The appellant eventually discovered that Sydnocarb was the apparent source of the amphetamines.

* * *

DISCUSSION

We are asked to determine whether the USOC owed the appellant a federal statutory or Texas common-law duty. In seven points of error, the appellant asserts: (1) the USOC owed her a federal statutory and Texas common-law duty; (2) there are fact issues whether the USOC had breached those duties; (3) fact issues exist whether damages can be limited; and (4) fact issues exist whether the USOC was grossly negligent.

Private Right of Action Under the Amateur Sports Act

Because no Texas court has considered this issue, we turn to federal cases for guidance. Federal courts have interpreted the Act and its legislative history not to imply private causes of action against the USOC.[2] *Oldfield v. The Athletic Congress,* 779 F.2d 505, 506-08 (9th Cir.1985); *Michels v. United States Olympic Committee,* 741 F.2d 155, 157-58 (7th Cir.1984); *DeFrantz v. United States Olympic Committee,* 492 F.Supp. 1181, 1190-92 (D.D.C.1980); *Martinez v. United States Olympic Committee,* 802 F.2d 1275, 1281 (10th Cir.1986). ***

The Ninth Circuit noted that the Act, as originally proposed, contained a provision referred to as the "Amateur Athletes' Bill of Rights," which expressly granted athletes the power to contest in federal court the actions of any sports organization that threatened to deny them the opportunity to participate. *See* §. 2036, 94th Cong. § 304(a) (1977); *Oldfield,* 779 F.2d at 507. The final version of the Act excluded the provision allowing athletes to sue in federal court and inserted it in the USOC's Constitution. *Oldfield,* 779 F.2d at 507. The court in *Oldfield* explained that the USOC's Constitution is not part of the Act, and thus, the provision did not allow private individuals to litigate in federal court. *Id.*

● *** Based on the Act's legislative history, the Seventh Circuit [in *Michels*] held that the Act contained no private right of action to require the USOC to hold a hearing. The court noted that Congress's refusal to insert the bill of rights provision into the final version indicates that it considered and then rejected a cause of action for athletes to enforce the Act's provisions. [741 F.2d] at 158. In concurrence, Judge Richard Posner suggested that in light of the Act's provisions to resolve disputes internally, the USOC is better equipped to handle disputes involving athletes. *Id.* He continued, "There can be few less suitable bodies than the federal courts for determining the eligibility, or the procedures for determining eligibility, of athletes to participate in the Olympic Games." *Id.*

The court in *DeFrantz* considered the case of 25 athletes and one executive member of the USOC who sought an injunction prohibiting the USOC from implementing USOC's House of Delegates' resolution to decline an invitation to 1980 Moscow Summer Olympics. 492 F.Supp. at 1183. The Court held the Act did not confer an enforceable right to an amateur athlete to compete in Olympic competition as the Act confers the broad authority to the USOC to make all decisions regarding competitions and participation. *Id.* at 1188. Furthermore, even if such a right to compete existed, the court noted that the Act does not imply a private cause of action to enforce such a right. *Id.* at 1192. The court noted that the Act sought to protect the opportunity for athletes to compete and prevent rivalries between sports organizations. *Id.* The court looked to 36 U.S.C. § 395 (1988) and found established procedures for the internal consideration and resolution of jurisdictional and eligibility issues. Id. The court also cited 36 U.S.C. § 395(c)

---

2 Actions against the USOC have proven successful in two scenarios: (1) disputes between organizations and the USOC, *United States Wrestling Fed'n v. Wrestling Division of the AAU, Inc.,* 545 F.Supp. 1053, 1061 (N.D.Ohio 1982); Edward E. Hollis, III, Note, *The United States Olympic Committee and the Suspension of Athletes: Reforming Grievance Procedures Under the Amateur Sports Act of 1978,* 71 Ind.L.J. 183, 188; and (2) breach of contract allegations. *Harding v. United States Figure Skating Ass'n,* 851 F.Supp. 1476, 1480 (D.Or.1994); *Reynolds v. International Amateur Athletic Fed'n,* 841 F.Supp. 1444, 1448 (S.D.Ohio 1992). Intervention is appropriate only in the most extraordinary circumstances, where the association has clearly breached its own rules, the breach will imminently result in serious and irreparable harm to the plaintiff, and the plaintiff has exhausted all internal remedies. *Harding,* 851 F.Supp. at 1479. As a general rule, courts should not intervene in the merits of the underlying dispute, but if they do, then they should limit injunctive relief to correcting the breach of the rules. Id.

(1), which grants any aggrieved party the right to review by arbitration after exhaustion of other USOC remedies, as confirming the Act's intent to handle disputes internally. *Id.*

*** The legislative history of the Act indicates that Congress did not intend to provide individual athletes a private cause of action. If Congress had so intended, then it would not have removed the bill of rights from the original version of the Act. ***

Voluntary Assumption of a Duty Under State Law

The appellant argues the Act imposes a duty upon the USOC or a duty exists through voluntary assumption of the hotline service. Since we have held there is no private cause of action under the Act, we must determine whether the USOC assumed a duty under state tort law. The appellant maintains that even absent a statutory duty under the Act, the USOC voluntarily undertook an affirmative course of action for her benefit. She asserts the USOC assumed the obligation to exercise reasonable care. The USOC claims it does not owe the appellant any duty under Texas tort law, because...the Act pre-empts any common-law negligence action.

In determining whether a private cause of action existed under state tort law, the Appellate Division of the New Jersey Superior Court felt bound to follow federal case law. *Dolan v. U.S. Equestrian Team, Inc.*, 257 N.J.Super. 314, 608 A.2d 434, 437 (App.Div.1992). The court noted:

> [W]e believe the Act should be uniformly interpreted; that it would be inappropriate to attribute different or unique meanings to its provisions in New Jersey and thus create a jurisdictional sanctuary from the Congressional determination that these types of disputes should be resolved outside the judicial process. *Id.* 608 A.2d at 437.

We agree with *Dolan*. The interest of maintaining consistent interpretations among jurisdictions requires the Act to pre-empt claims asserted under state tort law. To hold a common law duty exists outside the scope of the Act, thereby enabling an individual athlete to bring suit, threatens to override legislative intent and opens the door to inconsistent interpretations of the Act.

We hold that the USOC did not owe the appellant a duty under any of the theories pleaded. ****

We affirm.

NOTES & QUESTIONS

1. Exactly why is it that the courts conclude that athletes do not have a private cause of action under the Amateur Sports Act?

2. When law students learn about contracts, one doctrine that they study is promissory estoppel. Fundamentally, promissory estoppel allows parties to recover contract-like damages in circumstances where they have reasonably relied on another's promise. This doctrine is found in the Restatement of Contracts (Second) Section 90. Should promissory estoppel operate to provide a cause of action when the telephone hot-line operators give out advice upon which they must know that athletes place reasonable reliance? Explain why or why not.

3. Explain whether you think that this result is "fair." Why or why not?

4. Is there a clear cause and effect relationship between Walton-Floyd's taking Sydnocarb and failing the drug test? In civil law cases, we typically require that proof be shown by "a preponderance of the evidence." In other words, the trier of fact (typically the jury) must be convinced that the evidence relating to a given fact tips the scale at least 51% in order for that fact to be considered "proven." This is very different from the standard required in criminal law cases where proof of facts is required to be "beyond a reasonable doubt." There are also some types of civil law cases where proof must be greater than "by a preponderance of the evidence," and that standard is usually referred to as "by clear and convincing evidence." The "clear and convincing evidence" standard is not as high a burden as "beyond a reasonable doubt" but it is appreciably higher than "by a preponderance of the evidence." In cases involving athletes and drugs use, do you think that there should be a requirement of proof by a preponderance of evidence, clear and convincing evidence, or beyond a reasonable doubt? Explain your reasoning. Is the burden even relevant? Why or why not?

NOTE: THE COURT OF ARBITRATION FOR SPORT

In response to the growing number of sports-related disputes, the Court of Arbitration for Sport was created in 1984. The idea for such an arbitral body is credited to the president of the International Olympic Committee (IOC) H.E. Juan Antonio Samaranch who yearned to create a sports-specific jurisdiction. The CAS is located in Lausanne, Switzerland with additional courts in New York and Sydney as well as ad-hoc courts in Olympic host cities as necessary. The CAS has jurisdiction over two types of disputes: those that are commercial in nature, and those that are disciplinary in nature. Commercial disputes may include contractual disputes as well as those disputes that would result in civil liability. A large number of disciplinary disputes are doping-related. A dispute may be submitted to the CAS only if there is an arbitration agreement between the parties that specifies recourse to the CAS. "An international court like the CAS, which can offer specialist knowledge, low cost and rapid action, provides a means of resolving sports disputes adapted to the specific needs of the international sporting community."

CAS 2007/A/1416 WADA v/ USADA & SCHERF ARBITRAL AWARD
DELIVERED BY THE COURT OF ARBITRATION FOR SPORT

Sitting in the following composition:
President: The Hon. Hugh L. Fraser, Ottawa, Canada
Arbitrators: Mr. Peter Leaver, QC, Barrister-at-Law, London, England
Mr. Jeffrey G. Benz, Attorney-at-Law, Los Angeles, USA

In the arbitration between

WORLD ANTI-DOPING AGENCY (WADA), Montréal, Canada
Represented by Mr. Stephen Drymer, Montréal, Canada
First Appellant
and
INTERNATIONAL ASSOCIATION OF ATHLETICS FEDERATIONS
(IAAF), Monaco
Represented by Mr. Huw Roberts, London, England
Second Appellant
v.
UNITED STATES ANTI-DOPING AGENCY (USADA), Colorado, USA
Represented by Mr. William Bock III, Indianapolis, USA
First Respondent
and
LINDSEY SCHERF, New York, USA
Represented by Mr. Howard Jacobs, Los Angeles, USA
Second Respondent

1. PARTIES

The First Appellant, the World Anti-Doping Agency ("WADA"), is the international independent organisation created in 1999 to promote, coordinate and monitor the fight against doping in sport in all its forms. It coordinates the development and implementation of the World Anti-Doping Code ("the WADC). WADA has its headquarters in Montreal, Canada. The Second Appellant, the International Association of Athletics Federations ("IAAF"), governs the sport of athletics throughout the world. The IAAF has its seat in the Principality of Monaco. The First Respondent, the United States Anti-Doping Agency (USADA) is the national anti-doping organization for the Olympic Movement in the United States. USADA's primary focus is on the areas of Research, Education, Drug Testing and Results Management. The Second Respondent, Lindsey Scherf, is a 21 year old competitor in the sport of Athletics. She is a citizen of the United States.

2. FACTUAL BACKGROUND

● 2.1 Lindsey Scherf is a collegiate distance runner. She is scheduled to graduate from Harvard University in June 2008 with a B.A. in Psychology. During her freshman year at Harvard in 2005, she set an American Junior (under age 20) record for 10,000 meters and ran the 2nd fastest time ever by an American Junior female in the 5,000 meters. She has competed outside the United States on two occasions, the first being the 2005 IAAF World Junior Cross Country Championships, and the most recent being the 2007 Gold Coast Marathon in Australia.

2.2 Lindsey Scherf was first diagnosed with exercise-induced asthma in 2003. She applied for, and received, an Abbreviated Therapeutic Use Exemption ("ATUE") for her Flovent asthma medication from the IAAF in 2005 and from USADA in 2006 and 2007.

2.3 (…).

2.4 In January 2007, Lindsey Scherf traveled to Australia for a semester of study abroad. She decided to enter the Gold Coast Marathon, scheduled to be run in Brisbane, Australia on July 1, 2007, as this would provide her only opportunity to meet the US Olympic Marathon Trials qualifying time.

2.5 Ms. Scherf was of the belief that if she ever entered an international competition she would require an ATUE from her International Federation. Her father on her behalf contacted USADA and was advised that a separate IAAF ATUE would be needed, and that USADA would forward Ms. Scherf's application to the IAAF.

2.6 On April 26, 2007, more than nine (9) weeks prior to the Gold Coast Marathon, Ms. Scherf applied for an (ATUE) from the IAAF for Flovent (...).

2.7 By late June 2007, Ms. Scherf had still not received word from the IAAF concerning the status of her applications. She diligently followed up with USADA since she understood that this agency had submitted the applications on her behalf. No information was provided to Ms. Scherf or to USADA concerning the status of her TUE applications prior to the start of the Gold Coast Marathon.

2.8 Ms. Scherf was aware that if she stopped using her Flovent medication 10-12 days prior to a competition it would be totally out of her system by race day. However, she had contracted a serious throat and lung infection on June 12, 2007, which was three weeks prior to the marathon race.

2.9 On June 20, 2007, Ms. Scherf saw Dr. Maria Kowalczuk at the University of Queensland Student Health Office. Dr. Kowalczuk advised her to continue taking Flovent and also prescribed Singular and Ventalin since she had lost her voice and was not well. Dr. Kowalczuk advised Ms. Scherf not to compete in the Gold Coast Marathon due to concerns over her health. She was concerned that Ms. Scherf's respiratory condition, if untreated, could result in myocarditis, a potentially fatal illness.

2.10 On advice from USADA's TUE Coordinator, Ms. Scherf decided to check with officials responsible for the Gold Coast Marathon to determine if there would be drug testing. She had decided to continue taking her asthma medication due to her respiratory difficulties and had determined that she would not compete in the Marathon if there was to be drug testing, unless her TUE was granted prior to the commencement of the race.

2.11 Ms. Scherf continued to communicate with race officials until the day of the marathon. She was advised that there had been no drug testing in the three previous years, and that it was highly unlikely that there would be a last minute decision by the Australian Sports Anti-Doping Authority to carry out drug tests at this competition.

2.12 Ms. Scherf then asked the Elite Athlete Service Manager for the Gold Coast Marathon to advise her if he became aware that drug testing would be implemented at the race as stated earlier. She had decided that she would not run the race if so notified. After not receiving any further notification, Ms. Scherf ran the marathon and was the second female finisher in a time of 2:41:19 which was slower than she had hoped for, but good enough to qualify her for the U.S. Olympic trials.

2.13 Shortly after finishing the race Ms. Scherf was advised that she had been selected for drug testing. She believed that the drug test would be positive for Flovent and consulted her father in the United States as to what to do.

2.14 Mr. Scherf was furious with his daughter for competing without the appropriate TUE or a guarantee that there would be no drug testing following the race. He advised his daughter that she would most likely face a two year ban if she tested positive for Flovent without an IAAF TUE. He thought that the penalty for refusing to provide a drug test might be less, and that the potential to straighten things out after the fact would be better for a refusal, than it would be for a failed test. Ms. Scherf therefore decided that she would not submit to a drug test.

2.15 Ms. Scherf's father later realized that he had given his daughter bad advice and left messages for her to ask to be tested the next day. When Ms. Scherf made this request to race officials she was advised that it was too late.

2.16 In 2007, the IAAF had apparently posted a list of its international events on its website. This fact was not known to USADA prior to the running of the Gold Coast Marathon. As it turned out, The Gold Coast marathon was not an international event within the meaning of the IAAF rules. Therefore, Ms. Scherf's USADA TUE would have been valid for the Gold Coast Marathon on July 1, 2007.

3.0 PROCEDURAL HISTORY

* * *

3.4 USADA conducted an investigation of the facts of the case. The investigation included a review of the documents provided by ASADA, a review of the correspondence submitted by Ms. Scherf, a telephone interview with Dr. Maria Kowalczuk of the Queensland Health Service Department, electronic communications with representatives of the Gold Coast Marathon and telephone interviews of Ms. Scherf, and her father, John Scherf.

3.5 At the conclusion of the investigation, the relevant written documents, as well as a written report concerning the investigation were submitted to USADA's Anti-Doping Review Board (ADRB) pursuant to Article 9 of the Protocol. The ADRB is an independent body consisting of three individuals independent of USADA with expertise in sports and anti-doping matters. Notice was given to Ms. Scherf of USADA's review pursuant to article 8 of the Protocol and she made a written submission to the ADRB.

3.6 The ADRB recommended proceeding with the case as an anti-doping rule violation. Thereafter, Ms. Scherf was charged by USADA with a doping violation and notified that she could receive a period of ineligibility of up to two years.

3.7 ***

3.8 At the conclusion of their investigation USADA offered Ms. Scherf the opportunity to accept a sanction which included a period of ineligibility of one year which was calculated by considering the two year period of ineligibility for a refusal to submit to a drug test under the IAAF rules and a one year reduction in the period of ineligibility for exceptional circumstances consistent with the sanction provisions of the IAAF and USOC rules, and the mandatory provisions of the Code.

3.9 Ms. Scherf accepted this resolution by written agreement executed on October 31, 2007, which also provided that her sanction was subject to review and possible appeal by WADA and the IAAF.

3.10 On November 2, 2007, USADA informed WADA of the sanction accepted by Lindsey Scherf.

3.11 On November 12, 2007, WADA filed with the Court of Arbitration for Sport an appeal against USADA's decision.

* * *

3.18 On May 22, 2008, a hearing was convened at the CAS regional offices in New York, New York. At the hearing WADA, IAAF and Lindsay Scherf were represented. USADA did not have representation at the hearing but its counsel, William Bock, made brief submissions by telephone during the hearing.

* * *

5.0 APPLICABLE LAW

5.1 Article R58 of the CAS Code provides:

"The Panel shall decide the dispute according to the applicable regulations and the rules of law chosen by the parties or, in the absence of such a choice, according to the law of the country in which the federation, association or sports-related body which has issued the challenged decision is domiciled or according to the rules of law, the application of which the Panel deems appropriate. In the latter case, the Panel shall give reasons for its decision."

* * *

6.0 JURISDICTION

6.1 The Jurisdiction of the CAS in the present case is based on the USADA Protocol for Olympic Movement Testing and the IAAF Anti-Doping Rules, and is re-confirmed by the signature of the Procedural Order by the parties.

6.2 Article R57 of the CAS Code provides that on an appeal to CAS the Panel has full power to review the facts and the law.

7.0 ISSUES

7.1 In light of the admitted anti-doping rule violation by Lindsey Scherf, the sole issue is whether she should have been required to serve the customary two year period of ineligibility.

8.0 SUMMARY OF THE PARTIES' POSITIONS

WADA:

8.1 WADA argues that Lindsey Scherf in her letter to ASADA dated July 3, 2007 admitted that in refusing to submit to a drug test, she hoped that "the penalty for refusing a drug test would be less severe than the penalty for testing positive...". Furthermore WADA asserts that this violation of anti-doping rules should be construed as a severe offence. They add that, according to the revised WADC, scheduled to be introduced in 2009, the applicable sanction in cases of refusal to submit to sample collection could be increased to up to four years where aggravating circumstances exist.

8.2 WADA maintains that in order to benefit from a reduction of the sanction for No Significant Fault or Negligence, the athlete must establish that her fault or negligence, when viewed in the totality of the circumstances and taking into account the criteria for "no fault or negligence", was not significant in relation to the anti-doping rules violation.

8.3 WADA further submits that such a reduction is meant to occur only in cases where the circumstances are truly exceptional, i.e. when an athlete can show that the degree of fault or negligence in the totality of the circumstances was such that it was not significant in relationship to the doping offence (WADC, comment to Article 10.5.2).

8.4 WADA points out that alleged irregularities in the TUE procedure or uncertainty about the existence of a TUE can never justify a refusal to submit to sample collection. Furthermore says WADA, Ms. Scherf was fully aware of her obligations and she knowingly chose to refuse to submit to sample collection, accepting the possible consequences of such doping offence, which had been brought to her attention several times.

8.5 WADA also submits that allegations of physical illness, dehydration, a knee injury, emotional upset, and poor advice from her father do not diminish the athlete's responsibility to submit to drug testing.

8.6 In WADA's opinion therefore, Lindsey Scherf should not benefit from a reduction of the otherwise applicable sanction of two years.

IAAF:

8.7 IAAF Rule 40.1(b) provides that the sanction for a first violation for a refusal to submit to doping control is a minimum of two years.

In accordance with IAAF Rule 40.3, the minimum two year sanction may be reduced on account of there being exceptional circumstances such that the athlete can demonstrate that she bears no significant fault or no significant negligence for the violation; however, the reduced period may be no more than half the minimum period of ineligibility otherwise applicable.

8.8 No significant fault or no significant negligence is defined in the IAAF rules as follows:

"When exceptional circumstances have been determined in an athlete's case under Rule 38 to demonstrate that the athlete's fault or negligence, when viewed in the totality of the circumstances, was not significant in relationship to the anti-doping rule violation."

8.9 The IAAF submits that, in determining whether the present case is a truly exceptional case that warrants a reduction in the minimum 2 year sanction, the Panel should have regard to the following three factors:

(i) the seriousness of the violation of refusing to submit to doping control;

(ii) the nature of the conduct of an athlete who refuses a doping test; and

(iii) the specific conduct of the athlete in this case.

8.10 The IAAF argues that a refusal to submit to doping control is considered to be a particularly serious violation of the anti-doping rules. They maintain that if this offence is not punished as severely as testing positive for a prohibited substance, athletes would have every incentive to refuse to submit to testing, thereby undermining the very basis of any detection based testing regime.

8.11 The IAAF further submits that it should be a very rare circumstance for an athlete who knowingly or intentionally conducts himself in such a manner to receive a reduction in the otherwise applicable minimum 2 year sanction. It also notes that, in future, violations of the rule may result in an increased sanction of up to 4 years.

8.12 The IAAF argues that Ms. Scherf acted with significant fault and/or negligence when she refused to submit to doping control on 1 July, 2007.

8.13 To support this contention the IAAF maintains the following:

Ms. Scherf was an experienced athlete who was hoping to qualify for the Olympic trials; She had previously applied for and received a TUE from the IAAF; She could have easily accessed the IAAF rules and procedures for applying for a TUE by downloading them from the IAAF website; Ms. Scherf chose to rely on USADA to submit her TUE application to the IAAF on her behalf; She failed to make direct contact with the IAAF to obtain information about her TUE application; She was reckless in entering the Gold Coast Marathon without confirming her TUE status; She repeatedly ignored the advice of doping control officials; Her indication more than 24 hours after her refusal that she had changed her mind was irrelevant since it was no longer feasible to have her tested.

8.14 The IAAF adopted and agreed with the WADA submissions on the issue of no significant fault or negligence. It concluded that there were no exceptional circumstances that could lead to a finding of no significant fault or negligence and, therefore, this was not one of those "most exceptional of cases" referred to in the IAAF rules.

USADA:

8.15 USADA agrees philosophically with the WADA statement that "as a matter of principle it is clear that a refusal ought to be punished as severely if not more severely than a positive test." It goes on to point out, however, that the legal rules, which USADA is bound to apply, did not permit it to reject an exceptional circumstances analysis out of hand merely because the case involved a refusal.

8.16 USADA submitted that Lindsey Scherf did bear fault for not submitting to doping control, and that she should have informed herself of the rules pertaining to doping control.

8.17 Furthermore, USADA indicated in its brief that it did not, and does not, accept any contention that bad advice from Ms. Scherf's father or anyone else, her physical condition following the marathon, her emotional state, her inquiries regarding doping control, or the IAAF's failure to grant her a TUE in and of themselves could have constituted exceptional circumstances.

8.18 What USADA did consider was whether the error made by the IAAF in failing to process the ATUE application promptly, and by USADA in incorrectly advising her of the need for an IAAF TUE, could operate to mitigate or lessen Ms. Scherf's degree of fault.

8.19 USADA points to the basic principle reaffirmed in a number of sport arbitrations decisions that "where the conduct of one party has led to legitimate expectations on the part of a second party, the first party is estopped from changing its course of conduct to the detriment of the second party". *AEK Athens and SK Slavia Prague v. Union of European Football Associations, CAS 98/200 and IAAF v. USATF, CAS 2003.*

8.20 USADA further submitted that it found that the errors of the IAAF and USADA did not excuse Ms. Scherf's fault in refusing to submit to doping control, but they did help to create a chain of events which on a balance of probabilities appear to have significantly mitigated Lindsey Scherf's fault in refusing doping control. USADA's counsel, William Bock in his brief telephone submission to the hearing, acknowledged that the errors made by USADA put Lindsey Scherf in a position where she then applied bad judgement.

8.21 USADA maintained that under the circumstances revealed by its thorough investigation of the matter, it was highly improbable that any of the nefarious explanations for Ms. Scherf's conduct could be supported.

8.22 USADA also argued that its determination of exceptional circumstances was entitled to deference by the Panel.

8.23 USADA concluded therefore that while Ms. Scherf bore some fault it was not under the circumstances significant.

LINDSEY SCHERF:

8.24 The Respondent Lindsey Scherf adopted the explanation for the finding of no significant fault or negligence contained in the USADA brief.

8.25 Lindsey Scherf submits that USADA conducted an extremely thorough and detailed investigation prior to its finding that she was not significantly at fault and was not significantly negligent. ***

8.26 Ms. Scherf submits that she was at all times open, frank, and honest in her dealings with USADA, and with the Gold Coast Marathon officials. She stated that with the help of her father, she was doing her best to comply with the complicated and confusing TUE process.

8.27 Ms. Scherf argues that the criticism by the IAAF of her decision to submit her TUE applications through USADA is unfair in that this was a procedure encouraged by USADA and a procedure that she had followed when making previous applications.

8.28 Ms. Scherf also points out that USADA is in the business of anti-doping and yet it did not appreciate that she did not need a further TUE in order to compete in the Gold Coast Marathon. She submits that it should not be expected that a 21 year old athlete of limited international experience would understand completely rules that National anti-doping agencies have difficulty understanding.

8.29 To further underscore this point, Ms. Scherf notes that the IAAF may have been confused about their own rules since they mistakenly granted approval for the TUE for Flovent on July 12, 2007. The Gold Coast Marathon was not on the list of IAAF International competitions, and after realizing that this approval had been granted in error, the IAAF withdrew Ms. Scherf's TUE on August 1, 2007.

9.0 THE PANEL'S DECISION

9.1 The USADA Protocol and the USOC ADP both provide for a sanction of two years for a first doping offence. The IAAF Rules establish a minimum period of ineligibility of two years for a first doping offence.

9.2 The Second Respondent Lindsey Scherf acknowledged that she had committed an anti-doping rule violation by refusing to submit to doping control. She signed the USADA Acceptance of Sanction, which began as follows:

> "I, Lindsey Scherf, accept the following sanction as a result of my
> doping offence arising from my July 1, 2007, refusal to submit to
> sample collection. I acknowledge that I have violated applicable
> rules, including the USADA Protocol for Olympic Movement
> Testing ("Protocol"), the United States Olympic Committee Anti-
> Doping Policies and the International Association of Athletics
> Federations ("IAAF") Anti-Doping Rules, all of which have
> adopted the World Anti-Doping Code (the "Code"),...

9.3 The Panel heard from Ms. Scherf who impressed as an honest, open and conscientious young athlete. She testified that she is essentially a collegiate runner who does not have an agent and who has had to rely on her father to assist her with much of the paperwork and administrative details that her busy schedule prevents her from attending to.

9.4 The hearing was advised that Ms. Scherf submitted the IAAF ATUE application to USADA on April 26, 2007, nine (9) full weeks before the Gold Coast Marathon. She assumed that the documentation had been forwarded by e-mail in a timely fashion to the IAAF by Camila Zardo who at the time was USADA's TUE Coordinator.

9.5 Ms. Zardo testified that she had been under the impression that the e-mail with supporting documents had been sent to the IAAF on May 1, 2007. She discovered in preparation for the appeal that the e-mail with the TUE application was not sent to the IAAF until June 26, 2007 just a few days prior to the July 1, 2007 marathon race.

9.6 Ms. Scherf also testified that she diligently pursued the matter of drug testing for the Gold Coast marathon with the Elite Athlete Service Manager, Ryan McDonald. She apprised him of the fact that she was taking medication that could not be ceased for health reasons and needed to know prior to the race whether drug testing would take place. She believed that she had an understanding from Mr. McDonald that he would inform her as soon as he became aware that drug testing was to take place.

9.7 The Panel learned after hearing testimony from Ryan McDonald that he knew on June 27, 2007 that drug testing would be conducted by ASADA at the Gold Coast Marathon, but for reasons of confidentiality did not share that information with Ms. Scherf.

9.8 The Panel accepts Ms. Scherf's contention that she had previously submitted her applications for a TUE to USADA and saw no reason to depart from that practice on this occasion. In fact, Camila Zardo testified that the IAAF wanted USADA to take authority over the TUE application process for its National level athletes.

9.9 The IAAF also criticizes Ms. Scherf for not approaching that organization directly when she had concerns about the length of time that it was taking to process her TUE application. However, Camila Zardo also testified that she was aware of many occasions when athletes would not receive the same response as USADA did when they attempted to contact International Federations on their own behalf.

9.10 The Panel also acknowledges that the IAAF rules and procedures regarding the TUE application process are confusing even for those who have responsibility for those issues on a daily basis. Criticisms about the ease of accessing the relevant sections of the IAAF website also have some validity. Counsel for Ms. Scherf demonstrated for the panel that at 6:40 pm on the day of the hearing one could still not download the relevant information from the IAAF web site. USADA in its brief indicated that it had experienced the same difficulty.

9.11 Ms. Scherf naively believed that a race official would inform her of the certainty that drug testing would take place at the Gold Coast Marathon, and that her good faith in seeking such assurance would be respected. The Panel agrees that errors made by the IAAF, and by USADA placed the athlete in somewhat of a quandary. Her subsequent error in judgment was as a direct result of the errors made by agencies that should have provided better service to the athlete.

9.12 USADA thoroughly investigated the matter and was satisfied that this was a case of exceptional circumstances where an athlete's fault was not significant, and where her negligence if any was not significant.

9.13 The Panel finds that exceptional circumstances did exist in this case, and agrees that Ms. Scherf bears No Significant Fault or Negligence, because her fault or negligence when viewed in light of all the circumstances was not significant in relation to her anti-doping rule violation. The Panel would, however, wish to make it clear that this is a rare case in which an athlete who has failed or refused to provide a sample will be able to satisfy a CAS Panel that the sanction is to be reduced on the ground of No Significant Fault or Negligence. Such cases will not often occur.

9.14 This conclusion makes it unnecessary for the Panel to address the issue of deference with regard to USADA's decision of October 31, 2007.

10.0 COSTS

* * *

10.4 After taking into account the outcome of the proceedings, and the conduct and financial resources of the parties, the Panel orders WADA and the IAAF to each contribute the sum of $4,000 towards Ms. Scherf's costs. The Panel also orders that USADA contribute a further sum of $2,000 towards Ms. Scherf's costs.

* * *

Done in Lausanne, 11 August 2008

THE COURT OF ARBITRATION FOR SPORT
Hon. Hugh L. Fraser
President of the Panel
Jeffrey G. Benz Peter Leaver QC
Arbitrator Arbitrato

NOTES & QUESTIONS

1. Recent CAS cases have confronted the complex nature of situations where athletes – for various reasons – have refused to submit to drug testing after competition. Here are two examples. 1) *Viktor Troicki v. ITF*. Viktor Troicki / ITF CAS 2013/A/3279. CAS upheld a 12-month suspension and other sanctions when Serbian tennis player refused to allow medical technicians to draw a blood sample after he claimed to be feeling ill. 2) *WADA v. Ivan Mauricio Casas Buritrago & GCD*, CAS 2013/A/3077. CAS determined that the Colombian cyclist had no compelling justification for refusing a drug test, and imposed a two-year suspension.

SLANEY V. THE INTERNATIONAL AMATEUR ATHLETIC FEDERATION AND THE UNITED STATES OLYMPIC COMMITTEE
244 F 3D 580 (2001)
UNITED STATES COURT OF APPEALS, SEVENTH CIRCUIT

FLAUM, CHIEF JUDGE.

Former Olympic runner Mary Decker Slaney ("Slaney") brought suit against the International Amateur Athletic Federation ("IAAF") and the United States Olympic Committee ("USOC") shortly after an IAAF arbitration panel determined that Slaney had committed a doping offense. *** Slaney now appeals the district court's decision, arguing that: (1) the New York Convention does not bar adjudication of her claims against the IAAF [and] (2) the Amateur Sports Act does not preempt all state-law claims by a participating athlete against the USOC... *** For the reasons stated herein, we affirm the decision of the district court.

In the course of her storied career, middle-distance runner Mary Decker Slaney has captured a multitude of United States and world records. She is considered by many to be one of the most celebrated female athletes of the past century, as well as one of the greatest runners of all-time. While Slaney began running in 1969, it was not until fifteen years later that she received international attention. At the 1984 Los Angeles Games, Slaney was considered a favorite to medal in the 3000 meters competition. While the world watched on, halfway through the race, Slaney began jostling for position with Zola Budd, a South African born, barefooted runner. When the pair became entangled, Slaney was tripped up by Budd. Slaney tumbled onto the infield, injuring her hip. As she crashed to the infield, any chance for an Olympic medal came crashing down with her. To this day, an indelible picture of Slaney, fallen on the side of the track and writhing in pain, remains in the minds of many who witnessed the event.

Slaney rebounded from her Olympic defeat and continued to compete, overcoming countless injuries. In June of 1996, she competed in the 5000 and 1500 meter races in the national trials for the Atlanta Olympics. Following her 5000 meter race, Slaney provided the USOC with a urine sample, which was tested for prohibited substances including exogenous testosterone.

Because current technology cannot detect the presence of prohibited testosterone in the body, testing programs measure the ratio of testosterone to epitestosterone ("T/E") in the body. This test, referred to as the T/E test, assumes that an ordinary T/E ratio in humans is one to one, and thus any ratio of above six to one is consistent with "blood doping." The ratio was established at six to one in order to account for non-doping factors that might cause elevated ratios in female athletes. Factors which may influence T/E ratio include an individual changing birth control pills, age, menstrual cycle, bacterial contamination of the urine sample, and alcohol use.

Slaney's test was conducted at the University of California at Los Angeles ("UCLA") Laboratory. The test revealed that Slaney's T/E ratio was elevated significantly beyond the permitted six to one ratio.[1] *** Slaney claimed that her elevated level was the result of (1) her menstrual cycle, and (2) her changing of birth control pills. Furthermore, Slaney posited that there was no scientific validity to the hypothesis that a T/E ratio above six to one was not normal for female athletes. Nonetheless, on February 5, 1997, the IAAF adopted the investigating doctor's recommendation and found Slaney's specimen positive for the prohibited substance testosterone.

* * *

The IAAF...invoked arbitration.[2] Slaney and the USATF opposed arbitration, but both were represented before the IAAF Arbitral Panel ("the Tribunal"). In late January 1999, the Tribunal

---

[1] Specifically, Slaney's samples tested at ratios of 9.5:1 to 11.6:1.

[2] Because of indications, during the late 1970's, that some national track and field federations were turning blind eyes to their athletes' drug abuse, the IAAF established worldwide testing procedures and eligibility rules. Rules 21-23 require all disputes between the IAAF and members to be submitted to an arbitration panel.

issued an interlocutory decision upholding the IAAF's interpretation of how to adjudicate a testosterone doping offense, and found that the rules were neither vague nor inconsistent. Thus, once the IAAF showed that Slaney had a T/E ratio greater than six to one, Slaney had to come forth and show by clear and convincing evidence that the elevated ratio was attributable to a pathological or physiological condition. Believing that it was scientifically impossible to prove by clear and convincing evidence that her high T/E ratio was due to pathological or physiological factors, Slaney withdrew from the arbitration, followed by the USATF. Ultimately, the Tribunal ruled that Slaney had committed a doping offense.

Slaney filed suit in the District Court for the Southern District of Indiana raising numerous state-law contract and tort claims against both the IAAF and the USOC. *** On November 5, 1999, the district court entered a judgment and order dismissing Slaney's state-law claims against the IAAF and USOC pursuant to Fed.R.Civ.P. 12(b)(1), and dismissing Slaney's 18 U.S.C. §§ 1962(c) and (d) claims pursuant to Fed.R.Civ.P. 12(b)(6). Specifically, the district court held that the United Nations Convention on the Recognition and Enforcement of Foreign Arbitral Awards, 9 U.S.C. § 201 ("New York Convention"), barred Slaney's claims against the IAAF, as those claims had been the subject of a valid arbitration decision. With regard to Slaney's claims against the USOC, the court held that the Amateur Sports Act, 36 U.S.C. § 220501 *et seq.*, gives the USOC the exclusive right to determine disputes over eligibility and does not create a private right of action.***

Slaney now appeals the decision of the district court. She contends that (1) the New York Convention does not bar her claims against the IAAF [and] (2) the Amateur Sports Act does not preempt all state-law claims made by an athlete against the USOC.***

NEW YORK CONVENTION DEFENSES

* * *

Article V(1)(b) of the New York Convention states that recognition and enforcement of an award may be refused if the party against whom it is invoked furnishes proof that it "was not given proper notice of the appointment of the arbitrator or of the arbitration proceedings or *was otherwise unable to present his case.*" (emphasis added). A court of appeals reviews a district court's decision confirming an arbitration award under ordinary standards: accepting findings of fact that are not clearly erroneous and deciding questions of law *de novo*. [Case Citations Omitted] As we have noted, in order to comport with the requirement that a party to a foreign arbitration be able to present her case, we require that the arbitrator provide a fundamentally fair hearing. A fundamentally fair hearing is one that "meets the minimal requirements of fairness – adequate notice, a hearing on the evidence, and an impartial decision by the arbitrator." Nevertheless, parties that have chosen to remedy their disputes through arbitration rather than litigation should not expect the same procedures they would find in the judicial arena. Specifically, concerning evidentiary matters, the Supreme Court has noted that "[a]rbitrators are not bound by the rules of evidence." *Bernhardt v. Polygraphic Co.*, 350 U.S. 198, 203-04 n. 4, 76 S.Ct. 273, 100 L.Ed. 199 (1956). The extent of an arbitrator's latitude is such that an "arbitrator is not bound to hear all of the evidence tendered by the parties.... [H]e must [merely] give each of the parties to the dispute an adequate opportunity to present its evidence and arguments." It is when the exclusion of relevant evidence actually deprived a party of a fair hearing that it is appropriate to vacate an arbitral award. *See id.*

***[W]e [have] surveyed several cases in which an arbitrator's award was not enforced by the courts on the grounds raised now by Slaney. For example, in *Tempo Shain Corp. v. Bertek, Inc.*, 120 F.3d 16, 21 (2d Cir.1997), the court held that...an arbitration panel's refusal to continue hearings to allow a witness to testify, the only witness with evidence of fraud not found from other sources, was fundamental unfairness and misconduct sufficient to vacate the award. In *Iran Aircraft Indus. v. Avco Corp.*, 980 F.2d 141, 146 (2d Cir.1992), a court also vacated an arbitration award, in that instance because the tribunal changed evidentiary rules during the hearing and thus prevented a party from presenting its documentary evidence. [Case Citations Omitted] Our examination of these cases leads us to conclude that Slaney's allegation has no merit. *** Slaney was not denied an opportunity to present her evidence. *** As such, Slaney's complaint does not truly attack the procedure implemented by the arbitration panel, but rather an underlying evidentiary decision of the panel. Unfortunately for Slaney, as the Supreme Court has noted, arbitrators are not bound by the rules of evidence. *Bernhardt*, 350 U.S. at 203-04 n. 4, 76 S.Ct. 273. Thus, this attempted defense must fail.

* * *

Thus, having found that (1) Slaney participated in the IAAF arbitration, (2) her present state-law complaint seeks to relitigate issues decided by the IAAF Tribunal, (3) the New York Convention mandates enforcement of the arbitrator's decision, and (4) there is no defense that should bar enforcement of the arbitration decision, we find that the district court did not err in dismissing Slaney's state-law claims against the IAAF pursuant to Fed.R.Civ.P. 12(b)(1).

STATE-LAW CLAIMS AGAINST THE USOC

* * *

According to the Amateur Sports Act, one of the purposes of the USOC is to exercise exclusive jurisdiction over all matters pertaining to United States participation in the Olympic Games. *See* 36 U.S.C. § 220503(3). The Act also states that the USOC is designed "to provide swift resolution of conflicts and disputes involving amateur athletes, national governing bodies, and amateur sports organizations," and "to encourage and provide assistance to amateur athletic activities for women." *Id.* at §§ 220503(8), 220503(12).

Beginning with the often quoted language from the concurrence in *Michels v. United States Olympic Committee*, the district court reiterated that "there can be few less suitable bodies than the federal courts for determining the eligibility, or procedures for determining the eligibility, of athletes to participate in the Olympic Games." 741 F.2d 155, 159 (7th Cir.1984) (Posner, J., concurring). From there, the court cited numerous cases which have adopted the principle that eligibility decisions fall within the USOC's exclusive jurisdiction over all matters pertaining to United States participation in the Olympic Games. For example, in *Dolan v. United States Equestrian Team*, Inc., 257 N.J.Super. 314, 608 A.2d 434, 437 (App.Div.1992), the court focused on the need for uniformity in determining questions of eligibility, and held "that it would be inappropriate to attribute different or unique meanings to [the Amateur Sports Act's] provisions in New Jersey and thus create a jurisdictional sanctuary from the Congressional determination that these types of disputes should be resolved outside the judicial processes." Similarly, in *Walton-Floyd v. United States Olympic Committee*, 965 S.W.2d 35, 40 (Tex.Ct.App.1998), the court noted that "[t]he interest of maintaining consistent interpretations among jurisdictions requires the Act to pre-empt claims asserted under state tort law. To hold a common law duty exists outside the scope of the Act, thereby enabling an individual athlete to bring suit, threatens to override legislative intent and opens the door to inconsistent interpretations of the Act." We agree with the district court and the courts in *Dolan and Walton-Floyd* that strict questions of athletes' eligibility are preempted by the Amateur Sports Act's grant of exclusive jurisdiction to the USOC over all matters pertaining to United States participation in the Olympic Games. However, that conclusion does not end our analysis.

* * *

While there is no dispute that the USOC has exclusive jurisdiction when it comes to eligibility determinations, the courts can still play a role in ensuring that the organization follows its rules for determining eligibility. The extent of the courts' powers in this area was previously examined by way of a suit brought by an athlete who captured the world's attention for reasons other than her competitive achievements. In *Harding v. United States Figure Skating Ass'n*, 851 F.Supp. 1476, 1479 (D.Or.1994) *vacated on other grounds*, 879 F.Supp. 1053 (D.Or.1995), the court defined (we believe correctly), the limited role that federal courts should play in eligibility determinations. There, the court cautioned that "courts should rightly hesitate before intervening in disciplinary hearings held by private associations.... Intervention is appropriate only in the most extraordinary circumstances, where the association has clearly breached its own rules, that breach will imminently result in *serious* and irreparable harm to the plaintiff, and the plaintiff has exhausted all internal remedies." Yet, while carving out this limited exception to the preemption created by the Amateur Sports Act, the opinion forewarned that while examining whether internal rules had been complied with, the courts "should not intervene in the merits of the underlying dispute." *Id.*

With this understanding of the limits of preemption, we turn to Slaney's claims against the USOC. Slaney suggests that nothing in the Act precludes her from bringing her state-law claims regarding the USOC's administration of its drug testing program, and specifically "the unlawful manner in which the USOC conducts its doping program." Based on our analysis above, we disagree. An inspection of the state-law claims that Slaney brings against the USOC reveals that, despite her best efforts to suggest to the contrary, Slaney is challenging the method by which the USOC determines eligibility of its athletes. Slaney's first state-law cause of action against the USOC is a breach of contract claim. ***

[T]he USOC has exclusive jurisdiction, under the Amateur Sports Act, to determine all matters pertaining to eligibility of athletes. Yet, Slaney cannot escape the fact that her state-law claims, whether framed as breach of contract, negligence, breach of fiduciary duty, fraud, constructive fraud, or negligent misrepresentation, are actually challenges to the method by which the USOC determines eligibility of athletes. Slaney does not suggest that the organization contravened its own guidelines, and as Slaney freely admits, the Amateur Sports Act creates no private cause of action. Thus, the district court was correct in determining that it lacked subject matter jurisdiction over Slaney's state-law claims against the USOC and thus in dismissing those causes of action pursuant to Fed.R.Civ.P. 12(b)(1).

CONCLUSION

Slaney participated in a valid arbitration with the IAAF which, under the New York Convention, we are obligated to recognize. Thus, the issue decided in that arbitration cannot be relitigated. Because adjudication of the state-law claims alleged against the IAAF in Slaney's complaint would necessitate relitigation of the issue decided in the arbitration, the district court correctly determined that it lacked subject-matter jurisdiction over those claims. Likewise, the district court correctly determined that it lacked jurisdiction to adjudicate Slaney's state-law claims against the USOC, finding that those claims were preempted by Congress's grant of exclusive authority to the USOC to determine the eligibility of American athletes. ***

For the foregoing reasons, we AFFIRM the decision of the district court.

NOTES & QUESTIONS

1. Jurisdiction is the power (or authority) to decide any given issue. Certain courts have jurisdiction to decide certain types of cases. State courts, for example, typically have jurisdiction to decide contract and tort disputes. Federal courts have jurisdiction over matters of Federal Constitutional law. Is one aspect of this case simply a question about what entity has jurisdiction to decide factual issues? What entity has the authority to determine whether there has been a doping violation? Is the final arbiter USATF, the USOC, or the IAAF?

2. To what extent or degree should the courts be involved in reviewing the determinations of independent bodies such as USATF, the USOC, IAAF, or decisions made by arbitrators? Explain your answer. As you think about this question, focus in particular on the following statement made by the court:

> In *Harding v. United States Figure Skating Ass'n*, 851 F.Supp. 1476, 1479 (D.Or.1994) *vacated on other grounds*, 879 F.Supp. 1053 (D.Or.1995), the court defined (we believe correctly), the limited role that federal courts should play in eligibility determinations. There, the court

cautioned that "courts should rightly hesitate before intervening in disciplinary hearings held by private associations.... Intervention is appropriate only in the most extraordinary circumstances, where the association has clearly breached its own rules, that breach will imminently result in *serious* and irreparable harm to the plaintiff, and the plaintiff has exhausted all internal remedies."

In 2015-2017, many NFL fans (and certainly many New England Patriots fans) paid a great deal of attention to the so-called "Deflategate" case. The NFL Commissioner, Roger Goodell, using the authority granted to him under the NFL's collective bargaining agreement with the NFL Players Association, upheld the League's punishment (*i.e.,* a 4-game suspension) of Patriots quarterback, Tom Brady, for Brady's alleged role in using under-inflated footballs during the Patriots' win January 18, 2015 over the Indianapolis Colts during the AFC Championship Game. After the District Court judge overturned the suspension – allowing allowing Brady to play the following season –, on appeal, the Second Circuit Court of Appeals ultimately overruled the District Court. Judge Barrington Daniels Parker's opinion makes it clear that the Court was not in a position to rebuke the NFL and Goodell's decision, in part because the decision to suspend Brady resulted from a process established by the collective bargaining agreement (*Natl. Football League Mgt. Council v. Natl. Football League Players Ass'n*, 125 F. Supp. 3d 449 (S.D.N.Y. 2015), *rev'd*, 820 F.3d 527 (2d Cir. 2016). The same principle appears in footnote number two of the *Delisa Walton-Floyd* case, which also cites *Harding*. For a summary of Deflategate, *see* https://en.wikipedia.org/wiki/Deflategate.

3. Today many sports contracts as well as the constitutions and/or bylaws of many sports organizations and professional leagues stipulate that controversies will be decided by private arbitration (*e.g.,* American Arbitration Association/AAA) rather than litigated by the courts. As this case explains, arbitration panels typically need not follow the rules of evidence that apply in the regular state and federal court systems. As a rule, arbitration decisions are quicker and less expensive than litigation in the courts. The *Slaney* case illustrates a bedrock principle of our public policy regarding arbitration. As a rule, courts refuse to review the validity of arbitration decisions unless exceptional or egregious unfairness will result.

4. What should the relationship be between science (*i.e.,* the technology available to test for the presence of banned substances) and sports?

5. What level of scientific reliability should be required to render an athlete ineligible? Explain your answer.

6. The March 1982 issue of *Track & Field News* reported the following at page 54:
Getting around the IAAF's ban on anabolic steroids hasn't been too tough, as most users simply switch to testosterone, which has been legal. The "legality," however, has arisen only

because there was no reliable test to prove whether or not the testosterone, which aids in building muscle mass, was the body's own or had been induced.

That fly has been removed from the ointment, the IOC announced in early February, as Medical Commission Chairman Prince Alexandre de Merode revealed that West German Researcher Dr. Manfred Donicke had established a reliable testing procedure.

The method involves calculating the ratio between two naturally occurring substances – epitestosterone and testosterone. Apparently only certain ratios can occur naturally, and any administration of foreign testosterone will upset the balance.

7. Mary Decker Slaney was the only American runner, man or woman to hold all American records from 800 to 10,000-meters at the same time, and was inducted into the National Distance Running Hall of Fame in 2003.

Mary Decker Slaney, photo reprinted with permission of the National Distance Running Hall of Fame

Sports Court Rules American Gymnast Paul Hamm Can Keep His Disputed Olympic Gold

By Nancy Armour, AP Sports Writer Oct 21, 2004

Paul Hamm can keep his Olympic gold medal.

Sports' highest court rejected a South Korean appeal Thursday, ruling that Hamm is the rightful champion in the men's all-around gymnastics competition at the Athens Games.

"The decision from CAS confirms what I've always felt in my heart, which is that I was champion that night and Olympic gold medalist," Hamm said. "I was just pleased it's all over with."

The decision by a three-judge panel from the Court of Arbitration for Sport ends a saga that began more than two months ago, when South Korea's Yang Tae-young claimed a scoring error cost him the title. Yang finished with the bronze medal.

Yang asked the court to order international gymnastics officials to change the results, and adjust the medal rankings so he would get the gold and Hamm the silver. But the judges dismissed the appeal, leaving Hamm with the gold and Yang with his bronze. Kim Dae-eun of South Korea was the silver medalist.

The verdict is final and cannot be appealed.

"An error identified with the benefit of hindsight, whether admitted or not, cannot be a ground for reversing a result of a competition," the judges said.

Hamm won the gold Aug. 18, rallying from 12th place with only two events left to become the first American man to win gymnastics' biggest prize.

But two days later, gymnastics officials discovered that Yang had been wrongly docked a tenth of a point on his second-to-last routine, the parallel bars. Yang ended up with the bronze, 0.049 points behind Hamm. Add that extra 0.100, though, and Yang would have finished on top, 0.051 points ahead of the American.

That, however, assumes everything in the final rotation played out the same way - a big if.

The International Gymnastics Federation (FIG) acknowledged the error and suspended three judges. But it said repeatedly it would not change the results because the South Koreans didn't protest until after the meet.

In their ruling, the judges said the Korean protest was submitted too late - and added that the court was not in a position to correct results even if a mistake were admitted.

"The solution for error, either way, lies within the framework of the sport's own rules," the panel said.

In Athens, the South Koreans appealed to the U.S. Olympic Committee and the International Olympic Committee. It brought back memories of the figure skating scandal at the Salt Lake City Games in 2002, when Canadians Jamie Sale and David Pelletier were given duplicate gold medals after a French judge said she had been "pressured" to put a Russian couple ahead of them.

But there were no such signs of impropriety in this case, and IOC president Jacques Rogge flatly refused to even consider the idea of giving Yang a gold medal.

Then FIG president Bruno Grandi confused the issue, writing a letter to Hamm and asking him to surrender the gold medal. In the letter, Grandi wrote, "The true winner of the all-around competition is Yang Tae-young."

Buoyed by that statement, Yang filed an appeal on the final day of the games with CAS.

The panel praised both gymnasts, saying they "have comported themselves with dignity, despite the controversy."

"They were the victims of this unusual case because a shadow of doubts has been cast over Hamm's achievement in winning the sport's most prestigious prize and because Yang may have been deprived of an opportunity of winning it," CAS said.

The tug-of-war over the medal has overshadowed Hamm's performance, one of the greatest comebacks in gymnastics history.

The defending world champion appeared to lose a chance at any medal, let alone the gold, when he botched the landing of his vault and stumbled backward, plopping down on a judges' table. His score of 9.137 dropped him to 12th place with only two events left.

But one by one, the gymnasts above him faltered. And Hamm was spectacular, closing with a pair of 9.837s on the parallel bars and high bar to win the gold.

"I feel like I had to win my medal in three ways, really," Hamm said last month in an interview with The Associated Press. "Obviously, in competition. Then with the media. Then in court. It really feels like I've been battling this whole time."

NOTES & QUESTIONS

1. Presumably, judging and umpiring errors will always occur in sport. In addition to the simple subjective nature of judging some sports (*e.g.,* equestrian, diving, figure skating, gymnastics), some officiating will inevitably result in errors of judgment (e.g., a replay reveals that a runner at first base is safe not out, a line call in tennis, and the like). Some sports such as fencing use sophisticated electronic equipment to assist judges. The same is true when football referees consult an instant replay or when basketball officials review a replay in order to determine whether a shot was released before or after time had expired. But as the Hamm situation demonstrates, occasionally officials will make quantitative, mathematical errors that can seriously alter the outcome of a contest. Should courts be involved in reviewing any of these types of officiating errors? Appellate judges are accustomed to review the decisions of trial court judges for error. Why should courts not be permitted to review the decisions of sports judges as well?

2. If courts were to get into the business of reviewing sports officials, can you suggest what sort of standard of review ought to be applied? Are there certain types of determinations (mistakes about rules...like mistakes about law, mistakes about facts, mistakes about interpretations?), which lend themselves to judicial review better than others? Explain your answer.

3. The CAS recently reached a similar conclusion in *Behdad Salimi & NOCIRI v. IWF.,* CAS ad hoc Division OG 16/028. The CAS refused to overturn the internal-sport-jury (*i.e.,* not a court jury) competition decision to overturn a weightlifting referee's determination regarding whether a competitor's lift was valid. The CAS stated that it could not reverse a field-of-play decision unless that decision was made in bad faith.

4. As mentioned in note 1, controversial calls and non-calls frequently occur. When the stakes are particularly high – such as in a playoff or other high-profile situation, the consequences can be extreme. And it is not uncommon for some to speculate about the possibility of exploring legal action to appeal decisions of sports officials. For example, on January 20, 2019, in the NFC Championship game between the Los Angeles Rams and New Orleans Saints, the on-field officials failed to call pass interference on a play that is generally acknowledged to have been blatant pass interference. *See e.g.,* https://www.foxnews.com/sports/controversial-rams-saints-no-call-overshadows-nfc-championship. And on May 4, 2019, after reviewing video replay, Churchill Downs officials (stewards) disqualified apparent Kentucky Derby winner Maximum Security for intereference, and awarded the runner-up, Country House, the victory. *See e.g.,* https://www.cbsnews.com/news/2019-kentucky-derby-winner-country-

house-win-after-maximum-security-win-disqualification-official-results-payouts/. For a discussion of many of these issues, *see e.g.,* Russ VerSteeg and Kimberley Maruncic, *Instant Replay: A Contemporary Legal Analysis,* 4 Mississippi Sports L.Rev. 153 (2015).

THREE STRIKES AND YOU'RE (NOT NECESSARILY) OUT: HOW BASEBALL'S ERRATIC APPROACH TO CONDUCT VIOLATIONS IS NOT IN THE BEST INTEREST OF THE GAME

MATTHEW A. FOOTE

6 DEPAUL J. SPORTS L. & CONTEMPORARY PROBS. 1 (2009 FALL)

On-the-Field Drug Violations: Performance-Enhancing Drugs

Performance-enhancing drugs have created a major concern in both amateur and professional sports. The Mitchell Report[1] produced startling revelations about the wide spread use of steroids in Baseball and could instigate dramatic changes in MLB's approach to drug use in the game, particularly when the CBA is renegotiated after the current CBA expires in 2011. Indeed, the Mitchell Report concluded that it "has not been an isolated problem involving just a few players or a few clubs."[2] In fact, "each of the thirty clubs has had players who have been involved with performance enhancing substances at some time in their careers."[3] The impetus for the Mitchell investigation was "speculation . . . originally fueled by the testimony of players before a federal grand jury investigating" alleged performance-enhancing drugs supplied to players by a San Francisco company named BALCO.[4] It is believed that New York Yankee Jason Giambi admitted to steroid use while testifying before that grand jury.[5] A recent book entitled *Game of Shadows* alleges that MLB stars Barry Bonds, Giambi, Gary Sheffield and others have long used steroids.[6]

In 2002, Baseball implemented its first mandatory random drug testing of players.[7] The league tests for performance-enhancing drugs as well as recreational drugs, and as of 2005 the policy provides for "a 50-game suspension for a first positive test, a 100-game suspension for

---

1 George J. Mitchell, DLA Piper US LLC, Report to the Commissioner of Baseball of an Independent Investigation Into the Illegal Use of Steroids and Other Performance Enhancing Substances by Players in Major League Baseball, Dec. 13, 2007, http://assets.espn.go.com/media/pdf/071213/mitchell_report.pdf [hereinafter Mitchell Report].

2 Mitchell Report, at SR-1.

3 Id.

4 Barry M. Bloom, Selig Announces Steroid Investigation, MLB, Mar. 30, 2006, http://mlb.mlb.com/news/article. jsp?ymd=20060330&content_id=1374385&vkey=news_mlb&fext=.jsp&c_id=mlb.

5 Mark Fainaru-Wada & Lance Williams, Giambi Admitted Taking Steroids, S.F. Chron., Dec. 2, 2004, at A1, available at 2004 WLNR 12912648.

6 Mark Fainaru-Wada & Lance Williams, Game of Shadows 142-3 (Gotham Books 2006).

7 MLB, Drug Policy in Baseball Timeline, MLB, http:// mlb.mlb.com/mlb/news/drug_policy.jsp?content=timeline (last visited June 30, 2009).

a second positive test, and a permanent suspension for a third positive test."[8] All of these suspensions are without pay. The Mitchell Report concluded that Baseball's drug testing program has been successful in that "detectable steroid use appears to have declined."[9] Nevertheless, the laundry list of current and former players who have reportedly tested positive for steroids, human growth hormone (HGH) or other performance-enhancing drugs is growing daily. The list includes Rick Ankiel, Paul Byrd, Mike Cameron, Ken Caminiti, Troy Glaus, Jose Guillen, Gary Matthews, Jr., Rafael Palmeiro, Sammy Sosa, Manny Ramirez, Matt Williams and many others.[10] The news about Palmeiro, a potential Hall of Famer, was particularly appalling after his adamant, finger-pointing denial while testifying before Congress.

In addition to these positive tests, nearly ninety major leaguers were named in the Mitchell Report, including Bonds, Andy Pettitte and seven-time Cy Young Award-winner Roger Clemens. A-Rod, who many hoped would someday restore the integrity of the home run record from the Bonds' steroid taint, admitted in 2009 to using steroids.[11] According to the Mitchell Report, former MVP Caminiti once estimated that at least half of major leaguers were using steroids.[12] Part of the ongoing problem is that players have shrewdly switched from steroids to HGH. The Mitchell Report recognized that "the use of human growth hormone has risen because, unlike steroids, it is not detectable through urine testing."[13] While HGH was added to the CBA as a banned substance in 2005, this is meaningless without the ability to test for HGH.[14]

For obvious reasons, this type of conduct transgression negatively affects both the image and the integrity of the game. First, like other criminal activity, steroid use damages the image of the game because it is illegal.[15] The integrity of the game is also jeopardized whenever anything other than natural competitive spirit influences the outcome of games. The Mitchell Report also mentioned concerns about steroid use that are analogous to concerns raised about players' associations with gamblers. The Report concluded that because of the illegality involved, players "can place themselves in a position of vulnerability to drug dealers who might use their access

8   See Major League Baseball's Joint Drug Prevention and Treatment Program, § 6(E)(2006); Major League Baseball's Joint Drug Prevention and Treatment Program, § 6(E) (2005).

9   Mitchell Report at SR-1.

10 See Steroids Suspensions, Baseball Almanac, http://www.baseball-almanac.com/legendary/steroids_baseball.shtml (last visited June 30, 2009); see also Rick Morrissey, Truth Be Known, Roping Honest MLB Doper Tough, Chi. Trib., Nov. 11, 2007, available at 2007 WLNR 22293296. HGH has become a drug of choice because, thus far, it is undetectable by testing. Mitchell Report at SR-2.

11 A-Rod Admits, Regrets Use of PED, ESPN, Feb. 10, 2009, http:// sports.espn.go.com/mlb/news/story?id=3894847 (last visited June 30, 2009) [Hereinafter A-Rod].

12 MITCHELL REPORT, at SR-2.

13 Id. at SR-1.

14 Id at SR-13.

15 Id. at SR-10. "Anabolic steroids are ... controlled substances under the federal Controlled Substances Act ... it is illegal to use or possess steroids or steroid precursors without a valid physician's prescription. Violations ... carry penalties similar to those applicable to the illegal use or possession of narcotics. Human growth hormone is a prescription medication. It is illegal to issue a prescription for human growth hormone except for very limited purposes. Human growth hormone never has been approved ... to improve athletic performance. Issuing a prescription for human growth hormone for any of these unauthorized purposes is a violation of federal law. Id.

and knowledge of violations of law to their own advantage, through threats intended to affect the outcome of baseball games or otherwise."[16]

Additionally, performance-enhancing drugs, like steroids and HGH, give some players a chemically created advantage over other players. Thus, their use is considered cheating. The image of the game is tarnished if its stars are viewed as cheaters. Much of the appeal of sport is the competition to discover which athlete's natural athletic ability and hard work will prevail. The current era of Baseball has come to be known as the "Steroid Era," and there have been cries for records and statistics from this era to be marked with asterisks. Indeed, the Mitchell Report states that "the widespread use of these substances raises questions about the validity of records and their comparability across different eras."[17]

Bonds's use of performance-enhancing drugs is now well documented in his indictment and his inclusion in the Mitchell Report.[18] In fact, the indictment stated that "during the criminal investigation, evidence was obtained, including positive tests for the presence of anabolic steroids and other performance-enhancing substances, for Bonds."[19] Baseball's reaction to the Bonds prosecution will illustrate the seriousness with which Baseball views performance-enhancing drugs, particularly with regard to his Hall of Fame eligibility and the handling of Bonds in the record books.

Conclusions to Draw From the Mitchell Report

It may still be too early to draw conclusions about the long-term effects that the Mitchell Report may have on Baseball. As mentioned, renegotiation of the CBA in 2011 will reveal the measure of the Report's effect. However, one thing is known: Baseball will not likely be able to punish players for steroid use that occurred prior to 2002. Surprisingly, prior to the 2002-2006 CBA, performance-enhancing drugs were never specifically prohibited.[20] Indeed, A-Rod admitted to steroid use during this period and received no punishment.[21]

Therefore, even if Bonds used steroids while breaking the single-season home run record in 2001, Baseball would be hard-pressed to justify an asterisk next to his name in the record books

---

16 Mitchell Report, at 4.

17 Id.

18 Id. at 113.

19 Barry M. Bloom, Bonds Indicted on Federal Charges, MLB, Nov. 16, 2007, http://mlb.mlb.com/news/article.jsp?ymd=20071115&content_id=2301117&vkey=news_mlb&fext=.jsp&c_id=mlb [hereinafter Bonds Indicted].

20 Drug Policy in Baseball Timeline, supra note 7. The illegal use of prescription drugs has been prohibited in Baseball since 1971. See Notice No. 12, Memorandum from Major League Baseball Office of the Commissioner to Administrative Officials of Major and Minor League Ball Clubs Re: Drug Education and Prevention Program, Apr. 5, 1971, P 9 ("Baseball must insist its personnel comply with the federal and state drug laws. It is your obligation to be familiar with these drug laws."). However, punishing players named in the Mitchell Report for offenses prior to 2002 would require proof of illegality, and no players named have been punished. Additionally, the Mitchell Report recommended that the Commissioner forego disciplining players for past offenses revealed in the report. Mitchell Report, at SR-33.

21 A-Rod, supra note 11.

for that record.[22] In addition, the indictment concerns testimony Bonds gave in 2003 about his alleged steroid use from 1999-2002, before the most recent CBA.[23] Bonds has never tested positive for steroids in league testing. Therefore, Baseball may be forced to punish Bonds by using the "best interests of the game" clause rather than any specific drug provisions. Considering Bonds's stature in the game, this will be a landmark decision for Commissioner Selig or his successors. Like Pete Rose, Bonds is clearly one of the greatest to ever play the game. However, unlike Rose, Bonds's on-field accomplishments are also tainted, as any steroid use would have boosted his performance. Bonds will be a sure Hall of Famer unless the Commissioner takes action preventing his induction.

Many players, MLBPA officials and the media have criticized the Mitchell Report. Some questioned Senator Mitchell's neutrality because: he was hired by the Commissioner to investigate; he serves on the board of directors of the Boston Red Sox; the law firm where he was a senior partner was used to conduct the investigation; and notable Red Sox players like David Ortiz and Manny Ramirez, who subsequently were linked to steroid use, were omitted from the Mitchell Report.[24] Secondly, since this distrust contributed to the Mitchell investigation being stone-walled by the players and the MLBPA, its findings included no player testimony. Further, the overwhelming majority of the Mitchell Report's evidence was supplied by only two sources, both of whom were former employees of major league teams.[25] Some have argued that testimony from two disgruntled employees simply is not enough to publicly accuse such a high number of players. Thus, many have dismissed the Report's findings as "unsubstantiated allegations."[26] Nevertheless, the fact that testimony and evidence provided by only two witnesses produced nearly ninety names cannot help but fuel speculation that the actual number of steroid users was even higher. Therefore, the real importance of the Mitchell Report is not the list of players included, but will be determined by whether or not Baseball is "shocked into action" to aggressively address drug use.[27]

---

22 In 2007, Bonds broke the all-time home run record. Since he has never tested positive for steroids, those calling for an asterisk next to his name will be disappointed even hard evidence surfaces of steroid use by Bonds prior to 2002.

23 Bonds Indicted, supra note 19.

24 Howard Bryant, Friction and Fractures Erode Faith in Mitchell's Investigation, ESPN, Dec. 11, 2007, http://sports.espn. go.com/mlb/news/story? id=3142651 ("neither Mitchell nor Selig anticipated the degree to which [these] relationships ... affected the confidence level of team executives ... who view those relationships as conflicts of interest that should have disqualified Mitchell.") Id. Only Mitchell's conflict of interests, not his personal credibility, has been challenged. The former judge and senator is widely-respected as a knowledgeable baseball man with integrity. Id. Mitchell was even twice nearly President Clinton's Supreme Court nominee. See Jeffrey Toobin, The Nine: Inside the Secret World of the Supreme Court 64, 74-6 (2007). Tom Verducci, Latest News Makes This a Dark, Dirty Day for Red Sox, Sports Illust., July 20, 2009, http:// sportsillustrated.cnn.com/2009/writers/tom_ verducci/07/30/manny.ortiz.index.html (last visited September 8, 2009).

25 The two former employees are former Mets clubhouse employee Kirk Radomski, and former Yankees trainer Brian McNamee. See generally Mitchell Report.

26 Orioles Issue Statement in Response to Mitchell Report, ESPN, Dec. 16, 2007, http://sports.espn.go.com/mlb/news/story?id=3156785.

27 Mitchell Report, at SR-9.

"Zero Tolerance" to What Effect?: The Case of J. C. Romero

As with other types of conduct violations, Baseball's response to performance-enhancing drug violations can contradict common sense. In 2008, Phillies pitcher J. C. Romero tested positive for a banned substance days before he was due to pitch in Game 5 of the World Series.[28] The hearing took place during the World Series and it was announced he would serve a fifty game suspension. However, this was not the typical steroids case. Romero had purchased a supplement from a local General Nutrition Store (GNC) he believed was approved for use under Baseball's rules. He personally checked the label, obtained opinions from two different nutritionists and his strength and conditioning coach. All sources claimed the supplement was approved. Furthermore, Romero relied on a MLBPA memorandum stating that any supplements purchased over the counter at a GNC were approved. However, the manufacturer of the supplement omitted a banned ingredient from the label. Although Romero could not realistically have known, Baseball still found him negligent for not discovering the banned ingredient.

This zero tolerance policy seems ridiculous in Romero's case. "If I made a mistake, it was to put all my trust in my superiors, the people I thought knew what they were doing," Romero stated in May 2009.[29] Romero was misled by the manufacturers of the supplement who misrepresented the contents of their product. While strict penalties will presumably deter drug use, cases like Romero's demonstrate the need for fact-specific inquiries and punishments tailored to specific circumstances.

Curiously, a 2006 incident also involving Romero further exemplifies how erratic the process can be. Romero tested positive for high levels of hormones as a result of a fertility supplement his wife and he were taking. Baseball eventually cleared Romero. Oddly, Baseball found it fit to look at the circumstances and facts surrounding that violation but not the later violation involving the GNC supplement. These examples illustrate the need for consistent but common sense based governance of conduct violations in Baseball.

Conclusion – Some Suggested Solutions

While the Mitchell Report only addresses steroid use, the process of the investigation and its recommendations are instructive on the more general issue of conduct violations. For example, the resistance by the MLBPA to the Mitchell Report demonstrates that any plan aimed at disciplining players will be extremely difficult to implement. The Mitchell Report laments that the MLBPA was "largely uncooperative," in that it rejected requests for documents and interviews with witnesses and MLBPA officers, and discouraged players from cooperating with the investigation.[30] Indeed, nearly all players refused to meet with the Mitchell investigators. While it is surprising that the MLBPA does not see the importance of drug testing to protect its members,

---

28 Peter Gammons, Suspended Romero 'Didn't Cheat', ESPN, Jan. 6, 2009, http://sports.espn.go.com/mlb/news/story?id=3812334.

29 Jim Salisburg, J.C. Romero plunges back in, Phila. Inq., May 19, 2009, http://www.philly.com/inquirer/sports/20090519_J_C__Romero_plunges_back_ in.html.

30 Mitchell Report, at SR-7.

its cooperation is necessary since federal law generally requires that discipline plans be collectively bargained.

Nevertheless, aggressive action is required to stem the increase in all conduct violations in Baseball. Baseball, for example, has adopted appropriately stiff penalties for on-the-field conduct violations. As the Mitchell Report concludes, the harsh penalty for performance-enhancing drug use has helped curb the number of positive tests.[31]

One recommendation made by the Mitchell Report provides a potentially viable framework for Baseball to counteract the growing concern of conduct violations. First, the Mitchell Report recommends that Baseball form a "Department of Investigations."[32] While the Mitchell Report does not suggest the structure of this Department in great detail, it would be helpful if it were made up of former players and coaches, as well as MLB employees. Thus, investigations and disciplinary decisions – when discretion is needed – can be made with the utmost possible impartiality. The Department of Investigations should also include a full-time steroid czar, with expertise in the science of drug-testing and abuse. This would help Baseball stay ahead in the technological race between the production of performance-enhancing drugs and the ability to detect them, as well as prevent situations like the J. C. Romero incident. It is also important that the Department of Investigations be given the authority to investigate possible conduct violations that have not resulted in criminal investigations but nevertheless may tarnish the image of the game.

As the Mitchell Report shows, Baseball kept its head in the sand about steroid abuse for nearly two decades. Despite the fact that Commissioner Ueberroth warned that performance-enhancing drugs would damage the integrity of the game in 1985, Baseball did not "push hard" for testing until 2002.[33] If Baseball had addressed the drug problem sooner, there would not have been a need for the Mitchell Report. On a larger scale, if Baseball were to implement a uniform, systemic program for violations, inappropriate player conduct could be better enforced and prevented.

NOTES & QUESTIONS

1. Obviously, the place of performance-enhancing drugs (such as anabolic steroids) in sports has been a major topic of discussion in the national and international media during the past several years. As Foote's article suggests, Major League Baseball and the National Football League have been nearly turned upside-down examining the issue. Presumably, rule makers have decided to ban such substances on two grounds. First they provide users an "unfair advantage." Second, they pose serious health risks to their users. Therefore, in order to preserve the integrity of sport and to provide a level playing field among participants, and

---

31 Id. at SR-2. The Mitchell Report chronicles how MLBPA objection to drug testing caused a delay in implementation of nearly twenty years. Id. at SR-13.

32 Mitchell Report, at 287.

33 Id. at 307.

in order to prevent undue health risks to participants, such substances are prohibited. For an excellent summary and discussion of cases and issues relating to PED's and professional baseball, *see* Louis H. Schiff and Robert M. Jarvis, Baseball and the Law: Cases and Materials "Notes" 148-155 (2016).

2. What criteria should rule makers use to determine what substances are prohibited and what substances are permitted? Where do we draw the line between advanced nutrition versus "illegal" substances? Should there be a uniform standard among all major sports? Why or why not?

3. As is true with computer hackers, are not the cheaters always going to be just one step ahead of the enforcement officials?

4. Isn't this the type of problem that simply will never go away? Is the use of technology to enhance performance any different from the use of technology to enhance athletic equipment? Rule makers regulate the designs and materials of golf clubs, golf balls, baseball bats, football helmets, tennis racquets, and countless other types of sports equipment. Presumably, rule makers must constantly monitor technological progress to prohibit unfair advantage and to prevent safety hazards related to technological improvements in equipment also.

5. Historically, the NFL has placed recreational drugs such as marijuana in a category separate from steroids and other performance-enhancing drugs. While the policy on performance enhancing drugs is one of zero tolerance, for recreational drugs there have been graduated steps of punishment. After an athlete tests positive for recreational drugs, he is given a second test before suspension ensues. Fines and suspension are the result of a third violation. The NFL has treated recreational drugs as more of a medical problem and attempts to get the player professional help to deal with his addiction. *See* Collinsworth, Cris, *The Best Policy: NFL'S Drug Testing,* http://www.nfl.com/news/story/6744864 (last updated October 23, 2003) and O'Hara, Mike, *Rogers Leaves Big Void: Defensive Line is Forced to Scramble in Wake of Tackle's Suspension for Using Banned Substance,* The Detroit News http://detnews.com/apps/pbcs.dll/article?AID=/20061019/SPORTS0101/610190347/1004/ SPORTS (last updated October 19, 2006).

6. Ricky Williams, the notorious Miami Dolphins running back, was suspended for the 2006 season. As a result of being caught in possession of marijuana, his fourth offense, Williams was placed on the CFL negotiation list for the 2006 season. Williams played for the Toronto Argonauts in 2006, but returned to play for the Miami Dolphins for the 2007 season. See Battista, Judy, *Fourth Drug Violation Bars Dolphins' Williams for 2006,* http://select.nytimes. com/gst/abstract.html?res=FA0D17FE385B0C758EDDAD0894DE404482&n=Top%2fReferen ce%2fTimes%20Topics%2fPeople%2fW%2fWilliams%2c%20Ricky. However, he was injured (shoulder) in his first game back on Monday Night Football, November 26, 2007, and missed

the remainder of the season. He had an excellent 2009 season, rushing for over 1,000 yards. See http://en.wikipedia.org/wiki/Ricky_Williams (last visited April 15, 2010).

7. On August 21, 1991, the IAAF put into effect a stringent policy on performance-enhancing drugs. The policy established a minimum suspension of four years (an increase of two years from the previous term). "The suspension would be extended to include the same event from which the athlete was disqualified, which means if a violation occurred in the Olympics and the succeeding Games were scheduled more than four years later, the suspension would remain in effect until the subsequent Olympics ended." Many critics of the new policy claim that such a suspension could potentially end an athlete's career. *See* Janofsky, Michael, *TRACK AND FIELD; I.A.A.F Cracks Down on Use of Steroids*, www.newyorktimes.com, August 22, 1991. The IAAF policy is updated each year, presumably to stay current on new drugs and new regulations. The current policy mandates both in competition and out of competition testing and includes exemptions for therapeutic use. There is no advanced notice afforded to the athletes for out of competition testing with the exception of extenuating circumstances. The list of prohibited substances for out of competition testing ranges from anabolic substances to hormones and diuretics. In terms of in competition testing, the banned list includes stimulants, narcotics, recreational drugs, and glucocorticosteroids. The penalty incurred as a result of a positive test can be anywhere from two months to two years of ineligibility. The new WADA banned substances list, effective January 1, 2019 is available at: https://www.wada-ama.org/en/resources/science-medicine/prohibited-list-documents.

RESOLUTION OF DOPING DISPUTES IN OLYMPIC SPORT: CHALLENGES PRESENTED BY "NON-ANALYTICAL" CASES
CAMERON A. MYLER
40 NEW ENGLAND LAW REVIEW 747 (2006)

I did compete as an Olympic athlete. I never used any performance enhancing substances, and although I represent athletes now who have been charged with the use of substances, I certainly do not endorse it and I see the need for a strong anti-doping program both in Olympic and professional sports. I competed when there were still two Germanies and the women on the East German team seemed to grow by exponential factors every year. When I was sixteen or seventeen and competing, I did not quite understand what that was all about, but I definitely do now.

Most recently, an athlete whom I represented, Christy Gains, was charged with a number of anti-doping rule violations in connection with the Bay Area Laboratory Co-Operative ("BALCO"), and I am sure we have heard more about that than we might want to. For purposes of this discussion, I think BALCO is instructive on a number of issues that have arisen in Olympic sport anti-doping programs.

First, I will give you a little bit of an overview of the process in Olympic sport and how disputes are adjudicated and then I will talk about a couple of particular cases that deal with this notion of a non-analytical positive, *i.e.,* the charging of an athlete with a doping offense when the U.S. Anti-Doping Agency ("USADA") or other doping agency has no positive test.[1]

First, the World Anti-Doping Agency ("WADA") is basically the umbrella under which all anti-doping efforts in the Olympic sphere occur. It was formed in 1999,[2] basically at the behest of the International Olympic Committee and it since has become a more independent entity so it has more perceived fairness and independence. WADA's stated purposes are to protect the fundamental rights of athletes to participate in doping-free sport and thus promote health, fairness, and equality for athletes worldwide,[3] and secondly to ensure harmonized, coordinated, and effective anti-doping programs at the international and national level with regard to the protection, deterrence, and prevention of doping.[4] WADA was really a very big step forward in anti-doping efforts because...there are...more than 200 countries that are members of the International Olympic Committee. Before WADA was created, the countries all had different programs, each of the sports had different programs, and there was not a whole lot of coordination between them. WADA has as its primary document the World Anti-Doping Code (hereinafter "WADA Code"), and all of the stakeholders in the Olympic movement, including the International Olympic Committee, each of the National Olympic Committees, and all of the international federations for sport had to adopt and implement the WADA Code prior to the opening ceremonies of the Olympic Games last year in Athens.[5] Included in the WADA Code... is the definition of doping that has become standard throughout, and the burdens and standard of proof that are required in the adjudication of disputes as well as the types of evidence that can be used to prosecute athletes.

In this country, the U.S. Olympic Committee basically has contracted with the USADA (United States Anti-Doping Agency), which again like WADA is an independent agency. It was formed in 2000[6] to remove the function of drug testing from each of the different sports because of conflicts of interest. Unlike WADA, USADA conducts all of the testing and adjudicates disputes in Olympic sport.

There are a couple of different general types of doping offenses in Olympic sport. In all of the professional sports we are really dealing with just positive tests. In Olympic sport, in addition to the positive tests of a urine or blood sample for a variety of different substances, there is also

1   Sally Jenkins, This Agency Lacks the Inside Dope, WASH. POST, May 17, 2004, at D01, available at http://washingtonpost.com/wp-dyn/articles/A31738-2004 May16.html.

2   World Anti-Doping Agency, WADA History, http://www.wada-ama.org (follow "About WADA – History" hyperlink), (last visited Apr. 6, 2006).

3   World Anti-Doping Agency, Mission, http://www.wada-ama.org (follow "About WADA – Mission" hyperlink), (last visited Apr. 6, 2006).

4   See id.

5   Copenhagen Declaration on Anti-Doping in Sport, Mar. 2003, available at http://www.wada-ama.org/rtecontent/document/copenhagen_en.pdf; WORLD ANTI-DOPING AGENCY, WORLD ANTI-DOPING CODE 6 (2003), available at http://www.wada-ama.org/rtecontent/document/code_v3.pdf.

6   U.S. Anti-Doping Agency, What We Do, http://www.usantidoping.org/what/ (last visited Apr. 6, 2006).

the notion of a "non-analytical positive."[7] The "non-analytic positive" allows USADA to charge athletes with having violated a rule even if they do not have a positive test. It is not really a new concept, but BALCO has since raised some new issues. For example, included within these non-analytical positive cases, could be refusing to submit to drug testing, admitting to the use of a substance, tampering with any part of the drug testing process, missing three tests within an eighteen month period (this actually constitutes a positive test and an athlete would be banned for two years in Olympic sport for having missed three tests), possessing substances, trafficking, administering substances to other athletes (this is really more directed at coaches), encouraging, aiding, abetting, covering up, or any other type of complicity involving an anti-doping rule violation. So, the scope is really quite broad.

Prior to BALCO, some charges were brought based on the forgoing violations, but during the BALCO scandal, a number of Olympic athletes were charged with violations. USADA basically was trying to prove that the Olympic athletes had used substances based on documents that were seized by the federal government in BALCO.

The following are a few comments about the adjudication process itself. If an athlete's sample tests positive or if he or she is charged with some other offense, USADA will submit his or her information to the appropriate review board.[8] The review board decides on the papers alone with no oral argument whether there is evidence to proceed. Not surprisingly there is almost always enough evidence to proceed. At that point, the athlete is formally charged with an offense and a sanction is recommended. The athlete can accept the sanction or he or she can challenge it. Prior to the adoption of the WADA Code, an athlete had the choice of having a case heard under the modified American Arbitration Association (AAA) commercial rules[9] before a panel of one or three arbitrators who are members of the Court of Arbitration for Sport (CAS) in North America.[10] Alternatively, an athlete could go straight to the Court of Arbitration for Sport and pick from about 250 arbitrators worldwide.[11] However, now he or she must go to the AAA first.

It is clear that the anti-doping organization has the burden of proof to establish charges against the athlete. It used to be that many sports required the doping agency to prove its charges beyond a reasonable doubt, but now under the WADA Code the new standard to prove an allegation is "to the comfortable satisfaction of the hearing body bearing in mind the seriousness of the allegation which is made."[12] It is a relatively ambiguous standard, which is not something that a lot of American lawyers are necessarily familiar with, although we are certainly

---

7   Dave Kindred, Smoke, Fire and Tainted Olympic Dreams, SPORTING NEWS, May 31, 2004, at 64, available at http://findarticles.com/p/articles/mi_m1208/is_22_228/ai_n6126783.

8   See U.S. ANTI-DOPING AGENCY, PROTOCOL FOR OLYMPIC MOVEMENT TESTING 5 (2004), available at http://www.usantidoping.org/files/active/what/protocol.pdf.

9   Am. Arbitration Ass'n, Sports Arbitration Including Olympic Athlete Disputes Introduction, http://www.adr.org/SportsOlympic (last visited Apr. 6, 2006).

10 Id.

11 Id.

12 WORLD ANTI-DOPING AGENCY, supra note 5, at 12, art. 3.1.

becoming more so. The WADA Code enumerates the standard as between a balance of the probabilities but less than a reasonable doubt, which is basically a "clear and convincing standard."

In the case of a positive test, it is assumed that the laboratory has conducted its testing properly. In those circumstances, the USADA only needs to show that, according to the lab documents, there has been a positive test. Then the burden shifts to the athlete to show that there has been some error in the testing process. Then, if the athlete can do that, the burden shifts back to the doping agency. But in a non-analytical case, the doping agency bears the burden of proof the entire time; it has to prove its entire case.

As to the type of evidence that can be used in a positive test case, it is clear that all sorts of documents from the laboratory will be available. In a non-analytical case, the nature and scope of evidence are pretty vague. The WADA Code states that "[f]acts related to anti-doping rule violations may be established by any reliable means, including admissions."[13] That, however, is all the WADA Code says. There is really not a lot of guidance there and only a couple of cases have been decided so far. For example, consider the case of Michelle Collins.[14] She was an Olympic track athlete who broke a number of world and American records a couple of summers ago and who was then charged by the USADA with having violated basically everything. They essentially named every single rule that they could, and said she had violated them and [that she had] taken all sorts of different steroids and other prohibited substances. Michelle was prosecuted with no positive test, but USADA had emails between Michelle and Victor Conte. Michelle apparently admitted in some of those emails that she used substances. USADA also relied on a number of blood and urine tests from BALCO but none of those were positive. They tried to infer from the results that she had used steroids. What is new, a little disturbing, and something athletes should be concerned about, is that USADA tried to conclude that because her endogenous steroid profiles (the steroids that your own body makes including testosterone and epitestosterone) were suppressed, the only explanation could be that she was taking some external source of steroid. The WADA Code, and none of the rules currently in place in the Olympic movement, really contemplated such a use of a longitudinal study. They were looking at the results of Michelle's tests over a pretty long period of time. The panel found her guilty. They found that USADA had proved its case beyond a reasonable doubt, which they could have done based on the admissions alone. But what was a little more troubling was that they found the blood and urine tests did show that she had used prohibited substances. Unfortunately, her lawyer actually stipulated that all of the test results were correct, which was something that was highly contested in Christy Gaines's case and in another one similar to Christy's case.

These non-analytical positive cases really raise some issues that are a concern to Olympic athletes. If Congress decides to subject professional athletes to the same sorts of testing and anti-doping programs, then other athletes will also have this concern. The cost for the athlete could be enormous. Usually, the adjudication of a positive test case takes at most a couple of months,

---

13   Id. at 12, art. 3.2.

14   See, e.g., Michelle Collins Suspended for Doping, USATODAY.COM, Dec. 10, 2004, available at http://www.usatoday.com/sports/olympics/summer/track/2004-12-10-collins-suspended_x.htm.

partly because athletes are competing and want a quick resolution of their cases. Christy's case went on for a year and a half and the legal fees were nearly $400,000. USADA spent 2.5 million dollars to prosecute her case and some other BALCO cases. Most athletes cannot afford this.

A second issue is the mere inference of wrongdoing. Marion Jones was a great example of this. Marion was never charged with any kind of doping offense, but USADA inferred that she may have used some substances based on documents they saw from BALCO. Marion's career and her reputation were tarnished, even though she was never charged.[15] A third issue is the doping agency's authority in these cases. USADA often seems like a quasi-criminal-kind of investigatory body and I am not certain their powers go quite as far as they think they should.

The fourth and final issue relates to the costs. The time involved in resolving disputes is a big issue for athletes since Olympic and professional athletes have a limited time window in which they can compete. In protracted cases, the athlete is unofficially sanctioned from competing while the case is being heard. In the sport of track and field, and other sports, however, athletes can compete in meets only if the race director invites them.

There already have been a number of issues relating to these non-analytical positive cases that have arisen, and I think they will only continue to be more prevalent going forward.

NOTES & QUESTIONS

1. The following story regarding sprint coach, Trevor Graham, comes from Cherry, Gene, *Crawford Leaves Coach Graham*; http://abcnews.go.com/Sports/wireStory?id=2636561 (last updated November 7, 2006):

> Graham, who has coached some of the world's top sprinters, was indicted last week by a U.S. grand jury on three counts of making false statements related to steroid distribution. Graham helped unmask the BALCO doping scandal in 2003 by sending the U.S. Anti-Doping Agency (USADA) a used syringe with small amounts of the previously undetectable steroid THG. He is charged with lying to federal agents investigating the scandal. Graham is due to be arraigned in San Francisco on Nov. 16 and could face as much as

---

15 Editor's footnote: Subsequent to the publication of this article, Marion Jones's use of illegal performance-enhancing substances has become public. The Wikipedia article states:

> She won five medals at the 2000 Summer Olympics in Sydney, Australia but has since agreed to forfeit all medals and prizes dating back to September 2000 after admitting that she took performance-enhancing drugs.

> In October 2007, Jones admitted taking steroids before the Sydney 2000 Summer Olympics and acknowledged that she had, in fact, lied when she previously denied steroid use in statements to the press, to various sports agencies, and—most significantly—to two grand juries. One was impaneled to investigate the BALCO "designer steroid" ring, and the other was impaneled to investigate a check fraud ring involving many of the same parties from the BALCO case. As a result of these admissions, Jones accepted a two-year suspension from track and field competition, and announced her retirement from track and field on October 5, 2007.

> The United States Anti-Doping Agency stated that the sanction "also requires disqualification of all her competitive results obtained after September 1, 2000, and forfeiture of all medals, results, points and prizes". On October 5, 2007, Jones formally pled guilty to lying to federal agents in the BALCO steroid investigation in the U.S. District Court. On January 11, 2008, Jones was sentenced to 6 months in jail. She began her sentence on March 7, 2008, and was released on September 5, 2008. http://en.wikipedia.org/wiki/Marion_Jones.

five years in prison for each count if found guilty. His attorney has said Graham is not guilty. Graham also is under investigation by the International Association of Athletics Federations (IAAF) and USADA, and the U.S. Olympic Committee (USOC) has banned him from using its facilities. More than six athletes Graham has coached have been suspended for doping or tested positive for performance-enhancing drugs.

2. 2006 Tour De France winner, Floyd Landis, experienced similar woes:

> In 2006, Landis won the first edition of the Tour of California, before going on to finish first in the 2006 Tour de France. He was stripped of his Tour de France victory and fired from the Phonak team after a drug-control test demonstrated the presence of a skewed testosterone/epitestosterone ratio during stage 17.

> Landis maintained his innocence, and he mounted a vigorous defense. Although Landis's legal team documented inconsistencies in the handling and evaluation of his urine samples, the disqualification was upheld.

> He was suspended from professional competition through January 30, 2009, following an arbitration panel's 2-to-1 ruling on September 20, 2007. Landis appealed the result of the arbitration hearing to the Court of Arbitration for Sport, which subsequently upheld the panel's ruling. http://en.wikipedia.org/wiki/Floyd_Landis. Then in late May 2010, Landis admitted that he had used the blood booster EPO to increase his endurance as well as human growth hormone and blood transfusions. In addition to these admissions, he accused other cyclists, including Lance Armstrong, of similar wrongdoing. http://www.nytimes.com/2010/05/21/sports/cycling/21landis.html.

3. And in the wake of Landis's allegations, Lance Armstrong gained exceptional notoriety as he initially maintained his innocence, and then later admitted to serious wrongdoing, involving numerous doping violations over the course of many years during his career. In January 2013 he publicly admitted his doping past in a two-part interview with Oprah Winfrey. He was stripped of his seven Tour De France victories and banned from cycling for life. He has been the subject of both civil suits and criminal investigations. For current information *see* http://en.wikipedia.org/wiki/Lance_Armstrong.

Further Reading on Olympic Sports, Private Associations, Drug Testing:

Patrick S. Baldwin, *Keeping Them Down on the Farm: The Possibility of a Class Action By Former Minor League Baseball Players Against Major League Baseball for Allowing Steroid Abuse*, 43 Ga. L. Rev. 1195 (2009).

Ian S. Blackshaw, *Have the Wheels Already Been Invented: The Court for Arbitration in Sport*, TMC Asser Press (2002).

Barry Boss, Rebecca Brodey, *Immaculate Suspension: Non-Analytical Positive Doping Violations from Usada to MLB,* 30 Ent. & Sports Law 3 (2014).

Sarah P. Bryan, *Anti-doping Regulation in Professional and Olympic Sports,* 38 Lab. & Employ. L. 11 (Winter 2010).

Saroja Cuffey, *Passing the Baton: The Effect of the International Olympic Committee's Weak Anti-Doping Laws in Dealing with the 2016 Russian Olympic Team,* 43 Brook. J. Intl. L. 665 (2018).

Joe Fore, *Moving Beyond "Gene Doping": Preparing for Genetic Modification in Sport,* 15 Va. J.L. & Tech. 76 (2010).

Andrew L. T. Green, *Spreading the Blame: Examining the Relationship Between DSHEA and the Baseball Steroid Scandal,* 90 B.U. L. Rev. 399 (2010).

Christopher S. Groleau, *Weird Science: A Look at the World Ant-Doping Agency's Questionable Testing Methods and the Need for Change to Protect International Athletes,* 13 Quinnipiac Health L.J. 85 (2009).

Nicholas Hailey, *A False Start in the Race Against Doping in Sport: Concerns with Cycling's Biological Passport,* 61 Duke L.J. 393 (2011).

Matthew Hard, *Caught in the Net: Athletes' Rights and the World Anti-Doping Agency,* 19 S. Cal. Interdisc. L.J. 533 (2010).

Holli N. Heiles, *Baseball's "Growth" problem: Can Congress Require Major League Baseball to Test Its Athletes for Human Growth Hormone? A Proposal,* 62 Ark. L. Rev. 315 (2009).

Sarah R. Heisler, *Steroid Regulation in Professional Sports: Sarbanes-Oxley as a Guide,* 27 Cardozo Arts & Ent. L.J. 199 (2009).

Jolyn R. Huen, *Passing the Baton: Track Superstar Marion Jones' Duty and Liability to Her Olympic Relay Teammates,* 5 DePaul J. Sports L. & Contemp. Probs. 39 (2008).

Bryan T. Ikegami, *From Dumpster to Dicta: How the Balco Investigation Created Incurable Violations of Players' Rights and How to Prevent Them,* 34 Colum. J.L. & Arts 491 (2011).

Philip Jacques, *Is Congress' Latest Effort to De-Juice Professional Sports Unconstitutional?,* 6 DePaul J. Sports L. & Contemp. Probs. 97 (2009).

Zackary Kessinger, *"Strike Two, You're Out!" the Need for A More Stringent Drug Policy in Major League Baseball,* 10 Wash. U. Jurisprudence Rev. 257 (2018).

Dionne L. Koller, *Sports, Doping, and the Regulatory "Tipping Point",* 26 Marq. Sports L. Rev. 181 (2015).

Tiffany D. Lipscomb, *Can Congress Squeeze the "Juice" Out of Professional Sports? The Constitutionality of Congressional Intervention Into Professional Sports' Steroid Controversy,* 69 Ohio St. L.J. 303 (2008).

Kevin Mahoney, *Learning From the Mistakes of Others: Changing Major League Baseball's Substance Abuse Arbitration Procedure,* 24 Ohio St. J. on Disp. Resol. 613 (2009).

Matthew J. Mitten, *Judicial Review of Olympic and International Sports Arbitration Awards: Trends and Observations,* 10 Pepp. Disp. Resol. L.J. 51 (2009).

Laurence M. Rose, *Drug Testing in Professional and College Sports,* 36 U.Kan.L.Rev. 787 (1988).

John A. Scanlan, Jr., *Playing the Drug Testing Game: College Athletes, Regulatory Institutions and the Structures of Constitutional Argument;* 62 Ind. L.J. 863 (1987).

Steven M. Silverberg, *Safe at Home? Assessing U.S. Efforts to Protect Youths from the Effects of Performance Enhancing Drugs in Sports,* 35 Brook. J. Int'l L. 271 (2010).

E. Tim Walker, *Missing the Target: How Performance-Enhancing Drugs Go Unnoticed and Endanger the Lives of Athletes,* 10 Villanova Sports & Ent. L.J. 181 (2003).

John C. Weistart & Cym H. Lowell, Law of Sports, §1.03 Status of the Amateur Athlete (Bobbs-Merrill Company, Inc., 1979).

John C. Weistart & Cym H. Lowell, Law of Sports, §§ 1.25, 2.07 Drugs (Bobbs-Merrill Company, Inc., 1979).

CHAPTER 2
TORTS I: ATHLETE-TO-ATHLETE INJURIES; FACILITIES OPERATORS

Lawyers and law students are familiar with the law of Torts. First year students spend many hours learning about intentional torts, such as assault and battery, and various aspects of negligence, and perhaps product liability as well. For example, law students learn that in order to prove negligence, a plaintiff must prove, by a preponderance of the evidence, that the defendant: 1) owed a duty of reasonable care to the plaintiff; 2) breached that duty by failing to act as a reasonable person would have acted under those or similar circumstances; 3) proximately caused harm to the plaintiff (*i.e.*, the plaintiff's harm was a foreseeable consequence of the defendant's conduct); and, 4) the plaintiff suffered an injury as a result of the defendant's breach of duty.

torts negligence

The first two cases in this chapter, *Trujillo* and *Karas,* explore athlete-to-athlete injuries. Pay particular attention to how and why the courts treat these injuries differently from non-sports injuries. The next two cases, *Strickland* and *Turner,* consider the liability of owners of facilities. Law students often read cases that deal with the liability of property owners. Many courts have said, for example, that property owners owe a "higher duty of care" to persons who have been invited onto their property (*e.g.*, guests such as spectators) than persons who are trespassers. You may wish to ask yourself how the courts' reasoning in *Strickland* and *Turner* compares with the standard "invitor/invitee" analysis, and whether the fact that sports are involved makes any difference in the courts' decisions.

TRUJILLO V. YEAGER
642 F.SUPP.2D 86, 250 ED. LAW REP. 172 (2009)
D. CONNECTICUT

JANET C. HALL, J.

Plaintiff Kevin Trujillo alleges that he was severely injured during an NCAA Division III men's varsity soccer match between his team, Coast Guard Academy, and Trinity College. He alleges that [Phil] Yeager, acting with negligence and recklessness, caused him severe injury during the course of the game.

Plaintiff Trujillo was a cadet and varsity soccer player at the United States Coast Guard Academy in New London, Connecticut, and a citizen of California for the purposes of diversity jurisdiction. Defendant Yeager was a student and varsity soccer player at Trinity College in Hartford, Connecticut, and a citizen of Illinois for the purposes of diversity jurisdiction.

On or about September 12, 2006, Trujillo and Yeager were playing in a soccer match between the Coast Guard Academy and Trinity College. During the game, Trujillo was struck in the head by Yeager. According to Trujillo's allegations, Yeager was careless and negligent, as well as reckless, in using force against Trujillo.

As a result of defendant['s] negligence, and defendant Yeager's recklessness, Trujillo suffered serious and debilitating injuries, some or all of which may be permanent. Trujillo has incurred medical expenses and may incur similar expenditures in the future. Trujillo has suffered lost wages and an impairment of his ability to earn income.

Yeager has moved to dismiss...on the grounds that he cannot be held liable in negligence for injuries caused in the course of a competitive contact sport. Yeager relies on the Connecticut Supreme Court's decision in *Jaworski v. Kiernan*, 241 Conn. 399, 696 A.2d 332 (1997). Trujillo has not filed an opposition to Yeager's Motion.

In *Jaworski*, the Connecticut Supreme Court analyzed the duty owed among adult co-participants in team contact sports. *Id. Jaworski*, like the instant case, involved an adult soccer match. In analyzing the facts of that case, the court engaged in an extensive policy discussion about the tension between promoting vigorous athletic competition and protecting those who participate. It noted that the vast majority of states have adopted an intentional or reckless standard of care for injuries occurring during athletic contests. *Id.* at 410, 696 A.2d 332. Ultimately, the court concluded that "a participant in an athletic contest [may] ... maintain an action against a co-participant only for reckless or intentional conduct and not for merely negligent conduct." *Id.* at 409, 696 A.2d 332.

Trujillo's Count One is a negligence count against Yeager, Trujillo's co-participant in the adult soccer match. *Jaworski* squarely forecloses Trujillo's ability to recover from Yeager merely upon proof of negligence. *Id.* at 412, 696 A.2d 332. Accordingly, Yeager's Motion to Dismiss...is GRANTED, and Count One, Trujillo's negligence count against Yeager, is DISMISSED.

NOTES & QUESTIONS

1. Why should the rules of tort liability in an athletic context be any different from ordinary rules of tort liability?

2. First year law students learn the principle of "negligence per se." As was noted in the introduction to this chapter, the general rule regarding proof of negligence requires that a plaintiff prove four elements: duty, breach, proximate cause, and injury. However, when an action is characterized as negligence *per se*, a court waives the necessity for a plaintiff to produce certain types of evidence. The court simply demands less proof from the plaintiff.

   For example, most jurisdictions agree that if a defendant violates a written law (statute), and if the plaintiff is injured as a result of the defendant's violation of that statute, and if the plaintiff is a member of the class of persons whom the statute was designed to protect, then the doctrine of negligence *per se* is applicable. Fundamentally, in such circumstances, a plaintiff does not need to prove the standard negligence elements of duty and breach (elements that are often very difficult to prove). Rather, the doctrine of negligence *per se* allows a court to substitute proof that the defendant violated a statute and that the plaintiff was in the class of persons whom the statute was designed to protect in place of the ordinary requirements that the plaintiff must prove duty and breach. The theory is simple. Proof that a defendant violated a statute and that the plaintiff belongs to the protected class take the place of – or substitute for – proof that the defendant owed a duty to the plaintiff and that the defendant breached that duty. The violation of the statute by itself (*per se*) proves that the defendant breached a duty owed to the plaintiff.

Would a similar analysis be useful for sports? In other words, should courts consider that a rule violation (*e.g.,* in football pulling an opponent's facemask or running into a kicker or punter) is similar to violation of a statute for purposes of a negligence *per se* analysis? What would be the advantages of such an analysis? Disadvantages?

3. Now is a good time to begin thinking about the role of comparative negligence with respect to athlete-to-athlete injuries during competition. Similar legal theories such as the doctrines of assumption of risk, consent, and contributory negligence must be considered as well. What are the doctrinal choices that courts are faced with in these circumstances? The next case and several other subsequent cases in the chapters that follow address some of these issues and how courts may consider them in the context of athletic competition.

4. Soccer is a sport that involves a significant amount of physical contact (unlike golf). Is the "contact" factor relevant? Sports such as skydiving, gymnastics, ski jumping, and pole vaulting, technically speaking, are not contact sports in the traditional sense (like soccer and football). Do you think that the liability rules for injuries caused by participation in those sports should be any different from the rule articulated in this case? Why or why not?

KARAS V. STREVELL
227 ILL.2D 440, 884 N.E.2D 122, 318 ILL.DEC. 567 (2008)
SUPREME COURT OF ILLINOIS

BURKE, J.

BACKGROUND

In January of 2004, Benjamin Karas was a member of the Barrington High School Hockey Club's junior varsity hockey team. Russell Zimmerman and Joseph Strevell, the player defendants, were members of the Naperville junior varsity hockey team. Both teams were members of a hockey league...Amateur Hockey Association Illinois, Inc. (the Hockey Association), and were governed by hockey rules, which the Hockey Association promulgated. One of these rules was a prohibition against body checking players from behind.

On January 25, 2004, Barrington played Naperville. On the back of each player's jersey the word "STOP" had been sewn above or between the player's number to reinforce the rule against body checking players from behind. According to plaintiff's complaint, during the game, the player defendants struck Benjamin "from behind on his back area causing his head to strike the boards resulting in serious personal injury, including neck and head injuries."

On September 14, 2004, plaintiff filed an eight-count, second amended complaint in the circuit court of Du Page County. Count I of the complaint alleged that Benjamin's injuries were caused by the player defendants' willful and wanton conduct.

On July 1, 2005, the circuit court dismissed.... In a written order, the circuit court explained the reasons for the dismissal. The court noted the rule, adopted by this court in *Pfister v. Shusta,* 167 Ill.2d 417, 212 Ill.Dec. 668, 657 N.E.2d 1013 (1995), that a plaintiff who is injured by a co-participant while engaged in a contact sport may only recover if the injury was the result of intentional or willful and wanton conduct. The circuit court concluded that the ice hockey game at issue was a contact sport, and that plaintiff had failed to plead willful and wanton conduct on the part of the player defendants.

On appeal, the appellate court reversed the trial court's dismissal.... 369 Ill.App.3d 884, 308 Ill.Dec. 81, 860 N.E.2d 1163. With respect to the player defendants, the appellate court held that plaintiff had adequately pled willful and wanton conduct and, in particular, a "conscious disregard for [plaintiff's] safety"[.]***

Margin note: Circuit court reasoning

Player Defendants

[5][6] In general, every person owes a duty of ordinary care to guard against injuries to others. [Citation Omitted] A person who breaches this duty is deemed negligent and may be held financially liable if his conduct proximately causes injury to another. [Citation Omitted] However, in *Pfister v. Shusta,* 167 Ill.2d 417, 212 Ill.Dec. 668, 657 N.E.2d 1013 (1995), this court adopted an exception to the standard of ordinary care for participants engaged in contact sports. Under this exception, a participant in a contact sport may not be held liable for negligent conduct, which injures a co-participant. Instead, liability will arise only if a participant intentionally, or willfully and wantonly, injures a co-participant. Stated otherwise, in a contact sport the duty owed by a participant to a fellow participant is the "duty to refrain from willful and wanton or intentional misconduct." *Pfister,* 167 Ill.2d at 420, 212 Ill.Dec. 668, 657 N.E.2d 1013.

> *Pfister* explained the rationale for limiting participants' liability in contact sports:
> The contact sports exception strikes the appropriate balance between society's interest in limiting liability for injuries resulting from physical contact inherent in a contact sport and society's interest in allowing recovery for injuries resulting from willful and wanton or intentional misconduct by participants. Those who participate in soccer, football, softball, basketball, or even a spontaneous game of can kicking, choose to play games in which physical contact among participants is inherent in the conduct of the game. Participants in such games assume a greater risk of injury resulting from the negligent

conduct of co-participants. * * * The contact sports exception allows recovery for injuries resulting from willful and wanton and intentional misconduct while taking into account the voluntary nature of participation in games where physical contact is anticipated and where the risk of injury caused by this contact is inherent." *Pfister,* 167 Ill.2d at 426-27, 212 Ill.Dec. 668, 657 N.E.2d 1013. See also *Azzano v. Catholic Bishop of Chicago,* 304 Ill.App.3d 713, 718, 237 Ill.Dec. 694, 710 N.E.2d 117(1999)("the public policy underlying the contact sports exception today is the need to strike a balance between protecting participants in sporting activities and the voluntary nature of participation in games where physical contact is inherent and inevitable").

Pfister also noted that a rule limiting the liability of participants in contact sports was necessary to avoid a chilling effect on the way these sports are played. As the court observed, if a negligence standard were imposed on participants, contact sports would be fundamentally altered or, perhaps, eliminated altogether. Numerous other courts have voiced the same concern and have stated that a primary justification for limiting liability in the sports context is to avoid fundamentally altering, or discouraging participation in, the sport at issue. [Citations Omitted]

In addition, several courts have recognized a need for a rule limiting liability in the sports context in order to avoid a flood of litigation. As one court has stated:

> If simple negligence were adopted as the standard of care, every punter with whom contact is made, every midfielder high sticked, every basketball player fouled, every batter struck by a pitch, and every hockey player tripped would have the ingredients for a lawsuit if injury resulted. * * * See also *Savino v. Robertson,* 273 Ill.App.3d 811, 818, 210 Ill. Dec. 264, 652 N.E.2d 1240 (1995)("the practical effect of applying an ordinary negligence standard would be to open a legal Pandora's box, allowing virtually every participant in a contact sport, injured by another during a 'warm-up' or practice, to bring an action based on the risks inherent in virtually every contact sport. This is exactly the type of result the courts have sought to avoid").

[7] Importantly, although *Pfister* referred to the contact sports exception in terms of the risks assumed by the plaintiff (*Pfister,* 167 Ill.2d at 426, 212 Ill.Dec. 668, 657 N.E.2d 1013), the exception is not an affirmative defense, nor does it require the court to determine the plaintiff's subjective awareness of the risks associated with the sport. Rather, the contact sports exception is an objective doctrine that defines the scope of the defendant's duty. See Restatement (Third) of Torts: Apportionment of Liability § 2, Comment *j,* at 27 (2000)("What courts often call 'primary assumption of risk,' is actually a doctrine about the defendant's liability or duty"); *Barrett v. Fritz,* 42 Ill.2d 529, 535, 248 N.E.2d 111 (1969)(assumption of the risk concepts are generally duplicative of other doctrines, including scope of duty).

[8] When deciding whether the contact sports exception applies, the court must consider the nature of the sport at issue and determine, based on its inherent risks, whether it is a contact sport. When the court concludes that "physical contact among participants is inherent" in

the game (*Pfister*, 167 Ill.2d at 425, 212 Ill.Dec. 668, 657 N.E.2d 1013), a player owes no duty to a co-participant to avoid ordinary negligence. *See generally Knight v. Jewett*, 3 Cal.4th at 315, 834 P.2d at 708, 11 Cal.Rptr.2d at 14 (a court need not ask what risks a particular plaintiff subjectively knew of and chose to encounter, but instead must evaluate the fundamental nature of the sport and the defendant's role in or relationship to that sport in order to determine whether the defendant owes a duty to protect a plaintiff from the particular risk of harm).

In the case at bar, there is no dispute regarding the nature of the sport at issue. The parties agree that ice hockey, played in a game in which body checking is permitted, is a contact sport. Thus, pursuant to *Pfister*, the duty owed by the player defendants to Benjamin was the "duty to refrain from willful and wanton or intentional misconduct." *Pfister*, 167 Ill.2d at 420, 212 Ill.Dec. 668, 657 N.E.2d 1013.

Pfister defined willful and wanton conduct as "a course of action which shows actual or deliberate intent to harm or which, if the course of action is not intentional, shows an utter indifference to or conscious disregard for a person's own safety or the safety or property of others." *Pfister*, 167 Ill.2d at 421, 212 Ill.Dec. 668, 657 N.E.2d 1013, *citing Ziarko v. Soo Line R.R. Co.*, 161 Ill.2d 267, 273, 204 Ill.Dec. 178, 641 N.E.2d 402 (1994). The appellate court below concluded that plaintiff had pled conduct on the part of the player defendants that met this standard. According to the appellate court, because plaintiff alleged that the player defendants knowingly violated a rule against body checking from behind, and because they knew that Benjamin was in a position near the edge of the rink, or boards, when he was struck, plaintiff sufficiently pled a "conscious disregard" of Benjamin's safety by the player defendants. 369 Ill.App.3d at 892, 308 Ill.Dec. 81, 860 N.E.2d 1163. Before this court, plaintiff repeats this line of reasoning.

We note that Pfister did not consider the application of the traditional willful and wanton standard to full-contact sports such as ice hockey and tackle football where physical contact between players is not simply an unavoidable by-product of vigorous play, but is a fundamental part of the way the game is played. In these sports, holding participants liable for consciously disregarding the safety of co-participants is problematic.

Striking or body checking a person who is standing on two thin metal blades atop a sheet of ice is an inherently dangerous action. Even a cleanly executed body check, performed according to the rules of ice hockey, evinces a conscious disregard for the safety of the person being struck. Yet, in an ice hockey game where body checking is permitted, players are struck throughout the game. This conduct is an inherent, fundamental part of the sport. Similarly, in tackle football, players must necessarily disregard the risk of injury to others, simply because of the way the game is played.

In full-contact sports such as tackle football, and ice hockey where body checking is permitted, a conscious disregard for the safety of the opposing player is an inherent part of the game. D. Lazaroff, *Torts & Sports*, 7 U. Miami Ent. & Sports L.Rev. 191, 213 ("The infliction of pain with the knowledge of danger is inherent in certain sports such as football and hockey").

A standard of care that holds a player liable based on conduct that is inherent in the sport is contrary to the underlying rationale of *Pfister*. As noted, the rule announced in *Pfister* is based on the long-standing principle that certain sports contain inherent risks for which a defendant owes no duty of care. *Pfister,* 167 Ill.2d at 426-27, 212 Ill.Dec. 668, 657 N.E.2d 1013; *see also Murphy v. Steeplechase Amusement Co.,* 250 N.Y. 479, 166 N.E. 173 (1929) (Cardozo, J.). Although they evince a conscious disregard for the safety of other players, body checking and tackling are an inherent part of the sports of ice hockey and football. Pursuant to *Pfister,* a participant has no duty to avoid such conduct.

Moreover, imposing liability under the conscious disregard of safety standard would have a pronounced chilling effect on full-contact sports such as ice hockey and football. If liability could be established every time a body check or tackle resulted in injury – because that conduct demonstrates a conscious disregard for the safety of the opposing player – the games of ice hockey and football as we know them would not be played. *Pfister,* 167 Ill.2d at 427, 212 Ill. Dec. 668, 657 N.E.2d 1013, quoting *Pfister,* 256 Ill.App.3d at 191-92, 194 Ill.Dec. 618, 627 N.E.2d 1260 (Green, J., dissenting).

Finally, the conscious disregard of safety standard is unfair to defendants in full-contact sports such as ice hockey. As one commentator has noted, ice hockey, like football, is an example of a sport "in which body checking and physical play may foreseeably result in frequent injuries. It would be...unjust to predicate participant liability upon the participant's knowledge that a tough check or collision could result in injury. This type of conduct is inherent in the sport itself." 7 U. Miami Ent. & Sports L.Rev. at 214.

In full-contact sports, such as ice hockey where body checking is allowed, and tackle football, the traditional willful and wanton standard is both unworkable and contrary to the rationale underlying *Pfister.* To remain consistent with the reasoning of *Pfister,* a standard of care must be employed that more accurately accounts for the inherent risks associated with these sports.

In considering the appropriate standard of care to be followed, we note that a majority of courts have concluded that "rules violations are inherent and anticipated aspects of sports contests" and, thus, insufficient to establish liability by themselves. T. Davis, *Avila v. Citrus Community College District: Shaping the Contours of Immunity and Primary Assumption of the Risk,* 17 Marq. Sports L.Rev. 259, 274 (2006). As this court observed in *Pfister,* in numerous sports, "'players regularly commit contact beyond that which is permitted by the rules even as applied. In basketball, such an illegal contact is described as a foul for which a sanction is imposed. Sometimes the player fouled is injured. This is to be expected.'" *Pfister,* 167 Ill.2d at 427, 212 Ill. Dec. 668, 657 N.E.2d 1013, quoting *Pfister,* 256 Ill.App.3d at 191-92, 194 Ill.Dec. 618, 627 N.E.2d 1260 (Green, J., dissenting). *See also Lang v. Silva,* 306 Ill.App.3d 960, 968-69, 240 Ill.Dec. 21, 715 N.E.2d 708 (1999)("even in sports where there are rules governing the permissible degree of physical contact, rule infractions are inevitable and justify a lower standard of care than ordinary negligence"); *Jaworski,* 241 Conn. at 407-08, 696 A.2d at 337 ("In athletic competitions, the object obviously is to win. In games, particularly those...involving some degree of physical contact, it is reasonable to assume that the competitive spirit of the participants will result in some rules violations and injuries. That is why there are penalty boxes, fouls shots, free kicks, and yellow cards"); *Mark v. Moser,* 746 N.E.2d 410, 419 (Ind.App.2001).***

[9] Courts have expressed a standard of care that balances these concerns and, in particular, acknowledges the risks inherent in certain sports, in various ways. Perhaps the most frequently

cited standard is that adopted by the Supreme Court of California in *Knight v. Jewett,* 3 Cal.4th 296, 834 P.2d 696, 11 Cal.Rptr.2d 2 (1992). There, the court stated that a participant breaches a duty of care to a co-participant "only if the participant intentionally injures another player or engages in conduct that is so reckless as to be totally outside the range of the ordinary activity involved in the sport." *Knight,* 3 Cal.4th at 320, 834 P.2d at 711, 11 Cal.Rptr.2d at 17. Other authorities have adopted similar standards. See, *e.g., Turcotte v. Fell,* 68 N.Y.2d at 441, 502 N.E.2d at 970, 510 N.Y.S.2d at 55 (liability will lie for "flagrant infractions unrelated to the normal method of playing the game and done without any competitive purpose"); *Mark,* 746 N.E.2d at 422 ("liability will not lie where the injury-causing action amounts to a tactical move that is an inherent or reasonably foreseeable part of the game and is undertaken to secure a competitive edge"); 17 Marq. Sports L.Rev. at 283 (liability will lie for "extreme conduct that falls squarely outside of the customs or ordinary conduct that can be expected in a particular sport"). Regardless of the precise wording, these standards all draw a line in a way that permits recovery for extreme misconduct during a sporting event that causes injury, while at the same time foreclosing liability for conduct which, although it may amount to an infraction of the rules, is nevertheless an inherent and inevitable part of the sport. We agree with the standards set forth in the above authorities, and conclude that, in a full contact sport such as ice hockey or tackle football, a participant breaches a duty of care to a co-participant only if the participant intentionally injures the co-participant or engages in conduct "totally outside the range of the ordinary activity involved in the sport." *Knight,* 3 Cal.4th at 320, 834 P.2d at 711, 11 Cal.Rptr.2d at 17.

[10] As currently pled, nothing takes the play at issue in this case totally outside the range of ordinary activity associated with ice hockey in a game in which body checking is allowed. ***

The key allegation in plaintiff's complaint is that the player defendants violated a rule against body checking from behind when they struck Benjamin. However, as noted, rules violations are considered an inherent, unavoidable risk of playing a contact sport. As pled then, plaintiff's complaint fails to allege conduct totally outside the ordinary range of activity associated with ice hockey. ***

NOTES & QUESTIONS

1. This was a high school game. What difference, if any, would it make if type of injury were to occur in a professional game rather than an amateur game?

2. At what point does a hockey player's conduct go beyond that which is reasonably anticipated? Does the nature of the sport matter? For example, would this type of violence be considered within the bounds of reasonable anticipation in baseball or basketball? How about tennis, golf, track and field, equestrian, ice dancing?

WILLIAMS V. RUDOLPH S. STRICKLAND
251 NC 767 (1960)
SUPREME COURT OF NORTH CAROLINA

PARKER, J.

In 1957 two men and their wives[,] the...defendants[,] purchased a tract of land, which was conveyed to them in fee simple, and began the construction thereon of a stock car race track. On 14 August 1957, the... defendants organized Strickland Enterprises, Inc. to engage in the amusement business, including the operation of a stock car race track. The four individual defendants are the sole stockholders and officers of this corporation. ***

On 24 August 1957, the...defendants began holding stock car races on the premises and charging admission thereto under the name of Edgecombe Speedway. Edgecombe Speedway was and is open to the public as a place of amusement, and the operators of it invited the public to attend the stock car races. Large numbers of people attended the races.

On 22 September 1957, plaintiff [Frances Williams], with numerous other persons, purchased from the operators of Edgecombe Speedway admission tickets. There were no grandstand or bleacher seats provided, and plaintiff, with a crowd of other spectators, stood up beyond one end of the race track to watch the races. During the races, and while a number of racing cars were going around the race track at high speeds, a wheel came off one of the racing cars making a turn at the end of the race track near which plaintiff and a crowd of spectators were standing, and 'flew' toward plaintiff at a high speed, striking her and causing her serious injuries.

Defendants were negligent, which negligence was the proximate cause of her injuries, in that: One. They provided no seats of any kind for paid spectators, who were required to stand near the race track to see the races. Two. They failed to provide a fence, wall, or barricade of sufficient height and strength to protect plaintiff and other paid spectators from wheels that at times come off speeding stock car racers and fly through the air at high speeds, though defendants knew, or, in the exercise of due care, should have known, that it is not uncommon for wheels to come off such racing cars during a race, and might likely injure a spectator. In spite of this foreseeable danger, defendants only strung one cable about 18 inches high above the ground, separating the race track proper from the area in which plaintiff, and other paid spectators were standing watching the races. Three. They failed to inspect the racing cars prior to the race during which plaintiff was injured to see if the wheels of the racing cars were in safe condition for racing. Four. Defendants failed to warn plaintiff of the increased danger of standing near the end of the race track, and failed to fence off or rope off such area, though defendants knew, or should have known, such area was relatively more dangerous for spectators during a race than the area surrounding other parts of the race track.

* * *

Plaintiff prays that she have judgment against the...defendants...for $15,500....

Since plaintiff purchased an admission ticket, and entered on the race track premises, a business conducted for profit, in the character of a patron, he occupied the status of an invitee. *Hahn v. Perkins,* 228 N.C. 727, 46 S.E.2d 854.

"One who invites the public to attend a race between motor vehicles and charges an admission fee is bound to exercise reasonable care to make the place provided for spectators reasonably safe, but, although a spectator is injured, no liability may be imposed on the persons conducting the races, in the absence of a showing of negligence on their part." 61 C.J.S. Motor Vehicles s 577, p. 682.

The general rule is that the owner or operator of an automobile race track is charged with the duty of exercising reasonable care, under the circumstances present, for the safety of patrons, that is a care commensurate with the known or reasonably foreseeable danger. Annotation, 37 A.L.R.2d 393, where many cases are cited.

Smith v. Cumberland County Agricultural Society, 163 N.C. 346, 79 S.E. 632, 633, Ann.Cas.1915B, 544, was an action for injuries sustained by plaintiff, who was caught by his foot in the trail rope of a balloon which ascended from the fair grounds of defendant, and was carried in the air for some distance. Plaintiff paid his fare for entrance to the fair. The Court said: "The owner of a place of entertainment is charged with an affirmative positive obligation to know that the premises are safe for the public use and to furnish adequate appliances for the prevention of injuries which might be anticipated from the nature of the performance, and he impliedly warrants the premises to be reasonably safe for the purpose for which they are designed." "He is not an insurer of the safety of those attending the exhibition, but he must use care and diligence to prevent injury, and by policemen or other guards warn the public against dangers that can reasonably be foreseen."

* * *

This is said in Annotation, 37 A.L.R.2d 394: "If the need is obvious or experience shows that an automobile race of the character and in the place proposed requires, in order to afford reasonable protection to spectators, the erection of fences or similar barriers between the track and the places assigned to them, it becomes a part of the duty in exercising reasonable care for their safety to provide fences or barriers, the adequacy of which is dependent on the circumstances present, principally the custom of the business." In this same annotation...will be found a number of cases in respect to the absence or inadequacy of fences, barricades, or other protective devices, where under the circumstances of individual cases, a recovery has been upheld and denied.

* * *

We think that the complaint with its amendments contains a sufficient statement of a cause of action against the...defendants predicating their liability, at least, on their failure to exercise care commensurate with the known or reasonably foreseeable dangers incident to motor vehicles racing at high speeds for the reasonable protection and safety of plaintiff, a patron, and its other patrons, watching the race, in that no seats of any kind were provided for plaintiff and there was an absence or inadequacy of fences, barricades, or other protective devices around the race track for plaintiff's safety, while he was watching the racing automobiles.

NOTES & QUESTIONS

1. How can a racetrack owner balance the spectators' desire to be right on top of the action with the need for safety? At what point does law impinge upon the rights of venue owners and spectators by taking a role that is overly paternalistic? How is this issue related to state statutes requiring drivers and occupants of automobiles to wear seat belts or laws requiring motorcyclists to wear helmets?

2. What could the racetrack owners have done to avoid liability?

3. If you were giving advice to an entrepreneur who wanted to open a dirt motocross track for teenagers, how would you begin to determine what sorts of safety precautions would be necessary for spectators?

4. What is the relationship between industry standards for safety in these types of venues and legal liability?

5. For a recent case exploring similar issues, see e.g., *Deaver v. Bd. of County Com'rs of Lyon County,* 342 P.3d 970 (Kan. App. 2015). Appellate court remanded this case where a girl died after being struck by a mud-a-thon vehicle that veered off of the racetrack, instructing the trial court to assess whether the municipality's conduct was wanton or grossly negligent pursuant to the state recreational use statute.

Edgecombe Speedway late 1950's

TURNER V. MANDALAY SPORTS ENTERTAINMENT, LLC

180 P.3D 1172 (2008)

SUPREME COURT OF NEVADA

PARRAGUIRRE, J.

In this appeal, we address whether baseball stadium owners and operators have a duty to protect spectators against injuries caused by foul balls that are errantly projected into the stands. We conclude that stadium owners and operators have a limited duty to protect against such injuries and that respondent satisfied its duty as a matter of law under the facts presented in this case. Accordingly, we affirm the district court's judgment in respondent's favor.

FACTUAL AND PROCEDURAL BACKGROUND

At all times relevant to this appeal, respondent Mandalay Sports Entertainment, LLC, owned and operated the Las Vegas 51s, a minor league baseball team that plays its home games at Cashman Field in Clark County. From 2000 to 2002, appellants Kathleen and Michael Turner owned season tickets for home games played by the 51s.

Like most professional baseball teams, the 51s include a disclaimer on their tickets informing fans that the team is not responsible for injuries caused by foul balls.[1] In addition, the public address announcer at Cashman Field warns the crowd about the danger of foul balls hit into the stands before each 51s home game. The 51s also post warning signs at every Cashman Field entry gate, cautioning fans to stay alert because of the risks posed by foul balls. The Turners acknowledge that they were aware of these warnings.

On May 4, 2002, while attending a 51s game at Cashman Field, Mr. and Mrs. Turner left their assigned seats and walked to the "Beer Garden," a concessions area located in the upper concourse level above the stands. The Beer Garden-which is several hundred feet from the playing field-contains tables and chairs where patrons can eat and drink but also has a railing where patrons can stand and continue to watch the game. Unlike other concession areas at Cashman Field, the Beer Garden has no protective screen surrounding it.[2]

While at the Beer Garden, Mr. Turner purchased a beverage for himself and a sandwich for his wife. Mr. Turner then stood at the railing so that he could continue to watch the game. Mrs. Turner, on the other hand, took her sandwich and sat at one of the available tables. According to Mrs. Turner, she was unable to see any part of the field from her table.

---

1 Specifically, this notice provides that the "Holder assumes all danger incidental to the game whether occurring before, during or after the game, including the dangers of being injured by thrown bats or thrown or batted balls, and agrees that the TEAMS, their agents, and players are not liable for resulting injuries."

2 Two other concession areas at Cashman Field provide protection from stray balls: (1) the Party Zone, which has a protective screen; and (2) the Club Level Restaurant, which is fully enclosed by clear glass walls.

As Mrs. Turner sat in the Beer Garden, a foul ball struck her in the face. The force of the ball's impact rendered her unconscious, broke her nose, and lacerated her face. According to Mrs. Turner, she never saw the ball coming and had no opportunity to get out of the way.

The Turners subsequently filed a complaint in district court against the Las Vegas 51s, alleging...negligence.

* * *

DISCUSSION

Mrs. Turner's negligence claim

The district court concluded that Mrs. Turner's negligence claim failed because the Las Vegas 51s did not owe a duty to protect her from the foul ball in question. For the following reasons, we agree with the district court's conclusion.

[4] A claim for negligence in Nevada requires that the plaintiff satisfy four elements: (1) an existing duty of care, (2) breach, (3) legal causation, and (4) damages. [Citation Omitted] At issue in this case is whether the 51s owed a duty to protect Mrs. Turner from foul balls hit into the area where she was sitting. Although we have previously recognized that "a proprietor owes a general duty to use reasonable care to keep the premises in a reasonably safe condition for use," we have never specifically defined the scope of that duty as it pertains to baseball stadium owners and operators. [Citation Omitted]

[5] In addressing this issue, at least 12 jurisdictions have adopted the "limited duty rule," which places two important requirements on stadium owners and operators.[3] First, the rule requires stadium owners and operators to provide a sufficient amount of protected seating for those spectators "who may be reasonably anticipated to desire protected seats on an ordinary occasion."[4] Second, it requires stadium owners and operators to provide protection for all spectators located in the most dangerous parts of the stadium, that is, those areas that pose an unduly high risk of injury from foul balls (such as directly behind home plate).

As explained by the Michigan Court of Appeals, "the limited duty rule ... identifies the duty of baseball stadium proprietors with greater specificity than the usual ... standard provides."[5] In this sense, the limited duty rule does not eliminate the stadium owner's duty to exercise reasonable care under the circumstances to protect patrons against injury; rather, it defines that duty in detail.

---

3   *See* James L. Rigelhaupt, Jr., Annotation, *Liability to Spectator at Baseball Game Who Is Hit by Ball or Injured as Result of Other Hazards of Game*, 91 A.L.R.3d 24 (1979)(electronically updated as of 2008).

4   *Schneider v. American Hockey*, 342 N.J.Super. 527, 777 A.2d 380, 384 (Ct.App.Div.2001)(internal quotation marks and citation omitted).

5   *Benejam v. Detroit Tigers*, Inc., 246 Mich.App. 645, 635 N.W.2d 219, 223 (2001).

6   Id.

[6] [7] By defining the duty of a baseball stadium owner or operator with specificity, the limited duty rule shields the stadium owner or operator from the need to take precautions that are clearly unreasonable while also establishing the outer limits of liability. Once a stadium owner or operator complies with the rule's requirements by providing sufficient protected seating, the owner or operator has satisfied the legal duty of protection owed to its patrons. Having met this obligation, the stadium owner or operator simply has no remaining duty to protect spectators from foul balls, which are a known, obvious, and unavoidable part of all baseball games. This specificity with regard to the duty imposed on the baseball stadium owner or operator serves the important purpose of limiting expensive and protracted litigation that "might signal the demise or substantial alteration of the game of baseball as a spectator sport."[7]

* * *

CONCLUSION

Since the record demonstrates that the 51s satisfied the requirements of the limited duty rule as a matter of law, and thus no genuine issue of material fact remains with regard to Mrs. Turner's negligence claim, we conclude that the district court was correct to enter summary judgment in the 51s' favor on that claim.

NOTES & QUESTIONS

1. For a recent case articulating the same legal principle, *see Tarantino v. Queens Ballpark Co., LLC*, 1 N.Y.S.3d 216 (N.Y. App. Div. 2d Dept. 2014). Plaintiff struck by a foul ball while seated in a luxury suite (not located behind home plate) with the windows open was barred from recovery because the defendant is required only to provide protective screening in the area behind home plate where there is maximum risk of being injured by a foul ball.

2. Articulate the so-called "limited duty" rule in your own words? Does it apply only to baseball stadium owners? Or is it applicable to owners of other sporting venues?

3. Assuming that the limited duty rule is applicable in some fashion to other sporting venues, how might it be modified to apply to other types of sporting venues? Can you think of specific types of sporting venues that might pose particular difficulties in applying the limited duty rule?

4. As you reflect on these cases, begin thinking about the relationship between the limited duty rule and the doctrine of assumption of risk.

---

7 *Benejam*, 635 N.W.2d at 223.

5. Is there a fundamental difference between the duty owed by a venue owner to spectators versus the duty owed to participants? If so, explain the nature of that difference. If not, explain why not. For a recent case examining the scope of duty owed to spectators and the doctrine of primary implied assumption of risk – a doctrine covered in greater detail below in chapter 3 (especially in the *Kahn* and *Crace cases*) – *see Coomer v. Kan. City Royals Baseball Corp.*, 437 S.W.3d 184 (Mo. 2014). As part of an advertising promotion, the Kansas City Royals mascot threw a hotdog into the crowd and struck a fan in the eye. The court reasoned that the risk of being hit by a mascot-thrown hotdog was not inherent in the game of baseball – unlike the risk of being hit by a bat or ball, and thus primary implied assumption of risk did not bar the plaintiff's suit. *See* Joshua D. Winneker et. al., *Who Let the Dogs Out: Should A Stadium Owner Be Held Liable for Injuries Sustained from A Mascot's Errant Hot Dog Toss?*, 21 Jeffrey S. Moorad Sports L.J. 369 (2014).

For exceptionally dangerous activities such as equestrian sports and skiing, a number of state legislatures have passed special statutes providing immunity for the venue operators who provide venues for these types of recreational activities. *See generally* Terrence J. Centner, *Tort Liability for Sports and Recreational Activities: Expanding Statutory Immunity for Protected Classes and Activities*, 26 J. Legis. 1 (2000). For a recent case example construing this type of statute, *see Fleury v. IntraWest Winter Park Operations Corp.*, 411 P.3d 81 (Colo. App. 2014), aff'd, 372 P.3d 349 (Colo. 2016)(Court held that skier's death caused by an avalanche is an inherent skiing risk pursuant to the Colorado's Ski Safety Act, and thus the widow's negligence and wrongful death claims were barred). For more on this topic, see J. Russell VerSteeg, *A Case For a Bill Recognizing Primary Assumption of Risk as Limiting Liability for Persons and Providers Who Take Part in Sports & Recreational Activities*, 36 U.ARKANSAS LITTLE ROCK LR 56 (2013); and, *infra* Chapter 4.

Further Reading on Athlete-to-Athlete Injuries and Facilities Operators Liability:

Douglas E. Abrams, *Player Safety in Youth Sports: Sportsmanship and Respect as an Injury-Prevention Strategy,* 22 Seton Hall J. Sports & Ent. L. 1 (2012).

Roger I. Abrams, Two Sports Torts: *The Historical Development of the Legal Rights of Baseball Spectators,* 38 Tulsa L. Rev. 433 (2003).

Chris Breton, *The Seventh-Inning Stretch(Er)?: Analyzing the Antiquated "Baseball Rule" and How It Governs Fan Injuries at Major League Baseball Games,* 21 U. Den. Sports & Ent. L.J. 209 (2018).

Paul Caprara, *Surf's Up: The Implications of Tort Liability in the Unregulated Sport of Surfing,* 44 Cal. W. L. Rev. 557 (2008).

Dr. Tracey B. Carter, *It Is A Mindboggling Dilemma: To Play or Not to Play Youth Sports Due to Concussion Risks?,* 67 Cath. U.L. Rev. 1 (2018).

Walter T. Champion, *At the Old Ball Game and Beyond: Spectators and The Potential for Liability,* 14 Am. J. Trial Advoc. 495 (1991).

Matthew G. Cole, *No Blood No Foul: The Standard of Care in Texas Owed by Participants to One Another in Athletic Contests,* 59 Baylor L. Rev. 435 (2007).

Evan Steele Fensterstock, *Shin v. AHN Applies the Primary Assumption of Risk Doctrine to Injuries Sustained By Golfers in the Same Group: Negligence Goes Unpunished,* 43 New Eng. L. Rev. 87 (2008).

Phoebe Friesen, Bethany Saul, Lisa Kearns, Kathleen Bachynski, Arthur Caplan, *Overuse Injuries in Youth Sports: Legal and Social Responsibility,* 28 J. Leg. Aspects Sport 151 (2018).

Peter C. Gopleurd, *Allocation of Risk Between Hockey Fans and Facilities: Tort Liability After the Puck Drops,* III, 38 Tulsa L. Rev. 445 (2003).

Brian P. Harlan, *The California Supreme Court Should Take a Mulligan: How the Court Shanked by Applying the Primary Assumption of Risk Doctrine to Golf,* 29 Loy. L.A. Ent. L. Rev. 91 (2008-09).

Gordon J. Hylton, *A Foul Ball in the Courtroom: The Baseball Spectator Injury as a Case of First Impression,* 38 Tulsa L. Rev. 485 (2003).

Mohit Khare, *Foul Ball! The Need to Alter Current Liability Standards for Spectator Injuries at Sporting Events,* 12 Tex. Rev. Ent. & Sports L. 91 (2010).

Daniel E. Lazaroff, *Torts and Sports: Participant Liability to Co-Participants for Injuries Sustained During Competition,* 7 U. Miami Ent. & Sports L. Rev. 191 (1990).

David F. Tavella, *Duty of Care to Spectators at Sporting Events: A Unified Theory,* 5 Fla. A & M U. L. Rev. 181 (2010).

Benjamin C. Thompson, *Personal Foul . . . 15 Years in Jail: Sports' Problem with Excessive Violence and the Severe Punishment Solution,* 76 UMKC L. Rev. 769 (2008).

Patrick K. Thornton, *Rewriting Hockey's Unwritten Rules: Moore v. Bertuzzi,* 61 Me. L. Rev. 205 (2009).

Robert J. Thorpe, *Way Out in Left Field: Crespin v. Albuquerque Baseball Club Rejects Nearly One Hundred Years of American Jurisprudence by Declining to Adopt the Baseball Rule in New Mexico,* 17 Sports Law. J. 267 (2010).

Griffin Toronjo Pivateau, *Tackling the Competitive Sports Doctrine: A New Proposal for Sports Injuries in Texas,* Tex. Rev. Ent. & Sports L. 85 (2007).

Benjamin Trachman, *Going to Bat for the "Baseball Rule": Atlanta National League Baseball Club, Inc. v. F.F. et al.,* 7 Harv. J. Sports & Ent. L. 205 (2016).

Russ VerSteeg, *Consent in Sports & Recreational Activities: Using Contract Law Terminology to Clarify Tort Principles,* 12 DePaul J. Sports L. & Contemp. Probs. 1 (2016).

Aaron Wakamatsu, S*pectator Injuries: Examining Owner Negligence and the Assumption of Risk Defense,* 6 Willamette Sports L.J. 1 (2009).

John C. Weistart & Cym H. Lowell, *Law of Sports,* §8.02 Liability for Injury to Participants (Bobbs-Merrill Company, Inc., 1979).

John C. Weistart & Cym H. Lowell, *Law of Sports,* §8.03 Liability for Injury to Spectators (Bobbs-Merrill Company, Inc., 1979).

Joshua Winneker, *Protecting the Unprotected: Creating an Anti-Retaliation Policy for Professional Athletes That Exercise Their Legal Rights in Participant vs. Participant Liability Contact Sports,* 12 Va. Sports & Ent. L.J. 315 (2013).

Ray Yasser, *In the Heat of Competition: Tort Liability of One Participant to Another,* 5 Seton Hall J. Sport L. 253 (1995).

CHAPTER 3
TORTS II: COACH LIABILITY; EQUIPMENT

The Torts cases that you have read thus far have required you to think about injuries caused by co-participants and injuries caused by those responsible for providing a sports venue for athletes and spectators. *Moose v. MIT* introduces the topic of coach liability. This case also provides another platform for considering assumption of risk and contributory (and comparative) negligence. Here we consider the extent to which a coach or athlete him/herself should be considered legally responsible for injury. As we know, injuries are an ordinary part of athletics because all games involve varying degrees of risk. The fundamental question here is whether or under what circumstances a coach should be held liable for injuries to athletes. *Trujillo* suggests that it would be unwise, as a rule, to hold coaches liable for injuries caused by the players whom they coach. A related question is whether and to what degree an athlete should be deemed to have assumed to the risks involved in his/her sport, or to what degree an athlete can be considered responsible for his/her own injuries through contributory or comparative fault. *Khan* and *Crace* introduce a trend in the law of sports liability; namely the adoption of primary implied assumption of risk for sports-related injuries.

McCormick and *Pell* explore the extent to which equipment manufacturers and sellers are held responsible for sports injuries. These cases provide an opportunity to delve into the world of products liability. As such, they also require us to think about the roles played by sports equipment manufacturers and the potential effects that legal decisions may have on the sports equipment industry as a whole. The tension is easy to understand. If litigation and insurance costs are too high, manufacturers will be likely to quit. Obviously there are a number of exceptionally negative consequences that could flow from manufacturers fleeing the marketplace due to fears of litigation and rising insurance costs. As you read these cases, think about what steps courts might take in order to balance the consumers' needs for safety with the needs of the manufacturers to stay in business so that various sports (*i.e.,* sports that rely on specialized equipment) can continue to thrive. Consider also the special problems confronted by manufacturers of safety equipment such as football, baseball, bicycle, ski, and hockey helmets. *Pell* provides an excellent example of the kinds of obstacles that exist for suppliers of gymnastic equipment. The note that concludes this chapter summarizes and explains the legal theories (both tort and commercial law) that relate to sports equipment.

MOOSE V. MASSACHUSETTS INSTITUTE OF TECHNOLOGY

43 MASS.APP.CT. 420 (1997)

APPEALS COURT OF MASSACHUSETTS, MIDDLESEX

SMITH, JUSTICE.

The plaintiff, Garret Moose, filed a negligence action against the Massachusetts Institute of Technology (MIT) and two of its track and field coaches, Paul Slovenski and Halston Taylor, seeking damages for injuries sustained while Moose was practicing pole vaulting at the institution. The plaintiff alleged that the defendants were negligent with respect to their coaching techniques and the equipment they furnished to him at the time he was injured. [A] jury found that each defendant, as well as the plaintiff, was negligent and that the defendants' negligence was the proximate cause of the plaintiff's injuries. The jury assessed damages at $615,000. The percentages of negligence were attributed as follows: plaintiff – fifteen percent, MIT – forty-five percent, Taylor – twenty-five percent, Slovenski – fifteen percent. The court entered judgment in the sum of $522,750 after deducting fifteen percent from the award for the plaintiff's negligence. The judgment provided that MIT's liability was $20,000 plus interest and costs because it was a charitable organization.

* * * *

Pole vaulting is a sport in which the object is to obtain the maximum vertical lift in order to clear a horizontal bar set at some height above the ground. In competition, after vaulters have cleared the bar, it is then adjusted upwards until a winner emerges.

To be able to go over the bar, a vaulter takes an approach run towards the bar carrying a long pole. When the vaulter gets near to the bar, he places one end of the pole into the vaulting box – an indentation in the ground almost directly beneath the bar. The box slants downward at the bottom and has metal sides. Once the pole is planted in the box, the vaulter uses the momentum from his approach run to bend the pole. When the pole bends back, the vaulter is lifted upwards and hopefully over the bar. Once over the bar, the vaulter lands on a foam mattress called the landing pit which cushions the vaulter's fall.

The defendant Slovenski, who had been the pole vaulting coach since November, 1990, was coaching Moose at the time of the accident. The defendant Taylor was head track and field coach and responsible for supervising Slovenski's activities as pole vaulting coach. Taylor's functions as head track and field coach included supervising the sports equipment in order to make sure it was safe, recommending the purchase of new equipment, and providing a safe environment for MIT track athletes.

In January of 1991, the plaintiff was a senior at MIT, majoring in aeronautical engineering. He was also a member of MIT's men's track and field team and had been involved in pole vaulting since the spring of his freshman year. On January 21, 1991, the day of the accident, the plaintiff was practicing pole vaulting under Slovenski's direct supervision at MIT's indoor track and field facility. The plaintiff was injured when after executing a pole vault, his heels hooked on the back edge of the landing pit and he fell backward, striking his head on the hard track surface. The back of the pit abutted the indoor track; the back left corner of the pit was two to three inches from the inside lane of the indoor track and the right rear corner was about two feet from the running surface. The track was made of concrete, covered with a thin layer of rubber.

The pit was purchased in 1980 and was thirteen feet in length; the minimum length required by NCAA rules was twelve feet with a recommended length of sixteen feet. Pits with more length were available since at least 1981 but a budgeting crisis at MIT affected the track team and the coaches' ability to purchase new equipment. About a year and one-half after the accident, Taylor had the pit replaced with one that was seventeen feet long.

Both Slovenski and Taylor had witnessed, or at least were aware of, vaulters bouncing off the pit mattress and landing over the sides and front of the pit resulting in the vaulter sustaining second impact injuries. The day of the accident there were no pads at the back or sides of the pit, although in the past, the coaches had placed pads on the sides and sometimes at the back of the pit. Slovenski was aware that some colleges used supplemental padding at the back of the pit. Prior to the accident, Taylor never discussed the padding issue with Slovenski. At the time of the accident, supplemental padding was available and Taylor could have ordered that pads be placed in the area at the back of the pit.[1]

On January 21, 1991, pursuant to Slovenski's instructions, the plaintiff was using a training pole to practice pole vaulting drills. There was evidence that the training pole that was being used by the plaintiff was too light for the plaintiff's weight.[2] The selection of a soft training pole for a heavy, fast athlete places the athlete at serious risk of a "blow through."[3]

After performing a number of drill techniques, Slovenski instructed the plaintiff to combine two of the vaulting techniques and go through the full vaulting motions. The approach run for these vaults was fifty feet and the plaintiff was to make his approach at about one-half his normal speed. Slovenski told the plaintiff to use the same training pole for the full vaults.

The plaintiff performed the first two of the full vaults. After he performed each vault, Slovenski gave him pointers on his performance. Before each vault, except the last one, Slovenski told the plaintiff to keep his speed down. However, after at least one of these vaults, he landed on the center of the pit, beyond where he should have landed. That landing indicated that he

---

1   The plaintiff's expert, Earl Bell, testified that supplemental padding should always be used around the pit's entire perimeter, especially around the back of the pit where the most serious injuries occur. Bell also testified that in his opinion, it was an unsound practice to locate the pit so that it abutted the hard track surface and it was unreasonable to fail to pad the hard surfaces abutting the pit. Bell also criticized the instructions and supervision given to the plaintiff before the accident.

2   A training pole is a more flexible pole than a competition pole. Because it is more flexible, it is easier to bend; therefore, vaults may be practiced at slower speeds. Although there was a factual dispute as to the exact characteristics of the pole that the plaintiff was using when he was injured, the jury were free to accept the plaintiff's testimony that he was using a thirteen foot pole which was intended for persons weighing from 120-150 pounds. At the time of the accident, the plaintiff weighed 175 pounds.

3   A "blow through" is a term used in track and field circles to describe over penetration of the pole vault landing pit. It occurs when a vaulter uses a pole too soft and small for his weight, speed, and abilities. As the vaulter jumps, the pole overbends sending the vaulter to the back of the pit instead of upward to the bar.

needed either to use a heavier pole, raise his grip, or shorten his approach run. Although proper coaching technique requires that these adjustments be made, Slovenski did not order any of these adjustments nor did he warn the plaintiff that he was overpenetrating.

A coach who is teaching proper pole vaulting techniques should have a vaulter under observation during the vaulter's entire approach run. Once a coach notices that a vaulter is running too fast, the coach should order the vaulter to abort the vault. In the past, other coaches had interrupted the plaintiff's vaults at various stages due to safety concerns, including when he was twenty-five feet into the vault approach run.

Slovenski did not observe the plaintiff's final approach run until the plaintiff had completed twenty-five feet of that run. When Slovenski first observed the plaintiff, he thought the plaintiff was running too fast, and he knew the plaintiff was going to make a bad vault. Slovenski did not instruct the plaintiff to slow down or to abort his vault.

When the plaintiff made the vault, he went up about thirteen feet; when he landed, his heels hooked on the back edge of the pit and he fell backward, striking his head on the hard track surface. Immediately after the accident, Taylor found the plaintiff lying on the track unconscious and convulsing.

The plaintiff was taken to Massachusetts General Hospital where he was diagnosed as having sustained a skull fracture with associated contusions to the brain. While the plaintiff was hospitalized, Slovenski visited him and told him that he was having nightmares and he felt that the accident was his fault. Slovenski also told the plaintiff that when he saw him on his final approach it occurred to him that he had not reminded him to keep his speed down, but he did not say anything to the plaintiff because he did not want to break the plaintiff's concentration.

On appeal, the defendants claim that they are entitled to judgments notwithstanding the verdicts, because there was no evidence to support a finding that they should have reasonably foreseen that the plaintiff would land beyond the back of the pit and hit his head on the track surface.

The defendants appear to have misinterpreted the law pertaining to reasonable foreseeability. It is only the risk which results in the harm that must be reasonably foreseeable, not the precise manner of the accident or the extent of the harm. *Luz v. Stop & Shop, Inc., of Peabody,* 348 Mass. 198, 204, 202 N.E.2d 771 (1964)("To be held liable the defendant need not have foreseen the precise manner in which the injuries occurred."). *See* Restatement (Second) of Torts § 435(1) (1965)....

The question whether the risk of injury was foreseeable is almost always one of fact. *Simmons v. Monarch Mach. Tool Co.,* 413 Mass. 205, 211, 596 N.E.2d 318 (1992). From the evidence before the jury, the plaintiff's accident was reasonably foreseeable by the defendants. The length of the landing pit and its location very close to a hard surface did not provide a safe environment for pole vaulters. It was also reasonably foreseeable that a vaulter using a training pole too light for his weight and running too fast on his approach run, would be carried across the pit and upon landing, end up beyond the back of the pit thereby incurring injury. ****

There was evidence that as a result of the accident, the plaintiff had a lost earning capacity of $25,000 per year and based on that figure, there was testimony from the plaintiff's expert that the plaintiff's lifetime lost earning capacity, discounted to present value, was $1,309,835. Thus, in light of these facts, we hold that the judge did not abuse his discretion by refusing to grant a new trial on the issue of damages because the jury's award of $615,000 was neither greatly disproportionate to the injury proven nor do we think it represents a miscarriage of justice.

Judgments affirmed.

NOTES & QUESTIONS

1. Why doesn't the court merely conclude that Moose assumed the risk of pole vaulting? After all, he was a college senior majoring in aeronautical engineering at one of the most prestigious technical universities in the world (*i.e.*, he was a rocket scientist "in training"). If anyone can be assumed to have completely understood the physics and attendant risks of the sport of pole vaulting, wouldn't he have been the poster child? Isn't pole vaulting an obviously and inherently dangerous sport?

2. To what standard of conduct does the court hold coach Slovenski? Is he judged under ordinary negligence principles? A professional standard (coaches malpractice?)?

3. Is coach Slovenski held responsible for negligence? If so, why isn't he judged using the intentional or willful misconduct standard that the court applied in the athlete-to-athlete injury cases (*i.e.*, *Trujillo* and *Karas*)?

4. In a sport such as track and field, is it reasonable to expect a head coach constantly to supervise the practices for each event? Is it reasonable to hold a track and field coach liable for negligence if s/he fails to prevent an injury? How is that humanly possible, given the multiple events in track and field and limited resources at most high schools and colleges?

5. How important do you think the testimony of the plaintiff's expert witness, Earl Bell, was? Explain your answer.

6. If coach Slovenski had screamed at Moose, and told him to "abort!" just before he planted his pole, would he have been liable for Moose's injuries if Moose had been injured as a result of being abruptly distracted by the coach's scream at the most critical and intense moment of the vault? If so, then is the court right saying that Slovenski should have yelled and told him to abort? Isn't this just an impossible "Catch 22"?

7. For an analysis of the issues raised in this case and others related to pole vault safety, *see* Russ VerSteeg, *Negligence in the Air: Safety, Legal Liability and the Pole Vault,* 4 TEXAS REV. ENT. & SPORTS L. 109 (2003).

Today women and girls also compete in the pole vault, an exciting and dangerous sport. Kaylan Pickford, Former University of Rhode Island Indoor Record Holder: 12 feet 7.5 inches. Photo by Stephen Pickford.

JANET C. HALL, J.

[In *Trujillo v. Yeager* (Chapter 2), the plaintiff also sued Yeager's coach, Michael Pilger, and the coach's employer, Trinity College. The court, therefore, examined the issue of a coach's liability and the liability of the college itself.]

The Trinity [College] defendants acknowledge that Connecticut courts have not explicitly addressed the issue of whether a negligence cause of action is available to injured players against non-participants such as coaches, but contend that *Jaworski's* reasoning and logic is equally applicable to claims against non-participants. They also rely upon cases from other jurisdictions, particularly the Massachusetts case of *Kavanagh v. Trustees of Boston University,* 440 Mass. 195, 795 N.E.2d 1170 (2003), which have held that a plaintiff injured while playing a competitive contact sport must allege reckless or intentional conduct to hold a non-participant defendant liable. The facts of *Kavanagh* are quite similar to this case. In Kavanagh, the plaintiff alleged that the university and its coach were negligent in not taking steps to prevent the plaintiff from being punched by an opposing player during a scuffle during an intercollegiate basketball game. *Id.* at 195-96, 795 N.E.2d 1170.

* * *

[3] This court...first turns to the foreseeability inquiry. Determining foreseeability requires analyzing whether "a reasonable person in the defendant's position, knowing what he knew or should have known, would have anticipated the harm that resulted from his actions." *Id.* at 406, 696 A.2d 332. Certainly the injury could have been anticipated. As *Jaworski* pointed out, "[s]occer ... is ... replete with occasions when the participants make contact with one another during the normal course of the game.... If a player seeks to challenge another player who has possession of the ball or seeks to prevent another player from gaining possession of the ball, the resulting contact could reasonably be foreseen to result in injury to either player." *Id.* at 406-07, 696 A.2d 332. [Internal Citation Omitted] The instant case similarly involves an attempt by one player to prevent another player from gaining possession. Although the defendants...are a coach and college rather than the opposing player, a coach can reasonably foresee that negligent training of player might result in injuries of the type that occurred in this case. On the facts pled, the court concludes that the injury was foreseeable.

As to the factors beyond the foreseeability inquiry, the Connecticut Supreme Court made clear in *Jaworski* that the normal and reasonable expectations of participants in contact team sports include the potential for injuries, that utilizing simple negligence as the standard of care for athletic contests would lead to a flood of undesirable litigation, and that a majority of other jurisdictions have adopted a reckless or negligence standard of care for athletic contests. It expressed its concern that liability for simple negligence would have the effect of dampening enthusiasm for competition or participation in sporting activities for fear of liability. Similar concerns are present...against the Trinity defendants. Trujillo, like the plaintiff in *Jaworski*, had a normal and reasonable expectation that injuries might occur. Holding coaches liable for negligence in training athletes under their care who recklessly or intentionally injure other individuals could dampen coaches' willingness to aggressively coach their athletes. At the level of organized, intercollegiate sports conducted under the auspices of the NCAA, a system of rules and discipline exists to control the behavior of coaches and players alike. To impose an overlay of liability in tort for simple negligence over this internal system of regulation would run the risk of undermining that system and creating the flood of unwarranted litigation that the Connecticut Supreme Court was eager to avoid.

*** [T]he Connecticut Supreme Court has specifically looked in this context to the decisions of other jurisdictions. In other situations, as well, that court has looked to the decisions of the Massachusetts Supreme Judicial Court. Therefore, the Supreme Judicial Court's precedent in *Kavanagh*, while not binding, is highly persuasive on how the Connecticut Supreme Court might rule on the issue of coaches' liability.

In *Kavanagh*, the court discussed the standard to be applied "to claims that coaches are liable for causing their players to injure other players." 440 Mass. at 204, 795 N.E.2d 1170. It explained that the court had previously held that a player's negligence did not suffice to impose liability for injuries the player inflicted during competition. *Id.* at 204-05, 795 N.E.2d 1170. The court noted that the requirement to show recklessness furthered a policy that "vigorous and active participation in sporting events should not be chilled by the threat of litigation." *Id.* at 205, 795 N.E.2d 1170. It then reasoned that for similar reasons, a similar standard should apply to coaches:

> Just as players are entitled to play aggressively without fear of liability, a coach properly may encourage players to play aggressively. Indeed, a coach's ability to inspire players to compete aggressively is one of a coach's important attributes. The mere possibility that some players might overreact to such inspiration or encouragement should not, by itself, suffice to impose liability on a coach. As we do with the players themselves, we must impose liability only where a coach's behavior amounts to at least recklessness. *Id.*

*** [H]olding coaches liable in negligence, particularly to players on a different college's team, would unreasonably threaten to chill competitive play. Moreover, as the *Kavanagh* court points out, "[u]nder the rules of any sport, fouls or other violations carry their own penalties, and it is up to the officials refereeing the competition to enforce those rules and impose those penalties." *Id.* at 205-06, 795 N.E.2d 1170. The obligation is not on the coaches. This is particularly true in the context of intercollegiate or professional competition, which employ a professional staff of referees, as compared with the recreational competition at issue in *Jaworski*.

This court concludes that, with regard to injuries sustained in athletic competition, the Connecticut Supreme Court would look to its precedent in *Jaworski* and the decisions of other states regarding injuries sustained in athletic contests. Given that *Jaworski*, and the decisions of sister states, militate strongly against permitting negligence claims to redress injuries sustained by participants in adult contact sports, this court concludes that the Connecticut Supreme Court would find that the appropriate standard of care to be imposed on coaches for injuries caused by their players is one of reckless or intentional conduct.

As to Trinity College, Trujillo seeks to hold it liable as the employer of Pilger and for its own failure to train and educate Yeager. The allegations against Trinity College are identical to those against Pilger and fail for the same reasons. Because the college acts, in effect, through the coach in training or educating players, allowing negligence claims against colleges for a coach's failure to adequately train or educate a player would allow plaintiffs to evade the policy of not allowing negligence claims against coaches for injuries caused by their players. Accordingly, Pilger and Trinity College's Motion to Dismiss (Doc. No. 16) is GRANTED, and Count Three is DISMISSED.

NOTES & QUESTIONS

1. At the conclusion of this case, the court states: "As to Trinity College, Trujillo seeks to hold it liable as the employer of Pilger and for its own failure to train and educate Yeager." This statement addresses the issue of whether an employer may be liable for the torts of its employees: the principle of vicarious liability, or *respondeat superior*. Fundamentally, the doctrine of *respondeat superior* ("let the one above reply") imposes tort liability on employers for the torts of their employees. This doctrine only applies when an employee is acting within the scope of his or her employment. For example, when a pizza shop delivery driver, while in the process of making a pizza delivery, negligently causes an auto accident, the persons injured by the pizza shop driver's negligence will be successful in their lawsuit against the pizza shop (*i.e.*, the owners or the corporation). We say that the pizza shop is vicariously liable for the negligence of its employee while the employee was acting within the scope of his or her employment. On the other hand, courts might reach a different legal result if the delivery driver had not been in the process of delivering pizzas when the accident occurred. For example, if the delivery driver instead had decided to drive to the next county to visit a personal friend on his way back from a pizza delivery, a court may decide that the act of driving to the next county to visit a personal friend was so far removed from his employer's purpose, that such conduct should no longer be considered "within the scope of employment." In such circumstances, courts frequently state that the employee was on his own "frolic or detour," and therefore, the employer cannot be held vicariously liable under the doctrine of *respondeat superior*.

2. How might a court determine when an athlete's conduct constitutes a "frolic or detour," relieving the team, club, or organization of liability?

   For example, Tennessee Titans defensive lineman Albert Haynesworth made history for the NFL's longest suspension for on-field action. Haynesworth was suspended for five games as a result of a head stomp on a helmet-less Dallas Cowboys center Andre Gurode. The action began early in the third quarter in the Titans vs. Cowboys game on October 1, 2006, after a 5-yard touchdown run by the Cowboys' Julius Jones. Following the run, Gurode's helmet came off and he was on his back. Haynesworth was standing over him and proceeded to first kick Gurode's unprotected head and then scraped his cleats across Gurode's face and forehead. Officials threw a penalty flag and in protest Haynesworth removed his helmet and tossed it, earning Haynesworth a second personal foul and ejection. The suspension began immediately and was without pay, costing Haynesworth an estimated $190,000 of his $646,251.00 salary. *See* Weir, Tom, Titans' Haynesworth Suspended Five Games For Stomping Incident; http://www.usatoday.com/sports/football/nfl/titans/2006-10-02-haynesworth-suspension_x.htm, Oct. 2, 2006. Explain whether you think that either Haynesworth or the Tennessee Titans ought to be liable to Gurode for his injuries.

● For another recent examination of this issue *see Nathans v. Offerman*, 22 F. Supp. 2d 271 (D. Conn. 2013). The court opined that whether a professional baseball player charging the mound to attack an opposing pitcher is foreseeable is a question of fact for the jury, and that the team could be vicariously liable because such conduct could be within the scope of the player's employment.

3. Several recent cases held that coaches are not liable when student athletes are injured, especially in circumstances where the student athlete is aware of the open risks involved. *See e.g., Bellinger v. Ballston Spa C. Sch. Dist.*, 57 A.D.3d 126 (N.Y. App. Div. 3d Dept. 2008) (negligent supervision not the proximate cause of injuries); *Williams v. Clinton C. Sch. Dist.*, 59 A.D.3d 938 (N.Y. App. Div. 4th Dept. 2009)(cheerleader assumed obvious risks of injury on unprotected floor).

KAHN V. EAST SIDE UNION HIGH SCHOOL DISTRICT
75 P. 3D 30 (2003)
SUPREME COURT OF CALIFORNIA

GEORGE, C.J.

[The authors have deleted a substantial portion of this opinion and changed the order of multiple paragraphs in an effort to assist the reader]

This case presents a question concerning the proper application of the doctrine of primary assumption of risk. At the time of her injury, plaintiff [Olivia Kahn] was a 14–year–old novice member of defendant school district's junior varsity swim team. She was participating in a competitive swim meet when she executed a practice dive into a shallow racing pool that was located on defendant school district's property and broke her neck. She alleged that the injury was caused in part by the failure of her coach, a district employee, to provide her with any instruction in how to safely dive into a shallow racing pool. She also alleged lack of adequate supervision and further that the coach breached the duty of care owed to her by insisting that she dive at the swim meet despite her objections, her lack of expertise, her fear of diving, and the coach's previous promise to exempt her from diving.

In *Knight v. Jewett* (1992) 3 Cal.4th 296, 11 Cal.Rptr.2d 2, 834 P.2d 696 (*Knight*), we considered the proper duty of care that should govern the liability of a sports participant for an injury to a coparticipant. We concluded that, in recognition of the circumstance that some risk of injury is inherent in most sports, and in order to avoid the detriment to a sport that would arise from discouraging participants from vigorously engaging in the activity, it is appropriate to hold that a participant breaches a duty of care to a coparticipant only if he or she "intentionally injures another player or engages in conduct that is so reckless as to be totally outside the range of the ordinary activity involved in the sport." (*Id.* at p. 320, 11 Cal.Rptr.2d 2, 834 P.2d 696.)

* * *

Although persons generally owe a duty of due care not to cause an unreasonable risk of harm to others (Civ.Code, § 1714, subd. (a)), some activities – and, specifically, many sports – are inherently dangerous. Imposing a duty to mitigate those inherent dangers could alter the nature of the activity or inhibit vigorous participation. In a game of touch football, for example, there is an inherent risk that players will collide; to impose a general duty on coparticipants to avoid the risk of harm arising from a collision would work a basic alteration– or cause abandonment – of the sport. We addressed this problem in *Knight*....

* * *

Looking first at the nature of the sport, we observed that "[i]n the sports setting ... conditions or conduct that otherwise might be viewed as dangerous often are an integral part of the sport itself." [Citation Omitted] We explained that, as a matter of policy, it would not be appropriate to recognize a duty of care when to do so would require that an integral part of the sport be abandoned, or would discourage vigorous participation in sporting events. Accordingly, defendants generally do not have a duty to protect the plaintiff from the risks inherent in the sport, or to eliminate risk from the sport, although they generally do have a duty not to increase the risk of harm beyond what is inherent in the sport. [Citation Omitted]

* * *

To impose liability on a coparticipant for "normal energetic conduct" ...while playing – even careless conduct – could chill vigorous participation in the sport. *** Accordingly, we concluded that coparticipants breach a duty of care to each other only if they "intentionally injure[ ] another player or engage[ ] in conduct that is so reckless as to be totally outside the range of the ordinary activity involved in the sport." [Citation Omitted]

* * *

The general proposition that a sports instructor or coach owes a duty of due care not to increase the risk of harm inherent in learning an active sport is consistent with a growing line of Court of Appeal opinions that have applied the *Knight* ... analysis to claims against such defendants. In these cases, the reviewing courts examined the particular circumstances of the sport, its inherent risks, and the relationship of the parties to the sport and to each other. Most also examined the question whether imposing broader liability on coaches and instructors would harm the sport or cause it to be changed or abandoned. In each instance, the Courts of Appeal have agreed that although the coach or athletic instructor did not have a duty to eliminate the risks presented by a sport, he or she did have a duty to the student not to increase the risk inherent in learning, practicing, or performing in the sport. [Citations Omitted]

* * *

Subsequent decisions have clarified that the risks associated with *learning* a sport may themselves be inherent risks of the sport, and that an instructor or coach generally does not increase the risk of harm inherent in learning the sport simply by urging the student to strive to excel or to reach a new level of competence. This line of cases analyzes and articulates an important and appropriate limitation on the duty of a sports instructor. The cases point out that instruction in a sport frequently entails challenging or "pushing" a student to attempt new or more difficult feats, and that "liability should not be imposed simply because an instructor asked the student to take action beyond what, with hindsight, is found to have been the student's abilities." [Citation Omitted] As a general matter, although the nature of the sport and the relationship of the parties to it and to each other remain relevant, a student's inability to meet an instructor's legitimate challenge is a risk that is inherent in learning a sport. To impose a duty to mitigate the inherent risks of learning a sport by refraining from challenging a student, as these cases explain, could have a chilling effect on the enterprise of teaching and learning skills that are necessary to the sport. At a competitive level, especially, this chilling effect is undesirable.

* * *

"Instruction in an activity such as judo necessarily requires pushing a student to move more quickly, attempt a new move, or take some other action that the student previously may not have attempted. That an instructor might ask a student to do more than the student can manage is an inherent risk of the activity. *Absent evidence of recklessness, or other risk-increasing conduct, liability should not be imposed simply because an instructor asked the student to take action beyond what, with hindsight, is found to have been the student's abilities.* To hold otherwise would discourage instructors from requiring students to stretch, and thus to learn, and would have a generally deleterious effect on the sport as a whole." [Citation Omitted](italics added by Supreme Court)

* * *

"Any other rule would discourage instructors from asking their students to do anything more than they have done in the past, and would therefore have a chilling effect on instruction, and thus would have a negative impact on the very purpose for seeking instruction: mastering the activity." [Citation Omitted]

* * *

A number of Court of Appeal decisions agree with the...conclusion that pushing an athlete to compete, excel, or move to the next level of competence ordinarily does not form a basis for liability on the part of athletic instructors and coaches. (*See Rodrigo v. Koryo Martial Arts, supra*, 100 Cal.App.4th at pp. 954–956, 122 Cal.Rptr.2d 832 [tae kwon do drill necessarily involved risk of injury from being kicked; instructor did not increase the risks inherent in learning the sport]; *Kane v. National Ski Patrol System, Inc., supra*, 88 Cal.App.4th at pp. 211–212, 105 Cal.Rptr.2d 600 [instructor of aspiring ski patrol members may have misassessed their skill level and the hazards of the terrain, but did not recklessly increase the risk inherent in improving skills to the level required for ski patrol members]; *Lilley v. Elk Grove Unified School Dist., supra*, 68 Cal. App.4th at p. 944, 80 Cal.Rptr.2d 638 [wrestling coach was not liable to pupil he injured during a challenging practice]; *Balthazor v. Little League Baseball, Inc., supra*, 62 Cal.App.4th 47, 72 Cal. Rptr.2d 337 [coach did not increase the risks inherent in learning to play baseball by continuing practice in twilight or by failing to remove an errant pitcher]; *Allan v. Snow Summit, Inc., supra*, 51 Cal.App.4th at pp. 1368–1369, 59 Cal.Rptr.2d 813 [instructor of novice skier did not increase the risks inherent in learning the sport by directing the student to attempt a more difficult run]; see also *West v. Sundown Little League of Stockton, Inc., supra*, 96 Cal.App.4th at pp. 357–358, 116 Cal.Rptr.2d 849 [baseball coach did not increase the risk inherent in the sport by challenging students or by allowing them to practice when the sun was in their eyes]; *Lupash v. City of Seal Beach, supra*, 75 Cal.App.4th at pp. 1436–1439, 89 Cal.Rptr.2d 920 [no liability for asserted negligent instruction of junior lifeguard in safety procedures]; *Aaris v. Las Virgenes Unified School Dist.* (1998) 64 Cal.App.4th 1112, 1117–1118, 75 Cal.Rptr.2d 801 [cheerleading coach did not increase risks inherent in dangerous activity]; *Fortier v. Los Rios Community College Dist., supra*, 45 Cal. App.4th at pp. 435–437, 52 Cal.Rptr.2d 812 [coach/instructor may urge aggressive play in football practice without incurring liability].)

* * *

[C]oaches and instructors should not be held liable for injuries caused by encouraging athletes to perform beyond their existing level of competence. "Coaches must be free to push their players to levels that may, in hindsight, be beyond the students' abilities." (*West v. Sundown Little League of Stockton, Inc., supra*, 96 Cal.App.4th at p. 360, 116 Cal.Rptr.2d 849.)

* * *

The Court of Appeal [in *Kane v. National Ski Patrol System, Inc., supra,* 88 Cal.App.4th 204, 105 Cal.Rptr.2d 600] stated that "an instructor's assessment errors – either in making the necessarily subjective judgment of skill level or the equally subjective judgment about the difficulty of conditions – are in no way 'outside the range of the ordinary activity involved in the sport.' (Citing *Knight v. Jewett*) Instructors must of necessity make such judgments in order to sufficiently challenge skiers so that they will in fact improve their skills. [Citation Omitted] Moreover, the consequence of holding a ski patrol instructor liable for such errors would be calamitous. If a ski patrol instructor's assessment of skill and conditions will support liability, we are at a loss as to what organization or person would or could take on the responsibility of training skiers to rescue other skiers. Because the ability to second-guess an instructor's assessment is essentially limitless, so too would an instructor's liability be limitless. The likely absence of a competent ski patrol would in turn endanger every skier." [Citation Omitted] In conclusion, "[b]ecause the facts presented by the Kanes did not show recklessness or other conduct outside the inherent risk of training to be a ski patrol member, the trial court should have granted [the] motion for judgment [in favor of defendants]." [Citation Omitted]

These cases appropriately reason that, even keeping in mind the role of the coach or sports instructor, the imposition of a duty to avoid challenging a student to perform beyond his or her current capacity would have a chilling effect on the enterprise of teaching and learning skills that are necessary to the sport. These decisions properly emphasize that a coach or athletic instructor must challenge his or her students, and that learning itself can be a risky process, sometimes unavoidably so. These cases also properly recognize that while a student is engaged in the process of learning, he or she frequently is at greater risk than a proficient athlete would be, and a coach does not have a duty to eliminate all the risks presented by inexperience.

[5] We agree that the object to be served by the doctrine of primary assumption of risk in the sports setting is to avoid recognizing a duty of care when to do so would tend to alter the nature of an active sport or chill vigorous participation in the activity. This concern applies to the process of learning to become competent or competitive in such a sport. Novices and children need instruction if they are to participate and compete, and we agree with the many Court of Appeal decisions that have refused to define a duty of care in terms that would inhibit adequate instruction and learning or eventually alter the nature of the sport. Accordingly, we believe that the standard set forth in *Knight*...as it applies to coparticipants, generally should apply to sports instructors, keeping in mind, of course, that different facts are of significance in each setting. In order to support a cause of action in cases in which it is alleged that a sports instructor has required a student to perform beyond the student's capacity or without providing adequate instruction, it must be alleged and proved that the instructor acted with intent to cause a student's injury or that the instructor acted recklessly in the sense that the instructor's conduct was "totally outside the range of the ordinary activity"... involved in teaching or coaching the sport.

* * *

In the present case, we recognize that the relationship of a sports instructor or coach to a student or athlete is different from the relationship between coparticipants in a sport. But because a significant part of an instructor's or coach's role is to challenge or "push" a student or athlete to advance in his or her skill level and to undertake more difficult tasks, and because the fulfillment of such a role could be improperly chilled by too stringent a standard of potential legal liability, we conclude that the same general standard should apply in cases in which an instructor's alleged liability rests primarily on a claim that he or she challenged the player to perform beyond his or her capacity or failed to provide adequate instruction or supervision before directing or permitting a student to perform a particular maneuver that has resulted in injury to the student. A sports instructor may be found to have breached a duty of care to a student or athlete only if the instructor intentionally injures the student or engages in conduct that is reckless in the sense that it is "totally outside the range of the ordinary activity" (*ibid.*) involved in teaching or coaching the sport.

Applying this standard to the present case, we conclude that, on the basis of the declarations and deposition testimony filed in support of and in opposition to defendants' motion for summary judgment, the Court of Appeal majority erred in determining that the doctrine of primary assumption of risk warranted entry of summary judgment in defendants' favor.

* * *

As the dissenting justice in the Court of Appeal pointed out, plaintiff was inexperienced. "Plaintiff's evidence was that she was panicked by the prospect of having to dive into a shallow pool, had told her coach about her fears, and was promised that it would not be required. To then, in the midst of a competitive meet, demand that she execute that very dive," in conjunction with an absence of training, presented a triable issue requiring resolution by a jury. We agree that the following factors indicated a triable issue with respect to whether the coach's behavior was reckless: the lack of training in the shallow-water dive disclosed by plaintiff's evidence, especially in the face of the sequenced training recommended in the Red Cross manual submitted by plaintiff; the coach's awareness of plaintiff's deep-seated fear of such diving; his conduct in lulling her into a false sense of security through a promise that she would not be required to dive, thereby eliminating any motivation on her part to learn to dive safely; his last-minute breach of that promise under the pressure of a competitive meet; and his threat to remove her from the team or at least the meet if she refused to dive.

[7] Clearly, a disputed issue of fact exists as to whether the coach provided any instruction at all on shallow-water diving, and the nature of the coach's promises and threats to plaintiff also are in dispute. If a jury were to find that defendant coach directed plaintiff (a novice on the swim team) to perform a shallow racing dive in competition without providing any instruction, that he ignored her overwhelming fears and made a last-minute demand that she dive during competition, in breach of a previous promise that she would not be required to dive, we believe the trier of fact properly could determine that such conduct was reckless in that it was totally outside the range of the ordinary activity involved in teaching or coaching the sport of

competitive swimming. Accordingly, on this record, we conclude that the trial court erred in granting summary judgment in favor of defendants and that the Court of Appeal erred in affirming that determination (footnote omitted).

CRACE V. KENT STATE UNIVERSITY
924 N.E. 2D 906 (2009)
COURT OF APPEALS OF OHIO, TENTH APPELLATE DISTRICT, FRANKLIN COUNTY

CONNOR, J

Appellant[], Angela...Crace ("appellant"), appeal[s] the decision of the Ohio Court of Claims granting judgment to appellee, Kent State University ("KSU"), after a bench trial on the bifurcated issue of KSU's liability. The trial court granted judgment to KSU after finding that the defense of primary assumption of the risk barred appellant's negligence and loss of consortium claims. For the reasons that follow, we affirm the decision of the trial court.

On February 12, 2001, appellant was a junior at KSU and was a member and captain of KSU's varsity cheerleading team. During the team's practice on that date, the KSU coach, Lenee Buchman ("Buchman"), assigned participants to positions in a maneuver known as the Big K.

The Big K was essentially a human pyramid that consisted of: a base, a middle layer/base, and flyers. Additionally, spotters were positioned on the ground to catch the flyers when they came down. The pyramid was two and one-half people high and had the highest degree of difficulty permitted by the NCAA.

Appellant and several other members of the KSU team had performed the Big K successfully in the previous season. However, several other members of the KSU team had not performed nor even seen the Big K before the team attempted it on February 12, 2001. Indeed, KSU's team included cheerleaders with varying levels of experience and expertise.

On February 12, 2001, Buchman assigned appellant to the position of a flyer. The first two attempts at the mount failed, which resulted in appellant falling from around 15 feet in the air. After each of these two failed attempts, appellant's front spotter caught her when she fell. Before the third attempt, Buchman substituted Detrick Cobbin ("Cobbin") as appellant's rear spotter. Cobbin had neither seen nor participated in the Big K prior to February 12, 2001.

According to Cobbin, before the third attempt, he told Buchman that he was uncomfortable performing as a spotter in the Big K. According to Buchman, this statement never occurred.[4]

It is undisputed, however, that Cobbin participated in the third attempt, which again failed. As a result, appellant again fell from around 15 feet in the air. When appellant came down, Cobbin failed to catch her. Instead, he panicked, shielded his eyes, and moved out of the way. As a result, appellant's fall was unbroken and caused catastrophic injuries, including immediate paraplegia.

---

4 The trial court never reached a factual finding regarding this specific issue.

Accordingly, appellant filed this suit against KSU alleging claims of negligence and loss of consortium based upon Buchman's conduct. The bifurcated issue of KSU's liability proceeded to a bench trial on July 24, 2006. On November 12, 2008, the trial court issued a decision granting judgment to KSU. ***

Ohio courts routinely apply primary assumption of the risk to cases involving sporting events and recreational activities. [Citations Omitted] The applicability of the primary assumption of the risk defense presents an issue of law for the court to decide. [Citation Omitted]. We therefore review the trial court's decision to apply the defense de novo. [Citations Omitted]

Under primary assumption of the risk, an individual assumes the inherent risks of the recreational activity and cannot recover for injuries unless another individual acted recklessly or intentionally. *Santho v. Boy Scouts of Am.*, 168 Ohio App.3d 27, 2006 Ohio 3656, P12, 857 N.E.2d 1255; *see also Marchetti v. Kalish* (1990), 53 Ohio St.3d 95, 559 N.E.2d 699, syllabus. The rationale is that certain risks are so inherent in some activities that the risk of injury is unavoidable. [Citations Omitted]

The Supreme Court of Ohio has further described the underlying rationale. *See Thompson v. McNeill* (1990), 53 Ohio St.3d 102, 559 N.E.2d 705:

> Acts that would give rise to tort liability for negligence on a city street or in a backyard are not negligent in the context of a game where such an act is foreseeable and within the rules. For instance, a golfer who hits practice balls in his backyard and inadvertently hits a neighbor who is gardening or mowing the lawn next door must be held to a different standard than a golfer whose drive hits another golfer on a golf course. A principal difference is the golfer's duty to the one he hit. The neighbor, unlike the other golfer or spectator on the course, has not agreed to participate or watch and cannot be expected to foresee or accept the attendant risk of injury. Conversely, the spectator or participant must accept from a participant conduct associated with that sport. Thus a player who injures another player in the course of a sporting event by conduct that is a foreseeable, customary part of the sport cannot be held liable for negligence because no duty is owed to protect the victim from that conduct. Were we to find such a duty between co-participants in a sport, we might well stifle the rewards of athletic competition. *Id.* at 104.

As a result, primary assumption of the risk negates a negligence claim because no duty is owed to protect against the inherent risks of the recreational activity. [Citation Omitted], citing Prosser & Keeton, The Law of Torts (5th ed.1984) 496, Section 68.... Given this profound impact, courts should proceed with caution when deciding to apply primary assumption of the risk. [Citations Omitted].

Under primary assumption of the risk, the injured plaintiff's subjective consent to and appreciation for the inherent risks are immaterial to the analysis. [Citations Omitted]. Indeed, "those entirely ignorant of the risks of a sport, still assume the risk * * * by participating in a sport or simply by attending the game. The law simply deems certain risks as accepted by plaintiff regardless of actual knowledge or consent." (Footnotes omitted.) [Citation Omitted] *citing*

Susan M. Gilles, *From Baseball Parks to the Public Arena: Assumption of the Risk in Tort Law and Constitutional Libel Law* (2002), 75 Temple L.Rev. 231, 236. In accordance with these principles, our court has previously held:

> [P]rimary assumption of [the] risk requires an examination of the activity itself and not plaintiff's conduct. If the activity is one that is inherently dangerous and from which the risks cannot be eliminated, then a finding of primary assumption of [the] risk is appropriate. *Gehri v. Capital Racing Club, Inc.* (June 12, 1997), 10th Dist. No. 96APE10-1307, 1997 Ohio App. LEXIS 2527.

* * *

As a result, and based upon the arguments presented in this matter, we must first determine if suffering an injury due to a fall is an inherent risk of cheerleading. We must then determine if Buchman acted recklessly or intentionally.

* * *

In its decision, the trial court held that "the risk of injury due to a fall while performing a mounted stunt is a result of a foreseeable, customary part of the sport of cheerleading." Trial court's decision, at 5. ***

Appellee's experts opined that injuries are a part of cheerleading. As the head coach of a national championship caliber team, Jomo Thompson testified about the injuries that members of his squad suffered. Further, he opined, "all mounts are risky." (Tr. 1102.) Mr. Thompson also testified that the coach should make sure the degree of risk is minimized. (Tr. 1103.) Appellee's other expert, James Albert Lord, III, opined that pyramids never hit perfectly. (Tr. 1233.) Further, he testified that even qualified spotters make mistakes. (Tr. 1214.)

Appellant's expert, Dr. Steven George, testified about the precarious nature of elevated stunts and human pyramids when he provided:

> Cheerleading does hold a unique difference to that of gymnastics in that while both are acrosports, in gymnastics, when a performer goes to perform, they're performing on a -- on a piece of apparatus that is stationary, structured, still, solid, and has the exact same performance characteristics every time they use it. * * *
>
> But in cheerleading, in partner stunts and in pyramid building, what you have here is you have an interplay between two or more participants, so it becomes a bit more precarious ***.(Tr. 321-22.)[5]

---

5   Dr. George defined an acrosport as a sport involving motion, rotation, and height. (Tr. 308.)

Dr. George emphasized that coaches should follow the American Association of Cheerleading Coaches and Administrators ("AACCA") safety manual in order to reduce the risks of cheerleading to manageable levels. Additionally, the trial court aptly noted that the following quote is attributable to Dr. George: "Spotting is not 100% fail-safe. Even under the very best of conditions, the window of foreseeability is never fully opened and the element of risk is forever present." Trial court's decision, at 5.

Therefore, according to the experts, the risk of injury is inherent in cheerleading, particularly when performing elevated stunts and human pyramids. Even when a coach follows the AACCA safety guidelines, the risk is forever present and may only be reduced to manageable levels. Manageable risks are nevertheless risks. It necessarily follows that the risk of injury is incapable of being completely eliminated.

We therefore find that the trial court did not err by applying the primary assumption of the risk defense. As such, appellee owed no duty to protect appellant from the inherent risk of injury related to a fall while participating in a mounted stunt or human pyramid. Based upon the claims presented in this matter, appellant may only recover if Buchman acted recklessly or intentionally.

With regard to this issue, we note that there is neither an allegation nor any evidence supporting the position that Buchman intentionally caused appellant's injury. Instead, appellant argues that Buchman acted recklessly. The Supreme Court of Ohio has outlined the requisite analysis on this issue. See *Thompson v. McNeill* (1990), 53 Ohio St. 3d 102, 559 N.E.2d 705:

> The actor's conduct is in reckless disregard of the safety of others if he does an act or intentionally fails to do an act which it is his duty to the other to do, knowing or having reason to know of facts which would lead a reasonable man to realize, not only that his conduct creates an unreasonable risk of physical harm to another, but also that such risk is substantially greater than that which is necessary to make his conduct negligent.

> * * *

> What constitutes an unreasonable risk under the circumstances of a sporting event must be delineated with reference to the way the particular game is played, *i.e.,* the rules and customs that shape the participants' ideas of foreseeable conduct in the course of a game. Id. at 105, quoting Restatement (Second) of Torts (1965), 587, Section 500.

In this regard, the experts described the rules and customs of cheerleading by explaining their experiences and referencing the AACCA safety manual. They presented differing opinions regarding whether Buchman properly ensured that the members of the team, in addition to the team as a whole, were capable and ready to perform the Big K on February 12, 2001.

* * *

Dr. George opined that a specifically defined group must perform proper progressions before attempting a maneuver such as the Big K. He opined that it would be impossible to perform all of the necessary progressions in one day. Further, he opined that, by substituting Cobbin before the third attempt, Buchman no longer had a specifically defined group and should have started the progressions from the beginning. Additionally, he opined that a coach does not have the discretion to force an individual to perform a difficult and risky stunt when that person has expressed apprehension about his participation.[6] According to Dr. George, this is particularly true when the first two attempts at the maneuver have failed. For these reasons, Dr. George testified that the team, in addition to Cobbin individually, was not performer ready when it attempted the Big K on February 12, 2001. As a result, Dr. George opined that Buchman acted recklessly in directing her team to perform the Big K.

On the other side, Mr. Thompson and Mr. Albert testified that Buchman met the requirements under the AACCA guidelines. They emphasized Buchman's level of experience as a cheerleading coach. They noted that the injury occurred in February, after the team had cheered for an entire football season and half of a basketball season. They deferred to Buchman on the issue of performer readiness because they opined that only a coach knows when a team and its members are capable of performing a particular maneuver. They testified that the team performed proper progressions by attempting each side of the pyramid before attempting the pyramid as a whole. They testified that it is common and necessary to make substitutions in cheerleading. According to their testimony, a coach has discretion in choosing whether to start progressions from the beginning after a substitution. For all of these reasons, appellee's experts opined that Buchman did not act recklessly and, in fact, did not even act negligently.

Having the ability to consider the competing positions, the trial court found that the team was well-trained and had performed the proper progressions before attempting the Big K. Trial court's decision, at 7. Further, the trial court found that Buchman did not act recklessly or intentionally. Id. Therefore, the trial court simply accepted the position of appellee's experts rather than that of the appellant's. Because this matter proceeded to a bench trial, we must defer to the trial court's factual findings in this regard. See *Tejeda*, supra.

Based upon the foregoing analysis, we find that appellant was participating in the recreational activity of cheerleading when she was injured as a result of an inherent risk that was incapable of being completely eliminated. Further, because the trial court found that Buchman did not act recklessly or intentionally in causing appellant's injury, we find that the trial court did not err by finding that primary assumption of the risk barred appellant's negligence and loss of consortium claims against KSU. ***

Judgment affirmed.

FRENCH, P.J., and SADLER, J., concur.

---

6   Again, we note that the trial court never reached a factual determination on Cobbin's refuted testimony.

1) Recent cases have continued to apply the doctrine of primary implied assumption of risk to sports-realted injuries. For example: 1) *Cann v. Stefanec,* 158 Cal. Rptr. 3d 474 (Ct. App. 2013). Holding that primary implied assumption of risk barred a negligence claim when UCLA female swimmer was injured during team weight lifting. 2) *Eriksson v. Nunnink,* 183 Cal. Rptr. 3d 234 (Cal. Ct. App. 2015). Appeals court ruled that the horseback riding coach could not be liable for death of minor equestrian killed during competition, because the parents of the deceased had not proved gross negligence.

MCCORMICK V. LOWE & CAMPBELL ATHLETIC GOODS CO.
144 SW 2D 866 (1940)
KANSAS CITY COURT OF APPEALS, MISSOURI

CAMPBELL, COMMISSIONER.

The defendant, Lowe & Campbell Athletic Goods Company, furnished a vaulting pole which broke while plaintiff was using it in vaulting, and thus caused him to fall and be injured. He brought this suit to recover for his injuries, had a verdict and judgment in the amount of $7,500. The defendant has appealed.

* * * *

The facts are: Plaintiff, in March and April, 1937, was a high school student in the Deuel County High School at Chappell, Nebraska. He was a skilled high school pole vaulter. The defendant at that time and continuously for a long time prior thereto was engaged in manufacturing and selling various kinds of athletic goods, among which were vaulting poles. The Deuel County High School, on March 4, 1937, sent to the defendant an order as follows: "1-T14-vaulting pole (hand picked) vaulter only weighs 120 lb."

> This order was made from defendant's catalogue, reading in part as follows:
> No Guarantee on Vaulting Poles or Javelins Bamboo vaulting poles being a product of nature and subjected to various kinds of treatment cannot be guaranteed against splitting or breaking. Keep in a cool, dry place laid flat on a level floor. Avoid Heated basements and sudden change of temperature. ***
> The defendant, acting on that order, sent to the school a bamboo vaulting pole.... ***

George Miller, an experienced pole vaulter and coach of athletics and science teacher of the school, testified *** that he *** was not present at the time of the accident. However, he examined the pole, evidently in a few minutes thereafter, and found the pole did not bend or buckle; that it was "broken clear in two and that the break was almost smooth", no splitting or splintering.

In the cross-examination of the witness he testified that he saw nothing indicating the pole was dangerous.

"Q. And you thought it (pole) was all right? A. I had never gotten a pole that I was able to break before; there was no reason why I should suspicion it being a defective pole."

Mr. Miller further testified that he recalled seeing two instances in which a vaulter broke a bamboo pole; that in those instances the pole "did not break clear in two, the vaulter hanging on to the pole with one hand has pushed away from the vaulting pole and on top of that he supports his arms and head so that the feet come down first;" that the poles buckled, "they never break entirely in two," and that the pole here involved was the only pole which broke "completely."

Plaintiff's witness, G. Harry Clay, testified he had had experience in testing materials for strength and defects, was a graduate of Rose Polytechnic Institute with the degree of B. S.; that he took an engineering course in an engineering school, was a member of the American Chemical Society, and that he was local counselor of that society, had been a member of American Society for Testing Materials; that for 10 years he was connected with the Kansas City Testing Laboratory which specialized in the testing of engineering materials, construction materials, road materials, "and all that sort of thing;" that bamboo is used as a structural material in the Orient and in South America; that he had made a study of bamboo by searching literature and experimenting on his own account; that the literature he had read was the Encyclopedia Brittanica, the year books and bulletins of the Agricultural Department of the United States; that from his study and experiments he was familiar with the physical characteristics and properties of bamboo poles; that the principles of testing bamboo were the same as the principles used in testing other structural materials. He further testified he examined the pole, the breaking of which caused plaintiff to be injured, and found a defect therein; that his conclusion there was a defect was based on his examination of the break itself; "it (pole) was broken short off just as a piece of brittle oak breaks off," "from the fact that bamboo breaks in an entirely different way;" and that bamboo breaks by long splits and cracks from the distortion of the cross section.

"Q. Now, if a bamboo pole is not defective, tell the jury how the pole will break or buckle or bend if it is subjected to more stress and strain than it can stand? A. Well, I can probably illustrate that with a fishing pole or with any of these pieces if I had the strength, but it breaks first by being distorted. As the pole is bent that circle becomes an ellipse. That flattening of the section of the pole results in cracking, probably through one or two of the knobs. That weakens the whole pole and it breaks, but not in two. It will bend clear double before it will break in two."

"Q. That is when it is not defective. A. That is when it is not defective."

Plaintiff testified he had been pole vaulting for 10 years prior to the accident; that during that time he had not seen or heard of a pole breaking during a vault, but had heard of one splitting; that he took the pole in question from the school building to the athletic field and vaulted twice "successfully;" that at each of said times his hold was 8 feet, 2 inches from the butt of the pole;

that he then placed his hold 11 feet, 3 inches from the butt of the pole, and proceeded to vault in the usual manner and that in the vault the pole broke "completely apart."

The defendant's witness, Charles Regelbrugge, testified he had been in charge of the vaulting pole department of the defendant for eight years; that defendant each year obtains 4000 to 6000 bamboo poles "in the raw" which were harvested in Japan; that the poles when received were each 18 to 20 feet in length and that 15 to 50 per cent of them were defective; that the defective ones could in some instances be discovered by "merely looking" at them, other defective poles could be discovered only by testing them; that when the defendant received an order for a vaulting pole it sent to him a work ticket on which was stated the length and type of pole ordered and in some instances the weight of the person who would use the pole in vaulting; that in filling the order he selected a pole, cut it to the length stated on the work ticket, then tested it by throwing his weight upon it "in four different positions"; he then caused a maple-wood plug to be inserted in the butt of the pole; the pole was then painted and wrapped in numerous places with adhesive tape. In his cross-examination this witness said he had no recollection of testing any pole that was sent to Chappell, Nebraska.

* * * *

He further testified he tested a pole for the purpose of making sure it would hold the person for whom it was intended and for the purpose of discovering defects.

"Q. And would the test that you customarily made before you sent these poles out to customers disclose defects? A. Yes, sir, we could sure find that."

* * *

[W]e conclude the evidence...shows that it was the practice and custom of defendant to inspect and test each bamboo vaulting pole before sending it to the purchaser. In other words, defendant recognized it was under duty to inspect and test a vaulting pole before releasing it to be used in vaulting. The purpose of such test...was to "make sure" the pole would hold the weight stated in the work ticket (in the instant case 120 pounds), to discover defects; and that such testing as defendant customarily made would "sure" disclose any existing defect. It follows, of course, if the pole were defective, and that a reasonably careful test would have disclosed the defect, then the jury could find defendant failed to make such test.

* * *

From an examination of the numerous cases cited in the briefs relating to the so-called modern rule governing liability of a manufacturer in cases such as the present one, we conclude that a manufacturer of a product is under duty to exercise ordinary care to test the product to determine whether or not it has a defect which would render it unsafe when applied to its intended use; that a failure to perform such duty renders the manufacturer liable to a person injured in consequence of such failure while using such article in the ordinary and usual manner. [Citations Omitted]

Defendant at the time it sent the...pole to the school knew plaintiff intended to use that pole in vaulting. It was therefore its duty to exercise reasonable care in testing the pole to ascertain whether or not it was free of defects which would endanger plaintiff when he put the pole to the intended use.

The defendant insists there was no evidence showing that the pole was defective; that its evidence "demonstrates" the pole was inspected and tested. Neither of these contentions can be sustained. There was evidence to the effect the pole "snapped off". This was sufficient, when taken in connection with the evidence of Clay, to enable the jury to find the pole was brittle. The only evidence which it can be said tended to show the pole which broke was tested, was that of Regelbrugge who stated the manner in which he customarily tested bamboo vaulting poles. *** He was the only witness who knew whether the pole was or was not tested, and his evidence on that subject was not sufficient to conclusively show he tested the pole in question. The jury could very well find that if he had thrown his weight upon the pole in four different positions as he stated he customarily did, the pole would have "snapped off" because it was brittle. Regelbrugge further testified that in "some years" he broke one-half of the poles in testing them; that he tested the poles to make sure "they would hold the man they were ordered for."

"Q. If that man was a 150-pound man, you wouldn't give it any more of a test, would you? A. No, sir."

"Q. And if he was a 200-pound man you wouldn't give it any more of a test, would you? A. No, sir."

* * *

"Q. And you would give it the same kind of a test without regard to what size person it was being ordered for? A. Yes, sir."

Plainly, the court cannot say such a method of testing was a reasonably careful method. The question was one for the trier of the fact.

* * *

The facts stated above were sufficient to warrant the jury in finding the pole was defective and unsafe for its intended use; that if defendant had tested it in a reasonably careful manner the defect would have been discovered and the injury averted. Thus the failure of the defendant to properly test the pole was the direct cause of the accident.

Plaintiff assumed the ordinary risk of pole vaulting but he did not assume risks due to the negligence of the defendant. He did not, prior to the accident, know or have cause to believe the pole was not a safe one to use in vaulting. He vaulted three times in the usual and skillful manner. This was not negligence as a matter of law. In this connection it must be remembered Miller, an experienced pole vaulter, testified he had never had a pole which he could break, and that he had no cause to "suspicion" the pole in question was a defective pole. It may be the defendant's opinion evidence was sufficient to allow the jury to find plaintiff was guilty of contributory negligence, but the court could not tell the jury it must believe that evidence.

* * * *

The record is free of error prejudicial to the defendant. The judgment should be and it is affirmed.

Harry Cooper demonstrates why larger men struggled on Bamboo. London 1948

NOTES & QUESTIONS

1. This case was decided using ordinary negligence principles. It pre-dates the advent of modern strict products liability. After you have read the note at the end of this chapter about tort and commercial law theories relating to sports equipment, and after you have taken the time to digest and absorb the modern rubric of products liability, look back at the facts of this case and test yourself to see whether you are able to articulate a rule of the case more satisfactory than the one that this court in 1940 enunciated.

2. What sort of testing protocol do you think would be appropriate for a manufacturer of modern fiberglass vaulting poles? If you were asked to advise a pole manufacturer about testing procedures, what would you suggest in order to avoid liability? Currently the

manufacturers test poles at the factory using sophisticated equipment in order to assign a weight-rating to them (*i.e.,* what the maximum body weight of the vaulter using the pole should be), and the manufacturers also use machines to test the poles by bending them in excess of 90 degrees (a stress test) to be certain that the pole is unlikely to break due to some structural defect.

3. What warning labels, if any, would you advise a pole manufacturer to place on the poles that it sells? (an issue taken to interesting heights/lengths in the next case).

4. *See* Russ VerSteeg, *Pole Vault Injuries: Product Liability and Commercial Law Theories*, 5 TEXAS REV. ENT. *&* SPORTS L. 237 (2004); Russ VerSteeg, *Arresting Vaulting Pole Technology*, 9 Vanderbilt J. Ent. & Tech. L. 93 (2005).

PELL V. VICTOR J. ANDREW HIGH SCHOOL AND AMF
462 NE 2D 858 (1984)
APPELLATE COURT OF ILLINOIS, FIRST DISTRICT, FIFTH DIVISION

WILSON, JUSTICE:

This is an appeal by defendant AMF, Inc. ("AMF")...on a jury verdict for plaintiff Lauren M. Pell for permanent injuries plaintiff sustained during gym class while performing a somersault off a trampoline manufactured by AMF. Prior to trial, plaintiff and defendants School District 230 and Victor J. Andrew High School entered into a settlement agreement for $1.6 million. Thereafter, the jury awarded plaintiff $5 million against AMF on the theory of strict liability, which amount was set off by the $1.6 million settlement figure and resulted in a final judgment against AMF for $3.4 million.

* * *

On December 29, 1980, plaintiff, a 16-year-old sophomore and beginner gymnast at Victor J. Andrew High School, was injured as the result of a somersault she performed on a product manufactured by AMF, called a mini-trampoline or trampolette ("mini-tramp"). This equipment consists of a 37-inch, square-shaped metal frame holding a "bed" of polypropylene fabric with rubber cables which lace the "bed" to the frame. Two adjustable metal leg sections can be used to set the frame at any angle or to fold the equipment flat.

The mini-tramp was sold to School District 230 with a heat-laminated caution label affixed to the bed which stated:

> Caution. Misuse and abuse of this trampoline is dangerous and can cause serious injuries. Read instructions before using this trampoline. Inspect before using and replace any

worn, defective, or missing parts. Any activity involving motion or height creates the possibility of accidental injuries. This unit is intended for use only by properly trained and qualified participants under supervised conditions. Use without proper supervision can be dangerous and should not be undertaken or permitted.

When the mini-tramp was assembled by a faculty member at the high school, the bed was placed so that the caution label was on the bottom, facing the floor, as opposed to the top where it would be visible to a performer. There were printed warnings also on the frame of the mini-tramp, however they were covered by frame pads on each of the four sides.

On the day of the injury, plaintiff had first performed two somersaults off the mini-tramp. Both of the school's coaches, Charlene Nutter, the varsity gymnastics coach, and Cathi Miles, were present in the gymnasium. Miles, who worked primarily with the freshmen and sophomore students, witnessed plaintiff's third somersault from a distance of approximately 10 feet. Plaintiff testified that she took a few running steps up to the mini-tramp and jumped onto the bed. When she went into the air, at the point when her feet were straight up and down above her, plaintiff said she felt a sharp pain in her knee and was unable to properly complete her somersault. She collapsed onto a nearby mat, severing her spine.

* * *

OPINION

Initially, AMF maintains that...it cannot be held liable, as a matter of law, for failing to provide warnings and instructional materials for using the mini-tramp since the school district as well as the high school had all of the appropriate instructional materials. We find this reasoning unpersuasive, however, because it misstates the central issue presented to the trier of fact, which was the unreasonably dangerous condition of the mini-tramp which, plaintiff alleged, existed because AMF failed to *adequately* warn of the equipment's propensity to cause severe spinal cord injuries if used for somersaulting without a safety device operated by a trained instructor.

Warnings must be adequate to perform their intended function of risk reduction. Warnings may be inadequate, however, if they: (1) do not specify the risk presented by the product; (2) are inconsistent with how a product would be used; (3) if they do not provide the reason for the warnings; or (4) if they do not reach foreseeable users. [Case Citations Omitted]

Considering these principles, in our opinion there was sufficient evidence in the instant case from which the jury could conclude that AMF's warnings were ineffective. First, the warnings did not specify the risk of severe spinal cord injury which would result in permanent paralysis during somersaulting off the mini-tramp if performed without a spotter or safety harness. Charlene Nutter, head coach at the high school, testified that she did not know that the mini-tramp had any more risk involved in it than did any other gymnastic equipment and had she known, she would have taken precautions.

Coach Cathi Miles was also unaware of any rule that somersaults should not be performed on a mini-tramp without a spotter or overhead mechanical safety belt, although she had used the safety harness with a larger (full size) trampoline as well as the mini-tramp.

In addition, the jury could have reasonably determined that the warnings were inadequate because their location was inconsistent with the equipment's use. Plaintiff presented evidence that the assembly instructions failed to specify that the warning label should be placed in such a manner that it would be clearly visible to a gymnast. As a result, the warning label on the "bed" was placed underneath, facing the floor. The warnings on the sides of the metal frame were also ineffective because they were covered by frame pads.

* * *

In a strict liability action, a manufacturer may remain a contributing cause of an injury if the intervening acts or omissions of others were foreseeable. Foreseeability means that which is objectively reasonable to expect, not what might conceivably occur. This is ordinarily a question of fact for the jury. Liability will also attach if the defendant's conduct contributed in whole or in part to the injury, so long as it was *one* of the proximate causes.

In the case before us, there was sufficient evidence to support a finding that it was objectively foreseeable that mini-tramp users such as plaintiff would not always be under the direct supervision of a coach and that neither a gymnast nor a coach would have sufficient knowledge of the dangers of the mini-tramp because the warnings were inadequate. As we have previously explained, plaintiff submitted ample evidence which strongly suggested that AMF's warnings were inadequate. Additionally, the record shows that... coaches were not "told to put the kids in harnesses if they're using a mini-tramp to avoid crippling injuries from doing a somersault." In our judgment, therefore...the evidence...demonstrated that (1) the absence of direct supervision was reasonably foreseeable, and (2) that AMF's failure to adequately warn of the risk of serious injury was a proximate cause of plaintiff's injury. ***

* * *

Accordingly, for all of the foregoing reasons, the judgment of the circuit court of Cook County will be affirmed.

AFFIRMED.

NOTES & QUESTIONS

1. Must a manufacturer warn of obvious dangers? Why or why not? For example, must the manufacturer of carving knives warn users that the blades are sharp and might cut them?

2. Manufacturers now place multiple warning labels on products. Do consumers actually take them seriously? Or have we become so desensitized to them that we simply ignore them as

if they were saying "blah, blah, blah"? One might well ask whether frequent flyers pay any attention to the airline crew's safety instructions regarding seatbelts, oxygen masks, and seat cushions as flotation devices as they taxi toward the runway?

3. Given the context of this injury (occurring in a high school gym class), is the plaintiff's claim – that she would not have attempted the somersault if there had been a visible warning label on the mini-tramp – credible? Isn't it more likely that she simply would have complied with the instructions of her gym teacher, no matter what type of warning label was on the apparatus? If true, what bearing should that fact have on the outcome of this decision?

4. Does this case teach manufacturers that they must specify: "Be certain to affix this warning label in a location where its user will be able to read it."? Isn't this a bit ridiculous? In terms of proximate cause, isn't it more reasonable to believe that the person who assembled the mini-tramp with the warning label on the wrong side (*i.e.,* facing downwards) was really the proximate cause of the plaintiff's injury, not AMF?

5. In light of this case, how would you advise a manufacturer of sporting goods equipment to deal with warning labels?

6. In a portion of the case that does not appear in the textbook, the court addressed the defendant's claim that the plaintiff was contributorily negligent. What is the relationship between the doctrine of strict products liability, comparative negligence, misuse, and assumption of risk?

7. *DuRocher v. Riddell, Inc.,* 97 F. Supp. 3d 1006 (S.D. Ind. 2015) is another more recent case that addresses issues relating to the causal connection between warnings and products liability. The court allowed plaintiffs' product liability claims against football helmet manufacturer to proceed, based on a theory of alleged defective design (*i.e.,* claiming that alternative designs and warnings could have decreased injuries.

Generally, a person injured by an arguably defective, commercially supplied product has available at least three separate and distinct causes of action: negligence, breach of implied warranty, and strict liability in tort. In some cases, a fourth cause of action, breach of an express warranty, is available.[8]

I. Product Liability

A. General

The size of jury awards in sports-related product liability lawsuits can be substantial. Twenty years ago in a case involving a high school student who was injured on a mini-trampoline "the jury awarded plaintiff $5 million against AMF on the theory of strict liability...." The classic Sports Law treatise — *The Law of Sports* by Weistart and Lowell - articulates the general rule regarding sports equipment and product liability succinctly: "The suppliers of athletic equipment have a duty to exercise care for the protection of those who use their equipment or who may be endangered by its use." Another popular Sports Law treatise acknowledges: "In any sports-related accident, a products liability suit that puts the sports equipment under scrutiny should at least be considered." That same treatise explains further:

> Under a theory of strict liability in tort, a commercial supplier who sells a product 'in defective condition unreasonably dangerous to the user or consumer' is subject to liability for harm caused. Liability attaches even if the seller has exercised all possible care and even though the user or consumer has no contractual relation with the seller. The determination of whether a product is defective is made with reference to a reasonable consumer's expectations. Assumption of risk and misuse of the product are defenses.

The doctrine of product liability serves broad economic and social purposes. Because fault (*i.e.,* the failure to act like a reasonable person under similar circumstances) is not a criterion for a finding of liability in this context, product liability saddles manufacturers/sellers with the costs of injuries caused by their products. In one sense, manufacturers/seller are in a better position to guard against injury than are the individuals who wind up being hurt by their products.

---

7 Adapted from Russ VerSteeg, *Pole Vault Injuries: Product Liability and Commercial Law Theories*, 5 TEXAS REV. ENT. & SPORTS L. 237 (2004). I have deleted nearly all footnotes to make the note easier to read.

8 Gary Uberstine, Editor; Joel Corry, Jeffrey Pressman, Assistant Editors, LAW OF PROFESSIONAL AND AMATEUR SPORTS (VOL. 3 2002) § 15:14 at 15-23 (hereinafter "GARY UBERSTINE, EDITOR; JOEL CORRY, JEFFREY PRESSMAN, ASSISTANT EDITORS"). See also Douglas Houser, John Ashworth, Ronald Clark, *Product Liability in the Sports Industry* 23 TORT & INSURANCE LAW JOURNAL 44, 47 (1987)("Today a person injured by a defective product has a choice of distinct, yet related, theories of recovery upon which to base his action, e.g., strict liability, negligence, or breach of warranty.").

Hence, product liability imposes accident costs on the superior risk bearer. As Thomas Van Flein has stated:

> The touchstone of products liability is risk allocation. Liability imposed against the product manufacturer for economic and non-economic harm caused to consumers transfers the real costs of defective products to the manufacturers and retailers (who profit from the products) rather than the injured consumers or society as a whole.

Most American jurisdictions have adopted section 402A of the Restatement, Second, of Torts for their general definitions and general rules regarding products liability. Section 402A provides:

> (1) One who sells any product in a defective condition unreasonably dangerous to the user or consumer or to his property is subject to liability for physical harm thereby caused to the ultimate user or consumer, or to his property, if the seller is engaged in the business of selling such a product, and
>
> it is expected to and does reach the user or consumer without substantial change in the condition in which it is sold.
>
> (2) The rule stated in Subsection (1) applies although
>
> the seller has exercised all possible care in the preparation and sale of his product, and
>
> the user or consumer has not bought the product from or entered into any contractual relation with the seller.

According to one commentator, "Section 402A imposes strict liability upon one who sells a product in a defective condition which is unreasonably dangerous to the user or consumer. The liability is in tort rather than warranty and therefore the various contract rules, such as notice of breach, do not apply."

It is common to define a product "defect" by actually recognizing three distinct types of product defects: 1) manufacturing defects; 2) design defects; and, 3) failures to warn adequately.
***

Uberstein explains:

> A review of case law reveals that there are three basic types of defects: manufacturing flaws, design flaws, and marketing flaws. Manufacturing flaws can be described as individual product imperfections, such as a coffee roll with a pebble in it. Design flaws impugn the entire product line. In litigation concerning the Ford Pinto, it was contended that all the Pintos of a given year were defective because Ford placed the gas tank in

a dangerously vulnerable position behind the rear axle. This would be an example of an alleged design defect. Finally, marketing flaws arise when the seller fails to provide needed instructions regarding proper use, or to provide adequate warnings concerning less obvious dangers.

Another key component of this definition of a defective product is the issue of what renders a product "unreasonably dangerous." In their article "Product Liability in the Sports Industry," Houser, Ashworth, and Clark posit:

> A defective product is "unreasonably dangerous" when the product is "dangerous to an extent beyond that which would be contemplated by the ordinary consumer who purchases it, with the ordinary knowledge common to the community as to its characteristics." It can be argued that an allegedly defective product used for an extended period of time without injury is prima facie not "unreasonably dangerous." ***

Another important aspect of the law of product liability to bear in mind is that courts have gradually expanded the scope of potential plaintiffs. As Houser, Ashworth, and Clark note:

> Around 1965, the definitions of "user" and "consumer" began to broaden gradually so that today an injured plaintiff may bring an action in strict liability even though he was not literally 'using' the product. Examples of the relaxation of this requirement include a bystander who was injured by the explosion of a shotgun, the driver of a car struck by another car, and a bystander injured by the explosion of a beer keg.

B. Design Defects Introduction

According to Uberstein,

> The modern products liability case often revolves around a claim that the product is defectively designed. In such a case, the plaintiff impugns the conscious design choice of the manufacturer and attempts to show a safer, economically feasible design. In determining whether the manufacturer's choice of design renders the product in a "defective condition unreasonably dangerous," courts have been unable to agree on a single standard.

Houser, Ashworth, and Clark note:

> The nature of sports, however, is such that a great many of the products used serve the sole purpose of protecting the user. Face masks, batting helmets, releasable ski bindings, knee pads and braces, football helmets, goggles, railings, floor pads, mouthpieces, roll bars and shoulder pads are a few examples of such protective products. *A defect in a piece*

of protective sports equipment is more apt to make that product 'unreasonably dangerous' because its sole purpose is to protect the user.

C. Failure to Warn Adequately

One court succinctly summarized the applicable legal doctrine as follows:

> it is well established that a product, although virtually faultless in design, material, and workmanship, may nevertheless be deemed defective so as to impose liability upon the manufacturer for physical harm resulting from its use, where the manufacturer fails to discharge a duty to warn or instruct with respect to potential dangers in the use of the product. Generally, the duty to warn arises where the supplier knows or should have known of the danger involved in the use of its product, or where it is unreasonably dangerous to place the product in the hands of a user without a suitable warning. However, where the danger or potentiality of danger is known or should be known to the user, the duty does not attach.

Houser, Ashworth, and Clark emphasize two important points regarding the adequacy of product warnings. First, "There is, of course, no duty to warn of dangers that could have been readily recognized by the ordinary user." Furthermore, the appropriate standard for determining sufficiency of a warning would seem to be whether an ordinary consumer could read and understand the warnings so as to be able to take the necessary precautions. "Whether or not a given warning is adequate depends upon the language used and the impression that it is calculated to make upon the mind of an average user of the product."

D. Defenses

As is true in all litigation, it is generally useful to distinguish between direct defenses and affirmative defenses. A direct defense relies on an argument that directly refutes an element of a plaintiff's prima facie case. For example, in a product liability suit, one element that a plaintiff must prove by a preponderance of the evidence is that the product in question was "defective unreasonably dangerous." Therefore, one direct defense in a product liability suit would be for a defendant to marshal facts and reasoning that tend to show that the product was not more dangerous than a reasonable consumer would have expected (*i.e.,* and therefore not defective unreasonably dangerous). An affirmative defense, on the other hand, is an argument that does not attempt to refute an element of the plaintiff's prima facie case, but instead, seeks to show an alternative explanation for the plaintiff's injury or justification for the defendant's conduct.

In a product liability lawsuit, defendants commonly raise five different (but in some cases related) affirmative defenses: 1) Plaintiff misused the product or used the product in a manner that the manufacturer/seller did not intend (but the plaintiffs misuse must not have been reasonably foreseeable); 2) Manufacturer/seller provided proper instructions and/or warnings regarding the product's use which the plaintiff failed to heed (and if plaintiff had heeded those warnings the product would have been safe); 3) Use or normal wear and tear over time have significantly changed the product from the condition that it was in when it left the manufacturer's/seller's control; 4) Plaintiff assumed the risk of injury; 5) Unforeseeable superseding conduct by a third party (*e.g.,* a coach's negligence) was the proximate cause of the plaintiffs injury, not the defendant's product.

II. Commercial Law Theories

A. General

In addition to strict product liability, an injured athlete may also (or in the alternative) look to commercial law; specifically the Uniform Commercial Code ("UCC") for legal theories of recovery against manufacturers/sellers. Under the UCC, one theory of legal liability available to plaintiffs is warranty law. Nearly all jurisdictions in the United States have adopted Article Two of the UCC. Article Two provides at least three different warranties that are likely to apply in the sale of most sporting goods equipment. Specifically, the most obvious warranty theories are breach of: 1) express warranty (§ 2-313); 2) implied warranty of merchantability (§ 2-314); and, 3) implied warranty of fitness for a particular purpose (§ 2-315). In addition to these, another commercial law theory that an injured plaintiff should keep in mind arises under the warranties created pursuant to the Magnuson Moss Warranty Act. The UCC warranties may apply to the various types of sports equipment and apparatus which constitute "goods" as that term is defined in the UCC.

B. A Few Details

In order for the impled warranty of merchantability (UCC § 2-314) to apply, the seller must be a "merchant" as that term is defined as a term of art in the UCC. Suffice it to say that a sporting goods store, a sporting goods supply catalogue company, and manufacturing companies themselves will generally be considered "merchants" for purposes of this rule. In order to be considered a "merchant," triggering § 2-314, a seller must regularly deal in goods of the kind. A coach, a school, another athlete, or an occasional eBay seller will ordinarily not come within the scope of the "merchant" rule for purposes of section 2-314.

UCC §§ 2-715 and 2-719 provide that a breach of either express or implied warranties may impose liability for personal injury as part of incidental or consequential damages.

C. Defenses to Warranty Actions

1. Lack of Privity

A lack of privity may be one legal obstacle that could prove difficult for some plaintiffs. Traditionally, at common law, a person who was injured by a product was barred from bringing a contract action against a seller unless s/he (*i.e.,* the plaintiff) was in privity of contract with the seller. Although the common law has relaxed this privity rule somewhat, and although the UCC has a specific provision, § 2-318, designed to address the issue, the rule may present special problems in the context of sports equipment liability. Section 2-318 defines the scope of both plaintiffs and defendants contemplated by Article 2 for personal injury. ***

On the issue of potential plaintiffs, § 2-318 offers three different alternatives, gradually progressing from very restrictive to very expansive. Alternative A provides, in part, that a seller's warranty "extends to any natural person who is in the family or household of his buyer or who is a guest in his home if it is reasonable to expect that such person may use...or be affected by the goods and who is injured in person by breach of the warranty."

Comment Three to § 2-318 addresses the issue of "vertical privity." Comment Three provides, in part: "this section...is neutral and is not intended to enlarge or restrict the developing case law on whether the seller's warranties, given to his buyer who resells, extend to other persons in the distributive chain." Hence, § 2-318 makes it a matter of state law, for example, whether a plaintiff-buyer may sue a wholesaler and/or a manufacturer - in addition to a direct retailer from whom s/he bought the product. As a rule, the majority of American jurisdictions permit a plaintiff to sue a wholesaler and/or manufacturer, despite a technical lack of vertical privity between those entities and the typical buyer.

2. Limitation or Exclusion of Liability

To be sure, sellers may exclude or modify express and implied warranties by employing the mechanics of § 2-316.

If a manufacturer wishes to minimize its exposure to liability for breach of warranty, Language such as the following may be effective:

> **WARRANTY DISCLAIMER: THE MANUFACTURER EXPRESSLY DISCLAIMS ANY EXPRESS OR IMPLIED WARRANTIES, INCLUDING THE WARRANTY OF MERCHANTABILITY AND/OR THE WARRANTY OF FITNESS FOR A PARTICULAR PURPOSE. SALESPERSONS MAY HAVE MADE ORAL OR WRITTEN STATEMENTS ABOUT THE MERCHANDISE WHICH IS THE SUBJECT OF THIS SALE. THE MANUFACTURER HAS NOT AUTHORIZED SUCH STATEMENTS AND SUCH STATEMENTS DO NOT CONSTITUTE WARRANTIES, SHALL NOT BE RELIED ON BY THE BUYER, AND ARE NO PART OF THE CONTRACT FOR SALE.**

This disclaimer must be clearly labeled as a "Warranty Disclaimer" (so that a reasonable consumer should recognize that it is not "hidden" within a purported warranty). Also, in order to be valid, it must be "conspicuous."

Thus, it should be written prominently in some fashion which calls attention to it; such as a contrasting color or typeface (ALL CAPS and/or BOLDFACE should suffice). Note that although the disclaimer/exclusionary language purports to disclaim any express warranty, § 2-316 (1) of the Code creates a rule which, as a matter of fact, makes it virtually impossible to disclaim express warranties.

According to the rule of § 2-316(1), when faced with this issue, courts will compare the language which the plaintiff argues creates an express warranty with the language which the defendant claims to exclude an express warranty. Then, to the extent that the court considers the two to be inconsistent, the court construes that inconsistency as rendering the purported exclusion void. The standard treatise on commercial law takes the position that courts should enforce language in a warranty disclaimer which nullifies unauthorized verbal or written statements made by salespeople such as that suggested (*i.e.,* Sales persons may have....).

But even if courts are unwilling to enforce a warranty disclaimer of this type, occasionally language such as this will deter a lawsuit because a consumer will read the warranty disclaimer and assume that it is valid and binding. If a disclaimer prevents even one lawsuit against a manufacturer or seller, it will be cost effective.

Section 2-715 of the UCC provides that a seller may limit or exclude liability for consequential damages. Many sellers in today's marketplace commonly do just this sort of thing by stating, for example, "In no event shall seller be liable for incidental or consequential damages. Seller's liability is limited to refund, repair, or replacement of defective goods."

However, when the consequential loss complained of is personal injury, sellers have a much more difficult task in making such an exclusion or limitation stand up in court. Subsection (3) of § 2-719 states: "Consequential damages may be limited or excluded unless the limitation or exclusion is unconscionable. Limitation of consequential damages for injury to the person in the case of *consumer goods* is prima facie unconscionable...."

The unresolved question, then, is whether sports equipment is considered "consumer goods." The general definitions section of the UCC (§ 1-201) does not define "consumer goods" but it defines "consumer" as "an individual who enters into a transaction primarily for personal, family, or household purposes."[9] Although Article 2 does not define "consumer goods," Article 9 defines "consumer goods" as "goods that are used or bought for use primarily for personal, family, or household purposes." It strikes me as strange to think that whether this type of exclusionary language is considered "prima facie unconscionable," may depend on the specific facts of each case (*i.e.,* whether the actual buyer purchases the goods on an individual basis or for an institution, such as a school or club). For example, if a school were to purchase sports equipment for its athletes, arguably that equipment would *not* come within the definition of "consumer goods," whereas if an individual athlete or a athlete's parent were to purchase the same equipment, it *would* be considered "consumer goods." It simply seems strange to think that the burden of proving unconscionability would depend on the status of who happens to purchase any given piece of equipment. ***

---

9 UCC §1-201

Further Reading on Coach's Liability and Equipment:

William Anderson, Cheryl Falvey, *Crumb Rubber Turf Wars: The Synthetic Turf Fields Investigation*, 83 Def. Couns. J. 286 (2016).

A. David Austill, *When It Hits the Fan: Will There Be Liability for the Broken Bat?*, 24 Marq. Sports L. Rev. 83 (2013).

Timothy Davis, *Tort Liability of Coaches for Injuries to Professional Athletes: Overcoming Policy and Doctrinal Barriers*, 76 UMKC L. Rev. 571 (2008).

Brooke de Lench & Lindsey Barton Straus, *Standard-Setting by Non-Governmental Agencies in the Field of Sports Safety Equipment: Promoting the Interests of Consumers or Manufacturers?*, 10 J. Bus. & Tech. L. 47 (2015).

Erika A. Diehl, *What's All the Headache? Reform Needed to Cope with the Effects of Concussions in Football*, 23 J.L. & Health 83 (2010).

David Feingold, *Who Takes the Heat? Criminal Liability for Heat-Related Deaths in High School Athletics*, 17 Cardozo J.L. & Gender 359 (2011).

Thomas R. Hurst, *Coach's Liability for Athlete's Injuries and Deaths*, 13 Seton Hall J. Sports L. 27 (2003).

Mitch Koczerginski, *Who Is at Fault When A Concussed Athlete Returns to Action?*, 47 Val. U. L. Rev. 63 (2012).

David Marck, *Necessary Roughness?: An Argument for the Assignment of Criminal Liability in Cases of Student-Athlete Sustained Heat-Related Deaths*, 21 Seton Hall J. Sports & Ent. L. 177 (2011).

Jason Navia, *Comment, Sitting on the bench: the failure of youth football helmet regulation and the necessity of government intervention*, 64 Admin. L. Rev. 265 (2012).

John C. Weistart & Cym H. Lowell, *Law of Sports*, §§8.06, 8.09-11 (Bobbs-Merrill Company, Inc., 1979).

Joshua D. Winneker & Philip Schultze, *"School's Out": A Coach's Tortious Instructions to His Players to Harm Others Is Beyond the Scope of Employment for Imputing Liability to the Employer-Schools*, 17 Tex. Rev. Ent. & Sports L. 145 (2016).

Chapter 4
Torts III: Institutions, Officials, & Waivers

In this chapter we look at the liability of institutions. The principal issue is whether and/or to what extent a school, club, school board, etc. can be held responsible for injuries to athletes or spectators. What steps must an institution take to balance the need for safety and the risks that go hand-in-hand with vigorous competition? As was the case with liability for equipment manufacturers, again the law must balance the need for safety with the risks that are inherent in participation in certain sports. This issue has received extraordinary publicity and national attention during the past several years, with the NFL taking center stage in the controversy. In late August 2013, the NFL settled the class action lawsuit that had been brought by former players for $765 million. The players' suit alleged that the NFL had concealed its knowledge about the dangers of concussions and other traumatic brain injuries. In addition to this settlement, former players have filed other lawsuits in state courts such as Missouri and Illinois against the NFL and helmet manufacturer, Ridell. *See e.g.,* https://en.wikipedia.org/wiki/Concussions_in_American_football#Federal_NFL_concussion_litigation; https://www.nflconcussionsettlement.com/. The NHL also reached a settlement in the wake of litigation. *See e.g.,* http://www.espn.com/nhl/story/_/id/25256208/nhl-reaches-settlement-concussion-lawsuit. And additional litigation continues.[1] For example, the widow of former Anaheim and San Jose player Todd Ewen filed a CTE-related suit against the NHL in May 2019. *See e.g.,* https://www.thedailybeast.com/todd-ewens-widow-sues-nhl-over-brain-injury-she-blames-for-his-death. For outstanding analysis of many aspects of this matter (e.g., science, ethics, law), see Ken Dryden, Game Change: The Life and Death of Steve Montador and the Future of Hockey (2017).

Kleinknecht asks us to think about the provision of medical and emergency personnel. Costs and risks are again fundamental considerations. *Hammond* integrates questions about assumption of risk and obvious dangers. What is the scope of a school's duty to warn athletes and their parents about the dangers associated with various sports?

Santopietro raises another serious issue – the responsibility of officials for the safety of participants and spectators. As any casual sports fan is well aware, officials, referees, and umpires cannot see everything. But when rule violations occur and an injury results, it is only natural that some may point an accusatory finger at the officials who, perhaps, could have prevented the rule violation in the first place.

Hiett, Lund, and *Kirton* examine another important aspect of liability for sports injuries – the enforceability of liability waivers. These cases consider what role public policy should play in

---

[1] Among the numerous examples, *see e.g., In re: Natl. Collegiate Athletic Assn. Student-Athlete Concussion Injury Litig., 13 C 9116, 2016 WL 3854603 (N.D. Ill. July 15, 2016). Court approved modified settlement in concussion litigation brought by former and current student athletes.*

using contracts and express assumption of risk to allocate risks in athletic competition. These cases, because they involve the use of contracts to allocate risk of loss, also serve as a bridge to the next chapter, Contracts.

A. DUTY OF CARE OWED TO ATHLETES

KLEINKNECHT V. GETTYSBURG COLLEGE
989 F 2D 1360 (1993)
UNITED STATES COURT OF APPEALS, THIRD CIRCUIT

HUTCHINSON, CIRCUIT JUDGE.

Suzanne W. Kleinknecht and Richard P. Kleinknecht (collectively "the Kleinknechts") appeal an order of the United States District Court for the Middle District of Pennsylvania granting summary judgment to appellee Gettysburg College ("the College"). We will reverse the district court's order granting summary judgment to the College for the following reasons.

I. *Procedural History*

Drew Kleinknecht died of cardiac arrest on September 16, 1988, while a student at the College and during a practice session of its intercollegiate lacrosse team. His parents filed this wrongful death and survival action against the College. ***

Following oral argument on January 30, 1992, the district court reversed its earlier decision and entered summary judgment in favor of the College on March 12, 1992. *Kleinknecht v. Gettysburg College,* 786 F.Supp. 449 (M.D.Pa.1992). In its opinion, the court first held that the College had no duty to anticipate and guard against the chance of a fatal arrhythmia in a young and healthy athlete. *Id.* at 454. The court also held that the actions taken by school employees following Drew's collapse were reasonable, and thus the College did not negligently breach any duty that might exist. *Id.* at 456.

* * * *

The Kleinknechts filed a timely appeal on March 25, 1992.

II. *Factual History*

In September 1988, Drew Kleinknecht was a twenty-year old sophomore student at the College, which had recruited him for its Division III intercollegiate lacrosse team. The College is a private, four-year liberal arts school. In 1988, it had an enrollment of about two thousand students and supported twenty-one intercollegiate sports teams involving approximately 525 male and female athletes.

Lacrosse is a contact sport. In terms of sports-related injuries at the College, it ranked at least fourth behind football, basketball, and wrestling, respectively. Lacrosse players can typically suffer a variety of injuries, including unconsciousness, wooziness, concussions, being knocked to the ground, and having the wind knocked out of them. Before Drew died, however, no athlete at the College had experienced cardiac arrest while playing lacrosse or any other sport.

In September 1988, the College employed two full-time athletic trainers, Joseph Donolli and Gareth Biser. Both men were certified by the National Athletic Trainers Association, which requires, *inter alia,* current certification in both cardio-pulmonary resuscitation ("CPR") and standard first aid. In addition, twelve student trainers participated in the College's sports program. The trainers were stationed in the College's two training room facilities at Musselman Stadium and Plank Gymnasium.

Because lacrosse is a spring sport, daily practices were held during the spring semester in order to prepare for competition. Student trainers were assigned to cover both spring practices and games. Fall practice was held only for the players to learn "skills and drills," and to become acquainted with the other team members. No student trainers were assigned to the fall practices.

Drew participated in a fall lacrosse practice on the afternoon of September 16, 1988. Coaches [Hank] Janczyk and Anderson attended and supervised this practice. It was held on the softball fields outside Musselman Stadium. No trainers or student trainers were present. Neither coach had certification in CPR. Neither coach had a radio on the practice field. The nearest telephone was inside the training room at Musselman Stadium, roughly 200-250 yards away. The shortest route to this telephone required scaling an eight-foot high cyclone fence surrounding the stadium. According to Coach Janczyk, he and Coach Anderson had never discussed how they would handle an emergency during fall lacrosse practice.

The September 16, 1988 practice began at about 3:15 p.m. with jogging and stretching, some drills, and finally a "six on six" drill in which the team split into two groups at opposite ends of the field. Drew was a defenseman and was participating in one of the drills when he suffered a cardiac arrest. According to a teammate observing from the sidelines, Drew simply stepped away from the play and dropped to the ground. Another teammate on the sidelines stated that no person or object struck Drew prior to his collapse.

After Drew fell, his teammates and Coach Janczyk ran to his side. Coach Janczyk and some of the players noticed that Drew was lying so that his head appeared to be in an awkward position. No one knew precisely what had happened at that time, and at least some of those present suspected a spinal injury. Team captain Daniel Polizzotti testified that he heard a continuous "funny," "gurgling" noise coming from Drew, and knew from what he observed that something "major" was wrong. Other teammates testified that Drew's skin began quickly to change colors. One team member testified that by the time the coaches had arrived, "[Drew] was really blue."

According to the College, Coach Janczyk acted in accordance with the school's emergency plan by first assessing Drew's condition, then dispatching players to get a trainer and call for an ambulance. Coach Janczyk himself then began to run toward Musselman Stadium to summon help.

The Kleinknechts dispute the College's version of the facts. They note that although Coach Janczyk claims to have told two players to run to Apple Hall, a nearby dormitory, for help, Coach Anderson did not recall Coach Janczyk's sending anyone for help. Even if Coach Janczyk did send the two players to Apple Hall, the Kleinknechts maintain, his action was inappropriate because Apple Hall was not the location of the nearest telephone. It is undisputed that two other team members ran for help, but the Kleinknechts contend that the team members did this on their own accord, without instruction from either coach.

The parties do not dispute that Polizzotti, the team captain, ran toward the stadium, where he knew a training room was located and a student trainer could be found. In doing so, Polizzotti scaled a chain link fence that surrounded the stadium and ran across the field, encountering student trainer Traci Moore outside the door to the training room. He told her that a lacrosse player was down and needed help. She ran toward the football stadium's main gate, managed to squeeze through a gap between one side of the locked gate and the brick pillar forming its support, and continued on to the practice field by foot until flagging a ride from a passing car. In the meantime, Polizzotti continued into the training room where he told the student trainers there what had happened. One of them phoned Plank Gymnasium and told Head Trainer Donolli about the emergency.

Contemporaneously with Polizzotti's dash to the stadium, Dave Kerney, another team member, ran toward the stadium for assistance. Upon seeing that Polizzotti was going to beat him there, Kerney concluded that it was pointless for both of them to arrive at the same destination and changed his course toward the College Union Building. He told the student at the front desk of the emergency on the practice field. The student called his supervisor on duty in the building, and she immediately telephoned for an ambulance.

Student trainer Moore was first to reach Drew. She saw Drew's breathing was labored, and the color of his complexion changed as she watched. Because Drew was breathing, she did not attempt CPR or any other first aid technique, but only monitored his condition, observing no visible bruises or lacerations.

By this time, Coach Janczyk had entered the stadium training room and learned that Donolli had been notified and an ambulance called. Coach Janczyk returned to the practice field at the same time Donolli arrived in a golf cart. Donolli saw that Drew was not breathing, and turned him on his back to begin CPR with the help of a student band member who was certified as an emergency medical technician and had by chance arrived on the scene. The two of them performed CPR until two ambulances arrived at approximately 4:15 p.m. Drew was defibrillated and drugs were administered to strengthen his heart. He was placed in an ambulance and taken to the hospital, but despite repeated resuscitation efforts, Drew could not be revived. He was pronounced dead at 4:58 p.m.

As the district court observed, the parties vigorously dispute the amount of time that elapsed in connection with the events following Drew's collapse. The College maintains that "Coach Janczyk immediately ran to Drew's side, followed closely by assistant coach, Anderson." Team captain Polizzotti estimated that it took him no more than thirty seconds to get from the practice field to the training room. The College contends that it took Moore no more than two minutes to get from the training room to Drew's side. In fact, the College maintains, the lacrosse team was practicing on this particular field because of its close proximity to the training room and the student trainers. The College estimates that an ambulance was present within eight to ten minutes after Drew's collapse.

The Kleinknechts, on the other hand, assert that as much as a minute to a minute and a half passed before Coach Janczyk arrived at Drew's side. With the aid of an engineering firm, the Kleinknechts constructed a map for the district court showing the paths taken by Polizzotti and Kerney, including estimates of how long it took them to arrive at their respective destinations and relay their messages to those who could be of assistance. *** [T]he Kleinknechts contend that evidence exists from which a jury could infer that as long as twelve minutes elapsed before CPR was administered. They also estimate that roughly ten more minutes passed before the first ambulance arrived on the scene.

Prior to his collapse on September 16, 1988, Drew had no medical history of heart problems. The Kleinknechts themselves describe him as "a healthy, physically active and vigorous young man," with no unusual medical history until his death. In January 1988, a College physician had examined Drew to determine his fitness to participate in sports and found him to be in excellent health. The Kleinknecht's family physician had also examined Drew in August 1987 and found him healthy and able to participate in physical activity.

Medical evidence indicated Drew died of cardiac arrest after a fatal attack of cardiac arrhythmia. Post-mortem examination could not detect the cause of Drew's fatal cardiac arrhythmia. An autopsy conducted the day after his death revealed no bruises or contusions on his body. This corroborated the statements by Drew's teammates that he was not in play when he suffered his cardiac arrest and dispelled the idea that contact with a ball or stick during the practice might have caused the arrhythmia. The National Institutes of Health examined Drew's heart as part of the autopsy, but found no pathology. A later examination of the autopsy records by a different pathologist, and still further study by yet another physician after Drew's body was exhumed, also failed to reveal any heart abnormality which could have explained Drew's fatal heart attack.

III. *Issues on Appeal*

The Kleinknechts...first argue that the district court erred in determining that the College had no legal duty to implement preventive measures assuring prompt assistance and treatment in the event one of its student athletes suffered cardiac arrest while engaged in school-supervised intercollegiate athletic activity. Second, the Kleinknechts maintain that the district court erred in determining that the actions of school employees following Drew's collapse were reasonable and that the College therefore did not breach any duty of care. ****

IV. *Analysis*

1. *The Duty of Care Issue*

[2][3] Whether a defendant owes a duty of care to a plaintiff is a question of law. *See* Restatement (Second) of Torts § 328(B) (1965)(court determines whether facts give rise to any legal duty on part of defendant). [Case Citations Omitted] In order to prevail on a cause of action in negligence under Pennsylvania law, a plaintiff must establish: (1) a duty or obligation recognized by the law, requiring the actor to conform to a certain standard of conduct; (2) a failure to conform to the standard required; (3) a causal connection between the conduct and the resulting injury; and (4) actual loss or damage resulting to the interests of another. [Case Citation Omitted] (*citing* Prosser, Law of Torts § 30, at 143 (4th ed. 1971)).

The Kleinknechts assert...different theories upon which they predicate the College's duty to establish preventive measures capable of providing treatment to student athletes in the event of a medical emergency such as Drew's cardiac arrest: (1) existence of a special relationship between the College and its student athletes; [and] (2) foreseeability that a student athlete may suffer cardiac arrest while engaged in athletic activity....

a. *Special Relationship*

[4] The Kleinknechts argue that the College had a duty of care to Drew by virtue of his status as a member of an intercollegiate athletic team. The Supreme Court of Pennsylvania has stated that "[d]uty, in any given situation, is predicated on the relationship existing between the parties at the relevant time...." [Citation Omitted]. The Kleinknechts argue that... a college or university owes a duty to its intercollegiate athletes to provide preventive measures in the event of a medical emergency.

*   *   *   *

Drew chose to attend Gettysburg College because he was persuaded it had a good lacrosse program, a sport in which he wanted to participate at the intercollegiate level. Head Trainer Donolli actively recruited Drew to play lacrosse at the College. At the time he was stricken, Drew was not engaged in his own private affairs as a student at Gettysburg College. Instead, he was participating in a scheduled athletic practice for an intercollegiate team sponsored by the College under the supervision of College employees. On these facts we believe that...a special relationship existed between the College and Drew that was sufficient to impose a duty of reasonable care on the College. Other states have similarly concluded that a duty exists based on such a relationship. [Multiple Citations][1]

---

1   We recognize that most of these cases involve participation on sports sponsored by a public school system at the pre-college level. Arguably, the relationship between the injured participant and the sponsor is closer, and the need to import a duty based on the special nature of the relationship between a public school and its interscholastic athletes is therefore more compelling than the case of a private college and its students participating in an intercollegiate athletic program. Here, however, we think that that distinction is balanced out by Gettysburg's active recruitment of Drew to participate in its intercollegiate lacrosse program.

* * * *

Drew was not acting in his capacity as a private student when he collapsed. Indeed, the Kleinknechts concede that if he had been, they would have no recourse against the College. There is a distinction between a student injured while participating as an intercollegiate athlete in a sport for which he was recruited and a student injured at a college while pursuing his private interests, scholastic or otherwise. This distinction serves to limit the class of students to whom a college owes the duty of care that arises here. Had Drew been participating in a fraternity football game, for example, the College might not have owed him the same duty or perhaps any duty at all. There is, however, no need for us to reach or decide the duty question either in that context or in the context of whether a college would owe a duty towards students participating in intramural sports. On the other hand, the fact that Drew's cardiac arrest occurred during an athletic event involving an intercollegiate team of which he was a member does impose a duty of due care on a college that actively sought his participation in that sport. We cannot help but think that the College recruited Drew for its own benefit, probably thinking that his skill at lacrosse would bring favorable attention and so aid the College in attracting other students.

* * * *

In conclusion...the College owed Drew a duty of care in his capacity as an intercollegiate athlete engaged in school-sponsored intercollegiate athletic activity for which he had been recruited.

b. Foreseeability

* * * *

[I]n the context of duty, "[t]he concept of foreseeability means the likelihood of the occurrence of a general type of risk rather than the likelihood of the occurrence of the precise chain of events leading to the injury." *Suchomajcz v. Hummel Chem. Co.,* 524 F.2d 19, 28 n. 8 (3d Cir.1975) (*citing* Harper & James, The Law of Torts § 18.2, at 1026, § 20.5, at 1147-49 (1956)). ***

Although the district court correctly determined that the Kleinknechts had presented evidence establishing that the occurrence of severe and life-threatening injuries is not out of the ordinary during contact sports, it held that the College had no duty because the cardiac arrest suffered by Drew, a twenty-year old athlete with no history of any severe medical problems, was not reasonably foreseeable. Its definition of foreseeability is too narrow. Although it is true that a defendant is not required to guard against every possible risk, he must take reasonable steps to guard against hazards, which are generally foreseeable. *Kimble v. Mackintosh Hemphill Co.,* 359 Pa. 461, 59 A.2d 68, 71 (1948). Though the specific risk that a person like Drew would suffer a cardiac arrest may be unforeseeable, the Kleinknechts produced ample evidence that a life-threatening injury occurring during participation in an athletic event like lacrosse was reasonably foreseeable. In addition to the testimony of numerous medical and athletic experts, Coach Janczyk, Head Trainer Donolli, and student trainer Moore all testified that they were aware of instances in which athletes had died during athletic competitions. The foreseeability of a life-threatening injury to Drew was not hidden from the College's view. Therefore, the College did owe Drew a duty to take reasonable precautions against the risk of death while Drew was taking part in the College's intercollegiate lacrosse program.

Having determined that it is foreseeable that a member of the College's interscholastic lacrosse team could suffer a serious injury during an athletic event, it becomes evident that the College's failure to protect against such a risk is not reasonable. The magnitude of the foreseeable harm – irreparable injury or death to one of its student athletes as a result of inadequate preventive emergency measures – is indisputable. With regard to the offsetting cost of protecting against such risk, the College prophesied that if this Court accepts that the College owed the asserted duty, then it will be required "to have a CPR certified trainer on site at each and every athletic practice whether in-season or off-season, formal or informal, strenuous or light," and to provide similar cardiac protection to "intramural, club sports and gym class." This "slippery slope" prediction reflects an unwarranted extension of the holding in this case. First, the recognition of a duty here is limited to intercollegiate athletes. No other scenario is presented, so the question whether any of the other broad classes of events and students posited by the College merit similar protection is not subject to resolution. Second, the determination whether the College has breached this duty at all is a question of fact for the jury. *See Suchomajcz*, 524 F.2d at 27; *see also Dougherty v. Boyertown Times*, 377 Pa.Super. 462, 547 A.2d 778, 787 (1988). This Court recognizes *only* that under the facts of this case, the College owed a duty to Drew to have measures in place at the lacrosse team's practice on the afternoon of September 16, 1988 in order to provide prompt treatment in the event that he or any other member of the lacrosse team suffered a life-threatening injury. [emphasis added]

* * *

[One] court described the duty a school owes its athletes as "[T]ak[ing] the form of giving adequate instruction in the activity, supplying proper equipment, making a reasonable selection or matching of participants, providing non-negligent supervision of the particular contest, and taking proper post-injury procedures to protect against aggravation of the injury." [Citation Omitted](quoting Annot., 35 A.L.R.3d 725, 734 (1971) (footnotes omitted)). ***

Our holding is narrow. *** [T]he College had a duty to provide prompt and adequate emergency medical services to Drew, one of its intercollegiate athletes, while he was engaged in a school-sponsored athletic activity for which he had been recruited. Whether the College breached that duty is a question of fact. *See Suchomajcz*, 524 F.2d at 27; *see also Dougherty*, 547 A.2d at 787. If the factfinder concludes that such a breach occurred, we think that the question whether that breach was the proximate or legal cause of Drew's death would likewise be a question of fact.

[T]wo distinct theories establish that the College owed a duty of care to Drew as an intercollegiate athlete. A special relationship existed between the College and Drew in his capacity as a school athlete. His medical emergency was within a reasonably foreseeable class of unfortunate events that could arise from participation in an intercollegiate contact sport. ***

Under the facts of this case, the College owed a duty to Drew to have reasonable measures in place at the practice on the afternoon of September 16, 1988 to provide prompt treatment in the event that he or any other member of the lacrosse team suffered a life-threatening injury. The determination whether the College in fact breached this duty is a question of fact for the jury.

2. The Reasonableness of the College's Actions

*** The question of breach must be reconsidered on remand in light of this Court's holding that the College did owe Drew a duty of care to provide prompt and adequate emergency medical assistance to Drew while participating as one of its intercollegiate athletes in a school-sponsored athletic activity.

V. Conclusion

The district court's holding that the College's duty of care to Drew as an intercollegiate athlete did not include, prior to his collapse, a duty to provide prompt emergency medical service while he was engaged in school-sponsored athletic activity will be reversed. The district court's holding that the College acted reasonably and therefore did not breach any duty owed to Drew following his collapse will likewise be reversed. We will remand this matter to the district court for further proceedings consistent with this opinion.

*   *   *   *

NOTES & QUESTIONS

1. Lawyers have adopted an economic mode of analysis to evaluate whether a defendant has breached a duty of care in situations involving safety precautions and the advisability of safety rules. A famous judge, Learned Hand, put it this way. Before adopting a safety rule, we should determine whether the costs of adopting the rule outweigh the benefits of adopting that rule (or vice versa). In short, Judge Hand said that we should compare two costs. First we should try to determine the likelihood of the injury (*i.e.,* probability or the "risk" that a given type of injury might occur) that we are trying to prevent and also try to assess the magnitude of that potential injury. According to Judge Hand, the likelihood of the injury multiplied by the magnitude of the injury equals the "cost" of that injury. That is one "cost." Second, on the other side of the equation, we should determine the costs associated with preventing that potential harm. In short, if the costs of trying to prevent the harm are greater than the costs of the harm itself, then it does *not* make sense to adopt a rule requiring the

preventative measures. On the other hand if the costs of trying to prevent the harm are less than the costs of the injury, then it *does* make sense to adopt a rule requiring safety measures. The preventative measures are said to be cost-effective. When a defendant fails to avail himself of cost-effective safety measures and a plaintiff suffers injury as a result of that failure, the defendant has breached his duty of care.

Using Judge Hand's rule – which lawyers refer to as the "Hand Formula" – we typically analyze any given proposed safety rule as follows. First, in order to evaluate the "costs" associated with an injury (*i.e.,* the injury that we are trying to prevent), we first must assess the likelihood (*i.e.,* probability) of the harm. How does one go about doing that? Well this is where empirical research from the insurance industry or other statistical studies can help. For example, in the automobile industry, empirical research can give us a good idea of the probability of certain types of car crashes. What percentage of car crashes involves what types of injuries? And what percentage of drivers are involved in those types of accidents? Secondly, we must try to assess the "magnitude of the harm." With automobile crashes, for example, the "magnitude" of injury involves at least two factors: 1) the severity of the injury (*i.e.,* grave bodily harm or death); and, 2) the costs associated with that injury (*e.g.,* the insurance costs, medical costs, pain and suffering, loss of consortium, etc. associated with grave bodily harm or death). According to the Hand Formula (one way that lawyers evaluate the advisability of safety rules and determine whether a defendant has breached his duty of care), this is how we arrive at the "costs" of the injury: we multiply the probability of the injury occurring by the magnitude of the injury. So, using our empirical research we must arrive at some number to express probability (*i.e.,* a number between .000 and 1.000). Secondly, we must arrive at some number to express the "magnitude of harm" (*e.g.,* the costs associated with the grave bodily injury or death caused by certain types of automobile accidents). The next step in this Hand Formula analysis is to determine, as nearly as possible, the costs of preventing the harm. For example, in order to try to prevent grave bodily harm and death in automobile accidents, the auto industry has spent millions of dollars doing research and development for safety belts and air bags, and continues to study the effects of their use. In addition, the auto industry has spent millions of dollars manufacturing and installing safety belts and air bags in all motor vehicles. Prior to making safety belts and air bags mandatory in newly manufactured vehicles, legislators had to satisfy themselves that the costs associated with preventing grave bodily harm and death in certain types of crashes (the R & D, manufacturing and installation costs) were less than the costs of the harm (*i.e.,* "cost of the harm" defined as the probability multiplied by the costs incurred by the harm [insurance, medical, legal, etc.]). In short, legislators had to decide that it was going to cost less to prevent the injuries than the aggregate costs of the injuries themselves. Articulate how the Hand Formula might apply to the *Gettysburg College* case.

2. Is the court saying, if Drew had been a "walk-on" athlete rather than a "recruited athlete," that the college would not have owed him a duty of care? If so, is there any rational basis for such a rule? Shouldn't the school owe the same safety/medical obligations to all of a team's

members regardless of whether they are walk-ons or recruited athletes? College football teams, for example, typically have large practice squads comprised of walk-on players who rarely, if ever, even get to suit up for games. When they are injured, as they frequently are, do schools owe them a lesser duty of care than scholarship starters?

3. In light of this case, how would you advise a college athletic department regarding emergency personnel, equipment, and procedures? Should trainers be available at all team practices? Nurses? Doctors? EMT's? What equipment should be required? Of course today it is likely that coaches and players would have cell phones and would simply call 911 within seconds or a minute or two at most in the event of an emergency situation such as the one that occurred in *Gettysburg College.*

4. At what point would you say that the costs of providing emergency personnel and equipment for collegiate athletic practices and competitions become too burdensome? At what point do costs become prohibitive?

5. At age 23, Hank "The Bank" Gathers lost his life to a heart condition during the West Coast Conference tournament on March 4, 1990. Gathers had previously been diagnosed with a heart condition in December of 1989 when he fainted after missing a free throw during a conference game. Gathers was put on medication to regulate his heartbeat and missed only two games. *Gathers Dies After Collapse on the Court* www.sportingnews.com/ archives/ sports2000/moments/145134.html (last updated March 12, 1990).

   Three years later, the basketball community was in for another huge blow. Reggie Lewis of the Boston Celtics suffered a heart attack while shooting baskets at Brandeis University. Four months prior to his death, Lewis was disoriented and dizzy during a regular-season game. Only 4 weeks later Lewis collapsed during a playoff game. The doctors' reports were inconclusive as to whether the condition was serious, thus allowing Lewis to play. Reggie Lewis was 27 years old at the time of his death. Heller, Dick, *Celtics Fans Mourned Reggie Lewis' Death in '93* www.washtimes.com/sports/20040726-124206-5316r.htm.

6. "Affecting approximately 5,000-7,000 young people each year, sudden cardiac arrest in college athletes is sometimes caused by congenital cardiovascular conditions, such as Long QT Syndrome or Hypertrophic Cardiomyopathy (HCM). According to the Cleveland Clinic, HCM, a condition that causes excessive thickening of the heart muscle, affects as many as 1.5 million Americans, making it the most common cause of sudden cardiac arrest in people under age 30. Preventative measures such as cardiac screenings are needed to detect an individual's risk to these types of conditions. In fact, an ECG exam can help detect heart conditions that account for nearly 60 percent of sudden cardiac arrests in young athletes." *Philips join forces with A Heart For Sports to 'Save an Athlete,' furthering its commitment to help prevent sudden cardiac arrest in college athletes* www.medical.philips.com /us/news/ content/file_1267.html (Last updated September 26, 2006).

7. 7. For a recent case involving related issues, *see e.g., Hill v. Slippery Rock U.*, 138 A.3d 673 (Pa. Super. 2016). Slippery Rock basketball player who had Sickle Cell Trait died during a practice session; defendants (university, NCAA, health center, and nurse) may be subject to liability for failing to test student-athlete for Sickle Cell Trait before clearing him for this level of activity.

HAMMOND V. BOARD OF EDUCATION OF CARROLL COUNTY
639 A 2D 223 (1994)
COURT OF SPECIAL APPEALS OF MARYLAND

MOTZ, JUDGE.

On August 25, 1989, appellant, Tawana Hammond, the first female high school football player in Carroll County history, was injured in her team's initial scrimmage. Three years later, Tawana and her mother, appellant Peggy Hammond, (collectively, the Hammonds) filed suit in the Circuit Court for Carroll County against appellee, the Board of Education of Carroll County (the Board), seeking $1.25 million in compensatory damages. The Hammonds asserted (1) that the high school authorities negligently failed to warn them of the potential risk of injury inherent in playing football and (2) that if they had been so warned Tawana would not have chosen to play football and her mother would not have permitted her to do so. After the parties conducted discovery, the Board moved for summary judgment, which the circuit court ([Phyllis] Beck, J.) granted.

The record reveals that the underlying material facts are not disputed. Sixteen-year-old Tawana tried out for the Francis Scott Key High School varsity football team in the summer of 1989, prior to the beginning of her junior year in high school. Although Tawana had previously participated in a number of track events and played softball and soccer, she had never engaged in any contact sports. Tawana had watched football on television since she was six years old but did not become interested in football until her freshman year in high school; she had never observed any "really serious" injuries in these televised games, only a "twisted ankle or something." She saw a half dozen high school games during her freshman and sophomore years and saw no players hurt at those games. Tawana knew football was a "physical contact sport," and determined she wanted to play it because "[i]t was different."

In order for a student to play sports at Francis Scott Key High School, the student and the student's parent must sign a document entitled "Francis Scott Key High School Athletic Regulations and Permission Form." Both Tawana and her father, John Hammond (not a party herein), signed this form on June 18, 1989. The permission form states that the student has read the school handbook and regulations and agrees to abide by them and that the parent has read them and "consents" to the child's participation in the sport. One sentence in the permission form specifically states that "[w]e do our very best to avoid accidents, but we realize that in the normal course of events, some occur." In deposition, Tawana testified that she read the permission form and, in particular, this sentence before she started playing football and understood that she "could get a broken leg, [or] broken arm," as a result of playing varsity, tackle football.

The permission form also requires that "[e]ach participating athlete must have a special examination" by the family physician and "must be found physically fit" and "must also have parent/guardian permission to participate." Tawana submitted the required "Carroll County Public Schools Athletic Participation Health Examination Form," signed by her doctor on July 31, 1989; in it her doctor certified that she was "physically able" to compete in a list of sports, including football. Moreover, on that same date Tawana's mother, a certified nurse's aide, whose older son played football at Francis Scott Key High School until "he sprained his leg," signed the participation form. On that form, Ms. Hammond gave her "consent" for Tawana to play the several sports listed, including football. Ms. Hammond acknowledged in deposition that "injury was [her] biggest fear" for Tawana, *i.e.,* "like [a] broken leg, [or] broken arms," but that she never communicated her fears to Tawana and believed Tawana "should be allowed to do whatever it was she wanted to do."

Throughout the summer of 1989, Tawana participated in the team's weight lifting program along with the other varsity football players. She was happy with the progress that she was making in her strength training and had no concerns or fears that she would not be physically strong enough to compete on the playing field. Practice began in August. On the first day of practice, which involved some contact drills, Tawana, along with the rest of the team, was instructed by the head coach, not to tackle, block or "do anything" with the neck because "you could get a neck injury." After the first practice, a meeting was conducted for the parents of the players. Tawana and both of her parents attended that meeting, at which an official gave a presentation discussing the possibility of serious injury to the neck if the head were used for blocking or tackling.

As practices continued, Tawana had no difficulty in keeping up physically with the other players on the team. On August 25, 1989, Tawana, along with the rest of the Francis Scott Key High School varsity football team, traveled to Anne Arundel County for the team's first practice scrimmage. Prior to the scrimmage, Tawana was interviewed by a television reporter and stated that "[p]laying football is a tough sport. I do have to admit that." During the scrimmage, while carrying the ball, Tawana was tackled by a rival player and sustained multiple internal injuries including a ruptured spleen. Her spleen and part of her pancreas were removed, and she was hospitalized for some time.

On August 13, 1992, Tawana and her mother filed this suit. The circuit court granted summary judgment to the Board, concluding that (a) it had no duty to warn "of the risk of serious, disabling and catastrophic injury associated with playing on a high-school-varsity, tackle, football team;" (b) if there was a duty to warn the Hammonds, it was satisfied; and (c) Tawana and her mother assumed the risk of injury as a matter of law. ***

The central theory espoused by the Hammonds, that the school board had a duty to warn them of the severe injuries that might result from voluntarily[1] participating on a varsity high school tackle football team, is one that, as far as we can determine, has never been adopted by any court in this country.

There are, to be sure, numerous cases in which minors injured while playing in school sporting events have sued school officials (or others similarly situated) asserting that the officials' negligence caused the participant's injuries. [Case Citations Omitted] In none of these cases, however, have the plaintiffs successfully asserted that the school officials were negligent because of some failure to warn the plaintiffs of the possible dangers involved in voluntarily participating in the contact sport. In the past, plaintiffs have made claims of negligence because of asserted inadequate or improper supervision, and inadequate equipment, but the parties have not cited and we have not uncovered any case in which a plaintiff, in circumstances similar to the Hammonds, has successfully made a negligence claim based on a failure to warn of possible physical injury.

Perhaps this is because permeating the sports injury cases is the recognition that "[p]hysical contact in ... an athletic contest is foreseeable and expected." *Albers v. Independent Sch. Dist. No. 302 of Lewis County*, 487 P.2d at 939. The "general rule is that participants in an athletic contest accept the normal physical contact of the particular sport." *Id.* Absent evidence of "mental deficiency," and there is no claim that Tawana is not at least of average intelligence, minors are held to "sufficiently appreciate[ ] the dangers inherent in the game of football," *Whipple v. Salvation Army*, 495 P.2d at 743, to know that "football is a rough and hazardous game and that anyone playing or practicing such a game may be injured," *Hale v. Davies*, 70 S.E.2d at 925, and that "[f]atigue, and unfortunately, injury are inherent in team competitive sports, especially football." *Benitez v. New York City Bd. Of Educ.*, 543 N.Y.S.2d at 34, 541 N.E.2d at 34. Thus, it is "common knowledge that children participating in games ... may injure themselves and ... no amount of supervision ... will avoid some such injuries, and the law does not make a school the insurer of the safety of pupils at play." *Brackman v. Adrian*, 472 S.W.2d at 739. As the Supreme Court of Oregon explained in rejecting a similar claim by a fifteen-year-old injured in a football game,

> The playing of football is a body-contact sport. The game demands that the players come into physical contact with each other constantly, frequently with great force ... the ball-carrier ... must be prepared to strike the ground violently. Body contacts, bruises, and clashes are inherent in the game. There is no other way to play it. No prospective player need be told that a participant in the game of football may sustain injury. That fact is self-evident. *Vendrell v. School Dist. No. 26C*, 376 P.2d at 412-13.

---

1   We note that different considerations may apply when an injury occurs during compulsory physical education classes rather than during voluntary participation in school athletic contests because, while a student usually is required to attend physical education classes and drills, a participant chooses to participate in voluntary games, and so can avoid them if he or she is weak, slow, disabled, etc. [case citations omitted].

For these reasons, courts have been extremely inhospitable to claims that properly equipped, injured high school players should be able to recover from school officials for injuries sustained during an ordinary, voluntary contact sport game. Thus, in the vast majority of such cases,[2] it has been held that those asserting such claims cannot recover as a matter of law. [Case Citations Omitted]

[4] ****

Here...the hazard alleged – the possibility of injury to a voluntary participant in a varsity high school tackle, football game – was "the normal, obvious and usual incident[ ]" of the activity. Accordingly...there was no duty on the part of the defendant to warn of this possibility.

In light of our conclusion that the Board had no duty to warn the Hammonds, we need not reach the question of whether Tawana assumed the risk as a matter of law. We do note, however, that there is case law supporting the circuit court's conclusion that she did. *See e.g., Whipple,* 495 P.2d at 743; *Vendrell,* 376 P.2d at 414; *Kluka v. Livingston Parish Sch. Bd.,* 433 So.2d at 304; *Hale,* 70 S.E.2d at 925. *See also Nesbitt v. Bethesda Country Club, Inc.,* 20 Md.App. 226, 232, 314 A.2d 738 (1974)(quoting 4 Am.Jur.2d, *Amusements & Exhibitions* § 98 ("[a] voluntary participant in any lawful game, sport or contest, in legal contemplation by the fact of his participation, assumes all risks incidental to the game, sport or contest which are obvious and foreseeable.").[3]

Although she has not stated a cause of action against the Board, Tawana's injuries were serious, painful, and permanent. We regret them and sympathize with her. Our holding here, that school officials have no duty to warn a student or the student's parents that serious injury might result from the student's voluntary participation on a high school varsity tackle football team, does not mean that such a warning would not be a sound idea as a matter of public policy. Young men – and women – of the same age, who wish to participate in the same team contact sports, vary considerably in weight and size; unfortunately, the sport may occasionally pit the brawniest against the most slender.[4] In view of the very serious injuries suffered by Tawana, school officials may well want to consider issuing a warning of the possibility of such injuries—even though there is no legal obligation to do so.

JUDGMENT

AFFIRMED

---

1   2   The exceptions involve claims not made here and facts not remotely similar to those in the case at hand. *See e.g., Tepper v. City of New Rochelle Sch. Dist.,* 531 N.Y.S.2d at 368 (summary judgment for defendants reversed when it was asserted that a coach was negligent in permitting a lacrosse player "of slight build and very limited experience, to go head-to-head [during a practice drill] with the 260-pound senior varsity team member, a player possessing substantially greater experience").

2   3   Again, this situation is to be contrasted with a student's arguable lack of assumption of risk in compulsory physical education classes. *See Benitez,* 543 N.Y.S.2d at 33, 541 N.E.2d at 33; *Passantino v. Bd. Of Educ.,* 383 N.Y.S.2d at 641.

3   4   The Hammonds have not asserted that they were entitled to any additional warning or consideration because Tawana is a young woman and we do not suggest that there is any basis for such an argument. Moreover, there is nothing in this record to suggest that Tawana's injuries were different or more severe because of her sex.

1. How are the plaintiff's allegations in this case regarding the school's failure to warn any different from the allegations of failure to warn in *Pell*? In both cases the plaintiffs allege that if they had received proper warnings they would not have participated in the dangerous activity.

2. The court notes that Tawana's mother was "a certified nurse's aid, whose older son played football at Francis Scott Key High School until he 'sprained his leg....'" How important do you think that those facts are to the decision? If you think that they are important, why? If not, why not?

3. The court makes it clear that there is no duty to warn of the obvious dangers of contact sports and that voluntary participants are deemed to have assumed the normal risks inherent in such sports. If those are the normal legal rules applicable to sports injuries, why were similar arguments in *Pell* unavailing?

4. Does it matter that the plaintiff in *Hammond* was injured while playing an extracurricular, voluntary sport (football) while the plaintiff in *Pell* was injured while participating in a mandatory physical education class? Does it matter that product liability was the legal theory in *Pell* whereas the *Hammond* case was tried on a theory of negligence? Should those sorts of differences matter legally?

SANTOPIETRO V. CITY OF NEW HAVEN
239 CONN. 207 (1996)
SUPREME COURT OF CONNECTICUT

BORDEN, ASSOCIATE JUSTICE.

This appeal arises out of injuries incurred by a spectator at a softball game. [In addition to suing the City of New Haven, the plaintiff sued the umpires, alleging negligence.]

Certain facts are not in dispute. On October 16, 1988, the plaintiffs attended a softball game played at East Shore Park in New Haven by teams belonging to an organized league. The defendants David Brennan and Bruce Shepard served as the umpires for that game. ****

The plaintiff Raymond Santopietro, Jr. observed the softball game from a position behind the backstop and was not on the field of play. ****

In the sixth inning, [Mark] Piombino came to bat in the game that Santopietro, Jr. was watching and hit a fly ball. In frustration, he intentionally flung his bat toward the backstop. Somehow, the bat passed through the backstop and struck Santopietro, Jr. in the head. As a result, Santopietro, Jr. suffered a fractured skull and other serious injuries.

A review of the evidence in the light most favorable to the plaintiffs indicates that the jury might reasonably have found the following facts. During the course of the game that Santopietro, Jr. was watching when he was injured, there occurred several incidents of unruly behavior by players who were on the same team as Piombino. Some players used vulgar language in a loud and angry manner. Players taunted members of the other team in an attempt to intimidate them. Players threw their gloves and kicked the dirt, and one player kicked a garbage can, upsetting its contents and creating a loud noise. After his turn at bat resulted in an out, another player angrily threw a bat along the ground in the direction of the bats not in use. Another player threw his glove from the pitcher's mound into the dugout. A player inside the dugout repeatedly banged a bat against the dugout, producing a loud noise. Furthermore, the jury could have inferred from the evidence presented that Brennan and Shepard were aware or reasonably should have been aware of these incidents.

After passing a written examination, Brennan and Shepard were both trained and approved to be softball umpires by the Amateur Softball Association (Association), a national organization that regulates the conduct of organized amateur softball in the United States. Both Brennan and Shepard possessed years of experience and had umpired hundreds of games. Shepard had received an award honoring him for being the best umpire in New Haven. Brennan testified that, as an umpire, he possesses specialized knowledge about softball and softball rules that is greater than the average person's knowledge. Both Brennan and Shepard were familiar with the Association's rules governing the conduct of umpires.

Brennan and Shepard further testified that when they give a warning, it usually has the effect of stopping the disruptive behavior and preventing future improper acts. They testified that any player who tosses a bat should be ejected immediately, and Brennan testified that if he had seen a player toss a bat as described by the witnesses, he would have ejected that player without warning. They testified that such disciplinary action is an effective means by which to control the actions of players.

Shepard testified that, as an umpire, he had the duty to maintain control of the game to prevent harm to spectators, and that warnings constitute the primary means by which to maintain that control. Moreover, Brennan testified that umpires have the authority to suspend the game if necessary to keep order or to prevent harm to spectators.

Brennan and Shepard also testified that the decision of whether to impose discipline in any given instance of unruly behavior is a discretionary matter for the umpire. Brennan testified that the rule against unsportsmanlike conduct gives the umpire authority "at his discretion, to disqualify any player who exhibits unsportsmanlike conduct in the judgment of the umpire." He further testified that decisions whether to take disciplinary action in response to loud swearing, throwing a glove or kicking dirt "are umpire judgment or umpire discretion calls." Shepard testified that the question of whether unruly behavior, such as using loud and abusive language, throwing a glove or kicking a garbage can, constitutes unsportsmanlike conduct will depend on the particular situation. **** Brennan further testified concerning the subjective nature of the decision whether to discipline a player for unsportsmanlike conduct. Specifically, he stated that "the majority of the time you'll find that umpires are former players, and umpires will use the term unsportsmanlike conduct as some type of action which, had I been a player, I wouldn't like done to me, I wouldn't let another group do it to another player."

We note that this testimony confirms what is the common understanding of the umpire's task. In the absence of exceptional circumstances, a softball umpire, when confronted with unruly behavior by a player that arguably constitutes unsportsmanlike conduct, faces a spectrum of discretionary options. At one end of the spectrum is taking no action; at the other end is ejection of the player or suspension of the game. In between are warnings and other appropriate disciplinary action. The umpire has discretion, within the spectrum, to respond to the offensive behavior in the manner that the umpire finds to be most appropriate in the given circumstances.

* * * *

We conclude that the plaintiffs were required to establish by expert testimony that the failure of Brennan and Shepard to act in the present case constituted a breach of duty, and that the plaintiffs' evidence did not satisfy that burden.

"A breach of duty by the defendant and a causal connection between the defendant's breach of duty and the resulting harm to the plaintiff are essential elements of a cause of action in negligence." *Catz v. Rubenstein*, 201 Conn. 39, 44, 513 A.2d 98 (1986); *see RK Constructors, Inc. v. Fusco Corp.*, 231 Conn. 381, 384, 650 A.2d 153 (1994)("essential elements of a cause of action in negligence are well established: duty; breach of that duty; causation; and actual injury"). ****

"The existence of a duty is a question of law and [o]nly if such a duty is found to exist does the trier of fact then determine whether the defendant violated that duty in the particular situation at hand. *Petriello v. Kalman*, 215 Conn. 377, 382-83, 576 A.2d 474 (1990). If a court determines, as a matter of law, that a defendant owes no duty to a plaintiff, the plaintiff cannot recover in negligence from the defendant." (Internal quotation marks omitted.) *RK Constructors, Inc. v. Fusco Corp.*, supra, 231 Conn. at 384-85, 650 A.2d 153.

If the determination of the standard of care requires knowledge that is beyond the experience of an ordinary fact finder, expert testimony will be required. *Jaffe v. State Dept. of Health*, 135 Conn. 339, 349, 64 A.2d 330 (1949).

[12] We note that the plaintiffs' claims in the present case are akin to allegations of professional negligence or malpractice, which we have previously defined as "the failure of one rendering professional services to exercise that degree of skill and learning commonly applied under all the circumstances in the community by the average prudent reputable member of the profession with the result of injury, loss, or damage to the recipient of those services." (Internal quotation marks omitted.) *Davis v. Margolis*, 215 Conn. 408, 415, 576 A.2d 489 (1990). *** In such cases in which the fact finder's decision requires specialized knowledge, expert testimony is

necessary "to assist lay people, such as members of the jury and the presiding judge, to understand the applicable standard of care and to evaluate the defendant's actions in light of that standard." *Id.*, at 416, 576 A.2d 489; *see, e.g., Barrett v. Danbury Hospital,* 232 Conn. 242, 252, 654 A.2d 748 (1995)(medical malpractice); *Davis v. Margolis,* supra, at 416, 576 A.2d 489 (legal malpractice); *Matyas v. Minck,* supra, 37 Conn.App. at 327, 655 A.2d 1155 (negligence of engineer). ***

Therefore, for the purposes of this appeal, we assume, without deciding, that umpires such as Brennan and Shepard[1] have a duty, essentially as postulated by the plaintiffs, to exercise reasonable judgment as umpires in order to maintain control of a game so as to prevent an unreasonable risk of injury to others. ****

We conclude, in the present case, that the plaintiffs failed to produce sufficient evidence that Brennan and Shepard had breached the applicable standard of care. Brennan and Shepard testified that unsportsmanlike conduct is prohibited and that it is appropriate for an umpire to take action to prevent or stop such conduct. They further testified that the umpire possesses the authority to warn players, eject them or suspend the game if necessary to deter unsportsmanlike conduct or to maintain control of a game. Moreover, when questioned about specific incidents that allegedly had occurred during the game at which Santopietro, Jr., was injured, Brennan and Shepard testified that if they had seen the incidents described by the witnesses, they would have taken some disciplinary action. They also testified, however, that the umpire possesses discretion in the application of the rule prohibiting unsportsmanlike conduct and that the decision whether to take some action against a player is made according to the judgment of the umpire based on the specific circumstances. Neither Brennan nor Shepard testified that, in the specific circumstances of that game, a reasonable umpire would have been required to take action in response to those incidents, or that it would have been unreasonable for an umpire not to have taken such action. In other words, their testimony that, in the exercise of their discretion, they would have taken action does not establish that a failure to act constituted a breach of the standard of care. ***

The plaintiffs do not argue, and we do not assume, that Brennan and Shepard possess a duty to make every discretionary call that arises during the course of the game error free. Umpire liability, if it were to exist, must be predicated on facts sufficient to support the conclusion that their unreasonable actions or failure to act led to such a loss of control of the game as to imperil unreasonably the safety of others. ***

We conclude, therefore, that the plaintiffs have failed to prove by expert testimony that Brennan and Shepard breached a duty of care to prevent an unreasonable risk of the injuries suffered by Santopietro, Jr. ****

The judgment is affirmed.

---

1 We note that Brennan and Shepard had been formally trained and were paid to officiate the game at which Santopietro, Jr., was injured. Although this information does not affect the resolution of the present case, we acknowledge that it may be relevant if, in the future, we are required to decide whether such a duty exists. The existence or extent of a duty might be affected by whether the umpire is a paid professional or an unpaid volunteer without formal training.

1. What standard of care should apply to sports officials? Should ordinary principles of negligence apply? Or should there be a professional standard commensurate with their training? For example, would there be a different standard for a Little League umpire versus a Major League umpire?

2. Given the extreme instances of fan violence that have occurred in the past several years at youth games, is there an argument to be made that a higher level of precautions should be taken at youth sporting events?

3. How much practical control do officials actually have? Wouldn't it make more sense to require venue owners or league officials to provide security or police protection rather than putting that burden on the shoulders of game officials?

4. The court requires expert testimony to establish the standard of care applicable to the softball umpires who are defendants in this case. Why is expert testimony necessary?

5. Explain what the court means when it refers to the "discretion" of umpires? What is the relevance of "discretion" to the legal principles established in this case?

6. For a recent case examining the potential liability of a wrestling referee, *see Rispoli v. Long Beach Union Free Sch. Dist.* 975 N.Y.S.2d 107 (App. Div. 2013). Referee of a wrestling match in which the plaintiff was injured could not be liable for failure to halt the match, even though the position involved in the injury was a potentially dangerous position.

B. EXPRESS ASSUMPTION OF RISK

HIETT V. LAKE BARCROFT COMMUNITY ASSOCIATION, INC.
418 SE 2D 894 (1992)
SUPREME COURT OF VIRGINIA

KEENAN, JUSTICE.

The primary issue in this appeal is whether a pre-injury release from liability for negligence is void as being against public policy.

Robert D. Hiett sustained an injury, which rendered him a quadriplegic while participating in the "Teflon Man Triathlon," (the triathlon) sponsored by the Lake Barcroft Community Association, Inc. (LABARCA). The injury occurred at the start of the swimming event when

Hiett waded into Lake Barcroft to a point where the water reached his thighs, dove into the water, and struck his head on either the lake bottom or an object beneath the water surface.

Thomas M. Penland, Jr., a resident of Lake Barcroft, organized and directed the triathlon. He drafted the entry form, which all participants were required to sign. The first sentence of the form provided:

> In consideration of this entry being accept[ed] to participate in the Lake Barcroft Teflon Man Triathlon, I hereby, for myself, my heirs, and executors waive, release, and forever discharge any and all rights and claims for damages which I may have or m[a]y hereafter accrue to me against the organizers and sponsors and their representatives, successors, and assigns, for any and all injuries suffered by me in said event.

* * *

Hiett alleged in his third amended motion for judgment that LABARCA...had failed to ensure that the lake was reasonably safe, properly supervise the swimming event, advise the participants of the risk of injury, and train them how to avoid such injuries. ***

In a preliminary ruling, the trial court held that, absent fraud, misrepresentation, duress, illiteracy, or the denial of an opportunity to read the form, the entry form was a valid contract and that the pre-injury release language in the contract released the defendants from liability for negligence. The trial court also ruled that such a release was prohibited as a matter of public policy only when it was included: (1) in a common carrier's contract of carriage; (2) in the contract of a public utility under a duty to furnish telephone service; or (3) as a condition of employment set forth in an employment contract.

* * * *

Hiett first argues that the trial court erred in ruling that the pre-injury release provision in the entry form did not violate public policy. He contends that since the decision of this Court in *Johnson's Adm'x v. Richmond and Danville R.R. Co.*, 86 Va. 975, 11 S.E. 829 (1890), the law in Virginia has been settled that an agreement entered into prior to any injury, releasing a tortfeasor from liability for negligence resulting in personal injury, is void because it violates public policy. **** In response, LABARCA...argue[s] that the decisions of this Court since *Johnson* have established that pre-injury release agreements such as the one before us do not violate public policy. We disagree with LABARCA....

The case law in this Commonwealth over the past one hundred years has not altered the holding in *Johnson*. In *Johnson,* this Court addressed the validity of a pre-injury release of liability for future negligent acts. There, the decedent was a member of a firm of quarry workers, which had entered into an agreement with a railroad company to remove a granite bluff located on the company's right of way. The agreement specified that the railroad would not be liable for any injuries or death sustained by any members of the firm, or its employees, occurring from any cause whatsoever.

The decedent was killed while attempting to warn one of his employees of a fast-approaching train. The evidence showed that the train was moving at a speed of not less than 25 miles per hour, notwithstanding the railroad company's agreement that all trains would pass by the work site at speeds not exceeding six miles per hour.

In holding that the release language was invalid because it violated public policy, this Court stated:

> [T]o hold that it was competent for one party to put the other parties to the contract at the mercy of its own misconduct ... can never be lawfully done where an enlightened system of jurisprudence prevails. Public policy forbids it, and contracts against public policy are void.

This Court emphasized that its holding was not based on the fact that the railroad company was a common carrier. Rather, this Court found that such provisions for release from liability for personal injury, which may be caused by future acts of negligence, are prohibited "universally." 86 Va. at 978, 11 S.E. at 830.

As noted by Hiett, the cases following *Johnson* have not eroded this principle. ****

[C]ases decided by this Court since *Johnson* have upheld provisions for indemnification against future property damage claims. In none of these cases, however, did the Court address the issue whether an indemnification provision would be valid against a claim for personal injury.

* * * *

We agree with Hiett that the...cases have not modified or altered the holding in *Johnson.* Therefore, we conclude here, based on *Johnson,* that the pre-injury release provision signed by Hiett is prohibited by public policy and, thus, it is void. *Johnson,* 86 Va. at 978, 11 S.E. at 829.

* * *

LUND V. BALLY'S AEROBIC PLUS
78 CAL.APP. 4TH 733 (2000)
COURT OF APPEAL, SECOND DISTRICT, CALIFORNIA

YEGAN, J.

The modern health or fitness club is a place where a person can attain physical health and fitness. It is also a place where a person can get hurt. For this reason, most, if not all, health clubs require patrons to assume the risk of physical injury associated with body building and aerobic conditioning. As we shall explain, here the waiver and release of liability operates as an effective written assumption of the risk, which bars recovery.

Ellen Lund appeals from the judgment of nonsuit granted to respondents Bally's Aerobic Plus, Inc., and Bally's Total Fitness (collectively, Bally's) after the presentation of her evidence at the trial of this personal injury case. Lund unsuccessfully contends the trial court erred when it concluded her claims were barred by a waiver and release form she signed when she became a member of a Bally's gym.

Facts and Procedural History

In late 1989 or early 1990, Lund injured her cervical spine and had surgery to fuse two vertebrae in her neck. In February 1994, she joined a Bally's health club in Simi Valley. In December of 1994, she paid Bally's $375 in addition to the cost of her membership for 20 sessions with a personal trainer, Ron Ladd. Lund told Ladd that she previously had neck surgery and that her doctor told her not to lift weight over her head. Ladd assured her that he could show her how to use the weight machines without injuring her neck. Lund followed his advice. Admittedly, with the benefit of hindsight, Ladd's assurances and Lund's acceptance of his representations were foolish.

During their first session, Ladd showed Lund how to use an incline bench press machine with a 10-pound weight. Lund lifted the weight 15 times before she felt pressure in her neck. After she lifted it three more times, Lund felt a pain, " like the top of my head broke off." She had reinjured her cervical spine, requiring another surgery. Lund sued Bally's for personal injury, contending Ladd was negligent when he instructed her on how to use the incline bench press.

The trial court granted Bally's motion for nonsuit following the presentation of her evidence at trial. It concluded that a waiver and release included in Lund's membership contract barred her claim. The waiver and release is part of the form retail installment contract prepared by Bally's that Lund signed when she joined the club in February 1994. Lund testified that, although she reviewed the financial terms of the contract, she did not read its other provisions.

Near the signature line, the contract states: "Notice to Buyer: 1. Do Not Sign This Agreement Before You Read It or if It Contains Any Blank Spaces to Be Filled in...." Lund testified she did not read this portion of the contract. A few lines later, the contract states: "Waiver and Release: This contract contains a Waiver and Release in Paragraph 10 to which you will be bound." Lund did not read this sentence. Lund also acknowledged that she did not read the waiver and release paragraph itself.

The waiver and release paragraph, printed on a following page of the contract, provides,

> 10. Waiver and Release. You (Buyer, each Member and all guests) agree that if you engage in any physical exercise or activity or use any club facility on the premises, you do so at your own risk. This includes, without limitation, your use of the locker room, pool, whirlpool, sauna, steamroom, parking area, sidewalk or any equipment in the health club and your participation in any activity, class, program or instruction. You agree that you are voluntarily participating in these activities and using these facilities and premises

and assume all risk of injury, illness, damage or loss to you or your property that might result, including, without limitation, any loss or theft of any personal property. You agree on behalf of yourself (and your personal representatives, heirs, executors, administrators, agents and assigns) to release and discharge us (and our affiliates, employees, agents, representatives, successors and assigns) from any and all claims or causes of action (known or unknown) arising out of our negligence. This Waiver and Release of liability includes, without limitation, injuries which may occur as a result of (a) your use of any exercise equipment or facilities which may malfunction or break; (b) our improper maintenance of any exercise equipment or facilities, (c) our negligent instruction or supervision, and (d) you slipping and falling while in the health club or on the premises. You acknowledge that you have carefully read this Waiver and Release and fully understand that it is a release of liability. You are waiving any right that you may have to bring a legal action to assert a claim against us for our negligence.

* * * *

Waiver and Release

* * *

The dispositive question is whether the February 1994 waiver and release applies to Lund's use of Bally's weight lifting equipment under the supervision of a personal trainer employed by Bally's. (*Paralift, Inc. v. Superior Court* (1993) 23 Cal.App.4th 748, 754 [29 Cal.Rptr.2d 177].) To achieve that result, the release must "'be clear, unambiguous and explicit in expressing the intent of the parties.'" (*Id.,* at p. 755, quoting *Madison v. Superior Court* (1988) 203 Cal.App.3d 589, 597-598 [250 Cal.Rptr. 299].) Waiver and release forms are to be strictly construed against the defendant. Such a form is simply a written assumption of a known risk, *i.e.,* a risk reasonably anticipated by the plaintiff. (*Leon v. Family Fitness Center (#107), Inc.* (1998) 61 Cal.App.4th 1227, 1234 [71 Cal.Rptr.2d 923].) To be operative, the defendant's negligence, which results in the plaintiff's injury, must be reasonably related to the object or purpose for which the release is given. (*Id.,* at p. 1235; *Paralift, Inc. v. Superior Court, supra,* 23 Cal.App.4th at p. 757; *Madison v. Superior Court, supra,* 203 Cal.App.3d at p. 601.) (2b). Here, the trial court correctly concluded that the waiver and release clearly and unambiguously applied to bar Lund's claims.

Lund was injured while exercising with equipment provided by Bally's. Her membership contract expressly states that she engaged in these activities at her own risk, and "assume[s] all risk of injury ... that might result" from them. Moreover, the contract released Bally's from all claims arising out of its negligence, including, "injuries which may occur as a result of (a) [Lund's] use of any exercise equipment or facilities, ... [and] (c) our negligent instruction or supervision ...." The undisputed evidence demonstrates that Lund was injured while using Bally's equipment under the "instruction or supervision" of a Bally's employee. The waiver and release clearly, unambiguously and explicitly bars this claim. [Case Citations Omitted] ***

The judgment is affirmed. Costs to respondent.

NOTES & QUESTIONS

1. Describe facts that a Virginia court (*i.e., Hiett*) would consider NOT violative of public policy in a case involving a sports injury waiver.

2. Does the Virginia court's decision make it more likely or less likely that organizations will be willing to sponsor athletic contests such as road races? Explain your answer.

3. Is there any way to rectify the apparent contradiction regarding the validity of liability waivers between these two cases? If so, explain how. If not, explain why not. Do you think that the nature of the risks involved has any bearing on the outcomes? For example, in *Hiett*, there are countless unknown and unforeseeable risks lurking in the waters of a lake, on roads where cyclists will ride, and where runners will run. But in a gym, there are a limited number of risks over which the owners presumably have a fair degree of control.

4. If you were advising a non-profit youth baseball league in Virginia, what advice would you give the board of Directors concerning a waiver of liability on their registration form? How about in California?

5. For a more recent case involving facts and a resolution similar to *Lund, see e.g., Grebing v. 24 Hour Fitness USA, Inc.,* 184 Cal. Rptr. 3d 155 (Cal. Ct. App. 2015). Appellate Court affirmed trial court's decision that plaintiff fitness club member's signed, written waiver of liability against 24 Hour Fitness was valid and member assumed all risks relating to the facilities, services, equipment, and premises.

6. Two other troubling questions are whether a minor can validly waive liability and also whether a parent or guardian can effectively waive liability for a minor? *See Shaner v. State Sys. of Higher Educ.,* 40 Pa. D. & C.4th 308 (1998). The *Shaner* Court considered the enforceability of a waiver of liability signed by the parent of a 14-year old girl participating in a softball camp. The girl, Susan Shaner, suffered a broken leg during a softball game at Bloomsburg University summer softball camp. In order to participate in the camp the signature of her parent was required on a waiver that contained the following terms:

   I desire to enroll in the 1985 Bloomsburg University softball camp. Bloomsburg University, the director, and anyone connected with the clinic do not assume liability for any injuries incurred while at camp or on the way to and from camp. Parents should contact their own insurance company to get additional insurance for their daughter if necessary.

Campers will be required to attend all sessions and must comply to all camp rules. Failure to do so may result in dismissal from camp. After an application is accepted there will be no refund of the $50 deposit.

Parent's signature /s/Mahlon R. Shaner

Shaner brought suit against the Pennsylvania State System of Higher Education alleging negligence. The lower court ruled that the waiver barred her claim. On appeal Shaner argued that "her father cannot legally bind her to the clause and she did not understand or agree to it. . . ." The appeals court held for Shaner, explaining that except for contracts of necessity, a minor is not competent to enter into a valid contract. The court reasoned that the release could not be enforced against the plaintiff on the grounds that: (1) a 14-year old plaintiff was a minor and therefore incompetent to enter a contractual agreement; and, (2) her father lacked the requisite authority to release the claim against defendant. Courts routinely hold that a minor lacks the capacity to waive liability. The next case addresses the issue of whether a parent may waive liability on behalf of a minor child.

KIRTON V. FIELDS
997 SO.2D 349 (2008)
SUPREME COURT OF FLORIDA

QUINCE, C.J.

STATEMENT OF THE CASE AND FACTS

Pursuant to a final judgment of dissolution of marriage, Bobby Jones was the primary residential parent for his fourteen year old son, Christopher. On May 10, 2003, the father took Christopher to Thunder Cross Motor Sports Park to ride his all terrain vehicle (ATV). To gain entry to the facility and be allowed to participate in riding the ATV, Bobby Jones, as Christopher's natural guardian, signed a release and waiver of liability, assumption of risk, and indemnity agreement. While attempting a particular jump, Christopher lost control of his ATV, causing himself to be ejected. Tragically, he hit the ground with the ATV landing on top of him. He got up, walked a short distance, then collapsed and died. Christopher's mother, Bette Jones, was unaware that the father was permitting their son to engage in this activity. She was also unaware that approximately one month prior to the accident causing Christopher's death, he had attempted the same jump, resulting in a fractured rib and mild concussion.

Subsequently, Fields, as personal representative of the estate of Christopher Jones, filed suit for wrongful death against Spencer Kirton, Scott Corey Kirton, Dudley Kirton, and the Kirton Brother Lawn Service, Inc. ("the Kirtons"), as owners and operators of Thunder Cross Motor Sports. *** The Kirtons then filed an answer and affirmative defenses to the amended complaint. In one of the affirmative defenses, the Kirtons argued that the claims raised by Fields were barred by the release and waiver executed by Mr. Jones on behalf of his son. The Kirtons, thereafter, filed a motion for summary judgment based on the release and waiver.[1] The trial court entered an order granting the Kirtons' motion for summary judgment on the wrongful death claim, finding that there was no genuine issue of material fact because the release executed by Mr. Jones on behalf of his minor child, Christopher, barred the claim.

On appeal, the Fourth District reversed the trial court's order granting the motion for summary judgment. [T]he district court held that a parent could not bind a minor's estate by the parent's execution of a pre-injury release.

ANALYSIS

The Kirtons and the amicus curiae supporting their position assert that a parent has a fundamental right to make decisions relating to the care of a minor child, and that right includes executing a pre-injury release on behalf of the minor child. On the other hand, Fields contends that pre-injury releases are invalid because neither the common law nor the Legislature has given parents the authority to waive these substantive rights of a minor child.

[The court briefly discussed the need to balance two important interests: the freedom generally allowed to parents in raising their children and the occasional need for the State to intervene in some instances to protect children.]

Florida Courts & Out-of-State Precedent

A federal district court in Florida in two separate cases…found that pre-injury releases signed by parents on behalf of their minor children were invalid. *See In re Royal Carribean Cruises Ltd.,* 459 F.Supp.2d 1275 (S.D.Fla.2006); *In re Royal Caribbean Cruises, Ltd.,* 403 F.Supp.2d 1168 (S.D.Fla.2005)(where both the father and minor child were injured on a jet ski that was owned by Royal Caribbean on the island of Coco Cay, Bahamas). In both cases, the federal district court reviewed out-of-state precedent and found that in cases involving school-sponsored or community-run activities the courts upheld pre-injury releases, and in cases involving commercial activities the courts have found the releases unenforceable. *In re Carribean Cruises Ltd.,* 459 F.Supp.2d at 1280; *In re Royal Caribbean Cruises, Ltd.,* 403 F.Supp.2d at 1172.

Other states and federal courts have also addressed the propriety of a parent or guardian's execution of a pre-injury release on behalf of a minor child. In holding that pre-injury releases executed by parents on behalf of minor children are unenforceable for participation in commercial activities, we are in agreement with the majority of other jurisdictions. *See, e.g., Meyer v. Naperville Manner, Inc.,* 262 Ill.App.3d 141, 199 Ill.Dec. 572, 634 N.E.2d 411 (1994)(finding a parental pre-injury waiver unenforceable in a situation where the minor child was injured after

---

1   Mr. Jones filed an affidavit in support of the Kirtons' motion for summary judgment. In that affidavit, he admitted that he willfully and with full understanding executed the release on behalf of his minor child at Thunder Cross Motor Sports Park. He also stated that he understood that it was his intention to waive the right to sue for the death of Christopher and to be banned by the other terms as set forth in the general release. He further stated that he understood that by signing the general release, he was forever discharging the Kirtons for any and all loss or damage and any claim or demands on account of injury to Christopher, or his property, or resulting in the death of Christopher arising out of, or related to the events, whether caused by the negligence of the releasees or otherwise.

falling off a horse at a horseback riding school); *Hojnowski v. Vans Skate Park*, 187 N.J. 323, 901 A.2d 381, 383 (2006)(finding that where a child was injured while skateboarding at a skate park facility, "a parent may not bind a minor child to a pre-injury release of a minor's prospective tort claims resulting from the minor's use of a commercial recreational facility"); *Hawkins v. Peart*, 37 P.3d 1062, 1066 (Utah 2001)(concluding that "a parent does not have the authority to release a child's claims before an injury," where the child was injured as a result of falling off a horse provided by a commercial business); *Scott v. Pac. W. Mountain Resort*, 119 Wash.2d 484, 834 P.2d 6 (1992) (holding that the enforcement of an exculpatory agreement signed by a parent on behalf of a minor child participating in a ski school is contrary to public policy).

Although there are jurisdictions where pre-injury releases executed by parents on behalf of minor children have been found enforceable, we note that the only published decisions where they have been upheld involved a minor's participation in school-run or community-sponsored activities. *See, e.g., Sharon v. City of Newton*, 437 Mass. 99, 769 N.E.2d 738 (2002)(holding that a parent has the authority to bind a minor child to a waiver of liability as a condition of a child's participation in public school extracurricular sports activities); *Zivich v. Mentor Soccer Club, Inc.*, 82 Ohio St.3d 367, 696 N.E.2d 201, 205 (1998) (concluding that a parent may bind a minor child to a release of volunteers and sponsors of a nonprofit sports activity from liability for negligence because the threat of liability would strongly deter "many individuals from volunteering for nonprofit organizations" because of the potential for substantial damage awards).

While this particular case involves a commercial activity, we note that these jurisdictions that have upheld pre-injury releases have done so because community-run and school-sponsored type activities involve different policy considerations than those associated with commercial activities.

This Case

Although parents undoubtedly have a fundamental right to make decisions concerning the care, custody, upbringing, and control of their children, the question of whether a parent should be allowed to waive a minor child's future tort claims implicates wider public policy concerns. While a parent's decision to allow a minor child to participate in a particular activity is part of the parent's fundamental right to raise a child, this does not equate with a conclusion that a parent has a fundamental right to execute a pre-injury release of a tortfeasor on behalf of a minor child. It cannot be presumed that a parent who has decided to voluntarily risk a minor child's physical well-being is acting in the child's best interest. Furthermore, we find that there is injustice when a parent agrees to waive the tort claims of a minor child and deprive the child of the right to legal relief when the child is injured as a result of another party's negligence. When a parent executes such a release and a child is injured, the provider of the activity escapes liability while the parent is left to deal with the financial burden of an injured child. If the parent cannot afford to bear that burden, the parties who suffer are the child, other family members, and the people of the State who will be called on to bear that financial burden. Therefore, when a parent decides to execute a pre-injury release on behalf of a minor child, the parent is not protecting the welfare of the child, but is instead protecting the interests of the activity provider.

Moreover, a "parent's decision in signing a pre-injury release impacts the minor's estate and the property rights personal to the minor." [Citation Omitted]. For this reason, the state must assert its role under parens patriae to protect the interests of the minor children.

"parent of the nation"

Business owners owe their patrons a duty of reasonable care and to maintain a safe environment for the activity they provide. If pre-injury releases were permitted for commercial establishments, the incentive to take reasonable precautions to protect the safety of minor children would be removed. Moreover, as a provider of the activity, a commercial business can take precautions to ensure the child's safety and insure itself when a minor child is injured while participating in the activity. On the other hand, a minor child cannot insure himself or herself against the risks involved in participating in that activity. As the New Jersey Supreme Court stated in *Hojnowski*:

> The operator of a commercial recreational enterprise can inspect the premises for unsafe conditions, train his or her employees with regard to the facility's proper operation, and regulate the types of activities permitted to occur. Such an operator also can obtain insurance and spread the costs of insurance among its customers. Children, on the other hand, are not in a position to discover hazardous conditions or insure against risks. Moreover, the expectation that a commercial facility will be reasonably safe to do that which is within the scope of the invitation, is especially important where the facility's patrons are minor children. If we were to permit waivers of liability, we would remove a significant incentive for operators of commercial enterprises that attract children to take reasonable precautions to protect their safety. [Citations Omitted]

Based on these public policy concerns, it is clear that the pre-injury release executed by Bobby Jones on behalf of his now deceased son was unenforceable because it prevented the minor's estate from bringing a cause of action against the commercial establishment that provided the activity, which resulted in the minor's death.

CONCLUSION

For the reasons set forth above, we hold that a pre-injury release executed by a parent on behalf of a minor child is unenforceable against the minor or the minor's estate in a tort action arising from injuries resulting from participation in a commercial activity.

NOTES & QUESTIONS

1. Shortly after this decision, the Florida legislature amended its statutes, granting guardians the authority to waive liability for commercial activity providers. Section 744.301 of the Florida statutes reads, in part:

   (3) In addition to the authority granted in subsection (2), natural guardians are authorized, on behalf of any of their minor children, to waive and release, in advance, any claim or cause of action against a commercial activity provider, or its owners, affiliates, employees,

or agents, which would accrue to a minor child for personal injury, including death, and property damage resulting from an inherent risk in the activity.

2. A recent case upholding the validity of a waiver signed by the parent of a minor is *Squires v. Breckenridge Outdoor Educ. Ctr.* 715 F.3d 867 (10th Cir. 2013). The Tenth Circuit upheld the validity a mother's liability waiver when daughter was injured while skiing with defendant's ski instructor. *See also Eriksson v. Nunnink.,* 183 Cal. Rptr. 3d 234 (Cal. Ct. App. 2015). Appeals court upheld the validity of a parent-signed waiver against horseback riding coach after the accidental death of a minor equestrian during competition.

Further Reading on Institutions, Officials and Waivers;

Gina Pauline, Barbara Osborne, John J. Miller, *Do Entry Form Waivers Properly Inform Triathlon Participants of the Dangers of the Sport?,* 26 J. Leg. Aspects Sport 106 (2016).

John C. Weistart & Cym H. Lowell, Law of Sports, §8.04 Waiver and Release of Liability (Bobbs-Merrill Company, Inc., 1979).

John C. Weistart & Cym H. Lowell, Law of Sports, §8.05 Liability for Injuries in Educational Programs (Bobbs-Merrill Company, Inc., 1979).

John T. Wendt, John J. Miller, *Tragedy at Fujairah: Risk Management and Legal Issues on the Death of Fran Crippen,* 2012 Den. U. Sports & Ent. L.J. 71 (2012).

Jay M. Zitter, *Sports injuries based on negligent supervision,* 58 Med. Trial Tech. Q. 393 (2011).

Further Reading on Torts and Sports in General:

Roger I. Abrams, *Torts and Sports: Legal Liability in Professional and Amateur Athletics,* 54 U. Cin. L. Rev. 1237 (1986).

Lawrence Bershad, *Boxing in the United States: Reform, Abolition or Federal Control,* 19 Seton Hall L. Rev. 865 (1989).

Nicholas Bittner, *A Hazy Shade of Winter: The Chilling Issues Surrounding Hazing in School Sports and the Litigation That Follows,* 23 Jeffrey S. Moorad Sports L.J. 211 (2016).

Dr. Tracey B. Carter, *It Is A Mindboggling Dilemma: To Play or Not to Play Youth Sports Due to Concussion Risks?,* 67 Cath. U.L. Rev. 1 (2018).

Walter T. Champion, *Nonprofessional Sport-Related Injuries and Assumption of Risk in Pennsylvania,* 54 Pa. B.A. Q.43 (1983).

Walter T. Champion, *The Ball Bounces Back: Rutter Reverses Risk,* 82 Pa. L.J. Rep. 3 (March 7, 1982).

Phyllis G. Coleman, *Scuba Diving Injuries: Causes, Remedies, and Defenses,* 29 J. Mar. L. & Com. 519 (1998).

Logan P. Desmond & Leeann M. Lower, *Boogaard v. National Hockey League,* 21 U. Den. Sports & Ent. L.J. 7 (2018).

N. Jeremi Duru, *In Search of the Final Head Ball: The Case for Eliminating Heading from Soccer,* 83 Mo. L. Rev. 559 (2018).

Daniel E. Lazaroff, *Golfer's Tort Liability - A Critique of Emerging Standard,* 24 Hastings Comm. & Ent. L.J. 317 (2002).

Joshua Lens, *NCAA Head Coach Responsibilities Legislation*, 14 DePaul J. Sports L. 33, 34 (2018).

Heather MacGillivray, *Where Is the Awareness in Concussion Awareness: Can Concussed Players Really Assume the Risk in A Concussed State?*, 21 Jeffrey S. Moorad Sports L.J. 529 (2014).

Matthew J. Mitten, *AIDS and Athletics*, 3 Seton Hall J. Sport L. 5 (1993).

Matthew J. Mitten, *Emerging Legal Issues in Sports Medicine*, 52 Def. L.J. 265 (2003).

Matthew J. Mitten, *Enhanced Risk of Harm to One's Self as a Justification for Exclusion From Athletics*, 8 Marq. Sports L. Rev. 189 (1998).

Matthew J. Mitten, *Team Physicians and Competitive Athletes: Allocating Legal Responsibility for Athletic Injuries*, 55 U. Pitt. L. Rev. 129 (1993).

Francis X. Shen, *Are Youth Sports Concussion Statutes Working?*, 56 Duq. L. Rev. 7 (2018).

Russ VerSteeg, *Consent in Sports & Recreational Activities: Using Contract Law Terminology to Clarify Tort Principles*, 12 DePaul J. Sports L. & Contemp. Probs. 1 (2016).

Russ VerSteeg, *Negligence in the Air: Safety, Legal Liability, and the Pole Vault*, 4 Tex. Rev. Ent. & Sports L. 109 (2003).

Russ VerSteeg, *Running Scared: Negligence and the Running Boom*, 4 Seton Hall J. Sport L. 447 (1994).

Chapter 5
Contracts

A. INTRODUCTORY CONCEPTS

In many respects, contract law dominates much of Sports Law. Athletes and organizations structure a great many of their affairs by means of contracts, some simple and some complex. In youth sports, parents typically sign some type of contract and pay a fee as a registration for their children to participate. High school athletes may sign letters of intent to attend certain colleges. In collegiate athletics, student athletes receive grants in aid (scholarships) that take the form of contracts. And of course in professional sports there are individual player contracts, collective bargaining agreements forged by management and player unions, endorsement contracts, and agency contracts, just to name a few.

This chapter introduces several issues that frequently arise in sports contracts. The Cannon case poses a number of questions regarding the formation of contracts (*i.e.,* What constitutes an offer? What constitutes an acceptance?), as well as giving us an opportunity to consider the relative bargaining power ordinarily exercised by a professional sports franchise as compared to a college student. Typically, in order to have a valid contract, an offeree must accept an offeror's offer; and there must be some *quid pro quo* (*i.e.,* something that each is agreeing to exchange). Lawyers call that *quid pro quo* "consideration." Of course in an ordinary player contract the player's "consideration" is her promise to play for the team, while the team's "consideration" is its promise to pay money to the player. Each exchanges his/her promise in return for the other's reciprocal promise. That's consideration. *Cannon* also provides a glimpse of a fairly sophisticated topic in Contract Law, the distinction between conditions precedent and conditions subsequent.

Like *Cannon* the *Barnett* case also raises the issue of contract remedies. In the majority of typical contracts cases, an aggrieved party asks the court for money damages. Courts also frequently call money damages a "legal remedy." The most common money damages that a court grants in a breach of contract case are "expectation damages." Expectation damages are the amount of money that a non-breaching party would have received if the breaching party had not breached (also referred to as the "benefit of the bargain"). The goal of expectation damages is to put the non-breaching party in the economic position that she would have been in had the other party not breached. But in *Barnett*, the plaintiff doesn't ask for money (*i.e.,* a "legal" remedy), but rather asks for the "equitable remedy" of negative injunction. In other words, the club asks for a court order that will prohibit the player from playing for any other basketball team. When a court grants an "equitable remedy," it orders a party either to do something (*i.e.,* to take some action) or to refrain from doing something. Pay particular attention to *why* negative injunctions are so important for some sports law contracts.

DiNardo presents a case involving both contract formation issues as well as the construction (*i.e.*, interpretation), of liquidated damages. Liquidated damages, unlike expectation damages or injunctions, represent a sum of money to which the parties actually agreed in their contract (just in case either party later breached). All three cases illustrate contract principles applied in a unique Sports Law setting.

LOS ANGELES RAMS FOOTBALL CLUB V. BILLY CANNON
185 F.SUPP. 717 (1960)
UNITED STATES DISTRICT COURT S.D. CALIFORNIA, CENTRAL DIVISION

LINDBERG, DISTRICT JUDGE.

Plaintiff, Los Angeles Rams Football Club, a member of the National Football League, has brought this action seeking injunctive relief and a declaration of right against the defendant, Billy Cannon, a citizen and resident of the State of Louisiana. The matter in controversy exceeds the value of $10,000, exclusive of interests and costs, and is within the diversity jurisdiction of this court.

Specifically, plaintiff prays for an injunction to restrain defendant from playing football or engaging in related activities for anyone other than plaintiff without the plaintiff's consent during the term of a contract or contracts allegedly entered into by the parties on November 30, 1959, and an order declaring the existence of a valid written contract or contracts.

Defendant denies he ever entered into a contract or contracts as alleged....

* * * *

The defendant, Billy Cannon, is a remarkable football player who has just finished his collegiate career with Louisiana State University. The last intercollegiate game he participated in was the Sugar Bowl game on January 1, 1960. Prior to that time, however, on November 28, 1959, or early in the morning of the 29th, he was contacted by telephone by Pete Rozelle, now Commissioner of the National Football League, but who was then and at all times material to the dispute here involved General Manager for the Los Angeles Rams.

* * *

The telephone call mentioned occurred less than thirty-six hours before the annual selection meeting of the National Football League, which was held in Philadelphia, Pennsylvania.

The Rams, after sifting an astonishing amount of information through a complex scouting system, concluded that Billy Cannon was the player of the current graduating crop they would most like to see on their team. The Rams, by virtue of ten losses and only two wins last season were tied for last place in the League, but as every cloud has its silver lining this fact also tied them for first draft choice at the above-mentioned selection meeting. The tie was to be broken by the flip of a coin. Thus, it was that the Rams stood a fifty-fifty chance of having the first draft choice.

* * *

The Rams won the toss of the coin and selected Billy Cannon as its first draft choice.

Immediately following the [selection] meeting defendant and Mr. Rozelle got together, met with members of the press, and discussed for the benefit of the press the fact that the Rams had received the first draft choice and had selected Billy Cannon.

Following the press interview Cannon and Rozelle went to Rozelle's hotel room where Cannon signed three sets of National Football Player Contract forms covering the years 1960, 1961 and 1962, and took possession of two checks, one for $10,000 and the other for $500.

Mr. Rozelle, on or about December 1st, left one set of said forms as filled out – that set embracing the 1960 season – with the then acting Commissioner, Mr. Gunsel.

Some two weeks later Billy Cannon was contacted on behalf of a Mr. K. S. Adams, Jr., who is the owner or part owner of the Houston Oilers, a football club in the recently-formed American Football League. On or about December 22nd Cannon met with Mr. Adams and others in Baton Rouge and negotiations were had with respect to a so-called personal service contract including the playing of football.

On December 30, 1959, Billy Cannon sent to the Rams a letter wherein he announced that he no longer desired to play for the Rams, purportedly revoked any offer he may have made to play for the Rams, and returned therewith the two checks above mentioned uncashed and unendorsed.

Prior thereto, however, it is contended that Mr. Gunsel approved the contract for the 1960 season, and the exhibit as admitted, Exhibit A, bears the signature of Mr. Gunsel alongside of which the date December 1, 1959 was written in.

At this point I propose to treat the question of whether or not a contract or contracts ever came into existence, dealing first with the instruments themselves before getting into the difficult matter of what transpired prior to and at the time of signing. The question, then, is, what is the nature of the several documents signed by Billy Cannon November 30, 1959? Disregarding for the moment the interpretations of the parties, the court must look to the instruments themselves.

We have three sets of instruments, in triplicate, each denominated National Football League Standard Players Contract, admitted in evidence.... The first set has the year 1960 typed in the appropriate blank; the second, 1961; and the third, 1962.

Each form states that it is a contract between Los Angeles Rams Football Club, thereinafter called the Club, and Billy Cannon, thereafter called the player. It states that in consideration of the respective promises contained therein the parties agree to the following terms:

* * *

Paragraph 5 is the negative covenant whereby the player promises not to play football or engage in related activities during the term of the contract for anyone else without the permission of the Club and Commissioner.

* * *

In Paragraph 8 the player represents that he has exceptional skill as a football player and that money damages would not compensate the loss thereof and he therefore agrees that the Club may enjoin him by appropriate injunction in the event of breach.

* * *

Paragraph 13 reads, in full:

"13. This agreement contains the entire agreement between the parties and there are no oral or written inducements, promises or agreements except as contained herein. This agreement shall become valid and binding upon each party hereto only when, as and if it shall be approved by the Commissioner."

Paragraph 14 provides that California law shall control. Paragraph 14 is the last paragraph of the form, following which there is space for the name of the Club, the signature of the Club's agent, the signature of the player, the signatures of two witnesses and space for the Commissioner's signature following the printed word "Approved." There are three date blanks, one next to the blank for the Club agent's signature, one next to the blank for the player's signature, and one next to the Commissioner's approval.

I have tried to cover as fully as necessary, but as briefly as that would permit, the form used by the Rams in their negotiations with Billy Cannon.

As heretofore indicated three sets of these forms were used. In the appropriate blank in Paragraph 1 the years 1960, 1961 and 1962, respectively, were inserted in the three sets. Each set contains the signature of Pete Rozelle for the Rams, Billy Cannon and the two witnesses. (I might state at this point, parenthetically, that no law this court is aware of requires this type of contract to be witnessed, nor does the contract itself set up such a requirement.)

Only one of the sets bears the signature of the Commissioner with respect to approval, and the evidence is to the effect that until late in December, 1959 the Commissioner was unaware of the other two sets.

The question germane at this point is just how important to these contracts is the Commissioner's approval. On this point, of course, the parties to the action are at opposite poles, plaintiff taking the position that it is an unimportant ministerial act concerning only the League and the Club, while the defendant takes the position that it is an act absolutely essential to the formation of a contract.

[1] It is the opinion of this court that on this issue the defendant must prevail. Approval by the Commissioner is essential to the formation of a contract here and this is so because the terms of the document make it so.

Keeping in mind that these forms were furnished by the Rams and not Billy Cannon, the court calls particular attention to the words regarding approval:

"This agreement shall become valid and binding upon each party hereto only when, as and if it shall be approved by the Commissioner."

Paraphrasing: "Shall become valid...only when...and if...it shall be approved..."

The words "shall become valid" clearly compels the conclusion that – in the absence of approval – it is not yet a valid agreement.

The use of the word "if" clearly suggests that approval might not happen at all.

This clause is too definite to be ignored. It jumps out at you. The words employed are too strong to permit of ambiguity. Their selection was obviously made with great care so that there would be no dispute about their meaning, and this court attaches to them the only meaning it can – that is, that the agreement shall only become valid and binding if, as and when approved by the Commissioner.

If there were not reason enough for so holding there are further reasons inherent in the instruments themselves which makes this conclusion inescapable.

* * * *

It is my conclusion...that until approved, these instruments are, at most, only offers.

* * * *

We may conclude, therefore, that what we have been loosely referring to as the 1961 and 1962 contracts were, at most, only offers and are now unquestionably revoked. That leaves the question of whether the 1960 instrument became a contract.

Having concluded as a matter of law that the alleged contracts...when signed by the defendant on November 30, 1959, constituted no more than an offer by Cannon to play football for the Rams until accepted by them and approved by the Commissioner. I next consider what the terms of the offer were.

It has been plaintiff's contention that they made the offer to Cannon and that he accepted that offer. That, as I have already stated, was not the result as a matter of law under paragraph 13 of the alleged contracts.

* * *

The testimony of Cannon and Rozelle as to many of the facts is directly contradictory and I shall attempt to resolve their disagreement only as to the more pertinent facts and statements such as appear essential in deciding what the understanding between them was.

*** Whether or not Rozelle referred to his proposal as a 'package' or not, it is my conclusion that Rozelle conveyed and Cannon obtained the impression that the proposal to be submitted by the Rams in the event they won the toss of the coin was to cover a three year period with total compensation, including a bonus, of $50,000. On the other hand, it likewise seems clear that Rozelle had in mind at the time he presented the Standard Players Contract forms to Cannon for signing...that the transaction would result in three separate and distinct contracts – one for each season – to be submitted to the Commissioner for approval if the Rams so desired, as each succeeding year approached. It thus appears that there was never a meeting of the minds as between the parties with respect to the offer. Construing the Contract forms as I do, *i.e.* requiring not only the signing by the parties, but also the approval of the Commissioner, the forms as signed by Cannon – even though signed by the Rams – must be construed as an offer by him to play for the Rams for a period of three years. This offer was never accepted by the Rams inasmuch as they requested and received the approval of the Commissioner as to the first year, 1960, only.

[3] ***

While some, particularly those schooled – to use the vernacular – in the 'game for dough' may view my interpretation of the transaction as a 'Pollyanna' approach and entirely unrealistic, it should be borne in mind that Cannon, while having been a highly publicized college ball player, was, in fact, and still is, it would appear, a provincial lad of 21 or 22, untutored and unwise, I am convinced, in the way of the business world. While he had entertained ambitions for years to get into professional football the proposition submitted to him by the Rams came by telephone apparently without prior notice while he was away from home and in New York for the purpose of receiving one of many rapidly accumulating honors that were being bestowed upon him. He was without counsel or advice and the whole transaction, including the signing of the alleged contracts, was completed in less than 48 hours. When Cannon arrived at the Warwick Hotel on Monday morning he did not know whether the Rams had acquired the right to draft him. He was immediately brought before the press and, as Rozelle testified, he Rozelle, heard Cannon make the statement to the effect that he would sign a contract with the Rams following the L.S.U. and Mississippi game in the Sugar Bowl on New Year's Day.

***

In view of the foregoing, it is my conclusion that the accepting of possession of the check for $10,000 by Cannon was not an acceptance of payment under the alleged contract, Exhibit A.

* * * *

I have [reached] the conclusion that there did not come into existence a valid written contract or contracts binding upon plaintiff and defendant.... ****

It probably should be observed, however, that while I have already indicated that Cannon did not intentionally or knowingly make himself ineligible to play in the Sugar Bowl game because of his dealings with the Rams on November 30th, I did not reach the issue of what in fact would have made him ineligible to play under the rules of the N.C.A.A. ****

Judgment will be for defendant, with costs.

NOTES & QUESTIONS

1. In terms of "offer & acceptance," identify what facts the *Cannon* court considered an "offer." According to this court, what facts could have constituted an "acceptance" of that offer? By definition an offeree's counteroffer constitutes a rejection of the offeror's original offer.

2. The court refers to a lack of "meeting of the minds" ("It thus appears that there was never a meeting of the minds as between the parties with respect to the offer."). The phrase "meeting of the minds" is a standard part of the Contract law lexicon. But the problem is that it is really not descriptive of the concept for which it stands. As a result, many law students (and lawyers I fear!), are under the mistaken impression that both parties must somehow participate in something of a Vulcan "Mind-Meld" in order for a contract to be valid. The requirement that there be a "meeting of the minds" does not actually mean that both parties must be "thinking the same thing." Rather in modern Contract jurisprudence, we have come to accept an "objective theory" of contract formation. In order for there to be a "meeting of the minds" using the objective theory, we must ask the following questions. Would a reasonable person in the position of the offeree think that the offeror, based on the outward manifestations of the offeror's conduct, was intending to be bound by his offer? In order to answer this question, you must take into account the words (if any) used by the offeror as well as all of the surrounding circumstances (*e.g.,* tone of voice, hand gestures, facial expression, etc.). If the answer is "yes" then at least we know that, objectively speaking, the offeror *intended* to make a contract. Then we must ask one more question. Would a reasonable person in the position of the offeror think that the offeree, based on the outward manifestations of the offeree's conduct, was intending to be bound by his acceptance? As was the case with objectively interpreting the offeror's offer, in order to answer this question, you must take into account the words (if any) used by the offeree as well all of the surrounding circumstances (*e.g.,* the offeree's tone of voice, hand gestures, facial expression, etc.). *So in essence, the objective theory of contract relies upon the external indicia (outward manifestations of the parties' words and conduct), to determine whether a reasonable person standing in the other person's shoes would have perceived that the other intended to be bound by their offer and acceptance.*

    In sum, then, the so-called "objective theory of contracts" (*i.e.,* using the objective manifestations of the intent of the parties as a basis for determining the parties' intent to enter into a contract) has actually made the archaic and outmoded concept of "meeting of the minds" virtually obsolete. Using the objective theory of contract formation, explain the *Cannon* court's decision.

3. First year Contracts students usually learn about "conditions precedent" and "conditions subsequent." Essentially, a condition precedent is an event, which acts as an "on switch" or

a triggering mechanism. When two people make a bet on the outcome of a basketball game, for example, the result (*i.e.,* the winning by one team) triggers an obligation for one party to owe money to the other. The fact that one team wins and the other loses, then, is a condition precedent to an obligation for payment. The obligation of payment does not arise until one team wins and the other loses. A condition subsequent, on the other hand, acts as an "off switch". A condition subsequent ordinarily (but not always) is worded in such a way that the parties create an obligation, which may be "turned off" or extinguished if a certain event later occurs. You can usually recognize a condition subsequent by words such as "unless" or "if not." For example, I could agree to pay you $100 unless the Boston Red Sox win the World Series in 2035. The way that the agreement is worded, our agreement creates an obligation on my part to pay you $100. But if the Red Sox win the World Series in 2035, that occurrence will "turn off" or "extinguish" my obligation. But we have to wait until the conclusion of the 2035 World Series in order to determine whether I'll owe you the $100.

In *Cannon,* the court suggests that the Commissioner's signature is required in order for the contract even to come into existence. Explain the applicability of terms "condition precedent" and "condition subsequent" to the approval and signature of the NFL Commissioner on the *Cannon* contracts.

Indeed, in order to be considered valid, most professional player contracts need a league commissioner's approval. Write a sentence that would make a commissioner's approval a condition precedent. Then, see if you can write a sentence that would make the commissioner's approval (or refusal) a condition subsequent.

4. According to the court, the so-called 1961 and 1962 "contract" offers were revoked ("We may conclude, therefore, that what we have been loosely referring to as the 1961 and 1962 contracts were, at most, only offers and are now unquestionably revoked."). Exactly what facts constituted the revocation of those offers?

5. To what extent do you think that the court was simply being paternalistic and protecting Cannon, a wet-behind-the-ears kid from Louisiana, from the big-time, professional football franchise?

6. Billy Cannon is one of twenty players who played the entire ten years of the American Football League, and he is a member of the American Football League Hall of Fame. He later became a dentist and subsequently served federal prison time for counterfeiting.

Printed with permission by Topps

CENTRAL NEW YORK BASKETBALL, INC. V. RICHARD BARNETT AND CLEVELAND BASKETBALL CLUB, INC.

181 NE 2D 506 (1961)

COURT OF COMMON PLEAS OF OHIO, CUYAHOGA COUNTY

DANACEAU, JUDGE.

This is an action for injunctive relief brought by the plaintiff, Central New York Basketball, Inc., a New York corporation, against Richard Barnett and Cleveland Basketball Club, Inc., a corporation. Plaintiff owns and operates a professional basketball team under the name of Syracuse Nationals, having a franchise of the National Basketball Association, now in its 16th season.

The defendant, Richard Barnett, a professional basketball player, the No. 1 draft choice in 1959 of the plaintiff and who played for the plaintiff during the ensuing 1959 basketball season, played for the Syracuse club throughout the 1960 basketball season under a signed and executed Uniform Player Contract of the National Basketball Association under date of March 16, 1960 by and between the plaintiff and said defendant, a copy of said agreement is attached to the petition, and was received in evidence as plaintiff's Exhibit B.

The defendant, Cleveland Basketball Club, Inc., is a member of the American Basketball League, recently organized, and owns and operates a professional basketball team.

In July of 1961, the defendants, Barnett and Cleveland Basketball Club, Inc., made and entered into an American Basketball League Player Contract in which the club engaged the player to render his services as a basketball player for a term beginning on September 15, 1961 and ending on September 14, 1962, a copy of said contract having been received in evidence as plaintiff's Exhibit A. ***

Plaintiff claims that the defendant, Barnett, is a professional player of great skill and whose talents and abilities as a basketball player are of special, unique, unusual and extraordinary character; that the defendant, Cleveland Basketball Club, Inc., knew that he was under contract with the plaintiff; that in accordance with the terms and conditions of said contract the plaintiff exercised a right to renew said contract for an additional year as provided therein and so notified the defendant Barnett, that the defendant Barnett breached the said contract by failing and refusing to play with and for the said plaintiff during the 1961-1962 playing season, and that said breach of contract was committed with the knowledge and participation of the defendant, Cleveland Basketball Club, Inc. Plaintiff claims that it cannot reasonably or adequately be compensated for damages in an action at law for the loss of defendant Barnett's services as required by said contract and on oral agreement between plaintiff and Barnett made in May of 1961, and that plaintiff will suffer immediate and irreparable damages. Plaintiff, therefore, prays:

1. That defendant Richard Barnett be restrained and enjoined, during the pendency of this action and permanently, from playing basketball or engaging in any activities relating to basketball for The Cleveland Basketball Club, Inc., or any person, firm, club or corporation other than the plaintiff, during the 1961-1962 basketball season.

2. That defendant Cleveland Basketball Club, Inc. be restrained and enjoined, during the pendency of this action and permanently, from any interference or attempted interference with the performance by the said Richard Barnett of his contract with plaintiff.

* * * *

The written agreement under date of March 16, 1960 and signed by the plaintiff and the defendant Barnett provides in part as follows:

> 5. The Player promises and agrees (a) to report at the time and place fixed by the Club in good physical condition; and (b) to keep himself throughout the entire season in good physical condition; and (c) to give his best services, as well as his loyalty, to the Club, and to play basketball only for the Club unless released, sold or exchanged by the Club...

> 9. The Player represents and agrees that he has exceptional and unique skill and ability as a basketball player; that his services to be rendered hereunder are of a special, unusual and extraordinary character which gives them peculiar value which cannot be reasonably or adequately compensated for in damages at law, and that the Player's breach of this

contract will cause the Club great and irreparable injury and damage. The Player agrees that, in addition to other remedies, the Club shall be entitled to injunctive and other equitable relief to prevent a breach of this contract by the Player, including, among others, the right to enjoin the Player from playing basketball for any other person or organization during the term of this contract.

22. (a) On or before September 1st (or if a Sunday, then the next preceding business day) next following the last playing season covered by this contract, the Club may tender to the Player a contract for the term of that season by mailing the same to the Player at his address following his signature hereto, or if none be given, then at his last address of record with the Club. If prior to the November 1 next succeeding said September 1, the player and the Club have not agreed upon the terms of such contract, then on or before 10 days after said November 1, the Club shall have the right by written notice to the Player at said address to renew this contract for the period of one year on the same terms, except that the amount payable to the Player shall be such as the Club shall fix in said notice; provided, however, that said amount shall be an amount payable at a rate not less than 75% of the rate stipulated for the preceding year.
(b) The Club's right to renew this contract, as provided in subparagraph (a) of this paragraph 22, and the promise of the Player not to play otherwise than with the Club have been taken into consideration in determining the amount payable under paragraph 2 hereof.

Plaintiff contends that the foregoing provisions provide for two alternatives: 1) that the parties may agree upon a signed new contract for the next succeeding playing season and 2) in the event a signed agreement is not made, the club has the right to renew the contract for a period of one year on the same terms, except that the salary shall be fixed by the club and shall be payable at a rate not less than the stipulated minimum.

The plaintiff contends that under the second alternative, the terms are the same as in the preceding year except for the amount of salary and that at the close of the renewal year, the contract has been completed and is at an end.

The construction of the contract urged by plaintiff, to which it is committed in open court, is reasonable, rational, practical, just and in accordance with the foregoing principles, and is adopted by this Court.

The defendant Barnett had previously played for the Syracuse team during the greater part of the 1959-1960 season under a signed contract.

Daniel Biasone, the President and General Manager of the Syracuse club, testified that near the close of the 1960-1961 season in March of 1961, he told the defendant Barnett that Barnett was one of seven players he would keep exempt from the forthcoming draft of players from all National Basketball Association clubs to stock the new Chicago club and that Barnett was one of the seven players he was 'protecting.'

In the latter part of May, 1961, Mr. Biasone reached the defendant Barnett by telephone, and they discussed salary for the next season and agreed upon an increase of $3,000 which would bring the salary of Barnett to $11,500. He further testified that Barnett said, "You mail them (contracts) down and I will sign them and return them." On cross-examination Biasone said that he was not sure and did not know whether Barnett said "I will sign."

The defendant Barnett testified:

Q What did he say?

A Well, he called me up and said that he wanted to discuss contracts for the coming year.

Q What did you say?

A I said that I thought I was worth $3000 more.

Q And he said?

A He agreed. He said, "I think you are worth $3000 more myself."

I said, "Send the contracts and I will look them over."

New contracts with the signature of plaintiff thereon were mailed to the defendant Barnett on May 26, 1961; and they remained with Barnett unsigned ever since.

In June of 1961, there was a telephone conversation between Jerry Walser, the Business Manager of the Syracuse club, and the defendant Barnett in which Barnett asked for an advance. Barnett:

Q What else was said in this conversation?

A Well, I asked for an advance on my – I asked for an advance of $300.

Q $300?

A That's right.

Q Did he say he would send you $300?

A He said as soon as Mr. Biasone returned – that he was away and that as soon as he could get his signature that they would advance the $300.

On July 10, 1961, the plaintiff, through Jerry Walser, mailed to Barnett a letter enclosing a check for $3,000. Mr. Biasone testified:

Q * * * Was money sent to Barnett for the 61-62 season, the current season?

A Yes.

Q When was that sent?

A The early part of July.

Q Of this year?

A This year.

Q And why was it sent?

A It was asked for.

Q By whom?

A By Dick.

Q How much money was sent to Mr. Barnett?

A $3000.

The letter and check were received by Barnett and remained in the sealed envelope until produced in court during a hearing on an application for a preliminary injunction on October 9, 1961.

Finding that the contracts mailed to Barnett were not returned and not hearing from Barnett, Mr. Biasone made repeated attempts to contact or reach the defendant Barnett in July and August of 1961 by telephone, telegram and letter, to all of which there was no response. On November 6, 1961, a letter from the plaintiff to the defendant was written and mailed and received by Barnett which reads as follows:

> It is our position that your 1960-61 contract with us was renewed when we came to terms and we sent you an advance. However, to abide by the letter of the contract and to make the position of the Syracuse Nationals absolutely clear, we hereby notify you that pursuant to Paragraph 22(a) of said contract, we hereby renew the same for the period of one year ending October 1, 1962. The amount payable to you under such renewed contract is hereby fixed at $11,500.

Meanwhile, during the months of June and July of 1961, Barnett met and talked to his former coach and advisor, John B. McLendon, who was the Coach of the Cleveland Pipers Basketball team of the defendant Cleveland Basketball Club, Inc. Both Barnett and McLendon stated that Barnett did not want to play for Syracuse but did want to play for the Cleveland Pipers. ***

*** Barnett and McLendon proceeded to take the necessary steps culminating in a signed contract between Barnett and the Cleveland Pipers with McLendon signing the contract on behalf of the Cleveland club.

The request of Barnett for an advance, whether it was $300 or $3,000, renders strong support to the claim of plaintiff that an oral agreement on a salary had been reached and that Barnett would play for Syracuse during the 1961-1962 season. Manifestly, unless there was such an understanding, there could be no salary upon which such an advance could be made. The evidence is overwhelming, and this Court finds that the plaintiff and the defendant Barnett reached an understanding that Barnett would play for Syracuse during the 1961- 1962 season at a salary of $11,500. ***

Plaintiff claims that defendant Barnett is a professional basketball player of great skill and whose talents and abilities as a basketball player are of special, unique, unusual and extraordinary character.

*** Daniel Biasone, the General Manager of the Syracuse club for the past 16 years, testified that *** Barnett was a box office attraction and was asked on cross examination: "on what basis do you say he was a great box office attraction?" He answered:

A Because he, in my opinion, he is such a tremendous ball handler and he does things that have crowd appeal, he is noticeable. He appeals to the crowd because he does things extraordinary.

Coach McLendon of the Cleveland Pipers is not so generous in his appraisal. Barnett, in his opinion, is not in the class of the specifically named outstanding basketball players. McLendon concedes that both Barnett and Neuman, now playing for Syracuse in his first year as a professional, are both "pretty good."

The defendant Barnett was asked by his counsel:

Q Do you represent to this Court that you have exceptional and unique skill and ability as a basketball player?

A No.

Q Do you represent to this Court that your services are of a special, unusual and extraordinary character?

A No.

Q You do represent to the Court that you are a professional basketball player; is that correct?

A Yes.

Q Do you think you are as good as Oscar Robertson?

A No.

* * * *

That the defendant Barnett was 19th among the top 25 scorers in the National Basketball Association in the 1960-61 season is confirmed in the statistics published on page 113 of the official Guide (plaintiff's Exhibit 4). On page 190 of the Guide is the record of Richard Barnett which indicates that he played in 78 games (out of 79) in the 60-61 season for a total of 1,970 minutes; that his F.G.M. percentage was .452; that his F.T.M. percentage was .712 and that he scored 1,320 points for an average of 16.9. The Guide also indicates that Barnett was not among the players in the East-West All Star Game on January 17, 1961 (Guide 144), nor was he among the players named in the U. S. Basketball Writers' All-NBA Team for 1961 (Guide 184).

* * *

Whether Barnett ranks with the top basketball players or not, the evidence shows that he is an outstanding professional basketball player of unusual attainments and exceptional skill and ability, and that he is of peculiar and particular value to plaintiff.

* * * *

An important growth in the field of equity has been the use of injunctions against the breach of negative agreements, both express and implied. Pomeroy's Specific Performance of Contract, Third Ed. at page 75 reads:

> Another class of contracts stipulating for personal acts are now enforced in England by means of an injunction. Where one person agrees to render personal services to another, which require and presuppose a special knowledge, skill, and ability in the employee, so that, in case of a default, the same services could not easily be obtained from others,

although the affirmative specific performance of the contract is beyond the power of the court, its performance will be negatively enforced by enjoining its breach. This doctrine applies especially to contracts made by actors, public singers, artists and others possessing a special skill and ability. ***

The opinion of the Court in *Philadelphia Ball Club v. Lajoie, supra,* is summarized in 58 L.R.A., 227 in the head notes as follows:

* * * *

2. Injunction will issue to prevent a baseball player from violating his contract to serve a certain organization for a stipulated time, during which he is not to play for any other club, where he is an expert player, has been with the organization sufficiently long to have become thoroughly familiar with the team work, and is a most attractive drawing card for the public because of his great reputation for ability in the position which he fills.

* * * *

[4] Professional players in the major baseball, football, and basketball leagues have unusual talents and skills or they would not be so employed. Such players, the defendant Barnett included, are not easily replaced. ***

Damages at law would be speculative and uncertain and are practically impossible of ascertainment in terms of money. There is no plain, adequate and complete remedy at law and the injury to the plaintiff is irreparable. ***

The Court finds in favor of the plaintiff on all issues joined and permanent injunctions as requested for the 1961-1962 basketball playing season are decreed. Thereafter the said injunctions shall be dissolved.

NOTES & QUESTIONS

1. Why can't the court simply force Barnett to play for the Syracuse Nationals? Would that really be so bad?

2. On what facts does the court rely to determine that Barnett had entered into a contract with Syracuse? Where is the offer? Where is the acceptance?

3. Explain the significance of whether a player is deemed to have exceptional skills. Isn't it true that all professional basketball players, by definition, could be considered to possess exceptional skills?

4. Explain why the court says that there is no adequate remedy "at law." Hint: look back at the introduction to this chapter where the distinction between "legal remedies" and "equitable remedies" is discussed.

VANDERBILT UNIVERSITY V. GERRY DINARDO

174 F. 3D 751 (1999)

UNITED STATES COURT OF APPEALS, SIXTH CIRCUIT

GIBSON, CIRCUIT JUDGE.

Gerry DiNardo resigned as Vanderbilt's head football coach to become the head football coach for Louisiana State University. As a result, Vanderbilt University brought this breach of contract action. The district court entered summary judgment for Vanderbilt, awarding $281,886.43 pursuant to a damage provision in DiNardo's employment contract with Vanderbilt. DiNardo appeals, arguing that the district court erred in concluding: (1) that the contract provision was an enforceable liquidated damage provision and not an unlawful penalty under Tennessee law; [and,] (2) that Vanderbilt did not waive its right to liquidated damages.... We affirm the district court's ruling that the employment contract contained an enforceable liquidated damage provision and the award of liquidated damages under the original contract.***

On December 3, 1990, Vanderbilt and DiNardo executed an employment contract hiring DiNardo to be Vanderbilt's head football coach. Section one of the contract provided:

> The University hereby agrees to hire Mr. DiNardo for a period of five (5) years from the date hereof with Mr. DiNardo's assurance that he will serve the entire term of this Contract, a long-term commitment by Mr. DiNardo being important to the University's desire for a stable intercollegiate football program....

The contract also contained reciprocal liquidated damage provisions. Vanderbilt agreed to pay DiNardo his remaining salary should Vanderbilt replace him as football coach, and DiNardo agreed to reimburse Vanderbilt should he leave before his contract expired. Section eight of the contract stated:

> Mr. DiNardo recognizes that his promise to work for the University for the entire term of this 5-year Contract is of the essence of this Contract to the University. Mr. DiNardo also recognizes that the University is making a highly valuable investment in his continued employment by entering into this Contract and its investment would be lost were he to resign or otherwise terminate his employment as Head Football Coach with the University prior to the expiration of this Contract. Accordingly, Mr. DiNardo agrees that in the event he resigns or otherwise terminates his employment as Head Football Coach (as opposed to his resignation or termination from another position at the University

to which he may have been reassigned), prior to the expiration of this Contract, and is employed or performing services for a person or institution other than the University, he will pay to the University as liquidated damages an amount equal to his Base Salary, less amounts that would otherwise be deducted or withheld from his Base Salary for income and social security tax purposes, multiplied by the number of years (or portion(s) thereof) remaining on the Contract.

During contract negotiations, section eight was modified at DiNardo's request so that damages would be calculated based on net, rather than gross, salary.

Vanderbilt initially set DiNardo's salary at $100,000 per year. DiNardo received salary increases in 1992, 1993, and 1994.

In November 1994, Louisiana State University contacted Vanderbilt in hopes of speaking with DiNardo about becoming the head football coach for L.S.U. Hoolahan [Vanderbilt's Athletic Director] gave DiNardo permission to speak to L.S.U. about the position. On December 12, 1994, DiNardo announced that he was accepting the L.S.U. position.

Vanderbilt sent a demand letter to DiNardo seeking payment of liquidated damages under section eight of the contract. Vanderbilt believed that DiNardo was liable for three years of his net salary: one year under the original contract and two years under the Addendum. DiNardo did not respond to Vanderbilt's demand for payment.

* * *

I.

* * *

Contracting parties may agree to the payment of liquidated damages in the event of a breach. *See Beasley v. Horrell*, 864 S.W.2d 45, 48 (Tenn.Ct.App.1993). The term "liquidated damages" refers to an amount determined by the parties to be just compensation for damages should a breach occur. *See id.* Courts will not enforce such a provision, however, if the stipulated amount constitutes a penalty. *See id.* A penalty is designed to coerce performance by punishing default. *See id.* In Tennessee, a provision will be considered one for liquidated damages, rather than a penalty, if it is reasonable in relation to the anticipated damages for breach, measured prospectively at the time the contract was entered into, and not grossly disproportionate to the actual damages. *See Beasley*, 864 S.W.2d at 48; *Kimbrough & Co. v. Schmitt*, 939 S.W.2d 105, 108 (Tenn.Ct.App.1996). When these conditions are met, particularly the first, the parties probably intended the provision to be for liquidated damages. However, any doubt as to the character of the contract provision will be resolved in favor of finding it a penalty. *See Beasley*, 864 S.W.2d at 48.

The district court held that the use of a formula based on DiNardo's salary to calculate liquidated damages was reasonable "given the nature of the unquantifiable damages in the case." 974 F.Supp. at 642. The court held that parties to a contract may include consequential damages and even damages not usually awarded by law in a liquidated damage provision provided that they were contemplated by the parties. *Id.* at 643. The court explained:

> The potential damage to [Vanderbilt] extends far beyond the cost of merely hiring a new head football coach. It is this uncertain potentiality that the parties sought to address by providing for a sum certain to apply towards anticipated expenses and losses. It is impossible to estimate how the loss of a head football coach will affect alumni relations, public support, football ticket sales, contributions, etc.... As such, to require a precise formula for calculating damages resulting from the breach of contract by a college head football coach would be tantamount to barring the parties from stipulating to liquidated damages evidence in advance. *Id.* at 642.

* * *

The contract language establishes that Vanderbilt wanted the five-year contract because "a long-term commitment" by DiNardo was "important to the University's desire for a stable intercollegiate football program," and that this commitment was of "essence" to the contract. Vanderbilt offered the two-year contract extension to DiNardo well over a year before his original contract expired. Both parties understood that the extension was to provide stability to the program, which helped in recruiting players and retaining assistant coaches. Thus, undisputed evidence, and reasonable inferences therefrom, establish that both parties understood and agreed that DiNardo's resignation would result in Vanderbilt suffering damage beyond the cost of hiring a replacement coach.

* * * *

The stipulated damage amount is reasonable in relation to the amount of damages that could be expected to result from the breach. As we stated, the parties understood that Vanderbilt would suffer damage should DiNardo prematurely terminate his contract, and that these actual damages would be difficult to measure. *See Kimbrough & Co.,* 939 S.W.2d at 108.

* * * *

Vanderbilt hired DiNardo for a unique and specialized position, and the parties understood that the amount of damages could not be easily ascertained should a breach occur. Contrary to DiNardo's suggestion, Vanderbilt did not need to undertake an analysis to determine actual damages, and using the number of years left on the contract multiplied by the salary per year was a reasonable way to calculate damages considering the difficulty of ascertaining damages with certainty. *See Kimbrough & Co.,* 939 S.W.2d at 108. The fact that liquidated damages declined each year DiNardo remained under contract, is directly tied to the parties' express understanding of the importance of a long-term commitment from DiNardo. Furthermore, the liquidated damages provision was reciprocal and the result of negotiations between two parties, each of whom was represented by counsel.

* * *

II.

DiNardo next argues that Vanderbilt waived its right to liquidated damages when it granted DiNardo permission to discuss the coaching position with L.S.U. Under Tennessee law, a party may not recover liquidated damages when it is responsible for or has contributed to the delay or nonperformance alleged as the breach. *See V.L. Nicholson Co. v. Transcon Inv. and Fin. Ltd., Inc.,* 595 S.W.2d 474, 484 (Tenn.1980).

Vanderbilt did not waive its rights under section eight of the contract by giving DiNardo permission to pursue the L.S.U. position. *See Chattem, Inc. v. Provident Life & Accident Ins. Co.,* 676 S.W.2d 953, 955 (Tenn.1984)(waiver is the intentional, voluntary relinquishment of a known right). First, Hoolahan's permission was quite circumscribed. Hoolahan gave DiNardo permission to talk to L.S.U. about their coaching position; he did not authorize DiNardo to terminate his contract with Vanderbilt. Second, the employment contract required DiNardo to ask Vanderbilt's athletic director for permission to speak with another school about a coaching position,[1] and Hoolahan testified that granting a coach permission to talk to another school about a position was a "professional courtesy." Thus, the parties certainly contemplated that DiNardo could explore other coaching positions, and indeed even leave Vanderbilt, subject to the terms of the liquidated damage provision. *** Allowing DiNardo to talk to another school did not relinquish Vanderbilt's right to liquidated damages.

Accordingly, we affirm the district court's judgment that the contract contained an enforceable liquidated damage provision, and we affirm the portion of the judgment reflecting damages calculated under the original five-year contract.

NOTES & QUESTIONS

1. When the court says that "The liquidated damages are in line with Vanderbilt's estimate of its actual damages," is the court referring to an estimate at the time of the making of the contract? Or is the court referring to an estimate of the actual damages that Vanderbilt incurred after DiNardo's breach? Does it matter? If so, why? If not, why not?

---

[1] Section nine provided:

The parties agree that should another coaching opportunity be presented to Mr. DiNardo or should Mr. DiNardo be interested in another coaching position during the term of this Contract, he must notify the University's Director of Athletics of such opportunity or interest and written permission must be given to Mr. DiNardo by the Director of Athletics before any discussions can be held by Mr. DiNardo with the anticipated coaching-position principal.

2. The court articulates the state's rule regarding liquidated damages as follows: "In Tennessee, a provision will be considered one for liquidated damages, rather than a penalty, if it is reasonable in relation to the anticipated damages for breach, measured prospectively at the time the contract was entered into, and not grossly disproportionate to the actual damages." How does this rule compare and contrast with the Uniform Commercial Code (UCC) rule (which governs the sale of goods) in UCC 2-718(1)? UCC 2-718 (1) reads:

3. Damages for breach by either party may be liquidated in the agreement but only at an amount which is reasonable in the light of the anticipated or actual harm caused by the breach, the difficulties of proof of loss, and the inconvenience or nonfeasibility of otherwise obtaining an adequate remedy. A term fixing unreasonably large liquidated damages is void as a penalty.

4. A recent Ohio case reached a similar conclusion, based on many similar facts: *Kent State Univ. v. Ford*, 26 N.E.3d 868 (Ohio App. 11th Dist. 2015). The appellate court upheld liquidated damages in the amount of the balance of salary remaining on contract when Kent State football coach breached his contract by leaving for coaching position at Bradley University.

B. SAMPLE CONTRACTS

The four sample contracts in the following section provide an opportunity to scrutinize actual contracts used in the industry. As such, they offer tremendous opportunities to learn a great deal that is practical. The Babe Ruth contract from 1930 gives us a chance to peek into the past. Pay particular attention to the language as well as the types of provisions in the Ruth contract that have survived into the modern era, still present either in general or verbatim in the contemporary MLB or NBA contracts.

Also remember, that the MLB and NBA contracts are products of collective bargaining and, by their very nature, incorporate their respective league constitutions and bylaws. Hence, these documents not only introduce the basic *content* of a professional athlete's employment agreement, but they also indirectly teach a great deal about the *structure and governance* of professional sports teams and leagues (*e.g.*, the powers of a commissioner and the relationships among member teams). The Talent Services Agreement provides an opportunity to explore the provisions of an important type of contract for professional athletes – a sponsorship/endorsement contract. As will be covered in greater detail in Chapter 11, one of the most important revenue streams for a professional athlete often comes from sponsorship/endorsement deals. This particular sample illustrates a basic blueprint for a sponsorship deal involving an NBA player and a clothing company. You should read these documents carefully and critically. Use them to learn what you can about professional sports contracts, the business and corporate aspects of teams and leagues, and elements of labor law associated with collective bargaining. Some of the relationships between antitrust and labor law will be addressed in the next chapter.

1930 BABE RUTH CONTRACT

REGULATIONS

1. The Club's playing season for each year covered by this contract and all renewals hereof shall be as fixed by the American League of Professional Baseball Clubs, or, if this contract shall be assigned to a Club in another league, then by the league of which such assignee is a member.

2. The Player must keep himself in first-class physical condition and must at all times conform his personal conduct to standards of good citizenship and good sportsmanship.

3. The Player, when requested by the Club, must submit to medical examination at the expense of the Club and, if necessary, to treatment by a regular physician in good standing at the Player's expense. Disability directly resulting from injury sustained in playing baseball for the Club while rendering service under this contract shall not impair the right of the Player to receive his full salary for the season in which the injury was sustained, but only upon the express, prerequisite condition that written notice of such injury, including the time, place, cause and nature of the injury, is served upon and received by the Club within twenty days of the sustaining of said injury. Any other disability may be ground for suspending or terminating this contract at the discretion of the Club. *]injury on the job*

4. The Club will furnish the Player with two complete uniforms, exclusive of shoes, the Player making a deposit of $30.00 therefor, which deposit will be returned to him at the end of the season or upon the termination of this contract, upon the surrender of the uniforms by him to the Club. And the Club will provide and furnish the Player while "abroad" or traveling with the Club in other cities with proper board, lodging, and pay all proper and necessary traveling expenses, including Pullman accommodations and meals en route.

5. The Player, while under contract or reservation, shall not engage, without the consent of his Club, in any game or exhibition of baseball (except for the Club or for an assignee of this contract), football, basketball, or other athletic sport.

6. For violation by the Player of any regulation the Club may impose a reasonable fine and deduct the amount thereof from the Player's salary or may suspend the Player without salary for a period not exceeding thirty days, or both, at the discretion of the Club. Written notice of the fine or suspension or both and of the reasons therefor shall in every case be given to the Player.

7. In order to enable the Player to fit himself for his duties under this contract the Club may require the Player to report for practice at such places as the Club may designate and to participate in such exhibition contests as may be arranged by the Club for a period of ....*Forty-five*.............. days prior to the playing season without any other compensation than that herein elsewhere provided, the Club, however, to pay the traveling expenses, including Pullman accommodations, and meals en route, of the Player from his home city to the training place of the Club, whether he be ordered to go there direct or by way of the home city of the Club. In the event of the failure of the Player to report for practice or to participate in the exhibition games, as provided for, he shall be required to get in playing condition to the satisfaction of the Club's team manager, and at the Player's own expense, before his salary shall commence.

The attention of both Club and Player is specifically directed to the following excerpt from Article II, Section I, of the Major League Rules:

"No Club shall make a contract different from the uniform contract or a contract containing a non-reserve clause, except with the written approval of the Advisory Council. All contracts shall be in duplicate and the Player shall retain a counterpart original. The making of any agreement between a Club and Player not embodied in the contract shall subject both parties to discipline by the Commissioner."

American League of Professional Baseball Clubs
UNIFORM PLAYER'S CONTRACT

Parties   The _American League Base Ball Club of New York_

herein called the Club, and _GEORGE HERMAN RUTH_

of _New York, N. Y._, herein called the Player.

Recital   The club is a member of the American League of Professional Baseball Clubs. As such, and *jointly* with the other members of the League, it is a party to agreements and rules with the National League of Professional Baseball Clubs and its constituent clubs, and with the National Association of Professional Baseball Leagues. The purpose of these agreements and rules is to insure to the public wholesome and high-class professional baseball by defining the relations between Club and Player, between club and club, between league and league, and by vesting in a designated Commissioner broad powers of control and discipline, and of decision in case of disputes.

Agreement   In view of the facts above recited the parties agree as follows:

Employment   1. The Club hereby employs the Player to render skilled service as a baseball player in connection

with all games of the Club during the year S _1930_ and _1931_ including the Club's training season, the Club's exhibition games, the Club's playing season, and the World Series (or any other official series in which the Club may participate and in any receipts of which the player may be entitled to share); and the player covenants that he will perform with diligence and fidelity the service stated and such duties as may be required of him in such employment.

Salary   2. For the service aforesaid the Club will pay the Player an aggregate salary of $_80,000.00_ _for each of said years_, as follows:

In semi-monthly installments after the commencement of the playing season covered by this contract, unless the Player is "abroad" with the Club for the purpose of playing games, in which event the amount then due shall be paid on the first week-day after the return "home" of the Club, the terms "*home*" and "*abroad*" meaning, respectively, *at and away from* the city in which the Club has its baseball field.

If a monthly salary is stipulated above, it shall begin with the commencement of the Club's playing season (or such subsequent date as the Player's services may commence) and end with the termination of the Club's scheduled playing season, and shall be payable in semi-monthly installments as above provided.

If the Player is in the service of the Club for part of the playing season only, he shall receive such proportion of the salary above mentioned, as the number of days of his actual employment bears to the number of days in the Club's playing season.

Loyalty   3. (a) The Player will faithfully serve the Club or any other Club to which, in conformity with the agreements above recited, this contract may be assigned, and pledges himself to the American public to conform to high standards of personal conduct, of fair play and good sportsmanship.

(b) The Player represents that he does not, directly or indirectly, own stock or have any financial interest in the ownership or earnings of any Major League club, except as hereinafter expressly set forth, and covenants that he will not hereafter, while connected with any Major League club, acquire or hold any such stock or interest except in accordance with Section 23 (e), Article II, Major League Rules.

Service   4. The Player will not play during the period of this contract otherwise than for the Club or such other Clubs as may become assignees of this contract in conformity with said agreements; nor will he play any exhibition games after October 31st any year until the training season the following year, nor in any post-season exhibition game in which more than two other players of the Club participate.

Assignment   5. (a) In case of assignment of this contract to another Club, the Player shall promptly report to the assignee club within 72 hours from the date he receives written notice from the Club of such assignment, if not more than 1600 miles by most-direct available railroad route, plus an additional 24 hours for each additional 800 miles; accrued salary shall be payable when he so reports; and each successive assignee shall become liable to the Player for his salary during his term of service with such assignee, and the Club shall not be liable therefor. If the Player fails to report as above specified, he shall not be entitled to salary after the date he receives written notice of assignment. If the assignee is a member either of the National or American League, the salary shall be as above (paragraph 2) specified. If the assignee is any other Club the Player's salary shall be the same as that usually paid by said Club to other players of like ability.

Termination   (b) This contract may be terminated at any time by the Club or by any assignee upon ten days' written notice to the Player.

Regulations   6. The Player accepts as part of this contract the Regulations printed on the third page hereof, and also such reasonable modifications of them and such other reasonable regulations as the Club may announce from time to time.

Agreements and Rules   7. (a) The Major and Major-Minor League Agreements and Rules, and all amendments thereto hereafter adopted, are hereby made a part of this contract, and the Club and Player agree to accept, abide by and comply with the same and all decisions of the Commissioner pursuant thereto.

Publication   (b) It is further expressly agreed that, in consideration of the rights and interest of the public, the Club, the League President, and/or the Commissioner may make public the record of any inquiry, investigation or hearing held or conducted, including in such record all evidence or information given, received or obtained in connection therewith, and including further the findings and decisions therein and the reasons therefor.

Renewal   8. (a) On or before February 15th (or if Sunday, then the succeeding business day) of the year next following the last playing season covered by this contract, by written notice to the Player at his address following his signature hereto (or if none be given, then at his last address of record with the Club), the Club or any assignee hereof may renew this contract for the term of that year except that the salary shall be such as the parties may then agree upon, or in default of agreement the Player will accept such salary rate as the Club may fix, or else will not play baseball otherwise than for the Club or for an assignee hereof.

(b) The Club's right of reservation of the Player, and of renewal of this contract as aforesaid, and the promise of the Player not to play otherwise than with the Club or an assignee hereof, have been taken into consideration in determining the salary specified herein and the undertaking by the Club to pay said salary is the consideration for both said reservation, renewal option and promise, and the Player's service.

Disputes   9. In case of dispute between the Player and the Club or any Major League Club assignee hereof, the same shall be referred to the Commissioner as an umpire, and his decision shall be accepted by all parties as final; and the Club and the Player agree that any such dispute, or any claim or complaint by either party against the other, shall be presented to the Commissioner within one year from the date it arose.

Supplemental Agreements   10. The Club and Player covenant that this contract fully sets forth all understandings and agreements between them, and agree that no other understandings or agreements, whether heretofore or hereafter made, shall be valid, recognizable, or of any effect whatsoever, unless expressly set forth in a new or supplemental contract executed by the Player and the Club (acting by its president, or such other officer as shall have been thereunto duly authorized by the president or Board of Directors, in writing filed of record with the League President and Commissioner—and that no other Club officer or employe shall have any authority to represent or act for the Club in that respect), and complying with all agreements and rules to which this contract is subject.

Special Covenants

See "Important Notice" above.

This contract shall not be valid or effective unless and until approved by the League President or Advisory Council, as the case may be.

Signed in duplicate this ......*10th*...... day of ....*March*........., A. D. 193*0*.

[SEAL]

                     American League Base Ball Club of New York
                                                 (Club)

                 By *Jacob Ruppert*
                                         (President)

Witness:

Byrd daut Jr   *George Herman Ruth*
                                             (Player)

                                           (Home address of Player)

168

1. In the "Regulations," what do you think was meant by "first-class physical condition" and "good citizenship"? These same general tenets are addressed again in paragraph 3(a) of the contract, itself, where the player "pledges himself to the American public to conform to high standards of personal conduct, of fair play and good sportsmanship." Don't these phrases strike you as somewhat trite and archaic today? How did the Babe perform on those matters?

2. Why do you think that the club was willing to pay a player his full salary for the entire season if he was injured while playing?

3. What do you think is the purpose of paragraph 5 in the "Regulations"? Does this mean that the player cannot play basketball in the driveway at his house with his teenage son or daughter? What do you think is included within the scope of "other athletic sport"? Where should the line be drawn when an athlete is cross-training to get in shape for baseball?

   On February 27, 2004, the New York Yankees cut third baseman Aaron Boone from the roster after he tore a ligament in his knee during a pickup basketball game. Although seemingly innocent, Boone's participation in the basketball game was in violation of his contract with the Yankees, which expressly prohibited participation in such activities. The Yankees were faced with three options: take no action and pay Boone his $5.75 million salary; void the contract thereby releasing him; or, amend the contract and keep Boone on the roster. The Yankees voided the contract and Boone signed with the Cleveland Indians. "There is precedent for voiding a contract because of a player's off-field activity. In 1994, Atlanta saved about $4.6 million by releasing outfielder Ron Gant in spring training after he broke his leg in a dirt-bike accident." The Yankees, for their part, signed superstar Alex Rodriguez to replace Boone. *See* Kepner, Tyler, *BASEBALL; Boone's Injury Could Cost Him His Contract*, www.select.nytimes.com, January 27, 2004. Apparently if there were any hard feelings between Boone and the organization, they improved over time. In December 2017, the Yankees re-hired Boone; they made him the 33rd manager of the franchise!

4. Why do you think that the parties felt it necessary to include a statement in the "Recital" regarding the Commissioner's "broad powers of control and discipline, and of decision in case of disputes"?

5. Explain what you think the purposes were for the requirements in paragraph 5(a) of the contract? In sports what do we typically call "assignment" of a club's rights to another team?

6. Paragraph 8 of the contract came to be called the "reserve clause." Explain how the reserve clause operated in practical terms.

Photo printed with permission from Topps

APPENDIX A
MAJOR LEAGUE
UNIFORM PLAYER'S CONTRACT

Parties

Between _____, herein called the Club,

and _____

of _____, herein called the Player.

Recital

The Club is, along with other Major League Clubs, signatory to the Major League Constitution and has subscribed to the Major League Rules.

Agreement

In consideration of the facts above recited and of the promises of each to the other, the parties agree as follows:

Employment

1. The Club hereby employs the Player to render, and the Player agrees to render, skilled services as a baseball player during the year(s) _____ including the Club's training season, the Club's exhibition games, the Club's playing season, the Wild Card Game, the Division Series, the League Championship Series and the World Series (or any other official series in which the Club may participate and in any receipts of which the Player may be entitled to share).

Payment

2. For performance of the Player's services and promises hereunder the Club will pay the Player the sum of $ _____ in semi-monthly installments after the commencement of the championship season(s) covered by this contract except as the schedule of payments may be modified by a special covenant. Payment shall be made on the day the amount becomes due, regardless of whether the Club is "home" or "abroad." If a monthly rate of payment is stipulated above, it shall begin with the commencement of the championship season (or such subsequent date as the Player's services may commence) and end with the termination of the championship season and shall be payable in semi-monthly installments as above provided.

Nothing herein shall interfere with the right of the Club and the Player by special covenant herein to mutually agree upon a method of payment whereby part of the Player's salary for the above year can be deferred to subsequent years. The Club shall be permitted to deduct from the Player's salary only those amounts that are specifically authorized by the Basic Agreement, this contract, any mutually agreed upon special covenant hereto, or a separate authorization signed by the Player. Any special covenant or authorization for a deduction from the Player's salary must state with specificity the particular expense for which the deduction is authorized. All deductions from a Player's salary must be identified on the Player's paystub and, if necessary, a separate document.

If the Player is in the service of the Club for part of the championship season only, he shall receive such proportion of the sum above mentioned, as the number of days of his actual employment in the championship season bears to the number of days in the championship season. Notwithstanding the rate of payment stipulated above, the minimum rate of payment to the Player for each day of service on a Major League Club shall be at the applicable rate set forth in Article VI(A)(1) of the Basic Agreement between the Thirty Major League Clubs and the Major League Baseball Players Association, effective December 1, 2016 ("Basic Agreement"). The minimum rate of payment for Minor League service for all Players (a) signing a second Major League contract (not covering the same season as any such Player's initial Major League contract) or a subsequent Major League contract, or (b) having at least one day of Major League service, shall be at the applicable rate set forth in Article VI(A)(2) of the Basic Agreement. The minimum rate of payment for Minor League service for all Players signing a first Major League contract who are not covered by Article VI(A)(2) of the Basic Agreement shall be at the applicable rate set forth in Article VI(A)(3) of the Basic Agreement.

Payment to the Player at the rate stipulated above shall be continued throughout any period in which a Player is required to attend a regularly scheduled military encampment of the Reserve of the Armed Forces or of the National Guard during the championship season.

Loyalty
3.(a) The Player agrees to perform his services hereunder diligently and faithfully, to keep himself in first-class physical condition and to obey the Club's training rules, and pledges himself to the American public and to the Club to conform to high standards of personal conduct, fair play and good sportsmanship.

Baseball Promotion
3.(b) In addition to his services in connection with the actual playing of baseball, the Player agrees to cooperate with the Club and participate in any and all reasonable promotional activities of the Club and Major League Baseball, which, in the opinion of the Club, will promote the welfare of the Club or professional baseball, and to observe and comply with all reasonable requirements of the Club respecting conduct and service of its team and its players, at all times whether on or off the field.

Pictures and Public Appearances
3.(c) The Player agrees that his picture may be taken for still photographs, motion pictures or television at such times as the Club may designate and agrees that all rights in such pictures shall belong to the Club and may be used by the Club for publicity purposes in any manner

it desires. The Player further agrees that during the playing season he will not make public appearances, participate in radio or television programs or permit his picture to be taken or write or sponsor newspaper or magazine articles or sponsor commercial products without the written consent of the Club, which shall not be withheld except in the reasonable interests of the Club or professional baseball.

PLAYER REPRESENTATIONS

Ability

4.(a) The Player represents and agrees that he has exceptional and unique skill and ability as a baseball player; that his services to be rendered hereunder are of a special, unusual and extraordinary character which gives them peculiar value which cannot be reasonably or adequately compensated for in damages at law, and that the Player's breach of this contract will cause the Club great and irreparable injury and damage. The Player agrees that, in addition to other remedies, the Club shall be entitled to injunctive and other equitable relief to prevent a breach of this contract by the Player, including, among others, the right to enjoin the Player from playing baseball for any other person or organization during the term of his contract.

Condition

4.(b) The Player represents that he has no physical or mental defects known to him and unknown to the appropriate representative of the Club which would prevent or impair performance of his services.

Interest in Club

4.(c) The Player represents that he does not, directly or indirectly, own stock or have any financial interest in the ownership or earnings of any Major League Club, except as hereinafter expressly set forth, and covenants that he will not hereafter, while connected with any Major League Club, acquire or hold any such stock or interest except in accordance with Major League Rule 20(e).

Service

5.(a) The Player agrees that, while under contract, and prior to expiration of the Club's right to renew this contract, he will not play baseball otherwise than for the Club, except that the Player may participate in post-season games under the conditions prescribed in the Major League Rules. Major League Rule 18(b) is set forth herein.

Other Sports

5.(b) The Player and the Club recognize and agree that the Player's participation in certain other sports may impair or destroy his ability and skill as a baseball player. Accordingly, the Player agrees that he will not engage in professional boxing or wrestling; and that, except with the written consent of the Club, he will not engage in skiing, auto racing, motorcycle racing, sky diving, or in any game or exhibition of football, soccer, professional league basketball, ice hockey or other sport involving a substantial risk of personal injury.

Assignment

6.(a) The Player agrees that his contract may be assigned by the Club (and reassigned by any assignee Club) to any other Club in accordance with the Major League Rules. The Club and the Player may, without obtaining special approval, agree by special covenant to limit or elim- inate the right of the Club to assign this contract.

Medical Information

6.(b) The Player agrees:

(1) that the Club's physician and any other physician or medical professional consulted by the Player pursuant to Regulation 2 of this contract or Article XIII(D) of the Basic Agreement may furnish to the Club all relevant medical information relating to the Player. Except as permitted by Article XIII(G) of the Basic Agreement, which is incorporated herein by reference, the Club is prohibited from re-disclosing any such information without the express written consent of the Player. The Club's physician shall be the custodian of the medical records furnished to a Club pursuant to this Paragraph 6(b). The Club's trainers shall have access to all such records provided to the Club.

(2) that, should the Club contemplate an assignment of this contract to another Club or Clubs, the Club's physician may furnish to the physicians and officials of such other Club or Clubs all relevant medical information relating to the Player; provided, however, that said physicians and officials are prohibited from re-disclosing any such information without the express written consent of the Player. In addition, within thirty (30) days from the receipt of the Player's medical information, the physicians and officials of the Club which requested the medical information will return any and all documents received to the Player's Club, and will not keep copies of any documents it received or any other records indicating the substance of the medical information transmitted. If the Player's UPC is assigned before the information is returned in accordance with this subparagraph (2), the assignee Club may retain the information. A Player may, at the time that he is no longer under reserve to the Club or on December 1 of every other year, whichever is earlier, request that the Club notify him of the Clubs to which his medical information was provided pursuant to this Paragraph 6(b)(2).

No Salary Reduction

6.(c) The amount stated in paragraph 2 and in special covenants hereof which is payable to the Player for the period stated in paragraph 1 hereof shall not be diminished by any such assignment, except for failure to report as provided in the next subparagraph (d).

Reporting

6.(d) The Player shall report to the assignee Club promptly (as provided in the Regulations) upon receipt of written notice from the Club of the assignment of this contract. If the Player fails to so report, he shall not be entitled to any payment for the period from the date he receives written notice of assignment until he reports to the assignee Club.

Obligations of Assignor and Assignee Clubs

6.(e) Upon and after such assignment, all rights and obligations of the assignor Club hereunder shall become the rights and obligations of the assignee Club; provided, however, that

(1) The assignee Club shall be liable to the Player for payments accruing from the date of assignment and shall not be liable (but the assignor Club shall remain liable) for payments accrued prior to and including that date.

(2) If at any time the assignee is a Major League Club, it shall be liable to pay the Player at the full rate stipulated in paragraph 2 hereof for the remainder of the period stated in paragraph 1 hereof and all prior assignors and assignees shall be relieved of liability for any payment for such period.

(3) Unless the assignor and assignee Clubs agree otherwise, if the assignee Club is a Minor League Baseball Club, the assignee Club shall be liable only to pay the Player at the rate usually paid by said assignee Club to other Players of similar skill and ability in its classification and the assignor Club shall be liable to pay the difference for the remainder of the period stated in paragraph 1 hereof between an amount computed at the rate stipulated in paragraph 2 hereof and the amount so payable by the assignee Club.

(4) If performance and/or award bonuses are included as Special Covenants hereunder and an assignment is made during the championship season, the responsibility for such bonuses shall be as follows:

(i) All performance and/or award bonuses earned prior to the assignment shall be the responsibility of the assignor Club;

(ii) The responsibility for any and all performance bonuses earned after the assignment shall be prorated between the assignor and assignee Clubs in proportion to the total number of relevant events attained during the season with each Club involved; and

(iii) The responsibility for any and all award bonuses earned after the assignment shall be the full and exclusive responsibility of the Club for whom the Player was performing services at the end of the championship season. For purposes of this paragraph, an award bonus for election or selection to the All-Star Game shall be deemed to be earned on the day of the announcement of the election or selection, an award bonus for performance over the championship season shall be deemed earned on the last day of the championship season and an award bonus for performance in the post-season shall be deemed earned on the day of the announcement of the award.

Moving Allowances

6.(f) The Player shall be entitled to moving allowances under the circumstances and in the amounts set forth in Articles VII(E) and VIII of the Basic Agreement.

"Club"

6.(g) All references in other paragraphs of this contract to "the Club" shall be deemed to mean and include any assignee of this contract.

TERMINATION

By Player

7.(a) The Player may terminate this contract, upon written notice to the Club, if the Club shall default in the payments to the Player provided for in paragraph 2 hereof or shall fail to perform any other obligation agreed to be performed by the Club hereunder and if the Club shall fail to remedy such default within ten (10) days after the receipt by the Club of written notice of such default. The Player may also terminate this contract as provided in subparagraph (d)(4) of this paragraph 7. (See Article XV(J) of the Basic Agreement.)

By Club

7.(b) The Club may terminate this contract upon written notice to the Player (but only after requesting and obtaining waivers of this contract from all other Major League Clubs) if the Player shall at any time:

(1) fail, refuse or neglect to conform his personal conduct to the standards of good citizenship and good sportsmanship or to keep himself in first-class physical condition or to obey the Club's training rules; or

(2) fail, in the opinion of the Club's management, to exhibit sufficient skill or competitive ability to qualify or continue as a member of the Club's team; or

(3) fail, refuse or neglect to render his services hereunder or in any other manner materially breach this contract.

7.(c) If this contract is terminated by the Club, the Player shall be entitled to termination pay under the circumstances and in the amounts set forth in Article IX of the Basic Agreement. In addition, the Player shall be entitled to receive an amount equal to the reasonable traveling expenses of the Player, including first-class jet air fare and meals en route, to his home city.

Procedure

7.(d) If the Club proposes to terminate this contract in accordance with subparagraph (b) of this paragraph 7, the procedure shall be as follows:

(1) The Club shall request waivers from all other Major League Clubs. Such waivers shall be good for the periods specified in Major League Rule 10. Such waiver request must state that it is for the purpose of terminating this contract and it may not be withdrawn.

(2) Upon receipt of waiver request, any other Major League Club may claim assignment of this contract at a waiver price of $1.00, the priority of claims to be determined in accordance with the Major League Rules.

(3) If this contract is so claimed, the Club shall, promptly and before any assignment, notify the Player that it had requested waivers for the purpose of terminating this contract and that the contract had been claimed.

(4) Within five (5) days after receipt of notice of such claim, the Player shall be entitled, by written notice to the Club, to terminate this contract on the date of his notice of termination. If the Player fails to so notify the Club, this contract shall be assigned to the claiming Club.

(5) If the contract is not claimed, the Club shall promptly deliver written notice of termination to the Player at the expiration of the waiver period.

7.(e) Upon any termination of this contract by the Player, all obligations of both Parties hereunder shall cease on the date of termination, except the obligation of the Club to pay the Player's compensation to said date.

Regulations

8. The Player accepts as part of this contract the Regulations set forth herein.

Rules

9.(a) The Club and the Player agree to accept, abide by and comply with all provisions of the Major League Constitution, and the Major League Rules, or other rules or regulations in effect on the date of this Uniform Player's Contract, which are not inconsistent with the provisions of this contract or the provisions of any agreement between the Major League Clubs and the Major League Baseball Players Association, provided that the Club, together with the other Major League Clubs and Minor League Baseball, reserves the right to modify, supplement or repeal any provision of said Constitution, Major League Rules or other rules and regulations in a manner not inconsistent with this contract or the provisions of any then existing agreement between the Major League Clubs and the Major League Baseball Players Association.

Disputes

9.(b) All disputes between the Player and the Club which are covered by the Grievance Procedure as set forth in the Basic Agreement shall be resolved in accordance with such Grievance Procedure.

Publication

9.(c) The Club, the Chief Baseball Officer and the Commissioner, or any of them, may make public the findings, decision and record of any inquiry, investigation or hearing held or conducted, including in such record all evidence or information given, received, or obtained in connection therewith.

Renewal

10.(a) Unless the Player has exercised his right to become a free agent as set forth in the Basic Agreement, the Club may retain reservation rights over the Player by instructing the Office of the Commissioner to tender to the Player a contract for the term of the next year by including the Player on the Central Tender Letter that the Office of the Commissioner submits to the Players Association on or before December 2 (or, if December 2 is a Saturday or Sunday, then on or before the preceding business day) in the year of the last playing season covered by this contract. (See Article XX(A) of and Attachments 9 and 12 to the Basic Agreement.) If prior to the March 1 next succeeding said December 2, the Player and the Club have not agreed upon the terms of such contract, then on or before ten (10) days after said March 1, the Club shall have the right by written notice to the Player at his address following his signature hereto, or if none be given, then at his last address of record with the Club, to renew this contract for the period of one year on the same terms, except that the amount payable to the Player shall be such as the Club shall fix in said notice; provided, however, that said amount, if fixed by a Major League Club, shall be in an amount payable at a rate not less than as specified in Article VI, Section B, of the Basic Agreement. Subject to the Player's rights as set forth in the Basic Agreement, the Club may renew this contract from year to year.

10.(b) The Club's right to renew this contract, as provided in subparagraph (a) of this paragraph 10, and the promise of the Player not to play otherwise than with the Club have been taken into consideration in determining the amount payable under paragraph 2 hereof.

Governmental Regulation–National Emergency

11. This contract is subject to federal or state legislation, regulations, executive or other official orders or other governmental action, now or hereafter in effect respecting military, naval, air or other governmental service, which may directly or indirectly affect the Player, Club or the League and subject also to the right of the Commissioner to suspend the operation of this contract during any national emergency during which Major League Baseball is not played.

Commissioner

12. The term "Commissioner" wherever used in this contract shall be deemed to mean the Commissioner designated under the Major League Constitution, or in the case of a vacancy in the office of Commissioner, the Executive Council or such other body or person or persons as shall be designated in the Major League Constitution to exercise the powers and duties of the Commissioner during such vacancy.

Supplemental Agreements

The Club and the Player covenant that this contract, the Basic Agreement, the Agreement Re Major League Baseball Players Benefit Plan and Major League Baseball's Joint Drug Prevention and Treatment Program and applicable supplements thereto fully set forth all understandings and agreements between them, and agree that no other understandings or agreements, whether heretofore or hereafter made, shall be valid, recognizable, or of any effect whatsoever, unless expressly set forth in a new or supplemental contract executed by the Player and the Club (acting by its President or such other officer as shall have been thereunto duly authorized by the President or Board of Directors as evidenced by a certificate filed of record with the Commissioner) and complying with the Major League Rules.

Special Covenants

_____

_____

_____

_____

Approval

This contract or any supplement hereto shall not be valid or effective unless and until Approved by the Commissioner.

Signed in duplicate this _____ day of _____, A.D. _____

_____ _____
(Player) (Club)

_____ By _____
(Home address of Player) (Authorized Signature)

_____

FOR COMMISSIONER'S OFFICE USE ONLY

REGULATIONS

1. The Club's playing season for each year covered by this contract and all renewals hereof shall be as fixed by the Office of the Commissioner.

2. The Player, when requested by the Club, must submit to a complete physical examination at the expense of the Club, and if necessary to treatment by a physician, dentist, certified athletic trainer or other medical professional in good standing. Upon refusal of the Player to submit to a complete medical or dental examination, the Club may consider such refusal a violation of this regulation and may take such action as it deems advisable under Regulation 5 of this contract. Disability directly resulting from injury sustained in the course and within the scope of his employment under this contract shall not impair the right of the Player to receive his full salary for the period of such disability or for the season in which the injury was sustained (whichever period is shorter), together with the reasonable medical and hospital expenses incurred by reason of the injury and during the term of this contract or for a period of up to two years from the date of initial treatment for such injury, whichever period is longer, but only upon the express prerequisite conditions that (a) written notice of such injury, including the time, place, cause and nature of the injury, is served upon and received by the Club within twenty days of the sustaining of said injury and (b) the Club shall have the right to designate the health care facilities, physicians, dentists, certified athletic trainers or other medical professionals furnishing such medical and hospital services. Failure to give such notice shall not impair the rights of the Player, as herein set forth, if the Club has actual knowledge of such injury. All workmen's compensation payments received by the Player as compensation for loss of income for a specific period during which the Club is paying him in full, shall be paid over by the Player to the Club. Any other disability may be ground for suspending or terminating this contract.

3. The Club will furnish the Player with two complete uniforms, exclusive of shoes, unless the Club requires the Player to wear non-standard shoes in which case the Club will furnish the shoes. The uniforms will be surrendered by the Player to the Club at the end of the season or upon termination of this contract.

4. The Player shall be entitled to expense allowances under the circumstances and in the amounts set forth in Article VII of the Basic Agreement.

5. For violation by the Player of any regulation or other provision of this contract, the Club may impose a reasonable fine and deduct the amount thereof from the Player's salary or may suspend the Player without salary for a reasonable period or both. Written notice of the fine or suspension or both and the reason thereof shall in every case be given to the Player and the Players Association. (See Article XII of the Basic Agreement.)

6. In order to enable the Player to fit himself for his duties under this contract, the Club may require the Player to report for practice at such places as the Club may designate and to participate in such exhibition contests as may be arranged by the Club, without any other compensation than that herein elsewhere provided, for a period beginning not earlier than thirty-three (33) days prior to the start of the championship season; provided, however, that the Club may invite players to report at an earlier date on a voluntary basis in accordance with Article XIV of the Basic Agreement. The Club will pay the necessary traveling expenses, including the first-class jet air fare and meals en route of the Player from his home city to the training place of the Club, whether he be ordered to go there directly or by way of the home city of the Club. In the event of the failure of the Player to report for practice or to participate in the exhibition games, as required and provided for, he shall be required to get into playing condition to the satisfaction of the Club's team manager, and at the Player's own expense, before his salary shall commence.

7. In case of assignment of this contract, the Player shall report promptly to the assignee Club within 72 hours from the date he receives written notice from the Club of such assignment.

8. Upon signing this contract, the Player shall execute the enclosed Life Insurance Notice and Consent Form in connection with the Club's participation in the League-wide Player Life Insurance Program.

Post-Season Exhibition Games. Major League Rule 18(b) provides:

(b) EXHIBITION GAMES. No player shall participate in any exhibition game during the period between the close of the Major League championship season and the following training season, except that, with the consent of the player's Club and permission of the Commissioner, a player may participate in exhibition games for a period of not less than 30 days, such period to be designated annually by the Commissioner. Players who participate in barnstorming during this period cannot engage in any Winter League activities.

Player conduct, on and off the field, in connection with such post-season exhibition games shall be subject to the discipline of the Commissioner. The Commissioner shall not approve of more than three players of any one Club on the same team. The Commissioner shall not approve of more than three players from the joint membership of the World Series participants playing in the same game.

No player shall participate in any exhibition game with or against any team which, during the current season or within one year, has had any ineligible player or which is or has been during the current season or within one year, managed and controlled by an ineligible player or by any person who has listed an ineligible player under an assumed name or who otherwise has violated, or attempted to violate, any exhibition game contract; or with or against any team which, during said season or within one year, has played against teams containing such ineligible players, or so managed or controlled. Any player who participates in such a game in violation of this Rule 18 shall be fined not less than $50 nor more than $500, except that in no event shall such fine be less than the consideration received by such player for participating in such game.

PRINTED IN U.S.A. REVISED AS OF DECEMBER 2016

MAJOR LEAGUE BASEBALL CONTRACT NOTES & QUESTIONS *answer*

1. In paragraph 2., there is mention of the possibility of deferred payments. Why would a player wish to have deferred payments? (Ooops, we said in the Introduction that we wouldn't discuss tax law).

2. Are you surprised at the language of paragraph 3.(a)? Trite and archaic you say?

3. Explain why you think that the language in paragraph 5 (b) "Other Sports" is different from the analogous provision in paragraph 5 of the Regulations that governed the Babe Ruth Contract.

4. Explain how paragraph 6.(a) permits some players to to have a "no trade" clause?

5. Look closely at paragraph 7.(b). Give concrete examples of the types of conduct that you think could trigger the "failures" in (1-3).

6. How is the procedure contemplated by paragraph 10.(a) "Renewal" different from the analogous provision (paragraph 8) of Babe Ruth's contract?

7. In the section entitled "Special Covenants" a player may, for example, wish to ask for bonuses as a reward for making the All Star Team, Rookie of the Year, MVP, *etc.* Can you think of other examples of such covenants? Think of some types of rewards that ought not be permitted? Why not?

EXHIBIT A

NATIONAL BASKETBALL ASSOCIATION
UNIFORM PLAYER CONTRACT

THIS AGREEMENT made this _____ day of _____,
is by and between _____ (hereinafter called the "Team"), a member of
the National Basketball Association (hereinafter called the "NBA" or "League") and
_____ an individual whose address is shown below (hereinafter
called the "Player"). In consideration of the mutual promises hereinafter contained, the parties
hereto promise and agree as follows:

1.   **TERM.**

The Team hereby employs the Player as a skilled basketball player for a term of ____ year(s)
from the 1st day of September

2.   **SERVICES.**

(a) The services to be rendered by the Player pursuant to this Contract shall include: (i) training camp, (ii) practices, meetings, and conditioning sessions conducted by the Team during the Season, (iii) games scheduled for the Team during any Regular Season, (iv) Exhibition games scheduled by the Team or the League during and prior to any Regular Season, (v) the NBA's All-Star Game (including the Rookie Game) and every event conducted in association with such All-Star Game (including, but not limited to, a reasonable number of media sessions and any event that is part of an All-Star Skills Competition if the Player had previously agreed to participate in that Competition), if the Player is invited to participate therein, (vi) Playoff games scheduled by the League subsequent to any Regular Season, and (vii) promotional activities of the Team and the League as set forth in paragraph 13 herein.

(b) If the Player is a Veteran, the Player will not be required to attend training camp earlier than 2 p.m. (local time) on the twenty-ninth (29th) day prior to the first game of any Regular Season. Notwithstanding the foregoing, if the Team is scheduled during a particular NBA Season to participate outside of North America in an

Exhibition game or a Regular Season game during the first week of the Regular Season, such Veteran Player may be required to attend the training camp conducted in advance of that Regular Season by 2 p.m. (local time) on the thirty-second (32nd) day prior to the first game of the Regular Season. Rookies may be required to attend training camp at an earlier date, but no earlier than ten (10) days prior to the date that Veterans are required to attend.

(c) Exhibition games shall not be played on the three (3) days prior to the opening of the Team's Regular Season schedule, nor on the day prior to a Regular Season game, nor on the day prior to and the day following the All-Star Game. Exhibition games prior to any Regular Season shall not exceed eight (including intra-squad games for which admission is charged), and Exhibition games during any Regular Season shall not exceed three.

COMPENSATION.

(a) Subject to paragraph 3(b) below, the Team agrees to pay the Player for rendering the services described herein the Compensation described in Exhibit I or Exhibit IA hereto (less all amounts required to be withheld by federal, state, and local authorities, and exclusive of any amount(s) which the Player shall be entitled to receive from the Player Playoff Pool). Unless otherwise provided in Exhibit 1, such Compensation shall be paid in twelve (12) equal semi-monthly payments beginning with the first of said payments on November 15th of each year covered by the Contract and continuing with such payments on the first and fifteenth of each month until said Compensation is paid in full.

(b) The Team agrees to pay the Player $1,500 per week, pro rata, less all amounts required to be withheld by federal, state, and local authorities, for each week (up to a maximum of four (4) weeks for veterans and up to a maximum of five (5) weeks for Rookies) prior to the Team's first Regular Season game that the Player is in attendance at training camp or Exhibition games; provided, however, that no such payments shall be made if, prior to the date on which he is required to attend training camp, the Player has been paid $10,000 or more in compensation with respect to the NBA Season scheduled to commence immediately following such training camp. Any Compensation paid by the Team pursuant to this subparagraph shall be considered an advance against any Compensation owed to the Player pursuant to paragraph 3(a) above, and the first scheduled payment of such Compensation (or such subsequent payments, if the first scheduled payment is not sufficient) shall be reduced by the amount of such advance.

(c) The Team will not pay and the Player will not accept any bonus or anything of value on account of the Team's winning any particular NBA game or series of games or attaining a certain position in the standings of the League as of a certain date, other than the final standing of the Team.

4.   **EXPENSES.**

The Team agrees to pay all proper and necessary expenses of the Player, including the reasonable lodging expenses of the Player while playing for the Team "on the road" and during the training camp period (defined for this paragraph only to mean the period from the first day of training camp through the day of the Team's first Exhibition game) for as long as the Player is not then living at home. The Player, while "on the road" (and during the training camp period, only if the player is not then living at home and the Team does not pay for meals directly), shall be paid a meal expense allowance as set forth in the Collective Bargaining Agreement currently in effect between the NBA and the National Basketball Players Association (hereinafter "the NBA/NBPA Collective Bargaining Agreement"). No deductions from such meal expense allowance shall be made for meals served on an airplane. During the training camp period (and only if the player is not then living at home and the Team does not pay for meals directly), the meal expense allowance shall be paid in weekly installments commencing with the first week of training camp. For the purposes of this paragraph, the Player shall be considered to be "on the road" from the time the Team leaves its home city until the time the Team arrives back at its home city.

5.   **CONDUCT.**

(a) The Player agrees to observe and comply with all Team rules, as maintained or promulgated in accordance with the NBA/NBPA Collective Bargaining Agreement, at all times whether on or off the playing floor. Subject to the provisions of the NBA/NBPA Collective Bargaining Agreement, such rules shall be part of this Contract as fully as if herein written and shall be binding upon the Player.

(b) The Player agrees (i) to give his best services, as well as his loyalty, to the Team, and to play basketball only for the Team and its assignees; (ii) to be neatly and fully attired in public; (iii) to conduct himself on and off the court according to the highest standards of honesty, citizenship, and sportsmanship; and (iv) not to do anything that is materially detrimental or materially prejudicial to the best interests of the Team or the League.

(c) For any violation of Team rules, any breach of any provision of this Contract, or for any conduct impairing the faithful and thorough discharge of the duties incumbent upon the Player, the Team may reasonably impose fines and/or suspensions on the Player in accordance with the terms of the NBAINBPA Collective Bargaining Agreement.

(d) The Player agrees to be bound by Article 35 of the NBA Constitution, a copy of which, as in effect on the date of this Contract, is attached hereto. The Player acknowledges that the Commissioner is empowered to impose fines upon and/or suspend the Player for causes and in the manner provided in such Article, provided that such fines and/or suspensions are consistent with the terms of the NBAINBPA Collective Bargaining Agreement.

(e) The Player agrees that if the Commissioner, in his sole judgment, shall find that the Player has bet, or has offered or attempted to bet, money or anything of value on the outcome of any game participated in by any team which is a member of the NBA, the Commissioner shall have the power in his sole discretion to suspend the Player indefinitely or to expel him as a player for any member of the NBA, and the Commissioner's finding and decision shall be final, binding, conclusive, and unappealable.

(f) The Player agrees that he will not, during the term of this Contract, directly or indirectly, entice, induce, or persuade, or attempt to entice, induce, or persuade, any player or coach who is under contract to any NBA team to enter into negotiations for or relating to his services as a basketball player or coach, nor shall he negotiate for or contract for such services, except with the prior written consent of such team. Breach of this subparagraph, in addition to the remedies available to the Team, shall be punishable by fine and/or suspension to be imposed by the Commissioner.

(g) When the Player is fined and/or suspended by the Team or the NBA, he shall be given notice in writing (with a copy to the Players Association), stating the amount of the fine or the duration of the suspension and the reasons therefor.

6. **WITHHOLDING.**

   (a) In the event the Player is fined and/or suspended by the Team or the NBA, the Team shall withhold the amount of the fine or, in the case of a suspension, the amount provided in Article VI of the NBA/NBPA Collective Bargaining Agreement from any Current Cash Compensation due or to become due to the Player with respect to the contract year in which the conduct resulting in the fine and/or the suspension occurred (or a subsequent contract year if the Player has received all Current Cash Compensation due to him for the then current contract year). If, at the time the Player is fined and/or suspended, the Current Cash Compensation remaining to be paid to the Player under this Contract is not sufficient to cover such fine and/or suspension, then the Player agrees promptly to pay the amount directly to the Team. In no case shall the Player permit any such fine and/or suspension to be paid on his behalf by anyone other than himself.

   (b) Any Current Cash Compensation withheld from or paid by the Player pursuant to this paragraph 6 shall be retained by the Team or the League, as the case may be, unless the Player contests the fine and/or suspension by initiating a timely Grievance in accordance with the provisions of the NBA/NBPA Collective Bargaining Agreement. If such Grievance is initiated and it satisfies Article XXXI, Section 13 of the NBA/NBPA Collective Bargaining Agreement, the amount withheld from the Player shall be placed in an interest-bearing account, pursuant to Article XXXI, Section 9 of such Agreement, pending the resolution of the Grievance.

7. **PHYSICAL CONDITION.**

   (a) The Player agrees to report at the time and place fixed by the Team in good physical condition and to keep himself throughout each NBA Season in good physical condition.

   (b) If the Player, in the judgment of the Team's physician, is not in good physical condition at the date of his first scheduled game for the Team, or if, at the beginning of or during any Season, he fails to remain in good physical condition (unless such condition results directly from an injury sustained by the Player as a direct result of participating in any basketball practice or game played for the Team during such Season), so as to render the Player, in the judgment of the Team's physician, unfit to play skilled basketball, the Team shall have the right to suspend such Player until such time as, in the judgment of the Team's physician, the Player is in sufficiently good physical condition to play skilled basketball. In the event of such suspension, the Compensation (excluding any signing bonus or Incentive Compensation) payable to the Player for any Season during such suspension shall be reduced in the same proportion as the length of the period during which, in the judgment of the Team's physician, the Player is unfit to play skilled basketball, bears to the length of such Season.

(c) If, during the term of this Contract, the Player is injured as a direct result of participating in any basketball practice or game played for the Team, the Team will pay the Player's reasonable hospitalization and medical expenses (including doctor's bills), provided that the hospital and doctor are selected by the Team, and provided further that the Team shall be obligated to pay only those expenses incurred as a direct result of medical treatment caused solely by and relating directly to the injury sustained by the Player. Subject to the provisions set forth in Exhibit 3, if in the judgment of the Team's physician, the Player's injuries resulted directly from playing for the Team and render him unfit to play skilled basketball, then, so long as such unfitness continues, but in no event after the Player has received his full Compensation for the Season in which the injury was sustained, the Team shall pay to the Player the Compensation prescribed in Exhibit 1 to this Contract for such Season. The Team's obligations hereunder shall be reduced by (i) any workers' compensation benefits, which, to the extent permitted by law, the Player hereby assigns to the Team, and (ii) any insurance provided for by the Team whether paid or payable to the Player.

(d) The Player agrees to provide to the Team's coach, trainer, or physician prompt notice of any injury, illness, or medical condition suffered by him that is likely to affect adversely the Player's ability to render the services required under this Contract, including the time, place, cause, and nature of such injury, illness, or condition.

(e) Should the Player suffer an injury, illness, or medical condition as provided in this paragraph 7, he will submit himself to a medical examination and appropriate medical treatment by a physician designated by the Team. Such examination when made at the request of the Team shall be at its expense, unless made necessary by some act or conduct of the Player contrary to the terms of this Contract.

8.   **PROHIBITED SUBSTANCES.**

The Player acknowledges that this Contract may be terminated in accordance with the express provisions of Article XXXIII (Anti-Drug Program) of the NBA/NBPA Collective Bargaining Agreement, and that any such termination will result in the Player's immediate dismissal and disqualification from any employment by the NBA and any of its teams. Notwithstanding any terms or provisions of this Contract (including any amendments hereto), in the event of such termination, all obligations of the Team, including obligations to pay Compensation, shall cease, except the obligation of the Team to pay the Player's earned Compensation (whether Current or Deferred) to the date of termination.

9. **UNIQUE SKILLS.**

The Player represents and agrees that he has extraordinary and unique skill and ability as a basketball player, that the services to be rendered by him hereunder cannot be replaced or the loss thereof adequately compensated for in money damages, and that any breach by the Player of this Contract will cause irreparable injury to the Team, and to its assignees. Therefore, it is agreed that in the event it is alleged by the Team that the Player is playing, attempting or threatening to play, or negotiating for the purpose of playing, during the term of this Contract, for any other person, firm, corporation, or organization, the Team and its assignees (in addition to any other remedies that may be available to them judicially or by way of arbitration) shall have the right to obtain from any court or arbitrator having jurisdiction such equitable relief as may be appropriate, including a decree enjoining the Player from any further such breach of this Contract, and enjoining the Player from playing basketball for any other person, firm, corporation, or organization during the term of this Contract. The Player agrees that the Team may at any time assign such right to the NBA for the enforcement thereof. In any suit, action, or arbitration proceeding brought to obtain such equitable relief, the Player does hereby waive his right, if any, to trial by jury, and does hereby waive his right, if any, to interpose any counterclaim or set-off for any cause whatever.

10. **ASSIGNMENT.**

(a) The Team shall have the right to assign this Contract to any other NBA team and the Player agrees to accept such assignment and to faithfully perform and carry out this contract with the same force and effect as if it had been entered into by the Player with the assignee team instead of with the Team. The Player further agrees that, should the Team contemplate the assignment of this Contract to one or more NBA teams, the Team's physician may furnish to the physicians and officials of such other team or teams all relevant medical information relating to the Player.

(b) In the event that this Contract is assigned to any other NBA team, all reasonable expenses incurred by the Player in moving himself and his family to the home territory of the team to which such assignment is made, as a result thereof, shall be paid by the assignee team. Such assignee team hereby agrees that its acceptance of the assignment of this Contract constitutes agreement on its part to make such payment.

(c) In the event that this Contract is assigned to another NBA team, the Player shall forthwith be provided notice orally or in writing, delivered to the Player personally or delivered or mailed to his last known address, and the Player shall report to the assignee team within forty-eight (48) hours after said notice has been received (if the assignment is made during a Season), within one (1) week after said notice has been received (if the assignment is made between Seasons), or within such longer time for reporting as may be specified in said notice. The NBA shall also promptly notify the Players Association of any such assignment. The Player further agrees that, immediately upon reporting to the assignee team, he will submit upon request to a physical examination conducted by a physician designated by the assignee team.

(d) If the Player, without a reasonable excuse, does not report to the team to which this Contract has been assigned within the time provided in subsection (c) above, then, upon consummation of the assignment, the player may be suspended by the assignee team or, if the assignment is not consummated or is voided as a result of the Player's failure to so report, by the assignor Team. In either case, the Player's Compensation may be reduced by the NBA by the imposition of a fine in an amount equal to the lesser of (i) ten (10) percent of the Player's full Compensation for the then-current Season, or (ii) $50,000.

11. **VALIDITY AND FILING.**
(a) This Contract shall be valid and binding upon the Team and the Player immediately upon its execution.

(b) The Team agrees to file a copy of this Contract, and/or any amendment(s) thereto, with the Commissioner of the NBA as soon as practicable by facsimile and overnight mail, but in no event may such filing be made more than forty-eight (48) hours after the execution of this Contract and/or amendment(s).

(c) If pursuant to the NBA Constitution and By-Laws or the NBA/NBPA Collective

Bargaining Agreement, the Commissioner disapproves this Contract (or amendment) within ten (10) days after the receipt thereof in his office by overnight mail, this Contract (or amendment) shall thereupon terminate and be of no further force or effect and the Team and the Player shall thereupon be relieved of their respective rights and liabilities thereunder. If the Commissioner's disapproval is subsequently overturned in any proceeding brought under the arbitration provisions of the NBAINBPA Collective Bargaining Agreement (including any appeals), the Contract shall again be valid and binding upon the Team and the Player, and the Commissioner shall be afforded another ten-day period to disapprove the Contract (based on the Team's Room at the time the Commissioner's disapproval is overturned) as set forth in the foregoing sentence. The NBA will promptly inform the Players Association if the Commissioner disapproves this Contract.

12. **OTHER ATHLETIC ACTIVITIES.**

The Player and the Team acknowledge and agree that (i) the Player's participation in other sports may impair or destroy his ability and skill as a basketball player, and (ii) the Player's participation in basketball out of season may result in injury to him. Accordingly, the Player agrees that he will not, without the written consent of the Team, engage in (x) sports endangering his health or safety (including, but not limited to, professional boxing or wrestling, motorcycling, moped-riding, auto racing, sky-diving, and hang gliding), or (y) any game or exhibition of basketball, football, baseball, hockey, lacrosse, or other athletic sport, under penalty of such fine and/or suspension as may be imposed by the Team and/or the Commissioner of the NBA. Nothing contained herein shall be intended to require the Player to obtain the written consent of the Team in order to enable the Player to participate in, as an amateur, the sport of golf, tennis, handball, swimming, hiking, soft ball, or volleyball.

13. **PROMOTIONAL ACTIVITIES.**

(a) The Player agrees to allow the Team or the League to take pictures of the Player, alone or together with others, for still photographs, motion pictures, or television, at such times as the Team or the League may designate. No matter by whom taken, such pictures may be used in any manner desired by either the Team or the League for publicity or promotional purposes. The rights in any such pictures taken by the Team or by the League shall belong to the Team or to the League, as their interests may appear.

(b) The Player agrees that, during any year of this Contract, he will not make public appearances, participate in radio or television programs, permit his picture to be taken, write or sponsor newspaper or magazine articles, or sponsor commercial products without the written consent of the Team, which shall not be withheld except in the reasonable interests of the Team or the NBA.

(c) Upon request, the Player shall consent to and make himself available for interviews by representatives of the media conducted at reasonable times.

(d) In addition to the foregoing, and subject to the conditions and limitations set forth in Article II, Section 8 of the NBAINBPA Collective Bargaining Agreement, the Player agrees to participate, upon request, in all other reasonable promotional activities of the Team and the NBA. For each such promotional appearance made on behalf of a commercial sponsor of the Team, the Team agrees to pay the Player $1,000 or, if the Team agrees, such higher amount that is consistent with the Team's past practice and not otherwise unreasonable.

14. **GROUP LICENSE.**

(a) The Player hereby grants to NBA Properties, Inc. the exclusive rights to use the Player's Player Attributes as such term is defined and for such group licensing purposes as are set forth in the Agreement between NBA Properties, Inc. and the National Basketball Players Association, made as of September 18, 1995 and amended January 20, 1999 (the "Group License"), a copy of which will, upon his request, be furnished the Player; and the Player agrees to make the appearances called for by such Agreement.

(b) Notwithstanding anything to the contrary contained in the Group License or this Contract, NBA Properties may use, in connection with League Promotions, the Player's (i) name or nickname and/or (ii) the Player's Player Attributes (as defined in the Group License) as such Player Attributes may be captured in game action footage or photographs. NBA Properties shall be entitled to use the Player's Player Attributes individually pursuant to the preceding sentence and shall not be required to use the Player's Player Attributes in a group or as one of multiple players. As used herein, League Promotion shall mean any advertising, marketing, or collateral materials or marketing programs conducted by the NBA, NBA Properties (or any subsidiary of NBA Properties) or any NBA team that is intended to promote (x) any game in which an NBA team participates or game telecast or broadcast (including Pre-Season, Exhibition, Regular Season, and Playoff games), (y) the NBA, its teams, or its players, or (z) the sport of basketball.

15. **TEAM DEFAULT.**

In the event of an alleged default by the Team in the payments to the Player provided for by this Contract, or in the event of an alleged failure by the Team to perform any other material obligation that it has agreed to perform hereunder, the Player shall notify both the Team and the League in writing of the facts constituting such alleged default or alleged failure. If neither the Team nor the League shall cause such alleged default or alleged failure to be remedied within five (5) days after receipt of such written notice, the National Basketball Players Association shall, on behalf of the Player, have the right to request that the dispute concerning such alleged default or alleged failure be referred immediately to the Grievance Arbitrator in accordance with the provisions of the NBAINBPA Collective Bargaining Agreement. If, as a result of such arbitration, an award issues in favor of the Player, and if neither the Team nor the League complies with such award within ten (10) days after the service thereof, the Player shall have the right, by a further written notice to the Team and the League, to terminate this Contract.

16. **TERMINATION.**

(a) The Team may terminate this Contract upon written notice to the Player if the Player shall:

(i) at any time, fail, refuse, or neglect to conform his personal conduct to standards of good citizenship, good moral character (defined here to mean not engaging in acts of moral turpitude, whether or not such acts would constitute a crime), and good sportsmanship, to keep himself in first class physical condition, or to obey the Team's training rules; or

(ii) at any time commit a significant and inexcusable physical attack against any official or employee of the Team or the NBA (other than another player), or any person in attendance at any NBA game or event, considering the totality of the circumstances, including (but not limited to) the degree of provocation (if any) that may have led to the attack, the nature and scope of the attack, the player's state of mind at the time of the attack, and the extent of any injury resulting from the attack; or

(iii) at any time, fail, in the sole opinion of the Team's management, to exhibit sufficient skill or competitive ability to qualify to continue as a member of the Team; provided, however, (x) that if this Contract is terminated by the Team, in accordance with the provisions of this subparagraph, prior to January 10 of any Regular Season, and the Player, at the time of such termination, is unfit to play skilled basketball as the result of an injury resulting directly from his playing for the Team, the Player shall (subject to the provisions set forth in Exhibit 3) continue to receive his full Compensation, less all workers' compensation benefits (which, to the extent permitted by law, and if not deducted from the Player's Compensation by the Team, the Player hereby assigns to the Team) and any insurance provided for by the Team paid or payable to the Player by reason of said injury, until such time as the Player is fit to play skilled basketball, but not beyond the Season during which such termination occurred; and provided, further, (y) that if this Contract is terminated by the Team, in accordance with the provisions of this subparagraph, during the period from the January 10 of any Regular Season through the end of such Regular Season, the Player shall be entitled to receive his full Compensation for said Season; or

(iv) at any time, fail, refuse, or neglect to render his services hereunder or in any other manner materially breach this Contract.

(b) If this Contract is terminated by the Team by reason of the Player's failure to render his services hereunder due to disability caused by an injury to the Player resulting directly from his playing for the Team and rendering him unfit to play skilled basketball, and notice of such injury is given by the Player as provided herein, the Player shall (subject to the provisions set forth in Exhibit 3) be entitled to receive his full Compensation for the Season in which the injury was sustained, less all workers' compensation benefits (which, to the extent permitted by law, and if not deducted from the Player's Compensation by the Team, the Player hereby assigns to the Team) and any insurance provided for by the Team paid or payable to the Player by reason of said injury.

(c) Notwithstanding the provisions of subparagraph 16(b) above, if this Contract is terminated by the Team prior to the first game of a Regular Season by reason of the Player's failure to render his services hereunder due to an injury or condition sustained or suffered during a preceding Season, or after such Season but prior to the Player's participation in any basketball practice or game played for the Team, payment by the Team of any Compensation earned through the date of termination under paragraph 3(b) above, payment of the Player's board, lodging, and expense allowance during the training camp period, payment of the reasonable traveling expenses of the Player to his home city, and the expert training and coaching provided by the Team to the Player during the training season shall be full payment to the Player.

(d) If this Contract is terminated by the Team during the period designated by the Team for attendance at training camp, payment by the Team of any Compensation earned through the date of termination under paragraph 3(b) above, payment of the Player's board,

lodging, and expense allowance during such period to the date of termination, payment of the reasonable traveling expenses of the Player to his home city, and the expert training and coaching provided by the Team to the Player during the training season shall be full payment to the Player.

(e) If this Contract is terminated by the Team after the first game of a Regular Season, except in the case provided for in sub-paragraphs (a)(iii) and (b) of this paragraph 16, the Player shall be entitled to receive as full payment hereunder a sum of money which, when added to the salary which he has already received during such Season, will represent the same proportionate amount of the annual sum set forth in Exhibit I hereto as the number of days of such Regular Season then past bears to the total number of days of such Regular Season, plus the reasonable traveling expenses of the Player to his home.

(f) If the Team proposes to terminate this Contract in accordance with subparagraph (a) of this paragraph 16, it must first comply with the following waiver procedure:

(i) The Team shall request the NBA Commissioner to request waivers from all other clubs. Such waiver request may not be withdrawn.

(ii) Upon receipt of the waiver request, any other team may claim assignment of this Contract at such waiver price as may be fixed by the League, the priority of claims to be determined in accordance with the NBA Constitution and By-Laws.

(iii)If this Contract is so claimed, the Team agrees that it shall, upon the assignment of this Contract to the claiming team, notify the Player of such assignment as provided in paragraph 10(c) hereof, and the Player agrees he shall report to the assignee team as provided in said paragraph 10(c).

(iv) If the Contract is not claimed, the Team shall promptly deliver written notice of termination to the Player at the expiration of the waiver period.

(v) The NBA shall promptly notify the Players Association of the disposition of any waiver request.

(vi) To the extent not inconsistent with the foregoing provisions of this subparagraph (f), the waiver procedures set forth in the NBA Constitution and By-Laws, a copy of which, as in effect on the date of this Contract, is attached hereto, shall govern.

(g) Upon any termination of this Contract by the Player, all obligations of the Team to pay Compensation shall cease on the date of termination, except the obligation of the Team to pay the Player's Compensation to said date.

17. **DISPUTES.**

In the event of any dispute arising between the Player and the Team relating to any matter arising under this Contract, or concerning the performance or interpretation thereof (except for a dispute arising under paragraph 9 hereof), such dispute shall be resolved in accordance with the Grievance and Arbitration Procedure set forth in the NBA/NBPA Collective Bargaining Agreement.

18. **PLAYER NOT A MEMBER.**

Nothing contained in this Contract or in any provision of the NBA Constitution and By-Laws shall be construed to constitute the Player a member of the NBA or to confer upon him any of the rights or privileges of a member thereof.

19. **RELEASE.**

The Player hereby releases and waives every claim he may have against the NBA and its related entities and every member of the NBA, and against every director, officer, owner, stockholder, trustee, partner, and employee of the NBA and its related entities and/or any member of the NBA and their related entities (excluding persons employed as players by any such member), and against any person retained by the NBA and/or the Players Association in connection with the NBAINBPA Anti-Drug Program, the Grievance Arbitrator, the System Arbitrator, and any other arbitrator or expert retained by the NBA and/or the Players Association under the terms of the NBA/NBPA Collective Bargaining Agreement, arising out of or in connection with (i) any injury that is subject to the provisions of paragraph 7, (ii) any fighting or other form of violent and/or unsportsmanlike conduct occurring during the course of any practice and/or any Exhibition, Regular Season, and/or Playoff game (on or adjacent to the playing floor or in or adjacent to any facility used for practices or games), (iii) the testing procedures or the imposition of any penalties set forth in paragraph 8 hereof and in the NBA/NBPA Anti-Drug Program, or (iv) any injury suffered in the course of his employment as to which he has or would have a claim for workers~ compensation benefits. The foregoing shall not apply to any claim of medical malpractice against a Team-affiliated physician or other medical personnel.

20.   **ENTIRE AGREEMENT.**
       This Contract (including any Exhibits hereto) contains the entire agreement between the parties and sets forth all components of the Player's Compensation from the Team or any Team Affiliate, and there are no undisclosed agreements of any kind, express or implied, oral or written, promises, undertakings, representations, commitments, inducements, assurances of intent, or understandings of any kind that have not been disclosed to the NBA (a) involving consideration of any kind to be paid, furnished, or made available to the Player, or any person or entity controlled by or related to the Player, by the Team or any Team Affiliate, either during the term of this Contract or thereafter, or (b) concerning any future Renegotiation, Extension, or other amendment of this Contract or the entry into any new Player Contract.

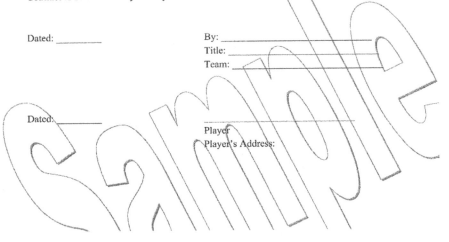

EXAMINE THIS CONTRACT CAREFULLY
BEFORE SIGNING IT.

THIS CONTRACT INCLUDES EXHIBITS _____, WHICH ARE
ATTACHED HERETO AND MADE A PART HEREOF.

IN WITNESS WHEREOF the Player has hereunto signed his name and the Team has caused this Contract to be executed by its duly authorized officer.

Dated: _____   By: _____
                          Title: _____
                          Team: _____

Dated: _____   _____
                          Player
                          Player's Address:

NBA Contract Notes & Questions

1. In paragraph 1., why do you suppose that the term "skilled basketball player" is used? Is this any different from what is expressed in paragraph 9 ("Unique Skills")? Explain.

2. In paragraph 5.(a), why should the players be asked to agree to certain parameters of conduct "at all times whether on or off the playing floor"?

3. Similarly, what types of conduct do you suppose would be considered a breach of paragraph 5.(b)(iii-iv) ("to conduct himself on and off the court according to the highest standards of honesty, citizenship, and sportsmanship; and not to do anything that is materially detrimental or materially prejudicial to the best interests of the Team or the League?") Given the track record of NBA players with domestic violence, drugs, and other types of criminal conduct over the past several years, how important is the interpretation of this language? What is the relationship between this provision and paragraph 16 ("Termination")?

4. Workers' compensation insurance provides an economically attractive alternative for employers. By providing workers' compensation benefits, employers are able to avoid costly lawsuits brought by injured employees. So if a worker in a lumber yard cuts his hand on a saw, the company's workers' compensation insurance policy pays the injured worker for his injury, based on factors such as the worker's age, experience, and the percentage of loss of function in the injured hand (*e.g.*, a 15% disability). Pursuant to paragraph 7.(c), explain how workers' compensation benefits are relevant to a professional basketball player's injury.

5. Paragraph 11.(c) addresses the possibility of the Commissioner's disapproval. Explain the Commissioner's disapproval in terms of either a condition precedent or a condition subsequent. Which term best describes the legal effect of the Commissioner's disapproval? Why?

TALENT SERVICES AGREEMENT

This TALENT SERVICES AGREEMENT (this "Agreement"), by and between COMPANY, LLC ("Company"), and _____ ("Agency") _____ ("Talent"), pursuant to which Agency shall provide Talent's Services (as defined below) to COMPANY on the terms and conditions set forth herein. COMPANY, Agency, and Talent may sometimes be referred to herein collectively as the "Parties" and individually as a "Party".

1.   TERM

1.1   Term. This Agreement shall commence upon full execution (the "**Effective Date**") and shall continue until June 30, 2019 (exclusive of the Wind Down Period contained in section 3.1 (d) below), unless earlier terminated as provided herein (the "**Initial Term**").

1.2   Option to Extend Term. The Parties shall have the option, exercisable subject to mutual agreement in writing, to extend the Initial Term for an additional twelve (12) month period (the "**Option Period**") subject to the same terms and conditions as governing the Initial Term. The option to extend the Term may be initiated by COMPANY by written notice given by COMPANY to the Agency at least one hundred twenty (120) days before the scheduled expiration of the Initial Term and shall be subject to mutual agreement in writing. The Initial Term together with the Option Period will be referred to as the "Term" provided however, in the event the Option Period is not exercised any reference to the Term hereunder shall solely apply to the Initial Term.

2.   SERVICES; PRODUCTS

2.1   Services Generally; Products. During the Term, the Agency shall cause Talent to render the Services for COMPANY and shall cause Talent to permit his name, voice, likeness, biography, image and any other identifying attributes of Talent, each as approved by Talent (the "**Publicity Rights**"), solely in connection with promoting COMPANY and the Products, subject to the terms and conditions of this Agreement.

     (a)   The term "**Products**" shall mean the following COMPANY-branded fashion clothing products: suiting, collared dressy and casual shirts, dressy sweaters, denim, dressy outerwear, casual pants and shorts made of khaki and/or woven material, and the following fashion accessories: dress shoes, scarves and belts, but specifically excluding t-shirts, polos, loungewear, underwear, watches, hats, and sunglasses.

     (b)   For avoidance of doubt, and notwithstanding Section 2.1(a) above, the Parties acknowledge and agreed that Talent may actually wear a watch in connection with the production of any Materials (as defined below) in Talent's sole discretion.

     (c)   The Video Materials, Print Materials and Behind the Scenes Materials (as such terms are defined below in Section 2.2) as well as any and all materials using the Publicity Rights produced in connection with, as a result of, the performance of Services by Talent under and in accordance with this Agreement are referred to herein collectively as the "**Materials**" and shall at all times be subject to Talent's written approval prior to use. COMPANY shall have the right, during the Term, to capture, create or produce the Materials hereunder by any process, technical means, instrumentation or device now known or hereinafter developed subject to the terms and conditions herein.

2.2   Services. During the Term and at the request of COMPANY, Agency shall cause Talent to provide the following personal services:

(a)   Shoot Days. Two (2) days of no more than six (6) consecutive hours from call time to release (inclusive of grooming/styling, production and reasonable breaks) in connection with the production of Materials exclusively for COMPANY for promoting COMPANY and the Products (each a "**Company Shoot Day**" or collectively, "**Company Shoot Days**"). The parties acknowledge that all aspects of each Work Day (including, without limitation, time, place, content and activities) shall be mutually agreed upon. Talent acknowledges that the Shoot Days may include other talent, with whom Talent may be captured in Materials.

(b)   Personal Appearances. Two (2) personal appearances lasting at least ninety (90) consecutive minutes but no more than three (3) consecutive hours (inclusive of reasonable breaks) each which may include activities to be mutually agreed upon, e.g., an in-store appearance, meet and greet with customers, and a reasonable amount of customer photo opportunities, content capture, media interviews and COMPANY interviews (each a "**Personal Appearance**" or collectively, "**Personal Appearances**"). For purposes of clarity, if Talent is invited to participate in All Star Weekend, Talent shall be available for one (1) Personal Appearance during such All Star Weekend, subject to Talent's professional availability for such All Star Weekend. COMPANY will make best efforts schedule one (1) of the personal appearances within 90 miles of Orlando, however, all event locations and appearances related to this agreement will be scheduled for dates, times and durations mutually agreeable to the parties.

(c)   NBA Event Days. Subject to NBA approval, which COMPANY shall solely be responsible for procuring, COMPANY shall have the right to capture Talent's Publicity Rights during NBA Event Days, which include but are not limited to NBA Tip-Off, October 2018, NBA Holiday/Season of Giving, November-December 2018, and NBA All-Star February 2019 ("**NBA Event Days**"), and use such captured Publicity Rights for the purpose of producing Materials hereunder for use in accordance with this Agreement; provided that the Parties acknowledge and agree that Talent shall have no obligation to provide Services to COMPANY on any such NBA Event Days.

(d)   Other. Talent shall provide his services to promote COMPANY through the Talent's personal social media platforms (further defined herein as "**Social Media Posts**"), and shall provide the Ancillary Services (as defined below). The Company Shoot Day, Personal Appearances, Social Media Posts and Ancillary Services shall be collectively referred to herein as "**Services**".

(e)   Print Materials. During the Company Shoot Days, Talent shall appear and sit for still photographs, as requested by COMPANY, that COMPANY may use for the purpose of producing the following print materials during the Term: (i) all COMPANY print media, including, but not limited to, all catalogues in both paper and digital form, newspapers, magazines, consumer and trade print, point-of-purchase displays, out-of-home advertising (e.g., in mall-kiosks, billboards, COMPANY operated Time Square LED screens, bus shelters and mobile ads), direct mail, shop-windows (but no standees or life size cutouts), in store décor or fixtures, placards, prints, model photos, gift cards, display units, boards; (ii) content for the Internet, Intranet, mobile broadcasts, e-mail programs or websites of COMPANY, COMPANY online advertising, social media sites (including but not limited to; www.Company.com, COMPANY Facebook, COMPANY Twitter, The Edit, COMPANY Pinterest, COMPANY Instagram, COMPANY Snapchat and COMPANY YouTube page), and other digital computer networks and all forms of COMPANY digital communication; and (iii) COMPANY public relations materials, internal communications, annual reports, investor relations materials and in-house events; subject to Talent's approval rights set forth herein. All of the foregoing, as approved by Talent, are collectively referred to herein as "**Print Materials**".

(f)   Video Materials. During the Company Shoot Days, Talent shall provide his on camera, voice-over and audio services, in connection with campaign shoots for the Products, as requested by COMPANY, that COMPANY may use for the purpose of producing the following video materials during the Term: (i) content for the Internet, Intranet, and e-mail programs or websites of COMPANY (including, but not limited to, www.Company.com), COMPANY online advertising, social media sites (including but not limited to; www.Company.com, COMPANY Facebook, COMPANY Twitter, COMPANY Blog, COMPANY Pinterest, COMPANY Instagram, COMPANY Snapchat and COMPANY YouTube page), downloads, streams (including but not limited to Youtube), and other digital computer networks and all forms of COMPANY digital communication; (ii) COMPANY in-store use (i.e., in-store closed-circuit TV); (iii) Company operated Time Square LED screens (but not in-taxi television of any kind) and (iv) COMPANY commercials for cinema, mobile broadcast, podcast, television (excluding pay TV), including cable, satellite, in-flight television; radio; in-store (e.g. in-store closed-circuit TV); COMPANY promotional and in-house audio services, and (v) COMPANY public relations materials, internal communications, annual reports, investor relations materials and in-house events; subject to Talent's approval rights set forth herein. All of the foregoing, as approved by Talent, are collectively referred to herein as "**Video Materials**." Subject to the terms and conditions herein, COMPANY shall also have the right to use any Print Materials (as hereinafter defined) and any Behind the Scenes Materials (as hereinafter defined) in the Video Material.

(g)   Behind the Scenes Access. COMPANY will have reasonable "behind the scenes" access to Talent (provided, however at no time when Talent is not "camera ready", on break, nude, eating, drinking, smoking, in private or otherwise has an expectation of privacy) during the Company Shoot Days, Ancillary Services and Personal Appearance. Talent shall allow film crews and photographers to capture reasonable behind-the scenes activity, including Talent interviews, for publicity purposes, so long as Talent would not reasonably be expected to be exposed to embarrassment or ridicule in connection with such activity and any such use of the footage remains subject to Talent's approval and the terms and conditions of this Agreement. If arranged by COMPANY, during the Services, Talent shall be available to participate in approved joint media interviews concerning Talent's relationship with COMPANY and shall permit select media personnel (as approved by Talent) that may also be granted access to the set. All such interviews shall occur during the performance of any Services and shall not require additional time. The materials produced in connection with such access, as approved by Talent, shall be referred to herein as the "**Behind the Scenes Materials**", and the Parties acknowledged and agreed that the following shall apply:

(i) COMPANY shall give Talent reasonable prior notice of any behind the scenes access to be given to a third-party, including the name of any entity being granted such access;

(ii) COMPANY may use any Behind the Scenes Materials for PR purposes in any and all media and in the Video Materials and/or Print Materials;

(iii) all uses of Behind the Scenes Materials must be consistent with the terms and conditions of this Agreement;

(iv) no Behind the Scenes Material, and no use or exploitation thereof, shall present Talent in a negative light or expose Talent to embarrassment or ridicule; and

(v) COMPANY will provide a minimum of twenty (20) photos from the Behind the Scenes Material which Talent will review and approve on-site one (1) photo (including caption), and will review and approve three (3) other photos and captions within forty-eight (48) hours for use by COMPANY in accordance with this Agreement.

(h)   Social Media. Talent shall promote COMPANY through the Talent's personal social media platforms (primarily Instagram and Twitter) at dates and times to be mutually agreed ("**Social Media Posts**"), and as set forth in more detail herein. All Social Media Posts required hereunder shall comply with the following guidelines: (1) Social Media Posts on Talent-owned channels must tap-tag @Companymen both on the photo and in the caption on Instagram, and @Company on all other applicable social media channels and must include the hashtags #CompanyPartner and #gamechangers; (2) Instagram Stories required hereunder on talent-owned channel must also mention and/or otherwise tag @Companymen and include the hashtags #CompanyPartner and #gamechangers; (3) posts must include all hashtags required by the FTC; (4)COMPANY and COMPANY franchises have the right to repost Talent's Social Media Posts related to COMPANY and use the content in both earned and paid digital campaigns; (4) Talent must wear a COMPANY [trademark-name ensemble] (i.e. jacket, blazer, jeans) in the majority of images or video posted in Social Media Posts (in any Social Media Posts in which Talent is not wearing a COMPANY [trademark-name ensemble], it is understood that Talent shall still wear COMPANY clothing); (5) Talent shall "like" COMPANY posts featuring Talent posted by COMPANY to its social media channels pursuant to this Agreement; (6) Talent shall not remove any Social Media Posts during the Term and for at least 90 days post-term unless Section 6.4 is triggered; and (7) Social Media Posts must not be disparaging, profane, derogatory, or offensive to the general public. In connection with each Social Media Post hereunder, COMPANY shall provide suggested post-date subject to Talent's schedule and commitments and COMPANY' marketing/promotion calendar, language and copy for Talent review and approval and COMPANY shall ensure that such copy complies with applicable rules and regulations. Any

Social Media Post approved by COMPANY shall be deemed in compliance with this Section. The parties agree to the following Social Media Posts during the Term:

(i)   Eight (8) Instagram posts, eight (8) Facebook posts, and five (5) Instagram Stories promoting Talent's relationship with COMPANY pursuant to this Agreement.

(ii)   One (1) of the aforementioned Instagram posts must promote Talent's relationship with COMPANY, in conjunction with COMPANY's announcement of the same and one (1) of the aforementioned Instagram posts must drive to the editorial feature of Talent.

(iii)   Talent shall post one (1) of the aforementioned Instagram Stories during each Shoot Day and during each Personal Appearance.

(a)   <u>Ancillary Services. Talent shall provide the following ancillary services, none of which will factor into the calculation of a Work Day</u>:

(i)   Prior to each Company Shoot Day, Talent shall participate in a wardrobe fitting which will not exceed two (2) consecutive hours each. The exact time, date and location to be mutually agreed upon.

(ii)   Talent shall participate in one (1) tech fitting session lasting no longer than one (1) consecutive hours, prior to the first Company Shoot Day on a mutually agreed upon time, date and location.

(iii)   Talent shall participate in one (1) media training session during the final fitting for an additional one (1) consecutive hour. If necessary, COMPANY shall travel to Talent to conduct said training.

(iv)   Talent shall wear a minimum of one mutually agreed upon COMPANY [trademark-name-ensemble] (i.e. jacket, blazer, jeans) a minimum of one (1) time per month (each a "**Wearing Occasion**"); provided however, Talent shall not wear headgear (sunglasses, headphones, hats) and/or outerwear as well as not wear any other [trademark-name] clothing or accessory items during the Wear Occasions. Wearing Occasions shall be tied to an arena tunnel arrival and/or departure for a nationally televised game or other pre-determined national appearance, as mutually approved by Talent, COMPANY and any necessary third parties in advance. During Wearing Occasions, Talent agrees to permit, subject to all necessary third party approvals, reasonable photography by Getty and NBA photographers for placement in publications and websites. Talent grants COMPANY and its franchisees the right to repurpose imagery of Talent during Wearing Occasions, on COMPANY (or its franchisee) owned digital channels, including paid social/digital advertising, subject to Talent's prior written approval. Talent shall use best efforts to provide COMPANY with a calendar of upcoming events for wardrobe dressing and cross-promotional opportunities (i.e. TV show appearances, non-NBA events, award ceremonies, foundation/volunteer events etc.) as reasonably requested by COMPANY.

(v)   If arranged by COMPANY, Talent shall participate in (1) up to three (3) media or COMPANY interviews that will take place on the COMPANY Shoot Days and (2) up to three (3) media or COMPANY interviews that will take place on during the Personal Appearances (all such interviews shall occur during the performance of any Services and shall not require additional time on such Work Days), with media approved by Talent, concerning

Talent's relationship with COMPANY and shall permit select media personnel that may also be granted access to event, subject to the following:

(1) Talent shall have reasonable approval in relation to the media outlets for interviews, which approval shall not unreasonably be withheld, conditioned or delayed. Proposed media outlets will be delivered to Talent's Representative approximately one (1) week prior to any media activities; provided that if COMPANY does not receive input/approval from Talent or Talent's Representative within three (3) business days of delivery, the media outlets will be deemed approved. However, Talent has agreed that, in certain circumstances, he may be asked to endeavor to provide input/approval within a shorter period (but in no event less than two (2) business days); provided that notice of such shortened time period shall be provided in writing to Talent's Representative.

(2) During interviews, Talent may state that he endorses and wears the COMPANY Products. In addition, during interviews arranged by COMPANY, Talent shall respond to questions concerning, discuss and comment on, in a favorable and positive manner, his association with Company.

(3) One (1) or two (2) of COMPANY interviews from each the Company Shoot Days and the Personal Appearances will be featured on Edit x Company as a pre-game ritual or Day-in-the-life piece.

(4) As an additional opportunity but not an obligation required by Talent, COMPANY may present additional COMPANY and media interview opportunities on non-Work Days to be mutually agreed upon by Talent and COMPANY with all media subject to Talent's approval.

(5) Talent shall provide COMPANY with fifty (50) autographed items (as approved by Talent using his reasonable discretion that will not be unreasonably withheld) including, but not limited to basketballs. The items are to be provided by COMPANY to the Talent for signature at COMPANY' sole expense. The items may be used in connection with advertising, publicizing, marketing and generally promoting COMPANY, but shall not be offered for sale or used for any other commercial purpose.

(i) Talent's team shall make reasonable efforts to attend monthly conference calls with COMPANY' team to discuss partnership details.

(j) Any Services not used or requested during the Term shall be waived and forfeited and shall not carry forward beyond the Term. Any Services not utilized by COMPANY shall not reduce the payments due Talent hereunder.

(k) In connection with the Services, COMPANY shall provide, at its sole cost and expense, make-up professionals, barber, and stylist.

(l) COMPANY understands that Agency and Talent's obligation to provide Agency and Talent's Services under this Agreement is subject to (i) the condition precedent that all monies due and owing hereunder have been paid and received by Agency in accordance with the schedule set forth herein; (ii) the condition precedent that travel reservations have been successfully made, completed and paid for by COMPANY as described herein, unless scheduled by Talent pursuant to this Agreement; (iii) all applicable NBA rules and regulations; and (iv) any group licensing agreement to which Talent is a party.

2.3   Work Sessions; Travel Time.

(a)   Work Days Defined. Any day on which Talent provides Services to COMPANY hereunder shall be a "**Work Day**." For the avoidance of doubt, time spent traveling to or from the location when Services are to be rendered, time spent participating in wardrobe fitting (outside of the Work Day), and time spent on Ancillary Services (unless otherwise Company set forth herein) will not be counted towards the hours of work performed for purposes of calculation of number of hours worked.

(b)   Rendering Services. Agency shall cause Talent to render his Services hereunder in a first-class, competent, prompt, diligent and professional manner, and to comply with all reasonable instructions, suggestions and recommendations that COMPANY may give him in connection with the rendering of such Services. Agency acknowledges that COMPANY may require Talent to perform more than one type of service on any given day, subject to Talent's approval.

(c)   Scheduling Work Days. COMPANY shall use reasonable effort to provide the Talent with at least thirty (30) days prior notice ("**Scheduling Notice**") of any Work Day it wishes to schedule. Talent shall use reasonable efforts to confirm his availability within two (2) business days thereafter, in accordance with the priority requirements set forth herein, to provide Services on the requested Work Day(s).

(i)   Priority. In connection with COMPANY efforts to schedule Talent's Services, Talent shall use best efforts to accommodate COMPANY' requests; provided that all scheduling shall be subject to Talent's prior-existing, personal and professional engagements (the "**Prior Engagements**").

(ii)   Excuses. Once a Work Day is scheduled by the parties, Talent shall be permitted to cancel the Work Day (such cancellation not to be deemed a breach) in the event of the following bona fide excuses: (A) Talent's physical illness, injury, disability or an immediate family member emergency, (B) a Force Majeure event (e.g., if by reason of any act of God, earthquake, flood, fire, epidemic, accident, explosion, casualty, labor controversy, riot, civil disturbance, war or armed conflict, delay of a common carrier, act or threat of terrorism, and/or (C) NBA and/or team obligations (each an "**Excuse**"). Talent shall use best efforts to inform COMPANY of any Excuse at least three (3) days prior to the scheduled Work Day (or as soon as practicable after the circumstances giving rise to such Excuse occur).

(iii)   If, at any time during this Agreement, Agency and/or Talent are prevented from or hampered or interrupted or interfered with in any manner whatever in fully performing Agency and/or Talent's duties hereunder, by reason of any present or future statute, law, ordinance, regulation, order, judgment or decree, whether legislative, executive or judicial (whether or not valid), act of God, earthquake, fire, flood, epidemic, accident, explosion, casualty, lockout, boycott, strike, labor controversy (including but not limited to threat of lockout, boycott or strike), riot, civil disturbance, war or armed conflict (whether or not there has been an official declaration of war or official statement as to the existence of a state of war), invasion, occupation, intervention of military forces, act of public enemy, embargo, delay of a common carrier, inability without default on COMPANY' part to obtain sufficient material, labor, transportation, power or other essential commodity required in the conduct of its business; or by reason of any cause beyond Agency and/or Talent's reasonable control; or by reason of any other cause of any similar nature (all of the foregoing being herein referred to as an "event of force majeure"), then Agency and Talent's obligations hereunder shall be suspended as often as any such event of force majeure occurs and during such periods of time as such events of force majeure exist and such non-performance shall not be deemed to be a breach of this Agreement.

3.   USE OF MATERIALS; APPROVAL RIGHTS

3.1   Use During the Term and Minimum Use of Materials Created During the Term.

(a)   During the Term, and subject in all respects to Talent's approval rights set forth in this Agreement (including Section 3.3 below), COMPANY and COMPANY franchisees (solely to display), shall have the right (subject to the terms hereof) to capture, stream, use, publicly display, edit, reproduce, publish, and/or exhibit throughout the world (the "**Territory**"), the Materials and Talent's approved Publicity Rights and/or frames, footage or film clips therefrom, solely to advertise, publicize, sell, market and promote COMPANY and the Products, in any and all media and iterations now known or hereinafter invented (each such use, a "**Permitted Use**"; collectively, the "**Permitted Uses**"). Notwithstanding the foregoing with respect to Print Materials created during the Term to sell a particular Product in catalog (digital or paper) or on the internet, for so long as the Product featured is for sale in catalog (digital or paper), but in no event more than three (3) months after the expiration or termination of this Agreement, COMPANY shall have the right within the Territory, on a non-exclusive basis, to use such Materials to sell or promote the applicable Product in the same manner permitted during the term (i) as content for the internet; (ii) in catalogs (paper and digital); and (iii) in direct mail (paper and digital). It is understood that whenever possible, Talent's name will be displayed with the mark COMPANY, such as "[Talent-name] For COMPANY", and that COMPANY shall have the right to incorporate Talent's name in an COMPANY branded hashtag and use the same in connection with the Permitted Use during the Term, subject to Talent's approval. Notwithstanding anything herein to the contrary, it is specifically agreed that Talent's Publicity Rights cannot be used in any traffic builder, tie-in program or other third party program involving COMPANY's use of a premium or a third party's product and/or service and shall include, among other things and without limitation (i) any program primarily designed to attract the consumer to purchase a product or service other than or in addition to Products themselves; and/or (ii) any cross promotion with a third party and/or its products or services. Further COMPANY shall not be entitled to use Talent's Publicity Rights in connection with COMPANY products which are not Products, except as Company set forth herein, as an endorsement of any entity, product or service, or to portray Talent in a defamatory, derogatory or negative light.

(b)   During the Term, and subject in all respects to Talent's approval rights set forth in section 3.3 below, COMPANY shall have the right to sublicense to NBA Properties, Inc. the right to stream, use, publicly display, edit, reproduce, publish, and/or exhibit throughout the world the Material captured and created by the NBA for promoting COMPANY and the Products in the context of the life of the Talent, provided COMPANY shall ensure that any use by NBA Properties, Inc. shall remain subject to the terms and conditions of this Agreement.

(c)   Notwithstanding anything to the contrary contained herein no Materials may be used pursuant to this Agreement if such Materials would reasonably and objectively be expected to expose Talent to embarrassment or ridicule. Agency and Talent acknowledges and agrees that it shall not during the Term of this Agreement, knowingly enter into any agreement that prevents COMPANY from exercising its rights hereunder.

(d)   Post Term Wind-Down Period. Following the expiration or termination of this Agreement all rights to use Talent's Property Rights shall immediately cease, provided however, COMPANY shall have the right, without additional compensation to the Agency, to use Materials approved during the Term for a three (3) month period, provided COMPANY' use shall remain subject to the terms and conditions of this Agreement. Following the Wind Down Use Period, COMPANY will not disseminate, use or authorize use of the Materials other than as so permitted under this Agreement; however, it is understood that any subsequent inadvertent de minimis use by COMPANY shall not constitute a breach by COMPANY hereunder and COMPANY agrees, upon discovery or notice thereof, to cease and desist from any such use.

(e)   The Parties acknowledge and agree that COMPANY and/or its affiliates is not required to take down any Materials posted to social media during the Term or the Wind Down Period (other than in the event of termination); provided that post-Term, COMPANY does not run any paid media to support/promote such Materials on the social media platforms, nor otherwise refresh, repost or draw attention to such Materials following the Term, as applicable.

3.2   Additional Use. Anything to the contrary notwithstanding, COMPANY, its parent and affiliates shall have the right to use, in perpetuity: (i) the Materials in their respective non-commercial, non-public, internal corporate reports and communications, and for any non-commercial, non-public, internal, archival and for historical retrospective use, provided no use implies an ongoing relationship.

3.3   Talent Approval Rights.

(a)   COMPANY shall: (i) furnish Talent with a copy of all materials utilizing Talent's Publicity Rights, including, without limitation, any Materials, at least three (3) business days prior to COMPANY' use thereof; and (ii) not release or use any such materials (including the Materials) without Talent's written approval, which may not be unreasonably withheld. If Talent does not explicitly disapprove any proposed materials within three (3) business days following receipt, such proposed materials shall be deemed to have been approved. Furthermore, Talent agrees that, in certain circumstances due to the exigencies of production, Talent may be required to provide approval within a shorter (i.e. less than 48 hours) period, provided that notice of such shortened time period shall be provided in writing to Talent's Representative. Under such circumstances, Talent agrees to use reasonable efforts to fully cooperate with

COMPANY in order to meet any such timelines set by COMPANY. In the event that COMPANY does not receive approval within the determined shorter time period, then the approval will be deemed given. In the event Talent does not approve any Material and COMPANY resubmits such Material ("**Resubmitted Material**") to Talent for his approval, if Talent does not explicitly disapprove the Resubmitted Material within forty-eight (48) hours following receipt, such Resubmitted Material shall be deemed to have been approved.

(b)   Talent acknowledges that COMPANY does not need to seek Talent's approval to acquire images from Getty or content secured from NBA, provided any such use shall remain subject to Talent's approval. For the sake of clarity, the parties acknowledge that COMPANY may seek and Talent may provide approval of the general use of images (e.g. in an email), and that under these circumstances COMPANY shall not have to seek approval over each variation of such use, provided such variation is substantially similar to the approved use and used in accordance with this Agreement.

(c)   Talent shall have reasonable approval in relation to the media outlets for Talent interviews, which will be delivered to Talent's Representative approximately one (1) week prior to any media activities; provided that should COMPANY not receive input/approval from Talent or Talent's representative within three (3) business days of delivery, the input/approval will be deemed given. Furthermore, Talent agrees that, in certain circumstances, Talent may be required to provide input/approval within a shorter period (but in no event less than 48-hours); provided that notice of such shortened time period shall be provided in writing to Talent's Representative. Under such circumstances, Talent agrees to make reasonable efforts to fully cooperate with COMPANY in order to meet any such timelines. In the event that COMPANY does not receive input/approval within the determined shorter time period, then the input/approval will be deemed given.

(d)   All requests for approval shall be sent to Talent and Talent's Representative:

Name & Address
Email:

4.   OWNERSHIP OF THE MATERIALS

4.1   "Work for Hire." All Materials, any revisions, versions, re-recordings and remakes thereof under this Agreement (whether performed before, on or after the effective date hereof), but Company excluding ownership, right, title or interest of each of the Agency, Talent and the Publicity Rights and all trademark rights, rights of publicity and rights of privacy relating to Talent and the Publicity Rights and all posts from Talent's social media accounts (other than COMPANY-related hashtags) (collectively, the "Talent Rights"), shall be and remain the absolute and exclusive property of COMPANY forever, regardless of whether or not any such material is published or otherwise used by COMPANY; provided that COMPANY shall have no rights to use or exploit any of the Materials, or the Talent Rights other than as Company set forth herein. Each of the Agency and Talent acknowledges and agrees that the results and proceeds of

Talent's Services (whether performed before, on or after the effective date hereof, but Company excluding the Talent Rights) constitute "work for hire" as that term is defined in the Copyright Law of the United States and under the Berne and Universal Copyright Conventions and COMPANY shall be deemed the owner thereof. Each of the Agency and Talent acknowledges and agrees that it forever waives any right, title, or interest of any kind or nature whatsoever, including, but not limited to the so-called "moral rights" or "droits morals" or any similar law, doctrine or principle however denominated, in connection with any of the Materials produced pursuant to this Agreement. During the Term or thereafter, COMPANY understands that it does not have the right to, and agrees that it will not, file any application for trademark registration or otherwise obtain or attempt to obtain ownership of any trademark or trade name within the Territory which consists of the Talent Rights or any mark, design or logo intended to make reference to Talent.

4.2   Assignment. To the extent that the results and proceeds of Talent's Services (whether performed before, on or after the effective date hereof) are not considered "work for hire" under the Copyright Law of the United States or under the Berne and the Universal Copyright Conventions, each of the Agency and Talent hereby irrevocably assigns to COMPANY all of its right, title and interest of any kind or nature whatsoever in all of the Materials produced pursuant to this Agreement, and in or to any component part, element, character or characterization thereof, except for the Talent Rights or any portion thereof, which shall remain Talent's property.

5.   COMPENSATION DAY RATES; EXCLUSIVITY RETAINER PAYMENT; GUARANTEE

5.1   Compensation; Service Fees
(a)   During the Initial Term, as full consideration for Agency causing Talent to perform his obligations in connection with the particular Service set for in Section 2.2, and for all the rights granted by each of the Agency and Talent hereunder, COMPANY shall pay Agency on a pay or play basis, and Agency shall accept, a guaranteed payment of $85,000 (the "Contract Fee"). The Contract Fee shall be payable to NAME & ADDRESS. The Contract Fee shall be due as follows: $10,000 within 5 business days after receiving a fully executed copy of the Agreement from Agency, and additional payments of $25,000 due to Agency on November 30, 2018, January 31, 2019, and March 31, 2019. COMPANY shall not withhold any amounts from payments to Agency. In addition to the foregoing, COMPANY shall provide Agency with ten (10) $500 COMPANY gift cards during the Term, as well as mutually agreed upon amount of Products to perform the Services.

5.2   Travel Expenses. If, in connection with the rendering of Talent's Services hereunder:
(a)   Long Distance Travel Expenses. If Talent is required to travel more than forty-five (45) miles ("**Long Distance Travel**"), COMPANY shall provide Talent with: (A) if Talent is required to travel by air, one (1) round-trip first class airplane ticket(s) for Talent and one (1) coach class airplane ticket for Talent designee (or, if COMPANY for any reason is unable to provide such ticket(s), Talent and/or Talent's designee shall obtain such ticket(s) and COMPANY

shall reimburse Talent in accordance with Section 5.4); (B) exclusive ground transportation to and from Service location(s) for Talent and Talent's designee; (C) first-class hotel accommodations for Talent and one (1) standard hotel accommodations for Talent designee (i.e., two rooms); and (D) a per diem of two hundred dollars ($200) per day for Talent.

(b)   Local Travel Expenses. If Talent is not required to travel pursuant to Section 5.2(a), then COMPANY shall provide: (A) exclusive local transportation between Talent's then-current location and the location where Services are to be performed for Talent and Talent designee; and (C) a per diem of two hundred dollars ($200) per day for Talent.

5.3   Travel Payments to Agency. Payments shall be made as follows:

(a)   Travel Expenses. Any travel expense reimbursable pursuant to Section 5.2 hereof, shall be payable to Talent within forty-five (45) days of COMPANY' receipt of an invoice for such compensation together with the reasonable proof therefor; and Talent shall use reasonable efforts to submit applicable invoice to COMPANY no later than sixty (60) days after the date on which the applicable expenses were incurred or the applicable Services were performed.

5.4   Change of Manager. In the event Talent changes Manager during the Term, no service fee shall be due to the new manager from COMPANY.

5.5   Exclusivity.

Talent shall be exclusive to COMPANY in the promotion of Men's Suiting, Dress Shirts, Denim, and Dressy Outerwear categories during the Term. Notwithstanding anything to the contrary herein, nothing herein shall preclude Talent from entering into an endorsement, license, sponsorship and/or other similar agreement with an athletic apparel and/or footwear Agency (e.g., Nike, Adidas, Under Armour, etc.) during the Term, regardless if Products are included in such Agency's product line ("Athletic Apparel Sponsor"). In the event Talent enters into an Athletic Apparel Sponsor agreement during the Term, nothing herein shall prevent Talent from complying with the terms and conditions of such Athletic Apparel Sponsor agreement, and COMPANY will exercise best efforts to work Talent's sponsored footwear into photo shoots and marketing campaigns.

6.   REPRESENTATIONS, WARRANTIES AND COVENANTS

6.1   Agency Representations and Warranties. Agency represents and warrants that (i) it has the right, power and authority to enter into this Agreement and to perform all his obligations hereunder; (ii) Talent shall act with respect and professionalism and Talent shall take all steps reasonably necessary to ensure that the health and safety of those Talent interacts with while providing the Services is protected and maintained and (ii) Talent shall comply, and cause his agents or representatives to comply, with all applicable laws, regulations, orders and ordinances applicable to the Services.

6.2   COMPANY Representations and Warranties. COMPANY represents and warrants that (i) COMPANY has the right, power and authority to enter into this Agreement and to perform all its obligations hereunder; (ii) COMPANY shall comply, and cause its employees, officers, directors, agents, licensees or representatives to comply, with all applicable laws, regulations, orders and ordinances applicable to its obligations hereunder, the Products and/or the use and exploitation of the Talent Publicity Rights and/or the results of Talent's services hereunder and/or the exploitation of any rights granted hereunder; (iii) Talent shall be treated with respect and professionalism and COMPANY shall take all steps reasonably necessary to ensure that the health and safety of Talent is protected and maintained at all times whilst providing Services hereunder; (iv) it shall ensure that all people and organizations engaged in connection with the Services and this Agreement are suitably qualified, experienced and professional; and (v) Talent shall not be required to commit any act or be involved in any activity which may be dangerous, degrading, unprofessional or demeaning. COMPANY shall not bind Talent to any third party obligation in any way without the prior written consent of Talent in each instance, and COMPANY shall not represent or otherwise hold itself out to third parties as having the authority to do so.

6.3   Valid Agreement. Upon execution and delivery of this Agreement by the Parties hereto, this Agreement shall constitute the legal, valid and binding obligation of each of COMPANY, Agency and Talent enforceable against it in accordance with its terms.

6.4   Conduct. Either Party shall have the right to immediately terminate this Agreement in the event that the other Party, in such Party's reasonable discretion, engages in illegal behavior that constitutes a criminal offense under federal, state or local laws, or constitutes indecent, immoral, harmful or scandalous behavior that brings the other party into public hatred, public disrepute, contempt, scandal, scorn, or ridicule, or that will tend to shock, insult or offend the community or public morals or decency and that may, directly or indirectly damage, such Party's reputation or goodwill or if such party commits an offense involving moral turpitude under Federal, state or local laws or ordinances, or otherwise violates any applicable rules or regulations. In addition, Talent or Agency shall not engage in any act or conduct and/or make any derogatory statements which denigrate the other party and/or its brand.

6.5   Representative. Talent's designated representative ("**Representative**") is _____ and any person acting on behalf of_____. Representative is the sole and exclusive representative authorized and empowered to act on behalf of Talent, as its and his representative, in connection with this Agreement. COMPANY shall not be liable for the payment of any commissions payable by Talent to Talent's Representative in connection with this Agreement and each of the Agency and Talent agrees to indemnify and hold harmless COMPANY from and against any claim to the such commissions of any portion thereof made to any person other than Representative eligible to receive same pursuant to this Agreement.

6.6   Interviews. During interviews, Talent may state that he endorses and wears the Products. In addition, during interviews Talent shall respond to questions concerning, discuss and comment on, in a favorable and positive manner, his association with COMPANY but at no time shall Talent intentionally authorize or release advertising or publicity materials that make reference to, or in interviews disclose, the confidential terms of Talent's engagement hereunder or under any prior arrangement between COMPANY and Talent without COMPANY's prior written approval.

6.7   Testimonial Affidavits. During the Term, if COMPANY requests, for the purpose of complying with legal requirements concerning the use of testimonials and endorsements in advertising, Talent shall furnish to COMPANY appropriate affidavits attesting to Talent's use of, and preference for, the Products.

6.8   Compliance with Laws. Each of COMPANY, Agency and Talent shall comply with all applicable laws, regulations, orders and ordinances in rendering their respective services required hereunder.

6.9   Independent Contractor. With respect to COMPANY, each of Agency and Talent is, and shall at all times be, an independent contractor and shall not be considered an employee of COMPANY. As a result, each of Agency and Talent shall not have entitlement to, or participate in, any health insurance, sick days, vacation or any other benefits provided by COMPANY for its employees.

6.10   Taxes. Each of COMPANY, Agency and Talent shall completely and accurately report all amounts received pursuant to this Agreement on such tax returns as may be required by law, which returns shall be filed by each of COMPANY, Agency and Talent on a timely basis. Each of COMPANY, Agency and Talent shall pay all taxes when due (including, but not limited to, any estimated income taxes, income taxes, and employment and social security taxes) attributable to such amounts as may be required by law.

7.   INDEMNITY

7.1   Indemnity by the Agency; Talent. Agency and Talent shall indemnify and hold harmless COMPANY and COMPANY's parent and affiliates and their respective directors, officers, employees, agents, representatives, attorneys, fiduciaries, stockholders, and their respective successors and assigns, from and against any loss, damage, liability (including any liability by reason of any settlement that is approved by Agency and/or Talent in advance in writing of a claim, action, suit or proceeding) or expense (including reasonable outside attorneys' fees and disbursements) which may be obtained against, imposed upon, or suffered by, COMPANY, to the extent arising out of, or in connection with, (a) any material breach or material inaccuracy of any representation, warranty, or covenant made by Talent or Agency, as the case may be, in this Agreement or (b) Agency and/or Talent's uncured material breach of this Agreement.

7.2   Indemnity by COMPANY. COMPANY shall indemnify, defend and hold harmless Agency, Talent and Representative from and against, any loss, damage, liability (including any liability by reason of any settlement of a claim, action, suit or proceeding) or expense (including reasonable attorneys' fees and disbursements) which may be obtained against, imposed upon, or suffered by, the Agency, Talent or Representative, respectively, as a result of, or connected with, any material breach or inaccuracy of any representation, warranty, or covenant made by COMPANY in this Agreement or as a result of any failure of COMPANY to fulfill any of its obligations hereunder in any material respect, or any product liability or other actions brought against the Talent, as the case may be, relating to COMPANY' Products, Services, catalogues or retail stores or in any way connected with, any advertising material furnished by, or on behalf of, COMPANY.

7.3 <u>Permanent Disability or Death</u>. In the event of Talent's permanent disability so as to prevent Talent from performing his services or death during the Term, then COMPANY may elect to either terminate with the Wind Down Use Period or to use the Materials as provided for herein during the remainder of the Term and through the Wind Down Use Period, if applicable, provided however, that COMPANY's sole financial obligation hereunder shall be to pay any amount due to Talent or his estate (which, for the avoidance of doubt, in the event COMPANY chooses to use the Materials during the remainder of the Term, such financial obligation shall be all compensation due hereunder for the entire Term as if Talent had fully performed hereunder), as applicable.

8. NOTICES

All notices, requests, consents, approvals and other communications required or permitted to be given hereunder shall be in writing and shall be deemed to have been duly given if delivered by email, personally, or by reputable overnight courier as follows (or to such other address as COMPANY, Agency or Talent shall designate by notice to the other party in accordance herewith):

If to COMPANY, to:	With a copy to:
Company Name & Address Email:	Company Name & Address Email:
If to Agency, to: Name & Address Email:	

Any notice delivered, mailed or transmitted pursuant to this Section 8 shall be deemed given on the date it is delivered personally or on the date it is actually received, if sent by email transmission.

9. DEFAULT

9.1 If either Party at any time during the Term shall (i) fail to make any payment of any sum of money herein specified to be made, or (ii) fail to observe or perform any of the material covenants, agreements or obligations hereunder (other than the payment of money), the non-defaulting party may terminate this Agreement as follows: as to subparagraph (i) if such payment is not made within ten (10) business days after the defaulting party shall have received written notice of such failure to make payment, or as to subparagraph (ii) if such default is not cured within thirty (30) days after the defaulting party shall have received written notice specifying in reasonable detail the nature of such default. In addition, Agency may terminate this Agreement thirty (30) days after giving written notice to COMPANY in the event that (i) COMPANY declares bankruptcy or becomes insolvent, (ii) COMPANY disparages Talent, or (iii) COMPANY (or any officer, director, senior or public representative thereof) engages in any conduct or activity that is reasonably determined to be damaging to the reputation of COMPANY, its affiliates, or their respective products or services. Except as otherwise Company set forth herein, the termination rights set forth in this section shall not constitute the exclusive remedy of the non-defaulting party hereunder, however, and if default is made by either Party hereunder, the other may resort to such other remedies as said Party would have been entitled to if this section had been omitted from this agreement. Termination under the provisions of this section shall be without prejudice to any rights or claims which the terminating party may otherwise have against the defaulting party.

10.   MISCELLANEOUS

10.1   Survival of Representations and Warranties. The representations, warranties, indemnification obligations of the Parties hereto, and the insurance obligations of COMPANY, shall survive the expiration or earlier termination of this Agreement and shall be unaffected by any investigation made by or on behalf of any Party hereto or by any notice of breach of, or failure to perform under, this Agreement except that each Party shall have the right to waive, in whole or in part, any of the terms and conditions set forth in this Agreement and/or any breach or failure to comply with the same, and on such waiver, such Party may proceed with the consummation of the transactions contemplated herein, it being understood that such waiver shall not constitute a waiver of any right which the waiving Party may have by reason of the breach by the other Party of any representation, warranty or agreement contained herein, or by reason of any misrepresentation made by the other Party herein.

10.2   Confidential Information. Except as required by law or legal process, and except to enforce the terms of this Agreement, COMPANY, Agency or Talent shall not disclose to any third party, or utilize for their own benefit or for the benefit of any third party, any confidential or proprietary information of the others obtained hereunder, including any of the terms of this Agreement; provided, however, that such obligation shall not apply to any information to the extent that it is or becomes part of public knowledge from authorized sources other than COMPANY or Talent, as the case may be, and; provided, further, that COMPANY, Agency and Talent shall have the right to review the terms of this Agreement with their respective attorneys and other business advisers and further provided that Agency or Talent may disclose confidential or proprietary information of COMPANY to Representative. If COMPANY or Talent is compelled by law or legal process to disclose any such confidential or proprietary information, such Party shall give prompt notice to the other Parties so that appropriate protective relief may be sought. Neither Party shall issue any press release or other public announcement regarding this Agreement or the Services without the other Party's prior written consent.

10.3   Further Assurances. From time to time after the date of this Agreement, Talent and COMPANY, at the request of the other, and without further consideration, shall execute and deliver such further legally required documents or instruments as the requesting party may reasonably request in order to effect complete consummation of the transactions contemplated by this Agreement.

10.4   Liability. Except in the event of a party's gross negligence, willful misconduct or indemnification obligations hereunder, under no circumstances will either Party be liable to the other for any special, consequential, indirect, exemplary and/or punitive damages, or for loss of good will or business profits. Notwithstanding the foregoing, Agency's and Talent's collective liability under or in connection with this Agreement, whether such liability arises in contract, tort (including without limitation negligence) or otherwise, shall be limited to and shall not in aggregate exceed the amounts actually paid to Agency/Talent hereunder.

10.5   Trademarks. Nothing contained herein shall be construed to convey to COMPANY any rights to use the trademarks, logos or indicia of the NBA, any other professional or amateur basketball association, or any team, association, group, Agency, sponsor or other entity associated with Talent in any way, in conjunction with the rights granted hereunder. All rights to the use of such trademarks, logos or indicia must be acquired from the NBA, or any other appropriate rights holder.

10.6   Insurance. COMPANY agrees to provide and maintain, at its own expense, general liability insurance and product liability insurance with limits of no less than $5,000,000 and within thirty (30) days from the date hereof, COMPANY will submit to Talent, upon written request, a fully paid policy or certificate of insurance naming Agency, Talent and Talent's Representative as insured Parties, requiring that the insurer shall not terminate or materially modify such without written notice to Talent at least twenty (20) days in advance thereof.

10.7   Use of Materials. COMPANY shall not be under any obligation to cause the Materials produced hereunder to be used, it being understood that the sole obligation of COMPANY hereunder is to make such payments as are required under this Agreement and to comply with all the other terms and conditions of this Agreement.

10.8   SAG-AFTRA. COMPANY acknowledges that Talent is not a member of SAG-AFTRA. In the event any materials produced hereunder featuring the Talent's name and/or likeness come within the purview, or are governed by the regulations, of SAG-AFTRA, or of any other applicable union ("Guild Production Materials"), COMPANY shall Taft-Hartley Talent at COMPANY' sole cost (and in no event shall Talent be required to become a member of SAG-AFTRA) and COMPANY shall pay any and all dues, assessments, contributions, or other amounts, necessary in order for Talent to participate in the production of the Guild Production Materials, or required in connection with COMPANY' use of the Guild Production Materials, including, without limitation, pension, health, and welfare contributions or assessments that may be required by such entities. For the purposes of any pension, health, and welfare contributions that may be required hereunder, the compensation to Talent provided for in this Agreement will be allocated fifty percent (50%) to Covered Services (as such term is defined in the SAG-AFTRA Commercials Contract) and fifty percent (50%) to Non-Covered Services. Such payments shall be made by COMPANY or its agency and shall be in addition to any payments owed to Talent hereunder.

10.9 <u>Assignment</u>. This Agreement may not be assigned by either Party hereto without the prior written consent of the other Party and any attempted assignment shall be null and void.

10.10 <u>Successors</u>. This Agreement shall be binding upon COMPANY and Talent and their respective successors, permitted assigns, heirs, guardians, representatives and executors.

10.11 <u>Governing Law</u>. This Agreement is made in the State of New York and shall be construed and interpreted in accordance with the internal laws of the State of New York and of the United States of America applicable to contracts made and performed entirely in New York. COMPANY and Talent irrevocably submit to the exclusive jurisdiction of any New York State or Federal court sitting in the City of New York over any suit, action or proceeding arising out of, or relating to, this Agreement.

10.12 <u>Entire Agreement; Modification</u>. This Agreement constitutes the entire agreement between the Parties hereto pertaining to the subject matter hereof, and it supersedes all prior undertakings, oral or written, with respect to the subject matter hereof. This Agreement shall be binding upon each of COMPANY, Agency and Talent upon execution and delivery by each of them of one or more counterparts hereof. This Agreement may be modified only by a written instrument executed by all of the Parties hereto.

10.13 <u>Severability and Savings Clause</u>. If any provision of this Agreement is determined to be invalid or otherwise unenforceable by a court of competent jurisdiction, then such provision shall be deemed amended to the extent necessary to render it enforceable, and the determination that any provision is invalid or otherwise unenforceable shall in no way affect the validity or enforceability of any other provision herein.

10.14 <u>Waiver</u>. Any failure or delay by COMPANY or Talent to enforce any right granted herein shall not be deemed a continuing waiver or a modification by such Party of any such right and COMPANY or Talent may, within the time provided by applicable law, commence appropriate legal or equitable proceedings to enforce any or all rights granted herein, and any prior failure to enforce or delay in enforcement shall not constitute a defense.

10.15 <u>Construction</u>. Headings used in this Agreement are for convenience only and shall not be used in the interpretation of this Agreement. Unless otherwise indicated, references to Sections and Schedules are to the sections and schedules of this Agreement. As used herein, the singular includes the plural and the masculine, feminine, and neuter gender each includes the others where the context so indicates.

10.16 <u>No Strict Construction</u>. Neither this Agreement nor any provision in this Agreement shall be construed for or against any Party hereto because the Agreement as a whole, or any provision of this Agreement, was requested or drafted by such Party.

10.17 <u>Non-Disparagement</u>. During the Term, no Party hereto shall publicly disparage the other Party or its affiliates, directors, officers, employees, agents, representatives, attorneys, fiduciaries, stockholders, and their respective successors and assigns.

10.18 <u>Counterparts</u>. This Agreement may be executed in multiple counterparts, each of which shall be deemed an original, but all of which together shall constitute one and the same instrument. Signature pages delivered in electronic form (e.g., PDF files, JPEG files, etc.) shall be deemed to constitute delivery of original copies.

IN WITNESS WHEREOF, this Agreement has been duly executed by all of the Parties all as of the day and year first above written.

AGENCY   COMPANY, LLC

_____   _____

                                                    Name:
                                                    Title:

ACKNOWLEDGED AND AGREED:

_____

TALENT

NOTES & QUESTIONS answer

1. Paragraph 2.1 refers to the right of publicity as the Talent's "name, voice, biography, image and any other identifying attribute of Talent." Chapter 11 examines this concept and legal nuances in more depth in the *O'Brien* and *Jabbar* cases.

2. Paragraph 2.1(a) spells out specific types of products that the Talent is expected to endorse, and limits the scope to "COMPANY-branded fashion clothing." This provision also exludes certain types of apparel: "but specifically excluding t-shirts...etc." Paragraph 2.1(c) identifies specific types of video and print materials covered by the contract. These provisions illustrate good examples of specificity and clarity in contract drafting. Explain how the specificity in these two sections benefits both the Company and the Talent.

3. Note the multiple forms of media encompassed by ¶ 2.2(d) and ¶ 2.2(f). These provisions illustrate the need for modern lawyers to stay abreast of new and emerging media such as Twitter, Instagram, Pinterest, Snapchat, Facebook, YouTube, and blogs. Note also how the drafters used the language "including but not limited to" in an effort to make the list illustrative not limitative. In today's world where novel forms of communication frequently burst onto the scene apparently without warning, drafting in a way to keep open such possibilities is wise. And note how the various new forms of media have created additional obligations for the Talent such as to "like" and "tag" on social media – obligations that simply didn't exist before.

4. What provisions give the Talent opportunities for input into the creative process? What provisions give the Talent opportunities for approval? Do you think that that those provisions strike a fair balance? What are the pros and cons of allowing the Talent creative input and/or approval?

5. What provisions show an awareness of the practical considerations that need to be considered for someone whose day-job is professional basketball? For example where do you see allowances for matters such as travel and games? After all, basketball must be the Talent's number one priority; and yet he must fit in interviews, filming, personal appearances, and time for social media interaction.

6. What provisions deal with the ownership and usage of property (*i.e.,* materials produced in association with this contract)? Try to articulate the balance struck between the Company's property ownership/usage rights and the ownership/usage rights of the Talent? Chapter 11 will examine these issues as they relate to Copyright (*e.g.,* especially the work-for-hire doctrine in Copyright illustrated by the *Monster Communications* case), Trademark, and the Right of Publicity in greater detail.

Further Reading on Contracts:

Roger I. Abrams, *Baseball Salary Arbitration From the Inside,* 1998 N.J.J. 24 (1998).

Gene W. Allen, *Negotiating, Drafting, and Implementing Naming Rights Agreements,* 86 N.D. L. Rev. 789 (2010).

Thomas A. Baker III et. al., *Consent Theory As A Possible Cure for Unconscionable Terms in Student-Athlete Contracts,* 22 Marq. Sports L. Rev. 619 (2012).

Mark R. Bandsuch, *The NBA Dress Code and Other Fashion Faux Pas under Title VII,* 16 Vill. Sports & Ent. L.J. 1 (2009).

Joshua Bernstein, *Smart Contract Integration in Professional Sports Management: The Imminence of Athlete Representation,* 14 DePaul J. Sports L. 88, 89 (2018).

Kira N. Buono, *Athletes Sacked by Moral Turpitude Clauses: Presumed Guilty Unless Proven Innocent,* 41 New Eng. J. on Crim. & Civ. Confinement 367 (2015).

Debra D. Burke & Angela J. Grube, *The NCAA Letter of Intent: A Voidable Agreement for Minors?,* 81 Miss. L.J. 265 (2011).

Bruce Burton, *New Remedies for Breach of Sports Facility Use Agreements,* 88 Iowa L. Rev. 809 (2003).

Mason Storm Byrd, *Concussions and Contracts: Can Concern over Long-Term Player Health Pave the Way to Greater Guarantees in NFL Contracts?,* 59 Ariz. L. Rev. 511, 511 (2017).

Timothy Davis, *Balancing Freedom of Contract and Competing Values in Sports,* 38 S. Tex. L. Rev. 1115 (1997).

Martin J. Greenberg & Steven D. Gruber, *You Get Hired to Get Fired,* 24 Marq. Sports L. Rev. 141 (2013).

Martin J. Greenberg & Djenane Paul, *Coaches' Contracts: Terminating A Coach Without Cause and the Obligation to Mitigate Damages,* 23 Marq. Sports L. Rev. 339 (2013).

Gordon J. Hylton, *The Historical Origins of Professional Baseball Grievance Arbitration,* 11 Marq. Sports L. Rev. 175 (2001).

Richard T. Karcher, *The Coaching Carousel in Big-Time Intercollegiate Athletics: Economic Implications and Legal Considerations,* 20 Fordham Intell. Prop. Media & Ent. L.J. 1 (2009).

Toni Lester, *"Finding the 'Public' in 'Public Disrepute" – Would the Cultural Defense Make a Difference in Celebrity and Sports Endorsement Contract Disputes? – The Case of Michael Vick and Adrian Peterson,* 6 Pace. Intell. Prop. Sports & Ent. L.F. 21 (2016).

John Lillig, *"Magic" or Misery?: HBCUS, Guarantee Contracts, and Public Policy,* 6 DePaul J. Sports L. & Contemp. Probs. 41 (2009).

Greg Lush, *Reclaiming Student Athletes' Rights to Their Names, Images, and Likenesses, Post O'bannon v. NCAA: Analyzing NCAA Forms for Unconscionability,* 24 S. Cal. Interdisc. L.J. 767 (2015).

Robert A. McCormick, *Baseball's Third Strike: The Triumph of Collective Bargaining in Professional Baseball,* 35 Vand. L. Rev. 1131 (1982).

Sean M. Neary, *Mediating Professional Athlete Contracts in the Wake of Darrelle Revis,* 9 Willamette Sports L.J. 81 (2011).

Richard M. Perlmuetter, *Boston, From Blueprints to Bricks: A Survey of Current Baseball Stadium Financing Projects,* 34 Urb. Law 335 (2002).

Fernando M. Pinguelo, Timothy D. Cedrone, *Morals? Who Cares About Morals? An Examination of Morals Clauses in Talent Contracts and What Talent Needs to Know,* 19 Seton Hall J. Sports & Ent. L. 347 (2009).

Michael J. Redding, Daniel R. Peterson, *Third and Long: The Issues Facing the NFL Collective Bargaining Agreement Negotiations and the Effects of an Uncapped Year,* 20 Marq. Sports L. Rev. 95 (2009).

Gary R. Roberts, *Interpreting the NFL Player Contract,* 3 Marq. Sports L.J. 29 (1992).

Stephen F. Ross, Lindsay Berkstresser, *Using Contract Law to Tackle the Coaching Carousel,* 47 U.S.F. L. Rev. 709 (2013).

Jan Stiglitz, *Player Discipline in Team Sports,* 5 Marq. Sports L.J. 167 (1995).

John C. Weistart, *Judicial Review of Labor Agreements: Lessons From the Sports Industry,* 44 Law & Contemp. Probs. 109 (1981).

John C. Weistart & Cym H. Lowell, Law of Sports, §3.02-3.14 Legal Relationships in Professional Sports (Bobbs-Merrill Company, Inc., 1979).

CHAPTER 6
ANTITRUST (AND SOME ASPECTS OF LABOR LAW)

Before a law student, with a straight face, tells practicing attorneys that she's taken a Sports Law class, she must first understand the basics of Antitrust Law, and how those basics relate to Sports. The principles apply to both professional and amateur sports, and therefore this book does not artificially separate them. Always bear in mind that the Sherman Antitrust Act was a product of an era in United States history (late 19th century) when large companies, typically oil and steel, were conspiring with one another in an effort to control markets and to stifle competition. As a result, large businesses were able to put smaller ones out of business and consumers were deprived of choices for products and services and often compelled them to pay supracompetitive prices (*i.e.*, artificially higher or monopolistic prices). Agreements to fix prices and salaries, and conspiracies to boycott certain suppliers were the kinds of agreements, which impeded free trade.

The Rodenberg, Gregg, and Fielding article introduces the basic tenets of Antitrust Law using the context of women's professional golf and age restrictions. *Law v. NCAA* serves as an effective first case law illustration of the rudiments of the Sherman Antitrust Act § 1, and the way that it can apply to sports. This case does a nice job of presenting the law and applying it to specific facts. *American Needle* analyzes the single entity defense in the case of NFL marketing. *Mackey v. NFL* introduces another piece of the puzzle by blending the relationship of labor law and policy with Antitrust. Specifically, *Mackey* teaches us about the statutory and nonstatutory labor exemption defenses, and in so doing, it provides insight into the role played by the collective bargaining process. And although the U.S. Supreme Court has overturned some aspects of *Mackey* (*e.g.*, the law regarding impasse in labor negotiations), the portions of the case analyzing the principles of the statutory and nonstatutory labor exemptions remain good law. *See Brown v. Pro Football, Inc.,* 518 U.S. 231, 238, 116 S.Ct. 2116, 135 L.Ed.2d 521 (1996).

Wood takes us a couple of more steps forward into the Sherman § 1 analysis and its relationship to Labor Law and collective bargaining. In *Wood* we see clearly that many aspects of the way that sports leagues operate (*e.g.*, the amateur draft) would, in fact, constitute Sherman § 1 violations but for the fact that they result from collective bargaining and are permissible under the non-statutory labor exemption.

John Wolohan's article summarizes the long history of Major League Baseball's storied, if not infamous, antitrust exemption. In addition to thoroughly explaining the relevant case law, Professor Wolohan also offers an innovative perspective on the potential ramifications of the Curt Flood Act.

Perhaps the best known sports cases concerning a § 2 Sherman Act claim are the American Football League's suit against the National Football League in the 1960's and the United States

Football League's lawsuit against the National Football League in the 1980's. The note at the end of the chapter summarizing these cases demonstrates the challenges that plaintiffs face in establishing the relevant market for a good or service and also the challenges in proving that the defendant possesses the requisite amount of monopoly power or dominance in the relevant market.

A. BASIC PRINCIPLES

Basic knowledge of Antitrust Law is important for understanding professional and amateur sports. Antitrust principles apply to both professional and amateur sports, and therefore, as was noted above, this book does not artificially separate them. Antitrust is a complex and interdisciplinary subject, incorporating economics, sociology, and political science with the study of domestic and international law. At the risk of oversimplification, this section highlights some key antitrust principles and rules to better understand antitrust law and its important role in shaping the world of sports. This section provides a starting point for understanding the increasingly complex world of Antitrust Law.

In one basic sense, Antitrust Law itself manipulates the rules of Contract Law by prohibiting the enforcement of certain types of agreements. This limitation on freedom of contract is certainly not unique. For example, laws in most states that prohibit prostitution, gambling, and usury are laws that render specific categories of contracts illegal and unenforceable. Antitrust laws do much the same.

Antitrust Law is designed to promote competition for goods and services and prohibit unfair business practices. Competition in a free market enhances consumer welfare through an efficient allocation of resources. Producers create goods and services that consumers demand (*i.e.,* allocative efficiency) at the lowest price using the fewest resources (*i.e.,* productive efficiency). A producer's price covers the cost of providing the good or service and a profit margin to incentivize further production. If a producer's price in a competitive market for a good or service becomes too high, the producer risks losing market share for that good or service to lower-priced competitors. A supracompetitve price for a good or service may encourage new competitors to enter the market to meet consumer demands for that good or service at a lower price. *See American Football League v. National Football League,* 323 F.2d 124 (1963)(concerning a new entrant, the AFL, in professional football). An open and competitive market also encourages producers to innovate and provide goods and services in a better, more efficient way in the hope of maximizing their profit margins and market share.

In addition to promoting competition, antitrust laws advance several other important goals. By prohibiting unfair business practices, antitrust laws encourage individuals to participate in the economy and promote a wider distribution of wealth in society – providing an opportunity for more persons to share in the nation's economic pie. An open and competitive market promotes consumer freedom to choose the products and services that consumers value.

In 1890 Congress enacted the first antitrust law, the Sherman Act (15 U.S.C. §§ 1-7), named for its sponsor, Ohio Senator John Sherman. The Sherman Act's scope is broad, potentially covering a wide variety of anticompetitive practices. Section 1 prohibits agreements by competitors and others – combinations – that restrain trade. Prohibited restraints include agreements to fix prices and salaries, arrangements tying the purchase of one product to another less desirable product, territorial restraints on the distribution of products and services, and conspiracies to boycott certain suppliers of goods and services. Under § 1 of the Act, plaintiffs are not required to prove the same high degree of market control or dominance, in excess of seventy percent, that is necessary to prove monopoly power under a § 2 claim. *See ABA SECTION OF ANTITRUST LAW, ANTITRUST LAW DEVELOPMENTS* 231 (7th ed. 2012).

Section 2 prohibits the unfair creation of and any attempt to create a monopoly by unfair means. Monopolists eliminate competition and artificially limit the supply of goods and/or services to increase the costs (*i.e.,* prices charged to consumers) of those goods and services. This limitation and corresponding increase in pricing (monopolistic pricing) harms consumer welfare. It distorts consumer preference for goods and services by forcing consumers to purchase other substitute goods and services. The monopolistic increase in the cost for goods and services also limits the ability of consumers to purchase additional desired goods and services or to invest that money.

The Sherman Act authorizes public bodies (*e.g.,* U.S. Department of Justice) and private individuals to enforce its provisions. Every citizen is empowered to act as a private attorney general under the Sherman Act to sue a party for anticompetitive practices that violate the Act. The Act also incentivizes enforcement by providing treble damages to successful litigants as well as the cost of attorney fees.

Eliminating competition is a goal of many businesses. If the Coca-Cola Company did not exist, PepsiCo would probably be delighted. But sports are unique among businesses. For example, if the Red Sox did not exist, the Yankees would no longer have an important source of revenue. Red Sox fans are valuable to the Yankees because Red Sox fans pay to watch the Yankees play against the Red Sox. This is important both in terms of ticket sales, radio, television, and other media platform-generated revenues. This simple example illustrates one reason why sports are unique in business. Although teams fiercely compete on the field of play, they must cooperate in order to establish schedules, rules of play, and myriad other details that allow the teams to compete. The competition is controlled though cooperation. This principle, however, does not necessarily apply in all sports law contexts. Adidas and Nike, like PepsiCo and Coca-Cola, would probably be delighted if the other were not around to compete.

Hence, due to the unique nature of sports and the admixture of cooperation that is necessary to compete, courts have had to take a flexible approach to the application of the Sherman Antitrust Act § 1, which prohibits contracts, combinations, or conspiracies that unreasonably restrain trade.

15 UNITED STATES CODE § 1 (SHERMAN ANTITRUST ACT § 1)

§ 1. Trusts, etc., in restraint of trade illegal; penalty

Every contract, combination in the form of trust or otherwise, or conspiracy, in restraint of trade or commerce among the several States, or with foreign nations, is declared to be illegal. Every person who shall make any contract or engage in any combination or conspiracy hereby declared to be illegal shall be deemed guilty of a felony, and, on conviction thereof, shall be punished by fine not exceeding $100,000,000 if a corporation, or, if any other person, $1,000,000, or by imprisonment not exceeding 10 years, or by both said punishments, in the discretion of the court.

AGE ELIGIBILITY RULES IN WOMEN'S PROFESSIONAL GOLF: A LEGAL EAGLE OR AN ANTITRUST BOGEY?

19 J. LEGAL ASPECTS SPORT 103 (SUMMER 2009)

RYAN M. RODENBERG

ELIZABETH GREGG

LAWRENCE W. FIELDING

INTRODUCTION

The issue of age eligibility rules in professional sports was thrust onto the front page of every major newspaper's sports section in 2003 when Maurice Clarett from The Ohio State University challenged the NFL's minimum age rule in federal court on antitrust grounds. The resulting legal opinions, *Clarett v. NFL* (2004a) and *Clarett v. NFL* (2004b), revealed the extent to which the law struggles with eligibility rules in the context of professional sports. At the district court level in *Clarett,* Judge Scheindlin granted Clarett's motion for summary judgment, finding that preventing the running back from earning a living in professional football was "precisely the type of injury that antitrust laws were designed to prevent" (2004a, p. 406). The NFL promptly appealed. The Second Circuit Court of Appeals reversed (*Clarett,* 2004b). Writing for a unanimous three-judge panel, Judge Sotomayor agreed with the NFL's argument that the NFL's eligibility rules should not be subject to antitrust review because of the non-statutory labor exemption. The court concluded that: "This lawsuit reflects simply a prospective employee's disagreement with the criteria, established by the employer and the labor union, that he must meet in order to be considered for employment" (2004b, p. 143).

There is a plethora of examples of teenagers excelling at the highest level in a variety of sports. LeBron James in basketball, Jennifer Capriati in tennis, Freddy Adu in soccer, and Michael Phelps in swimming are just a few such examples. In professional women's golf, Natalie Gulbis, Paula Creamer, and Morgan Pressel have achieved success on the LPGA Tour as evidenced by their presence among the top 60 players on the 2008 year-end LPGA money list.

Structure and Governance of the LPGA

The LPGA is a not-for-profit organization consisting of LPGA tour events, corporate sponsors, and LPGA touring professionals. In 2008, the LPGA operated a twelve month competitive tournament schedule consisting of 36 tour events in 10 different countries. Total prize money for the year was over $62 million, a record for the LPGA. The LPGA is governed by a Board of Directors, comprised of a Commissioner, who serves as an ex-officio member, six independent directors, the LPGA Player Executive Committee, and the national president of the T&CP. In addition, three active LPGA tour players serve on the Board, but do not have voting rights. Duties of the Board of Directors include evaluating the organizational goals and policies of the LPGA, strategic planning, cultivating and maintaining relationships with sponsors, providing oversight in financial matters, offering legal guidance for the tour, and other responsibilities stipulated in the LPGA Constitution.

LPGA Tour Age Eligibility Rule

The LPGA Constitution specifically outlines player eligibility for the Tournament Division. Article IX, Section 2 of the LPGA Constitution states:

> Membership may be obtained only by making application, successful completion of qualifying competition as provided in Article VII of the Bylaws, and payment of requisite dues. Any female (at birth) 18 years of age or over shall be eligible to apply for membership in the Association's Tournament Division. Females (at birth) between the ages of 15 and 18 may be granted special permission to apply for membership by satisfactorily demonstrating to the Commissioner their capacity to assume the professional and financial responsibilities required of the Association's Tournament Division Members.

Rule

LPGA officials estimate that their minimum age rule was added to the constitution in the early 1970s (J. Dickinson, personal communication, October 10, 2008).

The LPGA minimum age rule is primarily designed to protect young elite athletes from entering the tour prior to legal adulthood. While few athletes have petitioned for early entrance into the LPGA, there have been instances where exceptionally talented and mature athletes have been granted full membership prior to their 18th birthday. Aree Song received a waiver granting her early membership in the LPGA at the age of 17 in 2003. Arguably the most remarkable example is that of Morgan Pressel, who successfully lobbied for a waiver granting her full membership in the LPGA Tournament Division. After her first petition was denied, Pressel submitted a second request for a waiver after Carolyn Bivens became commissioner in 2005. Following extensive conversations with the Pressel family and observation of her performance in LPGA events, Bivens concluded that Pressel possessed the intelligence and emotional maturity to successfully cope with the pressures of the tour.

Antitrust law has significantly affected the sports industry. This section outlines how antitrust doctrine was formed and how such laws have been applied to professional sports generally and golf specifically.

Formation of Antitrust Doctrine

Since its adoption in 1890, the Sherman Antitrust Act ("Sherman Act") has served as the prevailing antitrust statute in the United States. The Sherman Act prohibits "[e]very contract, combination. . .or conspiracy, in restraint of trade or commerce among the several states" (15 U.S.C. § 1, 2008). One of the first major Supreme Court cases interpreting the Sherman Act was *Standard Oil v. United States* (1911). *Standard Oil* deemed contracts, combinations, or conspiracies that "unreasonably" restrain trade to be illegal (p. 63). In *Chicago Board of Trade v. United States* (1918), the Court enunciated the guidelines to follow when analyzing an alleged restraint of trade:

> The court must ordinarily consider the facts peculiar to the business to which the restraint is applied; its condition before and after the restraint was imposed; the nature of the restraint, and its effect, actual or probable. The history of the restraint, the evil believed to exist, the reason for adopting the particular remedy, the purpose or end sought to be attained, are all relevant facts (p. 238).

Such guidelines resulted in courts balancing the procompetitive and anticompetitive effects of the restraint at issue. This balancing is known as the "rule of reason" test. An exception to the judicial balancing act was carved out in *Northern Pacific Railway v. United States* (1958). In this case, the Supreme Court declared that blatantly anticompetitive restraints with no redeeming virtues could be declared illegal per se without any inquiry into the reasonableness.

Antitrust Law's Application to Professional Sports Generally

The Sherman Act's substantive interaction with professional sports has been relatively short. This relatively abbreviated legal history is primarily attributable to the Supreme Court's *Federal Baseball Club of Baltimore v. National League of Professional Baseball Clubs* (1922) decision. In *Federal Baseball*, the Court held that major league baseball was exempt from antitrust scrutiny. The Court reasoned that the sport of professional baseball was not part of interstate commerce. Fifty years later, the Supreme Court revisited the issue in *Flood v. Kuhn* (1972). *Flood* described the *Federal Baseball* decision as "an aberration" and "an anomaly," but did not explicitly overrule it despite concluding that baseball "is a business and is engaged in interstate commerce" (p. 282). It was not until 1998 that Congress passed the appropriately named Curt Flood Act (15 U.S.C. § 27, 2008) which partially overruled *Federal Baseball*.

After *Federal Baseball* (1922), however, courts determined that numerous professional sports other than baseball should be subject to federal antitrust laws. Included here were the major team sports of basketball (*Haywood v. National Basketball Association*, 1971), football (*Radovich v. National Football League*, 1957), and hockey (*Philadelphia World Hockey Club, Inc. v. Philadelphia Hockey Club, Inc.*, 1972). In addition, courts considered antitrust issues related to individual, non-team sports such as boxing and tennis. In *International Boxing Club v. United States* (1958), the Supreme Court found that there was nothing particularly unique about professional boxing to warrant that the industry be exempt from federal antitrust laws. In the context of tennis, the U.S. Court of Appeals for the Second Circuit in the case of *Volvo North American Corp. v. Men's International Professional Tennis Council* (1988) specifically outlined the need for a determination of whether the rule of reason or per se test should apply. However, prior to any such determination, the parties reached an out-of-court settlement.

Antitrust Law's Application to Professional Golf Specifically

Although, the sport of golf has not been implicated in antitrust cases to the extent of major American team sports, two major antitrust cases have focused on professional golf: *Blalock v. Ladies Professional Golf Association* (1973) (decided under the per se test) and *Deesen v. Professional Golfers Association* (1966)(evaluated under the rule of reason test). Both cases shed light on how courts might treat an antitrust challenge to the LPGA's age eligibility rule.

The *Blalock* (1973) case involved a professional golfer who had been suspended by the LPGA Tour for one year. The player was suspended after she was found to have impermissibly moved her ball on multiple occasions during competitive play. She sued under Section One of the Sherman Act, arguing that the suspension amounted to a group boycott. The court agreed with Blalock's arguments, characterizing the suspension as being per se illegal and a "naked restraint of trade" (1973, p. 1265). The court's rationale was two-fold. First, the court found the suspension decision to be a result of the LPGA Tour executive board's "unfettered, subjective discretion" (p. 1265). Second, the court took note that the executive board was comprised of other LPGA Tour players with voting power. This fact was notable because plaintiff's direct competitors had a financial incentive to keep the plaintiff excluded from the market of professional golfers.

In contrast to *Blalock*'s finding of per se illegality, the *Deesen* (1966) court adopted the rule of reason test. The plaintiff in *Deesen* sued under Section One of the Sherman Act after having his golf tournament entry form rejected on several occasions. The Professional Golfers Association (PGA) stated that his entries were denied because of prolonged poor play. The court found the PGA's requirements regarding minimum performance standards to be reasonable. The court also concluded that the PGA's rules pertaining to the maximum number of players eligible for tournament play to be a reasonable measure.

PROFESSIONAL SPORTS' ELIGIBILITY RULES UNDER THE ANTITRUST MICROSCOPE

Courts have analyzed a number of sport-specific eligibility rules from an antitrust perspective. In addition to an overview of group boycotts and concerted refusals to deal, this section reviews how certain courts have ruled when deciding the legality of such rules. This section concludes by offering a proposed analytical framework for independent contractor individual sports such as golf.

Group Boycotts and Concerted Refusals to Deal

Legal challenges to minimum age rules in professional sports typically label such eligibility rules as "group boycotts" and/or "concerted refusals to deal." Andersen and Rogers (1992) provide the following definition: "concerted refusals to deal or group boycotts typically involve collective action by a group of competitors for the purpose of excluding or otherwise interfering with other competitors" (p. 356). Early Supreme Court decisions such as *Fashion Originators' Guild of America v. Federal Trade Commission* (1941) and *Klor's v. Broadway Hale Stores* (1959) deemed group boycotts and concerted refusals to deal to be per se illegal. In contrast, the case of *Silver v. New York Stock Exchange* (1963) represented the Supreme Court's move towards the rule of reason test when interpreting group boycotts and concerted refusals to deal. Although not a sports-related case, the Supreme Court in *Silver* outlined a general exception to per se illegality that has been adopted by at least one lower court charged with deciding the legality of a player eligibility rule.

In *Mackey v. National Football League* (1976), the Eighth Circuit...declared: "[t]he term 'group boycott'. . .is in reality a very broad label for divergent types of concerted activity. To outlaw certain types of business conduct merely by attaching the 'group boycott' and 'per se' labels obviously invited the chance that certain types of reasonable concerted activity will be proscribed" (*Mackey*, p. 619).

Nine years after *Mackey* (1976), the Supreme Court made a profound move away from the per se standard in the case of group boycotts and concerted refusals to deal. In *Northwest Wholesale Stationers v. Pacific Stationary and Printing* (1985), the Court ruled that a plaintiff seeking to attach the per se label must show that the activity in question has a predominantly anticompetitive effect that is not justified by efficiency.

Professional Sports Eligibility Rules in the Courts

Eligibility rules in professional sports have been decided under both the *per se* and the rule of reason test. The NBA's four-year college rule was declared per se illegal in *Denver Rockets v. All-Pro Management* (1971). The *Denver Rockets* court pointed towards the overly broad nature of the NBA's rule (*Denver Rockets*, 1971, pp. 1067-1068). *Linseman v. World Hockey Association* (1977) addressed the World Hockey Association's (WHA) rule mandating that all players be at least 20 years old. Adopting similar reasoning as that found in *Denver Rockets*, the *Linseman* court declared the WHA's minimum age rule to be completely arbitrary. In granting the plaintiff's motion for a preliminary injunction, the court pinpointed how the rule did not consider Linseman's talent level when barring him from playing in the WHA. *Blalock* (1973) also adopted the per se rule when the court declared the LPGA Tour to have impermissibly barred the plaintiff from competition.

In addition to the aforementioned *Deesen* (1966) case, a number of other antitrust cases have adopted the rule of reason test in sport eligibility cases. *Molinas v. National Basketball*

Association (1961) involved a challenge to the NBA's expulsion of a player who had wagered on his own team. After being suspended, Molinas sued the NBA, alleging that his indefinite suspension constituted an illegal group boycott. The court disagreed, generally finding that a sport governing body such as the NBA needs to be able to adopt reasonable rules. More specifically, the *Molinas* court found that the NBA's anti-gambling rule was "about as reasonable a rule as could be imagined" (p. 244). *Smith v. Pro Football, Inc.* (1978) and *Neeld v. National Hockey League* (1979) reached similar results in their adoption of the rule of reason test. Smith found that "the 'anticompetitive evils' of the challenged practice must be carefully balanced against its 'procompetitive virtues' to ascertain whether the former outweigh the latter" (p. 1183). More pointedly, the *Smith* court declared that a "restraint is unreasonable only if it has the 'net effect' of substantially impeding competition" (p. 1183). *Neeld* involved a lawsuit by a one-eyed player who had been declared ineligible by the National Hockey League (NHL). In rejecting the plaintiff's group boycott claim, the *Neeld* court specifically rejected the per se rule and instead found that safety was the primary impetus for NHL's eligibility rule where "the record amply supports the reasonableness of the by-law" (p. 1300).

Clarett (2004a) and *Clarett* (2004b) illustrate how major team sports with labor unions are treated differently than individual sports such as golf and tennis when under antitrust scrutiny. In unionized team sports, governing bodies defend challenges to their eligibility rules in two ways. First, if analyzed under the rule of reason test, the leagues can argue that the procompetitive effects of such rules outweigh any anticompetitive results. Second, they can appeal to the non-statutory labor exemption to the antitrust laws. Unlike team sports, individual sports such as golf, tennis, and track and field do not have player unions. As such, there is no non-statutory labor exemption to the antitrust laws.

Proposed Analysis of Age Eligibility Rules in Independent Contractor Individual Sports

Although not an age eligibility rule case, *National Collegiate Athletic Association ("NCAA") v. Board of Regents* (1984) illustrates how the Supreme Court might evaluate an antitrust challenge to a minimum age rule in professional sports, using the rule of reason test, not the per se test. The Court adopted the rule of reason test, at least in part, because of the unique nature of sports. In *NCAA*, the justices found that the "case involve[d] an industry in which horizontal restraints on competition are essential if the product is to be available at all" (p. 101). One year after *NCAA* (1984), the Supreme Court further limited the use of the per se test to cases where the "challenged activity falls into a category likely to have predominantly anticompetitive effects" (*Northwest Stationers*, 1985, p. 298). Given these precedents, the rule of reason should control antitrust challenges to the LPGA Tour's age eligibility rule.

An underage golfer seeking to compete on the LPGA Tour would probably file her antitrust claim under Section One of the Sherman Act. Such a claim would almost certainly result in a rule of reason judicial balancing test between procompetitive and anticompetitive effects of the LPGA's minimum age rule. Like all sports leagues, women's professional golf is a unique industry. Players compete against each other on the golf course, but collaborate on certain governance issues and mutually agree to be bound by a set of rules. The LPGA Tour has a justifiable need to manage the pool of eligible players and ensure uniform treatment for the women who compete on tour.

The LPGA Tour can also argue that its minimum age rule is reasonable. Unlike rigid age rules in other professional leagues, the LGPA Tour's policy is flexible. The LGPA's deliberations in the case of Morgan Pressel show that the Tour is willing to evaluate applications for early entry on a case-by-case basis. The press release announcing Pressel's successful application indicates that the LPGA Tour's decision-making process includes, at a minimum, an evaluation of the prospective applicant's playing ability, intelligence, maturity, and financial stability. This case-specific calculus clearly distinguishes the LPGA Tour's age rule from the NBA's rigid rule that was invalidated in *Denver Rockets* (1971).

Although a litigant might attempt to rely on *Blalock* (1973) for precedent, for at least two reasons a litigant seeking to invalidate the Tour's age rule would also not be able to persuasively rely on this case. First, subsequent to the decision in *Blalock*, the LPGA Board of Directors has discontinued the practice of having current players serve on the Board with voting power. Currently, the three players on the Board serve in an advisory capacity only and do not possess voting privileges. As such, it would be exceedingly difficult for an antitrust plaintiff to argue that concerted action among competitors resulted in the exclusion of the prospective player. Second, as demonstrated by *NCAA* (1984), the clear trend in sports cases is to adopt the rule of reason test, not per se rule applied in *Blalock*. These reasons, coupled with the necessity and reasonableness of the age policy, provide the LPGA Tour's minimum age rule with an extra layer of legal protection, and shield the organization from an antitrust lawsuit filed by an aggrieved teenager frustrated with her inability to compete on the LPGA Tour.

CONCLUSION

Like other sports governing bodies, the LPGA Tour has adopted minimum age eligibility rules to deal with precocious teenagers looking to compete at the highest level of women's professional golf. While some professional leagues have stringent age rules that may violate antitrust laws, the LPGA has demonstrated progressive thought in the development of its eligibility rule. Because the LPGA allows for a multi-faceted evaluation in specific petitions for early entry to the Tour, it is likely that LPGA Tour would prevail if the antitrust legality of its age restriction were challenged in court and evaluated under the rule of reason test.

LAW V. NATIONAL COLLEGIATE ATHLETIC ASSOCIATION
134 F 3D 1010 (1998)
UNITED STATES COURT OF APPEALS, TENTH CIRCUIT.

EBEL, CIRCUIT JUDGE.

Defendant-Appellant the National Collegiate Athletic Association ("NCAA") promulgated a rule limiting annual compensation of certain Division I entry-level coaches to $16,000. Basketball coaches affected by the rule filed a class action [Norman Law, Named Plaintiff] challenging the restriction under Section 1 of the Sherman Antitrust Act. The district court granted summary judgment on the issue of liability to the coaches and issued a permanent injunction restraining the NCAA from promulgating this or any other rules embodying similar compensation restrictions. The NCAA now appeals, and we affirm.

I. Background

The NCAA is a voluntary unincorporated association of approximately 1,100 educational institutions.[1] The association coordinates the intercollegiate athletic programs of its members by adopting and promulgating playing rules, standards of amateurism, standards for academic eligibility, regulations concerning recruitment of student athletes, rules governing the size of athletic squads and coaching staffs, and the like. The NCAA aims to "promote opportunity for equity in competition to assure that individual student-athletes and institutions will not be prevented unfairly from achieving the benefits inherent in participation in intercollegiate athletics."

The NCAA classifies sports programs into separate divisions to reflect differences in program size and scope. NCAA Division I basketball programs are generally of a higher stature and have more visibility than Division II and III basketball programs. Over 300 schools play in Division I, and each Division I member hires and employs its own basketball coaches.

During the 1980s, the NCAA became concerned over the steadily rising costs of maintaining competitive athletic programs, especially in light of the requirements imposed by Title IX of the 1972 Education Amendments Act to increase support for women's athletic programs. The NCAA observed that some college presidents had to close academic departments, fire tenured faculty, and reduce the number of sports offered to students due to economic constraints. At the same time, many institutions felt pressure to "keep up with the Joneses" by increasing spending on recruiting talented players and coaches and on other aspects of their sports programs in order to remain competitive with rival schools. In addition, a report commissioned by the NCAA known as the "Raiborn Report" found that in 1985 42% of NCAA Division I schools reported deficits in their overall athletic program budgets, with the deficit averaging $824,000 per school. The Raiborn Report noted that athletic expenses at all Division I institutions rose more than 100% over the eight-year period from 1978 to 1985. Finally, the Report stated that 51% of Division I

---

[1] Because this appeal stems from the grant of a motion for summary judgment, we review the facts taken in the light most favorable to the NCAA, the non-moving party. *See Kaul v. Stephan*, 83 F.3d 1208, 1212 (10th Cir.1996).

schools responding to NCAA inquiries on the subject suffered a net loss in their basketball programs alone that averaged $145,000 per school.

Part of the problem identified by the NCAA involved the costs associated with part-time assistant coaches. The NCAA allowed Division I basketball teams to employ three full-time coaches, including one head coach and two assistant coaches, and two part-time coaches. The part-time positions could be filled by part-time assistants, graduate assistants, or volunteer coaches. The NCAA imposed salary restrictions on all of the part-time positions. A volunteer coach could not receive any compensation from a member institution's athletic department. A graduate assistant coach was required to be enrolled in a graduate studies program of a member institution and could only receive compensation equal to the value of the cost of the educational experience (grant-in-aid) depending on the coach's residential status (*i.e.* a non-resident graduate assistant coach could receive greater compensation to reflect the higher cost of out-state tuition than could an in-state student). The NCAA limited compensation to part-time assistants to the value of full grant-in-aid compensation based on the value of out-of-state graduate studies.

Despite the salary caps, many of these part-time coaches earned $60,000 or $70,000 per year. Athletic departments circumvented the compensation limits by employing these part-time coaches in lucrative summer jobs at profitable sports camps run by the school or by hiring them for part-time jobs in the physical education department in addition to the coaching position. Further, many of these positions were filled with seasoned and experienced coaches, not the type of student assistant envisioned by the rule.

In January of 1989, the NCAA established a Cost Reduction Committee (the "Committee") to consider means and strategies for reducing the costs of intercollegiate athletics "without disturbing the competitive balance" among NCAA member institutions. The Committee included financial aid personnel, inter-collegiate athletic administrators, college presidents, university faculty members, and a university chancellor. In his initial letter to Committee members, the Chairman of the Committee thanked participants for joining "this gigantic attempt to save intercollegiate athletics from itself." It was felt that only a collaborative effort could reduce costs effectively while maintaining a level playing field because individual schools could not afford to make unilateral spending cuts in sports programs for fear that doing so would unduly hamstring that school's ability to compete against other institutions that spent more money on athletics. In January of 1990, the Chairman told NCAA members that the goal of the Committee was to "cut costs and save money." It became the consensus of the Committee that reducing the total number of coaching positions would reduce the cost of intercollegiate athletic programs.

The Committee proposed an array of recommendations to amend the NCAA's bylaws, including proposed Bylaw 11.6.4 that would limit Division I basketball coaching staffs to four members – one head coach, two assistant coaches, and one entry-level coach called a "restricted-earnings coach." The restricted-earnings coach category was created to replace the positions of part-time assistant, graduate assistant, and volunteer coach. The Committee believed that doing so would resolve the inequity that existed between those schools with graduate programs that could hire graduate assistant coaches and those who could not while reducing the overall amount spent on coaching salaries.

A second proposed rule, Bylaw 11.02.3, restricted compensation of restricted-earnings coaches in all Division I sports other than football to a total of $12,000 for the academic year and $4,000 for the summer months (the "REC Rule" for restricted-earnings coaches). The Committee determined that the $16,000 per year total figure approximated the cost of out-of-state tuition for graduate schools at public institutions and the average graduate school tuition at private institutions, and was thus roughly equivalent to the salaries previously paid to part-time graduate assistant coaches. The REC Rule did allow restricted-earnings coaches to receive additional compensation for performing duties for another department of the institution provided that (1) such compensation is commensurate with that received by others performing the same or similar assignments, (2) the ratio of compensation received for coaching duties and any other duties is directly proportional to the amount of time devoted to the two areas of assignment, and (3) the individual is qualified for and actually performs the duties outside the athletic department for which the individual is compensated. The REC Rule did not prevent member institutions from using savings gained by reducing the number and salary of basketball coaches to increase expenditures on other aspects of their athletic programs.

****

The NCAA adopted the proposed rules, including the REC Rule, by majority vote in January of 1991, and the rules became effective on August 1, 1992.[2] The rules bind all Division I members of the NCAA that employ basketball coaches. The schools normally compete with each other in the labor market for coaching services.

In this case, plaintiffs-appellees were restricted-earnings men's basketball coaches at NCAA Division I institutions in the academic year 1992-93. They challenged the REC Rule's limitation on compensation under section 1 of the Sherman Antitrust Act, 15 U.S.C. § 1 (1990), as an unlawful "contract, combination ... or conspiracy, in restraint of trade."

The district court addressed the issue of liability before addressing issues of class certification and damages. [T]he court found the NCAA liable for violating section 1. **** On January 5, 1996, the district court, pursuant to 15 U.S.C. § 26, permanently enjoined the NCAA from enforcing or attempting to enforce any restricted-earnings coach salary limitations against the named plaintiffs, and it further enjoined the NCAA from "reenacting the compensation limitations embodied in [the REC Rule]." The NCAA appeals the permanent injunction.

---

2   Other cost-saving measures were adopted that, *inter alia,* limited:
* the number of coaches who could recruit off campus.
* off-campus contacts with prospective student-athletes.
* visits by prospective student-athletes.
* printed recruiting materials.
* the number of practices before the first scheduled game.
* the number of games and duration of seasons.
* team travel and training table meals.
* financial aid grants to student-athletes.

III. Rule of Reason Analysis

Section 1 of the Sherman Act provides, "Every contract, combination in the form of trust or otherwise, or conspiracy, in restraint of trade or commerce among the several States, or with foreign nations, is hereby declared to be illegal." 15 U.S.C. § 1. Because nearly every contract that binds the parties to an agreed course of conduct "is a restraint of trade" of some sort, the Supreme Court has limited the restrictions contained in section 1 to bar only "unreasonable restraints of trade." *NCAA v. Board of Regents*, 468 U.S. 85, 98, 104 S.Ct. 2948, 2959, 82 L.Ed.2d 70 (1984); *see also Standard Oil Co. v. United States*, 221 U.S. 1, 52-60, 31 S.Ct. 502, 512-16, 55 L.Ed. 619 (1911). To prevail on a section 1 claim under the Sherman Act, the coaches needed to prove that the NCAA (1) participated in an agreement that (2) unreasonably restrained trade in the relevant market. *See Reazin v. Blue Cross & Blue Shield of Kan., Inc.*, 899 F.2d 951, 959 (10th Cir.1990). The NCAA does not dispute that the REC Rule resulted from an agreement among its members. However, the NCAA does contest the district court's finding...that the REC Rule is an unreasonable restraint of trade.

Two analytical approaches are used to determine whether a defendant's conduct unreasonably restrains trade: the *per se* rule and the rule of reason. *See SCFC ILC, Inc. v. Visa USA, Inc.*, 36 F.3d 958, 963 (10th Cir.1994). The *per se* rule condemns practices that "are entirely void of redeeming competitive rationales." *Id.* Once a practice is identified as illegal *per se*, a court need not examine the practice's impact on the market or the procompetitive justifications for the practice advanced by a defendant before finding a violation of antitrust law. Rule of reason analysis, on the other hand, requires an analysis of the restraint's effect on competition. *See National Soc'y of Prof'l Engineers v. United States*, 435 U.S. 679, 695, 98 S.Ct. 1355, 1367, 55 L.Ed.2d 637 (1978). A rule of reason analysis first requires a determination of whether the challenged restraint has a substantially adverse effect on competition. *See SCFC*, 36 F.3d at 965; *United States v. Brown Univ.*, 5 F.3d 658, 668 (3d Cir.1993). The inquiry then shifts to an evaluation of whether the procompetitive virtues of the alleged wrongful conduct justify the otherwise anticompetitive impacts. *See Brown Univ.*, 5 F.3d at 669. The district court applied the rule of reason standard to its analysis of the REC Rule.

Horizontal price-fixing is normally a practice condemned as illegal *per se*. *See FTC v. Superior Court Trial Lawyers Ass'n*, 493 U.S. 411, 436 n. 19, 110 S.Ct. 768, 782 n. 19, 107 L.Ed.2d 851 (1990) ("horizontal price-fixing ... has been consistently analyzed as a *per se* violation for many decades"); *United States v. Socony-Vacuum Oil Co.*, 310 U.S. 150, 223, 60 S.Ct. 811, 844, 84 L.Ed. 1129 (1940). By agreeing to limit the price which NCAA members may pay for the services of restricted-earnings coaches, the REC Rule fixes the cost of one of the component items used by NCAA members to produce the product of Division I basketball. As a result, the REC Rule constitutes the type of naked horizontal agreement among competitive purchasers to fix prices usually found to be illegal *per se*. ****

However, the Supreme Court recognized in *Broadcast Music, Inc. v. Columbia Broadcasting Sys., Inc.*, 441 U.S. 1, 23, 99 S.Ct. 1551, 1564, 60 L.Ed.2d 1 (1979), that certain products require horizontal restraints, including horizontal price-fixing, in order to exist at all. Faced with such a product – the ASCAP blanket music license which could not exist absent an agreement among artists to sell their rights at uniform prices – the Court held that a rule of reason analysis should be applied to the restraint. *Id.* at 24, 99 S.Ct. at 1564-65.

Subsequently, the Supreme Court in *NCAA v. Board of Regents* departed from the general treatment given to horizontal price-fixing agreements by refusing to apply a *per se* rule and instead adopting a rule of reason approach in reviewing an NCAA plan for televising college football that involved both limits on output and price-fixing. *See* 468 U.S. at 99-103, 104 S.Ct. at 2959-61. The Court explained:

> Horizontal price fixing and output limitation are ordinarily condemned as a matter of law under an "illegal *per se*" approach because the probability that these practices are anticompetitive is so high; a *per se* rule is applied "when the practice facially appears to be one that would always or almost always tend to restrict competition and decrease output." In such circumstances a restraint is presumed unreasonable without inquiry into the particular market context in which it is found. Nevertheless, we have decided that it would be inappropriate to apply a *per se* rule to this case. This decision is not based on a lack of judicial experience with this type of arrangement, on the fact that the NCAA is organized as a nonprofit entity, or on our respect for the NCAA's historic role in the preservation and encouragement of intercollegiate amateur athletics. *Rather, what is critical is that this case involves an industry in which horizontal restraints on competition are essential if the product is to be available at all.* 468 U.S. at 100-101, 104 S.Ct. at 2959-60 (quoting *Broadcast Music,* 441 U.S. at 19-20, 99 S.Ct. at 1562-63)(footnotes omitted and emphasis added).

The "product" made available by the NCAA in this case is college basketball; the horizontal restraints necessary for the product to exist include rules such as those forbidding payments to athletes and those requiring that athletes attend class, etc. *See id.* at 101-02, 104 S.Ct. at 2960- 61 (what a sports league and its members "market ... is competition itself.... Of course, this would be completely ineffective if there were no rules ... to create and define the competition to be marketed."). Because some horizontal restraints serve the procompetitive purpose of making college sports available, the Supreme Court subjected even the price and output restrictions at issue in *Board of Regents* to a rule of reason analysis. *See id.* at 103, 104 S.Ct. at 2961; *see also Hairston v. Pacific 10 Conference,* 101 F.3d 1315, 1318-19 (9th Cir.1996)(employing rule of reason analysis and finding that imposing sanctions for violations of NCAA rules did not violate section 1 of the Sherman Act); *Banks v. NCAA,* 977 F.2d 1081, 1088-94 (7th Cir.1992)(upholding no-draft and no-agent eligibility rules for student athletes under rule of reason analysis); *Justice v. NCAA,* 577 F.Supp. 356, 379-82 (D.Ariz.1983)(NCAA sanctions against member institution imposed for violations of NCAA rule barring compensation of student athletes did not violate antitrust laws under rule of reason analysis).

Other courts also have applied a rule of reason analysis to sports league rules, *see* I ABA Section of Antitrust Law, *Antitrust Law Developments* 115-16 (4th ed.1997), (citing cases), including restraints otherwise given *per se* treatment, *see, e.g., M & H Tire Co., Inc. v. Hoosier Racing Tire*

Corp., 733 F.2d 973, 980 (1st Cir.1984)(applying rule of reason standard to a rule requiring all auto racing competitors to use the same tire and stating that "in the sports area various agreed-upon procedures may be essential to survival"). *See also* Phillip E. Areeda, *Antitrust Law* ¶ 1478d, at 359 (1986)(noting that courts "have not woodenly applied the *per se* prohibitions developed for ordinary business situations" to sports leagues).

[In addition], the Supreme Court has made it clear that the *per se* rule is a "demanding" standard that should be applied only in clear cut cases. *See Continental T.V., Inc. v. GTE Sylvania Inc.,* 433 U.S. 36, 50, 97 S.Ct. 2549, 2557-58, 53 L.Ed.2d 568 (1977). As a result, courts consistently have analyzed challenged conduct under the rule of reason when dealing with an industry in which some horizontal restraints are necessary for the availability of a product, even if such restraints involve horizontal price-fixing agreements. *See* I ABA Section of Antitrust Law, *supra,* at 49 (citing cases). Thus, we apply the rule of reason approach in this case.

[9] Courts have imposed a consistent structure on rule of reason analysis by casting it in terms of shifting burdens of proof. *See* I ABA Section of Antitrust Law, *supra,* at 53 (citing cases). Under this approach, the plaintiff bears the initial burden of showing that an agreement had a substantially adverse effect on competition. [Citations Omitted] If the plaintiff meets this burden, the burden shifts to the defendant to come forward with evidence of the procompetitive virtues of the alleged wrongful conduct. [Citations Omitted] If the defendant is able to demonstrate procompetitive effects, the plaintiff then must prove that the challenged conduct is not reasonably necessary to achieve the legitimate objectives or that those objectives can be achieved in a substantially less restrictive manner. [Citations Omitted] Ultimately, if these steps are met, the harms and benefits must be weighed against each other in order to judge whether the challenged behavior is, on balance, reasonable.

[The court determined that there was a substantially adverse effect on competition and then turns to consider the pro-competitive aspects of the NCAA rule].

B. Procompetitive Rationales

[15] Under a rule of reason analysis, an agreement to restrain trade may still survive scrutiny under section 1 if the procompetitive benefits of the restraint justify the anticompetitive effects. [Case citations omitted]; *see also* I ABA Section of Antitrust Law, *supra,* at 53, 66. Justifications offered under the rule of reason may be considered only to the extent that they tend to show that, on balance, "the challenged restraint enhances competition." *Board of Regents,* 468 U.S. at 104, 104 S.Ct. at 2961.

In *Board of Regents* the Supreme Court recognized that certain horizontal restraints, such as the conditions of the contest and the eligibility of participants, are justifiable under the antitrust laws because they are necessary to create the product of competitive college sports. *Id.* at 117, 104 S.Ct. at 2968-69. Thus, the only legitimate rationales that we will recognize in support of the REC Rule are those necessary to produce competitive intercollegiate sports. The NCAA advanced three justifications for the salary limits: retaining entry-level coaching positions; reducing costs; and maintaining competitive equity. We address each of them in turn.

1. Retention of Entry-Level Positions

The NCAA argues that the plan serves the procompetitive goal of retaining an entry-level coaching position. The NCAA asserts that the plan will allow younger, less experienced coaches entry into Division I coaching positions. While opening up coaching positions for younger people may have social value apart from its affect on competition, we may not consider such values unless they impact upon competition. [Citations Omitted]

The NCAA also contends that limiting one of the four available coaching positions on a Division I basketball team to an entry level position will create more balanced competition by barring some teams from hiring four experienced coaches instead of three. However, the REC Rule contained no restrictions other than salary designed to insure that the position would be filled by entry-level applicants; it could be filled with experienced applicants. In addition, under the REC Rule, schools can still pay restricted-earnings coaches more than $16,000 per year by hiring them for physical education or other teaching positions. In fact, the evidence in the record tends to demonstrate that at least some schools designated persons with many years of experience as the restricted-earnings coach. The NCAA did not present any evidence showing that restricted-earnings positions have been filled by entry-level applicants or that the rules will be effective over time in accomplishing this goal. Nothing in the record suggests that the salary limits for restricted-earnings coaches will be effective at creating entry-level positions. Thus, the NCAA failed to present a triable issue of fact as to whether preserving entry-level positions served a legitimate procompetitive end of balancing competition.

2. Cost Reduction

The NCAA next advances the justification that the plan will cut costs. However, cost-cutting by itself is not a valid procompetitive justification. If it were, any group of competing buyers could agree on maximum prices. Lower prices cannot justify a cartel's control of prices charged by suppliers, because the cartel ultimately robs the suppliers of the normal fruits of their enterprises. Further, setting maximum prices reduces the incentive among suppliers to improve their products. Likewise, in our case, coaches have less incentive to improve their performance if their salaries are capped. As the Supreme Court reiterated in *Superior Court Trial Lawyers*, 493 U.S. at 423, 110 S.Ct. at 775, "the Sherman Act reflects a legislative judgment that ultimately competition will produce not only lower prices, but also better goods and services ... This judgment recognizes that all elements of a bargain – quality, service, safety, and durability – and not just the immediate cost, are favorably affected by the free opportunity to select among alternative offers." (internal quotations omitted).

* * * *

Reducing costs for member institutions, without more, does not justify the anticompetitive effects of the REC Rule.

* * * *

3. Maintaining Competitiveness

We note that the NCAA must be able to ensure some competitive equity between member institutions in order to produce a marketable product: a "team must try to establish itself as a winner, but it must not win so often and so convincingly that the outcome will never be in doubt, or else there will be no marketable 'competition.'" Michael Jay Kaplan, Annotation, *Application of Federal Antitrust Laws to Professional Sports*, 18 A.L.R. Fed. 489 § 2(a) (1974). The NCAA asserts that the REC Rule will help to maintain competitive equity by preventing wealthier schools from placing a more experienced, higher-priced coach in the position of restricted-earnings coach. ***

While the REC Rule will equalize the salaries paid to entry-level coaches in Division I schools, it is not clear that the REC Rule will equalize the experience level of such coaches.[3] Nowhere does the NCAA prove that the salary restrictions enhance competition, level an uneven playing field, or reduce coaching inequities. **** The undisputed record reveals that the REC Rule is nothing more than a cost-cutting measure.... Thus, on its face, the REC Rule is not directed towards competitive balance nor is the nexus between the rule and a compelling need to maintain competitive balance sufficiently clear on this record to withstand a motion for summary judgment.[4]

IV. Conclusion

For the reasons discussed above, we AFFIRM the district court's order granting a permanent injunction barring the NCAA from reenacting compensation limits such as those contained in the REC Rule based on its order granting summary judgment to the plaintiffs on the issue of antitrust liability.

NOTES & QUESTIONS

1. Explain the difference between the "per se rule" and the "rule of reason."

2. The NCAA argued in *Law* that its "restricted earnings" policy for coaching was a necessary cost reduction and noted the NCAA's "Raiborn Report." It found that, in 1985, 42 percent of Division I schools reported athletic programs with budget deficits. *See* Daniel L. Fulks, Executive Summary, Revenues and Expenses of NCAA Div. I Intercoll. Athletics Progs. (2013)

---

3 For example, some more-experienced coaches may take restricted-earnings coach positions with programs such as those at Duke or North Carolina, despite the lower salary, because of the national prominence of those programs. In fact, absent the REC Rule, the market might produce greater equity in coaching talent, because a school with a less-prominent basketball program might be able to entice a more-experienced coach away from a prominent program by offering a higher salary.

4 Because we hold that the NCAA did not establish evidence of sufficient procompetitive benefits, we need not address question of whether the plaintiffs were able to show that comparable procompetitive benefits could be achieved through viable, less anticompetitive means. See I ABA Section of Antitrust Law, *supra,* at 66 (collecting cases); Areeda, *supra,* ¶ 1502, at 372 (if the defendant proves procompetitive justifications, the plaintiff must demonstrate that less restrictive means could have been used to achieve the same results to prevail under the rule of reason analysis).

(reporting that similar to 2011, only 23 athletic programs in the Football Bowl Subdivision (FBS) reported a positive net revenue, no athletic programs in the Football Championship Subdivisions (FCS) reported a positive net revenue, and no athletic program in Division I without football reported net revenue for its athletics as a whole); Interview with Athletic Director Thomas Wistrcill, University of Akron, (Mar. 26, 2014)(confirming that 23 of the total 351 Division I athletic programs operated in the black for the academic year, 2012-13); Amanda Leone, *Buying Influence in College Athletics: How Much Does It Cost to Put In Your Two Cents?*, 23 Seton Hall J. Sports & Ent. L. 221, 225 (2013)(reporting that a substantial majority of NCAA Division I athletic programs lose money annually, while the expenses necessary to maintain competitiveness continue to increase each year). *See also* David Welch Suggs, *College Sports,* Presidency, Spring 2012, at 19 (reporting that subsidies for Division I FBS athletic programs rose by 53% at the median from 2005-2009, whereas subsidies for education and related functions rose only 22% for the same period). Given the increase in expenses and the recent data about the overwhelming majority of athletic programs operating in the red on an annual basis, should courts reconsider the position that "mere profitability or cost savings" do not "qualif[y] as a defense under antitrust laws" to salary caps? As the *Law* court suggested, does the use of salary caps necessarily mean that Division I athletic programs are inefficient? Can salary caps ever be justified?

3. In the case *NHLPA v Plymouth Whalers Hockey Club,* 419 F.3d 462 (6th Cir. 2005) the Sixth Circuit addressed a unique antitrust issue, the little known Van Ryn rule. The OHL, or Ontario Hockey League, consists of 20 teams with players aged 16 to 20. The league is a major source of players for the NHL entry draft. OHL eligibility permits each team to carry only three 20 year olds. Also, no player can be signed by an OHL team unless he was previously on a CHA, Canadian Hockey Association or USA Hockey Player's Registration the previous season. However, the NCAA does not permit players holding either registration to play for an NCAA team. Combining these rules prevents the OHL from signing any 20 year old NCAA players. This rule is often referred to as the Van Ryn rule. Mike Van Ryn was a University of Michigan hockey player, and was drafted by the New Jersey Devils NHL Team in 1998. In doing this, the Devils obtained the rights to him for one year, and at that point, if the Devils failed to sign him, he would become an unrestricted free agent. Under the terms of the Collective Bargaining Agreement, those rights could be extended only if Van Ryn remained in NCAA competition or went to play for a non-affiliated hockey league. Van Ryn did remain in NCAA competition for one year following the draft, which extended the Devil's rights to him. He then signed with an OHL club, and because the OHL is affiliated with the NHL, the Devil's rights to him were not extended. He then became a free agent and signed with the NHL's St. Louis Blues in 2000. Had he not played for the OHL team, his only route to free agency would have been to sit the season out. Thus, the Van Ryn rule was adopted by the OHL. The OHL argues the rule gives those who have been playing for their league the advantage, while opponents argue it is to prevent NCAA players from becoming free agents. The Plaintiffs claimed that this rule was anti-competitive, in violation of the Sherman Antitrust

rule. However, the court disagreed. The Court explained factors to consider when weighing circumstantial evidence of a conspiracy claim: 1) whether the defendant's actions, if taken independently, would be contrary to their economic self interest; 2) whether the defendants have been uniform in their actions; 3) whether the defendants have exchanged or had the opportunity to exchange information relative to the alleged conspiracy; and, 4) whether defendants have a common motive to conspire. The court found that under this standard, there was no conspiracy. It should also be kept in mind that, as the court acknowledged, the circumstances may change with the new collective bargaining agreement.

4. An important threshold question for any inquiry about a potential Sherman Act § 1 violation is whether the alleged restraint resulted from a contract, combination or conspiracy. By definition there must be at least two parties involved in order for a contract, combination, or conspiracy to exist, since a single entity is incapable of contracting, combing, or conspiring with itself. In *Fraser v. Major League Soccer, L.L.C.,* 284 F.3d 47, 53 (1st Cir. 2002) eight professional soccer players sued the MLS, some of its investor/owners who controlled a portion of the teams, and the national soccer league governing body. They alleged that the MLS's control over player employment violated §§ 1 and 2 of the Sherman Act and § 7 of the Clayton Act, which prohibits stock or asset acquisitions that lessen competition or tend to create a monopoly. The MLS owned all of the teams (12 prior to the 2012 season). "In a nutshell, [the] MLS recruits the players, negotiates their salaries, pays them from league funds, and to a large extent, determines where each of them will play . . . . However, the MLS also relinquished some control over the team operations" (*e.g.,* permitting investors/owners to: hire local staff at their expense, license local broadcast rights, and conduct all local marketing on behalf of the MLS without prior MLS approval, also, "the operators/owners play a limited role in selecting some players for their teams"). *Id.* 53-54. The district court granted partial summary judgment for the MSL on the Clayton Act and Sherman Act § 1 counts. The district court found that the MSL was a single entity and as such did not "conspire" with others under § 1 which requires an agreement between two or more parties. *Id.* at 55. The First Circuit Court of Appeals did not agree that the MSL was a single-entity, describing it instead as a "hybrid arrangement, somewhere between a single company . . . and a cooperative arrangement between existing competitors." *Id.* at 58. The appellate court said that even if § 1 applies to the MLS arrangement, the MLS conduct "cannot be condemned under *per se* rules and presents at best a debatable case [for condemnation] under the rule of reason analysis." As in any other non-*per se* case, the plaintiffs can only succeed if they show that the "MLS exercised significant market power in a properly defined market [and] that the practices in question adversely affected competition in that market and that the adverse effects on competition outweighed the competitive benefits." *Id.* at 59. Here, the plaintiffs failed to establish that the group composed of Division I soccer players in the U.S. was the relevant market. The jury found that "neither the U.S. nor Division I delimited the relevant market – imply[ing] that [the] MLS faced significant competition for player services both from outside the United States and from non-Division I teams." *Id.* at 59.

5. For a recent case considering Sherman § 1 claims as they relate to NCAA transfer policies, *see Pugh v. NCAA*. No. 1:15-cv-01747-TWP-DKL, 2016 U.S. Dist. LEXIS 132122 (S.D. Ind. Sept. 27, 2016)(Court upheld NCAA eligibility rule requiring transfer football student athlete to sit out one year, reasoning that such a rule is presumptively pro-competitive). This issue is also relevant to issues addressed later in *English v. NCAA* in chapter 9.

6. In an effort to avoid Sherman § 1, some emerging sports businesses such as the WNBA and MLS (as was mentioned in the previous note) have adopted a "single entity" corporate structure, on the theory that, if all of the league's teams are part of the same corporate entity, then, by definition, there can be no contract, combination, or conspiracy since only one corporate entity is involved.

On May 24, 2010, the U.S. Supreme Court decided *American Needle, Inc. v. NFL,* 130 S. Ct. 2201(2010). The Seventh Circuit Court of Appeals had held that the NFL was a single entity for purposes of licensing its trademarks. American Needle challenged the NFL's right to grant an exclusive license to Reebok, on grounds that such an agreement violated § 1 of the Sherman Antitrust Act. The Court, Justice Stevens writing for a unanimous Court, held that the NFL's 32 teams *may* be subject to liability because they are sufficiently independent. They compete in ways that make them capable of coming within the reach of § 1 of the Sherman Antitrust Act. The Court reversed and remanded the case since it was up to the lower court to determine whether the NFL's conduct was reasonable under the Rule of Reason test. *See* Michael A. McCann, *American Needle v. NFL: An Opportunity to Reshape Sports Law,* 119 Yale L. J. 726, 777-81 (2010)(arguing that the Court should reject the NFL's single-entity claim and recommending instead that Congress enact targeted sports-related exemptions to Section 1's prohibitions).

The excerpt below provides the lion's share of the Court's anaysis relating to the single entity issue.

AMERICAN NEEDLE V. NATIONAL FOOTBALL LEAGUE
130 S.CT. 2201 (2010)
UNITED STATES SUPREME COURT

STEVENS, JUSTICE

"Every contract, combination in the form of a trust or otherwise, or, conspiracy, in restraint of trade" is made illegal by § 1 of the Sherman Act, 15 U.S.C. § 1. The question whether an arrangement is a contract, combination, or conspiracy is different from and antecedent to the question whether it unreasonably restrains trade. This case raises that antecedent question about the business of the 32 teams in the National Football League (NFL) and a corporate entity that they formed to manage their intellectual property. We conclude that the NFL's licensing activities constitute concerted action that is not categorically beyond the coverage of § 1. The legality of that concerted action must be judged under the Rule of Reason.

I

Originally organized in 1920, the NFL is an unincorporated association that now includes 32 separately owned professional football teams. Each team has its own name, colors, and logo, and owns related intellectual property. Like each of the other teams in the league, the New Orleans Saints and the Indianapolis Colts, for example, have their own distinctive names, colors, and marks that are well known to millions of sports fans.

Prior to 1963, the teams made their own arrangements for licensing their intellectual property and marketing trademarked items such as caps and jerseys. In 1963, the teams formed National Football League Properties (NFLP) to develop, license, and market their intellectual property. Most, but not all, of the substantial revenues generated by NFLP have either been given to charity or shared equally among the teams. However, the teams are able to and have at times sought to withdraw from this arrangement.

Between 1963 and 2000, NFLP granted nonexclusive licenses to a number of vendors, permitting them to manufacture and sell apparel bearing team insignias. Petitioner, American Needle, Inc., was one of those licensees. In December 2000, the teams voted to authorize NFLP to grant exclusive licenses, and NFLP granted Reebok International Ltd. an exclusive 10–year license to manufacture and sell trademarked headwear for all 32 teams. It thereafter declined to renew American Needle's nonexclusive license.

American Needle filed this action in the Northern District of Illinois, alleging that the agreements between the NFL, its teams, NFLP, and Reebok violated §§ 1 and 2 of the Sherman Act. In their answer to the complaint, the defendants averred that the teams, NFL, and NFLP were incapable of conspiring within the meaning of § 1 "because they are a single economic enterprise, at least with respect to the conduct challenged." After limited discovery, the District Court granted summary judgment on the question "whether, with regard to the facet of their operations respecting exploitation of intellectual property rights, the NFL and its 32 teams are, in the jargon of antitrust law, acting as a single entity." The court concluded "that in that facet of their operations they have so integrated their operations that they should be deemed a single entity rather than joint ventures cooperating for a common purpose."

The Court of Appeals for the Seventh Circuit affirmed. Relying on Circuit precedent, the court limited its inquiry to the particular conduct at issue, licensing of teams' intellectual property. The court . . . discounted the significance of potential competition among the teams regarding the use of their intellectual property because the teams "can function only as one source of economic power when collectively producing NFL football." The court noted that football itself can only be carried out jointly. Moreover, "NFL teams share a vital economic interest in collectively promoting NFL football ... [to] compet[e] with other forms of entertainment." "It thus follows," the court found, "that only one source of economic power controls the promotion of NFL football," and "it makes little sense to assert that each individual team has the authority, if not the responsibility, to promote the jointly produced NFL football." [T]he court held that § 1 did not apply.

We granted certiorari.

II

As the case comes to us, we have only a narrow issue to decide: whether the NFL respondents are capable of engaging in a "contract, combination ..., or conspiracy" as defined by § 1 of the Sherman Act or, as we have sometimes phrased it, whether the alleged activity by the NFL respondents "must be viewed as that of a single enterprise for purposes of § 1."

Taken literally, the applicability of § 1 to "every contract, combination ... or conspiracy" could be understood to cover every conceivable agreement, whether it be a group of competing firms fixing prices or a single firm's chief executive telling her subordinate how to price their company's product. But even though, "read literally," § 1 would address "the entire body of private contract," that is not what the statute means.

The meaning of the term "contract, combination ... or conspiracy" is informed by the " 'basic distinction' " in the Sherman Act " 'between concerted and independent action'" that distinguishes § 1 of the Sherman Act from § 2. *Copperweld Corp. v. Independence Tube Corp.*, 467 U.S., at 767 (1984). Section 1 applies only to concerted action that restrains trade. Section 2, by contrast, covers both concerted and independent action, but only if that action "monopolize[s]," or "threatens actual monopolization," *id.* at 767, a category that is narrower than restraint of trade. Monopoly power may be equally harmful whether it is the product of joint action or individual action.

* * *

Thus, in § 1 Congress "treated concerted behavior more strictly than unilateral behavior." *Id.,* at 768. This is so because unlike independent action, "[c]oncerted activity inherently is fraught with anticompetitive risk" insofar as it "deprives the marketplace of independent centers of decisionmaking that competition assumes and demands." *Id.,* at 768–769. *** [A]n arrangement must embody concerted action in order to be a "contract, combination ... or conspiracy" under § 1.

III

We have long held that concerted action under § 1 does not turn simply on whether the parties involved are legally distinct entities. Instead, we have eschewed such formalistic distinctions in favor of a functional consideration of how the parties involved in the alleged anticompetitive conduct actually operate.

As a result, we have repeatedly found instances in which members of a legally single entity violated § 1 when the entity was controlled by a group of competitors and served, in essence, as a vehicle for ongoing concerted activity. In *United States v. Sealy, Inc.,* 388 U.S. 350 (1967), for example, a group of mattress manufacturers operated and controlled Sealy, Inc., a company that licensed the Sealy trademark to the manufacturers, and dictated that each operate within a specific geographic area. The Government alleged that the licensees and Sealy were conspiring in violation of § 1, and we agreed. ****

IV

"[S]ubstance, not form, should determine whether a[n] ... entity is capable of conspiring under § 1." This inquiry is sometimes described as asking whether the alleged conspirators are a single entity. That is perhaps a misdescription, however, because the question is not whether the defendant is a legally single entity or has a single name; nor is the question whether the parties involved "seem" like one firm or multiple firms in any metaphysical sense. The key is whether the alleged "contract, combination ..., or conspiracy" is concerted action—that is, whether it joins together separate decisionmakers. The relevant inquiry, therefore, is whether there is a "contract, combination ... or conspiracy" amongst "separate economic actors pursuing separate economic interests," such that the agreement "deprives the marketplace of independent centers of decisionmaking," and therefore of "diversity of entrepreneurial interests." *Frasier v. Major League Soccer, L.L.C,* 284 F.3d 47, 57 (CA 1 2002).

* * *

If it does, the entities are capable of conspiring under § 1, and the court must decide whether the restraint of trade is an unreasonable and therefore illegal one.

V

The NFL teams do not possess either the unitary decisionmaking quality or the single aggregation of economic power characteristic of independent action. Each of the teams is a substantial, independently owned, and independently managed business. "[T]heir general corporate actions are guided or determined" by "separate corporate consciousnesses," and "[t]heir objectives are" not "common." The teams compete with one another, not only on the playing field, but to attract fans, for gate receipts and for contracts with managerial and playing personnel.

Directly relevant to this case, the teams compete in the market for intellectual property. To a firm making hats, the Saints and the Colts are two potentially competing suppliers of valuable trademarks. When each NFL team licenses its intellectual property, it is not pursuing the "common interests of the whole" league but is instead pursuing interests of each "corporation itself," *Copperweld,* 467 U.S., at 770; teams are acting as "separate economic actors pursuing separate economic interests," and each team therefore is a potential "independent cente[r] of decisionmaking," Decisions by NFL teams to license their separately owned trademarks collectively and to only one vendor are decisions that "depriv[e] the marketplace of independent centers of decisionmaking," and therefore of actual or potential competition. ****

In defense, respondents argue that by forming NFLP, they have formed a single entity, akin to a merger, and market their NFL brands through a single outlet. But it is not dispositive that the teams have organized and own a legally separate entity that centralizes the management of their intellectual property. An ongoing § 1 violation cannot evade § 1 scrutiny simply by giving the ongoing violation a name and label.

The NFL respondents may be similar in some sense to a single enterprise that owns several pieces of intellectual property and licenses them jointly, but they are not similar in the relevant functional sense. Although NFL teams have common interests such as promoting the NFL brand, they are still separate, profit-maximizing entities, and their interests in licensing team trademarks are not necessarily aligned. Common interests in the NFL brand "*partially* unit[e] the economic interests of the parent firms,", but the teams still have distinct, potentially competing interests.

*   *   *   *

[D]ecisions by the NFLP regarding the teams' separately owned intellectual property constitute concerted action. Thirty-two teams operating independently through the vehicle of the NFLP are not like the components of a single firm that act to maximize the firm's profits. The teams remain separately controlled, potential competitors with economic interests that are distinct from NFLP's financial well-being. ****

VI

Football teams that need to cooperate are not trapped by antitrust law. "[T]he special characteristics of this industry may provide a justification" for many kinds of agreements. *Brown,* 518 U.S., at 252. The fact that NFL teams share an interest in making the entire league successful and profitable, and that they must cooperate in the production and scheduling of games, provides a perfectly sensible justification for making a host of collective decisions. But the conduct at issue in this case is still concerted activity under the Sherman Act that is subject to § 1 analysis.

When "restraints on competition are essential if the product is to be available at all," *per se* rules of illegality are inapplicable, and instead the restraint must be judged according to the flexible Rule of Reason. *NCAA,* 468 U.S., at 101. Our decision not to apply a *per se* rule to this case rests in large part on our recognition that a certain degree of cooperation is necessary if the type of competition that petitioner and its member institutions seek to market is to be preserved". In such instances, the agreement is likely to survive the Rule of Reason. And depending upon the concerted activity in question, the Rule of Reason may not require a detailed analysis; it "can sometimes be applied in the twinkling of an eye." *NCAA,* 468 U.S., at 109, n. 39.

Other features of the NFL may also save agreements amongst the teams. We have recognized, for example, "that the interest in maintaining a competitive balance" among "athletic teams is legitimate and important," *NCAA*, 468 U.S., at 117. While that same interest applies to the teams in the NFL, it does not justify treating them as a single entity for § 1 purposes when it comes to the marketing of the teams' individually owned intellectual property. It is, however, unquestionably an interest that may well justify a variety of collective decisions made by the teams. What role it properly plays in applying the Rule of Reason to the allegations in this case is a matter to be considered on remand.

* * *

Accordingly, the judgment of the Court of Appeals is reversed, and the case is remanded for further proceedings consistent with this opinion.

NOTES AND QUESTIONS

1. What test did the *American Needle* Court apply to determine whether the NFL's conduct violated the Sherman Act?

2. The Court states that in general, NFL teams "do not possess either the unitary decision making quality or the single aggregation of economic power characteristic of independent action." Considering that statement, what is the future of the single entity defense to the Sherman Act for not just the NFL, but all professional sports teams after *American Needle*?

3. The NBA emphasized in its amicus brief that under its constitution and bylaws, the NBA has authority to "assert full control over the conduct of [NBA] teams if their conduct does not serve the best interests of the League as a whole." Brief of Nat'l Basketball Ass'n and NBA Props. as Amici Curiae Supporting Respondents at 14, *Am. Needle, Inc. v. Nat'l Football League*, 130 S. Ct. 2201 (2010). At least one author argues that this authority would render the NBA closer to the parent-subsidiary distinction considered in *Copperweld*, 467 U.S. 752 (1984), and thus more likely to be deemed a single entity not subject to § 1 of the Sherman Antitrust Act. Nathaniel Grow, *American Needle and the Future of the Single Entity Defense Under Section One of the Sherman Act*, 48 Am. Bus. L.J. 449 (2011). Do you think, based on the amount of control the NBA has in its bylaws, the single entity defense would be available to it in a case similar to *American Needle*?

4. The Court recognized that NFL teams must cooperate in the production and scheduling of games and that § 1 would not prohibit those kinds of collective activities. What other kinds of collective activities by the NFL might be necessary for the production of football and not violate § 1?

5. For a recent case considering a realated issue, *see Kelsey K. v. NFL Enterprises, LLC*, 254 F. Supp. 3d 1140 (N.D. Cal. 2017), *aff'd*, 757 Fed. Appx. 524 (9th Cir. 2018)(unpublished). The

district court dismissed NFL cheerleaders-plaintiffs' Sherman § 1 claim alleging collusion to suppress cheerleader salaries, because plaintiffs were unable to show that there was an agreement (*i.e.,* contract, combination, or conspiracy).

MACKEY V. NATIONAL FOOTBALL LEAGUE

543 F 2D 606 (1976)

UNITED STATES COURT OF APPEALS, EIGHTH CIRCUIT

LAY, CIRCUIT JUDGE.

This is an appeal by the National Football League (NFL), twenty-six of its member clubs, and its Commissioner, Alvin Ray "Pete" Rozelle, from a district court judgment holding the "Rozelle Rule"[5] to be violative of § 1 of the Sherman Act, and enjoining its enforcement.

This action was initiated by a group of present and former NFL players [John Mackey, Named Plaintiff], appellees herein, pursuant to ss 4 and 16 of the Clayton Act, 15 U.S.C. §§ 15 and 26, and § 1 of the Sherman Act, 15 U.S.C. § 1. Their complaint alleged that the defendants' enforcement of the Rozelle Rule constituted an illegal combination and conspiracy in restraint of trade denying professional football players the right to freely contract for their services. Plaintiffs sought injunctive relief and treble damages.

The district court, the Honorable Earl R. Larson presiding, conducted a plenary trial which consumed 55 days and produced a transcript in excess of 11,000 pages. At the conclusion of trial, the court entered extensive findings of fact and conclusions of law. The court granted the injunctive relief sought by the players and entered judgment in their favor on the issue of liability. This appeal followed.

The district court held that the defendants' enforcement of the Rozelle Rule constituted a concerted refusal to deal and a group boycott, and was therefore a per se violation of the Sherman Act. Alternatively, finding that the evidence offered in support of the clubs' contention that the Rozelle Rule is necessary to the successful operation of the NFL insufficient to justify the restrictive effects of the Rule, the court concluded that the Rozelle Rule was invalid under the Rule of Reason standard. Finally, the court rejected the clubs' argument that the Rozelle Rule was immune from attack under the Sherman Act because it had been the subject of a collective bargaining agreement between the club owners and the National Football League Players Association (NFLPA).

The defendants raise two basic issues on this appeal: (1) whether the so-called labor exemption to the antitrust laws immunizes the NFL's enforcement of the Rozelle Rule from antitrust

---

5 The Rozelle Rule essentially provides that when a player's contractual obligation to a team expires and he signs with a different club, the signing club must provide compensation to the player's former team. If the two clubs are unable to conclude mutually satisfactory arrangements, the Commissioner may award compensation in the form of one or more players and/or draft choices as he deems fair and equitable.

liability; and (2) if not, whether the Rozelle Rule and the manner in which it has been enforced violate the antitrust laws. ****

HISTORY

We first turn to a brief examination of the pertinent history and operating principles of the National Football League.

The NFL, which began operating in 1920, is an unincorporated association comprised of member clubs which own and operate professional football teams. It presently enjoys a monopoly over major league professional football in the United States. The League performs various administrative functions, including organizing and scheduling games, and promulgating rules. A constitution and bylaws govern its activities and those of its members. Pete Rozelle, Commissioner of the NFL since 1960, is an employee of the League and its chief executive officer. His powers and duties are defined by the NFL Constitution and Bylaws.

Throughout most of its history, the NFL's operations have been unilaterally controlled by the club owners. In 1968, however, the NLRB recognized the NFLPA as a labor organization, within the meaning of 29 U.S.C. § 152(5), and as the exclusive bargaining representative of all NFL players, within the meaning of 29 U.S.C. § 159(a). Since that time, the NFLPA and the clubs have engaged in collective bargaining over various terms and conditions of employment. Two formal agreements have resulted. The first, concluded in 1968, was in effect from July 15, 1968 to February 1, 1970. The second, entered into on June 17, 1971, was made retroactive to February 1, 1970, and expired on January 30, 1974. Since 1974, the parties have been negotiating; however, they have not concluded a new agreement.

For a number of years, the NFL has operated under a reserve system whereby every player who signs a contract with an NFL club is bound to play for that club, and no other, for the term of the contract plus one additional year at the option of the club. The cornerstones of this system are s 15.1 of the NFL Constitution and Bylaws, which requires that all club-player contracts be as prescribed in the Standard Player Contract adopted by the League, and the option clause embodied in the Standard Player Contract.[6] Once a player signs a Standard Player Contract, he is bound to his team for at least two years. He may, however, become a free agent at the end of the option year by playing that season under a renewed contract rather than signing a new one. A player "playing out his option" is subject to a 10% salary cut during the option year.

Prior to 1963, a team which signed a free agent who had previously been under contract to another club was not obligated to compensate the player's former club. In 1963, after R. C. Owens

---

6 Paragraph 10 of the Standard Player Contract contains the following option clause:
The Club may, by sending notice in writing to the Player, on or before the first day of May following the football season referred to in P 1 hereof, renew this contract for a further term of one (1) year on the same terms as are provided by this contract, except that (1) the Club may fix the rate of compensation to be paid by the Club to the Player during said further term, which rate of compensation shall not be less than ninety percent (90%) of the sum set forth in P 3 hereof and shall be payable in installments during the football season in such further term as provided in P 3; and (2) after such renewal this contract shall not include a further option to the Club to renew the contract. The phrase "rate of compensation" as above used shall not include bonus payments or payments of any nature whatsoever and shall be limited to the precise sum set forth in P 3 hereof.

played out his option with the San Francisco 49ers and signed a contract with the Baltimore Colts, the member clubs of the NFL unilaterally adopted the following provision, now known as the Rozelle Rule, as an amendment to the League's Constitution and Bylaws:

Any player, whose contract with a League club has expired, shall thereupon become a free agent and shall no longer be considered a member of the team of that club following the expiration date of such contract. Whenever a player, becoming a free agent in such manner, thereafter signed a contract with a different club in the League, then, unless mutually satisfactory arrangements have been concluded between the two League clubs, the Commissioner may name and then award to the former club one or more players, from the Active, Reserve, or Selection List (including future selection choices) of the acquiring club as the Commissioner in his sole discretion deems fair and equitable; any such decision by the Commissioner shall be final and conclusive.

This provision, unchanged in form, is currently embodied in s 12.1(H) of the NFL Constitution. The ostensible purposes of the rule are to maintain competitive balance among the NFL teams and protect the clubs' investment in scouting, selecting and developing players.

During the period from 1963 through 1974, 176 players played out their options. Of that number, 34 signed with other teams. In three of those cases, the former club waived compensation. In 27 cases, the clubs involved mutually agreed upon compensation. Commissioner Rozelle awarded compensation in the four remaining cases.

We turn now to the contentions of the parties.

THE LABOR EXEMPTION ISSUE

We review first the claim that the labor exemption immunizes the Commissioner and the clubs from liability under the antitrust laws. Analysis of this contention requires a basic understanding of the legal principles surrounding the labor exemption and consideration of the factual record developed at trial.

History

The concept of a labor exemption from the antitrust laws finds its basic source in §§ 6 and 20 of the Clayton Act, 15 U.S.C. § 17 and 29 U.S.C. § 52, and the Norris-LaGuardia Act, 29 U.S.C. §§ 104, 105 and 113. Those provisions declare that labor unions are not combinations or conspiracies in restraint of trade, and specifically exempt certain union activities such as secondary picketing and group boycotts from the coverage of the antitrust laws. *See Connell Co. v. Plumbers & Steamfitters,* 421 U.S. 616, 621-22, 95 S.Ct. 1830, 44 L.Ed.2d 418 (1975). The *statutory* exemption was created to insulate legitimate collective activity by employees, which is inherently anticompetitive but is favored by federal labor policy, from the proscriptions of the antitrust laws. (emphasis added) *See Apex Hosiery Co. v. Leader,* 310 U.S. 469, 60 S.Ct. 982, 84 L.Ed. 1311 (1940).

The *statutory* exemption extends to legitimate labor activities unilaterally undertaken by a union in furtherance of its own interests. (emphasis added) *See United States v. Hutcheson,* 312 U.S. 219, 61 S.Ct. 463, 85 L.Ed. 788 (1941). It does not extend to concerted action or agreements between unions and non-labor groups. The Supreme Court has held, however, that in order to properly accommodate the congressional policy favoring free competition in business markets with the congressional policy favoring collective bargaining under the National Labor Relations Act, 29 U.S.C. s 151 et seq., certain union-employer agreements must be accorded a limited *nonstatutory* exemption from antitrust sanctions. (emphasis added) *See Connell Co. v. Plumbers & Steamfitters, supra; Meat Cutters v. Jewel Tea,* 381 U.S. 676, 85 S.Ct. 1596, 14 L.Ed.2d 640 (1965). *See* generally Morris, The Developing Labor Law 807-16 (1971).[7]

* * *

The clubs and the Commissioner claim the benefit of the *nonstatutory* labor exemption here, arguing that the Rozelle Rule was the subject of an agreement with the players union and that the proper accommodation of federal labor and antitrust policies requires that the agreement be deemed immune from antitrust liability. (emphasis added) The plaintiffs assert that the Rozelle Rule was the product of unilateral action by the clubs and that the defendants cannot assert a colorable claim of exemption.

To determine the applicability of the nonstatutory exemption we must first decide whether there has been any agreement between the parties concerning the Rozelle Rule.

The Collective Bargaining Agreements

The district court found that neither the 1968 nor the 1970 collective bargaining agreement embodied an agreement on the Rozelle Rule, and that the union has never otherwise agreed to the Rule. ****

The 1968 Agreement

At the outset of the negotiations preceding the 1968 agreement, the players did not seek elimination of the Rozelle Rule but felt that it should be modified. During the course of the negotiations, however, the players apparently presented no concrete proposals in that regard and there was little discussion concerning the Rozelle Rule. At trial, Daniel Shulman, a bargaining representative of the players, attributed their failure to pursue any modifications to the fact that the negotiations had bogged down on other issues and the union was not strong enough to persist.

The 1968 agreement incorporated by reference the NFL Constitution and Bylaws, of which the Rozelle Rule is a part. Furthermore, it expressly provided that free agent rules shall not be amended during the life of the agreement.

---

7 As the Supreme Court stated in *Connell Co. v. Plumbers & Steamfitters,* 421 U.S. 616, at 622, 95 S.Ct. 1830, at 1835, 44 L.Ed.2d 418 (1975): "(t)he nonstatutory exemption has its source in the strong labor policy favoring the association of employees to eliminate competition over wages and working conditions."

The 1970 Agreement

At the start of the negotiations leading up to the 1970 agreement, it appears that the players again decided not to make an issue of the Rozelle Rule. The only reference to the Rule in the union's formal proposals presented at the outset of the negotiations was the following:

> The NFLPA is disturbed over reports from players who, after playing out their options, are unable to deal with other clubs because of the Rozelle Rule. A method should be found whereby a free agent is assured the opportunity to discuss contract with all NFL teams.

There was little discussion of the Rozelle Rule during the 1970 negotiations.

* * * *

Since the beginning of the 1974 negotiations, the players have consistently sought the elimination of the Rozelle Rule. The NFLPA and the clubs have engaged in substantial bargaining over that issue but have not reached an accord. Nor have they concluded a collective bargaining agreement to replace the 1970 agreement which expired in 1974.

Based on the fact that the 1968 agreement incorporated by reference the Rozelle Rule and provided that free agent rules would not be changed, we conclude that the 1968 agreement required that the Rozelle Rule govern when a player played out his option and signed with another team. Assuming, without deciding, that the 1970 agreement embodied a similar understanding, we proceed to a consideration of whether the agreements fall within the scope of the nonstatutory labor exemption.

Governing Principles

Under the general principles surrounding the labor exemption, the availability of the nonstatutory exemption for a particular agreement turns upon whether the relevant federal labor policy is deserving of pre-eminence over federal antitrust policy under the circumstances of the particular case. *See Connell Co. v. Plumbers & Steamfitters, supra; Meat Cutters v. Jewel Tea, supra; Mine Workers v. Pennington,* 381 U.S. 657, 85 S.Ct. 1585, 14 L.Ed.2d 626 (1965).

Although the cases giving rise to the nonstatutory exemption are factually dissimilar from the present case, certain principles can be deduced from those decisions governing the proper accommodation of the competing labor and antitrust interests involved here.

We find the proper accommodation to be: First, the labor policy favoring collective bargaining may potentially be given pre-eminence over the antitrust laws where the restraint on trade primarily affects only the parties to the collective bargaining relationship. [Case Citations Omitted] Second, federal labor policy is implicated sufficiently to prevail only where the agreement sought to be exempted concerns a mandatory subject of collective bargaining. [Case Citations Omitted] Finally, the policy favoring collective bargaining is furthered to the degree necessary to override the antitrust laws only where the agreement sought to be exempted is the product of bona fide arm's-length bargaining. [Case Citations Omitted]

Application

Applying these principles to the facts presented here, we think it clear that the alleged restraint on trade effected by the Rozelle Rule affects only the parties to the agreements sought to be exempted. Accordingly, we must inquire as to the other two principles: whether the Rozelle Rule is a mandatory subject of collective bargaining, and whether the agreements thereon were the product of bona fide arm's-length negotiation.

Mandatory Subject of Bargaining

Under s 8(d) of the National Labor Relations Act, 29 U.S.C. § 158(d), mandatory subjects of bargaining pertain to "wages, hours, and other terms and conditions of employment. . . ." *See NLRB v. Borg-Warner Corp.,* 356 U.S. 342, 78 S.Ct. 718, 2 L.Ed.2d 823 (1958). Whether an agreement concerns a mandatory subject depends not on its form but on its practical effect. *See Federation of Musicians v. Carroll,* 391 U.S. 99, 88 S.Ct. 1562, 20 L.Ed.2d 460 (1968). Thus, in *Meat Cutters v. Jewel Tea, supra,* the Court held that an agreement limiting retail marketing hours concerned a mandatory subject because it affected the particular hours of the day which the employees would be required to work. In *Teamsters Union v. Oliver,* 358 U.S. 283, 79 S.Ct. 297, 3 L.Ed.2d 312 (1959), an agreement fixing minimum equipment rental rates paid to truck owner-drivers was held to concern a mandatory bargaining subject because it directly affected the driver wage scale.

* * * *

On its face, the Rozelle Rule does not deal with "wages, hours and other terms or conditions of employment," but with inter-team compensation when a player's contractual obligation to one team expires and he is signed by another. Viewed as such, it would not constitute a mandatory subject of collective bargaining. The district court found, however, that the Rule operates to restrict a player's ability to move from one team to another and depresses player salaries. There is substantial evidence in the record to support these findings. Accordingly, we hold that the Rozelle Rule constitutes a mandatory bargaining subject within the meaning of the National Labor Relations Act.

Bona Fide Bargaining

The district court found that the parties' collective bargaining history reflected nothing which could be legitimately characterized as bargaining over the Rozelle Rule; that, in part due to its recent formation and inadequate finances, the NFLPA, at least prior to 1974, stood in a relatively weak bargaining position vis-à-vis the clubs; and that "the Rozelle Rule was unilaterally imposed by the NFL and member club defendants upon the players in 1963 and has been imposed on the players from 1963 through the present date."

On the basis of our independent review of the record, including the parties' bargaining history as set forth above, we find substantial evidence to support the finding that there was no bona fide arm's-length bargaining over the Rozelle Rule preceding the execution of the 1968 and

1970 agreements. The Rule imposes significant restrictions on players, and its form has remained unchanged since it was unilaterally promulgated by the clubs in 1963. ****

In view of the foregoing, we hold that the agreements between the clubs and the players embodying the Rozelle Rule do not qualify for the labor exemption. The union's acceptance of the status quo by the continuance of the Rozelle Rule in the initial collective bargaining agreements under the circumstances of this case cannot serve to immunize the Rozelle Rule from the scrutiny of the Sherman Act.

ANTITRUST ISSUES

We turn, then, to the question of whether the Rozelle Rule, as implemented, violates s 1 of the Sherman Act, which declares illegal "every contract, combination * * * or conspiracy, in restraint of trade or commerce among the several States." 15 U.S.C. § 1. The district court found the Rozelle Rule to be a per se violation of the Act. Alternatively, the court held the Rule to be violative of the Rule of Reason standard.[8]

* * * *

Per Se Violation

* * * *

The express language of the Sherman Act is broad enough to render illegal nearly every type of agreement between businessmen. The Supreme Court has held, however, that only those agreements which "unreasonably" restrain trade come within the proscription of the Act. *See Northern Pac. R. Co. v. United States,* 356 U.S. 1, 78 S.Ct. 514, 2 L.Ed.2d 545 (1958); *Chicago Board of Trade v. United States,* 246 U.S. 231, 38 S.Ct. 242, 62 L.Ed. 683 (1918); *Standard Oil Co. v. United States,* 221 U.S. 1, 31 S.Ct. 502, 55 L.Ed. 619 (1911). The "Rule of Reason" emerged from these cases.

As the courts gained experience with antitrust problems arising under the Sherman Act, they identified certain types of agreements as being so consistently unreasonable that they may be deemed to be illegal per se, without inquiry into their purported justifications. As the Supreme Court stated in *Northern Pac. R. Co. v. United States, supra,* 356 U.S. at 5, 78 S.Ct. at 518:

> (T)here are certain agreements or practices which because of their pernicious effect on competition and lack of any redeeming virtue are conclusively presumed to be unreasonable and therefore illegal without elaborate inquiry as to the precise harm they have caused or the business excuse for their use.

---

8 It is undisputed that the NFL operates in interstate commerce. It is also recognized that the business of professional football enjoys no special exemption from the antitrust laws. *See Radovich v. National Football League,* 352 U.S. 445, 77 S.Ct. 390, 1 L.Ed.2d 456 (1957).

Among the practices which have been deemed to be so pernicious as to be illegal per se are group boycotts and concerted refusals to deal. [Case Citations Omitted] The term "concerted refusal to deal" has been defined as "an agreement by two or more persons not to do business with other individuals, or to do business with them only on specified terms." *Note, Concerted Refusals to Deal Under the Antitrust Laws,* 71 Harv.L.Rev. 1531 (1958). The term "group boycott" generally connotes "a refusal to deal or an inducement of others not to deal or to have business relations with tradesmen." Kalinowski, supra, 11 U.C.L.A.L.Rev. at 580 n. 49. *See also Worthen Bank & Trust Co. v. National BankAmericard Inc., supra,* 485 F.2d at 124-25.

The district court found that the Rozelle Rule operates to significantly deter clubs from negotiating with and signing free agents. By virtue of the Rozelle Rule, a club will sign a free agent only where it is able to reach an agreement with the player's former team as to compensation, or where it is willing to risk the awarding of unknown compensation by the Commissioner. The court concluded that the Rozelle Rule, as enforced, thus constituted a group boycott and a concerted refusal to deal, and was a per se violation of the Sherman Act.

There is substantial evidence in the record to support the district court's findings as to the effects of the Rozelle Rule. We think, however, that this case presents unusual circumstances rendering it inappropriate to declare the Rozelle Rule illegal per se without undertaking an inquiry into the purported justifications for the Rule.

[T]he line of cases which has given rise to per se illegality for the type of agreements involved here generally concerned agreements between business competitors in the traditional sense. *See generally Worthen Bank & Trust Co. v. National BankAmericard Inc., supra.* Here, however, as the owners and Commissioner urge, the NFL assumes some of the characteristics of a joint venture in that each member club has a stake in the success of the other teams. No one club is interested in driving another team out of business, since if the League fails, no one team can survive. See *United States v. National Football League,* 116 F.Supp. 319, 323 (E.D.Pa.1953). Although businessmen cannot wholly evade the antitrust laws by characterizing their operation as a joint venture, we conclude that the unique nature of the business of professional football renders it inappropriate to mechanically apply per se illegality rules here, fashioned in a different context. This is particularly true where, as here, the alleged restraint does not completely eliminate competition for players' services. ****

In view of the foregoing, we think it more appropriate to test the validity of the Rozelle Rule under the Rule of Reason.

Rule of Reason

The focus of an inquiry under the Rule of Reason is whether the restraint imposed is justified by legitimate business purposes, and is no more restrictive than necessary. *See Chicago Board of Trade v. United States, supra; Worthen Bank & Trust Co. v. National BankAmericard Inc., supra.*

In defining the restraint on competition for players' services, the district court found that the Rozelle Rule significantly deters clubs from negotiating with and signing free agents; that it acts as a substantial deterrent to players playing out their options and becoming free agents; that it significantly decreases players' bargaining power in contract negotiations; that players are thus denied the right to sell their services in a free and open market; that as a result, the salaries paid by each club are lower than if competitive bidding were allowed to prevail; and that absent the Rozelle Rule, there would be increased movement in interstate commerce of players from one club to another.

We find substantial evidence in the record to support these findings. Witnesses for both sides testified that there would be increased player movement absent the Rozelle Rule. Two economists testified that elimination of the Rozelle Rule would lead to a substantial increase in player salaries. Carroll Rosenbloom, owner of the Los Angeles Rams, indicated that the Rams would have signed quite a few of the star players from other teams who had played out their options, absent the Rozelle Rule. Charles De Keado, an agent who represented Dick Gordon after he played out his option with the Chicago Bears, testified that the New Orleans Saints were interested in signing Gordon but did not do so because the Bears were demanding unreasonable compensation and the Saints were unwilling to risk an unknown award of compensation by the Commissioner. Jim McFarland, an end who played out his option with the St. Louis Cardinals, testified that he had endeavored to join the Kansas City Chiefs, but was unable to do so because of the compensation asked by the Cardinals. Hank Stram, then coach and general manager of the Chiefs, stated that he probably would have given McFarland an opportunity to make his squad had he not been required to give St. Louis anything in return.[9]

In support of their contention that the restraints effected by the Rozelle Rule are not unreasonable, the defendants asserted a number of justifications. First, they argued that without the Rozelle Rule, star players would flock to cities having natural advantages such as larger economic bases, winning teams, warmer climates, and greater media opportunities; that competitive balance throughout the League would thus be destroyed; and that the destruction of competitive balance would ultimately lead to diminished spectator interest, franchise failures, and perhaps the demise of the NFL, at least as it operates today. Second, the defendants contended that the Rozelle Rule is necessary to protect the clubs' investment in scouting expenses and player developments costs. Third, they asserted that players must work together for a substantial period of time in order to function effectively as a team; that elimination of the Rozelle Rule would lead to increased player movement and a concomitant reduction in player continuity; and that the quality of play in the NFL would thus suffer, leading to reduced spectator interest, and financial detriment both to the clubs and the players. Conflicting evidence was adduced at trial by both sides with respect to the validity of these asserted justifications.

The district court held the defendants' asserted justifications unavailing. As to the clubs' investment in player development costs, Judge Larson found that these expenses are similar to

---

9 Among other examples which support Judge Larson's findings are:
Marlin Briscoe indicated that he had to sign a three-year contract with Miami even though he would have preferred a single-year contract. He stated that "they would not accept anything less than a three-year contract because of what they would have to give up. . . ." Alan Page testified that the Rozelle Rule was a hindrance to free player movement, but that the principal effect is on players' salaries. Steven Falk, an attorney for Bob Hayes, testified that Dallas told the Redskins that "they (Dallas) were not trading Hayes to anybody within their own division. . . ." William Sullivan president of the Patriots, said he didn't want to sign Joe Kapp, Minnesota's quarterback, and then take a chance on what Minnesota would demand.

those incurred by other businesses, and that there is no right to compensation for this type of investment. With respect to player continuity, the court found that elimination of the Rozelle Rule would affect all teams equally in that regard; that it would not lead to a reduction in the quality of play; and that even assuming that it would, that fact would not justify the Rozelle Rule's anticompetitive effects. As to competitive balance and the consequences which would flow from abolition of the Rozelle Rule, Judge Larson found that the existence of the Rozelle Rule has had no material effect on competitive balance in the NFL. **** In conclusion the court held that the Rozelle Rule was unreasonable in that it was overly broad, unlimited in duration, unaccompanied by procedural safeguards, and employed in conjunction with other anticompetitive practices such as the draft, Standard Player Contract, option clause, and the no-tampering rules.

* * *

We do recognize, as did the district court, that the NFL has a strong and unique interest in maintaining competitive balance among its teams. The key issue is thus whether the Rozelle Rule is essential to the maintenance of competitive balance, and is no more restrictive than necessary. The district court answered both of these questions in the negative.

We need not decide whether a system of inter-team compensation for free agents moving to other teams is essential to the maintenance of competitive balance in the NFL. Even if it is, we agree with the district court's conclusion that the Rozelle Rule is significantly more restrictive than necessary to serve any legitimate purposes it might have in this regard. *** It operates as a perpetual restriction on a player's ability to sell his services in an open market throughout his career. *** [T]he player may be unaware of the precise compensation demanded by his former team, and that other teams might be interested in him but for the degree of compensation sought.[10]

Judge Frank emphasized the harshness of a rule in the field of professional baseball similar to the Rozelle Rule:

As one court, perhaps a bit exaggeratedly, has put it, "While the services of these baseball players are ostensibly secured by voluntary contracts a study of the system as * * * practiced under the plan of the National Agreement, reveals the involuntary character of the servitude which is imposed upon players by the strength of the combination controlling the labor of practically all of the players in the country. * * *" (I)f the players be regarded as quasi-peons, it is of no moment that they are well paid; only the totalitarian-minded will believe that high pay excuses virtual slavery. *Gardella v. Chandler,* 172 F.2d 402, 410 (2nd Cir. 1949).

---

10 The conclusion that the Rozelle Rule constitutes an unreasonable restraint of trade was reached in *Kapp v. National Football League, supra,* even without the prolonged inquiry which has been undertaken in this case. The court stated:

We conclude that such a rule imposing restraint virtually unlimited in time and extent, goes far beyond any possible need for fair protection of the interests of the club-employers or the purposes of the NFL and that it imposes upon the player-employees such undue hardship as to be an unreasonable restraint and such a rule is not susceptible of different inferences concerning its reasonableness; it is unreasonable under any legal test and there is no genuine issue about it to require or justify trial. 390 F.Supp. at 82.

In sum, we hold that the Rozelle Rule, as enforced, unreasonably restrains trade in violation of s 1 of the Sherman Act.

*   *   *

CONCLUSION

In conclusion...we find that...the [nonstatutory labor] exemption cannot be invoked where, as here, the agreement was not the product of bona fide arm's-length negotiations. Thus, the defendants' enforcement of the Rozelle Rule is not exempt from the coverage of the antitrust laws. Although we disagree with the district court's determination that the Rozelle Rule is a per se violation of the antitrust laws, we do find that the Rule, as implemented, contravenes the Rule of Reason and thus constitutes an unreasonable restraint of trade in violation of s 1 of the Sherman Act.

****

With the exception of the district court's finding that implementation of the Rozelle Rule constitutes a per se violation of s 1 of the Sherman Act and except as it is otherwise modified herein, the judgment of the district court is AFFIRMED. The cause is remanded to the district court for further proceedings consistent with this opinion.

Photo reprinted with permission by Topps

1. A five-time Pro Bowl choice and member of two Super Bowl teams (one winner), Mackey was voted the Tight End on the NFL's 50th Anniversary Team in 1969. In Super Bowl V on January 17, 1971, he caught a pass from Johnny Unitas and scored on (at the time) a controversial 75-yard touchdown pass. http://www.youtube.com/watch?v=xrg6rhKq27w The Colts won that game 16-13. In 1992, Mackey became the first pure tight end to be inducted into the Pro Football Hall of Fame.

2. What is the significance of the fact that the court finds "substantial evidence to support the finding that there was no bona fide arm's-length bargaining over the Rozelle Rule"?

3. Explain the difference between the "statutory labor exemption" and the "nonstatutory labor exemption."

4. Explain the significance of collective bargaining agreements and "wages, hours, and other terms and conditions of employment," to the nonstatutory labor exemption.

5. In terms of legal principles, describe the similarities and differences between *Mackey* and *Law v. NCAA*.

6. The past several decades have witnessed numerous power struggles and labor disputes involving work stoppages between the owners and players of the four major professional leagues in North America. Generally speaking, the players' strikes and owners' lockouts have resulted from an inability to reach mutually satisfactory collective bargaining agreements.

   The 1994 MLB players' strike had significant ramifications for the sport. The ensuing seasons experienced an appreciable decline in game attendance and a lack of fan interest. In 1998-99 the NBA experienced an owners' lockout that shortened the season to 50 games instead of 82, and then again as recently as 2011, another owners' lockout shortened the season to 66 games.

   As for the NFL, the 2011 situation was rather complex. The 2011 NFL lockout was pre-empted in 2008 when the NFL owners opted out of the previous Collective Bargaining Agreement (CBA), leaving the 2010 season without a salary cap and setting the expiration of the CBA for March 1, 2011. On the date set for expiry, the players determined it would not be in their best interests to remain unionized if the existence of such a union would serve to allow the NFL to impose anticompetitive restrictions. Thus, the NFLPA decertified as a union. Consequently, the owners imposed a lockout. A group of players, represented mainly by quarterbacks, filed an antitrust lawsuit against the league and asked the court to prevent a lockout by invoking the Sherman Act. The players alleged that the NFL had agreed and conspired to coerce the Players to agree to a new anticompetitive system of player restraints that would economically harm the Players. The Players also claimed that the anticompetitive agreement, the lockout, was aimed at shutting down the entire free agent marketplace. The district court ruled for the owners under the Norris-LaGuardia Act, which prevents federal courts from issuing injunctions during labor disputes to end work stoppages. However, in early July, the 8th Circuit Court of Appeals ruled that even without a union, employees may engage in activities for the purpose of mutual aid and protection. The Court of Appeals allowed the owners and players to settle their differences outside of court. The NFL and the NFLPA agreed to a ten-year collective bargaining agreement on July 25, 2011, ending the NFL's 132-day lockout. *Brady v. NFL,* 779 F. Supp. 2d 992 (2011).

And in 2012, the NHL suffered a similar fate. The Wikipedia entry summarizes the 2012 NHL lockout as follows:

The 2012–13 NHL lockout was a labour dispute that began at 11:59 pm EDT on September 15, 2012. A tentative deal on a new collective bargaining agreement (CBA) was reached on January 6, 2013, with its ratification and signing of a memorandum of understanding on the agreement completed by January 12, 2013, 119 days after the expiry of the previous CBA.[1][2]

The owners of the league's franchises, led by National Hockey League commissioner Gary Bettman, declared a lockout of the members of the National Hockey League Players' Association (NHLPA) after a new agreement could not be reached before the expiry of the NHL collective bargaining agreement on September 16, 2012. The lockout shortened the 2012–13 NHL season, originally scheduled to begin on October 11, 2012, from 82 to 48 games, a reduction of 41.5 percent. The revised season started on January 19, 2013 and ended on April 28, 2013.[3]

At issue for the owners were desires to reduce the players' guaranteed 57% share of hockey-related revenues, introduce term limits on contracts, eliminate salary arbitration, and change free agency rules. The union's initial offers focused on increased revenue sharing between owners and a fixed salary cap that is not linked to league revenues. As the deadline for a work stoppage approached, the union unsuccessfully challenged the league's ability to lock out players of three Canadian teams – the Edmonton Oilers and Calgary Flames (in the jurisdiction of Alberta), and the Montreal Canadiens (in the jurisdiction of Quebec).

The dispute was the third lockout in the 19 years since Bettman became Commissioner in 1993, following player lockouts in 1994–95 and 2004–05, with the latter case leading to the cancellation of the entire season. This was also the third labour dispute for NHLPA executive director Donald Fehr who, as head of the Major League Baseball Players' Association, led his union through a lockout in 1990 and a strike in 1994–95.

During the lockout, many NHL players went to other leagues in North America and Europe. Many businesses in the United States and Canada located near NHL arenas lost money as a result of the games not played. http://en.wikipedia.org/wiki/2012_NHL_lockout

B. FURTHER CONSIDERATIONS

WOOD V. NATIONAL BASKETBALL ASSOCIATION
809 F. 2D 954 (1987)
UNITED STATES COURT OF APPEALS, SECOND CIRCUIT

WINTER, CIRCUIT JUDGE:

O. Leon Wood, an accomplished point-guard from California State University at Fullerton and a member of the gold medal-winning 1984 United States Olympic basketball team, appeals from Judge Carter's dismissal of his antitrust action challenging certain provisions of a collective bargaining agreement between the National Basketball Association ("NBA"), its member-teams, and the National Basketball Players Association ("NBPA"). Wood contends that the "salary cap," [and]...college draft...violate Section 1 of the Sherman Act, 15 U.S.C. § 1 (1982), and are not exempt from the Sherman Act by reason of the non-statutory "labor exemption." We disagree and affirm.

* * * *

The Memorandum [*i.e.,* the Memorandum of Understanding between the NBA and the NBPA dated April 18, 1983, which functionally serves as the operative collective bargaining agreement between them] continued the college draft and free agency/first refusal provisions of the earlier agreements and, like those agreements, included provisions for fringe benefits such as pensions and medical and life insurance. However, the Memorandum also established a minimum for individual salaries and a minimum and maximum for aggregate team salaries. The latter are styled the salary cap provisions, even though they establish a floor as well as a ceiling. Under the salary cap, a team that has reached its maximum allowable team salary may sign a first-round draft choice like Wood only to a one-year contract for $75,000. An integral part of the method by which the floor and ceiling on aggregate team salaries were to be determined was a guarantee that the players would receive 53 percent of the NBA's gross revenues, including new revenues, in salaries and benefits. This combination of fringe benefits, draft, free agency, a floor and a ceiling on aggregate team salaries, and guaranteed revenue sharing was unique in professional sports negotiations.

* * * *

The Philadelphia 76ers drafted Wood in the first round of the 1984 college draft. At the time of the draft, the 76ers' team payroll exceeded the amount permitted under the salary cap. The 76ers therefore tendered to Wood a one-year $75,000 contract, the amount stipulated under the salary cap. This offer was a formality, however, necessary to preserve its exclusive rights to sign him. In fact, the team informed Wood's agent of its intention to adjust its roster so as to enable it to negotiate a long-term contract with Wood for substantially more money. Wood understandably did not sign the proffered contract.

On September 13, 1984, he turned from the basketball court to the district court and sought a preliminary injunction restraining enforcement of the agreement between the NBA and NBPA and compelling teams other than the 76ers to cease their refusal to deal with him except on the terms set out in the collective bargaining agreement and Memorandum.

Judge Carter denied Wood's motion. *Wood v. National Basketball Ass'n,* 602 F.Supp. 525 (S.D.N.Y.1984). He found that both the salary cap and college draft provisions

> affect only the parties to the collective bargaining agreement – the NBA and the players – involve mandatory subjects of bargaining as defined by federal labor laws, and are the result of bona fide arms-length negotiations. Both are proper subjects of concern by the Players Association. As such these provisions come under the protective shield of our national labor policy and are exempt from the reach of the Sherman Act. *Id.* at 528.

* * * *

Meanwhile, Wood signed a contract with the 76ers that provided for $1.02 million in total compensation over a four-year period, including a $135,000 signing bonus. Wood has since been traded.

In January 1986, the parties made an evidentiary submission to Judge Carter for a decision on the merits. This consisted of papers submitted with the motion for a preliminary injunction and a stipulation of additional facts. On February 5, 1986, Judge Carter granted judgment to the defendants. This appeal followed.

DISCUSSION

Plaintiff views the salary cap...[and] college draft...as an agreement among horizontal competitors, the NBA teams, to eliminate competition for the services of college basketball players. As such, he claims, they constitute *per se* violations of Section 1 of the Sherman Act.

**** We may assume for purposes of this decision that the individual NBA teams and not the league are the relevant employers and that Wood would obtain considerably more favorable employment terms were the draft and salary cap eliminated so as to allow him to offer his services to the highest bidder among NBA teams. We may further assume that were these arrangements agreed upon by the NBA teams in the absence of a collective bargaining relationship with a union representing the players, they would be illegal and plaintiff would be entitled to relief.

The draft and salary cap are not, however, the product solely of an agreement among horizontal competitors but are embodied in a collective agreement between an employer or employers and a labor organization reached through procedures mandated by federal labor legislation. ****

Although the combination of the college draft and salary cap may seem unique in collective bargaining (as are the team salary floor and 53 percent revenue sharing agreement), the uniqueness is strictly a matter of appearance. The nature of professional sports as a business and professional sports teams as employers calls for contractual arrangements suited to that unusual commercial context. However, these arrangements result from the same federally mandated processes as do collective agreements in the more familiar industrial context. ***

Federal labor policy… allows employees to seek the best deal for the greatest number by the exercise of collective rather than individual bargaining power. Once an exclusive representative has been selected, the individual employee is forbidden by federal law from negotiating directly with the employer absent the representative's consent, *NLRB v. Allis-Chalmers Mfg. Co.*, 388 U.S. 175, 180, 87 S.Ct. 2001, 2006, 18 L.Ed.2d 1123 (1967), even though that employee may actually receive less compensation under the collective bargain than he or she would through individual negotiations. *J.I. Case Co. v. NLRB*, 321 U.S. 332, 338-39, 64 S.Ct. 576, 580-81, 88 L.Ed. 762 (1944).

The gravamen of Wood's complaint, namely that the NBA-NBPA collective agreement is illegal because it prevents him from achieving his full free market value, is therefore at odds with, and destructive of, federal labor policy.

*   *   *   *

Wood further attacks the draft and salary cap as disadvantaging new employees. However, newcomers in the industrial context routinely find themselves disadvantaged vis-à-vis those already hired. A collective agreement may thus provide that salaries, layoffs, and promotions be governed by seniority, *Ford Motor Co. v. Huffman*, 345 U.S. at 337-39, 73 S.Ct. at 685-87, even though some individuals with less seniority would fare better if allowed to negotiate individually.

Finally, Wood argues that the draft and salary cap are illegal because they affect employees outside the bargaining unit. However, that is also a commonplace consequence of collective agreements. Seniority clauses may thus prevent outsiders from bidding for particular jobs, and other provisions may regulate the allocation or subcontracting of work to other groups of workers. *See Fibreboard Paper Products Corp. v. NLRB*, 379 U.S. 203, 210-15, 85 S.Ct. 398, 402-05, 13 L.Ed.2d 233 (1964). Indeed, the National Labor Relations Act explicitly defines "employee" in a way that includes workers outside the bargaining unit. 29 U.S.C. § 152(3).[1]

If Wood's antitrust claim were to succeed, all of these commonplace arrangements would be subject to similar challenges, and federal labor policy would essentially collapse unless a wholly unprincipled, judge-made exception were created for professional athletes. Employers would have no assurance that they could enter into any collective agreement without exposing themselves to an action for treble damages. ****

---

[1] The definition provides, in pertinent part, that "[t]he term 'employee' shall include any employee, *and shall not be limited to the employees of a particular employer,* unless this subchapter explicitly states otherwise." 29 U.S.C. § 152(3)(emphasis added). *See also Reliance Ins. Cos. v. NLRB*, 415 F.2d 1, 6 (8th Cir.1969) (job applicants are "employees" within meaning of 29 U.S.C. § 152(3)); *Time-O-Matic, Inc. v. NLRB*, 264 F.2d 96, 99 (7th Cir.1959)(same); *John Hancock Mut. Life Ins. Co. v. NLRB*, 191 F.2d 483, 485 (D.C.Cir.1951).

Freedom of contract is particularly important in the context of collective bargaining between professional athletes and their leagues. Such bargaining relationships raise numerous problems with little or no precedent in standard industrial relations. As a result, leagues and player unions may reach seemingly unfamiliar or strange agreements. If courts were to intrude and to outlaw such solutions, leagues and their player unions would have to arrange their affairs in a less efficient way. It would also increase the chances of strikes by reducing the number and quality of possible compromises.

The issues of free agency and entry draft are at the center of collective bargaining in much of the professional sports industry. It is to be expected that the parties will arrive at unique solutions to these problems in the different sports both because sports generally differ from the industrial model and because each sport has its own peculiar economic imperatives. The NBA/NBPA agreement is just such a unique bundle of compromises. The draft and the salary cap reflect the interests of the employers in stabilizing salary costs and spreading talent among the various teams. Minimum individual salaries, fringe benefits, minimum aggregate team salaries, and guaranteed revenue sharing reflect the interests of the union in enhancing standard benefits applicable to all players.

We also agree with the district court that all of the above matters are mandatory subjects of bargaining under 29 U.S.C. § 158(d). Each of them clearly is intimately related to "wages, hours, and other terms and conditions of employment." Indeed, it is precisely because of their direct relationship to wages and conditions of employment that such matters are so controversial and so much the focus of bargaining in professional sports. Wood's claim for damages, for example, is based on an allegation of lost wages. ****

It is true that the combination of the draft and salary cap places new players coming out of college ranks at a disadvantage. However, as noted earlier, that is hardly an unusual feature of collective agreements. In the industrial context salaries, promotions, and layoffs are routinely governed by seniority, with the benefits going to the older employees, the burdens to the newer. ***

Affirmed.

NOTES & QUESTIONS

1. What is the significance of the fact that the NBA salary cap and college draft were all arrived at through the process of collective bargaining?

2. Wood's argument "that the draft and salary cap...affect[ed] employees outside of the bargaining unit" was correct was it not? It did, after all, affect rookies, who, by definition, could not have been involved in the bargaining unit. How, then, does the court explain away the principle articulated in *Mackey* that, in order to be enforceable, this type of horizontal agreement must affect only the parties who were involved in an arm's-length bargaining process?

3. The court discussed "freedom of contract." What is the point that it is trying to make about freedom of contract in this context?

4. Congress enacted the National Labor Relations Act (NLRA) in 1935 as a means to promote industrial harmony in the U.S. by providing for a collective bargaining process between employers and employees. *See* 29 U.S.C. §§ 159-61; www.nlrb.gov/resources/national-labor-relations-act (last visited March 2014)("Congress enacted the [NLRA] to protect the rights of employees and employers, to encourage collective bargaining, and to curtail certain private sector labor and management practices, which can harm the general welfare of workers, business, and the U.S. economy."). Section 7 of the NLRA recognizes the right of employees to "self-organization, to form, join, or assist labor organizations, to bargain collectively through representatives of their own choosing, and to engage in other concerted activities for the purpose of collective bargaining or other mutual aid or protections, and shall also have the right to refrain from any or all of such activities except to the extent that such right may be affected by an agreement requiring membership in a labor organization as a condition of employment as authorized in section 158 (a)(3) . . . ."

It is an unfair labor practice under § 8 (a)(1) of the NLRA for an employer to "interfere with, restrain, or coerce" employees engaged in "concerted activities," as defined in § 7 of the Act. An example of such unfair labor practice can be found in *Elmer Nordstrom, Et. Al, d/b/a Seattle Seahawks v. National Football Players Association,* 292 N.L.R.B. 899 (1989). In that case, the Seattle Seahawks released Sam McCullum after the Seahawks acquired another wide receiver to replace McCullum. McCullum sued the Seahawks, claiming that he was discriminated against because he was the team's union representative. *See* 15 U.S.C. § 8(a)(3) (prohibiting an employer from "discriminat[ing] in regard to hire or tenure of employment . . ." including dismissal, as an unfair labor practice). Prior to his dismissal, McCullum was a staunch defender of players' rights and held a prominent role in union activities leading to the 1982 players' strike. Management became upset with McCullum's critical and public statements regarding the team (*e.g.,* that team doctors released injured players too soon to play) and his orchestration of a "solidarity handshake" by his teammates with members of the opposing team at the first preseason game in 1982. The Seahawks obtained wide receiver Roger Carr and released McCullum before the 1982 training camp ended. In order to prove this unfair labor practice, McCullum was first required to show that his union activities were a motivating factor in the Seahawk's decision to release him. The Seahawks could defend their actions by demonstrating that McCullum would have been released even if he had not engaged in union activities. The Seahawks were unable to show that McCullum would have been replaced by Carr even without McCullum's union-activity. The NLRB thought that McCullum's termination stemmed from anti-union animus as reflected in Seahawks coach Petera's threat to heavily fine McCullum if he went ahead with the handshake. Also, Petera failed to consult with any scouts or position coaches before acquiring Carr. Their assessment of McCullum and other receivers in training camp diminished the need to acquire Carr. The NLRB ultimately found that "antiunion considerations were a motivating factor in . . .

McCullum's release." Do you agree with this *Nordstrom* result? McCullum finally obtained a $250,000 back pay award eleven years later. *See Nordstrom v. NLRB*, 984 F.2d 479 (D.C. Cir. 1993). Retaliation for union activities is often difficult to discern since employers are adept at masking their actions with legitimate business concerns about a player's abilities. Do you think there ought to be a presumption in favor of discriminatory retaliation if someone like McCullum, a player representative – tantamount to a shop steward – is dismissed?

5. A highly publicized case underscored the important role of labor law in amateur sports. Several football players who received grant-in-aid scholarships from Northwestern University claimed they were employees of Northwestern. *See Northwestern University and College Athletes Players Association,* No. 13-RC-121359 at 2 (N.L.R.B. 2014). They formed the College Players Association (CAPA), contending it was a labor organization (union) under the NLRA. *Id.* at 3. In a landmark decision on March 26, 2014, the NLRB Regional Director held they were employees under NLRA § 2(3). The Regional Director rejected Northwestern's argument that they were "primarily students" because scholarship players spend more time per-week on football-related activities than school-related activities and are subject to strict control (*e.g.,* supervision by coaches) all year. *Id.* at 18. He characterized the scholarships as "a transfer of economic value" totaling as much as $76,000 per year and result[ing] in each player receiving total compensation" of more than $250,000 throughout their four or five years of "perform[ing] football duties for the Employer." *Id.* at 14. He described the "tender" – scholarship offer – as a contract detailing the duration and conditions under which the compensation is provided to the players. Non-scholarship athletes or "walk-ons" are not employees because they do not sign a tender. The Regional Director noted that Northwestern's football program generated approximately $235 million in ticket sales, television contracts, merchandise sales, and licensing agreements, during the nine-year period of 2003-12. *Id.* at 18. Less quantifiable in terms of an economic benefit is the team's positive impact on the school's reputation and related increases in alumni giving and applications for admission. The Regional Director ordered an immediate election in which all grant-in-aid players were entitled to vote on whether they desire to be represented by CAPA for collective bargaining purposes. *Id.* at 23.

An election was held on April 24, 2014 but the results were impounded as Northwestern petitioned for review of the director's decision by the full Board. *Northwestern University and College Athletes Players Association (CAPA),* 362 NLRB No. 167 (Aug. 11, 2015). The Board vacated the regional director's ruling "without deciding whether the scholarship players are statutory employees under Section 2(3)." *Id.* at 26. Instead the Board declined to assert jurisdiction in this case because it would "not effectuate the policies of the [NLRA]" in promoting uniformity and stability in labor relations, given the nature of league sports and the NCAA's oversight [that] renders individual team bargaining problematic. . . . *Id.* at 21. Also, "[d]espite the similarities between FBS football and professional sports leagues," all but 17 "of the roughly 125 FBS [schools] are state run institutions. *Id.* at 21. As a result, the Board cannot assert jurisdiction over the vast majority of FBS teams because they are not operated by 'employers' within the meaning of [NLRA] Section 2((2)." *Id.* at 21. [I]n all our past cases involving professional sports, the Board was able to regulate all, or at least most, of the teams in the relevant league or association." *Id.* at 21-22. "[A]sserting jurisdiction in this case would not promote stability in labor relations [since] the Board cannot regulate most FBS teams. *Id.* at 23. The Board nevertheless distinguished football players from "graduate student assistants or student janitors and cafeteria workers." *Id.* at 12. Players are materially different from other kinds of student roles because student athletes receive a scholarship to participate in an extracurricular, voluntary activity. Do you agree with the Regional Director's decision? What are some of the effects that player unionization would have on the NCAA? For example, could the player unions negotiate for greater compensation, fewer and shorter practice sessions, and first-class travel and accommodations for away games? Should scholarship athletes in other sports (e.g., basketball) be entitled to organize in light of the Regional Director's ruling? Do you agree with the Board's decision to decline jurisdiction in this case? Does the Board's decision promote the economic and educational interests of scholarship players? Does the Board's decision enhance consumer welfare by promoting a better quality and less expensive product, namely amateur college football?

6. Student-athletes have argued that they are employees under the Fair Labor Standards Act (FLSA). *See Berger v. Nat'l Collegiate Ass'n.,* 843 F.3d 285 (7th Cir. 2016)(former student athletes unsuccessfully sued Penn, the NCAA and more than 120 other Division I NCAA schools claiming they were employees under FLSA and thus entitled to a minimum wage; the court held that NCAA-regulated sports are 'extracurricular,' 'interscholastic athletic' activities and that the Department of Labor did not intend the FLSA to apply to student-athletes. *Berger,* at 293.). Under FLSA, the plaintiff bears the burden of showing that he or she must perform work for an employer to qualify as an "employee" and if that burden is met, the employer must pay employees a minimum wage. *See Id.* at 290-91; 29 U.S.C.A. § 203(d), e(1), (g). The *Berger* court held the plaintiff's argument did not adequately "take into account [the NCAA's] tradition of amateurism or the reality of the student-athlete experience." *Id.* at 291. "Simply put, student-athletic 'play' is not 'work,' at least as that term is used in FLSA" and are not entitled to a minimum wage. *Id.* 293. *See Dawson, v. NCAA,* 250 F. Supp. 3d. 401 (N.D. Cal. 2017)(finding the *Berger* decision persuasive and dismissing a student-athlete FLSA claim).

7. The NFL's effort to address bullying among players is a prime example of non-adversarial ways in which leagues and players' associations can work together to resolve issues. The controversy surrounding bullying in the NFL began in 2013 when Jonathan Martin, the 6-foot-5-inch starting left tackle for the Miami Dolphins, exited the Dolphins' practice facility and checked himself into a nearby hospital. Martin requested psychological treatment as a result of persistent bullying and harassment from his teammates. The Dolphins asked the NFL to investigate the allegations of misconduct. The league commissioned an independent report in which the NFL, the National Football League Players Association, and the Miami

Dolphins fully cooperated. The report concluded that three starters on the Dolphins offensive line engaged in a pattern of harassment directed at Martin, another offensive lineman, and a member of the training staff. The report does not "tone[] down the racist, sexually explicit, misogynistic or homophobic references." It concluded by stating: "As all must surely recognize, the NFL is not an ordinary workplace. Professional football is a rough, contact sport played by men of exceptional size, speed, strength and athleticism. But even the largest, strongest and fleetest person may be driven to despair by bullying, taunting and constant insults. We encourage the creation of new workplace conduct rules and guidelines that will help ensure that players respect each other as professionals and people." Theodore V. Wells, Jr. et al., Report To The National Football League Concerning Issues Of Workplace Conduct At The Miami Dolphins at 140 (February 14, 2014). Can you think of other examples of non-adversarial collaboration between professional sports leagues and players' associations?

THE CURT FLOOD ACT OF 1998 AND MAJOR LEAGUE BASEBALL'S FEDERAL ANTITRUST EXEMPTION

JOHN T. WOLOHAN

9 MARQ. SPORTS L.J. 347 (1999)

INTRODUCTION

In 1922, Justice Oliver Wendell Holmes writing for the United States Supreme Court held that organized baseball was "purely a state affair," and while money was involved, baseball "would not be called trade or commerce in the commonly accepted use of those words." Since Justice Holmes' decision in *Federal Baseball Club of Baltimore v. National League of Professional Baseball Clubs*, organized baseball has cherished its antitrust exemption and rigorously protected and fought over it in the courts. One of the individuals who challenged baseball's unique legal position was Curt Flood, in *Flood v. Kuhn.* In 1969, Curt Flood was traded from the St. Louis Cardinals to the Philadelphia Phillies, without his knowledge or consent. When informed of the trade, Flood petitioned Bowie Kuhn, the Commissioner of Baseball at the time, requesting that he be declared a free agent. When his request was denied and with help from the Major League Baseball Players Association (MLBPA), Flood filed a federal antitrust lawsuit against Major League Baseball (MLB) claiming that baseball's reserve rule violated federal antitrust law. In 1972, the Supreme Court, for the third time in 50 years, upheld baseball's antitrust exemption even though it acknowledged that "professional baseball is a business and it is engaged in interstate commerce." In holding organized baseball exempt from federal antitrust law, the Supreme Court blindly followed Justice Holmes' decision and held that if there were "any inconsistency or illogic" in the decision it was up to Congress to remedy it, not the Court.

It took twenty-six years, but Congress has finally acted to remedy the inconsistency or illogic in baseball's antitrust exemption. Although too late to help his playing career, Flood may have finally won his victory against MLB when on October 27, 1998, President Bill Clinton signed into law the Curt Flood Act of 1998. The Curt Flood Act, which overturns part of base-ball's 76-year-old antitrust exemption, grants to major league baseball players, for the first time, the same rights under antitrust law as other professional athletes. Congress also hopes that by passing the Curt Flood Act and making the playing field between the owners and players more equal, it will bring some stability to baseball's labor relations.

Although baseball has traditionally fought hard to keep its antitrust exemption, the Curt Flood Act would never have unanimously passed in Congress if it were not for the support and urging it received from both MLB and the Players' Association. In the last Collective Bargaining Agreement (CBA), both MLB and the Players' Association agreed to "jointly request and cooperate in lobbying the Congress to pass a law that will clarify that Major League Baseball Players are covered under the antitrust laws."

* * * *

I. History of Baseball and Federal Antitrust Law

Although the National League began playing professional baseball before Congress passed the Sherman Antitrust Act in 1890, baseball more than any other sport has had to continuously defend itself against antitrust allegations. This section of the paper examines how the courts... historically treated organized baseball under Federal antitrust laws. *** [T]he courts...relied on stare decisis to let stand baseball's antitrust exemption even though the legal theory upon which the original decision was based is no longer valid.

* * * *

B. Baseball Supreme Court Trilogy

The most famous antitrust challenge concerning baseball, and the case that provides it with an antitrust exemption, is the first case in baseball's Supreme Court trilogy, *Federal Baseball*. The Federal League declared its intention to establish itself as a third major league in 1913 and began play in 1914. After two years of direct competition for players and fans, both the Federal League and Major League Baseball were ready to reach some form of settlement. In December of 1915, the leagues entered into a "Peace Agreement" which resulted in the dissolution of the Federal League and all of its constituent clubs. As part of the settlement, the Federal League received $600,000.00, two of its owners were allowed to buy existing major league teams, and the contracts of some Federal League players were sold to the highest bidders among the major league teams.

However, the settlement made no provisions for the Federal League team in Baltimore. With no league to play in and no where to go after the Federal League dissolved, the Baltimore team folded and its owners filed an antitrust suit alleging that organized baseball conspired to monopolize the baseball business in violation of the Sherman Act. The Baltimore franchise claimed that MLB "destroyed the Federal League by buying up some of the constituent clubs and in one way or another inducing all those clubs except the plaintiff to leave their League." A federal district court agreed with Baltimore's argument and awarded them $240,000.00 in treble damages, costs, and attorney fees.

Baltimore's victory was short lived. The District Court's decision was overturned by the Court of Appeals. In reaching its decision, the Court of Appeals, citing *American League Baseball Club of Chicago v. Chase*, 149 N.Y. Supp. 6 (Sup. Ct. 1914) held that baseball was a game and "did not constitute trade or commerce." The Court of Appeals also noted that the giving of exhibitions of baseball "is local in its beginning and in its end" and therefore not interstate.

Disappointed with the Court of Appeals' decision, Baltimore appealed to the United States Supreme Court. The Supreme Court, in upholding the Court of Appeals' decision, also held that the business of baseball was purely a state affair and did not involve interstate commerce within the meaning of the Sherman Antitrust Act. In delivering the Supreme Court's decision, Justice Holmes stated that although "competitions must be arranged between clubs from different cities and States ... the transport is a mere incident, not the essential thing."[1] Justice Holmes also found that "a baseball exhibition, although made for money, is not trade or commerce in the commonly accepted use of those words, since personal effort not related to production is not a subject of commerce."[2]

This decision to exempt baseball from federal antitrust law, would survive repeated challenges for the next seventy-six years until Congress passed the Curt Flood Act. Although not part of baseball's Supreme Court trilogy, the first case after *Federal Baseball* to challenge baseball's antitrust immunity and the one that came closest to overturning it was *Gardella v. Chandler*.[3]

Daniel Gardella was a journeyman baseball player who played baseball for the New York Giants during the 1944 and 45 seasons and was under contract with them for the 1946 season. During the 1946 spring training, with the World War II veterans having returned to the States, Gardella signed a contract to play professional baseball in Mexico. Gardella, a minor league player before the war, did not believe that he had a chance to make the Giants. Upon returning to the United States, Gardella, who only played one year in Mexico, was blacklisted from organized baseball.

The Commissioner of Baseball, Albert B. "Happy" Chandler, in an attempt to avert another war over players' salaries, declared that any player who jumped to the Mexican League would be barred from organized baseball. No longer able to make a living by playing organized baseball professionally, Gardella filed a lawsuit challenging baseball's reserve clause and the Supreme Court's decision in *Federal Baseball*.

The Federal District Court in New York, citing *Federal Baseball*, dismissed the case for failure to state a cause of action and Gardella appealed to the Second Circuit Court. In a 2-1 decision, the Second Circuit ruled that due to the use of radio and television the game of baseball is now interstate commerce. The Second Circuit, noted that the game of baseball and the Supreme Court's expending definition of interstate commerce had changed so much since *Federal Baseball*, decided that there was enough merit in the case to warrant a trial.

---

1 *Federal Baseball*, 259 U.S. at 208.

2 *Id.*

3 *Gardella v. Chandler*, 172 F.2d 402 (2d Cir. 1949), rev'g 79 F. Supp. 260 (S.D.N.Y. 1948).

In rejecting organized baseball's argument that it was exempt from federal antitrust law under *Federal Baseball*, Judge Frank stated that "the Supreme Court's recent decisions have completely destroyed the vitality of *Federal Baseball* ... and have left that case but an impotent zombie."[4] In distinguishing *Gardella* from *Federal Baseball*, the Second Circuit found baseball's reserve clause "shockingly repugnant to moral principles"[5] which "results in something resembling peonage of the baseball player."[6] The Second Circuit also noted that unlike the situation in the *Federal Baseball* case, organized baseball now had "lucratively contracted for the interstate communication, by radio and television, of the playing of the games."[7] Finally, while acknowledging that it could not overturn a Supreme Court decision, the court stated that it was not required to "wait for a formal retraction in the face of changes plainly foreshadowed."[8]

Although remanded back to the district court for trial, the case never made it back to court. A week before the case was scheduled to be heard, organized baseball settled with *Gardella* for $60,000.00. Although organized baseball received a scare in Gardella, the next case, the second in baseball's Supreme Court trilogy, is more indicative of how the courts have treated organized baseball's antitrust immunity. The case, *Toolson v. New York Yankees*,[9] which is actually three cases, reaffirmed that Congress had no intention of including baseball within the scope of federal antitrust law.

In *Toolson*, George Toolson, a minor league player within the Yankee farm system refused to report to the team's Eastern League affiliate after he had been demoted from the

Yankees' International League team. In an attempt to free himself from his contract, Toolson filed an antitrust lawsuit against organized baseball arguing that its reserve clause and farm system denied him the opportunity to improve his livelihood.

Having lost in both the District Court and the Ninth Circuit Court of Appeal, Toolson appealed to the United States Supreme Court. *Toolson*, therefore, was the Supreme Court's first opportunity to correct *Federal Baseball* by including baseball within the scope of federal antitrust law. The Supreme Court, however, in a one page decision, upheld its decision in *Federal Baseball* ruling that Congress had no intention of including the business of baseball within the scope of the federal antitrust laws. In support of this decision, the Supreme Court noted that Congress had thirty years since *Federal Baseball* to bring the business of baseball under the scope of federal antitrust law and that during that time baseball had been allowed to develop with the belief that it was not subject to antitrust law. The Supreme Court concluded that it was the obligation of Congress to bring baseball within the scope of federal antitrust law, not the courts.

---

1   4   *Gardella*, 172 F.2d at 403, 408-9.

2   5   *Id.* at 409.

3   6   *Id.*

4   7   In *Federal Baseball*, the Supreme Court held that the traveling across state lines was but an incidental means of enabling games to be played locally and therefore insufficient to constitute interstate commerce. The Second Circuit, however, found that the interstate communication by radio and television is in no way a means, incidental or otherwise, of performing the intra-state activities and thus constituted interstate commerce. *See id.* at 410.

5   8   "This Court's duty is to divine as best it can, what would be the event of the appeal in the case before it." *Id.* at 409, n. 1.

6   9   *Toolson*, 346 U.S. 356.

The last case in baseball's Supreme Court trilogy was *Flood v. Kuhn*.[10] Curt Flood, an all-star outfielder with the St. Louis Cardinals, was traded to the Philadelphia Phillies in 1969, without Flood's knowledge or consent. When informed of the trade, Flood complained to Commissioner Bowie Kuhn and requested that Kuhn declare him a free agent, thereby allowing him to negotiate with any major league team he wished. When Kuhn denied his request, Flood filed a lawsuit claiming that organized baseball's reserve rule violated federal antitrust law.

In rejecting Flood's lawsuit, the District Court and the Second Circuit Court of Appeals found that *Federal Baseball* and *Toolson* were controlling and felt compelled to uphold them. Flood appealed, and "for the third time in 50 years," the Supreme Court agreed to examine whether organized baseball was within the reach of federal antitrust law.

After an extensive history of the game and some of its players, the Supreme Court held that the "longstanding exemption of professional baseball's reserve system from federal antitrust laws is an established aberration in which Congress has acquiesced, is entitled to [the] benefit of stare decisis, and any inconsistency or illogic is to be remedied by the Congress and not by the Supreme Court." Therefore, the Court held that although baseball enjoyed an exemption from the federal antitrust laws, it was an "aberration" confined to baseball.

The Supreme Court did acknowledge in *Flood* that baseball was a trade or commerce engaged in interstate commerce, but it still refused to overturn baseball's antitrust exemption. In support of its decision, the Supreme Court noted that "baseball with full and continuing congressional awareness, has been allowed to develop and to expand unhindered by federal legislative action." The Court reasoned that since Congress had failed to revoke baseball's antitrust exemption, Congress must have intended for baseball to be outside the reach of the antitrust laws.

[T]he Supreme Court's decision was not unanimous. In his dissent, Justice Douglas held that if the Supreme Court were to consider the question of baseball for the first time upon a clean slate, there would be no doubt that the Court would hold baseball subject to federal antitrust regulation.[11] As for the failure of Congress to pass legislation overruling *Federal Baseball* and subjecting baseball to federal antitrust laws, Justice Douglas argued that "the unbroken silence of Congress should not prevent us from correcting our own mistakes." If in making its decision the Court was to rely upon congressional inaction, Justice Douglas noted that Congress also failed to pass any legislation exempting professional sports from antitrust regulation.

II. The Curt Flood Act of 1998

As mentioned in the introduction, as part of the 1997 Basic Agreement between MLB and the MLBPA both sides agreed that they would jointly request and lobby for the passage of a law clarifying that professional baseball players are covered under antitrust law. The result of this joint effort is the Curt Flood Act.

---

10   *Flood*, 407 U.S. 258.

11   *Flood*, 407 U.S. at 289.

An important aspect of the Curt Flood Act, which amends the Clayton Act by adding a new section at the end, is that it only applies to Major League Baseball players. Therefore any antitrust issues covering minor league baseball, the amateur draft, the relationship between the major leagues and the minors, franchise relocation, intellectual property, the Sports Broadcasting Act, and umpires are specifically excluded from coverage under the Curt Flood Act.

*　*　*　*

[S]ix sections of the Act specifically identify areas excluded from coverage under the Act. The first two sections, §§ 27 (b)(1) and (2), are designed to protect the relationship between Major League Baseball and the minor leagues. ***

[I]t was important for the Senate Judiciary Committee to accommodate the concerns of the minor leagues, and these sections accomplish this goal by "direct[ing] a court's attention to only those practices, or aspects of practices, that affect major league players." *** Therefore, as long as a player is in the minor leagues, the Curt Flood Act will not apply to them or their relationship with their minor league team and league.

After addressing the minor league issue, the next area excluded from coverage is franchise expansion, relocation, or ownership issues. ***

Section 27 (b)(3), makes it clear that the conduct, acts, practices, or agreements relating to or affecting franchise expansion, location or relocation, franchise ownership issues, including ownership transfers are specifically excluded from coverage under the Act. ****

The fourth area excluded from coverage under the Curt Flood Act is the Sports Broadcasting Act of 1961. The Sports Broadcasting Act of 1961 exempts professional football, baseball, basketball, and hockey leagues from antitrust laws in the area of network TV contracts.[12] *** After hearing from each of the professional sports leagues, Congress passed the Sports Broadcast Act, thereby allowing professional sports leagues to pool and sell television rights as a package.

The fifth area excluded from coverage under the Act is the relationship between organized baseball and umpires. Although Major League Umpires have their own union and their

---

[12] Before the passage of the Sports Broadcast Act of 1961, professional sports teams sold the television rights of their games individually. In 1960, the American Football League (AFL) negotiated a four-year television contract for the rights to the entire league with ABC for $1.7 million per year. The AFL's deal was unique in that for the first time an entire professional sports league pooled its television rights and sold them to a single network. The NFL fearing that the deal would provide the AFL with a competitive advantage also sought to pool its television rights. The NFL however was barred from pooling its television rights by the court in *United States v. National Football League*, 196 F. Supp. 445 (E.D. Pa. 1961). Believing that the NFL was at a competitive disadvantage, Pete Rozelle, the NFL Commissioner, approached Congress seeking special legislation, which would allow the league to pool its members' television rights. After hearing from Rozelle and the heads of the other professional sports leagues, Congress passed the Sports Broadcast Act of 1961. The Act exempts professional sports leagues from antitrust litigation in the limited area of pooling and selling the league's television rights as a package. The Act also restricts the ability of the leagues to define the geographical area into which the pooled telecasts may be broadcast. For more information on the Sports Broadcasting Act of 1961 See David S. Neft & Richard M. Cohen, THE FOOTBALL ENCYCLOPEDIA: THE COMPLETE HISTORY OF PROFESSIONAL NFL FOOTBALL FROM 1892 TO THE PRESENT (1991); Gary R. Roberts, *Pirating Satellite Signals of Blacked-Out Sports Events: A Historical and Policy Perspective*, 11 COLUMBIA--VLA JOURNAL OF LAW & THE ARTS, 363-386 (1987); Robert A. Garrett & Philip R. Hochberg, *Sports Broadcasting and the Law*, 59 INDIANA LAW JOURNAL, 155-192 (1984); and John T. Wolohan, *NFL Broadcasts and the Home System Defense of the Federal Copyright Act*, 5, JOURNAL OF LEGAL ASPECTS OF SPORT 35 (1995).

relationship with baseball has been almost as combative as that of the players, umpires are excluded from coverage under the Curt Flood Act. ***

The last area specifically excluded from coverage under the Curt Flood Act is all persons not in the business of organized professional major league baseball. *** Congress failed to include an important group under coverage of the Curt Flood Act - Individual, partnerships, corporations, trusts, or unincorporated associations who are attempting to purchase Major League Baseball teams.

After identifying what type of conduct, acts and practices are specifically excluded from coverage under the Curt Flood Act, Section 27 (c) states that only major league baseball players have standing to sue Major League Baseball under the Act. This limitation of standing seems to be directed at depriving the Justice Department, which opposed the Curt Flood Act, and the Federal Trade Commission the ability to sue Major League Baseball over player restraints.

*   *   *

The final section of note is § 27 (d)(4), which states that:

Nothing in this section shall be construed to affect the application to organized professional baseball of the nonstatutory labor exemption from antitrust laws.

*   *   *   *

Conclusion

To determine the importance of the Curt Flood Act, we must first determine what the current status of organized baseball's antitrust exemption is after the passage of the Act. Odd as it may sound, by passing the Curt Flood Act, Congress may have actually saved baseball's antitrust exemption. After the Supreme Court's decision in *Flood,* there was a trend among some courts to limit baseball's antitrust exemption to the reserve system only. *** In...these cases, the courts interpreted the Supreme Court's decision in *Flood* as placing limits on baseball's antitrust exemption, narrowly applying the exemption only to baseball's player reserve system.

Still, not every court interpreted *Flood* as placing limits on baseball's antitrust exemption. [Other] courts, for example, upheld an industry wide antitrust exemption when they held that until Congress acted to limit baseball's antitrust exemption, the exemption encompassed the entire business of baseball.

With the passage of the Curt Flood Act, baseball can now argue that Congress has acted. As discussed above, the Act is specifically designed to repeal baseball's antitrust exemption as it applies to Major League Baseball players. A reasonable interpretation of Congress' decision to only include Major League Baseball players, therefore would be that Congress did not want the entire business of baseball to be covered under a blanket antitrust exemption. Congress could have included minor league baseball, the amateur draft, the relationship between the major leagues and the minors, franchise relocation, intellectual property, the Sports Broadcasting Act, umpires or any other area it wanted in the Curt Flood Act, but it specifically excluded them.

It only stands to reason, therefore, that Congress in its actions, by failing to include the entire business of baseball in the Curt Flood Act, wanted everything not having to do with player relations exempt from antitrust laws.

If you accept this interpretation of the Curt Flood Act, the argument... that baseball's antitrust exemption is just limited to the reserve system, no longer ha[s] any value. Therefore, the Act, instead of weakening baseball's antitrust exemption, actually makes it stronger.

NOTES & QUESTIONS

1. In the famous *Federal Baseball* decision, what was the court's basis for holding that Major League Baseball was not involved in interstate commerce?

2. Had the *Gardella* case been appealed to the U.S. Supreme Court rather than settled, do you think that the Supreme Court might have affirmed the Second Circuit's opinion? If so why? If not why not?

3. In *Toolson* and in *Flood* the Supreme Court held that Congress, not the judiciary, has the authority to determine whether baseball ought to be exempt from antitrust. What criteria should be considered in determining whether such issues ought to be resolved by the legislative or the judicial branch? In his dissent in *Flood,* Justice Douglas argued that the Supreme Court ought to have the authority to correct its own mistakes. What's wrong, if anything, with that logic?

4. Do you think that Wolohan is right? Has the Curt Flood Act actually strengthened Major League Baseball's position by preserving certain aspects of the antitrust exemption? Explain your answer. See note 6 below for summaries of recent relevant cases.

5. Congress specifically stated that the Curt Flood Act did not apply to certain activities of Major League Baseball (MLB), such as operating a minor league system and controlling franchise relocations. After *American Needle,* should baseball be concerned about retaining its exemption in the areas not covered under the Curt Flood Act? Keep in mind, *American Needle* was the "first time in 26 years [that] the Court . . . addressed the scope of Section One and the delineation between concerted and independent conduct." Nathanial Grow, *American Needle and the Future of the Single Entity Defense Under Section One of the Sherman Act,* 48 Am. Bus. L.J. 449, 454-55 (2011). Can *American Needle* be interpreted as a signal of the Court's willingness to address antitrust issues in professional sports? What pro-competitive arguments would you expect the MLB to advance in retaining its antitrust exemption? What anti-competitive arguments would you expect opponents of the exemption to raise?

6. Recent cases suggest that courts are narrowly construing the Curt Flood Act. Here are a few examples. 1) *City of San Jose v. Off. of Commr. of Baseball,* C-13-02787 RMW, 2013 WL

5609346, at *1 (N.D. Cal. Oct. 11, 2013), *aff'd sub nom. City of San Jose v. Off. of the Com'r of Baseball,* 776 F.3d 686 (9th Cir. 2015). Characterizing the MLB antitrust exemption as "unrealistic, inconsistent, and illogical," the district court nevertheless held that the antitrust exemption applies generally to the business of baseball. Affirmed on appeal, the Ninth Circuit determined that *the* MLB antitrust exemption after the Curt Flood Act applies to franchise relocation. 2) *Miranda v. Selig,* 860 F.3d 1237 (9th Cir. 2017), *cert. denied,* 138 S. Ct. 507 (2017), *reh'g denied,* 138 S. Ct. 1045 (2018). Payment restrictions applicable to minor league players come within the antitrust exemption still in place after the Curt Flood Act. Affirmed on appeal by the Ninth Circuit in *Miranda v. Selig.* 860 F.3d 1237 (9th Cir. 2017)(The Curt Flood Act expressly exempts "anything related to the employment of minor league baseball players," and thus defendants cannot be subject to antitrust liability for activities related to minor league baseball. 3) *Wyckoff v. Off. of the Commr. of Baseball,* 211 F. Supp. 3d 615 (S.D.N.Y. 2016), *aff'd sub nom. Wyckoff v. Off. of Commr. of Baseball,* 705 Fed. Appx. 26 (2d Cir. 2017)(unpublished). Upholding MLB's position that its antitrust exemption relates to scouts.

7. In their book, Baseball and the Law: Cases and Materials, Louis Schiff and Robert Jarvis include nicely edited versions (along with informative notes) of *Federal Baseball, Toolson,* and *Flood.* Louis H. Schiff and Robert M. Jarvis, Baseball and the Law: Cases and Materials 50-77 (2016).

15 UNITED STATES CODE § 2

§ 2. Monopolizing trade a felony; penalty

Every person who shall monopolize, or attempt to monopolize, or combine or conspire with any other person or persons, to monopolize any part of the trade or commerce among the several States, or with foreign nations, shall be deemed guilty of a felony, and, on conviction thereof, shall be punished by fine not exceeding $100,000,000 if a corporation, or, if any other person, $1,000,000, or by imprisonment not exceeding 10 years, or by both said punishments, in the discretion of the court.

NOTES & QUESTIONS

1. In the 1960's when the American Football League challenged the National Football League in terms of popularity, it also challenged the NFL in court, arguing that the NFL's monopoly had run afoul of Sherman section 2. *See AFL v. NFL,* 323 F. 2d 124 (4th Cir. 1963). In the 1980's the United States Football League made similar arguments against the NFL. *See USFL v. NFL,* 842 F.2d. 1335 (2d Cir. 1988). The USFL filed suit alleging violations of the Sherman Antitrust Act. The jury of the lower court awarded plaintiffs one dollar in damages after finding that defendants had willfully acquired or maintained monopoly power in a market consisting

of major league professional football in the U.S. and that such monopolization had injured plaintiffs. On appeal, the lower court's verdict was affirmed. The anti-competitive activities on which the jury based its verdict did not justify a large damages verdict or sweeping injunctive relief. What types of conduct by the NFL might have been considered violative of the Sherman Act, section 2?

Further Reading on Antitrust and Labor Law

Charlotte S. Alexander & Nathaniel Grow, *Gaming the System: The Exemption of Professional Sports Teams from the Fair Labor Standards Act*, 49 U. Cal. Davis L. Rev. 123 (2015).

Sean W.L. Alford, *Dusting off the AK-47: An Examination of the NFL Players' Most Powerful Weapon in an Antitrust Lawsuit Against the NFL*, 88 N.C. L. Rev. 212 (2009).

Thomas A. Baker III, J.D., Ph.D. et. al., *Debunking the NCAA's Myth That Amateurism Conforms with Antitrust Law: A Legal and Statistical Analysis*, 85 Tenn. L. Rev. 661 (2018).

Thomas A. Baker III & Natasha T. Brison, *From Board of Regents to O'bannon: How Antitrust and Media Rights Have Influenced College Football*, 26 Marq. Sports L. Rev. 331 (2016).

William W. Barry III, *Employee-Athletes, Antitrust, and the Future of College Sports*, 28 Stanf. L. & Pol'y Rev. 245 (2017).

Alexandra Baumann, *Play Ball: What Can Be Done to Prevent Strikes and Lockouts in Professional Sports and Keep the Stadium Lights on*, 32 J. Nat'l Ass'n Admin. L. Judiciary 251, 253 (2012).

Joy Blanchard, *Flag on the Play: A Review of Antitrust Challenges to the NCAA. Could the New College Football Playoff Be Next?*, 15 Va. Sports & Ent. L.J. 1 (2015).

Timothy S. Bolen, *Singled Out: Application and Defense of Antitrust Law and Single Entity Status to Non-Team Sports*, 15 Suffolk J. Trial & App. Advoc. 80 (2010).

Kevin W. Brooks, *"Physically Ready to Compete": Can Players' Unions Bar Potential Draftees Based on Their Age?*, 21 Sports Law. J. 89 (2014).

Michael A. Carrier, *How Not to Apply the Rule of Reason: The O'bannon Case*, 114 Mich. L. Rev. First Impressions 73 (2015).

Walter T. Champion, Jr., *"Mixed Metaphors," Revisionist History and Post-Hypnotic Suggestions on the Interpretation of Sports Antitrust Exemptions: The Second Circuit's Use in Clarett of a Piazza-Like "Innovative Reinterpretation of Supreme Court Dogma*, 20 Marq. Sports L. Rev. 55 (2009).

Walter T. Champion, Jr., *The Second Circuit Takes a Look at the Non-Statutory Labor Exemption in Professional Sports: A Review of Wood v. National Basketball Association, Caldwell v. American Basketball Association, National Basketball Association. Williams, and Clarett v. National Football League*, 27 Hofstra Lab. & Emp. L.J. 83 (2009).

Christine Colwell, *Playing for Pay or Playing to Pay: Student-Athletes as Employees under the Fair Labor Standards Act*, 79 La. L. Rev. 899 (2019).

Christopher L. Cook, *American Needle, Inc. v. National Football League and Its Effect on Professional Sports*, 12 J. Bus. & Tech. L. 297 (2017).

Jason J.Cruz, *Rethinking the Use of Antitrust Law in Combat Sports*, 28 J. Legal Aspects Sport 63 (2018).

Ross E. Davies, *Along Comes the Players Association: The Roots and Rise of Organized Labor in Major League Baseball*, 16 N.Y.U. J. Legis. & Pub. Policy 321 (2013).

James R. Devine, *Baseball's Labor Wars in Historical Context*, 5 Marq. Sports L.J. 1 (1994).

Marc Edelman, *Are Commissioner Suspensions Really Different From Illegal Group Boycotts? Analyzing Whether the NFL Personal Conduct Policy Illegally Restrains Trade*, 58 Cath. U. L. Rev. 631 (2009).

Marc Edelman, *How Antitrust Law Could Reform College Football: Section 1 of the Sherman Act and the Hope for Tangible Change*, 68 Rutgers U.L. Rev. 809 (2016).

Marc Edelman, *In Defense of Sports Antitrust Law: A Response to Law Review Articles Calling for the Administrative Regulation of Commercial Sports*, 72 Wash. & Lee L. Rev. Online 210 (2015).

Marc Edelman, *A Short Treatise on Amateurism and Antitrust Law: Why the NCAA's No-Pay Rules Violate Section 1 of the Sherman Act*, 64 Case W. Res. L. Rev. 61 (2013).

Matthew C. Garner, *Time to Move On? Franchise Relocation in MLS, Antitrust Implications... And the Hope that FIFA is Not Watching*, 16 Sports Law. J. 159 (2009).

Lee Goldman, *Sports, Antitrust, and the Single Entity Theory*, 63 Tul. L. Rev. 751 (1989).

Nathaniel Grow, *The Curiously Confounding Curt Flood Act*, 90 Tul. L. Rev. 859 (2016).

Jill S. Harris, *The Demand For Student-Athlete Labor and the Supply of Violations in the NCAA*, 26 Marq. Sports L. Rev. 41 (2016).

Daniel E. Lazaroff, *The Antitrust Implications of Franchise Relocation Restrictions in Professional Sports*, 53 Fordham L. Rev. 157 (1984).

M. Scott LeBlanc, *American Needle, Inc. v. NFL: Professional Sports Leagues and "Single-Entity Antitrust Exemption*, 5 Duke J. Const. L. & Pub. Pol'y Sidebar 148 (2010).

Michael Lydakis, *Andrew Zapata, Tackling the Issues: The History of the National Football League's 2011 Collective Bargaining Agreement and What It Means for the Future of the Sport*, 10 Willamette Sports L.J. 17 (2012).

Michael A. McCann, *American Needle v. NFL: An Opportunity to Reshape Sports Law*, 119 Yale L.J. 726 (2010).

Robert A. McCormick, *Professional Football's Draft Eligibility Rule: The Labor Exemption and the Antitrust Laws*, 33 Emory L.J. 375 (1984).

Theodore McDowell, *Changing the Game: Remedying the Deficiencies of Baseball's Antitrust Exemption in the Minor Leagues*, 9 Harv. J. Sports & Ent. L. 1 (2018).

Marvin Miller, *Remarks: Reflections on Baseball and the Mlbpa*, 16 N.Y.U. J. Legis. & Pub. Policy 352 (2013).

Matthew J. Mitten, *University Price Competition For Elite Students and Athletes: Illusions and Realities*, 36 S. Texas L. Rev. 59 (1995).

Peter R. Morrison, *Shutting Down the Offense: Why the Supreme Court Should Designate the NFL a Single Entity for Antitrust Purposes*, 3 J. Bus. Entrepreneurship & L. 97 (2009).

Sheldon D. Pollack & Daniel V. Johns, *Northwestern Football Players Throw A "Hail Mary" but the National Labor Relations Board Punts: Struggling to Apply Federal Labor Law in the Academy*, 15 Va. Sports & Ent. L.J. 77 (2015).

Christopher Pruitt, *Debunking a Popular Antitrust Myth: The Single Entity Rule and Why College Football's Bowl Championship Series Does Not Violate the Sherman Antitrust Act*, 11 Tex. Rev. Ent. & Sports L. 125 (2009).

Michael J. Redding, Daniel R. Peterson, *Third and Long: The Issues Facing the NFL Collective Bargaining Agreement Negotiations and the Effects of an Uncapped Year*, 20 Marq. Sports L. Rev. 95 (2009).

Gary Roberts, *On the Scope and Effect of Baseball's Antitrust Exclusion*, 4 Seton Hall J. Sport L. 321 (1994).

Geoffrey J. Rosenthal, *College Play and the FLSA: Why Student-Athletes Should be Classified as "Employees" Under the Fair Labor Standards Act*, 36 Hofstra Lab. & Em. L. J. 133 (2017).

Stephen F. Ross, *Antitrust Options to Redress Anticompetitive Restraints and Monopolistic Practices by Professional Sports Leagues*, 52 Case W. Res. L. Rev. 133 (2001).

Stephen F. Ross, *Monopoly Sports Leagues*, 73 Minn. L. Rev. 643 (1989).

Stephen F. Ross, *Open Competition in League Sports*, 2002 Wis. L. Rev. 49 (2002).

Stephen F. Ross, *The Misunderstood Alliance Between Sports Fans, Players and the Antitrust Laws*, 1997 U. Ill. L. Rev. 519 (1997).

John P. Sahl, *College Athletes and Due Process Protection*, 21 Ariz. St. L. J. 621 (1989).

Louis H. Schiff and Robert M. Jarvis, *Baseball and the Law: Cases and Materials 50-77 (2016).*

Steven Semeraro, *Is the National Football League a "Single Entity" Incapable of Conspiring Under the Sherman Act? The Supreme Court Will Decide*, 32 T. Jefferson L. Rev. 1 (2009).

Christopher Smith, *A Necessary Game Changer: Resolving the Legal Quagmire Surrounding Expiration of the Nonstatutory Labor Exemption in Sports*, 14 U. Pa. J. Bus. L. 1191 (2012).

Cyntrice Thomas et. al., *The Treatment of Non-Team Sports Under Section One of the Sherman Act*, 12 Va. Sports & Ent. L.J. 296 (2013).

John C. Weistart, *League Control of Market Opportunities: A Perspective on Competition and Cooperation in the Sports Industry*, 1984 Duke L.J. 1013 (1984).

John C. Weistart & Cym H. Lowell, Law of Sports, Chapter 5 (Bobbs-Merrill Company, Inc., 1979).

Alexander C. Krueger-Wyman, *Collective Bargaining and the Best Interests of Basketball*, 12 Va. Sports & Ent. L.J. 171 (2012).

CHAPTER 7
SOME CONSTITUTIONAL LAW CONCERNS

These cases illustrate a number of Constitutional issues that frequently arise in Sports Law. As a rule, the cases require application of fairly elementary Constitutional Law. Plaintiffs typically argue that a right guaranteed either by the federal or a state constitution has been violated. Two issues that often arise are: 1) whether a person's right to exercise speech or religion freely has been violated (First Amendment), and 2) whether a person's liberty or property has been taken without due process of law (Fourteenth Amendment). As such, courts must determine whether state action was involved.

Courts must also determine what level of "scrutiny" will be applied: rational basis; middle tier; or, strict scrutiny. There are three basic rules that one must keep in mind when analyzing cases such as these. First, as a rule, when a state law affects a fundamental right (such as freedom of religion or speech, protected by the First Amendment), in order to be held constitutional, courts say that the rule must be designed to promote a **compelling governmental objective** *and* it must be **narrowly drafted** (by the **least restrictive means**) in a fashion to achieve that compelling governmental objective (**strict scrutiny**). Second, if a state law affects a "suspect class," courts say that, in order to be held constitutional, the rule must be designed to promote an **important governmental objective** *and* it must be **closely drafted** in a fashion to achieve that important governmental objective (**middle tier**). Third, in all cases where the state law at issue does not affect either a fundamental right or a suspect class, courts say that, in order to held constitutional, the challenged law must be designed merely to promote a **legitimate governmental objective** *and* it must be **rationally related** to achieving that legitimate governmental objective (**rational basis**).

Brentwood Academy analyzes the state action requirement as it applies to the 14th Amendment. *Spring Branch* is a case construing the Texas State Constitution and its guarantees of equal protection and due process. *James*, like *Spring Branch*, considers the issue of whether a high school student's participation in extracurricular sports activities should be deemed a constitutionally protectable "property interest." *Jordan* also looks at this same issue, but does so in the emotionally-charged context of teenage alcohol consumption, school discipline, and the scholarship opportunities of a high school football player. *Vernonia* examines the Fourth and Fourteenth Amendment claims of a seventh grader who was denied permission to play football because his parents refused to sign a drug testing consent form. The Court discusses the special role of athletes in the school setting and their related privacy concerns.

In *Hart*, we see First Amendment concerns raised in the context of video games that use the likeness of professional and college athletes. Courts have to balance the public's interest in free expression guaranteed by the First Amendment against the athlete's right of publicity.

Chapter 11, titled "Intellectual Property," will further discuss issues related to an athlete's right of publicity.

As you read these cases, you may find it helpful to consider the following two constitutional amendments and 42 USC ("United States Code") § 1983. Plaintiffs routinely invoke 42 USC § 1983, which provides a cause of action for rights secured by the Constitution. Plaintiffs often plead a violation of this federal statute in an effort to secure redress for violations of civil rights.

First Amendment

Congress shall make no law respecting an establishment of religion, or prohibiting the free exercise thereof; or abridging the freedom of speech, or of the press; or the right of the people peaceably to assemble, and to petition the government for a redress of grievances.

Fourteenth Amendment (pertinent part)

No state shall make or enforce any law which shall abridge the privileges or immunities of citizens of the United States; nor shall any state deprive any person of life, liberty, or property, without due process of law; nor deny to any person within its jurisdiction the equal protection of the law.

42 USC § 1983

Every person who, under color of any statute, ordinance, regulation, custom, or usage, of any State or Territory or the District of Columbia, subjects, or causes to be subjected, any citizen of the United States or other person within the jurisdiction thereof to the deprivation of any rights, privileges, or immunities secured by the Constitution and laws, shall be liable to the party injured in an action at law, suit in equity, or other proper proceeding for redress, except that in any action brought against a judicial officer for an act or omission taken in such officer's judicial capacity, injunctive relief shall not be granted unless a declaratory decree was violated or declaratory relief was unavailable. For the purposes of this section, any Act of Congress applicable exclusively to the District of Columbia shall be considered to be a statute of the District of Columbia.

BRENTWOOD ACADEMY V. TENNESSEE SECONDARY SCHOOL ATHLETIC ASSOCIATION

531 US 288 (2001)

SUPREME COURT OF THE UNITED STATES

JUSTICE SOUTER DELIVERED THE OPINION OF THE COURT.

The issue is whether a statewide association incorporated to regulate interscholastic athletic competition among public and private secondary schools may be regarded as engaging in state action when it enforces a rule against a member school. The association in question here includes most public schools located within the State, acts through their representatives, draws its officers from them, is largely funded by their dues and income received in their stead, and has historically been seen to regulate in lieu of the State Board of Education's exercise of its own authority. We hold that the association's regulatory activity may and should be treated as state action owing to the pervasive entwinement of state school officials in the structure of the association, there being no offsetting reason to see the association's acts in any other way.

I.

Respondent Tennessee Secondary School Athletic Association (Association) is a not-for-profit membership corporation organized to regulate interscholastic sport among the public and private high schools in Tennessee that belong to it. No school is forced to join, but without any other authority actually regulating interscholastic athletics, it enjoys the memberships of almost all the State's public high schools (some 290 of them or 84% of the Association's voting membership), far outnumbering the 55 private schools that belong. A member school's team may play or scrimmage only against the team of another member, absent a dispensation.

The Association's rulemaking arm is its legislative council, while its board of control tends to administration. The voting membership of each of these nine-person committees is limited under the Association's bylaws to high school principals, assistant principals, and superintendents elected by the member schools, and the public school administrators who so serve typically attend meetings during regular school hours. Although the Association's staff members are not paid by the State, they are eligible to join the State's public retirement system for its employees. Member schools pay dues to the Association, though the bulk of its revenue is gate receipts at member teams' football and basketball tournaments, many of them held in public arenas rented by the Association.

The constitution, bylaws, and rules of the Association set standards of school membership and the eligibility of students to play in interscholastic games. Each school, for example, is regulated in awarding financial aid, most coaches must have a Tennessee state teaching license, and players must meet minimum academic standards and hew to limits on student employment. ***

Ever since the Association was incorporated in 1925, Tennessee's State Board of Education (State Board), has (to use its own words), acknowledged the corporation's functions "in providing standards, rules and regulations for interscholastic competition in the public schools of Tennessee." More recently, the State Board cited its statutory authority, Tenn.Code Ann. § 49-1-302 (1996), when it adopted language expressing the relationship between the Association and the State Board. Specifically, in 1972, it went so far as to adopt a rule expressly "designat[ing]" the Association as "the organization to supervise and regulate the athletic activities in which the public junior and senior high schools in Tennessee participate on an interscholastic basis." Tennessee State Board of Education, Administrative Rules and Regulations, Rule 0520-1-2-.26 (1972) (later moved to Rule 0520-1-2-.08). ****

The action before us responds to a 1997 regulatory enforcement proceeding brought against petitioner, Brentwood Academy, a private parochial high school member of the Association. The Association's board of control found that Brentwood violated a rule prohibiting "undue influence" in recruiting athletes, when it wrote to incoming students and their parents about spring football practice. The Association accordingly placed Brentwood's athletic program on probation for four years, declared its football and boys' basketball teams ineligible to compete in playoffs for two years, and imposed a $3,000 fine. When these penalties were imposed, all the voting members of the board of control and legislative council were public school administrators.

Brentwood sued the Association and its executive director in federal court under Rev. Stat. § 1979, 42 U.S.C. § 1983, claiming that enforcement of the Rule was state action and a violation of the First and Fourteenth Amendments. The District Court entered summary judgment for Brentwood and enjoined the Association from enforcing the Rule. *Brentwood Academy v. Tennessee Secondary Schools Athletic Association,* 13 F.Supp.2d 670 (M.D.Tenn.1998). In holding the Association to be a state actor under § 1983 and the Fourteenth Amendment, the District Court found that the State had delegated authority over high school athletics to the Association, characterized the relationship between the Association and its public school members as symbiotic, and emphasized the predominantly public character of the Association's membership and leadership. The court relied on language in *National Collegiate Athletic Assn. v. Tarkanian,* 488 U.S. 179, 193, n. 13, 109 S.Ct. 454, 102 L.Ed.2d 469 (1988), suggesting that statewide interscholastic athletic associations are state actors, and on other federal cases in which such organizations had uniformly been held to be acting under color of state law.

The United States Court of Appeals for the Sixth Circuit reversed. 180 F.3d 758 (1999). *** It said the District Court was mistaken in seeing a symbiotic relationship between the State and the Association, it emphasized that the Association was neither engaging in a traditional and exclusive public function nor responding to state compulsion, and it gave short shrift to the language from *Tarkanian* on which the District Court relied. ***

We granted certiorari, 528 U.S. 1153, 120 S.Ct. 1156, 145 L.Ed.2d 1069 (2000), to resolve the conflict[1] and now reverse.

II.

A.

[1][2] Our cases try to plot a line between state action subject to Fourteenth Amendment scrutiny and private conduct (however exceptionable) that is not. *Tarkanian, supra,* at 191, 109 S.Ct. 454; *Jackson v. Metropolitan Edison Co.,* 419 U.S. 345, 349, 95 S.Ct. 449, 42 L.Ed.2d 477 (1974). *** If the Fourteenth Amendment is not to be displaced...its ambit cannot be a simple line between States and people operating outside formally governmental organizations, and the deed of an ostensibly private organization or individual is to be treated sometimes as if a State

---

1   A number of other courts have held statewide athletic associations to be state actors. *Griffin High School v. Illinois High School Assn.,* 822 F.2d 671, 674 (C.A.7 1987); *Clark v. Arizona Interscholastic Assn.,* 695 F.2d 1126, 1128 (C.A.9 1982), cert. denied, 464 U.S. 818, 104 S.Ct. 79, 78 L.Ed.2d 90 (1983); *In re United States ex rel. Missouri State High School Activities Assn.,* 682 F.2d 147, 151 (C.A.8 1982); *Louisiana High School Athletic Assn. v. St. Augustine High School,* 396 F.2d 224, 227-228 (C.A.5 1968); *Oklahoma High School Athletic Assn. v. Bray,* 321 F.2d 269, 272-273 (C.A.10 1963); *Indiana High School Athletic Assn. v. Carlberg,* 694 N.E.2d 222, 229 (Ind.1997); *Mississippi High School Activities Assn., Inc. v. Coleman,* 631 So.2d 768, 774-775 (Miss.1994); *Kleczek v. Rhode Island Interscholastic League, Inc.,* 612 A.2d 734, 736 (R.I.1992); see also *Moreland v. Western Penn. Interscholastic Athletic League,* 572 F.2d 121, 125 (C.A.3 1978) (state action conceded).

had caused it to be performed. Thus, we say that state action may be found if, though only if, there is such a "close nexus between the State and the challenged action" that seemingly private behavior "may be fairly treated as that of the State itself." *Jackson, supra,* at 351, 95 S.Ct. 449.[2]

[3] ***

Our cases have identified a host of facts that can bear on the fairness of such an attribution. We have, for example, held that a challenged activity may be state action when it results from the State's exercise of "coercive power," *Blum v. Yaretsky,* 457 U.S., at 1004, 102 S.Ct. 2777, when the State provides "significant encouragement, either overt or covert," *ibid.,* or when a private actor operates as a "willful participant in joint activity with the State or its agents," *Lugar, supra,* at 941, 102 S.Ct. 2744 (internal quotation marks omitted). We have treated a nominally private entity as a state actor when it is controlled by an "agency of the State," *Pennsylvania v. Board of Directors of City Trusts of Philadelphia,* 353 U.S. 230, 231, 77 S.Ct. 806, 1 L.Ed.2d 792 (1957)(*per curiam*), when it has been delegated a public function by the State, cf., *e.g., West v. Atkins, supra,* at 56, 108 S.Ct. 2250; *Edmonson v. Leesville Concrete Co.,* 500 U.S. 614, 627-628, 111 S.Ct. 2077, 114 L.Ed.2d 660 (1991), when it is "entwined with governmental policies," or when government is "entwined in [its] management or control," *Evans v. Newton,* 382 U.S. 296, 299, 301, 86 S.Ct. 486, 15 L.Ed.2d 373 (1966).

[4] Amidst such variety, examples may be the best teachers, and examples from our cases are unequivocal in showing that the character of a legal entity is determined neither by its expressly private characterization in statutory law, nor by the failure of the law to acknowledge the entity's inseparability from recognized government officials or agencies. *Lebron v. National Railroad Passenger Corporation,* 513 U.S. 374, 115 S.Ct. 961, 130 L.Ed.2d 902 (1995), held that Amtrak was the Government for constitutional purposes, regardless of its congressional designation as private; it was organized under federal law to attain governmental objectives and was directed and controlled by federal appointees. *Pennsylvania v. Board of Directors of City Trusts of Philadelphia, supra,* held the privately endowed Gerard College to be a state actor and enforcement of its private founder's limitation of admission to whites attributable to the State, because, consistent with the terms of the settlor's gift, the college's board of directors was a state agency established by state law. Ostensibly the converse situation occurred in *Evans v. Newton, supra,* which held that private trustees to whom a city had transferred a park were nonetheless state actors barred from enforcing racial segregation, since the park served the public purpose of providing community recreation, and "the municipality remain[ed] entwined in [its] management [and] control," *id.,* at 301, 86 S.Ct. 486.

These examples of public entwinement in the management and control of ostensibly separate trusts or corporations foreshadow this case, as this Court itself anticipated in *Tarkanian. Tarkanian* arose when an undoubtedly state actor, the University of Nevada, suspended its basketball coach, Tarkanian, in order to comply with rules and recommendations of the National

---

2 If a defendant's conduct satisfies the state-action requirement of the Fourteenth Amendment, the conduct also constitutes action "under color of state law" for § 1983 purposes. *Lugar v. Edmondson Oil Co.,* 457 U.S. 922, 935, 102 S.Ct. 2744, 73 L.Ed.2d 482 (1982).

Collegiate Athletic Association (NCAA). The coach charged the NCAA with state action, arguing that the state university had delegated its own functions to the NCAA, clothing the latter with authority to make and apply the university's rules, the result being joint action making the NCAA a state actor.

To be sure, it is not the strict holding in *Tarkanian* that points to our view of this case, for we found no state action on the part of the NCAA. ***

But, dictum in Tarkanian pointed to a contrary result on facts like ours, with an organization whose member public schools are all within a single State. "The situation would, of course, be different if the [Association's] membership consisted entirely of institutions located within the same State, many of them public institutions created by the same sovereign." *Id.*, at 193, n. 13, 109 S.Ct. 454. To support our surmise, we approvingly cited two cases: *Clark v. Arizona Interscholastic Assn.,* 695 F.2d 1126 (C.A.9 1982), cert. denied, 464 U.S. 818, 104 S.Ct. 79, 78 L.Ed.2d 90 (1983), a challenge to a state high school athletic association that kept boys from playing on girls' interscholastic volleyball teams in Arizona; and *Louisiana High School Athletic Assn. v. St. Augustine High School,* 396 F.2d 224 (C.A.5 1968), a parochial school's attack on the racially segregated system of interscholastic high school athletics maintained by the athletic association. In each instance, the Court of Appeals treated the athletic association as a state actor.

B.

[5] Just as we foresaw in *Tarkanian,* the "necessarily fact-bound inquiry,"…leads to the conclusion of state action here. The nominally private character of the Association is overborne by the pervasive entwinement of public institutions and public officials in its composition and workings, and there is no substantial reason to claim unfairness in applying constitutional standards to it.

The Association is not an organization of natural persons acting on their own, but of schools, and of public schools to the extent of 84% of the total. Under the Association's bylaws, each member school is represented by its principal or a faculty member, who has a vote in selecting members of the governing legislative council and board of control from eligible principals, assistant principals, and superintendents.

*** Interscholastic athletics obviously play an integral part in the public education of Tennessee, where nearly every public high school spends money on competitions among schools. Since a pickup system of interscholastic games would not do, these public teams need some mechanism to produce rules and regulate competition. The mechanism is an organization overwhelmingly composed of public school officials who select representatives (all of them public officials at the time in question here), who in turn adopt and enforce the rules that make the system work. Thus, by giving these jobs to the Association, the 290 public schools of Tennessee belonging to it can sensibly be seen as exercising their own authority to meet their own responsibilities. Unsurprisingly, then, the record indicates that half the council or board meetings documented here were held during official school hours, and that public schools have largely provided for the Association's financial support. A small portion of the Association's revenue comes from membership dues paid by the schools, and the principal part from gate receipts at tournaments among the member schools. *** The Association thus exercises the authority of the predominantly public schools to charge for admission to their games; the Association does not receive this money from the schools, but enjoys the schools' moneymaking capacity as its own.

In sum, to the extent of 84% of its membership, the Association is an organization of public schools represented by their officials acting in their official capacity to provide an integral element of secondary public schooling. There would be no recognizable Association, legal or tangible, without the public school officials, who do not merely control but overwhelmingly perform all but the purely ministerial acts by which the Association exists and functions in practical terms. Only the 16% minority of private school memberships prevents this entwinement of the Association and the public school system from being total and their identities totally indistinguishable.

To complement the entwinement of public school officials with the Association from the bottom up, the State of Tennessee has provided for entwinement from top down. State Board members are assigned ex officio to serve as members of the board of control and legislative council, and the Association's ministerial employees are treated as state employees to the extent of being eligible for membership in the state retirement system.

* * *

[6] The entwinement down from the State Board is therefore unmistakable, just as the entwinement up from the member public schools is overwhelming. Entwinement will support a conclusion that an ostensibly private organization ought to be charged with a public character and judged by constitutional standards; entwinement to the degree shown here requires it. ***

The judgment of the Court of Appeals for the Sixth Circuit is reversed, and the case is remanded for further proceedings consistent with this opinion.

It is so ordered.

Justice THOMAS, with whom THE CHIEF JUSTICE, Justice SCALIA, and Justice KENNEDY join, dissenting.

We have never found state action based upon mere "entwinement." Until today, we have found a private organization's acts to constitute state action only when the organization performed a public function; was created, coerced, or encouraged by the government; or acted in a symbiotic relationship with the government. The majority's holding – that the Tennessee Secondary School Athletic Association's (TSSAA) enforcement of its recruiting rule is state action – not only extends state-action doctrine beyond its permissible limits but also encroaches upon the realm of individual freedom that the doctrine was meant to protect. I respectfully dissent.

1. There are multiple levels of analysis that must be considered when analyzing constitutional claims in a Sports Law context. As this case demonstrates, in order to prove a violation of the plaintiff's First or Fourteenth Amendment Rights, there must be "state action" present. For a moment, stop and reflect. What rights are guaranteed by the First and Fourteenth Amendments in the first place? How might rights such as these be violated in the context of sports? Give examples.

2. The Tennessee Secondary School Athletic Association, it seems, could be deemed to have been involved with "state action" pursuant to the "agency of the state" theory, "public function" doctrine, or the concept of "entwinement with government policies." On which of these theories did the Court rely, and why?

3. Before *Tarkanian,* student-athletes relied on two theories when arguing that state action existed when the NCAA or a member institution deprived or attempted to deprive them of eligibility. Some courts adopted the public function theory, which held that a private party is subject to the same constitutional due process constraints as the state if it is performing public functions that are typically exercised by the government. The Supreme Court, however, abandoned this theory and held that neither the conduct nor coordination of amateur sports is a traditional and exclusive function of the state. *San Francisco Arts & Athletics, Inc. v United States, Olympic Committee,* 483 U.S. 522, 542, 545 (1987)(rejecting a trademark infringement claim that the USOC enforced its exclusive right under the Amateur Sports Act to use the word "Olympic" and related symbols in an unconstitutionally discriminatory manner because the USOC is not a governmental actor subject to the Fifth Amendment's equal protection guarantees). The second, more popular, state action theory was the entanglement doctrine. Under this doctrine, courts found that "the NCAA and its member public instrumentalities are joined in a mutual beneficial relationship, . . . [forming] a symbiotic relationship between public and private entities, triggering constitutional scrutiny." *Howard University v. NCAA,* 510 F.2d 213, 216 (D.C. Cir. 1975)(involving a claim for injunctive relief by athletes and Howard University alleging their constitutional rights were violated when the NCAA declared soccer players ineligible and the soccer team was placed on probation for one year and barred from postseason play). In *Howard,* Judge Tamm opined that the NCAA was "impregnated with a governmental character," because approximately half of the NCAA's institutional members were state or federally funded, contributed the largest amounts of dues and served as the dominant political force in formulating NCAA policy. *Id.* at 220. However, in 1988, the Supreme Court took a different approach in *Tarkanian.* The Court found that the University of Nevada Las Vegas' impact on NCAA policy was minimal because it was only one of several hundred other public and private institutions that similarly affected that policy, and most of them were located in other states and not acting under color of Nevada law when they assisted in formulating NCAA policy. As a

result, the Court concluded that NCAA policy was independent of any particular state and, therefore, the NCAA's involvement could not be considered state action. *See* John P. Sahl, *College Athletes and Due Process Protection: What's Left After National Collegiate Athletic Association v. Tarkanian,* __ U.S.__, 109 S.Ct. 454 (1988), 21 Ariz. St. J. L. 622, 642-652, 660-61 (1989)(arguing, in part, that the NCAA's enforcement policy and rules were inadequate to protect the eligibility interests of student-athletes — although the NCAA has since adopted some of the author's suggested reforms — and criticizing the Court's "formalistic approach to defining state action" as "frustrating societal expectations of fairness" for athletes and others). Explain the significance of the *Tarkanian* case on the outcome of the *Brentwood Academy* case.

4. *Borden v. School District of the Township of East Brunswick,* 523 F.3d 153 (3d Cir. 2008). High school football coach brought action against school district, seeking declaration that district's policy prohibiting faculty participation in student-initiated prayer was unconstitutionally overbroad and vague, and violated his federal and state constitutional rights to freedom of speech, academic freedom, freedom of association, and due process. The United States District Court for the District of New Jersey, Dennis M. Cavanaugh, J., 2006 WL 4844119, entered judgment in favor of coach, and district appealed.

The Court of Appeals for the Third Circuit, Fisher, Circuit Judge, reversed and held that:

(1) the policy was not unconstitutionally overbroad;

(2) the policy was not void for vagueness;

(3) the coach's acts of bowing his head and taking a knee with his team while they prayed did not address matters of public concern, and thus did not trigger his First Amendment free speech rights;

(4) the policy did not violate coach's right to academic freedom;

(5) the policy did not violate coach's right to freedom of association;

(6) the policy did not violate coach's due process rights; and

(7) the coach was in violation of the Establishment Clause of the First Amendment when he bowed his head and took a knee while his team prayed.

And for a somewhat similar, recent case, *see Kennedy v. Bremerton Sch. Dist.,* 869 F.3d 813 (9th Cir. 2017), *cert. denied,* 139 S. Ct. 634 (2019). Reasoning that plaintiff's requested injunction to allow him to kneel and pray after public high school football games would violate the First Amendment's Establishment Clause, the Ninth Circuit upheld district court's refusal to grant the injunction. And for another recent sports-related freedom of speech case, *see Donnelly v. U. of N. Carolina,* 763 S.E.2d 154 (N.C. App. 2014). When the university banned a fan from its athletic facilities because of the fan's belligerent and harassing behavior directed at student athletes and staff, the appellate court, affirming the trial court, ruled that such conduct was not protected by the First Amendment's Freedom of Speech guarantee.

695 S.W.2D 556 (1985)

SUPREME COURT OF TEXAS

RAY, JUSTICE.

This is a direct appeal brought by the Attorney General, representing the Texas Education Agency, and others, seeking immediate appellate review of an order of the trial court which held unconstitutional, and enjoined enforcement of, a provision of the Texas Education Code. **** We hold that the statutory provision is not unconstitutional and reverse the judgment of the trial court.

Chris Stamos and others brought this suit on behalf of Nicky Stamos and others, seeking a permanent injunction against enforcement of the Texas "no pass, no play" rule by the Spring Branch and Alief Independent School Districts. ***

THE "NO PASS, NO PLAY" RULE

The Second Called Session of the 68th Legislature adopted a package of educational reforms known as "H.B. 72." Act of July 13, 1984, Chapter 28, 1984 Tex.Gen. Laws, 2nd Called Session 269. A major provision of these educational reforms was the so-called "no pass, no play" rule, which generally requires that students maintain a "70" average in all classes to be eligible for participation in extracurricular activities. *See* Tex.Educ.Code Ann. § 21.920(b) (Vernon Supp.1985). The rule is incorporated in section 21.920 of the Texas Education Code and provides as follows:

§ 21.920. Extracurricular Activities

(a) ***

(b) A student, other than a mentally retarded student, enrolled in a school district in this state shall be suspended from participation in any extracurricular activity sponsored or sanctioned by the school district during the grade reporting period after a grade reporting period in which the student received a grade lower than the equivalent of 70 on a scale of 100 in any academic class. The campus principal may remove this suspension if the class is an identified honors or advanced class. A student may not be suspended under this subsection during the period in which school is recessed for the summer or during the initial grade reporting period of a regular school term on the basis of grades received in the final grade reporting period of the preceding regular school term.

(c) In this section, "mentally retarded" has the meaning assigned by Section 21.503(b)(5) of this code.

(d) ***

ISSUES RAISED

The sole issue before this court is the constitutionality of the no pass, no play rule. The district court held the rule unconstitutional on the grounds that it violated equal protection and due process guarantees. The burden is on the party attacking the constitutionality of an act of the legislature. *Texas Public Building Authority v. Mattox,* 686 S.W.2d 924, 927 (Tex.1985). There is a presumption in favor of the constitutionality of an act of the legislature. *See Sax v. Votteler,* 648 S.W.2d 661, 664 (Tex.1983).

This court has long recognized the important role education plays in the maintenance of our democratic society. Article VII of the Texas Constitution "discloses a well-considered purpose on the part of those who framed it to bring about the establishment and maintenance of a comprehensive system of public education, consisting of a general public free school system and a system of higher education." *Mumme v. Marrs,* 120 Tex. 383, 40 S.W.2d 31, 33 (1931). *** The Constitution leaves to the legislature alone the determination of which methods, restrictions, and regulations are necessary and appropriate to carry out this duty, so long as that determination is not so arbitrary as to violate the constitutional rights of Texas' citizens. *Id.*

Equal Protection

Stamos challenges the constitutionality of the "no pass, no play" rule on the ground that it violates the equal protection clause of the Texas Constitution. The first determination this court must make in the context of equal protection analysis is the appropriate standard of review. When the classification created by a state regulatory scheme neither infringes upon fundamental rights or interests nor burdens an inherently suspect class, equal protection analysis requires that the classification be rationally related to a legitimate state interest. *Sullivan v. University Interscholastic League,* 616 S.W.2d 170, 172 (Tex.1981). Therefore, we must first determine whether the rule burdens an inherently suspect class or infringes upon fundamental rights or interests.

The no pass, no play rule classifies students based upon their achievement levels in their academic courses. We hold that those students who fail to maintain a minimum level of proficiency in all of their courses do not constitute the type of discrete, insular minority necessary to constitute a "suspect" class. *See United States v. Carolene Products Co.,* 304 U.S. 144, 152 n. 4, 58 S.Ct. 778, 783 n. 4, 82 L.Ed. 1234 (1938). Thus, the rule does not burden an inherently "suspect" class.

* * *

Stamos also argues that the rule is subject to strict scrutiny under equal protection analysis because it impinges upon a fundamental right, *i.e.,* the right to participate in extracurricular activities. We note that the overwhelming majority of jurisdictions have held that a student's right to participation in extracurricular activities does *not* constitute a fundamental right. *See, e.g., Hardy v. University Interscholastic League,* 759 F.2d 1233, 1235 (5th Cir.1985); *Walsh v. Louisiana High School Athletic Ass'n,* 616 F.2d 152, 160-61 (5th Cir.1980); *Pennsylvania Interscholastic Athletic Ass'n, Inc. v. Greater Johnstown School District,* 76 Pa.Commw. 65, 463 A.2d 1198, 1202 (1983); and *Smith v. Crim,* 240 Ga. 390, 240 S.E.2d 884, 885 (1977).

Fundamental rights have their genesis in the express and implied protections of personal liberty recognized in federal and state constitutions. A student's "right" to participate in extracurricular activities does not rise to the same level as the right to free speech or free exercise of religion, both of which have long been recognized as fundamental rights under our state and federal constitutions. We adopt the majority rule and hold that a student's right to participate in extracurricular activities *per se* does *not* rise to the level of a fundamental right under our constitution.

Because the no pass, no play rule neither infringes upon fundamental rights nor burdens an inherently suspect class, we hold that it is *not* subject to "strict" or heightened equal protection scrutiny. Rather, the rule must be judged by the [rational basis] standard....

The no pass, no play rule distinguishes students based upon whether they maintain a satisfactory minimum level of performance in each of their classes. Students who fail to maintain a minimum proficiency in all of their classes are ineligible for participation in school-sponsored extracurricular activities for the following six-week period, with no carry over from one school year to the next. The rule provides a strong incentive for students wishing to participate in extracurricular activities to maintain minimum levels of performance in all of their classes. In view of the rule's objective to promote improved classroom performance by students, we find the rule rationally related to the legitimate state interest in providing a quality education to Texas' public school students. ***

Procedural Due Process

We begin our analysis of the due process arguments in this cause by recognizing that the strictures of due process apply only to the threatened deprivation of liberty and property interests deserving the protection of the federal and state constitutions. [Case Citations Omitted] The federal courts have made it clear that the federal constitution's due process guarantees do not protect a student's interest in participating in extracurricular activities. *See Niles v. University Interscholastic League,* 715 F.2d 1027, 1031 (5th Cir.1983); *Mitchell v. Louisiana High School Athletic Ass'n,* 430 F.2d 1155, 1158 (5th Cir.1970); *see also, Hamilton v. Tennessee Secondary School Athletic Ass'n,* 552 F.2d 681, 682 (6th Cir.1976); and *Albach v. Odle,* 531 F.2d 983, 984-85 (10th Cir.1976). We must, then, examine our state constitution to determine whether its due process guarantees extend to a student's desire to participate in school-sponsored extracurricular activities.

A property or liberty interest must find its origin in some aspect of state law. *See Board of Regents v. Roth,* 408 U.S. at 577-78, 92 S.Ct. 2709. Nothing in either our state constitution or statutes entitles students to an absolute right to participation in extracurricular activities. We are in agreement, therefore, with the overwhelming majority of jurisdictions that students do not possess a constitutionally protected interest in their participation in extracurricular activities. [Citations Omitted] Therefore, the strictures of procedural due process do *not* apply to the determination by a campus principal, pursuant to section 21.920(b) of the Texas Education Code, as to whether a student who fails an identified honors or advanced course shall be permitted to participate in extracurricular activities.

[The Court's discussion of Substantive Due Process has been omitted].

Accordingly, we reverse the district court's judgment with regard to the constitutionality of section 21.920 of the Texas Education Code....

NOTES & QUESTIONS

1. Explain the significance of the court's determination that the students affected by the no pass, no play rule are not an inherently suspect class, and the significance of the court's determination that a student's right to participate in extracurricular activities is not a fundamental right.

2. The public announcements from homosexual professional athletes, such as NFL prospect Michael Sam and NBA player Jason Collins, have highlighted the concern about equal treatment for all athletes, including homosexuals. The announcements have produced support for these athletes and policy directives prohibiting discrimination on sexual orientation. For example, the NFL released a statement "welcoming and supporting Michael Sam in 2014." In 2013, the NFL Commissioner Roger Goodell "sent the NFL's sexual orientation anti-discrimination and harassment policy to all club presidents, coaches and general managers who made it available to all players and staff."NFL Statement on Michael Sam, http://nflcommunications.com/2014/02/09/nfl-statement-on-michael-sam/, February 9, 2014.

   Transgender athletes present related issues. Various athletic organizations and governing bodies have made a concerted effort to find ways to accommodate male athletes who identify as women (MTF) and women athletes who identify as men (FTM). Organizations have tried to strike a balance between accommodation and maintaining fairness for competition. The NCAA for example, has adopted a policy that permits MTF athletes to compete as females after one year of testosterone suppression therapy (a policy first adopted in 2011).

   And then a perhaps even more complex gender-related issue is posed by athletes such as South African middle distance runner, Castor Semenya. Semenya is a woman who possesses an unusually high level of testosterone. On May 1, 2019, the Court of Arbitration for Sport upheld (2-1) an IAAF rule requiring that, to compete legally, female athletes must have testosterone levels below a certain chemical level (*i.e.,* 5 nanomoles per liter of blood).

   What other important social issues, such as prohibiting sexual orientation discrimination, are reflected in contemporary sports? Do professional and amateur sports play a special role in advancing the discussion about equality and other important societal values (*e.g.,* being a good spouse or parent, avoiding illegal drug use)? Consider the impact of Jackie Robinson on the Civil Rights movement.

   And for more recent examples, consider these three matters.

   1) During the 2014 NCAA's Basketball Tournament (*i.e.,* "March Madness"), Ervin "Magic" Johnson, LeBron James and other professional athletes appeared on TV commercials encouraging persons to sign up for the Affordable Care Act (sometimes called Obamacare) to meet an important registration deadline. Not having six million registrants by this deadline would

have disappointed many of the Act's supporters. More than six million applicants ultimately registered before the March 31st 2014 deadline. Some commentators attribute that achievement, in part, to the government's promotional campaign that included professional athletes in the final days before the deadline.

2) A firestorm erupted in the wake of racist comments made by Donald Sterling, owner of the Los Angeles Clippers. The NBA acted swiftly and banned Sterling for life, as a consequence.

3) Public debate nearly reached a boiling point in response to Colin Kaepernick's political statement of "taking-a-knee" – as an expression of protest relating to various forms of racial injustice – during the playing of the National Anthem at NFL games. Dozens of others joined Kaepernick by following his example, and in May 2018 the NFL issued a new policy in response. The NFL's policy would have imposed fines but allowed that players who didn't wish to stand during the anthem were permitted to remain in the locker room. President Trump then added to the controversy when he weighed in, condemning the protesting players' conduct. Then after the NFL Players association filed a grievance in July, the NFL agreed to hit the "pause button," and put the policy on hold. *See e.g.,* http://static2.businessinsider.com/nfl-halts-national-anthem-policy-2018-7.

Should athletes and other entertainers (*e.g.,* recording artists, actors) actively participate in the public debate about important and sometimes controversial issues? Have sports helped to advance societal awareness about equality concerns in the past? Is it unfair to expect athletes to play a special role in promoting equality and other important values? Is it even possible today for athletes to promote important values given the front-page scandals involving athletes (*e.g.,* the controversy involving Alex Rodriquez and the use of performance enhancing drugs, the Pete Rose betting case, and Kobe Bryant's and Tiger Woods's marital indiscretions)?

JAMES V. TALLASSEE HIGH SCHOOL
907 F.SUPP. 364 (1995)
UNITED STATES DISTRICT COURT, M.D. ALABAMA, NORTHERN DIVISION

DE MENT, DISTRICT JUDGE.

STATEMENT OF FACTS

This is an action for declaratory and injunctive relief and damages on behalf of the plaintiff, Nancy James ("Ms. James"), who is, and was at all relevant times, a student at Tallassee High School. In 1993, the Tallassee City Board of Education adopted rules and regulations contained in a student handbook which established, among other things, guidelines for cheerleader selection, cheerleader eligibility, and the selection of a head and co-head cheerleader of the cheerleading squad for Tallassee High School. Specifically, these rules, printed in the 1994-95 Tallassee High School Student Handbook, provided that the head and co-head cheerleaders of the football and basketball cheerleading squads would be chosen by a majority of the cheerleaders on the respective squads.

In March, 1995, Carol Lowe ("Ms. Lowe"), in her capacity as the sponsor of the cheerleaders at Tallassee High School, adopted rules that differed from those in the handbook for selection of the head and co-head cheerleaders. Ms. Lowe's rules, given to each potential cheerleader, provided that Ms. Lowe would choose the head and co-head cheerleaders based on her discretion and the cheerleaders' scores in the try-outs.

After try-outs, Ms. James was selected to be a member of the Tallassee High School cheerleading squad. Once the cheerleading squad was named, Ms. James was chosen by Ms. Lowe to be the co-head cheerleader of the basketball squad; however, Ms. James was not chosen to be the head or co-head cheerleader of the football squad. James appealed the sponsor's decision because Ms. Lowe did not choose her as the head or co-head cheerleader of the football squad. Thereafter, a hearing was held on June 19, 1995, wherein the Tallassee Board of Education considered the selection process of the head and co-head cheerleading squads and rejected the plaintiff's appeal.

On August 15, 1995, Ms. James filed this action claiming that she deserves a remedy in federal court because Tallassee High School failed to follow the rules in the Tallassee High School student handbook. Specifically, Ms. James claims that the defendants violated her Fifth Amendment right to due process and her Fourteenth Amendment right to equal protection under the laws by denying her the opportunity to be head or co-head cheerleader of the football team. Ms. James further contends that she was "possibly denied" the opportunity to continue her education in college because she might have had a better chance of obtaining a college cheerleading scholarship. Therefore, Ms. James requests the court, among other things, to award her damages pursuant to 42 U.S.C. § 1983 for the violation of her constitutional rights, and to direct the defendants to hold an election of the head and co-head cheerleaders of the football and basketball squads by a majority of the cheerleading squad.

*** [The court discussed the appropriate standard of review for a motion to dismiss]

DISCUSSION

A. Due Process Clause Under the Fifth Amendment

Ms. James first alleges that she has been deprived of her due process rights under the Fifth Amendment. In order to prevail on this claim, Ms. James must show that the defendants have deprived her of either a liberty interest or a property interest. James raises her due process claim based on a denial of an alleged property interest in being selected as head or co-head cheerleader of the football cheerleading squad.

"To have a property interest in a benefit, a person clearly must have more than an abstract need or desire for it. He [or she] must have more than a unilateral expectation of it. He [or she] must, instead have a legitimate claim of entitlement to it." *Board of Regents v. Roth*, 408 U.S. 564, 577, 92 S.Ct. 2701, 2708, 33 L.Ed.2d 548 (1972). It is clear that a majority of the federal courts addressing the question have determined that a student does not have a cognizable property interest in participating in extracurricular activities at public institutions.

In *Mitchell v. Louisiana High School Athletic Association,* the former Fifth Circuit held that a high school student did not have a right to challenge his eligibility for high school athletics in federal court. 430 F.2d 1155, 1158 (5th Cir.1970).[1] In its holding, the *Mitchell* court noted that the privilege of participating in such an extracurricular activity did not rise to the level of a federal property interest that could be protected by the Constitution. *Id.* Similarly, the Tenth Circuit dismissed a student athlete's complaint challenging a rule that barred any athlete who transferred from his or her home district to a boarding school from participating in interscholastic athletics for a year, stating that "[p]articipation in interscholastic athletics is not a constitutionally protected civil right." *Albach v. Odle,* 531 F.2d 983, 984-85 (10th Cir.1976).

Moreover, at least one federal district court has specifically addressed the due process rights of a high school cheerleader. *See Haverkamp v. Unified School District Number 380,* 689 F.Supp. 1055 (D.C.Kan.1986). The *Haverkamp* court held that a high school cheerleader's position as head cheerleader, or even as a member of the cheerleading squad, did not constitute a property interest for the purposes of determining whether a plaintiff's due process rights had been violated. *Id.* at 1058. In fact, in *Haverkamp,* the plaintiff had already been selected to the cheerleading squad and had been removed for disciplinary reasons.

In the present case, Ms. James has not lost a position as head or co-head cheerleader of the football cheerleading squad; rather, she was never selected to serve in that position. Thus, Ms. James has only a mere expectation of being chosen as the head or co-head of the football cheerleading squad. Furthermore, Ms. James was selected by Ms. Lowe to be the co-head basketball cheerleader. Thus, the court is not convinced that Ms. James' allegation that her opportunity to obtain a college cheerleading scholarship was substantially harmed. While the court does not wish to imply that it condones Ms. Lowe's unilateral action to change the rules governing the selection of head and co-head cheerleaders at Tallassee High School, the court believes that Ms. James does not have a federally-protected property interest in having the opportunity to be selected as the head or co-head cheerleader of the football cheerleading squad. Accordingly, the court finds that Ms. James' due process claim is due to be dismissed.

B. Equal Protection Clause Under the Fourteenth Amendment

Ms. James also alleges a violation of the Equal Protection Clause of the Fourteenth Amendment. To establish an equal protection claim, a plaintiff must initially show that he or she was treated differently from other individuals similarly situated. *Cleburne v. Cleburne Living Ctr.,* 473 U.S. 432, 439, 105 S.Ct. 3249, 3254, 87 L.Ed.2d 313 (1985)("The Equal Protection Clause of the Fourteenth Amendment commands that no State shall 'deny to any person within its jurisdiction the equal protection of the laws,' which is essentially a direction that all persons similarly situated should be treated alike."). Thus, to survive a motion to dismiss on her equal protection claim, Ms. James must allege that she was treated differently than others who were similarly

---

1   Decisions of the former Fifth Circuit filed prior to October 1, 1981, constitute binding precedent in the Eleventh Circuit. *Bonner v. City of Prichard,* 661 F.2d 1206, 1209 (11th Cir.1981) (en banc).

situated, *i.e.,* any other Tallassee High School students who were members of the cheerleading squad from which the head and co-head cheerleaders were chosen.

It is clear that Ms. James' complaint fails to state a claim upon which relief can be granted because it does not contain even a hint of an allegation that Ms. James was similarly situated to other Tallassee cheerleaders, yet treated more harshly or differently by the defendants than the other Tallassee cheerleaders. Therefore, even assuming the allegations in the complaint as true, it is abundantly clear to the court that Ms. James' equal protection claim must be dismissed pursuant to Rule 12(b)(6) because she has failed to allege sufficient facts to support an equal protection claim.

CONCLUSION

For the foregoing reasons, the court finds that defendants' motion to dismiss is due to be granted. A judgment in accordance with this memorandum opinion will be entered separately.

NOTES *&* QUESTIONS

1. In the field of Labor Law, employee handbooks are often treated as contracts. How might you articulate an argument on James's behalf, arguing that the Student Handbook, which contained written procedures for cheerleader selection, ought to have been treated as a contract? Develop the argument that James should win on a breach of contract theory.

2. Even if James didn't have a property interest in being appointed head cheerleader, isn't it true that she at the very least had a right to expect the school to follow its own written procedures? If so, why? If not, why not?

3. To what extent do you think that the court was concerned that other disgruntled cheerleaders and athletes who were cut from a team or demoted to JV might open the floodgates of litigation if it had ruled in James's favor?

4. For recent cases involving gender discrimination where the courts reasoned that there was a valid claim of a violation of equal protection, *see:* 1) *Beattie v. Line Mt. Sch. Dist.,* 992 F. Supp. 2d 384 (M.D. Pa. 2014). Granting a preliminary injunction, prohibiting school district from preventing a 12 year-old girl from participating on the school's boys-only wrestling team, the court ruled that the gender-based, discriminatory policy likely violated Equal Protection and the state's Equal Rights Amendment – even though the district argued that its reasons for the policy (including safety, prevention of inappropriate physical contact, and sexual harassment) justified it. 2) *Hayden ex rel. A.H. v. Greensburg Community Sch. Corp.,* 743 F.3d 569 (7th Cir. 2014). The Seventh Circuit Court of Appeals held that the public school's short-hair-cut policy for its boys basketball team (but not for the girls) violated both Equal Protection and Title IX because the policy treated genders in a non-justifiable discriminatory manner.

JORDAN V. O'FALLON TOWNSHIP HIGH SCHOOL
706 NE 2D 137 (1999)
APPELLATE COURT OF ILLINOIS, FIFTH DISTRICT

This case examines how O'Fallon Township High School (O'Fallon) officials withheld a student's participation in interscholastic athletics as punishment for his violation of the school's zero-tolerance conduct code. Before they are allowed to participate in any extracurricular activity, all O'Fallon students must agree in writing to abide by the code's ban on alcohol and drug use. Students who violate the code's ban are disciplined by school officials under procedures that do not necessarily comport with due process. School officials imposed discipline in this case without affording the student a formal hearing. The student was not allowed to confront witnesses who provided the evidence upon which the discipline was based. Nor was the student permitted to present witnesses to rebut that evidence.

The student sued to enjoin the disciplinary action. The trial court refused to grant an injunction, and the student appealed.

On appeal, the student claims that O'Fallon school officials violated the procedural due process component of the fourteenth amendment. U.S. Const., amend. XIV. He argues that school officials were constitutionally obliged to afford him a minimal due process hearing before discipline could be administered. ***

We now decide whether a talented high school football player with college athletic scholarship opportunities possesses an interest in playing high school football that due process protects. *** We conclude that O'Fallon school officials dispensed that process which was due and acted reasonably under the circumstances presented.

The 1997 O'Fallon High School football season highlighted the skills of a young man named Kevin Jordan. Jordan's ability to break tackles and find daylight brought several postseason honors, including his selection as team captain for the ensuing 1998 season. Jordan's ability also drew the attention of several universities. College coaches from across the country wrote to Jordan and expressed their interest in his future. Although the coaches did not extend scholarship offers, they clearly suggested that such offers would be forthcoming provided Jordan continued to excel as a high school football player in his senior season.

Thus, the 1998 season appeared to offer Jordan a legitimate chance to earn an athletic scholarship to a major university. The season's promise ended, however, when Jordan's playing privileges surrendered to enforcement of O'Fallon's zero-tolerance conduct code. School officials determined that Jordan violated the code's ban on alcohol use. As a result, the captain of O'Fallon's football team was suspended from play for the entire 1998 season. Kevin Jordan never played another down of high school football.

The suspension stemmed from an early morning encounter with O'Fallon police officers. The officers answered Jordan's 9-1-1 emergency call from a phone booth near an O'Fallon convenience store. When they arrived at the convenience store, they found a disheveled and shoeless Jordan standing in the parking lot. It was 3 o'clock in the morning, and according to the officers, Jordan evidenced obvious signs of inebriation. His eyes were glazed, his speech was slurred,

spicy facts

and he smelled of alcohol. Jordan's condition was confirmed when, according to the officers, he admitted to alcohol consumption.

The officers, pursuant to a reciprocal reporting agreement with the school, reported the incident to O'Fallon school officials. An assistant principal reviewed their report, discussed it with them, and confronted Jordan. Jordan denied alcohol use. He also denied any admission to the contrary. He explained that his condition resulted from an attack by unknown assailants who threw beer bottles at him during the assault. He insisted that the smell of alcohol detected by the officers was misconstrued.

The assistant principal weighed what the officers and Jordan told him and decided that Jordan violated his commitment to remain alcohol – and drug – free. Jordan had a prior violation of the code's alcohol ban. Therefore, the assistant principal cited him for a second violation and informed him that he was suspended from participation in high school athletics for a period that encompassed the entire football season.

The assistant principal's action was reviewed by the O'Fallon Activity Council (Activity Council). The Activity Council is a body comprised of the principal, all assistant principals, the dean of students, the athletic director, the assistant athletic director, the band director, the head of speech activities, and the student council sponsor. The Activity Council reviews discipline only to determine whether the conduct code is interpreted consistently and applied uniformly. Its members agreed unanimously that the code was properly applied in Jordan's case.

Jordan's stepfather appealed to the school superintendent, who was empowered to review and override the disciplinary action. After agreeing to review the matter, the superintendent met with Jordan, his attorney, and his stepfather. Jordan, assisted by counsel, reiterated his version of the early morning encounter with O'Fallon police officers. Jordan was afforded the opportunity to present any information or make any comment he deemed important to the superintendent's review.

The superintendent listened to everything Jordan presented and reserved judgment until he could meet with the officers involved in the incident. Jordan's attorney was apprised of a planned meeting with the officers and was invited to attend. His schedule did not permit attendance, and the meeting was held without him.

The superintendent told the officers of Jordan's claims. The officers questioned the veracity of those claims, noting that Jordan's story had significantly changed from what he had earlier told them. They insisted that Jordan admitted to them that he had been drinking alcohol. They also expressed their opinion that Jordan's glassy eyes and slurred speech were the result of alcohol consumption. The possibility that the smell of alcohol resulted from an assault with beer bottles did not alter their opinion of Jordan's inebriated condition.

The superintendent told Jordan's attorney what the officers conveyed to him. He advised Jordan's attorney that he would not overrule the suspension and invited him to appeal to the O'Fallon Board of Education, the final arbiter of student discipline.

Throughout this process, Jordan's stepfather and attorney repeatedly requested a more formal proceeding. They wanted to confront the police officers and to call witnesses who could account for most of Jordan's activities on the night in question. Their call for a formal hearing went unheard.

Jordan did not appeal to the O'Fallon Board of Education. Instead, he commenced this action. He obtained a temporary restraining order that enjoined the suspension. The matter proceeded to a hearing on Jordan's request for a preliminary injunction pending a trial on the merits of the underlying lawsuit. Jordan argued that the disciplinary action was arbitrary and capricious and that the procedures employed were constitutionally infirm. The trial judge found that the evidence failed to establish a protected property or liberty interest. Therefore, the judge did not determine whether the process afforded met minimal constitutional procedural standards. He did hold, however, that the disciplinary action was neither arbitrary nor capricious. This appeal ensued.

Jordan challenges the school's power to sideline him in the manner employed. He argues that school officials cannot suspend him from participation in interscholastic athletics without first affording him a minimal due process hearing to contest the disciplinary action. At a minimum, he claims a right to confront his accusers and to present witnesses who could corroborate his denial of alcohol use.

[1][2] The fourteenth amendment forbids the State to deprive any person of life, liberty, or property without due process of law. U.S. Const., amend. XIV. Therefore, any person who raises a procedural due process claim must demonstrate that a protectable property or liberty interest is at stake. *Hawkins v. National Collegiate Athletic Ass'n*, 652 F.Supp. 602, 610 (C.D.Ill.1987). Protected property interests are created "'and their dimensions are defined' by an independent source such as State statutes or rules entitling * * * citizen[s] to certain benefits." *Goss v. Lopez*, 419 U.S. 565, 572-73, 95 S.Ct. 729, 735, 42 L.Ed.2d 725, 733 (1975), quoting *Board of Regents of State Colleges v. Roth*, 408 U.S. 564, 577, 92 S.Ct. 2701, 2709, 33 L.Ed.2d 548, 561 (1972). In *Board of Regents of State Colleges*, the Supreme Court addressed the parameters of a constitutionally protected property interest. In reviewing several cases that defined protected property interests in different contexts, the Supreme Court wrote:

> Certain attributes of "property" interests protected by procedural due process emerge from these decisions. To have a property interest in a benefit, a person clearly must have more than an abstract need or desire for it. He must have more than a unilateral expectation of it. He must, instead, have a legitimate claim of entitlement to it. *Board of Regents of State Colleges*, 408 U.S. at 577, 92 S.Ct. at 2709, 33 L.Ed.2d at 561.

Based upon this definition, courts have repeatedly held that there is no property or liberty interest in taking part in interscholastic athletics. *Clements v. Board of Education of Decatur Public School District No. 61*, 133 Ill.App.3d 531, 533, 88 Ill.Dec. 601, 478 N.E.2d 1209, 1210 (1985).

Students can need, want, and expect to participate in interscholastic athletics, but students are not *entitled* to participate in them. Football is neither an integral part of a quality education nor a requirement under any rule or regulation governing education in this State. Consequently, not every public high school in this State fields a football team. Those students who attend

O'Fallon Township High School thus enjoy an opportunity that many other high school students are not permitted to enjoy. Simply put, playing high school football is a privilege rather than a right. *Todd v. Rush County Schools,* 133 F.3d 984, 986 (7th Cir.1998).

Jordan concedes that, standing alone, participation in interscholastic athletics does not rise to the level of a protected interest. Most students can be suspended from play without a constitutional right to a due process hearing. Notwithstanding, Jordan thinks that he should be treated differently. His reasoning follows.

Since he possesses athletic prowess, his participation in high school football can develop into something of substantial economic value. Unlike his less talented teammates, Jordan can turn participation in interscholastic athletics into a college scholarship. His participation thus rises to a protectable property interest that commands procedural due process. It follows that school officials could not ban him from a playing field where scholarship opportunities awaited, without first conducting a minimal due process hearing.

This argument is untenable. Since Jordan possessed no independent right to participate in high school football, the existence of a protected property interest depends upon whether he can legitimately claim the right to participate in order to earn college financial assistance. This in turn depends upon whether the hope of earning a college scholarship rises to the level of a protectable property interest. Under the circumstances presented, it does not.

Scholarship opportunities do not elevate participation in interscholastic athletics into an interest that due process protects because such opportunities are themselves mere expectancies. The acquisition of a scholarship remains contingent on far more than simply maintaining playing privileges.

* * * *

In holding that the opportunity to earn an athletic scholarship is too speculative to elevate participation in high school football to the level of a constitutionally protected interest, we note several contingencies that impact scholarship hopes. Here, Jordan would have had to again excel on the playing field. He would have had to meet academic and entrance exam requirements. He would have had to overcome the unreliable image that his disciplinary problems conveyed. And, most importantly, he would have had to stay healthy.

* * *

[E]ven a player with obvious college-level skills can harbor no more than an expectation of college financial assistance so long as he is still playing high school football. Football can exact a swift and permanent toll on any player's scholarship hopes. The vagaries of the game do not spare talented players and have crushed the aspirations of some of the very best. An athletic scholarship offer can vanish from a running back's future as swiftly as a healthy knee. Therefore, athletic scholarships remain expectancies, regardless of a player's talent level, until that player completes high school football with his health firmly intact. A player's hopes, no matter how justified, cannot elevate his high school playing privileges to a protectable property interest at any stage where disciplinary action would be taken against those privileges.

Jordan did not possess the right to participate in interscholastic athletics. Nor did his scholarship opportunities confer such a right. Therefore, a protectable property interest was not at stake when the school imposed discipline, and a due process hearing was not required.

* * *

We are consistently reluctant to intrude upon the disciplinary decisions of school districts. *Donaldson v. Board of Education for Danville School District No. 118,* 98 Ill.App.3d 438, 439, 53 Ill. Dec. 946, 424 N.E.2d 737, 738- 39 (1981). If the opportunity to earn college financial assistance were to elevate participation in interscholastic athletics into a protected property right, school districts would have to afford procedural due process in practically all disciplinary actions where student participation in outside activities was at stake. We cannot accept a notion that would invite a due process claim by every student engaged in interscholastic athletics and extracurricular activities. Judicial intervention in school discipline would become the rule rather than the exception unless school districts provided due process hearings in all such disciplinary actions.

* * *

For the reasons stated, we affirm the trial court's order denying a preliminary injunction. Affirmed.

NOTES & QUESTIONS

1. As regards legal principles, discuss the similarities and differences between *James* and *Jordan*.

2. Suppose that the coach had decided not to allow Jordan to play because he had heard a rumor that Jordan had smoked cigarettes at a weekend party. Would that change the outcome of the case? Suppose instead that the coach had heard a rumor that Jordan had been drinking beer and smoking marijuana at a weekend party? The court states, "Of course, school officials cannot impose student punishment in a completely arbitrary and capricious manner." Give examples of the types of things that you believe would constitute "a completely arbitrary and capricious manner."

3. Kevin Jordan returned to school and played the following year, graduating with the class of 1999. He went on to play collegiate football at Millikin University in Decatur, Illinois.

JUSTICE SCALIA

The Student Athlete Drug Policy adopted by School District 47J in the town of Vernonia, Oregon, authorizes random urinalysis drug testing of students who participate in the District's school athletics programs. We granted certiorari to decide whether this violates the Fourth and Fourteenth Amendments to the United States Constitution.

I A

Petitioner Vernonia School District 47J (District) operates one high school and three grade schools in the logging community of Vernonia, Oregon. As elsewhere in small-town America, school sports play a prominent role in the town's life, and student athletes are admired in their schools and in the community.

In the mid-to-late 1980's, . . . teachers and administrators observed a sharp increase in drug use. Students began to speak out about their attraction to the drug culture, and to boast that there was nothing the school could do about it. Along with more drugs came more disciplinary problems. Between 1988 and 1989 the number of disciplinary referrals in Vernonia schools rose to more than twice the number reported in the early 1980's, and several students were suspended....

Not only were student athletes included among the drug users but, as the District Court found, athletes were the leaders of the drug culture. This caused the District's administrators particular concern, since drug use increases the risk of sports-related injury. Expert testimony at the trial confirmed the deleterious effects of drugs on motivation, memory, judgment, reaction, coordination, and performance. The high school football and wrestling coach witnessed a severe sternum injury suffered by a wrestler, and various omissions of safety procedures and misexecutions by football players, all attributable in his belief to the effects of drug use.

Initially, the District responded to the drug problem by offering special classes, speakers, and presentations designed to deter drug use. It even brought in a specially trained dog to detect drugs, but the drug problem persisted.***

District officials began considering a drug-testing program. They held a parent "input night" to discuss the proposed Student Athlete Drug Policy (Policy), and the parents in attendance gave their unanimous approval. The school board approved the Policy for implementation in the fall of 1989. Its expressed purpose is to prevent student athletes from using drugs, to protect their health and safety, and to provide drug users with assistance programs.

B

The Policy applies to all students participating in interscholastic athletics. Students wishing to play sports must sign a form consenting to the testing and must obtain the written consent of their parents. Athletes are tested at the beginning of the season for their sport. In addition, once each week of the season the names of the athletes are placed in a "pool" from which a student, with the supervision of two adults, blindly draws the names of 10% of the athletes for random testing. Those selected are notified and tested that same day, if possible.

The student to be tested completes a specimen control form which bears an assigned number. Prescription medications that the student is taking must be identified by providing a copy of the prescription or a doctor's authorization. The student then enters an empty locker room accompanied by an adult monitor of the same sex. Each boy selected produces a sample at a urinal, remaining fully clothed with his back to the monitor, who stands approximately 12 to 15 feet behind the student. Monitors may (though do not always) watch the student while he produces the sample, and they listen for normal sounds of urination. Girls produce samples in an enclosed bathroom stall, so that they can be heard but not observed. After the sample is produced, it is given to the monitor, who checks it for temperature and tampering and then transfers it to a vial.

The samples are sent to an independent laboratory, which routinely tests them for amphetamines, cocaine, and marijuana. Other drugs, such as LSD, may be screened at the request of the District, but the identity of a particular student does not determine which drugs will be tested. The laboratory's procedures are 99.94% accurate. The District follows strict procedures regarding the chain of custody and access to test results. The laboratory does not know the identity of the students whose samples it tests. It is authorized to mail written test reports only to the superintendent and to provide test results to District personnel by telephone only after the requesting official recites a code confirming his authority. Only the superintendent, principals, vice-principals, and athletic directors have access to test results, and the results are not kept for more than one year.

If a sample tests positive, a second test is administered as soon as possible to confirm the result. If the second test is negative, no further action is taken. If the second test is positive, the athlete's parents are notified, and the school principal convenes a meeting with the student and his parents, at which the student is given the option of (1) participating for six weeks in an assistance program that includes weekly urinalysis, or (2) suffering suspension from athletics for the remainder of the current season and the next athletic season. The student is then retested prior to the start of the next athletic season for which he or she is eligible. The Policy states that a second offense results in automatic imposition of option (2); a third offense in suspension for the remainder of the current season and the next two athletic seasons.

C

In the fall of 1991, respondent James Acton, then a seventh grader, signed up to play football at one of the District's grade schools. He was denied participation, however, because he and his parents refused to sign the testing consent forms. The Actons filed suit, seeking declaratory and injunctive relief from enforcement of the Policy on the grounds that it violated the *Fourth and Fourteenth Amendments to the United States Constitution and Article I, § 9, of the Oregon Constitution.* After a bench trial, the District Court entered an order denying the claims on the merits and dismissing the action. The United States Court of Appeals for the Ninth Circuit reversed, holding that the Policy violated both the *Fourth* and Fourteenth Amendments and Article I, § 9, of the Oregon Constitution. We granted certiorari.

II

The *Fourth Amendment to the United States Constitution* provides that the Federal Government shall not violate "the right of the people to be secure in their persons, houses, papers, and effects, against unreasonable searches and seizures . . . ." We have held that the Fourteenth Amendment extends this constitutional guarantee to searches and seizures by state officers, *Elkins v. United States,* 364 U.S. 206, 213 (1960), including public school officials, *New Jersey v. T. L. O.,* 469 U.S. 325, 336-337 (1985). In *Skinner v. Railway Labor Executives' Assn.,* 489 U.S. 602 (1989), we held that state-compelled collection and testing of urine, such as that required by the Policy, constitutes a "search" subject to the demands of the *Fourth Amendment.* As the text of the *Fourth Amendment* indicates, the ultimate measure of the constitutionality of a governmental search is "reasonableness". At least in a case such as this, where there was no clear practice, either approving or disapproving the type of search at issue, at the time the constitutional provision was enacted, whether a particular search meets the reasonableness standard "'is judged by balancing its intrusion on the individual's *Fourth Amendment* interests against its promotion of legitimate governmental interests.'" *Skinner, supra,* at 619. A search unsupported by probable cause can be constitutional, we have said, "when special needs, beyond the normal need for law enforcement, make the warrant and probable-cause requirement impracticable." *Griffin v. Wisconsin,* 483 U.S. 868, 873.

We have found such "special needs" to exist in the public school context. There, the warrant requirement "would unduly interfere with the maintenance of the swift and informal disciplinary procedures [that are] needed," and "strict adherence to the requirement that searches be based on probable cause" would undercut "the substantial need of teachers and administrators for freedom to maintain order in the schools." *T. L. O.,* 469 U.S. at 340, 341. The school search we approved in *T. L. O.,* while not based on probable cause, *was* based on individualized *suspicion* of wrongdoing. As we explicitly acknowledged, however, "'the *Fourth Amendment* imposes no irreducible requirement of such suspicion,'" *id.,* at 342, n. 8.

We have upheld suspicionless searches and seizures to conduct drug testing of railroad personnel involved in train accidents, to conduct random drug testing of federal customs officers who carry arms or are involved in drug interdiction, and to maintain automobile checkpoints looking for illegal immigrants and contraband, and drunk drivers, *Michigan Dept. of State Police v. Sitz,* 496 U.S. 444 (1990).

III

The first factor to be considered is the nature of the privacy interest upon which the search here at issue intrudes. The Fourth Amendment does not protect all subjective expectations of privacy, but only those that society recognizes as "legitimate." T. L. O., 469 U. S., at 338. What expectations are legitimate varies, of course, with context, depending, for example, upon whether the individual asserting the privacy interest is at home, at work, in a car, or in a public park. In addition, the legitimacy of certain privacy expectations vis à vis the State may depend upon the individual's legal relationship with the State. **** Central, in our view, to the present case is the fact that the subjects of the Policy are (1) children, who (2) have been committed to the temporary custody of the State as schoolmaster.

"[A] proper educational environment requires close supervision of schoolchildren, as well as the enforcement of rules against conduct that would be perfectly permissible if undertaken by an adult." 469 U. S., at 339. While we do not, of course, suggest that public schools as a general matter have such a degree of control over children as to give rise to a constitutional "duty to protect," we have acknowledged that for many purposes "school authorities ac[t] *in loco parentis*," with the power and indeed the duty to "inculcate the habits and manners of civility[.] Thus, while children assuredly do not "shed their constitutional rights . . . at the schoolhouse gate," *Tinker v. Des Moines Independent Community School Dist.*, 393 U.S. 503, 506 (1969), the nature of those rights is what is appropriate for children in school.

Fourth Amendment rights, no less than First and Fourteenth Amendment rights, are different in public schools than elsewhere; the "reasonableness" inquiry cannot disregard the schools' custodial and tutelary responsibility for children. For their own good and that of their classmates, public school children are routinely required to submit to various physical examinations, and to be vaccinated against various diseases..... Particularly with regard to medical examinations and procedures, therefore, "students within the school environment have a lesser expectation of privacy than members of the population generally."

Legitimate privacy expectations are even less with regard to student athletes. School sports are not for the bashful. They require "suiting up" before each practice or event, and showering and changing afterwards. Public school locker rooms, the usual sites for these activities, are not notable for the privacy they afford. The locker rooms in Vernonia are typical: no individual dressing rooms are provided; shower heads are lined up along a wall, unseparated by any sort of partition or curtain; not even all the toilet stalls have doors. As the United States Court of Appeals for the Seventh Circuit has noted, there is "an element of `communal undress' inherent in athletic participation[.]"

There is an additional respect in which school athletes have a reduced expectation of privacy. By choosing to "go out for the team," they voluntarily subject themselves to a degree of regulation even higher than that imposed on students generally. In Vernonia's public schools, they must submit to a preseason physical exam, they must acquire adequate insurance coverage or sign an insurance waiver, maintain a minimum grade point average, and comply with any "rules of conduct, dress, training hours and related matters as may be established for each sport by the head coach and athletic director with the principal's approval." Somewhat like adults who choose to participate in a "closely regulated industry," students who voluntarily participate in school athletics have reason to expect intrusions upon normal rights and privileges, including privacy. See *Skinner,* 489 U. S., at 627.

IV

Having considered the scope of the legitimate expectation of privacy at issue here, we turn next to the character of the intrusion that is complained of. We recognized in *Skinner* that collecting the samples for urinalysis intrudes upon «an excretory function traditionally shielded by great privacy.» *Skinner,* 489 U. S., at 626. We noted, however, that the degree of intrusion depends upon the manner in which production of the urine sample is monitored. Under the District›s Policy, male students produce samples at a urinal along a wall. They remain fully clothed and are only observed from behind, if at all. Female students produce samples in an enclosed stall, with a female monitor standing outside listening only for sounds of tampering. These conditions are nearly identical to those typically encountered in public restrooms, which men, women, and especially school children use daily. Under such conditions, the privacy interests compromised by the process of obtaining the urine sample are in our view negligible. The other privacy invasive aspect of urinalysis is, of course, the information it discloses concerning the state of the subject's body, and the materials he has ingested. In this regard it is significant that the tests at issue here look only for drugs, and not for whether the student is, for example, epileptic, pregnant, or diabetic. Moreover, the drugs for which the samples are screened are standard, and do not vary according to the identity of the student. And finally, the results of the tests are disclosed only to a limited class of school personnel who have a need to know; and they are not turned over to law enforcement authorities or used for any internal disciplinary function.

Respondents argue, however, that the District's Policy is in fact more intrusive than this suggests, because it requires the students, if they are to avoid sanctions for a falsely positive test, to identify *in advance* prescription medications they are taking. We agree that this raises some cause for concern. In *Von Raab,* we flagged as one of the salutary features of the Customs Service drug testing program the fact that employees were not required to disclose medical information unless they tested positive, and, even then, the information was supplied to a licensed physician rather than to the Government employer. On the other hand, we have never indicated that requiring advance disclosure of medications is *per se* unreasonable. Indeed, in *Skinner* we held that it was not «a significant invasion of privacy.» *Skinner,* 489 U. S., at 626, n. 7. It can be argued that, in *Skinner,* the disclosure went only to the medical personnel taking the sample, and the Government personnel analyzing it, and that disclosure to teachers and coaches – to persons who personally *know* the student – is a greater invasion of privacy. Assuming for the sake of argument that both those propositions are true, we do not believe they establish a difference that respondents are entitled to rely on here.

***Accordingly, we reach the same conclusion as in *Skinner:* that the invasion of privacy was not significant.

V

Finally, we turn to consider the nature and immediacy of the governmental concern at issue here, and the efficacy of this means for meeting it. It is a mistake to think that the phrase "compelling state interest," in the Fourth Amendment context, describes a fixed, minimum quantum of governmental concern, so that one can dispose of a case by answering in isolation the question: Is there a compelling state interest here? Rather, the phrase describes an interest which appears *important enough* to justify the particular search at hand, in light of other factors which show the search to be relatively intrusive upon a genuine expectation of privacy. Whether that relatively high degree of government concern is necessary in this case or not, we think it is met.

That the nature of the concern is important – indeed, perhaps compelling – can hardly be doubted. Deterring drug use by our Nation's schoolchildren is at least as important as enhancing efficient enforcement of the Nation's laws against the importation of drugs, which was the governmental concern in *Von Raab*, or deterring drug use by engineers and trainmen, which was the governmental concern in *Skinner*. School years are the time when the physical, psychological, and addictive effects of drugs are most severe. And of course the effects of a drug infested school are visited not just upon the users, but upon the entire student body and faculty, as the educational process is disrupted. In the present case, moreover, the necessity for the State to act is magnified by the fact that this evil is being visited not just upon individuals at large, but upon children for whom it has undertaken a special responsibility of care and direction. Finally, it must not be lost sight of that this program is directed more narrowly to drug use by school athletes, where the risk of immediate physical harm to the drug user or those with whom he is playing his sport is particularly high. Apart from psychological effects, which include impairment of judgment, slow reaction time, and a lessening of the perception of pain, the particular drugs screened by the District's Policy have been demonstrated to pose substantial physical risks to athletes. Amphetamines produce an "artificially induced heart rate increase, [p]eripheral vasoconstriction, [b]lood pressure increase, and [m]asking of the normal fatigue response," making them a "very dangerous drug when used during exercise of any type." *Hawkins, Drugs and Other Ingesta: Effects on Athletic Performance,* in H. Appenzeller, Managing Sports and Risk Management Strategies 90, 90-91 (1993). Marijuana causes "[i]rregular blood pressure responses during changes in body position," "[r]eduction in the oxygen carrying capacity of the blood," and "[i]nhibition of the normal sweating responses resulting in increased body temperature." *Id.,* at 94. Cocaine produces "[v]asoconstriction[,] [e]levated blood pressure," and "[p]ossible coronary artery spasms and myocardial infarction."

*** As to the efficacy of this means for addressing the problem: It seems to us self-evident that a drug problem largely fueled by the "role model" effect of athletes' drug use, and of particular danger to athletes, is effectively addressed by making sure that athletes do not use drugs. Respondents argue that a "less intrusive means to the same end" was available, namely, "drug testing on suspicion of drug use." Brief for Respondents 45-46. We have repeatedly refused to declare that only the "least intrusive" search practicable can be reasonable under the Fourth Amendment.

*   *   *

Taking into account all the factors we have considered above – the decreased expectation of privacy, the relative unobtrusiveness of the search, and the severity of the need met by the search – we conclude Vernonia's Policy is reasonable and hence constitutional.

NOTES & QUESTIONS

1. Do you agree with the Court's conclusion that "school athletes have a reduced expectation of privacy [b]y going out for a team" because they voluntarily submit to a higher degree of regulation than the general student body? The Court states that this higher degree of regulation includes "rules of conduct [and] dress." What if the coach prohibits the wearing of a yarmulke or head-scarf during practice and competition? Should the Court defer to the coach's dress regulation in this instance, given one's First Amendment right to freely practice his or her religion?

2. Do you agree with the *Vernonia* Court's finding that the "character of the intrusion," regarding the manner and production of the urine sample, was "negligible"?

3. The NCAA adopted a comprehensive drug-testing program in 1986. Stanford University student athletes sued the NCAA claiming its drug-testing program violated their right to privacy under the Article I, § 1 of the California Constitution that expressly recognizes certain inalienable rights, including the "pursu[it of] safety, happiness and privacy." *Hill v. National Collegiate Athletic Assn.*, 865 P.2d 633, 641 (CA 1994). The trial court ruled the testing program violated the students' right to privacy and permanently enjoined the NCAA from testing the athletes. It further found that the university lacked a compelling need for the program. The Court of Appeals affirmed the trial court's judgment. The California Supreme Court reversed and held that the NCAA's drug testing policy did not violate the state constitutional right to privacy because the student athletes had a diminished expectation of privacy by participating in athletic activity that *by its nature* required frequent physical examinations. In addition, the Court found that the student athletes had advanced notice of the testing and the ability to consent to it. Despite the fact that refusing to consent meant disqualification from competition, the Court did not find the consent to be involuntary because the student athletes had no legal right to participate in sports. Should there be greater restrictions on the ability of schools to conduct drug-testing programs for student athletes? Should university athletes be treated differently than high school athletes when it comes to drug-testing? The *Hill* Court noted there is no explicit reference to a privacy right in the federal constitution, although "[t]he Fourth Amendment's search and seizure clause is sometimes referred to as a privacy provision." *Id.* at 650. Thus, the *Hill* decision rests squarely on the California Supreme Court's interpretation of an express provision in its state constitution. What arguments would you advance on behalf of the Stanford athletes if Article I, § 1 of the California statute did not expressly protect privacy?

GREENAWAY, JR., CIRCUIT JUDGE.

* * *

I. Facts

[Ryan] Hart was a quarterback, player number 13, with the Rutgers University NCAA Men's Division I Football team for the 2002 through 2005 seasons. As a condition of participating in college-level sports, Hart was required to adhere to the National Collegiate Athletic Association's ("NCAA") amateurism rules as set out in Article 12 of the NCAA bylaws. *See,* e.g., NCAA, *2011-12 NCAA Division I Manual* § 12.01.1 (2011)("Only an amateur student-athlete is eligible for inter-collegiate athletics participation in a particular sport."). In relevant part, these rules state that a collegiate athlete loses his or her "amateur" status if (1) the athlete "[u]ses his or her athletics skill (directly or indirectly) for pay in any form in that sport," *id.* § 12.1.2, or (2) the athlete "[a]ccepts any remuneration or permits the use of his or her name or picture to advertise, recommend or promote directly the sale or use of a commercial product or service of any kind," *id.* § 12.5.2.1.2. In comporting with these bylaws, Hart purportedly refrained from seizing on various commercial opportunities. On the field, Hart excelled. At 6'2", weighing 197 pounds, and typically wearing a visor and armband on his left wrist, Hart amassed an impressive list of achievements as the Scarlet Knights' starting quarterback. As of this writing, Hart still holds the Scarlet Knights' records for career attempts, completions, and interceptions. Hart's skill brought success to the team and during his senior year the Knights were invited to the Insight Bowl, their first Bowl game since 1978.

Hart's participation in college football also ensured his inclusion in EA's successful NCAA *Football* videogame franchise. EA, founded in 1982, is "one of the world's leading interactive entertainment software companies," and "develops, publishes, and distributes interactive software worldwide" for consoles, cell phones, and PCs. EA's catalogue includes *NCAA Football,* the videogame series at issue in the instant case. . . . New editions in the series are released annually, and "allow[] users to experience the excitement and challenge of college football" by interacting with "over 100 virtual teams and thousands of virtual players."

* * *

In no small part, the *NCAA Football* franchise's success owes to its focus on realism and detail — from realistic sounds, to game mechanics, to team mascots. This focus on realism also ensures that the "over 100 virtual teams" in the game are populated by digital avatars that resemble their real-life counterparts and share their vital and biographical information. Thus, for example, in *NCAA Football 2006,* Rutgers' quarterback, player number 13, is 6'2" tall, weighs 197 pounds and resembles Hart. Moreover, while users can change the digital avatar's appearance and most of the vital statistics (height, weight, throwing distance, etc.), certain details remain immutable: the player's home state, home town, team, and class year.

*** [O]n October 12, 2010, Appellant filed his second amended complaint, again alleging a claim pursuant to the right of publicity based on Appellee's purported misappropriation of Appellant's identity and likeness to enhance the commercial value of *NCAA Football.* Specifically, Appellant alleges that (1) Appellee replicated his likeness in *NCAA Football 2004, 2005,* and *2006* (complete with biographical and career statistics) and that (2) Appellee used Appellant's image "in the promotion for [*NCAA Football*] wherein [Appellant] was throwing a pass with actual footage from Rutgers University's Bowl Game against Arizona State University."

*** The District Court . . . ruled in favor of [the] Appellee, holding that *NCAA Football* was entitled to protection under the *First Amendment.* Appellant timely appealed, arguing that the District Court erred in granting summary judgment prematurely and, in the alternative, erred in holding that *NCAA Football* was shielded from right of publicity claims by the *First Amendment.* . . .

III. Discussion

We begin our analysis by noting the self-evident: video games are protected as expressive speech under the *First Amendment. Brown v. Entm't Merchs. Ass'n,* 131 S. Ct. 2729, 2733 (2011). As the Supreme Court has noted, "video games communicate ideas — and even social messages — through many familiar literary devices (such as characters, dialogue, plot, and music) and through features distinctive to the medium (such as the player's interaction with the virtual world)." *Id.* As a result, games enjoy the full force of *First Amendment* protections. As with other types of expressive conduct, the protection afforded to games can be limited in situations where the right of free expression necessarily conflicts with other protected rights.

The instant case presents one such situation. Here, Appellee concedes, for purposes of the motion and appeal, that it violated Appellant's right of publicity; in essence, misappropriating his identity for commercial exploitation. However, Appellee contends that the *First Amendment* shields it from liability for this violation because *NCAA Football* is a protected work. To resolve the tension between the *First Amendment* and the right of publicity, we must balance the interests underlying the right to free expression against the interests in protecting the right of publicity. *See Zacchini v. Scripps-Howard Broad. Co.,* 433 U.S. 562, 574-75 (1977). . . . In our discussion below, we first consider the nature of the interests we must balance and then analyze the different approaches courts have taken to resolving the tension between the First Amendment and the right of publicity.

A. The Relevant Interests at Issue

* * *

1. Freedom of Expression

Freedom of expression is paramount in a democratic society, for "[i]t is the function of speech to free men from the bondage of irrational fears." *Whitney v. California,* 274 U.S. 357, 376 (1927). As Justice Louis Brandeis wrote nearly a century ago:

> Those who won our independence believed that the final end of the state was to make men free to develop their faculties . . . . They valued liberty both as an end and as a means. They believed liberty to [be] the secret of happiness and courage to be the secret of liberty. They believed that freedom to think as you will and to speak as you think are means indispensable to the discovery and spread of political truth; that without free speech and assembly discussion would be futile; that with them, discussion affords ordinarily adequate protection against the dissemination of noxious doctrine; that the greatest menace to freedom is an inert people; that public discussion is a political duty; and that this should be a fundamental principle of the American government. *Id.* at 375.

In keeping with Justice Brandeis' eloquent analysis, the great legal minds of generations past and present have recognized that free speech benefits both the individual and society. The Supreme Court in *Procunier v. Martinez* noted that the protection of free speech serves the needs "of the human spirit — a spirit that demands self-expression," adding that "[s]uch expression is an integral part of the development of ideas and a sense of identity." *416 U.S. 396, 427 (1974).* Suppressing such expression, therefore, is tantamount to rejecting "the basic human desire for recognition and [would] affront the individual's worth and dignity." *Id.* Indeed, *First Amendment* protections have been held applicable to not only political speech, but to "entertainment [including, but certainly not limited to,] motion pictures, programs broadcast by radio and television, and live entertainment, such as musical and dramatic works." *Tacynec v. City of Phila.,* 687 F.2d 793, 796 (3d Cir. 1982). Thus, "[t]he breadth of this protection evinces recognition that freedom of expression is not only essential to check tyranny and foster self-government but also intrinsic to individual liberty and dignity and instrumental in society's search for truth." *Dun & Bradstreet, Inc. v. Greenmoss Builders, Inc.,* 472 U.S. 749, 787 (1985) (Brennan, J., dissenting).

The interest in safeguarding the integrity of these protections therefore weighs heavily in any balancing inquiry. Still, instances can and do arise where *First Amendment* protections yield in the face of competing interests. *See, e.g., Eldred v. Ashcroft,* 537 U.S. 186, 219-203 (2003)(discussing the interplay between copyright law and *First Amendment* protections); *Dun & Bradstreet, Inc.,* 472 U.S. at 757-61 (determining that a state may allow recovery of damages in certain defamation cases after balancing "the State's interest in compensating private individuals for injury to their reputation against the *First Amendment* interest in protecting this type of expression"). Ultimately, we must determine whether the interest in safeguarding the right of publicity overpowers the interest in safeguarding free expression.

* * *

IV. Analysis of the Transformative Use Test

[The Third Circuit considered three possible tests to apply in balancing the interest protected by the right of publicity against those interests preserved by the *First Amendment*.] In our view, the Transformative Use Test appears to strike the best balance because it provides courts with a flexible yet uniformly applicable — analytical framework.

* * *

[T]he Transformative Use Test is the most consistent with other courts' ad hoc approaches to right of publicity cases. For example, a majority of the Supreme Court of California in *Guglielmi v. Spelling-Goldberg Productions* argued that the "fictionalized version" of a late actor's life, "depicting the actor's name, likeness and personality without obtaining . . . prior consent" was entitled to protection from a right of publicity claim. *603 P.2d at 455, 457-59.* In essence, the actor's identity was sufficiently transformed by the fictional elements in the book so as to tip the balance of interests in favor of the *First Amendment.* . . . Additionally, in *Cardtoons, L.C. v. Major League Baseball Players Ass'n,* 95 F.3d 959 (10th Cir. 1996), which focused on the use of baseball players' identities for parody trading cards, the transformative nature of the caricatures on the cards (and the parodic text about the players' "statistics") was sufficient to quash any right of publicity claim. *Id.* at 972-73 ("Because celebrities are an important part of our public vocabulary, a parody of a celebrity does not merely lampoon the celebrity, but exposes the weakness of the idea or value that the celebrity symbolizes in society."). ***

* * *

C. Application

In applying the Transformative Use Test to the instant case, we must determine whether Appellant's identity is sufficiently transformed in *NCAA Football.* *** [W]e use the term "identity" to encompass not only Appellant's likeness, but also his biographical information. It is the combination of these two parts — which, when combined, identify the digital avatar as an in-game recreation of Appellant — that must be sufficiently transformed.

Having thus cabined our inquiry to the appropriate form of Appellant's identity, we note that — based on the combination of both the digital avatar's appearance and the biographical and identifying information — the digital avatar does closely resemble the genuine article. Not only does the digital avatar match Appellant in terms of hair color, hairstyle and skin-tone, but the avatar's accessories mimic those worn by Appellant during his time as a Rutgers player. The information, as has already been noted, also accurately tracks Appellant's vital and biographical details. And while the inexorable march of technological progress may make some of the graphics in earlier editions of *NCAA Football* look dated or overly-computerized, we do not believe that video game graphics must reach (let alone cross) the uncanny valley to support a right of publicity claim. If we are to find some transformative element, we must look somewhere other than just the in-game digital recreation of Appellant.

Considering the context within which the digital avatar exists — effectively, looking at how Appellant's identity is "incorporated into and transformed by" *NCAA Football,* — provides little support for Appellee's arguments. The digital Ryan Hart does what the actual Ryan Hart did while at Rutgers: he plays college football, in digital recreations of college football stadiums, filled with all the trappings of a college football game. This is not transformative; the various digitized sights and sounds in the video game do not alter or transform the Appellant's identity in a significant way. . . .

Even here, however, our inquiry is not at an end. For as much as the digital representation and context evince no meaningful transformative element in NCAA Football, a third avatar-specific element is also present: the users' ability to alter the avatar's appearance. *** Indeed, the ability for users to change the avatar accounted, in large part, for the District Court's deciding that *NCAA Football* satisfied the Transformative Use Test. *See Hart,* 808 F. Supp. 2d at 785. We must therefore consider to what extent the ability to alter a digital avatar represents a transformative use of Appellant's identity.

At the outset, we note that the mere presence of this feature, without more, cannot satisfy the Transformative Use Test. True, interactivity is the basis upon which *First Amendment* protection is granted to video games in the first instance. However, the balancing test in right of publicity cases does not look to whether a particular work *loses First Amendment* protection. Rather, the balancing inquiry looks to see whether the interests protected by the right of publicity are sufficient to *surmount* the already-existing *First Amendment* protections. *** To hold, therefore, that a video game should satisfy the Transformative Use Test simply because it includes a particular interactive feature would lead to improper results. Interactivity cannot be an end onto itself.

Moreover, we are wary of converting the ability to alter a digital avatar from mere feature to talisman, thereby opening the door to cynical abuse. If the mere presence of the feature were enough, video game companies could commit the most blatant acts of misappropriation only to absolve themselves by including a feature that allows users to modify the digital likenesses. We cannot accept that such an outcome would adequately balance the interests in right of publicity cases. . . .

* * *

For these reasons, we hold that the broad application of the Transformative Use Test represents an inappropriate application of the standard. Consequently, we shall not credit elements of *NCAA Football* that do not, in some way, affect the use or meaning of Appellant's identity.

As a final point, we note that the photograph of Appellant that appears in NCAA Football 2009 does not bear on our analysis above. On that subject, we agree with the District Court that the photograph is "but a fleeting component part of the montage" and therefore does not render the entire work nontransformative. *Hart,* 808 F. Supp. 2d at 786. The reasoning from *ETW* is sufficiently applicable: the context of Appellant's photograph — the montage — imbues the image with additional meaning beyond simply being a representation of the player. *See ETW,* 332 F.3d at 938 (holding that the photographs in a collage were "combined to describe, in artistic form, a historic event in sports history and to convey a message about the significance of [Tiger] Woods's achievement in that event"). Consequently, this particular use of Appellant's likeness *is* shielded by the *First Amendment* and therefore can contribute nothing to Appellant's claim for violation of his right of publicity.

IV. Conclusion

We therefore hold that the *NCAA Football 2004, 2005* and *2006* games at issue in this case do not sufficiently transform Appellant's identity to escape the right of publicity claim and hold that the District Court erred in granted summary judgment in favor of Appellee. While we do hold that the only apparent use of Appellant's likeness in *NCAA Football 2009* (the photograph) is protected by the *First Amendment,* Appellant's overall claim for violation of his right of publicity should have survived Appellee's motion for summary judgment. . . . We shall reverse the District Court's grant of summary judgment and remand this case back to the court below . . . .

NOTES & QUESTIONS

1. For a case that distinguished *Hart, see Mitchell v. Cartoon Network, Inc.,* No.15-5668 2015 U.S. Dist. LEXIS 157737 (D.N.J. Nov. 20, 2015). There the court applied the Transformative Use test and dismissed the plaintiff's right of publicity claim. Mitchell is a "well-known figure in the video gaming community, recognizable by his long black hair and black beard, black suit or dress shirt, and American flag tie." *Id.* *1-2. He is well known because of his world records in various arcade games like Pac-Man and Donkey Kong. Mitchell claimed "The Regular Show" on Cartoon Network violated his right to publicity by creating an animated character, "GBF." GBF has long black hair and a black beard, but GBF is a floating head from outer space. The court distinguished this case from *Hart* because there the football player avatar was basically a recreation of the real football player; here, a floating head from outer space who happens to hold "universe records" in arcade games is not the same as the real-life gamer. *Id.* at *15. "GBF is not a literal recreation of Plaintiff at all: GBF looks different from Plaintiff, comes from a different planet, plays a different game, holds a different record, and uses different methods to secure his high score. While at the highest level of generality, both Plaintiff and GBF compete at video games, this broad commonality does not make GBF and Plaintiff similar enough to make GBF non-transformative. *** Because they have added something new, Defendants' appropriation of Plaintiff's identity passes the Transformative Use Test, and thus receives [First Amendment] protection . . . ." *Id.* at *17.

2. For another recent case presenting similar right of publicity issues, *see Daniels v. FanDuel, Inc.,* 116CV01230TWPDKL, 2017 WL 4340329 (S.D. Ind. Sept. 29, 2017), *aff'd,* 909 F.3d 876 (7th Cir. 2018). Court determined that the Indiana right of publicity statute's exceptions relating

to public interest and newsworthiness shielded defendant (*i.e.,* a gambling website) from college football players' claims relating to defendant's use of their names.

3. For additional thoughts regarding the right of publicity issue raised in this case, refer to Note 4 following *Bloom v. NCAA* in Chapter 9. *See also* Section C. "Right of Publicity" in Chapter 11.

Further Reading on Constitutional Law:

Sarah Brown & Natasha Brison, *More Than an Athlete: Constitutional and Contractual Analysis of Activism in Professional Sports,* 7 Ariz. St. Sports & Ent. L.J. 249, 249 (2018).

Walter T. Champion, *No Pass, No Play - Texas Style,* 5 Ent. & Sports Law 5 (1986).

Jonathan G. Finck, *Can NFL Players Be Punished for Kneeling? An Analysis of the Banter Surrounding the Star-Spangled Banner,* 21 U. Den. Sports & Ent. L.J. 125 (2018).

J. Wes Gay, *Hands Off Twitter: Are NCAA Student-Athlete Social Media Bans Unconstitutional?,* 39 Fla. St. U. L. Rev. 781 (2012).

Ray D. Hacke, *"Girls Will Be Boys, and Boys Will Be Girls": The Emergence of the Transgender Athlete and A Defensive Game Plan for High Schools That Want to Keep Their Playing Fields Level-for Athletes of Both Genders,* 18 Tex. Rev. Ent. & Sports L. 131 (2018).

Tyler C. Haslam, *Leveling the Playing Field: Using Rational Basis with A Bite As Means of Overcoming the NCAA's Violation of Equal Protection,* 37 Ohio N.U. L. Rev. 283 (2011).

James Hefferan, *Picking Up the Flag? The University of Missouri Football Team and Whether Intercollegiate Student-Athletes May Be Penalized for Exercising Their First Amendment Rights,* 12 DePaul J. Sports L. & Contemp. Probs. 44 (2016).

Christopher J. Kaufman, *Unsportsmanlike Conduct: 15-Yard Penalty and Loss of Free Speech in Public University Sports Stadiums,* 57 U. Kan. L. Rev. 1235 (2009).

Ronald S. Katz & Robert W. Luckinbill, *Changing Sex/gender Roles and Sport,* 28 Stan. L. & Policy Rev. 215 (2017).

Lewis Kurlantzick, *John Rocker and Employee Discipline for Speech,* 11 Marq. Sports L. Rev. 185 (2001).

Carmen Maye, *Public-College Student-Athletes and Game-Time Anthem Protests: Is There A Need for A Constitutional-Analytical Audible?,* 24 Comm. L. & Policy 55 (2019).

Matthew J. Mitten & Timothy Davis, *Athlete Eligibility Requirements and Legal Protection of Sports Participation Opportunities,* 8 Va. Sports & Enter. L.J. 71 (2008).

Mathew J. Parlow, *Race, Speech, and Sports,* 52 U. Rich. L. Rev. 923 (2018).

Jon Perrelle, *An Opportunity for Reform: Tennessee Secondary School Athletic Association v. Brentwood Academy and NCAA Recruiting,* 74 Brook. L. Rev. 1213 (2010).

Robert E. Shepherd, Jr., *Why Can't Johnny Read or Play,* 1 Soviet L. & Bus. News 163 (1991).

Russ VerSteeg, *Blackhawk Down or Blackhorse Down? The Lanham Act's Prohibition of Trademarks That "May Disparage" & the First Amendment,* 68 Okla. L. Rev. 677 (2016).

CHAPTER 8

TITLE IX, THE REHABILITATION ACT, AND THE AMERICANS WITH DISABILITIES ACT

This chapter examines three important and controversial topics in Sports Law today: 1) Title IX; 2) the Rehabilitation Act of 1973; and, 3) the Americans with Disabilities Act of 1990 ("ADA"). Part A of the chapter begins with Glenn George's article summarizing the basic rules of Title IX and its application to athletics through formative case law. The first case, *Daniels,* reviews Title IX's rules and expands upon them by interpreting the relevant Code of Federal Regulations provisions in light of the disparate treatment afforded a high school girls' softball team. The second case, *Mercer,* adds additional perspective in a case involving a collegiate contact sport, football. *Boucher* illustrates the types of struggles that colleges and universities have experienced in their efforts to comply with the proportionality requirements of Title IX. The final two cases, *Boulahanis* and *Equity in Athletics,* take that issue further, examining financial decisions and the potential for reverse discrimination that institutions face.

While reading these cases you might want to give some thought to other instances of sports-related gender discrimination. For example, in recent years, a number of women's professional teams, such as the United States women's ice hockey and soccer teams, have fought for equality in pay and other working conditions – and and have gained some success. *See e.g.,* https://thinkprogress.org/womens-soccer-secures-new-deal-ffe06dc4b9e1/.

Part B discusses the Rehabilitation Act of 1973 and the Americans with Disabilities Act of 1990. It begins with Maureen Weston's article that examines both Acts and identifies primarily three types of cases involving athletes and disability rights issues. Three cases follow Weston's article and demonstrate, in part, the scope and complexity of these Acts in providing disabled athletes with greater access to compete in sports. The first case, *Knapp,* considers rules restricting the eligibility of athletes with enhanced health risks. The second case, *Ganden,* discusses a disabled athlete who failed to meet a "neutral" eligibility requirement. The final case, *Martin,* illustrates an example of a disabled athlete pursuing an accommodating rule change under the ADA.

A. TITLE IX

TITLE IX AND THE SCHOLARSHIP DILEMMA

B. GLENN GEORGE

9 MARQ. SPORTS L. J. 273 (1999)

I. A Brief History of Title IX

Although...[enacted June 23, 1972], Title IX...only developed as a driving force in intercollegiate athletics during the [1990's]. Title IX's prohibition, included in the Education Amendments of 1972, states in straight-forward terms that no one "shall, on the basis of sex, be excluded from participation in, be denied the benefits of, or be subjected to discrimination under any education program or activity receiving Federal financial assistance." Some schools responded immediately, and there were significant early gains in the participation rates of women in intercollegiate athletic programs. Prior to Title IX, women accounted for only fifteen percent of intercollegiate student athletes; the participation rate for women doubled by 1984.

The application of this prohibition to intercollegiate athletics, however, was not secured until 1988. Some early interpretations of the legislation had limited its application to *the particular university programs actually receiving federal dollars.*(emphasis added). In 1984, the Supreme Court took the same position in the case of *Grove City College v. Bell.*[1] Congress acted four years later to overturn the result in *Grove City College.* The Civil Rights Restoration Act of 1987 (1988 Amendments)[2] amended Title IX to extend its prohibition against sex discrimination to the entire institution as long as a single program within the institution received federal funds. Thus, Title IX did not come into its own as a force in the world of intercollegiate athletics until [the late 1980's].

In spite of Title IX's questionable application to intercollegiate athletics in its early days, the Secretary of the Department of Health, Education and Welfare moved ahead under statutory mandate to issue regulations governing college sports programs.[3] Those regulations were issued in 1975 and, interestingly enough, included a section on the allocation of financial aid:

(1) To the extent that a recipient awards athletic scholarship or grants-in-aid, it must provide reasonable opportunities for such award for members of each sex in proportion to the number of students of each sex participating in interscholastic or intercollegiate athletics.

(2) Separate athletic scholarships or grants-in-aid for members of each sex may be provided as part of separate athletic teams for members of each sex to the extent consistent with this paragraph and § 106.41.[4]

---

1 465 U.S. 555 (1984).

2 20 U.S.C. § 1687 (1988).

3 See Education Amendments of 1974, Pub. L. No. 93-380, § 844, 88 Stat. 612 (1974). The Javits Amendment, adopted by Congress in 1974, required the Department of Health, Education and Welfare to issue regulations under Title IX concerning intercollegiate athletic activities.

4 34 C.F.R. § 106.37(c) (1997).

Another section of the 1975 regulations defined the concept of "equal opportunity" in college sports programs by listing ten factors for consideration. Four years later, the Secretary provided further enlightenment in the 1979 Policy Interpretation which focused exclusively on the application of Title IX to intercollegiate athletics. In 1980, enforcement authority was transferred to the newly created Department of Education and its Office for Civil Rights (OCR).

A. The First Wave: Proportionality in Participation Rates

Soon after the application of Title IX to intercollegiate athletics was secured in 1988, frustrated women athletes and their advocates turned to the judicial system for relief. A wave of litigation in the early 1990s focused primarily on the issue of participation rates, disputes which were often prompted by the institution's decisions to eliminate both men's and women's teams as part of general budget cuts. The question of participation opportunities understandably took precedent – issues like financial aid, equipment budgets, and practice facilities were irrelevant unless women's teams existed to enjoy those benefits.

OCR's definition of equity in participation rates, generally adopted by the courts, made most of these cases clear winners for the complaining women athletes. OCR's Policy Interpretation offered three avenues for demonstrating compliance in this area, yet only one option was available as a practical matter. In the 1975 regulations, the first factor in the consideration of equal opportunity was "[w]hether the selection of sports and levels of competition effectively accommodate the interests and abilities of members of both sexes." The 1979 Policy Interpretation elaborated on that requirement by establishing three possible measures:

(1) Whether intercollegiate level participation opportunities for male and female students are provided in numbers substantially proportionate to their respective enrollments; or

(2) Where the members of one sex have been and are underrepresented among intercollegiate athletes, whether the institution can show a history and continuing practice of program expansion which is demonstrably responsive to the developing interest and abilities of the members of that sex; or

(3) Where the members of one sex are underrepresented among intercollegiate athletes, and the institution cannot show a continuing practice of program expansion such as that cited above, whether it can be demonstrated that the interests and abilities of the members of that sex have been fully and effectively accommodated by the present program.

As a practical matter, the first option under the Policy Interpretation – the proportionality standard – became the only relevant issue. The expansion of women's teams in the 1970s was followed by the elimination of both men's and women's teams in the 1990s as budgets tightened. Thus, few schools could point to any recent history of expanding opportunities for women, as required by the second option. The very uncertainty of defining and measuring what it means to "effectively accommodate the interests of both sexes" in option three apparently caused most courts to avoid that standard altogether. By default, the only safe harbor became the proportionality standard. Consequently, school after school lost on (or chose not to dispute), the simple calculation of comparing the percentage of women in the student body to the percentage of women in the intercollegiate athletic program.

Cohen v. Brown University,[5] perhaps one of the best known Title IX cases, is a good example. In 1991, Brown University decided to eliminate women's volleyball and gymnastics, as well as men's golf and water polo, in a belt-tightening move. The women sued and obtained a preliminary injunction to restore the women's teams. The plaintiff's proof was simple – both before and after the cuts, the number of female intercollegiate athletes at Brown University continued to lag behind the percentage of women in the general student body. After two appeals to the First Circuit and a denial of certiorari by the Supreme Court, Brown University finally threw in the towel. Brown University's failure to convince the Supreme Court to reexamine the mechanical approach of the proportionality standard was understood by most as the loss of both the battle and the war.

Given the almost universal success of the proportionality standard, most institutions had a clear understanding of their participation obligations under Title IX and began moving toward compliance.

* * *

NOTES *&* QUESTIONS

1. Explain in your own words the significance of *Grove City College v. Bell*.

2. What role has the Office for Civil Rights played in the current status of Title IX?

3. Explain what the "proportionality standard" is.

4. Title IX requirements apply to any school or university receiving "federal financial assistance." Where the university as a whole receives federal monies, for example, financial aid for students, is its athletic department governed by Title IX even if the department does not directly receive earmarked federal funds? In *Haffer v. Temple University*, 688 F.2d 14 (3d Cir. 1982), eight undergraduate women sued Temple claiming that its intercollegiate athletics program discriminated against them on the basis of sex. *Id.* at 15. The *Haffer* court held that congress intended Title IX to apply to the university as a whole whenever students directly receive federal grants or loans irrespective of direct federal aid for the athletic department. *Id.* at 16-17. "[F]ederal money sent to the University itself frees nonfederal funds which can be allocated to intercollegiate athletics . . . ." *Id.* at 17.

5. Is the NCAA a recipient of federal financial assistance and thus subject to Title IX because the NCAA gets dues from member institutions that receive federal funds? In *Smith v. NCAA*, 525 U.S. 459 (1999), the Supreme Court held that it is not. Smith was a student-athlete who completed her undergraduate work in 2.5 years at St. Bonaventure and during that time

---

5   809 F. Supp. 978 (D.R.I. 1992).

played intercollegiate volleyball for two years. Smith then enrolled in post-graduate work at two different schools and wanted to continue playing intercollegiate volleyball. The NCAA would not provide her a waiver of its rule that permitted postgraduate participation in intercollegiate athletics at only the institution that awarded the student-athlete's undergraduate degree. Smith claimed the NCAA implicitly discriminated against women by allowing more waivers from eligibility restrictions to male than female postgraduate student-athletes. *Id.* at 64. However, the Supreme Court held that the NCAA is not subject to Title IX requirements even though it receives dues from members who receive federal funding. *Id* at 470.

DANIELS V. SCHOOL BOARD OF BREVARD COUNTY
985 F. SUPP. 1458 (1997)
UNITED STATES DISTRICT COURT, M.D. FLORIDA, ORLANDO DIVISION

CONWAY, DISTRICT JUDGE.

I. INTRODUCTION

The Plaintiffs in this action are Jessica and Jennifer Daniels, and their father, Daniel Daniels. Jessica and Jennifer are seniors at Merritt Island High School ("MIHS"). They both are members of the girls' varsity softball team.

Plaintiffs have sued the Defendant, School Board of Brevard County, based on disparities between the MIHS girls' softball and boys' baseball programs. They assert claims pursuant to 20 U.S.C. § 1681 ("Title IX") and the Florida Educational Equity Act, Fla.Stat. § 228.2001 ("the Florida Act").

Plaintiffs seek a preliminary injunction. On November 24, 1997, the Court heard oral argument on the motion. After considering the parties' evidentiary submissions, legal memoranda and arguments, the Court determines that the Plaintiffs are entitled to a preliminary injunction.

II. PRELIMINARY INJUNCTION STANDARD

"A plaintiff moving for a preliminary injunction must show: (1) a substantial likelihood of success on the merits; (2) a substantial threat of irreparable injury; (3) that the threatened injury to the plaintiff outweighs the injury to the nonmovant; and (4) that the injunction would not disserve the public interest." *Statewide Detective Agency v. Miller,* 115 F.3d 904, 905 (11th Cir.1997).

III. TITLE IX AND THE FLORIDA ACT

Subject to exceptions not pertinent here, Title IX provides:
No person in the United States shall, on the basis of sex, be excluded from participation in, be denied the benefits of, or be subjected to discrimination under any education program or activity receiving Federal financial assistance[.] 20 U.S.C. § 1681(a).

"Congress enacted Title IX in response to its finding – after extensive hearings held in 1970 by the House Special Subcommittee on Education – of pervasive discrimination against women with respect to educational opportunities." *Cohen v. Brown University,* 101 F.3d 155, 165 (1st Cir.1996), *cert. denied,* 520 U.S. 1186, 117 S.Ct. 1469, 137 L.Ed.2d 682 (1997). "Title IX was passed with two objectives in mind: 'to avoid the use of federal resources to support discriminatory practices,' and 'to provide individual citizens effective protection against those practices.'" *Id.* (quoting *Cannon v. University of Chicago,* 441 U.S. 677, 704, 99 S.Ct. 1946, 1961, 60 L.Ed.2d 560 (1979)).

Title IX is implemented with respect to athletic activities by 34 C.F.R. § 106.41. Section § 106.41(a) generally provides:

> No person shall, on the basis of sex, be excluded from participation in, be denied the benefits of, be treated differently from another person or otherwise be discriminated against in any interscholastic, intercollegiate, club or intramural athletics offered by a recipient, and no recipient shall provide any such athletics separately on such basis.

Section 106.41(c) provides:

> A recipient which operates or sponsors interscholastic, intercollegiate, club or intramural athletics shall provide equal athletic opportunity for members of both sexes. In determining whether equal opportunities are available the Director will consider, among other factors:
> (1) Whether the selection of sports and levels of competition effectively accommodate the interests and abilities of members of both sexes;
> (2) The provision of equipment and supplies;
> (3) Scheduling of games and practice times;
> (4) Travel and per diem allowance;
> (5) Opportunity to receive coaching and academic tutoring;
> (6) Assignment and compensation of coaches and tutors;
> (7) Provision of locker rooms, practice and competitive facilities;
> (8) Provision of medical and training facilities and services;
> (9) Provision of housing and dining facilities and services;
> (10) Publicity.
> Unequal aggregate expenditures for members of each sex or unequal expenditures for male and female teams if a recipient operates or sponsors separate teams will not constitute noncompliance with this section, but the Assistant Secretary may consider the failure to provide necessary funds for teams for one sex in assessing equality of opportunity for members of each sex.

The Florida Act also prohibits, *inter alia,* gender discrimination in public education. It extends protection to those enrolled in public educational institutions which receive or benefit from either state or federal financial assistance. *See* Fla.Stat. § 228.2001(2)(a). The Florida Act lists the identical factors for assessing discrimination in athletics set forth in 34 C.F.R. § 106.41(c)(1)-(10). See Fla.Stat. § 228.2001(3)(d)(1)-(10).

IV. ANALYSIS

A. Substantial Likelihood of Success on the Merits

[1] Plaintiffs assert that the following inequalities exist at the MIHS softball and baseball facilities, and that these disparities violate Title IX and the Florida Act.

Electronic Scoreboard

It is undisputed that the boys' baseball field has an electronic scoreboard, and that the girls' field has no scoreboard at all. At the preliminary injunction hearing, Defendant's counsel argued that a scoreboard is inessential to varsity softball play. The Court disagrees. A scoreboard is of obvious benefit to players who must keep track of the score, the innings, and the numbers of outs, balls and strikes at any given moment. The prestige factor of a scoreboard is also obvious. As with all the differences the Court addresses in this Order, the fact that the boys have a scoreboard and the girls do not sends a clear message to players, fellow students, teachers and the community at large, that girls' varsity softball is not as worthy as boys' varsity baseball.

Batting Cage

It is also undisputed that the boys' baseball team has a batting cage and the girls' softball team does not. The use of a batting cage sharpens hitting skills. The girls' softball team is technically disadvantaged by the absence of such equipment. At the hearing, Plaintiffs' counsel represented that it would be difficult for the two teams to share one batting cage as a result of differences in the pitching machines each team uses. Accordingly, it appears that sharing the existing batting cage is not feasible.

Bleachers

Photographs submitted by Plaintiffs starkly illustrate that the bleachers on the girls' softball field are in worse condition, and seat significantly fewer spectators, than the bleachers on the boys' field. In fact, at the preliminary injunction hearing, Defendant's counsel admitted that the girls' bleachers are actually "hand-me-downs" that the boys' team passed on to the girls' team after the boys' team received new bleachers. Again, the message this sends the players, spectators and community about the relative worth of the two teams is loud and clear.

Signs

A sign reading "Merritt Island Baseball" is emblazoned in very large letters on the side of a portable structure adjacent to the boys' baseball field. The sign faces MIHS' student parking lot. This sign clearly publicizes only the boys' baseball team. Another sign is located just outside the left field fence of the boys' field. This billboard-type sign reads "Home of the Mustangs;" it faces toward the boys' field. Due to its location, the effect of this second sign is to advertise the boys' baseball team. There are no signs publicizing the girls' softball team.

Bathroom Facilities

There are no restrooms located on the girls' softball field. Restrooms are located on the boys' baseball field. A fence separates the girls' field from the restrooms. There is a dispute concerning whether the coach of the girls' team has been provided with a key to a gate in the fence. Equal access to restroom facilities is such a clearly established right as to merit no further discussion.

Concession Stand/Press Box/Announcer's Booth

A combination concession stand/press box/announcer's booth is located on the boys' baseball field. There is no such structure on the girls' softball field. These facilities affect player and spectator enjoyment of a sport, as well as attendance.

Field Maintenance

The photographs submitted by Plaintiffs facially suggest that the girls' softball field is not as well-maintained as the boys' baseball field. However, at the preliminary injunction hearing, Defendant's counsel stated that the photographs were misleading because MIHS was in the process of reconditioning the girls' field at the time the photographs were taken. Defense counsel maintains that the reconditioning process continues. Accordingly, at this juncture, it is difficult for the Court to evaluate the comparative level of field maintenance.

Lighting

The boys' baseball field is lighted for nighttime play; the girls' softball field is not. Apparently, this single factor was the impetus for this lawsuit.

Nighttime play affects spectator attendance, parental involvement, and player and spectator enjoyment. Nighttime games have a "big league" quality not associated with daytime play. Additionally, lighting affords more flexibility regarding practice scheduling. The absence of lighting on the girls' softball field detrimentally affects the girls' team in all these respects.

After Plaintiffs filed suit, the Brevard County School Board voted to install lighting at MIHS' girls softball field. Plaintiffs contend that they have not received assurance that the lighting will be in place by January 26, 1998, the beginning of the girls' season. Defendant's counsel stated at the preliminary injunction hearing that there is every reason to believe that lighting would be installed by that date. Unless the lighting is in place by January 26, 1998, MIHS will be enjoined from using the lights on the boys' baseball field.

The Court determines that the cumulative effect of the inequalities in the two athletic programs is so significant as to give Plaintiffs a substantial likelihood of success on the merits of the Title IX and Florida Act claims. The Defendant has chosen to favor the boys' baseball team with a lighted playing field, a scoreboard, a batting cage, superior bleachers, signs publicizing the team, bathroom facilities, and a concession stand/press box/announcer's booth, but has not seen fit to provide the girls softball team with any of these things. This disparity implicates several of the considerations listed in 34 C.F.R. § 106.41. *See* §106.41(2) ("provision of equipment and supplies"), (3) ("[s]cheduling of games and practice times"), (7) ("[p]rovision of ... practice and competitive facilities"), (8) ("[p]rovision of ... training facilities"), and (10) ("[p]ublicity"). A balance of the relevant factors favors the Plaintiffs.

[2] The Defendant seeks to avoid liability on the basis that it provides equal funding for the boys' and girls' programs. According to the Defendant, each team has a separate booster club which engages in separate fund-raising activities. The Defendant suggests that it cannot be held responsible if the fund-raising activities of one booster club are more successful than those of another. The Court rejects this argument. It is the Defendant's responsibility to ensure equal athletic opportunities, in accordance with Title IX. This funding system is one to which Defendant has acquiesced; Defendant is responsible for the consequences of that approach.

B. Substantial Threat of Irreparable Injury

[3] Plaintiffs have also demonstrated a substantial threat of irreparable injury. Each day these inequalities go unredressed, the members of the girls' softball team, prospective members, students, faculty and the community at large, are sent a clear message that girls' high school varsity softball is not as worthy as boys' high school varsity baseball, *i.e.,* that girls are not as important as boys. In that regard, Plaintiffs have filed two expert affidavits detailing the effects of such unequal treatment on girls. Further, Jessica and Jennifer are seeking athletic scholarships, many of which, Plaintiffs maintain, are not decided until after the softball season is over. Accordingly, it is critical that the two girls do their best during their final season.

C. Relative Harm/Public Interest

[4] Since these inequalities should have long ago been rectified, the Court is unsympathetic to Defendant's claims that it will be unduly harmed by the expenditure of funds necessary to level the playing field for girls' softball athletes. For too long, the girls' softball team has been denied athletic opportunity equal to the boys' baseball team. The harm associated with that treatment as second-class athletes is significant. In short, the balance of harms favors Plaintiffs. The players and all others associated with these programs, the school system as a whole, and the public at large, will benefit from a shift to equal treatment.

* * * *

V. CONCLUSION

[6] After careful analysis, the Court determines that Plaintiffs are entitled to a preliminary injunction. ***

> As the Court of Appeals for the First Circuit recently observed in *Cohen:*
> There can be no doubt that Title IX has changed the face of women's sports as well as our society's interest in and attitude toward women athletes and women's sports. In addition, there is ample evidence that increased athletics participation opportunities for women

and young girls, available as a result of Title IX enforcement, have had salutary effects in other areas of societal concern.

One need look no further than the impressive performances of our country's women athletes in the 1996 Olympic Summer Games to see that Title IX has had a dramatic and positive impact on the capabilities of our women athletes, particularly in team sports. These Olympians represent the first full generation of women to grow up under the aegis of Title IX. The unprecedented success of these athletes is due, in no small measure, to Title IX's beneficent effects on women's sports, as the athletes themselves have acknowledged time and again. What stimulated this remarkable change in the quality of women's athletic competition was not a sudden, anomalous upsurge in women's interest in sports, but the enforcement of Title IX's mandate of gender equity in sports. 101 F.3d at 188 [Citations Omitted]

Based on the foregoing, it is ORDERED as follows:

1. Plaintiffs' Application for Preliminary Injunction and Request for Prompt Hearing (Dkt.3), filed October 9, 1997, is GRANTED.

2. Not later than December 15, 1997, Defendant shall serve and file a plan concerning how Defendant proposes to remedy the inequalities identified in this Order, given the Court's determination that a preliminary injunction should issue. ****

NOTES & QUESTIONS

1. The court compares the boys varsity baseball program to the girls varsity softball program. Are there other pairs of high school boys and girls sports to which the logic of the *Daniels* court might also be applied? Give examples, and discuss the pros and cons of requiring complete equality as regards facilities and equipment.

2. On an abstract level of principle, it is easy to understand the court's decision regarding equality in this case. Does the court satisfactorily explain why funds that come directly from the booster club are treated the way that they are? Parent booster clubs at high schools across America routinely hold fundraisers of various sorts (*e.g.*, bake sales, car washes, raffles, auctions) on behalf of bands, glee clubs, drama clubs, and sports teams. Does this case teach us that schools cannot allow those booster clubs to be entitled to use those funds for the their respective organizations? Explain.

3. *See also Cruz ex rel. Cruz v. Alhambra Sch. Dist.,* 601 F. Supp. 2d 1183 (CD. Cal. 2009) (award of attorneys' fees in excess of $720,000 were reasonable in case involving female students who prevailed in Title IX litigation).

190 F. 3D 643 (1999)

UNITED STATES COURT OF APPEALS, FOURTH CIRCUIT

LUTTIG, CIRCUIT JUDGE:

[1] Appellant Heather Sue Mercer challenges the federal district court's holding that Title IX provides a blanket exemption for contact sports and the court's consequent dismissal of her claim that Duke University discriminated against her during her participation in Duke's intercollegiate football program. For the reasons that follow, we hold that where a university has allowed a member of the opposite sex to try out for a single-sex team in a contact sport, the university is, contrary to the holding of the district court, subject to Title IX and therefore prohibited from discriminating against that individual on the basis of his or her sex.

I.

Appellee Duke University operates a Division I college football team. During the period relevant to this appeal (1994-98), appellee Fred Goldsmith was head coach of the Duke football team and appellant Heather Sue Mercer was a student at the school.

Before attending Duke, Mercer was an all-state kicker at Yorktown Heights High School in Yorktown Heights, New York. Upon enrolling at Duke in the fall of 1994, Mercer tried out for the Duke football team as a walk-on kicker. Mercer was the first--and to date, only--woman to try out for the team. Mercer did not initially make the team, and instead served as a manager during the 1994 season; however, she regularly attended practices in the fall of 1994 and participated in conditioning drills the following spring.

In April 1995, the seniors on the team selected Mercer to participate in the Blue-White Game, an intrasquad scrimmage played each spring. In that game, Mercer kicked the winning 28-yard field goal, giving the Blue team a 24-22 victory. The kick was subsequently shown on ESPN, the cable television sports network. Soon after the game, Goldsmith told the news media that Mercer was on the Duke football team, and Fred Chatham, the Duke kicking coach, told Mercer herself that she had made the team. Also, Mike Cragg, the Duke sports information director, asked Mercer to participate in a number of interviews with newspaper, radio, and television reporters, including one with representatives from "The Tonight Show."

Although Mercer did not play in any games during the 1995 season, she again regularly attended practices in the fall and participated in conditioning drills the following spring. Mercer was also officially listed by Duke as a member of the Duke football team on the team roster filed with the NCAA and was pictured in the Duke football yearbook.

During this latter period, Mercer alleges that she was the subject of discriminatory treatment by Duke. Specifically, she claims that Goldsmith did not permit her to attend summer camp, refused to allow her to dress for games or sit on the sidelines during games, and gave her fewer opportunities to participate in practices than other walk-on kickers. In addition, Mercer claims that Goldsmith made a number of offensive comments to her, including asking her why she was interested in football, wondering why she did not prefer to participate in beauty pageants rather than football, and suggesting that she sit in the stands with her boyfriend rather than on the sidelines.

At the beginning of the 1996 season, Goldsmith informed Mercer that he was dropping her from the team. Mercer alleges that Goldsmith's decision to exclude her from the team was on the basis of her sex because Goldsmith allowed other, less qualified walk-on kickers to remain on the team. Mercer attempted to participate in conditioning drills the following spring, but Goldsmith asked her to leave because the drills were only for members of the team. Goldsmith told Mercer, however, that she could try out for the team again in the fall.

* * *

From the district court's order dismissing her Title IX claim for failure to state a claim upon which relief can be granted and its order denying the motion to alter judgment, Mercer appeals.

II.

Title IX prohibits discrimination on the basis of sex by educational institutions receiving federal funding. *See* 20 U.S.C. § 1681(a) ("No person in the United States shall, on the basis of sex, be excluded from participation in, be denied the benefits of, or be subjected to discrimination under any education program or activity receiving Federal financial assistance...."). Soon after enacting Title IX, Congress charged the Department of Health, Education, and Welfare (HEW) with responsibility for developing regulations regarding the applicability of Title IX to athletic programs. *See* Pub.L. No. 93-380, § 844, 88 Stat. 484 (1974). Acting upon that charge, HEW duly promulgated 34 C.F.R. § 106.41, which reads in relevant part as follows:

> Athletics.
> (a) General. No person shall, on the basis of sex, be excluded from participation in, be denied the benefits of, be treated differently from another person or otherwise be discriminated against in any interscholastic, intercollegiate, club or intramural athletics offered by a recipient, and no recipient shall provide any such athletics separately on such basis.
> (b) Separate teams. Notwithstanding the requirements of paragraph (a) of this section, a recipient may operate or sponsor separate teams for members of each sex where selection for such teams is based upon competitive skill or the activity involved is a contact sport. However, where a recipient operates or sponsors a team in a particular sport for members of one sex but operates or sponsors no such team for members of the other sex, and athletic opportunities for members of that sex have previously been limited, members of the excluded sex must be allowed to try out for the team offered unless the sport involved is a contact sport. For the purposes of this part, contact sports include boxing, wrestling, rugby, ice hockey, football, basketball and other sports the purpose or major activity of which involves bodily contact. 34 C.F.R. § 106.41(a)-(b).

The district court held, and appellees contend on appeal, that, under this regulation, "contact sports, such as football, are specifically excluded from Title IX coverage." We disagree.

* * *

Standing alone...subsection (a) would require covered institutions to integrate all of their sports teams. In order to avoid such a result – which would have radically altered the face of intercollegiate athletics – HEW provided an explicit exception to the rule of subsection (a) in the first sentence of subsection (b), allowing covered institutions to "operate or sponsor separate teams for members of each sex where selection for such teams is based upon competitive skill or the activity involved is a contact sport." By its terms, this sentence permits covered institutions to operate separate teams for men and women in many sports, including contact sports such as football, rather than integrating those teams.

The first sentence of subsection (b), however, leaves unanswered the question of what, if any, restrictions apply to sports in which a covered institution operates a team for one sex, but operates no corresponding team for the other sex. HEW addressed this question in the second sentence of subsection (b).

* * *

The second sentence of subsection (b) does not purport in any way to state an exemption, whether for contact sports or for any other subcategory, from the general anti-discrimination rule stated in subsection (a). And HEW certainly knew how to provide for a complete exemption had it wished, Congress itself having provided a number of such exemptions in the very statute implemented by the regulation. Rather, the sentence says, and says only, that covered institutions must allow members of an excluded sex to try out for single-sex teams in non-contact sports. Therefore, the "unless" phrase at the end of the second clause of the sentence cannot (logically or grammatically) do anything more than except contact sports from the tryout requirement that the beginning of the second clause of the sentence imposes on all other sports.

Contrary to appellees' assertion, this reading of the regulation is perfectly consistent with the evident congressional intent not to require the sexual integration of intercollegiate contact sports. If a university chooses not to permit members of the opposite sex to tryout for a single-sex contact-sports team, this interpretation respects that choice. At the same time, however, the reading of the regulation we adopt today, unlike the one advanced by appellees, ensures that the likewise indisputable congressional intent to prohibit discrimination in all circumstances where such discrimination is unreasonable – for example, where the university itself has voluntarily opened the team in question to members of both sexes – is not frustrated.

We therefore construe the second sentence of subsection (b) as providing that in non-contact sports, but not in contact sports, covered institutions must allow members of an excluded sex to try out for single-sex teams. Once an institution has allowed a member of one sex to try out for a team operated by the institution for the other sex in a contact sport, subsection (b) is simply no longer applicable, and the institution is subject to the general anti-discrimination provision of subsection (a). ***

Accordingly, because appellant has alleged that Duke allowed her to try out for its football team (and actually made her a member of the team), then discriminated against her and ultimately excluded her from participation in the sport on the basis of her sex, we conclude that she has stated a claim under the applicable regulation, and therefore under Title IX. We take to heart appellees' cautionary observation that, in so holding, we thereby become "the first Court in United States history to recognize such a cause of action." Br. of Appellees at 20. Where, as here, however, the university invites women into what appellees characterize as the "traditionally all-male bastion of collegiate football," *id.* at 20 n. 10, we are convinced that this reading of the regulation is the only one permissible under law.

The district court's order granting appellees' motion to dismiss for failure to state a claim is hereby reversed, and the case remanded for further proceedings.

REVERSED AND REMANDED

Heather Mercer, published courtesy Donnan

NOTES & QUESTIONS

1. The court quotes C.F.R. sect. 106.41 (b), which states that a school "may operate or sponsor separate teams for members of each sex where selection for such teams is based upon competitive skill or the activity involved is a contact sport." Can you think of varsity sports at the high school or college level where selection is *not* "based upon competitive skill"? Just what is this "based upon competitive skill" language supposed to mean?

2. Suppose that, because a school does not field a male gymnastics team, a male gymnast wants to try out for his high school's girls' gymnastics team. How does C.F.R. sect. 106.41 (b) apply to this situation?

3. Is the practical effect of the *Mercer* decision likely to be that institutions simply will be disinclined to permit females to try out for contact sports, in order to avoid allegations of discrimination? Explain why or why not.

4. Suppose that a talented female high school athlete wants to try out for the boys baseball or wrestling team. How does C.F.R. sect. 106.41 (b) apply to this situation? Suppose that the sport is golf?

5. For recent cases considering similar issues, see: 1) *Beattie v. Line Mountain Sch. Dist.* 992 F. Supp. 2d 384 (M.D. Pa. 2014). Granting a preliminary injunction, prohibiting school district from preventing a 12 year-old girl from participating on the school's boys-only wrestling team, the court ruled that the gender-based, discriminatory policy likely violated Equal Protection and the state's Equal Rights Amendment – even though the district argued that its reasons for the policy (including safety, prevention of inappropriate physical contact, and sexual harassment) justified it. 2) *Hayden ex rel A.H. v. Greensburg Cmty. Sch. Corp.* 743 F.3d 569 (7th Cir. 2014). The Seventh Circuit Court of Appeals held that the public school's short-hair-cut policy for its boys basketball team (but not for the girls) violated both Equal Protection and Title IX because the policy treated genders in a non-justifiable discriminatory manner.

BOUCHER V. SYRACUSE UNIVERSITY
164 F. 3D. 113 (1999)
UNITED STATES COURT OF APPEALS, SECOND CIRCUIT

CALABRESI, CIRCUIT JUDGE:

Former female club athletes at Syracuse University ("Syracuse" or "the University") appeal from an April 3, 1998 judgment of the United States District Court for the Northern District of New York (Frederick J. Scullin, Jr., J.) granting summary judgment to Syracuse on a Title IX accommodation claim. Plaintiffs also appeal two orders of June 12, 1996. The first such order dismissed their Title IX equal treatment claims, and the second conditionally certified a class.

We affirm in part, dismiss the appeal in part, and vacate and remand in part.

FACTS AND PROCEDURAL HISTORY

Plaintiff students "individually and on behalf of all others similarly situated" filed suit in May of 1995 against Syracuse University, alleging numerous violations of Title IX of the Education

Amendments of 1972, 20 U.S.C. § § 1681-1688, and its governing regulations. Seven of the eight named plaintiffs were at that time members of Syracuse's club lacrosse team and the eighth was a member of the University's club softball team. All plaintiffs have since graduated from the University.

The plaintiffs argued that Syracuse discriminated against female athletes in its allocation of participation opportunities (which includes decisions regarding which varsity teams to field as well as how many opportunities for participation by female varsity athletes are thereby created as a result of those decisions).[1] Plaintiffs also alleged that Syracuse provided unequal benefits to varsity female athletes as compared to varsity male athletes, and provided unequal scholarship funding to varsity female athletes as compared to varsity male athletes.[2]

* * *

Just over 50% of the Syracuse's student population is female, yet, when this complaint was filed, women made up only 32.4% of its athletes. In its 1993-94 National Collegiate Athletic Association submission, Syracuse stated that of its 681 varsity student-athletes, 217 were women, while 464 were men. These numbers reflected a 19% disparity between the percentage of varsity athletes who were female and the percentage of the University's students who were female.[3]

At the time that this suit was begun in May of 1995, the University funded eleven men's varsity teams and nine women's varsity teams. Just prior to the filing of the complaint, Syracuse announced a plan to add two new varsity women's teams to its athletic program – women's varsity soccer and women's varsity lacrosse. These teams began to play, respectively, in the 1996-97 and the 1997-98 academic years, thus bringing the number of varsity teams funded by the school to eleven men's and eleven women's.[4]

The University established five of its nine women's varsity teams in 1971[5] – when it first funded women's varsity sports. It dropped one of these sports (fencing) in 1972, and replaced it with field hockey. Crew was added as a women's varsity team in 1977. Three additional women's

---

1   This kind of Title IX claim is commonly referred to as an "accommodation" claim because it derives from the Title IX implementing regulations, which provide that in determining whether equal athletic opportunities for members of both sexes are available, the Office of Civil Rights of the Department of Education (the office charged with enforcement of Title IX) will consider, among other factors, "[w]hether the selection of sports and levels of competition effectively accommodate the interests and abilities of members of both sexes." 34 C.F.R. § 106.41(c)(1); *see also Cohen v. Brown Univ.*, 991 F.2d 888, 897 (1st Cir.1993) (*"Cohen I"*)(noting three major areas of regulatory compliance under Title IX: athletic financial assistance (scholarships), equivalence in other athletic benefits and opportunities, and effective accommodation of student interests and abilities).

2   These types of Title IX claims are generally referred to as "equal treatment" claims because they derive from the Title IX regulations found at 34 C.F.R. § 106.37(c) and 106.41(c)(2)-(10), which call for equal provision of athletic scholarships as well as equal provision of other athletic benefits and opportunities among the sexes.

3   Between 1990 and the time of the filing of this suit, the disparity between the percentage of varsity athletes who are female as compared to the percentage of the University's students who are female ranged from 19 to 22%.

4   It is the case, however, that for Title IX accommodation purposes, it is the aggregate number of opportunities provided for each sex, and not the number of teams funded for each sex, that matters. *Cf. Cohen I*, 991 F.2d at 897.

5   These were basketball, fencing, swimming, tennis, and volleyball.

sports were added to the varsity roster in 1981.[6] After 1981, no new women's varsity team was created by the University until the addition of the varsity soccer team in 1997. Thus, until the filing of this complaint in 1995, fourteen years passed by without the University creating any new women's varsity teams. In the course of this litigation, Syracuse announced plans to institute a varsity women's softball team which, according to the University's representations at oral argument, will begin play in the 1999-2000 academic year.

* * * *

After a period of limited discovery, the district court granted summary judgment to the University on plaintiffs' accommodation claim. It found that although opportunities to participate in varsity athletics at Syracuse were not allocated equally between the sexes, the University nevertheless fell within one of the safe harbors set forth in the governing regulations of Title IX. [Citation Omitted] Under the implementing regulations, there are three safe harbor defenses to a claim of unequal accommodation of student interest in varsity athletics. *See* 34 C.F.R. § 106.41(c)(1); 44 Fed.Reg. 71413 (1979). The district court held that Syracuse met the requirements of the second safe harbor because it had "continued a practice of program expansion which is responsive to the abilities and interests of its student body."[7]

Specifically, the district court found that (1) Syracuse had a "strong history of adding women's sports programs"; (2) although between 1982 and 1995, the University had added no new varsity women's teams, it did fund additional scholarships and provide enhanced facilities, coaching, and support services for its women varsity athletes; (3) between 1982 and 1995, the absolute number of female participants in varsity sports had increased from 148 to 217; and (4) Syracuse had established two new varsity women's teams since 1995 and planned to add a third in 1999-2000. *Id.*

Finally, the district court noted that in conducting the safe harbor analysis, a court "may consider whether there are any formal policies in place which might indicate that the institution is monitoring the pulse of its students' interests in anticipation of expansion." *Id.* Despite recognizing that the school had not established that it had any formal policy to allow students to voice their interests, the court concluded that "the best evidence of continued expansion is expansion itself." *Id.* Accordingly, it granted summary judgment to the University.

---

6 These were indoor track, outdoor track, and cross country.

7 The court observed:

   Where a university has a practice of expanding its athletic program, approaching proportionality and meeting the needs of the under-represented gender; and continues to expand in response to its student body's interest and abilities, as well as that of secondary feeder schools; symmetry in athletic programs is not required under Title IX, and liability may be avoided. Under this "safe harbor" of a continuing practice of program expansion, courts look to the institution's past and continuing remedial efforts to provide nondiscriminatory participation opportunities through program expansion. 1998 WL 167296, at *3 (citing *Cohen I*, 991 F.2d at 898; *Bryant v. Colgate University*, 1996 WL 328446, at *10; 44 Fed.Reg. 71,413).

DISCUSSION

A. Lacrosse.

Syracuse argues that this appeal is moot because it has already implemented a varsity women's lacrosse team and that there is, therefore, nothing left for the certified class to pursue. ***

We...hold that insofar as plaintiffs' complaint sought a varsity lacrosse team, the claim is now moot, given that the team has been created and is already participating in intercollegiate play. *See County of Los Angeles v. Davis*, 440 U.S. 625, 631-32, 99 S.Ct. 1379, 59 L.Ed.2d 642 (1979) (finding case moot where there was no reasonable expectation that the alleged violation would recur). ***

B. Softball.

Plaintiffs also contest the district court's failure to certify a sub-class of current and future women interested in playing varsity softball. They argue that this issue is not moot because such a team has not yet begun play. We agree with both contentions. ***

[T]he University represented both to the district court and to this Court that a varsity women's softball team is in the process of being established, and that the team will begin play during the 1999-2000 academic year. Because full implementation of a varsity women's softball team would render the remaining live aspect of this case moot, we again choose not to reach the merits of the University's safe harbor defense, and prefer instead to remand the case to the district court with instructions to dismiss the case if the University completes its plan to institute a varsity women's softball team by the date indicated. Should the University not live up to its representations, the district court is ordered to certify a class of current and future women students interested in playing varsity softball and to revisit the merits of the case at that time. ***

NOTES & QUESTIONS

1. Given the slow pace of federal litigation, isn't it true that mootness will always be a problem for plaintiffs in Title IX litigation?

2. The Syracuse University women's lacrosse and softball programs have enjoyed considerable success. For updates on the lacrosse team go to: https://cuse.com/index.aspx?path=wlacrosse. For updates on softball go to: https://cuse.com/index.aspx?path=softball.

3. Recent cases have continued to uphold female collegiate student athletes' rights to equal treatment. One example is *Biediger v. Quinnipiac U.*, 691 F.3d 85, 90 (2d Cir. 2012)(affirmed D. Conn). The Second Circuit affirmed the district court's injunction and ruling that the university failed to provide women genuine athletic participation opportunities substantially proportionate to the university's female student body.

BOULAHANIS V. BOARD OF REGENTS

198 F. 3D. 633 (1999)

UNITED STATES COURT OF APPEALS, SEVENTH CIRCUIT

FLAUM, CIRCUIT JUDGE.

The plaintiffs-appellants, a group of former and prospective athletes at Illinois State University (the "University"), appeal the district court's grant of summary judgment to the University, alleging that the actions of the University in eliminating its men's wrestling and men's soccer programs constitute a violation of Title IX of the Education Amendments of 1972, 20 U.S.C. § 1681. *** For the reasons set out below, we agree with the judgment of the district court and affirm.

I. Facts

In the fall of 1993, the Gender Equity Committee of Illinois State University undertook a year-long investigation of gender equity and Title IX compliance at the University. The results of this study indicated that enrollment at the University was 45% male and 55% female, while athletic participation was 66% male and 34% female. The study concluded that these numbers did not constitute equitable participation opportunities for women. In response to this conclusion, the University began to consider ways to bring itself into compliance with Title IX.

Under Title IX, Illinois State University is required to "provide equal athletic opportunity" for men and women. 34 C.F.R. § 106.41(c). Equal opportunities are to be evaluated according to the following ten factors:

(1) Whether the selection of sports and levels of competition effectively accommodate the interests and abilities of members of both sexes;
(2) The provision of equipment and supplies;
(3) Scheduling of games and practice time;
(4) Travel and per diem allowance;
(5) Opportunity to receive coaching and academic tutoring;
(6) Assignment and compensation of coaches and tutors;
(7) Provision of locker rooms, practice and competitive facilities;
(8) Provision of medical and training facilities and services;
(9) Provision of housing and dining facilities and services; and
(10) Publicity. *Id.*

In addition to these considerations, an "institution may violate Title IX solely by failing to accommodate the interests and abilities of student athletes of both sexes." *Kelley v. Board of Trustees,* 35 F.3d 265, 268 (7th Cir.1994)(citing *Roberts v. Colorado St. Bd. of Agric.,* 998 F.2d 824, 828 (10th Cir.1993); *Cohen v. Brown Univ.,* 991 F.2d 888, 897-98 (1st Cir.1993)).

In order to effectively accommodate the athletic interests of both male and female students, the University had three options under the policy interpretations of Title IX promulgated by the Office of Civil Rights: (1) provide participation opportunities for men and women that are substantially proportionate to their respective rates of enrollment as full-time undergraduate students; or (2) demonstrate a history and continuing practice of program expansion for the under-represented sex; or (3) fully and effectively accommodate the interests and abilities of the under-represented sex. 44 Fed.Reg. 71,418 (1979). Because the University had not added a women's sports program in over ten years, and because it did not believe it could accommodate effectively the interests and abilities of its women students, the University focused on achieving the goal of substantial proportionality. ***

The University considered ten options to achieve compliance with Title IX. These options included: (1) dropping men's wrestling; (2) dropping men's wrestling and men's soccer; (3) dropping men's wrestling, men's soccer, and men's tennis; (4) dropping men's wrestling and adding women's soccer; (5) dropping men's wrestling and men's soccer and adding women's soccer; (6) dropping men's wrestling, men's soccer, and men's tennis and adding women's soccer; (7) adding women's soccer; (8) adding women's soccer and bringing women to full funding; (9) dropping men's wrestling and men's soccer, adding women's soccer, and adjusting men's rosters and women's grants in aid; and (10) dropping men's wrestling and men's soccer, adding women's soccer, and adjusting men's rosters and grants in aid for both men and women. After careful consideration of these options, the University ultimately chose and implemented option number ten. This resulted in the addition of women's soccer and the elimination of men's soccer and men's wrestling. The implementation of this plan increased the athletic participation of women to 51.72% and decreased the athletic participation of men to 48.29%, thereby bringing the disparity between enrollment and participation to within three percentage points.

The plaintiffs-appellants are former members of the men's soccer and men's wrestling teams at Illinois State University who, as a consequence of the University's elimination of those programs under its gender equity plan, were no longer able to participate in those sports at the University. They contend that the University's decision to eliminate the programs in which they participated was based on sex, and is therefore a violation of Title IX. *** The district court granted the University summary judgment....

II. Analysis

* * *

A.

Title IX states that "No person in the United States shall, on the basis of sex, be excluded from participation in, be denied the benefits of, or be subjected to discrimination under any education program or activity receiving Federal financial assistance." 20 U.S.C. § 1681(a). The plaintiffs-appellants contend that the University's actions in eliminating the men's soccer and men's wrestling programs were based solely on the sex of the participants. According to the plaintiffs-appellants, because these discriminatory actions would not have been taken "but for" the sex of the participants, the actions violate Title IX on its face. *See International Union v. Johnson*

Controls, Inc., 499 U.S. 187, 200, 111 S.Ct. 1196, 113 L.Ed.2d 158 (1991)(quoting *Los Angeles Dep't of Water and Power v. Manhart*, 435 U.S. 702, 711, 98 S.Ct. 1370, 55 L.Ed.2d 657 (1978) [Citation Omitted](stating that the simple test for discrimination is "whether the evidence shows 'treatment of a person in a manner which but for that person's sex would have been different'")).

The plaintiffs-appellants' argument is similar to one this Court has already considered in *Kelley v. Board of Trustees*, 35 F.3d 265 (7th Cir.1994). The plaintiffs in *Kelley* were members of the men's swimming team at the University of Illinois. That program was eliminated in an attempt by that university to cut its athletic budget by getting rid of teams that were not competitive on a national level. Although the men's swimming team at the University of Illinois was eliminated on this basis, the women's swimming program was maintained because of concerns about compliance with Title IX. *Id.* at 269. Members of the University of Illinois's men's swimming team, like the plaintiffs-appellants in this case, challenged the university's cancellation of the athletic program in which they participated as a violation of Title IX. We rejected that challenge, holding that the elimination of men's swimming did not violate Title IX because "men's participation in athletics [continued] to be more than substantially proportionate to their presence in [the University of Illinois's] student body." *Id.* at 270.

The plaintiffs-appellants contend that our decision in *Kelley* is distinguishable from the facts of this case, and is therefore not controlling. In attempting to distinguish *Kelley*, the plaintiffs-appellants rely on the financial and budgetary considerations that motivated the University of Illinois's athletic department to eliminate men's swimming. *See id.* at 269. According to the plaintiffs-appellants, a decision that is motivated by financial concerns, even if it includes sex-based considerations, does not violate Title IX. In contrast, a decision like the one in this case, that is motivated by the sex of the participants, does violate Title IX. In short, the plaintiffs-appellants attempt to draw a distinction between decisions in which sex is a consideration (as in *Kelley*), and decisions in which sex serves as the motivating factor (as in the present case).

We are not persuaded by the plaintiffs-appellants' attempt to distinguish decisions to eliminate athletic programs motivated by financial concerns from those based on considerations of sex. That distinction ignores the fact that a university's decision as to which athletic programs to offer necessarily entails budgetary considerations. For universities, decisions about cutting or adding athletic programs are based on a consideration of many factors including: the total size of the athletic department, which is governed by budgetary considerations, and the distribution of programs among men and women, which is governed by Title IX concerns. To say that one decision is financial, while another is sex-based, assumes that these two aspects can be neatly separated. They cannot. Absent financial concerns, Illinois State University presumably would rather have added women's programs while keeping its men's programs intact. Similarly, in the absence of Title IX concerns, the University of Illinois in *Kelley* would have cut both its men's and women's swimming programs in order to save money.[1] Ultimately, both the decision of the

---

1 This is clearly illustrated by the fact that the University of Illinois "did not eliminate the women's swimming program because the school's legal counsel advised that such action would put the [u]niversity at risk of violating Title IX." *Kelley*, 35 F.3d at 269.

University in this case and the decision of the University of Illinois at issue in *Kelley* were based on a combination of financial and sex-based concerns that are not easily distinguished.

* * *

[A] holding that universities cannot achieve substantial proportionality by cutting men's programs is tantamount to a requirement that universities achieve substantial proportionality through additional spending to add women's sports programs. This result would ignore the financial and budgetary constraints that universities face. *See Roberts v. Colorado St. Bd. of Agric.*, 998 F.2d 824, 830 (10th Cir.1993). ("[I]n times of economic hardship, few schools will be able to satisfy Title IX's effective accommodation requirement by continuing to expand their women's athletic programs."). Unless we are willing to mandate such spending, the agency's substantial proportionality rule must be read to allow the elimination of men's athletic programs to achieve compliance with Title IX.

* * *

As we noted in *Kelley,* the elimination of men's athletic programs is not a violation of Title IX as long as men's participation in athletics continues to be "substantially proportionate" to their enrollment. *See Kelley,* 35 F.3d at 270. After the elimination of men's soccer and men's wrestling at the University, the athletic participation of men remained within three percentage points of enrollment. *** Because the University has achieved substantial proportionality between men's enrollment and men's participation in athletics, it is presumed to have accommodated the athletic interests of that sex. [Case Citations Omitted] Under such circumstances, Illinois State University's actions in eliminating the programs at issue do not constitute a violation of Title IX.
AFFIRMED

NOTES & QUESTIONS

1. Instead of deciding to cut teams summarily, would it be preferable for schools to phase them out gradually over the course of several years, so that scholarship players and others who were recruited would not be left out in the cold when a team is abruptly discontinued? Clearly, if a school were to adopt a "phase-out" approach, walk-ons would become essential during any phase-out period.

2. According to the court in *Boulahanis,* "a holding that universities cannot achieve substantial proportionality by cutting men's programs is tantamount to a requirement that universities achieve substantial proportionality through additional spending to add women's sports programs. This result would ignore the financial and budgetary constraints that universities face." To what extent do you believe the court simply does not wish to second-guess and micromanage a university's decisions regarding how it will achieve substantial

proportionality? Would a contrary holding open the proverbial floodgates of litigation? Explain why or why not.

EQUITY IN ATHLETICS, INC. V. U.S. DEPT. OF EDUCATION[2]
291 FED.APPX. 517, 2008 WL 4104235 (C.A.4 (VA.))
4TH CIR. CA(2008) NO. 07-1914

HANSEN, SENIOR CIRCUIT JUDGE:

Equity in Athletics, Inc. ("EIA") sought a preliminary injunction to prevent James Madison University ("JMU") from eliminating seven men's sports and three women's sports from its intercollegiate athletic program. EIA claimed that JMU intentionally discriminated against male athletes in violation of ... Title IX of the Education Amendments of 1972. Because the district court did not abuse its discretion...we affirm the district court's denial of EIA's motion for a preliminary injunction.

I.

Title IX provides that "[n]o person in the United States shall, on the basis of sex, be excluded from participation in, be denied the benefits of, or be subjected to discrimination under any education program or activity receiving Federal financial assistance." 20 U.S.C. § 1681(a). Title IX did not specifically address its application to athletics, and in 1974, Congress directed the Secretary of Health, Education, and Welfare ("HEW") to promulgate regulations, "which shall include with respect to intercollegiate athletic activities reasonable provisions considering the nature of particular sports." *McCormick v. Sch. Dist. of Mamaroneck,* 370 F.3d 275, 287 (2d Cir.2004)(quoting Education Amendments of 1974, Pub.L. No. 93-380, § 844, 88 Stat. 484, 612 (1974)). HEW followed the rulemaking procedures in promulgating 45 C.F.R. § 86.41 in 1975, which provides that "[a] recipient which operates or sponsors interscholastic, intercollegiate, club or intramural athletics shall provide equal athletic opportunity for members of both sexes." § 86.41(c). One of the ten factors listed as assisting in that determination is "[w]hether the selection of sports and levels of competition effectively accommodate the interests and abilities of members of both sexes." § 86.41(c)(1).[3]

* * *

---

2   This case was not selected for publication in the Federal Reporter. Not for Publication in West's Federal Reporter See Fed. Rule of Appellate Procedure 32.1 generally governing citation of judicial decisions issued on or after Jan. 1, 2007. See also Fourth Circuit Rule 32.1 (Find CTA4 Rule 32.1).

3   Congress divided HEW into two agencies in 1979, the Department of Health and Human Services and the Department of Education ("DOE"). "HEW's functions under Title IX were transferred ... to the [DOE]." *N. Haven Bd. of Educ. v. Bell,* 456 U.S. 512, 516 n. 4, 102 S.Ct. 1912, 72 L.Ed.2d 299 (1982)(citing 20 U.S.C. § 3441(a)(3)). The DOE subsumed functions from five separate departments and subsequently consolidated the regulations of those five departments into one title of the Code of Federal Regulations at Title 34. DOE recodified 45 C.F.R. § 86.41 at 34 C.F.R. § 106.41.

James Madison University (JMU) is a state-sponsored university in Virginia and receives federal funds. In an effort to comply with Title IX with respect to its athletic program, JMU's Board of Visitors voted on September 29, 2006, to eliminate seven men's sports (archery, cross country, gymnastics, indoor and outdoor track, swimming, and wrestling) and three women's sports (archery, fencing, and gymnastics) to obtain proportionality between the gender makeup of its athletic programs and its undergraduate enrollment. At the time, JMU's undergraduate population was divided 61% female and 39% male, while its student athletes were 51% female and 49% male. The proposed cuts relied on the first part of the Three-Part Test and were designed to put JMU's student-athlete population in a similar male/female ratio as its general student population. The Board issued a press release explaining its decision the same day. It also issued a "Title IX Statement" on February 8, 2007, further addressing the reasoning behind the cuts, which were to be effective as of July 1, 2007.

Athletes, coaches, and fans formed EIA, a not-for-profit organization, to fight the proposed cuts. ***

II.

*** We focus our attention on assessing whether EIA has sufficiently established a likelihood of success on the merits to entitle it to a preliminary injunction against JMU.

Courts have consistently rejected EIA's underlying claim that equal opportunity under § 86.41 should be tied to expressed interest rather than actual participation. *See Neal v. Bd. of Trs. of Cal. State Univ.,* 198 F.3d 763, 767 (9th Cir.1999)(reversing grant of preliminary injunction, noting that "Appellees' argument that equal opportunity is achieved when each gender's athletic participation roughly matches its interest in participating is hardly novel," and that "[s]everal courts of appeals have considered and rejected Appellees' approach as fundamentally inconsistent with the purpose of Title IX"); *Boulahanis v. Bd. of Regents,* 198 F.3d 633, 638-39 (7th Cir.1999)("[T]he elimination of men's athletic programs is not a violation of Title IX as long as men's participation in athletics continues to be 'substantially proportionate' to their enrollment."), *cert. denied,* 530 U.S. 1284, 120 S.Ct. 2762, 147 L.Ed.2d 1022 (2000); *Cohen v. Brown Univ.,* 101 F.3d 155, 174 (1st Cir.1996)(*Cohen II*)....

* * *

[T]he cases discussed above raise a serious doubt about whether... JMU violated Title IX... in using gender to select which athletic programs to cut. *See Kelley,* 35 F.3d at 272 ("[I]nsofar as the University actions were taken in an attempt to comply with the requirements of Title IX, plaintiffs' attack on those actions is merely a collateral attack on the statute and regulations and is therefore impermissible."). *** [N]early every circuit in the country has rejected challenges similar to EIA's underlying complaint against JMU, i.e., that JMU violated Title IX...when it used gender to determine which athletic programs to cut. We agree with the district court that EIA has failed to establish a likelihood of success on its claims against JMU sufficient to entitle it to a preliminary injunction.

The final factor to be considered on a motion for a preliminary injunction is the public interest. The district court sympathized with the student-athletes affected by the cuts, characterizing them as "innocent victims" of Title IX's remedial effects. Given the current state of the law related to Title IX's effect on athletic programs, however, the district court did not clearly err in determining that the public interest favored JMU's ability "to chart [its] own course in providing athletic opportunities without judicial interference or oversight, absent a clear showing that [it is] in violation of the law." 504 F.Supp.2d at 112 (internal marks omitted).

III.

EIA has failed to establish that the district court abused its discretion in... rejecting EIA's motion for a preliminary injunction. We affirm the district court's judgment.

NOTES & QUESTIONS

1. Compare and contrast *Equity in Athletics* and *Boulahanis*.

2. *Portz v. St. Cloud State U.*, 297 F. Supp. 3d 929 (D. Minn. 2018). Ruling that the aggrieved players had demonstrated a likelihood of success on the merits of their Title IX and Equal Protection claims and that they would probably suffer irreparable harm, the court enjoined St. Cloud State University from eliminating the women's tennis team, pending the outcome of litigation.

B. THE REHABILITATION AND AMERICANS WITH DISABILITIES ACTS

1. OVERVIEW

THE INTERSECTION OF SPORTS AND DISABILITY: ANALYZING REASONABLE ACCOMMODATIONS FOR ATHLETES WITH DISABILITIES
MAUREEN A. WESTON
50 ST. LOUIS U. L.J. 137 (2005)

I. Introduction

When thinking about athletes participating in competitive or organized sports, typically the public rarely contemplates the inclusion of players with medical impairments or other physical, mental, and learning disabilities. Yet many athletes with disabilities, whether visible or hidden, have achieved success in both amateur and professional sports. Although deaf, Kenny Walker attained All-American status as a defensive tackle at the University of Nebraska and went on to play professionally with the Denver Broncos. Jim Abbot, who has only one arm as a result of a birth defect, successfully pitched in the professional baseball leagues. The sporting public has applauded the accomplishments of these athletes who are able to compete presumably "despite" their disabilities or by "overcoming" them. The awe turned to apprehension when Hank Gathers, who was medically cleared to play college basketball despite a heart rhythm disorder, died on the court, or when twelve-year old Michael Montalvo, who has AIDS, sought to enroll in karate classes, and even when Magic Johnson returned to professional basketball after revealing that he was HIV positive.

The rights of athletes with medical impairments or disabilities to participate in competitive sports are also increasingly controversial. Because of a medical impairment or disability, some athletes cannot satisfy certain eligibility requirements set by the governing sporting organizations or they need accommodation in order to participate.

* * *

Athletes who have been effectively excluded from sports participation because of a medical impairment or disability have invoked the stringent anti-discrimination standards of federal disability laws in asserting rights to participate and to reasonable modifications of eligibility standards in sports programs at the interscholastic, intercollegiate, and professional levels.

Federal disability legislation, primarily through the Rehabilitation Act of 1973, which applies to federally funded programs, and the Americans with Disabilities Act of 1990 (ADA), whose broader coverage reaches most private employers and private entities constituting places of public accommodations, prohibits discrimination on the basis of disability and further obligates these entities to provide reasonable accommodations, modifications, or auxiliary aids that will enable qualified individuals with disabilities to access and to participate in the program or activity. 29 U.S.C. § 794; 42 U.S.C. § 12101. In enacting the ADA, Congress found, inter alia, that individuals with disabilities continually encounter various forms of discrimination, including "outright intentional exclusion, the discriminatory effects of architectural, transportation, and communication barriers, overprotective rules and policies, failure to make modifications to existing facilities, programs and practices, exclusionary qualification standards and criteria, segregation, and relegation to lesser services, programs, activities, benefits, jobs or other opportunities." A goal of these laws, which apply to virtually all sports teams and organizations, is to assure the equality of opportunity and full participation for individuals with disabilities.

Federal disability laws have had and continue to have a significant impact in sports, raising complicated and controversial medico-legal questions surrounding the rights of individuals with disabilities to participate in athletics and the concomitant rights and obligations of the entities regulating athletic competition to set and enforce eligibility and safety rules. Many of the cases involving disability law in sports have garnered intense public attention, raising questions about the impact on the competitive nature of sports and the ability of sporting organizations to enforce rules of participation.

II. Prohibitions on Disability-Based Discrimination and Requirements for Reasonable Accommodation

A. Historical Treatment of Athletes with Disabilities

Historically, athletes with medical impairments and disabilities had minimal legal recourse to assert rights to participate in competitive sports. No such rights were recognized at common law, and Constitutional claims against exclusion met limited success. In *City of Cleburne v. Cleburne Living Center,* the Supreme Court held that individuals with disabilities were not a quasi-suspect class. As a result, public schools and institutions (as "state actors") could discriminate against or exclude disabled athletes from participation if rationally related to a legitimate objective, such as to guard the health and safety of athletes. On a due process level, there is no fundamental or constitutional right to participate in competitive sports.

B. Federal Laws Prohibiting Disability-Based Discrimination and Requiring Reasonable Accommodation

The need to recognize the rights of the disabled population began to emerge on a national scale in the early 1970s, motivating Congress to enact major federal legislation to recognize the civil rights of individuals with disabilities.

1. The Rehabilitation Act and the ADA

Federal legislation, beginning with the Rehabilitation Act of 1973 and followed by the Americans with Disabilities Act of 1990, provides qualified disabled individuals with protection against discrimination on the basis of disability and requires covered entities to provide reasonable accommodations and to modify eligibility criteria that unfairly screen out persons with disabilities. Recourse may also be available under state law disability-related discrimination statutes, but enforcement and remedies vary by state. As a result, most disability discrimination claims are based on the federal statutes rather than on the U.S. Constitution.

2. Basic Non-discrimination Mandate

The general prohibition of discrimination provides that "[n]o individual shall be discriminated against on the basis of disability in the full and equal enjoyment of the goods, services, facilities, privileges, advantages, or accommodations of any place of public accommodation by any person who owns, leases (or leases to), or operates a place of public accommodation."

Unlike other civil rights statutes that prohibit discrimination (for example, on the basis of race, age, or gender), federal disability laws also impose an affirmative obligation upon covered entities to comply with requests for reasonable accommodations, as well as for modification of non-essential eligibility criteria. For example, discrimination is defined by the statute to include, inter alia, the imposition or application of eligibility criteria that screen out or tend to screen out an individual with a disability . . . [and] a failure to make reasonable modifications in policies, practices, or procedures, when such modifications are necessary to afford such goods, services, facilities, privileges, advantages, or accommodations to individuals with disabilities.

The ADA further requires that these "[g]oods, services, facilities, privileges, advantages, and accommodations shall be afforded to an individual with a disability in the most integrated setting appropriate to the needs of the individual." Exceptions are warranted only where the entity can demonstrate that such criteria are necessary or that "making such modifications would fundamentally alter the nature of such goods, services, facilities, privileges, advantages, or accommodations."

3. Purposes

Participation in sports was not a specific focus of the federal legislation, whose primary intent was to address employment and physical access issues. However, implementing regulations expressly require institutions to provide qualified individuals with disabilities an equal opportunity to participate in educational and nonacademic activities, including inter-collegiate athletics. Moreover, the legislation's overarching purpose, to eradicate unfounded stereotypes and exclusion resulting from overprotective rules and exclusionary criteria, and to assert equal opportunity and full participation for persons with disabilities, is equally applicable in the sports area.

C. Stating a Disability Rights Claim: An Athlete's Prima Facie Case

Athletes with disabilities may seek protection under, and athletic programs are required to comply with, either of the two primary federal laws that prohibit disability-based discrimination. To obtain such protection under either the ADA or Rehabilitation Act, an athlete must establish four elements. First, the program is a "covered entity" under the law. Second, the athlete is "disabled" within the meaning of the statute. Third, the athlete is "otherwise qualified" to participate, with or without reasonable accommodation. Finally, the athlete was discriminated against (excluded from participation) because of disability.

1. Athletic Programs, Leagues, and Organizations as "Covered Entities"

The initial element of an athlete's claim must establish that the defendant, school, program, or entity is a "covered entity" as defined under either the Rehabilitation Act or the ADA. The Rehabilitation Act applies to recipients of federal funds, which generally include public programs, schools, colleges, or universities. The ADA broadens the scope of coverage to private entities and places of public accommodation. The ADA is codified under five titles. Title I applies to employment. Title II applies to public programs and services, here governing entities that are publicly funded at the state or local level. Title III applies to private entities constituting places of public accommodation. Public schools and universities are unquestionably covered under the mandates of Title II or of the Rehabilitation Act, and private universities are also covered under Title III as places of public accommodation.

A highly litigated issue has involved determining whether private sports leagues, associations, or athletic standard-setting or membership organizations are "places of public accommodation" subject to the ADA. The ADA defines the term "public accommodation" by listing a host of "private entities" with operations that affect commerce. The list of private entities includes twelve categories, which in turn contain over fifty examples of covered facilities, including "a gymnasium, health spa, bowling alley, golf course, or other place of exercise or recreation."

Some courts strictly interpret the statutory language, holding that the terms "facility" and "place" in the ADA require a physical structure. For example, in *Elitt v. U.S.A. Hockey*, a Missouri federal district court held that a youth hockey league and its national governing body did not constitute places of public accommodation. In that case, the league refused to permit a child with Attention Deficit Disorder to play hockey. In dismissing the claim, the court reasoned that the plaintiff had failed to show he was denied access to a place of public accommodation simply by alleging that he could not play in the league; that is, he had not shown that he was denied access to the ice rink itself. The Sixth Circuit has reached a similar conclusion, holding that neither a state high school athletic association nor the National Football League ("NFL") were "places" of public accommodation, even though association and NFL events were held at "places" of public accommodations.

Other courts take a broader view, holding that Title III is not limited to physical structures. For example, in *Shultz v. Hemet Youth Pony League, Inc.*, a California federal district court held that a youth baseball league and its organizing body were covered by the ADA. In so doing, the court ruled that "Title III's definition of 'place of public accommodation' is not limited to actual physical structures with definite physical boundaries." The court in *Bowers v. NCAA* came to a similar conclusion. Although acknowledging that the NCAA is an unincorporated and voluntary membership organization of approximately 1,200 postsecondary educational institutions, and not a "place" of public accommodation, the *Bowers* court emphasized that the ADA prohibits more than just discrimination based on physical access. As the chief entity responsible for governing intercollegiate athletics, the NCAA was found to control, manage, and regulate participation in intercollegiate sports through, inter alia, its eligibility rules. Accordingly, the court found the NCAA subject to Title III by interpreting "operating" a place of public accommodations in terms of the entity's power to control, manage, or regulate the place and conditions causing the alleged discrimination.

* * *

2. The "Disabled" Athlete

Assuming an athlete overcomes the initial hurdle of establishing that the particular entity or organization is covered by federal law, the athlete seeking protection under the ADA must be "disabled" within the meaning of the statute. This requires that the athlete has "a physical or mental impairment that substantially limits one or more of the major life activities of such individual." The ADA's regulations describe "major life activities" as "functions such as caring for one's self, performing manual tasks, walking, seeing, hearing, speaking, breathing, learning, and working." This definition excludes individuals with temporary injuries, medical impairments, or disabilities that do not substantially limit a major life activity.

With respect to athletes excluded from sports participation based on permanent medical ineligibility, a critical inquiry is whether sports participation is a "major life activity." An athlete may also argue that the list of major life activities is non-exhaustive, leading the parties to argue whether participation in sports is a major life activity or integral to learning. For example, the Seventh Circuit has held that although a student was medically ineligible to play college basketball because of a heart condition, he was not "disabled" because he was only limited in playing intercollegiate athletics, by itself not a major life activity. Perhaps where the exclusion from athletics is framed as substantially limiting the major life activity of learning or working, the disability prong is more easily satisfied. For example, athletes with learning disabilities are covered because their impairments restrict the major life activity of learning. A professional athlete excluded because of disability could also link the limitation to the life activity of working. However, exclusion from working at a particular job has not been considered a substantial limitation on working.

A person is also "disabled" under the ADA where such individual has a "record of such impairment; or . . . [is] regarded as having such an impairment." This definition may cover athletes excluded on the basis of a record of a medical impairment or genetic predisposition for a medical risk.

3. Who is "Otherwise Qualified with or Without Reasonable Accommodation?"

An apparent irony is that the athlete pursuing an ADA claim must not only be "disabled," but also "otherwise qualified" to participate in the athletic program. Such an athlete is qualified if he or she can meet essential program eligibility requirements "with or without reasonable modifications to [the program's] rules, policies, or practices."

4. Excluded Because of Disability

Finally, the athlete must prove that he or she was discriminated against or excluded from participation because of disability. As mentioned previously, discrimination is defined to include the imposition or application of eligibility criteria that screen out or tend to screen out an individual with a disability . . . from fully and equally enjoying any good, services, facilities, privileges, advantages, or accommodations, unless such criteria can be shown to be necessary . . . [and] a failure to make reasonable modifications in policies, practices, or procedures . . . to individuals with disabilities, unless the entity can demonstrate that making such modifications would fundamentally alter the nature of such [programs].

D. In Defense, Legally Valid Justifications for Exclusion

In defense, exclusion is permissible where the requested accommodation or modification is unreasonable, requires the elimination of essential eligibility requirements, poses an undue hardship on the program, or fundamentally alters the nature of the sport or competition. More recently, courts have ruled that an entity need not permit participation where such poses a direct threat to the player or others. Whether participation would pose a risk of harm to the player or to others is a recurring issue facing many athletic programs when an athlete has an increased risk of injury.

III. Type of Legal Challenges by Athletes with Disabilities

The disability rights issue arises primarily in three types of cases. The first occurs where athletes with high medical risk seek to participate. Liability and safety concerns prevail where such players obtain medical clearance and die or are injured while participating in the sports program, or where the players are denied medical clearance to play and sue claiming disability-based discrimination. The second category involves athletes who fail to meet a "neutral" eligibility requirement, such as age or academic standards and are denied participation in athletics. A third category involves athletes who need accommodation or modification to the rules of play in the particular sport. ***

IV. Conclusion

The federal disability laws provide athletes with a vital mechanism to ensure that decisions regarding their rights to participate in athletics are thoughtfully considered, medically justified, and not disregarded simply upon notions of undue administrative burdens, false notions of competitive advantage, or paternalism. The common thread among ... cases involving challenges by athletes with disabilities illustrates that sporting organizations should be prepared to explain the purpose of their eligibility requirements and rules of competition, to articulate the connection between the requirements and purpose, and to evaluate on an individual basis whether modification of such rules can be made without undermining this legitimate purpose or fundamentally altering the nature of the game....

NOTES & QUESTIONS

1. For a recent case examining some of these issues, *see Steines ex rel. Steines v. Ohio High Sch. Athletic Ass'n,* 68 F. Supp. 3d 768 (S.D. Ohio 2014), *vacated sub nom. C.S. v. Ohio High Sch. Athletic Assn.,* 1:14-CV-525, 2015 WL 4575217 (S.D. Ohio July 29, 2015). The court held that the state high school athletic association's refusal to grant a waiver for an out-of-state student with learning disabilities violated the ADA, because the association is a public entity within the scope of the Act and the waiver-refusal constituted a failure to provide a reasonable modification of the state's in-state residency rule.

2. ATHLETES WITH A HIGH MEDICAL RISK

KNAPP V. NORTHWESTERN UNIVERSITY

101 F.3D 473 (1996)

UNITED STATES COURT OF APPEALS, SEVENTH CIRCUIT

TERRENCE EVANS, CIRCUIT JUDGE.

Nicholas Knapp wants to play NCAA basketball for Northwestern University – so badly that he is willing to face an increased risk of death to do so. Knapp is a competent, intelligent adult capable of assessing whether playing intercollegiate basketball is worth the risk to his heart and possible death, and to him the risk is acceptable. Usually, competent, intelligent adults are allowed to make such decisions. This is especially true when, as here, the individual's family approves of the decision and the individual and his parents are willing to sign liability waivers regarding the worst-case scenario should it occur.

Northwestern, however, refuses to allow Knapp to play on or even practice with its men's basketball team. Knapp, currently a sophomore at Northwestern, has the basketball skills to play at the intercollegiate level, but he has never taken the court for his team. Although Northwestern does not restrict him from playing pick-up basketball games, using recreational facilities on campus, or exerting himself physically on his own, the university disqualified Knapp from playing on its intercollegiate basketball team. The issue in this case boils down to whether the school – because of § 504 of the Rehabilitation Act of 1973, as amended, 29 U.S.C. § 794 – will be forced to let Knapp don a purple uniform and take the floor as a member of Northwestern's basketball team.

Prior to his senior year of high school Knapp was rated among the best basketball players in Illinois. He was recruited by numerous universities, including Northwestern. At the end of Knapp's junior year at Peoria's Woodruff High School, Northwestern orally offered him an athletic scholarship to play basketball. Knapp orally accepted the offer.

A few weeks into his senior year, Knapp suffered sudden cardiac death – meaning his heart stopped-during a pick-up basketball game. Paramedics used cardiopulmonary resuscitation, defibrillation (*i.e.,* electric shocks), and injections of drugs to bring Knapp back to life. A few weeks later, doctors implanted an internal cardioverter-defibrillator in Knapp's abdomen. The device detects heart arrhythmia and delivers a shock to convert the abnormal heart rhythm back to normal. In other words, if Knapp's heart stops again the device is supposed to restart it.

On the day following his sudden cardiac death, Northwestern informed Knapp and his family that whatever the ultimate medical decision, Northwestern would honor its commitment for a scholarship. Seven weeks after his collapse Knapp signed a national letter of intent to attend Northwestern.

Knapp did not play basketball during his senior year in high school, but he was always a superb student, and in June 1995 he graduated as the valedictorian of his class. In September 1995 he enrolled as a Northwestern student.

On November 7, 1995, Dr. Howard Sweeney, Northwestern's head team physician, declared Knapp ineligible to participate on Northwestern's men's basketball team for the 1995-96 school year. Dr. Sweeney based his decision on Knapp's medical records in which several treating physicians recommended that Knapp not play competitive basketball, the report of team physician Dr. Mark Gardner following a physical examination of Knapp, published guidelines and recommendations following two national medical conferences known as the Bethesda Conferences regarding eligibility of athletes with cardiovascular abnormalities, and recommendations of physicians with whom Dr. Gardner and Dr. Sweeney consulted. After the basketball season ended, Northwestern and the Big Ten declared Knapp permanently medically ineligible to play basketball. Northwestern's athletic director, Rick Taylor, later confirmed that Northwestern will never voluntarily let Knapp play intercollegiate basketball as a Wildcat.

As a result, Knapp has never practiced with the Northwestern team nor played in a college game. His scholarship nevertheless continues and he attends practices (though he is not allowed to do anything but watch, apparently). He also receives other benefits afforded to athletes (such as tutoring, counseling, and training table), in addition to the full range of academic and non-academic offerings the university provides to all students.

On the same day Dr. Sweeney declared him ineligible, Knapp filed a complaint in federal district court asserting that Northwestern's actions violated the Rehabilitation Act. The suit sought declaratory relief, preliminary and permanent injunctive relief, and compensatory damages. Knapp's undisputed goal is to force Northwestern to allow him to play varsity basketball.

In May 1996 Northwestern filed a motion for summary judgment, and Knapp thereafter requested a permanent injunction. The district court held a hearing on September 6, 1996, solely to determine whether Knapp presently is medically eligible to play intercollegiate basketball. Presented with conflicting evidence, the district court found Knapp medically eligible and Northwestern in violation of the Rehabilitation Act. After subsequent hearings on the issue of reasonable accommodation, the district court denied Northwestern's motion for summary judgment and entered a permanent injunction prohibiting Northwestern from excluding Knapp from playing on its basketball team for any reason related to his cardiac condition.

The district court's decision was based on the affidavit of Knapp and the testimony and affidavits of two experts presented by Northwestern and three experts presented by Knapp. All the experts agreed Knapp had suffered sudden cardiac death due to ventricular fibrillation; even with the internal defibrillator, playing intercollegiate basketball places Knapp at a higher risk for suffering another event of sudden cardiac death compared to other male college basketball players; the internal defibrillator has never been tested under the conditions of intercollegiate basketball; and no person currently plays or has ever played college or professional basketball after suffering sudden cardiac death and having a defibrillator implanted. Northwestern's experts, cardiologists who participated in at least one of the Bethesda conferences, testified that playing intercollegiate basketball significantly and unacceptably increases Knapp's risk of death. At least one of Northwestern's experts stated that individuals with internal defibrillators should not play intercollegiate basketball. Knapp's expert cardiologists, one of whom, Dr. Lawrence Rink, is Knapp's treating cardiologist and an Indiana University basketball team physician, testified that although Knapp is at an increased risk for sudden cardiac death, that risk, especially with the internal defibrillator in place, is insubstantial or at least acceptable.

After tasting defeat in the district court, Northwestern filed an emergency notice of appeal on September 27, 1996. It also sought a stay of enforcement of the injunction. We expedited the proceedings, granted the stay pending this decision, and heard oral arguments on November 7, 1996, ironically one year to the day after Dr. Sweeney first declared that Knapp could not play basketball for Northwestern.

We review the district court's grant of a permanent injunction for abuse of discretion. *United States v. Kaun*, 827 F.2d 1144, 1148 (7th Cir. 1987). Factual determinations are reviewed under a clearly erroneous standard and legal conclusions are given *de novo* review. A factual or legal error may be sufficient to establish an abuse of discretion. *Id.* Interpretation of the Rehabilitation Act presents legal questions calling for *de novo* review.

The Rehabilitation Act, which is the sole basis for Knapp's claim, ensures that "[n]o otherwise qualified individual with a disability in the United States, ... shall, solely by reason of her or his disability, be excluded from the participation in, be denied the benefits of, or be subjected to discrimination under any program or activity receiving Federal financial assistance...." 29 U.S.C. § 794(a). To prevail on his claim for discrimination under the Act, Knapp must prove that: (1) he is disabled as defined by the Act; (2) he is otherwise qualified for the position sought; (3) he has been excluded from the position solely because of his disability; and (4) the position exists as part of a program or activity receiving federal financial assistance. Northwestern does not dispute that it receives federal financial assistance and that it has excluded Knapp from its intercollegiate basketball program solely because of his cardiac condition, so our focus is on whether Knapp is an "otherwise qualified individual with a disability."

* * *

Even if we were inclined to find Knapp disabled under the Rehabilitation Act, he would still come up short because we also hold as a matter of law that he is not, under the statute, "otherwise qualified" to play intercollegiate basketball at Northwestern. A qualified disabled person, with respect to postsecondary education services, is a "person who meets the academic and technical standards requisite to admission or participation in the [school's] education program or activity." An explanatory note to the regulations states that the term "technical standards" means "all nonacademic admissions criteria that are essential to participation in the program in question."

Section 794 does not compel educational institutions to disregard the disabilities of disabled persons. It requires only that an "otherwise qualified" disabled person not be excluded from participation in a federally funded program solely because of the disability. In other words, although a disability is not a permissible ground for assuming an inability to function in a particular context, the disability is not thrown out when considering if the person is qualified for the position sought. "An otherwise qualified person is one who is able to meet all of a program's requirements in spite of his handicap," with reasonable accommodation.

Legitimate physical qualifications may in fact be essential to participation in particular programs. Paragraph (k) of § 84.3 defines the term "qualified handicapped person." Throughout the regulation, this term is used instead of the statutory term "otherwise qualified handicapped person." The Department believes that the omission of the word "otherwise" is necessary in order to comport with the intent of the statute because, read literally, "otherwise" qualified handicapped persons include persons who are qualified except for their handicap, rather than in spite of their handicap. Under such a literal reading, a blind person possessing all the qualifications for driving a bus except sight could be said to be "otherwise qualified" for the job of driving. Clearly, such a result was not intended by Congress. In all other respects, the terms "qualified" and "otherwise qualified" are intended to be interchangeable.

A significant risk of personal physical injury can disqualify a person from a position if the risk cannot be eliminated. But more than merely an elevated risk of injury is required before disqualification is appropriate. *Mantolete v. Bolger*, 767 F.2d 1416, 1424 (9th Cir. 1985). Any physical qualification based on risk of future injury must be examined with special care if the Rehabilitation Act is not to be circumvented, since almost all disabled individuals are at a greater risk of injury.

In *Mantolete,* the Ninth Circuit addressed the standard to apply in determining if an individual is otherwise physically qualified to perform an activity when the possibility of future injury exists:

> [I]n some cases, a job requirement that screens out qualified handicapped individuals on the basis of possible future injury is necessary. However, we hold that in order to exclude such individuals, there must be a showing of a reasonable probability of substantial harm. Such a determination cannot be based merely on an employer's subjective evaluation or, except in cases of a most apparent nature, merely on medical reports. The question is whether, in light of the individual's work history and medical history, employment of that individual would pose a reasonable probability of substantial harm. . . . In applying this standard, an employer must gather all relevant information regarding the applicant's work history and medical history, and independently assess both the probability and severity of potential injury. This involves, of course, a case-by-case analysis of the applicant and the particular job.

We agree this is the appropriate standard. We now turn, however, to who should make such an assessment.

In this case, the severity of the potential injury is as high as it could be-death. In regard to the probability of injury, Dr. John H. McAnulty, one of Knapp's experts, testified at the injunction hearing that the annual risk of death to Knapp as a result of his cardiac condition under a worst-case scenario is 2.4 percent and that playing intercollegiate basketball would elevate this annual risk to 2.93 percent, or 1 in 34. In other words, if 34 Nick Knapp played basketball for a year, chances are one would die. Dr. Brian Olshansky, another expert for Knapp, put Knapp's risk of death for the 1996-97 basketball season at no greater than 1 in 100. These estimates took into account Knapp's internal defibrillator, apparently the only "accommodation" possible for Knapp's condition. Although the doctors indicated that these numbers were merely estimates, all agreed that the risk to Knapp is higher than to the average male collegiate basketball player. Knapp's experts believed it was an acceptable level of risk.

Northwestern's experts agreed with the school's team doctors that Knapp's participation in competitive Big Ten basketball presented an unacceptable level of risk. ***

Knapp's and Northwestern's experts disagreed on the effect of the passage of time on the likelihood that Knapp would suffer another sudden cardiac death. Almost all experts agreed that the internal defibrillator had never been tested under conditions like an intercollegiate basketball game or practice and that it was unclear whether the device would actually work under the stress and physical conditions of a high-intensity sport. ***

* * *

We disagree with the district court's legal determination that such decisions are to be made by the courts and believe instead that medical determinations of this sort are best left to team doctors and universities as long as they are made with reason and rationality and with full regard to possible and reasonable accommodations. In cases such as ours, where Northwestern has examined both Knapp and his medical records, has considered his medical history and the relation between his prior sudden cardiac death and the possibility of future occurrences, has considered the severity of the potential injury, and has rationally and reasonably reviewed consensus medical opinions or recommendations in the pertinent field — regardless whether conflicting medical opinions exist — the university has the right to determine that an individual is not otherwise medically qualified to play without violating the Rehabilitation Act. The place of the court in such cases is to make sure that the decision-maker has reasonably considered and relied upon sufficient evidence specific to the individual and the potential injury, not to determine on its own which evidence it believes is more persuasive.

* * *

We do not believe that, in cases where medical experts disagree in their assessment of the extent of a real risk of serious harm or death, Congress intended that the courts — neutral arbiters but generally less skilled in medicine than the experts involved — should make the final medical decision. Instead, in the midst of conflicting expert testimony regarding the degree of serious risk of harm or death, the court's place is to ensure that the exclusion or disqualification of an individual was individualized, reasonably made, and based upon competent medical evidence. So long as these factors exist, it will be the rare case regarding participation in athletics where a court may substitute its judgment for that of the school's team physicians.

In this case, the district court found that if "as a matter of law and fact, all that is required ... is that Northwestern make a rational decision that Knapp's risk is substantial based on reasonable evidence to which courts must defer, then I find Northwestern has done this."

Because we hold today as a matter of law that a court must allow Northwestern to make its own determinations of substantial risk and severity of injury if they are based on reliable evidence, the district court's order forcing Northwestern to let Knapp play must be reversed.

* * *

In closing, we wish to make clear that we are *not* saying Northwestern's decision necessarily is the right decision. We say only that it is not an illegal one under the Rehabilitation Act. On the same facts, another team physician at another university, reviewing the same medical history, physical evaluation, and medical recommendations, might reasonably decide that Knapp met the physical qualifications for playing on an intercollegiate basketball team. Simply put, all universities need not evaluate risk the same way. What we say in this case is that if substantial evidence supports the decision-maker — here Northwestern — that decision must be respected.

Section 794 prohibits authorities from deciding without significant medical support that certain activities are too risky for a disabled person. Decisions of this sort cannot rest on paternalistic concerns. Knapp, who is an adult, is not in need of paternalistic decisions regarding his health, and his parents — more entitled to be paternalistic toward him than Northwestern — approve of his decision.... But here, where Northwestern acted rationally and reasonably rather than paternalistically, no Rehabilitation Act violation has occurred. The Rehabilitation Act "is carefully structured to replace ... reflexive actions to actual or perceived handicaps with actions based on reasoned and medically sound judgments...."

REVERSED.

NOTES & QUESTIONS

1. Do you agree with the court's decision in *Knapp*?

2. When reviewing an adverse determination concerning an athlete's intercollegiate eligibility, how much significance should a court attach to a liability-waiver agreement executed by the athlete or a family member? Should the significance depend on the setting: for example, high school or professional sports?

3. In *Pakula v. University of Kansas*, 897 F. Supp. 1387 (D. Kan. 1995), the court refused to substitute its judgment for KU's physicians who rationally and reasonably found – supported by substantial competent evidence – that an intercollegiate football player was ineligible to play because of an increased neurological risk of injury. And for another more recent but similar case, *see Class v. Towson U.*, 806 F.3d 236 (4th Cir. 2015). Towson University football player Gavin Class alleged a violation of the ADA, but the Fourth Circuit upheld the university's decision (via its football team doctor) not to allow plaintiff to return to play, following on-field collapse from heatstroke that resulted in Class being in a coma for over a week and multiple surgeries (including a liver transplant).

GANDEN V. NATIONAL COLLEGIATE ATHLETIC ASSOCIATION
NO. 96 C 6953, 1996 WL 680000
UNITED STATES DISTRICT COURT, NORTHERN DISTRICT OF ILLINOIS

MANNING, DISTRICT JUDGE.

[Plaintiff Chad Ganden filed this motion for a preliminary injunction to compel the National Collegiate Athletic Association (NCAA) to waive its core course and minimum grade point average requirements. To be eligible for Division I competition, a student must have taken 13 core courses and attained a minimum GPA determined by a sliding scale based on the student's standardized college entrance examination – the higher test score, the lower the GPA score. A core course offered fundamental instructional components in a specified area, such as reading or math, and did not include remedial, special education or compensatory courses. Ganden was diagnosed with a learning disability and received an Individualized Education Plan (IEP) in high school to help him prepare for college. IEPs often include remedial courses making it more difficult for learning disabled students to meet the NCAA's "core course" requirement which was the case with Ganden when the NCAA did not accept some of his remedial courses. Ganden was one of the nation's fastest swimmers so despite his academic record, Michigan State University offered him a swimming scholarship contingent on his receiving a waiver from the NCAA modifying its core course requirement. When the NCAA refused to grant the waiver, Ganden brought this action.]

* * *

CONCLUSIONS OF LAW

To obtain a preliminary injunction, a movant must first establish (1) some likelihood of his success on the merits, and (2) that, without the injunction, he will suffer "irreparable harm" for which he has "no adequate remedy at law." *** The movant need only demonstrate a "reasonable likelihood" of prevailing at trial in that his "chances are better than negligible."

* * * *

B. *Ganden's Substantive Claim.*

Ganden contends that the NCAA's denial of his waiver application violated Title III because (1) the NCAA relied upon an eligibility criterion that "screened" him out on the basis of his disability as prohibited under section 12182(b)(2)(A)(i), and (2) the NCAA refused to make reasonable modifications to its eligibility requirements that discriminated against him on the basis of his disability as required under section 12182(b)(2)(A)(ii) 9. Because the NCAA computes GPA only from "core courses," its "core course" definition may determine whether a student satisfies its minimum GPA/ACT requirement. As learning disabilities such as Ganden's significantly restrict the student's opportunity to take "core courses," Ganden argues that the "core course" requirement screened him out on the basis of this disability.

In addition, Ganden argues that the NCAA was required to make reasonable modifications to either its "core course" criterion or its GPA standard to provide him with a waiver in light of his disability. First, Ganden asserts that the refusal to modify its "core course" definition to consider his two LRC [Learning Resource Center] courses as "core" violated Title III which would have allowed him to satisfy the minimum GPA requirements. Second, Ganden argues more generally that the NCAA should have modified its minimum GPA standard in light of his difficulty meeting the "core course" requirement with his disability, his improving academic record, and other indications of his ability to succeed at college. Ganden also argues that the NCAA waiver process did not permit it to consider whether modifications to its eligibility criteria would be reasonable. In particular, Ganden argues that its insulated review process did not permit the direct participation of either himself or other his counselors and parents. Ganden asserts that this additional information was necessary for a full consideration of his ability to succeed at college.

The NCAA responds that; (1) Ganden cannot demonstrate a causal link between his disability and the NCAA's denial of his waiver application, (2) Title III does not require the NCAA to modify its eligibility requirements because those requirements are "necessary for the provision" of the privilege Ganden seeks and the proposed modifications would "fundamentally alter" the nature of that privilege, and (3) the NCAA has already provided Ganden with reasonable modifications to its review process and eligibility requirements. Because it considered some of Ganden remedial courses as "core courses," the NCAA argues that it did not deny his waiver on the basis of his disability but simply because he failed to meet the minimum required GPA. In addition, the NCAA argues that its eligibility criteria are "necessary" to accomplish the purpose of its intercollegiate program, to promote and develop both educational leadership and athletic excellence. Similarly, the NCAA contends that Ganden's proposed modifications to those criteria would "fundamentally alter" the nature of its dual purpose intercollegiate program. ***

1. *Discrimination on the Basis of Disability.*
The court rejects the NCAA's contention that Ganden cannot establish a causal link between its denial of Ganden's waiver application and his learning disability. The NCAA asserts that it denied Ganden's waiver application because he failed to meet the minimum eligibility requirements through his combined GPA and ACT scores. ***

The court respectfully disagrees with this analysis. In implementing civil rights legislation for the disabled, Congress recognized that discrimination on the basis of a disability is "most often the product, not of invidious animus, but rather of thoughtlessness and indifference — of benign neglect." *** In the instant case, the evidence strongly suggests that Ganden failed to take the requisite "core courses" or satisfy the remaining eligibility criteria because of his disability.

When they reviewed his waiver application, the NCAA Subcommittee was aware of this condition and how it affected his ability to meet their eligibility requirements. Consequently, Ganden has presented a strong prima facie case that there is a causal link between the NCAA refusal to certify Ganden a "qualifier" and his learning disability.

2. Reasonable Modifications.

The court next addresses whether Ganden's requested modifications are reasonable or would "fundamentally alter" the nature of the privilege or accommodation to which he has been denied access. *** This analysis requires that the court examine the particular eligibility criteria and the nature of the privilege that it monitors. The criteria at issue are the minimum GPA requirements and the "core course" definition that is instrumental in computing a student's GPA. The privilege at issue is the NCAA's intercollegiate athletic program. *** [T]he eligibility requirements (1) insure that student-athletes are representative of the college community and not recruited solely for athletics (2) insure that a student-athlete is academically prepared to succeed at college; and (3) preserve amateurism in intercollegiate sports.

* * *

[T]he NCAA has an important interest in insuring that its student-athletes are prepared to succeed at college. Whatever criticism one may level at GPA and the national standardized tests, these provide significant objective predictors of a student's ability to succeed at college. The "core course" criteria further serves the dual interest of insuring the integrity of that GPA and independently insuring that the student has covered the minimum subject matter required for college.

However, in the case of learning disabled students, the NCAA may be able to serve these purposes and insure that a student has the necessary academic capabilities through consideration of additional factors. In fact, through its waiver application process, the NCAA provides such individualized consideration. In the case of learning disabled students, a generally improving academic record may indicate that prior remedial courses adequately substituted for earlier "core courses," even if not qualitatively and quantitatively identical to other "core courses." In such circumstances, some remedial courses may have served the same role as approved "core courses" to other students. Therefore, the record indicates that Title III requires the NCAA to consider a students' progress in his or her IEP courses and overall high school career.

* * *

As Ganden argues, Title III requires the NCAA to individually assess his request for modifications. However, the NCAA provided such an assessment. The Subcommittee reviewed Ganden's case for over one hour. It received an application prepared by a member institution with a strong interest in procuring a waiver on his behalf. This package included his academic record, a psychological report focusing on his disability as well as his efforts and successes in overcoming it, and arguments on his behalf from MSU. In addition, the record indicates that the Subcommittee was aware of the Department of Justice's efforts and arguments on his behalf. After this review, the Subcommittee accommodated Ganden through granting him "partial qualifier" status.

While there is some doubt whether the NCAA actually counted Ganden's three "Basic" courses as "core" in consideration of his disability or MSU's reliance argument, the record reveals that the Subcommittee did consider Ganden's disability, his efforts to overcome it, and his impressive academic gains during his final two years of high school. Even though he did not meet the minimum GPA, it still granted Ganden "partial qualifier" status. Title III does not require the NCAA to simply abandon its eligibility requirements, but only to make reasonable modifications to them. The record reveals that the NCAA did precisely that.

3. *Necessity of Eligibility Criteria.*

Presuming Ganden's adequate prima facie case that the NCAA's "core course" and GPA requirements discriminate against him on the basis of his learning disability, the NCAA denial of his waiver discriminates against Ganden unless those requirements are "necessary for the provision of the goods, services, facilities, privileges, advantages or accommodations offered ..." There is little case law interpreting this provision of Title III. *** The court must determine whether the modifications to the eligibility criteria are reasonable or would require "a modification of the essential nature of the program."

Consistent with the analysis above, the present record reveals that the "core course" definition is "necessary to the provision" of the privilege to the extent that it excludes Ganden's courses for LRC Typing and LRC Computers. Similarly, the analysis above reveals that the NCAA GPA minimum is also "necessary."

4. *Conclusion.*

Although Ganden has demonstrated some likelihood of success on the merits...the court finds that he has not shown a reasonable likelihood of success on the critical allegation that the NCAA's denial of his waiver application constituted "discrimination" under section 12182(b)(2) of Title III. Looking at the case as a whole, the court concludes that Ganden has failed to satisfy the minimum threshold of demonstrating a reasonable likelihood of success at trial.

CONCLUSION

For the reasons set forth above, the court denies Ganden's motion for a preliminary injunction.

NOTES & QUESTIONS

1. One expert suggests that athletes with learning disabilities have not been more successful in having organizations like the NCAA modify academic eligibility standards because courts and sporting programs are suspicious of the diagnosis, or cause of the athlete's failure to

meet the eligibility requirements, Maureen Weston, *The Intersection of Sports and Disability: Analyzing Reasonable Accommodations for Athletes with Disabilities,* 50 St. Louis U. L.J. 137, 155 (2006). *See also Tantum v. NCAA,* 992 F. Supp. 1114 (E.D. Mo. 1998)(reflecting that even experts may disagree about the cause of a student's ineligibility). *In Tantum,* the student sought a temporary restraining order against the defendants, the NCAA and St. Louis University (SLU). He claimed the NCAA violated the ADA by discriminating against him on the basis of a mental disability when "it refused to recognize a nonstandard, untimed ACT score for purposes" of deciding his intercollegiate athletic eligibility. *Id.* at 1116. His high school counselor advised Tantum in his senior year to be examined for a learning disability because he risked losing his SLU basketball scholarship if he was ineligible. Tantum was examined on two occasions by different experts with conflicting diagnoses about whether he had a mental disability *Id.* at 1123. Tantum also admitted that he had "not put the requisite effort into his school work until his junior year." *Id.* The court denied Tantum's claim because, in part, he failed to demonstrate a substantial likelihood of success on the merits – that he suffered from a "mental impairment that substantially limits one or more of [his] major life activities." *Id.* (citing 28 C.F.R. § 36.104.).

2. The *Ganden* court discussed *Sandison v. Michigan High School Athletic Association,* which upheld age restrictions in high school sports. Under these restrictions, students who are held back academically in school because of learning disabilities eventually exceed the age requirements of participating in sports. Should older students who are held back because of learning disabilities be allowed to compete in high school sports, even though they may not meet the age requirements? *Cf. Cruz v. Pennsylvania Interscholastic Athletic Association,* 157 F. Supp. 2d 485 (E.D. Penn. 2001)(holding that a learning disabled high school student seeking a waiver of the Pennsylvania Interscholastic Athletic Association (PIAA) age requirement rule was entitled to an individual assessment by the PIAA of whether the waiver is consistent with the rule's purpose of promoting the safety of athletes and protecting against any unfair advantage to or displacement of other athletes).

4. ATHLETES NEEDING ACCOMMODATION OR MODIFICATION TO THE RULES OF PLAY

PGA TOUR, INC. V. MARTIN
532 U.S. 661 (2001)
UNITED STATES SUPREME COURT

STEVENS, JUSTICE

This case raises two questions concerning the application of the Americans with Disabilities Act of 1990, to a gifted athlete: first, whether the Act protects access to professional golf tournaments by a qualified entrant with a disability; and second, whether a disabled contestant may be denied the use of a golf cart because it would "fundamentally alter the nature" of the tournaments, to allow him to ride when all other contestants must walk.

I

Petitioner PGA TOUR, Inc., a nonprofit entity formed in 1968, sponsors and cosponsors professional golf tournaments conducted on three annual tours [that produce revenues of] about $300 million a year, much of which is distributed in prize money.

There are various ways of gaining entry into particular tours. *** Most participants, however, earn playing privileges in the PGA TOUR or NIKE TOUR by way of a three-stage qualifying tournament known as the "Q–School." Any member of the public may enter the Q–School by paying a $3,000 entry fee and submitting two letters of reference from, among others, PGA TOUR or NIKE TOUR members. The $3,000 entry fee covers the players' greens fees and the cost of golf carts, which are permitted during the first two stages, but which have been prohibited during the third stage since 1997. ***

II

Casey Martin is a talented golfer. As an amateur, he won 17 Oregon Golf Association junior events before he was 15, and won the state championship as a high school senior. He played on the Stanford University golf team that won the 1994 National Collegiate Athletic Association (NCAA) championship. As a professional, Martin qualified for the NIKE TOUR in 1998 and 1999, and based on his 1999 performance, qualified for the PGA TOUR in 2000. In the 1999 season, he entered 24 events, made the cut 13 times, and had 6 top-10 finishes, coming in second twice and third once.

Martin is also an individual with a disability as defined in the Americans with Disabilities Act of 1990 (ADA or Act). Since birth he has been afflicted with Klippel-Trenaunay-Weber Syndrome, a degenerative circulatory disorder that obstructs the flow of blood from his right leg back to his heart. The disease is progressive; it causes severe pain and has atrophied his right leg. During the latter part of his college career, because of the progress of the disease, Martin could no longer walk an 18-hole golf course. Walking not only caused him pain, fatigue, and anxiety, but also created a significant risk of hemorrhaging, developing blood clots, and fracturing his tibia so badly that an amputation might be required. For these reasons, Stanford made written requests to the Pacific 10 Conference and the NCAA to waive for Martin their rules requiring players to walk and carry their own clubs. The requests were granted.

When Martin turned pro and entered petitioner's Q-School, the hard [*i.e.*, rules] card permitted him to use a cart during his successful progress through the first two stages. He made a request, supported by detailed medical records, for permission to use a golf cart during the third stage. Petitioner refused to review those records or to waive its walking rule for the third stage. Martin therefore filed this action. A preliminary injunction entered by the District Court made it possible for him to use a cart in the final stage of the Q-School and as a competitor in the NIKE TOUR and PGA TOUR. Although not bound by the injunction, and despite its support for petitioner's position in this litigation, the USGA voluntarily granted Martin a similar waiver in events that it sponsors, including the U.S. Open.

III

At trial, petitioner did not contest the conclusion that Martin has a disability covered by the ADA, or the fact "that his disability prevents him from walking the course during a round of golf." Rather, petitioner asserted that the condition of walking is a substantive rule of competition, and that waiving it as to any individual for any reason would fundamentally alter the nature of the competition.

Rejecting petitioner's argument that an individualized inquiry into the necessity of the walking rule in Martin's case would be inappropriate, the District Court stated that it had "the independent duty to inquire into the purpose of the rule at issue, and to ascertain whether there can be a reasonable modification made to accommodate plaintiff without frustrating the purpose of the rule" and thereby fundamentally altering the nature of petitioner's tournaments. The judge found that the purpose of the rule was to inject fatigue into the skill of shotmaking, but that the fatigue injected "by walking the course cannot be deemed significant under normal circumstances." Furthermore, Martin presented evidence, and the judge found, that even with the use of a cart, Martin must walk over a mile during an 18-hole round, and that the fatigue he suffers from coping with his disability is "undeniably greater" than the fatigue his able-bodied competitors endure from walking the course. As the judge observed: "[P]laintiff is in significant pain when he walks, and even when he is getting in and out of the cart. With each step, he is at risk of fracturing his tibia and hemorrhaging. The other golfers have to endure the psychological stress of competition as part of their fatigue; Martin has the same stress plus the added stress of pain and risk of serious injury. As he put it, he would gladly trade the cart for a good leg. To perceive that the cart puts him—with his condition—at a competitive advantage is a gross distortion of reality."

As a result, the judge concluded that it would "not fundamentally alter the nature of the PGA Tour's game to accommodate him with a cart." The judge accordingly entered a permanent injunction requiring petitioner to permit Martin to use a cart in tour and qualifying events.

* * *

On the merits, because there was no serious dispute about the fact that permitting Martin to use a golf cart was both a reasonable and a necessary solution to the problem of providing him access to the tournaments, the Court of Appeals regarded the central dispute as whether such permission would "fundamentally alter" the nature of the PGA TOUR or NIKE TOUR. Like the District Court, the Court of Appeals viewed the issue not as "whether use of carts generally would fundamentally alter the competition, but whether the use of a cart by Martin would do so." That issue turned on "an intensively fact-based inquiry," and, the court concluded, had been correctly resolved by the trial judge. In its words, "[a]ll that the cart does is permit Martin access to a type of competition in which he otherwise could not engage because of his disability."

The day after the Ninth Circuit ruled in Martin's favor, the Seventh Circuit came to a contrary conclusion in a case brought against the USGA by a disabled golfer who failed to qualify for "America's greatest – and most democratic – golf tournament, the United States Open." *Olinger v. United States Golf Assn.*, 205 F.3d 1001 (C.A. 7 2000). The Seventh Circuit endorsed the conclusion of the District Court in that case that "the nature of the competition would be fundamentally altered if the walking rule were eliminated because it would remove stamina (at least a particular type of stamina) from the set of qualities designed to be tested in this competition." In the Seventh Circuit's opinion, the physical ordeals endured by Ken Venturi and Ben Hogan when they walked to their Open victories in 1964 and 1950 amply demonstrated the importance of stamina in such a tournament. As an alternative basis for its holding, the court also concluded that the ADA does not require the USGA to bear "the administrative burdens of evaluating requests to waive the walking rule and permit the use of a golf cart."

Although the Seventh Circuit merely assumed that the ADA applies to professional golf tournaments, and therefore did not disagree with the Ninth on the threshold coverage issue, our grant of certiorari encompasses that question as well as the conflict between those courts.

IV

* * *

Our conclusion is consistent with case law in the analogous context of Title II of the Civil Rights Act of 1964, 78 Stat. 243.... These cases support our conclusion that, as a public accommodation during its tours and qualifying rounds, petitioner may not discriminate against either spectators or competitors on the basis of disability.

V

As we have noted, 42 U.S.C. § 12182(a) sets forth Title III's general rule prohibiting public accommodations from discriminating against individuals because of their disabilities. The question whether petitioner has violated that rule depends on a proper construction of the term "discrimination," which is defined by Title III to include:

"a failure to make reasonable modifications in policies, practices, or procedures, when such modifications are necessary to afford such goods, services, facilities, privileges, advantages, or accommodations to individuals with disabilities, *unless the entity can demonstrate that making such modifications would fundamentally alter the nature* of such goods, services, facilities, privileges, advantages, or accommodations." (emphasis added).

*** In this case...the narrow dispute is whether allowing Martin to use a golf cart, despite the walking requirement that applies to the PGA TOUR, the NIKE TOUR, and the third stage of the Q–School, is a modification that would "fundamentally alter the nature" of those events.

* * *

Petitioner...distinguishes the game of golf as it is generally played from the game that it sponsors in the PGA TOUR, NIKE TOUR, and (at least recently) the last stage of the Q-School – golf at the "highest level." According to petitioner, "[t]he goal of the highest-level competitive athletics is to assess and compare the performance of different competitors, a task that is meaningful only if the competitors are subject to identical substantive rules." The waiver of any possibly "outcome-affecting" rule for a contestant would violate this principle and therefore, in petitioner's view, fundamentally alter the nature of the highest level athletic event. The walking rule is one such rule, petitioner submits, because its purpose is "to inject the element of fatigue into the skill of shot-making," and thus its effect may be the critical loss of a stroke. As a consequence, the reasonable modification Martin seeks would fundamentally alter the nature of petitioner's highest level tournaments even if he were the only person in the world who has both the talent to compete in those elite events and a disability sufficiently serious that he cannot do so without using a cart.

The force of petitioner's argument is, first of all, mitigated by the fact that golf is a game in which it is impossible to guarantee that all competitors will play under exactly the same conditions or that an individual's ability will be the sole determinant of the outcome. For example, changes in the weather may produce harder greens and more head winds for the tournament leader than for his closest pursuers. ***

Further, [t]he District Court credited the testimony of a professor in physiology and expert on fatigue, who concluded . . . golf is a low intensity activity [and that] fatigue from the game is primarily a psychological phenomenon in which stress and motivation are the key ingredients ... rather than exercise from walking. Moreover, when given the option of using a cart, the majority of golfers in petitioner's tournaments have chosen to walk, often to relieve stress or for other strategic reasons.

* * *

[P]etitioner's claim that all the substantive rules for its "highest-level" competitions are sacrosanct and cannot be modified under any circumstances is effectively a contention that it is exempt from Title III's reasonable modification requirement. But that provision carves out no exemption for elite athletics, and given Title III's coverage not only of places of "exhibition or entertainment" but also of "golf course[s]," its application to petitioner's tournaments cannot be said to be unintended or unexpected.

Under the ADA's basic requirement that the need of a disabled person be evaluated on an individual basis, we have no doubt that allowing Martin to use a golf cart would not fundamentally alter the nature of petitioner's tournaments. As we have discussed, the purpose of the walking rule is to subject players to fatigue, which in turn may influence the outcome of tournaments. Even if the rule does serve that purpose, it is an uncontested finding of the District Court that Martin "easily endures greater fatigue even with a cart than his able-bodied competitors do by walking." The purpose of the walking rule is therefore not compromised in the slightest by allowing Martin to use a cart. A modification that provides an exception to a peripheral tournament rule without impairing its purpose cannot be said to "fundamentally alter" the tournament. What it can be said to do, on the other hand, is to allow Martin the chance to qualify for, and compete in, the athletic events petitioner offers to those members of the public who have the skill and desire to enter. That is exactly what the ADA requires. As a result, Martin's request for a waiver of the walking rule should have been granted.

The ADA admittedly imposes some administrative burdens on the operators of places of public accommodation that could be avoided by strictly adhering to general rules and policies that are entirely fair with respect to the able-bodied but that may indiscriminately preclude access by qualified persons with disabilities. But surely, in a case of this kind, Congress intended that an entity like the PGA not only give individualized attention to the handful of requests that it might receive from talented but disabled athletes for a modification or waiver of a rule to allow them access to the competition, but also carefully weigh the purpose, as well as the letter, of the rule before determining that no accommodation would be tolerable.

The judgment of the Court of Appeals is affirmed.

SCALIA and THOMAS, Justices, Dissenting

* * *

Either out of humility or out of self-respect (one or the other) the Court should decline to answer this incredibly difficult and incredibly silly question [: is someone riding around a golf course from shot to shot really a golfer"]. To say that something is "essential" is ordinarily to say that it is necessary to the achievement of a certain object. But since it is the very nature of a game to have no object except amusement (that is what distinguishes games from productive activity), it is quite impossible to say that any of a game's arbitrary rules is "essential." Eighteen-hole golf courses, 10-foot-high basketball hoops, 90-foot baselines, 100-yard football fields – all are arbitrary and none is essential. The only support for any of them is tradition and (in more modern times) insistence by what has come to be regarded as the ruling body of the sport – both of which factors support the PGA TOUR's position in the present case. (Many, indeed, consider walking to be the central feature of the game of golf – hence Mark Twain's classic criticism of the sport: "a good walk spoiled.")

My belief that today's judgment is clearly in error should not be mistaken for a belief that the PGA TOUR clearly ought not allow respondent to use a golf cart. That is a close question, on which even those who compete in the PGA TOUR are apparently divided; but it is a different question from the one before the Court. Just as it is a different question whether the Little League ought to give disabled youngsters a fourth strike, or some other waiver from the rules that makes up for their disabilities. In both cases, whether they ought to do so depends upon (1) how central to the game that they have organized (and over whose rules they are the master) they deem the waived provision to be, and (2) how competitive – how strict a test of raw athletic ability in all aspects of the competition – they want their game to be. But whether Congress has said they must do so depends upon the answers to the legal questions I have discussed above – not upon what this Court sententiously decrees to be "'decent, tolerant, [and] progressive,'"[.]

* * *

NOTES & QUESTIONS

1. Does the accommodation of allowing a disabled golfer to use a cart during tournaments fundamentally change the rules of golf? Should this be the Court's decision or the PGA's?

2. For a recent case exploring similar issues in the context of a high school athlete, *see K. L. v. Missouri State High Sch. Activities Assn.,* 178 F. Supp. 3d 792 (E.D. Mo. 2016). Court denied injunctive relief when high track & field para-athlete alleged violation of the Rehabilitation Act and ADA because the state high school athletic association would not allow the athlete to use a racing chair and to be given time accommodations. The court determined that such accommodations *would* fundamentally change the competition.

Further Reading on Title IX, The Rehabilitation Act, and The Americans with Disabilities Act:

Brenda L. Ambrosius, *Title IX: Creating Unequal Equality Through Application of the Proportionality Standard in Collegiate Athletics,* 46 Val. U. L. Rev. 557 (2012).

Paul Anderson, *Title IX at Forty An Introduction and Historical Review of Forty Legal Developments That Shaped Gender Equality Law,* 22 Marq. Sports L. Rev. 325 (2012).

Zachary W. Anderson, *Title IX Compliance: In the Name of Financial Stability or Gender Equality? An in-Depth Review of Title IX and the University of Nebraska at Omaha Athletic Department's Compliance,* 10 Willamette Sports L.J. 33 (2012).

Lisa Borders, *Inspiring and Empowering Women: The Wnba Leading the Way into the 21st Century,* 28 J. Leg. Aspects Sport 121 (2018).

Deborah L. Brake, *Lessons from the Gender Equality Movement: Using Title IX to Foster Inclusive Masculinities in Men's Sport*, 34 L. & Inequal. 285 (2016).

Deborah L. Brake, *Wrestling with Gender: Constructing Masculinity by Refusing to Wrestle Women*, 13 Nev. L.J. 486 (2013).

Erin E. Buzuvis, *"As Who They Really Are": Expanding Opportunities for Transgender Athletes to Participate in Youth and Scholastic Sports*, 34 L. & Inequal. 341 (2016).

Erin E. Buzuvis, *Athletic Compensation for Women Too? Title IX Implications of Northwestern and O'Bannon*, 41 J.C. & U.L. 297 (2015).

Jessica Constance Caggiano, *Girls Don't Just Wanna Have Fun: Moving Past Title IX's Contact Sports Exception*, 72 U. Pitt. L. Rev. 119 (2010).

Michael Cottingham, *Michael Carroll, Don Lee, Deborah Shapiro, Brenda Pitts, The Historical Realization of the Americans with Disabilities Act on Athletes with Disabilities*, 26 J. Leg. Aspects Sport 5 (2016).

Lisa Davis, *Jacqueline Paradee Mette, Title IX: Its History and Impact on Female Athletes*, Del. Law. 18 (Winter 2012/2013).

Jared A. Fiore, *Playing Between the Lines: The Legality of Male Athletes in Interscholastic Field Hockey*, 10 Willamette Sports L.J. 1 (2013).

Ephraim Glatt, *Defining "Sport" Under Title IX: Cheerleading, Biediger v. Quinnipiac University, and the Proper Scope of Agency Deference*, 19 Sports Law. J. 297, 298 (2012).

James J. Hefferan, Jr., *A Sporting Chance: Biediger v. Quinnipiac University and What Constitutes A Sport for Purposes of Title IX*, 26 Marq. Sports L. Rev. 583 (2016).

Nancy Hogshead-Makar, *Playing Unfair: Commission's Opposition to Title IX Shows Bias Against Women's Sports*, L.A. Daily J. 6, Col 3 (March 11, 2003).

Maliha Ikram, *When Local Governments Waiver: Giving Bite to Students with Disabilities' Federal Right to Avail Physical Education*, 15 Rutgers J.L. & Pub. Pol'y 345 (2018).

Margaret E. Juliano, *Forty Years of Title IX: History and New Applications*, 14 Del. L. Rev. 83 (2013).

Dionne L. Koller, *Not Just One of the Boys: A Post-Feminist Critique of Title IX's Vision for Gender Equity in Sports*, 43 Conn. L. Rev. 401 (2010).

Victoria Langton, *Stop the Bleeding: Title IX and the Disappearance of Men's Collegiate Athletic Teams*, 12 Vand. J. Ent. & Tech. L. 183 (2010).

Daniel R. Marburger, *Is Title IX Really to Blame for the Decline in Intercollegiate Men's Nonrevenue Sport*, 14 Marq. Sports L. Rev. 65 (2003).

Alfred Dennis Mathewson, *Remediating Discrimination Against African American Female Athletes at the Intersection of Title IX and Title VI*, 2 Wake Forest J.L. & Pol'y 295 (2012).

Patrick J. McAndrews, *Keeping Score: How Universities Can Comply with Title IX Without Eliminating Men's Collegiate Athletic Programs*, 2012 B.Y.U. Educ. & L.J. 111 (2012).

Michael A. McCann, *Do You Believe He Can Fly? Royce White and Reasonable Accommodations Under the Americans with Disabilities Act for NBA Players with Anxiety Disorder and Fear of Flying*, 41 Pepp. L. Rev. 397 (2014).

Wes R. McCart, *Simpson v. University of Colorado: Title IX Crashes the Party in College Athletic Recruiting*, 58 DePaul L. Rev. 153 (2008).

Matthew J. Mitten, *Amateur Athletes With Handicaps or Physical Abnormalities*, 71 Neb. L. Rev. 987 (1992).

Matthew J. Mitten, *Sports Participation by Handicapped Athletes*, 10 Ent. & Sports Law 15 (1982).

Barbara Osborne, *Failing to Fund Fairly: Title IX Athletics Scholarships Compliance*, 6 Tenn. J. Race Gender & Soc. Just 83 (2017).

Barbara Osborne, *Pay Equity for Coaches and Athletic Administrators: An Element of Title IX*, 34 Univ. Mich. J.L. Reform 231 (2001).

Katrina A. Pohlman, *Have We Forgotten K-12? The Need for Punitive Damages to Improve Title IX Enforcement*, 71 U. Pitt. L. Rev. 167 (2009).

Colton Puckett, *American Sports Council v. United States Department of Education: Forty Years of Title IX and Still Standing (or Not)*, 20 Sports Law. J. 261 (2013).

Brianna J. Schroeder, Note, *Power Imbalances in College Athletics and an Exploited Standard: Is Title IX Dead?* 43 Val. U. L. Rev. 1483 (2009).

Scott Skinner-Thompson, *Ilona M. Turner, Title IX's Protections for Transgender Student Athletes*, 28 Wis. J.L. Gender & Soc'y 271 (2013).

Rodney K. Smith, *Solving the Title IX Conundrum With Women's Football*, 38 S. Tex. L. Rev. 9 (1997).

Bethany Swaton, *Girls Can Play Too: Has the Lack of female Leadership in NCAA Athletics Become an Afterthought?*, 20 Seton Hall J. Sports & Ent. L. 1(2010).

Symposium, *Competing in the 21st Century: Title IX, Gender Equity and Athletics*, 31 Univ. Mich. J.L. Reform 1 (2001).

Yuri Walker, *Playing the Game of Academic Integrity vs. Athletic Success: The Americans with Disabilities Act (ADA) and Intercollegiate Student-Athletes with Learning Disabilities*, 15 Marq. Sports L. Rev. 601 (2005).

Andrew Warden, *Driving the Green: The Impact of PGA Tour, Inc. v. Martin on Disabled Athletes and the Future of Competitive Sports*, 80 N.C. L. Rev. 643 (2002).

Andrew J. Weissler, *Unasked Questions: Applying Title IX's Effective Accommodation Mandate to Interscholastic Athletics*, 19 Sports Law. J. 71 (2012).

John C. Weistart & Cym H. Lowell, Law of Sports, § 2.10 Sex Discrimination (Bobbs-Merrill Company, Inc., 1979).

Darryl C. Wilson, *Title IX's Collegiate Sports Application Raises Serious Questions Regarding the Role of the NCAA*, 31 J. Marshall L. Rev. 1303 (1998).

Darryl C. Wilson, *Parity Bowl IX: Barrier Breakers v. Common Sense Makers; The Serpentine Struggle for Gender Diversity in Collegiate Athletics*, 27 Cumb. L. Rev. 397 (1996-1997).

Glenn Wong, Kyle Skillman, Chris Deubert, *The NCAA's Infractions Appeals Committee: Recent Case History, Analysis and the Beginning of a New Chapter*, 9 Va. Sports & Ent. L.J. 47 (2009).

CHAPTER 9
NCAA

The three introductory articles provide an overview of the history, organization, structure, and governance of the NCAA, and a number of the most important legal and non-legal issues facing the NCAA and intercollegiate athletics today. The excerpts from Smith's article introduce the background and governance. Mitten's article focuses on antitrust concerns. And Lynch's article takes a provocative look at the difficult balance between the educational goals and the athletic and financial aspects of modern college sports.

The cases illustrate some of the concerns raised in the articles. *Ross v. Creighton* underscores the significant challenges that universities face in educating some athletes and the serious consequences that result when they fail in this regard. *English v. NCAA* reflects the NCAA's regulatory efforts to limit student-athletes moving from one institution to another, often for athletic reasons, such as additional playing time. In *Bloom v. NCAA,* we see how student-athletes are severely limited in monetizing their athletic talents. All three cases concern important social issues, for example educating students and protecting the amateurism of college athletes. These cases emphasize, in part, the important role the NCAA plays promoting social values, albeit in the context of athletics.

When reading these materials, it is best to read them actively, with specific goals in mind. First, you should read them with an eye to uncovering any pertinent laws and legal rules applicable to the NCAA. Similarly, you should be on the lookout for any administrative regulations also (*i.e.,* the NCAA's own regulations). You should also adjust your reading radar in an effort to discern policy. In particular try to think about what *values* are being promoted by the laws and regulations discussed. In addition, think about whose *interests* are being protected by laws and regulations (*e.g.,* coaches, alumni, student athletes, corporations). Lastly, try to decide whether you think that the author of the article or judge who wrote the opinion has a specific point of view. Is the author or judge biased? Does the author or judge have a particular axe to grind?

A BRIEF HISTORY OF THE NATIONAL COLLEGIATE ATHLETIC ASSOCIATION'S ROLE IN REGULATING INTERCOLLEGIATE ATHLETICS

RODNEY K. SMITH

11 MARQ. SPORTS L. REV. 9 (2000)

I. Introduction

As one whose scholarship focuses on religious liberty and sport, I am often asked why I write in such seemingly disparate areas. My typical response is that given my interest in the role of religion in society, I certainly should be interested in sport, the religion of the American people. This response invariably engenders a slight smile and chuckle. I fear that there is some truth to the statement. Although I do not have the statistics necessary to prove it, my impression is that as many adults are zealously devoted to "the game" on any given day as are devoted to a worship service at a religious institution. As a people, we seem almost fixated on sport and devote much space in newspapers and newscasts to sport, with little space being allocated to religion. Yet, the discourse regarding sport is generally just description of events occurring, and rarely peers more deeply into the ramifications of specific issues, or of the general issue of our virtually thoughtless zeal for sport in contemporary society. While I find this to be personally troubling, it is just such thoughtless zeal as to sport, and the desire to see one's team win at virtually any cost, that contributes to the increasing regulation of athletics at virtually all levels.

Devotees of a given team, including coaches and fans alike, often strive mightily to find clever ways to unbalance the playing field in their team's favor through questionable recruiting techniques or other devices. This propensity to seek undue advantages in sport has made regulation of intercollegiate athletics a necessity in order to maintain even a semblance of a balanced playing field. Each new, creative way of bending the rules to create an undue advantage has necessarily led to the development of new rules and regulations. In turn, the growth in the number of rules has required development of an extensive structure to ensure that the rules are enforced.

In this essay, I will briefly examine the historical development of the National Collegiate Athletic Association (hereinafter NCAA), and the regulation of intercollegiate athletics. I will also offer some general comments regarding the history and future of the regulation of intercollegiate athletics.

II. A Brief History of the National Collegiate Athletic Association

A. 1840-1910

The need for regulation of intercollegiate athletics in the United States has existed for at least a century and a half. One of the earliest interschool athletic events was a highbrow regatta between Harvard and Yale Universities, which was commercially sponsored by the then powerful Elkins Railroad Line. Harvard University sought to gain an undue advantage over its academic rival Yale by obtaining the services of a coxswain who was not a student. Thus, the commercialization and propensity to seek unfair advantages existed virtually from the beginning of organized intercollegiate athletics in the United States. The problem of cheating, which was no doubt compounded by the increasing commercialization of sport, was a matter of concern. Initially, these concerns led institutions to move the athletic teams from student control to faculty oversight. Nevertheless, by the latter part of the nineteenth century, two leading university presidents were voicing their fears that intercollegiate athletics were out of control. President Eliot at Harvard was very concerned about the impact that commercialization of intercollegiate athletics was having, and charged that "lofty gate receipts from college athletics had turned amateur contests into major commercial spectacles." In the same year, President

Walker of the Massachusetts Institute of Technology bemoaned the fact that intercollegiate athletics had lost its academic moorings and opined that "[i]f the movement shall continue at the same rate, it will soon be fairly a question whether the letters B.A. stand more for Bachelor of Arts or Bachelor of Athletics." In turn, recognizing the difficulty of overseeing intercollegiate athletics at the institutional level, whether through the faculty or the student governance, conferences were being created both to facilitate the playing of a schedule of games and to provide a modicum of regulation at a broader level.

Despite the shift from student control to faculty oversight and some conference regulation, intercollegiate athletics remained under-regulated and a source of substantial concern. Rising concerns regarding the need to control the excesses of intercollegiate athletics were compounded by the fact that in 1905 alone, there were over eighteen deaths and one hundred major injuries in intercollegiate football. National attention was turned to intercollegiate athletics when President Roosevelt called for a White House conference to review football rules. President Roosevelt invited officials from the major football programs to participate. Deaths and injuries in football persisted, however, and Chancellor Henry MacCracken of New York University called for a national meeting of representatives of the nation's major intercollegiate football programs to determine whether football could be regulated or had to be abolished at the intercollegiate level. Representatives of many major intercollegiate football programs accepted Chancellor MacCracken's invitation and ultimately formed a Rules Committee. President Roosevelt then sought to have participants in the White House conference meet with the new Rules Committee. This combined effort on the part of educators and the White House eventually led to a concerted effort to reform intercollegiate football rules, resulting in the formation of the Intercollegiate Athletic Association (hereinafter IAA), with sixty-two original members. In 1910, the IAA was renamed the NCAA. Initially, the NCAA was formed to formulate rules that could be applied to the various intercollegiate sports.

In the years prior to the formation of the NCAA, schools wrestled with the same issues that we face today: the extreme pressure to win, which is compounded by the commercialization of sport, and the need for regulations and a regulatory body to ensure fairness and safety. In terms of regulation, between 1840 and 1910, there was a movement from loose student control of athletics to faculty oversight, from faculty oversight to the creation of conferences, and, ultimately, to the development of a national entity for governance purposes.

B. 1910-1970

In its early years, the NCAA did not play a major role in governing intercollegiate athletics. It did begin to stretch beyond merely making rules for football and other games played, to the creation of a national championship event in various sports. Indeed, students, with some faculty oversight, continued to be the major force in running intercollegiate athletics. By the 1920s, however, intercollegiate athletics were quickly becoming an integral part of higher education in the United States. Public interest in sport at the intercollegiate level, which had always been high, continued to increase in intensity, particularly as successful and entertaining programs developed, and also with increasing access to higher education on the part of students from all segments of society.

With this growing interest in intercollegiate sports and attendant increases in commercialization, outside attention again focused on governance and related issues. In 1929, the highly respected Carnegie Foundation for the Advancement of Education issued a significant report regarding intercollegiate athletics and made the following finding:

> [A] change of values is needed in a field that is sodden with the commercial and the material and the vested interests that these forces have created. Commercialism in college athletics must be diminished and college sport must rise to a point where it is esteemed primarily and sincerely for the opportunities it affords to mature youth.

The Carnegie Report, echoing themes that appear ever so relevant in the year 2000, concluded that college presidents could reclaim the integrity of sport. College administrators "could change the policies permitting commercialized and professionalized athletics that boards of trustees had previously sanctioned."

While the NCAA made some minor attempts to restructure rules to increase integrity in the governance of intercollegiate athletics, those efforts were insufficient to keep pace with the growing commercialization of, and interest in, intercollegiate athletics. Recruitment of athletes was not new, but the rising desire to win, with all its commercial ramifications, contributed to recruitment being raised to new heights. *** Public interest in intercollegiate athletics continued to increase with support from the federal government during the 1930s. The capacity of the NCAA to regulate excesses was not equal to the daunting task presented by the growth of, interest in, and commercialization of sport.

After World War II, with a dramatic increase in access to higher education on the part of all segments of society, largely through government support for returning military personnel to attend college, public interest expanded even more dramatically than it had in the past. Increased interest, not surprisingly, led to even greater commercialization of intercollegiate athletics. With the advent of television, the presence of radios in the vast majority of homes in the United States, and the broadcasting of major sporting events, these pressures further intensified. More colleges and universities started athletic programs, while others expanded existing programs, in an effort to respond to increasing interest in intercollegiate athletics. These factors, coupled with a series of gambling scandals and recruiting excesses, caused the NCAA to promulgate additional rules, resulting in an expansion of its governance authority.

In 1948, the NCAA enacted the so-called "Sanity Code," which was designed to "alleviate the proliferation of exploitive practices in the recruitment of student-athletes." To enforce the rules in the Sanity Code, the NCAA created the Constitutional Compliance Committee to interpret rules and investigate possible violations. Neither the Sanity Code with its rules, nor the Constitutional Compliance Committee with its enforcement responsibility, were successful because their only sanction was expulsion, which was so severe that it rendered the Committee impotent and the rules ineffectual. Recognizing this, the NCAA repealed the Sanity Code in

1951, replacing the Constitutional Compliance Committee with the Committee on Infractions, which was given broader sanctioning authority. Thus, in 1951, the NCAA began to exercise more earnestly the authority which it had been given by its members.

Two other factors are worth noting in the 1950s: (1) Walter Byers became Executive Director of the NCAA, and contributed to strengthening the NCAA, and its enforcement division, over the coming years to televise intercollegiate football; and (2) the NCAA negotiated its first contract valued in excess of one million dollars, opening the door to increasingly lucrative television contracts in the future. The NCAA was entering a new era, in which its enforcement authority had been increased, a strong individual had been hired as executive director, and revenues from television were beginning to provide it with the wherewithal to strengthen its capacity in enforcing the rules that were being promulgated. Through the 1950s and 1960s, the NCAA's enforcement capacity increased annually.

C. 1971-1983

By 1971, as its enforcement capacity had grown yearly in response to new excesses arising from increased interest and commercialization, the NCAA was beginning to be criticized for alleged unfairness in the exercise of its enhanced enforcement authority. Responding to these criticisms, the NCAA formed a committee to study the enforcement process, and ultimately, in 1973, adopted recommendations developed by that committee designed to divide the prosecutorial and investigative roles of the Committee on Infractions. In the early 1970s, as well, the membership of the NCAA decided to create divisions, whereby schools would be placed in divisions that would better reflect their competitive capacity. Despite these efforts, however, by 1976, when the NCAA was given additional authority to enforce the rules by penalizing schools directly, and, as a result, athletes, coaches, and administrators indirectly, criticism of the NCAA's enforcement authority grew even more widespread. Indeed, in 1978, the United States House of Representatives Subcommittee on Oversight and Investigation held hearings to investigate the alleged unfairness of the NCAA's enforcement processes. Once again, the NCAA responded by adopting changes in its rules designed to address many of the criticisms made during the course of the hearings. While concerns were somewhat abated, the NCAA's enforcement processes continued to be the source of substantial criticism through the 1970s and 1980s.

The NCAA found itself caught between two critiques. On the one hand, it was criticized for responding inadequately to the increased commercialization of intercollegiate athletics, with all its attendant excesses; while on the other hand, it was criticized for unfairly exercising its regulatory authority. Another factor began to have a major impact as well. University and college presidents were becoming more directly concerned with the operation of the NCAA for two major reasons: (1) as enrollments were beginning to drop, and expenses were increasing in athletics and elsewhere, presidents began, with some ambivalence, to see athletics as an expense, and as a potential revenue and public relations source; and (2) they personally came to understand that their reputations as presidents were often tied to the success of the athletic program and they were, therefore, becoming even more fearful of the NCAA's enforcement authority.

D. 1984-1999

In difficult economic times for higher education in the 1980s, university presidents increasingly found themselves caught between the pressures applied by influential members of boards of trustees and alumni, who often demanded winning athletic programs, and faculty and educators, who feared the rising commercialization of athletics and its impact on academic values. Many presidents were determined to take an active, collective role in the governance of the NCAA, so they formed the influential Presidents Commission in response to these pressures. In 1984, the Presidents Commission began to assert its authority, and by 1985, it took dramatic action by exercising their authority to call a special convention to be held in June of 1985. This quick assertion of power led one sports writer to conclude that "There is no doubt who is running college sports. It's the college presidents."

The presidents initially were involved in a number of efforts to change the rules, particularly in the interest of cost containment. These efforts were not all successful. Over time, however, the presidents were gaining a better understanding of the workings of the NCAA, and they were beginning to take far more interest in the actual governance of intercollegiate athletics. A little over a decade later, the presidents' involvement grew to the extent that they had changed the very governance structure of the NCAA, with the addition of an Executive Committee and a Board of Directors for the various divisions, both of which are made up of presidents or chief executive officers.

In *NCAA v. Tarkanian,* in a 5-4 decision, the United States Supreme Court held that the NCAA was not a state actor, freeing the NCAA from defending against due process allegations brought by Coach Jerry Tarkanian. Despite this victory, concerns persisted regarding due process in the NCAA's enforcement processes. In time, the presidents decided to take action in reforming the enforcement process. The presidents were involved in forming a Special Committee to Review the NCAA Enforcement and Infractions Process, and supported the naming of one of their own, President Rex E. Lee of Brigham Young University, as Chairman. This distinguished committee, which included other luminaries such as former Chief Justice of the United States Supreme Court Warren E. Burger, issued a report in 1991. The Committee made the following basic recommendations: (1) "Enhance the adequacy of the initial notice of an impending investigation and assure a personal visit by the enforcement staff with the institution's chief executive officer;" (2) "Establish a 'summary disposition' procedure for treating major violations at a reasonably early stage in the investigation;" (3) "Liberalize the use of tape recordings and the availability of such recordings to involved parties;" (4) "Use former judges or other eminent legal authorities as hearing officers in cases involving major violations and not resolved in the 'summary disposition' process;" (5) "Hearings should be open to the greatest extent possible;" (6) "Provide transcripts of all infractions hearings to appropriate involved parties;" (7) "Refine and enhance the role of the Committee on Infractions and establish a limited appellate process beyond that committee;" (8) "Adopt a formal conflict-of-interest policy;" (9) "Expand the public reporting of infractions cases;" (10) "Make available a compilation of previous committee decisions;" and (11) "Study the structure and procedures of the enforcement staff." These recommendations have been taken seriously, and, as implemented, are helping to improve the enforcement processes.

During this time period, there were a number of additional developments that had an impact on the role of the NCAA in fulfilling its enforcement and governance of responsibilities. Even in a short history, like this one, a few of those developments are noteworthy.

As the role of television and the revenue it brings to intercollegiate athletics has grown in magnitude, the desire for an increasing share of those dollars has become intense. The first television event in the 1950s was a college football game, and the televising of college football games remained under the NCAA's control for a number of years. In time, however, a group of powerful intercollegiate football programs were determined to challenge the NCAA's handling of the televising of games involving their schools. In *NCAA v. Board of Regents*, the United States Supreme Court held that the NCAA had violated antitrust laws. This provided an opening for those schools, and the bowls that would ultimately court them, to directly reap the revenues from the televising of their football games. This shift has effectively created a new division in football called the College Football Association, which is made up of the football powerhouses in Division I. Because these schools have been able to funnel more television revenues in their direction, which has led to increases in other forms of revenue, they have gained access to resources that have unbalanced the playing field in football and other sports.

Another matter that has dramatically impacted intercollegiate athletics during the past two decades is Title IX, with its call for gender equity in intercollegiate athletics. With some emphasis on proportionality in opportunities and equity in expenditures for coaches and other purposes in women's sports, new opportunities have been made available for women in inter-collegiate athletics. The cost of these expanded opportunities has been high, however, particularly given that few institutions have women's teams that generate sufficient revenue to cover the cost of these added programs. This increase in net expenses has placed significant pressure on intercollegiate athletic programs, particularly given that the presidents are cost-containment conscious, desiring that athletic programs be self-sufficient. Revenue producing male sports, therefore, have to bear the weight of funding women's sports. This, in turn, raises racial equity concerns because most of the revenue producing male sports are made up predominantly of male student-athletes of color, who are expected to deliver a product that will not only produce sufficient revenue to cover its own expenses, but also a substantial portion of the costs of gender equity and male sports that are not revenue producing.

The gender equity and television issues have been largely economic in their impact, but they do indirectly impact the role of the NCAA in governance. Since football funding has been diverted from the NCAA to the football powerhouses, the NCAA for the most part has had to rely even more heavily on its revenue from the lucrative television contract for the Division I basketball championship. Heavy reliance on this funding source raises racial equity issues, since student-athletes of color, particularly African-American athletes, are the source of those revenues. Thus, the very governance costs of the NCAA are covered predominantly by the efforts of these student-athletes of color. This inequity is exacerbated by the fact that schools and conferences rely heavily on revenues from the basketball tournament to fund their own institutional and conference needs.

Generally, developments during the past two decades have focused on governance and economic issues. There have been some efforts, however, to enhance academic integrity and revitalize the role of faculty and students in overseeing intercollegiate athletics. *** This process helps institutions focus on academic values and related issues. These efforts also provide the chief executive officers with additional information and a potentially enhanced role in intercollegiate athletics at the campus level.

The past [several] decades have been active ones for the NCAA. With meteoric rises in television and related revenues, the commercialization of intercollegiate athletics has continued to grow at a pace that places significant strain on institutions and the NCAA. These commercial pressures, together with increasing costs related to non-revenue producing sports, costly gender equity requirements, and other resource demands (*e.g.,* new facilities), make it challenging to maintain a viable enforcement process and a balanced playing field.

III. The Future

Over the past 150 years, the desire to win at virtually any cost, combined with the increases in public interest in intercollegiate athletics, in a consumer sense, have led inexorably to a highly commercialized world of intercollegiate athletics. These factors have created new incentives for universities and conferences to find new ways to obtain an advantage over their competitors. This desire to gain an unfair competitive advantage has necessarily led to an expansion in rules and regulations. This proliferation of rules and the development of increasingly sophisticated regulatory systems necessary to enforce those rules, together with the importance that attaches to enforcement decisions, both economically and in terms of an institution's reputation (and derivatively its chief executive officer's career), places great strain on the capacity of the NCAA to govern intercollegiate athletics. This strain is unlikely to dissipate in the future because the pressures that have created the strain do not appear to be susceptible, in a practical sense, to amelioration. Indeed, the one certainty in the future of the NCAA is the likelihood that big-time intercollegiate athletics will be engaged in the same point-counterpoint that has characterized its history; increased commercialization and public pressure leading to more sophisticated rules and regulatory systems.

As rules and regulatory systems continue along the road of increased sophistication, the NCAA will more closely resemble its industry counterparts. It will develop an enforcement system that is more legalistic in its nature, as regulatory proliferation leads to increasing demands for fairness. In such a milieu, chief executive officers will have to take their responsibilities for intercollegiate athletics even more seriously. It can be hoped, as well, that their involvement, and the increased involvement on the part of faculty and staff, through the certification process and otherwise, will lead to a more responsible system in terms of the maintenance of academic values. If the NCAA and those who lead at the institutional and conference levels are unable to maintain academic values in the face of economics and related pressures, the government may be less than a proverbial step away.

1. Explain the relationship between money and the pressure that college athletic directors, coaches, and players feel to win.

2. What are the pros and cons of the increased commercialism of intercollegiate sports? Consider an example given by Matthew Mitten, James Musselman, and Bruce Burton: "On New Years Day 2007, steep underdog Boise State University ran a daring Statue of Liberty play for a two-point conversion and posted a 43-42 overtime upset against the favored University of Oklahoma Sooners. This soon resulted in millions of dollars in new pledges for the university's business and nursing schools, growth in the number of graduate school inquiries, increased political recognition among Idaho legislatures, Hollywood inquiries about film rights, national recognition on ESPN and other cable sports shows, leaps in alumni giving and other fundraising not solely directed toward athletics, and local retail business boosts. Officials believe that the energizing bounce to the school and to the community of Boise 'will pay off for years.'" *Targeted Reform of Commercialized Intercollegiate Athletics,* 47 San Diego L. Rev. 779, 793 (2010).

3. To what extent does it matter that the so-called revenue producing sports "foot the bill" for all of the other sports at the intercollegiate level? Should that affect legal relationships or regulations? If so why, if not why not?

4. For a detailed analysis of *Tarkanian, see* John Sahl, *College Athletes and Due Process Protection: What's Left After National Collegiate Athletic Association v. Tarkanian,* 28 Ariz. St. L. J. 621 (1989)(also arguing, in part, for greater due process protections for those charged with an infraction in the NCAA disciplinary process).

APPLYING ANTITRUST LAW TO NCAA REGULATION OF "BIG TIME" COLLEGE ATHLETICS: THE NEED TO SHIFT FROM NOSTALGIC 19TH AND 20TH CENTURY IDEALS OF AMATEURISM TO THE ECONOMIC REALITIES OF THE 21ST CENTURY

MATTHEW J. MITTEN

11 MARQ. SPORTS L. REV. 1 (2000)

The original purpose of intercollegiate athletics was to provide an extracurricular activity for talented students who attended college primarily to earn an academic degree that would enable them to pursue a career outside of professional athletics. According to the National Collegiate Athletic Association ("NCAA"), "[s]tudent-athletes shall be amateurs in an intercollegiate sport, and their participation should be motivated primarily by education and by the physical, mental and social benefits to be derived. Student participation in intercollegiate athletics is an avocation, and student-athletes should be protected from exploitation by professional and commercial enterprises." Today, this concept of an "amateur" athlete and the student-athlete model still applies for most sports and most students, especially women's sports and men's non-revenue sports.

Not all NCAA sponsored sports fit neatly within this amateur model. Athletes participating in NCAA Division I football and basketball often are more interested in developing their skills in hope of a future professional playing career than in earning a college degree. In fact, universities sponsoring "big-time" football and basketball programs effectively serve as a farm system for the National Football League and National Basketball Association by providing the training environment and playing field for talented football and basketball players to hone their physical talents.

The tremendous public popularity of men's college football and basketball creates a substantial revenue-generating capacity and the prospect of increased visibility for universities. The significant economic rewards of winning have generated fierce off-field competition among universities for inputs necessary to produce winning teams (*e.g.,* coaches and players), as well as efforts to fully exploit the economic value of their athletic products by maximizing fan and booster support, television revenues, and commercial sponsorships. The economic realities of this environment contrast sharply with the nostalgic ideal of the college amateur athlete whose participation in a sport is merely incidental to a university's provision of higher education in an academic environment.

The NCAA's basic regulatory objective is "to maintain intercollegiate athletics as an integral part of the educational program and the athlete as an integral part of the student body and, by so doing, retain a clear line of demarcation between intercollegiate athletics and professional sports." In other words, the NCAA seeks to: 1) preserve the amateur nature of college sports; 2) as a component part of higher education; and 3) to ensure competitive balance on the playing field. Although these are laudable objectives, they are quite difficult to achieve given the economic reality of "big-time" college athletics, namely an existing "athletics arms race" fueled by the multi-million dollar economic rewards of winning teams fielded by members operating "big time" programs.

The NCAA effectively determines the permissible nature and scope of virtually all aspects of both on-field and off-field competition among its members. It appears to function as an economic cartel in its regulation of Division I football and basketball programs. The NCAA's member schools are economic competitors that collectively possess monopsony power over the demand for college football and basketball players and monopoly power over the supply of college football and basketball games. They frequently agree to limit (or prohibit), free market forces from determining input prices for players, output of games, and other aspects of economic competition among themselves. The NCAA polices and enforces its rules and agreements by disciplining violators. Although individual NCAA members have an incentive to gain a competitive advantage by not complying with the association's rules, there is an economic necessity to remain a part of this national organization to reap the economic rewards of "big-time" college sports.

Given the economic realities of "big-time" college athletics, many NCAA rules limiting economic competition among universities appear to violate the federal antitrust laws. However, although there have been several antitrust suits challenging the legality of NCAA imposed restraints affecting Division I football and basketball, most litigation has been unsuccessful. In analyzing judicial treatment of the NCAA and its rules for antitrust purposes, it is important to look at the historical evolution of antitrust jurisprudence concerning intercollegiate athletics. Courts initially held that NCAA rule-making, regulatory, or enforcement activities do not sufficiently impact interstate trade or commerce to establish Sherman Act jurisdiction. NCAA rules designed to promote amateurism and protect academic integrity were deemed to constitute regulation of noncommercial activity that does not trigger antitrust scrutiny. Beginning in the mid-1970s, courts began recognizing that the provision and regulation of "big-time" intercollegiate athletics is business activity subject to the Sherman Act, but were reluctant to find that NCAA regulations violated the antitrust laws.

In 1984, in *NCAA v. Board of Regents*,[1] the Supreme Court held that the NCAA does not have a blanket exemption from the antitrust laws, although it is a nonprofit entity with educational objectives, because the "NCAA and its member institutions are in fact organized to maximize revenues." The Court invalidated NCAA restrictions on its members' sale of television rights to football games that prevented economic competition among them. However, the Court acknowledged the NCAA's role "as the guardian of an important American tradition," and its "historic role in the preservation and encouragement of intercollegiate amateur athletics." The Court's majority strongly suggested that primarily noncommercial NCAA rules to preserve amateurism, academic integrity, and competitive balance do not violate the antitrust laws.

After *Board of Regents*, courts generally have rejected antitrust challenges to NCAA rules by providing great deference and discretion to the NCAA. These courts have assumed that NCAA rules are ancillary noncommercial restraints necessary to produce intercollegiate athletics and/or to further legitimate higher education objectives. ***

On the one hand, courts have held that agreements among NCAA member schools that directly fix prices in input or output markets for college sports are illegal. The *Board of Regents* Court ruled that the NCAA's exclusive football television rights plan violates the antitrust laws because it effectively establishes a set price for televised football games without any offsetting procompetitive justification, such as preserving competitive balance or the integrity of intercollegiate athletics. Consistent with *Board of Regents*, in *Law v. NCAA*, the Tenth Circuit...held that an NCAA imposed cap of $16,000.00 on Division I entry-level basketball coaches' salaries is an unreasonable restraint of trade as a matter of law.[2] ***

At the other end of the spectrum, courts have uniformly upheld NCAA eligibility standards that athletes must satisfy to participate in intercollegiate athletics. Athlete eligibility requirements promulgated by the NCAA appear to be virtually per se legal under the antitrust laws. Courts have rejected antitrust challenges to NCAA regulations designed to preserve the

---

1   *NCAA v. Board of Regents*, 468 U.S. 85 (1984).

2   *Law v. NCAA*, 134 F.3d 1010 (10th Cir. 1998).

amateur nature of college sports, such as the "no draft" and "no agent" rules and the imposition of disciplinary sanctions on institutions for violation of the NCAA's amateurism rules.

* * *

Adidas's recent antitrust challenge to NCAA restrictions on its members' sale of promotional rights to sponsors illustrates judicial unwillingness to acknowledge that universities engage in economic competition among themselves off the playing field and that some NCAA rules may restrain trade. In *Adidas America, Inc. v. NCAA,* Adidas alleged that NCAA limits on the size of manufacturer logos on uniforms and playing equipment unreasonably restrained competition among NCAA member institutions for the sale of advertising rights. The court initially denied Adidas's motion for a preliminary injunction against enforcement of this rule. Observing that *Law* provides no guidance regarding the line between commercial and noncommercial activities, the court characterized the subject NCAA regulation as noncommercial because it does not have the purpose or effect of giving NCAA members a direct economic benefit. Rather, it found the rule furthered the NCAA's legitimate objective of preventing the commercialization of college sports, notwithstanding that patches identifying football bowl game sponsors on player uniforms are not subject to the size limits of this rule (not to mention that athletes may be required to wear a particular manufacturer's shoes as part of a sponsorship agreement with an NCAA university).

Subsequently, the court granted the NCAA's motion to dismiss Adidas's complaint. **** [T]he court concluded that the NCAA's rule restricting the size of manufacturer logos on uniforms has no significant anticompetitive effect as a matter of law.

The *Adidas* trial court's disposition of the case is another example of unwarranted judicial deference to NCAA regulation of economic competition among its member institutions. The *Adidas* holding is inconsistent with the *Board of Regents* and *Law* precedent establishing a framework of antitrust analysis for NCAA regulatory activity with a commercial impact. Adidas's allegations, at the very least, raise a factual issue for discovery regarding the anticompetitive effects of this NCAA rule. If the limitation on logo size has the effect of reducing economic competition among NCAA members, the NCAA must prove that it furthers a valid procompetitive objective that cannot be accomplished by a substantially less restrictive means.

There is no valid justification for permitting the NCAA to determine arbitrarily the permissible degree of economic competition among its members or, in light of these universities significant economic self-interest, for courts to defer to the NCAA's judgment. Courts should abandon anachronistic precedent based on unrealistic ideals of the "amateur" nature of "big-time" college athletics and develop a principled antitrust jurisprudence more consistent with the economic realities of college sports in the 21st century.

I am not advocating that all NCAA regulation of competition violates the antitrust laws. However, courts should not continue to make unrealistic or unwarranted assumptions about the economic effects of NCAA rules reducing or eliminating competition among its approximately 1,100 member schools. NCAA regulation that has anticompetitive, intrabrand effects should be proven to be the least restrictive means of promoting interbrand competition as a matter of fact, rather than being presumed to do so as a matter of law.

NOTES & QUESTIONS

1. The International Olympic Committee used to treat amateurism as something sacrosanct, like the NCAA currently does. The IOC, however, has sharply curtailed its position on this matter, now permitting professionals to compete in the Olympic Games. If the NCAA were to change its rules to permit athletes to earn money from their sport during their period of eligibility, what might be the pros and cons?

2. Are there plausible legal remedies for the "arms race" that currently exists in big time college athletics? If so, articulate what they might be and how they might alleviate the problem.

3. Do all of the NCAA's activities "preserve amateurism?" In *In re NCAA I-A Walk-On Football Players Litigation,* 398 F. Supp. 2d 1144 (W.D. WA 2005), the court denied the NCAA's Motion for Judgment on the Pleadings in a class action brought by former walk-on student athletes alleging the NCAA's scholarship cap violated the Sherman Act. The court held that "courts have found the award of financial aid to college students to be 'trade or commerce' and therefore subject to the Sherman Act." The court ultimately denied class certification in that case, but does it leave the door open to potential antitrust violations based on the NCAA's per-sport scholarship limitations?

QUID PRO QUO: RESTORING EDUCATIONAL PRIMACY TO COLLEGE BASKETBALL
TANYON T. LYNCH
12 MARQ. SPORTS L. REV. 595 (2002)

II. OVERVIEW OF THE ORGANIZATIONAL STRUCTURE OF COLLEGE ATHLETICS

Colleges and universities providing athletics programs typically belong to regional and national governing bodies that provide administrative, legislative, and promotional support for their members. Conferences provide this support at the regional level. At the national level, this support is provided by either the NCAA or the National Association of Intercollegiate Athletics. This article's analysis will be limited to the NCAA, the most influential regulator of college athletics.

Although the NCAA's principle of institutional control requires university presidents to assume ultimate responsibility for athletics programs, this authority is usually delegated to the institution's athletics director, who reports to either the university president or a vice president. Coaches and administrative staff in the athletics department report to the athletics director whose daily responsibilities may include generating revenue in addition to managing facilities, media relations, and academic affairs. Therefore, in reality, the athletics director bears most of the burden for assuring that the athletics department's goals remain consistent with the overall purpose of the university.

University presidents also delegate responsibilities for their athletics programs to collegiate conferences. In most major conferences, university presidents serve as the board of directors, which ultimately retains authority over conference operations. Historically, conferences existed primarily to provide schools with a reliable source of competitors. The modern conference's operations include monitoring compliance with conference and NCAA policies, managing conference championships, structuring broadcasting contracts, and redistributing revenues. The conference's commissioner either oversees or performs these functions.

Despite its voluntary nature, the NCAA is the leading regulatory body for intercollegiate athletics. Formed in 1906 with only 39 charter members, the NCAA now consists of over 1200 institutions, conferences, and organizations. The association is divided into three major membership categories: Division I, II, and III. *** In 1997, the NCAA restructured its organizational scheme to provide for greater divisional autonomy. As a result, each division now has its own governing body.

III. THREATS TO EDUCATIONAL PRIMACY

The United States stands alone in combining higher education with athletic development. College athletics programs offer countless benefits to sponsoring institutions and participating students. At the institutional level, college athletics can play a role in increasing the institution's visibility and unifying the university community. Furthermore, these programs generate revenues from a variety of sources, including gate receipts, corporate sponsorships, and television rights fees. At the student level, athletics programs can provide educational opportunities for students who otherwise could not afford to attend college. Participation in college athletics can also facilitate the development of valuable attributes such as, leadership, competitiveness, discipline, and teamwork. To reap these and other substantial benefits, colleges and universities pour millions of dollars into their athletics programs. Ideally, all college athletics programs would place student-athletes' educational priorities first. Yet, in practice, this does not occur. Under the current regime, competitive pressure to win games, commercialism, and professionalism often lead to the subordination of educational primacy. ***

A. Competitive Pressure

Successful basketball teams generate millions of dollars in revenue from ticket sales, guarantees, payouts from tournaments, television rights fees, licensed merchandise, and corporate sponsorships. Additional benefits thought to accrue to athletically successful schools include additional tuition and fees from increased enrollments and an increase in alumni donations. However, when costs enter the equation, the vast majority of universities lose money on athletics programs. Still, many programs subscribe to the philosophy that "the team that spends the most wins the most."

When the team wins consistently, coaches reap substantial benefits from the team's success. This occurs because, increasingly, coaches' job security and base salaries are tied to their competitive records. In addition to high base salaries, successful coaches might also receive home loans, automobiles, deferred compensation, and bonuses for winning. Winning coaches can further supplement their university income with income from shoe contracts, sports camps, and appearances on radio and television talk shows.

Competitive pressure constitutes the first major threat to educational primacy. Competitive pressure may be generated either internally by inherently competitive coaches or externally by the financial incentives to win games. But regardless of its origin, this pressure eventually trickles down to student-athletes. As such, the pressure to win, if left unchecked, usually manifests itself in ways that seriously conflict with the principle of educational primacy. That is, perverse incentives at either the institutional or coach level can result in the intentional subordination of educational primacy. ***

Many basketball players enter college academically deficient. Add to this deficiency, forty to sixty hours per week of athletic activities, and missed classes, and the result is an athlete unlikely to graduate. In fact, only forty-three percent of all NCAA basketball players graduate within six years and, of those athletes who do graduate, many do not receive a meaningful degree. As a result, some critics condemn Division I basketball programs for exploiting athletes until the end of their eligibility and then summarily discarding them. This exploitation is often facilitated by coaches, who exert considerable influence over the administrative processes governing student-athlete affairs. The areas in which coaches may exert the most influence are admissions, financial aid, and academic services.

To build and sustain successful programs, coaches frequently recruit student-athletes that fall decisively below their schools' regular admissions standards. Athletes who fail to meet a school's regular admissions standards may still be admitted through "special" or "wild-card" admissions processes. The "wild card" admissions process gives a coach a limited number of "no questions asked" admits. Therefore, the wild card process places the admit decision completely within the coach's discretion, limited only by NCAA eligibility standards. "Special admissions" is the process by which the admissions office admits athletes who, although they do not meet the school's regular admissions standards, enrich the student body nonetheless. Although this process is also available to legacies, musicians, and other students with desirable characteristics, a study conducted in 1991 shows that football and men's basketball players in elite sports programs are six times more likely than other students to have been special admits.

To successfully recruit a blue-chip athlete, a coach might find it necessary to exaggerate the athlete's educational prospects. For example, in *Ross v. Creighton University*, the coaching staff recruited Kevin Ross to play basketball at "an academically superior university," despite his severely deficient academic background. To obtain his commitment, Ross was assured that he "would receive a meaningful education." Yet after four years as a student-athlete, Ross dropped out of the university with the language skills of a fourth grader. Under the NCAA's current rules, Ross would not have met the initial eligibility standards and, therefore, he probably would not have been admitted to Creighton.

After an athlete enrolls in school, coaches can exert substantial influence over the athlete's academic future. The key source of this influence resides in a coach's ability to cancel an athlete's scholarship. Before the one-year renewable athletic scholarship came into existence in 1973, athletes received four-year scholarships that continued even after they withdrew from their sports. Today, NCAA rules permit expedited cancellation for athletes who voluntarily withdraw from their sports. Thus, cancellation power gives coaches a powerful tool that can be used to alter a student-athlete's academic priorities.

NCAA rules limit an athlete's participation in "countable athletically related activities" to four hours per day and twenty hours per week. However, many student-athletes complain that the "voluntary workout" exception swallows this rule. That is, to the extent that coaches use time spent on voluntary workouts to determine an athlete's status on the team, the workouts are not truly voluntary. Consequently, some athletes still spend forty to sixty hours per week on their sports, which invariably limits the amount of time that the athletes spend studying and attending classes.

Given athletes' rigorous game and workout schedules, similarly demanding academic programs would present a constant threat to NCAA eligibility. This threat would be even more pronounced for marginal students. To protect against the risk of an athlete becoming ineligible for competition, coaches often steer athletes into less demanding majors or courses. At some schools, these less demanding majors might include general studies, physical education, or sports management. Although most athletics departments provide extensive academic support services for student-athletes, in the absence of sufficient time to indulge these services, even a hollow major can threaten an athlete's eligibility.

When legitimate attempts to keep athletes on the court prove futile, competitive pressure and perverse incentives can combine to produce academic scandals, as was the case at the University of Minnesota from 1994 through 1999. During this time period, the head men's basketball coach, an academic counselor, and a secretary engaged in the most egregious academic fraud that the NCAA Committee on Infractions had seen since the early 1980s. Specifically, with the head coach's knowledge, a secretary completed four hundred assignments for student-athletes and the secretary's sister, a tutor, authored forty-eight papers for student-athletes. The NCAA's institutional sanctions for these and other violations included placing the university on probation for four years, vacating team and individual records, and decreasing grants-in-aid, official visits, and evaluation opportunities in men's basketball. As for the wrongdoers, the head coach was forced to resign and the contracts of his two accomplices were never renewed.

* * *

B. Commercialism

The commercial model of college athletics gives priority to the spectators' entertainment needs, rather than to the student-athletes' educational needs. Corporate sponsorships, broadcasting contracts, product value, and market share dominate this model, where student-athletes and coaches are viewed as entertainment products. The Final Four exemplifies the commercial model of college athletics.

Commercialism constitutes the second major threat to educational primacy. In addition to subordinating educational primacy, commercialism increases the pressure to win. [D]ependence on revenues from gate receipts, corporate sponsorships, and television contracts intensifies external pressures to win. ***

Media-driven schedules for athletic contests can assist in the subordination of educational primacy. [M]id-week and late-night games scheduled to accommodate media demands often conflict with student-athletes' academic obligations. For instance, bowl game scheduling forces athletes to practice during final exam periods. Moreover, the "Final Four" teams of the NCAA tournament will miss at least three weeks of classes during March. Although such academically intrusive schedules can maximize television revenues and media exposure, these gains often come at the expense of the athletes' academic success.

Commercialism also raises concerns of financial exploitation for student-athletes. At most college games, corporate logos can be seen on uniforms, hats, and scoreboards among other places. *** Although these arrangements enrich athletics departments, coaches, and sponsors, many student-athletes, whose incomes are restricted by NCAA amateurism rules, feel that they are being exploited by such arrangements.

Few athletics departments generate sufficient revenue to cover the full cost of their programs. Although booster club donations, corporate sponsorships and the like provide additional revenues for athletics departments, most college athletics programs still require financial support from general university funds. Sympathizers of commercialized college sports cite the precarious financial condition of college athletics programs as support for the present and continued commercialization of college athletics.

C. Professionalism

As early as the late-nineteenth century, the desire to produce winning athletic teams led universities to seek out highly skilled athletes, many of whom had little interest in academics. In fact, some of these early college athletes were not even students. In return for their athletic services, early student-athletes received "scholarships, sinecure jobs, gifts from alumni and citizens, and a hundred other types of financial compensation." Current NCAA amateurism rules forbid all but the first category of compensation for student-athletes.

Modern universities attract athletes with promises of free tuition, room and board, and academic support services. All of which are sanctioned by NCAA regulations. As an additional incentive, a few universities have resorted to the use of prohibited "extra benefits" to lure the best athletes. The use of financial incentives in recruiting, whether NCAA-sanctioned or prohibited, allows college teams to attract higher quality athletes, thereby improving the teams' revenue potential. Yet recruiting such highly qualified athletes also requires a corresponding commitment to provide the academic services, coaching staffs, and facilities necessary to support these athletes. The ability to provide the requisite support services helps to explain why well-funded athletics programs generally field the most competitive teams.

Professionalism poses the third threat to educational primacy. As an inherent form of pay-for-play, the athletic scholarship can be viewed as a manifestation of the professionalism that characterizes "amateur" college athletics. Accordingly, educational primacy is subverted because student-athletes cannot withdraw from their sports, even for academic reasons, without suffering the detrimental economic consequences of such a decision.

Further evidence of the professionalization of college sports lies in the fact that college athletics programs have become training grounds for professional sports careers. Indeed some athletes attend college for the sole purpose of advancing their professional sports careers. Professionalized college athletics demand that its participants train and perform at the highest possible level. *** [Furthermore,] professionalized athletes usually abandon the team when they reach a level of play sufficiently high to attract opportunities from major professional leagues.

Competitive pressure, commercialism, and professionalism constitute the three main threats to educational primacy. If left unchecked, these threats can combine to overshadow the academic purpose of institutions of higher education. The threats are interrelated in that commercialism intensifies competitive pressure and competitive pressure encourages professionalism. Hence, any attempt to safeguard the principle of educational primacy must address all three of its major threats.

IV. GOVERNANCE OF THE PRINCIPLE EDUCATIONAL PRIMACY

The principle of educational primacy requires that a student-athlete's status as a student take precedence over his or her status as an athlete. In the world of college athletics, this principle competes with the demands of competitive pressure, commercialism, and professionalism. Various governance structures exist to safeguard the principle of educational primacy against these competing interests. These structures may be divided into two broad categories: (1) internal and (2) external. The internal governance structure consists of universities, conferences, and the NCAA, whereas the legislature and courts comprise the external governance structure. External involvement in the regulation of college athletics is very limited. Consequently, college athletics is dominated by internal governance structures, which are plagued by self-interest and conflicting goals.

A. Internal Governance

Internal governance of the principle of educational primacy has two main benefits. First, internal governance saves the government the cost of regulation. Second, internal governance structures can detect and remedy problems more quickly than external governance structures. To the extent that internal governance structures fail to adequately safeguard the principle of educational primacy, external governance structures can provide a meaningful oversight function.

* * *

Self-interest and perverse incentives can prevent individual universities from effectively policing the principle of educational primacy. College admissions standards vary and, as previously noted, schools lower these standards for elite athletes to build successful teams. Furthermore, universities alone determine what constitutes good academic standing once a student enrolls. Thus, a school may relax both its admissions standards and its standards for good academic standing to accommodate an athlete's eligibility. Lenient academic policies for student-athletes clearly conflict with the goals of higher education. ***

Conferences share common eligibility standards, which might be higher than those required by the NCAA. To this extent, conferences can regulate their members' academic standards to ensure that they do not fall to unacceptable levels. However, a conference that sets its academic standards too high might find itself at a competitive disadvantage in inter-conference competition.

In addition to the regulation of academic policies, conferences promote their respective athletic contests and redistribute revenues among their members. Historically, conference members aligned themselves because of shared geography and competitive and academic philosophies. More recently, members' revenue potential has become the most important common denominator. To maximize revenues, conferences become parties to broadcasting contracts, which often require academically intrusive schedules. Absent external pressure to do so, a single conference has very little incentive to oppose its own policies regarding the scheduling of televised athletic contests. To do so would decrease its revenue potential and hence its attractiveness to present and future members.

* * * *

The NCAA also acts as a promoter and economic regulator of collegiate athletics. Indeed, the promotion and economic regulation of college athletics are the NCAA's dominant functions. In this capacity, the NCAA experiences role conflict similar to that experienced by universities and conferences. ***

Although the NCAA manual contains hundreds of pages of rules, the small size of the NCAA's enforcement staff impairs its ability to detect violations of those rules. As a result, the NCAA relies mainly on informants and institutional self-reporting to apprise it of alleged violations. Once the NCAA becomes aware of potential violations, lack of judicially enforceable discovery power limits its ability to gather and verify pertinent information. To lessen the impact of these limitations, the NCAA encourages schools to cooperate with NCAA investigators in return for reduced penalties. NCAA penalties for the most flagrant violations usually result only in the loss of scholarships and recruiting visits and perhaps probation for the offending university. ***

The NCAA's national character makes it the ideal institution to promulgate and enforce uniform rules that encourage educational primacy. However, as an entity, the NCAA profits from activities that threaten educational primacy. In fact, the NCAA is financially dependent upon its basketball tournament, which capitalizes upon all three threats to educational primacy. Strict enforcement of the principle of educational primacy by the NCAA would force the organization into financial ruin.

Since a university's primary purpose is to educate its students, the university is the ideal entity to police the principle of educational primacy. However, historically, and even today, universities have not adequately done this, absent outside intervention. Since conferences and the NCAA are financially dependent on activities that compete with the principle of educational primacy, they do not and cannot be expected to vigorously police or enforce the principle of educational primacy. To summarize, self-interest and conflicting goals have prevented all three internal governance structures from adequately policing the principle. The next section discusses how external governance structures have dealt with these problems.

B. External Governance

Internal governance structures regulate both the economic and educational aspects of intercollegiate athletics. This conflicting role, in which economic concerns often take precedence over student-athletes' educational concerns, supports an increased role for external regulation. Yet, courts and legislatures have largely declined invitations to intervene in university/student-athlete relations.

With the exception of Title IX, Congress does not interfere with the NCAA's regulation of the university/student-athlete relationship. To further insure this relationship against congressional intervention, the NCAA maintains an office in Washington, D.C., which employs full-time lobbyists. At the state level, legislative intervention is generally limited to the regulation of student-athlete relationships with sports agents and funding restrictions for college athletics programs.

Although the threat of litigation might enhance the status of educational primacy in college athletics programs, courts have been reluctant to hold universities liable for the failure to educate individual student-athletes. To this end, courts uniformly deny negligent admissions and educational malpractice claims. Difficulties in establishing educational standards, injury, causation, and remedies are cited as reasons for courts' hostility towards these claims. In addition, courts fear that allowing such claims would induce floods of litigation by disgruntled students.

Contract claims can provide an alternative to educational malpractice and negligent admissions claims. In Ross, the court noted that if Ross could establish that the university failed to honor a specific contractual promise, a breach of contract action might exist. ***

Courts and legislatures have, for the most part, chosen to play a passive role in the regulation of college athletics. This passiveness has, in effect, given the NCAA virtually unlimited power over the future of college athletics. Therefore, any serious attempts to reform college athletics must focus on the NCAA.

As the most powerful regulator of college athletics programs, the NCAA is in a unique position to strengthen the principle of educational primacy. Yet any attempt to strengthen educational primacy must also minimize its major threats, *i.e.* competitive pressures, commercialism, and professionalism. Even if institutional interests militate against the NCAA implementing legislation that directly strengthens educational primacy, the NCAA should, at the very least, take steps to ensure that future legislative amendments do not further weaken the principle. ***

NOTES & QUESTIONS

1. Men's college basketball today generates millions of dollars. Given the the pressures articulated in Lynch's article and the enormous sums of money involved, it is not surprising that scores of individuals and companies have been accused of a variety of forms of bribery and corruption. One of the most recent scandals has made headlines since 2017, involving allegedly illicit payments to coaches and players by Adidas and other companies. In the wake of this scandal, University of Louisville basketball coach, Rick Pitino, was fired; recent surveillance video evidence that has come to light, however, suggests that Pitino was actually not aware of much of the corrupt activities going on around him. *See e.g.,* https://www.courier-journal.com/story/sports/college/louisville/2019/04/24/college-basketball-trial-new-evidence-supports-rick-pitino/3566206002/; https://en.wikipedia.org/wiki/2017%E2%80%9318_NCAA_Division_I_men's_basketball_corruption_scandal.

ROSS V. CREIGHTON UNIVERSITY
957 F.2D 410 (1992)
UNITED STATES COURT OF APPEALS, SEVENTH CIRCUIT

KENNETH RIPPLE, CIRCUIT JUDGE

OPINION

Kevin Ross filed suit against Creighton University (Creighton or the University) for negligence and breach of contract arising from Creighton's alleged failure to educate him. The district court dismissed Mr. Ross' complaint for failure to state a claim. For the following reasons we affirm in part and reverse in part the judgment of the district court.

I. BACKGROUND

A. *Facts*

In the spring of 1978, Mr. Ross was a promising senior basketball player at Wyandotte High School in Kansas City, Kansas. Sometime during his senior year in high school, he accepted an athletic scholarship to attend Creighton and to play on its varsity basketball team.

Creighton is an academically superior university. Mr. Ross comes from an academically disadvantaged background. At the time of his enrollment at Creighton, Mr. Ross was at an academic level far below that of the average Creighton student. For example, he scored in the bottom fifth percentile of college-bound seniors taking the American College Test, while the average freshman admitted to Creighton with him scored in the upper twenty-seven percent. According to the complaint, Creighton realized Mr. Ross' academic limitations when it admitted him, and, to induce him to attend and play basketball, Creighton assured Mr. Ross that he would receive sufficient tutoring so that he "would receive a meaningful education while at Creighton."

Mr. Ross attended Creighton from 1978 until 1982. During that time he maintained a D average and acquired 96 of the 128 credits needed to graduate. However, many of these credits were in courses such as Marksmanship and Theory of Basketball, and did not count towards a university degree. Mr. Ross alleges that he took these courses on the advice of Creighton's Athletic Department, and that the department also employed a secretary to read his assignments and prepare and type his papers. Mr. Ross also asserts that Creighton failed to provide him with sufficient and competent tutoring that it had promised.

When he left Creighton, Mr. Ross had the overall language skills of a fourth grader and the reading skills of a seventh grader. Consequently, Mr. Ross enrolled, at Creighton's expense, for a year of remedial education at the Westside Preparatory School in Chicago. At Westside, Mr. Ross attended classes with grade school children. He later entered Roosevelt University in Chicago, but was forced to withdraw because of a lack of funds. In July 1987, Mr. Ross suffered what he terms a "major depressive episode," during which he barricaded himself in a Chicago motel room and threw furniture out the window. To Mr. Ross, this furniture "symbolized" Creighton employees who had wronged him.

II

ANALYSIS

* * *

B. *The Negligence Claims*

Mr. Ross advances...separate theories of how Creighton was negligent towards him: educational malpractice for not educating him ...[and] a new tort of "negligent admission" to an educational institution.... We believe that, on the facts of this case, Illinois law would deny Mr. Ross recovery on...[these] theories.

1. Educational malpractice

Illinois courts have never ruled on whether a tort cause of action exists against an institution for educational malpractice. However, the overwhelming majority of states that have considered this type of claim have rejected it. Only Montana allows these claims to go forward, and its decision was based on state statutes that place a duty of care on educators, a circumstance not present here.

Courts have identified several policy concerns that counsel against allowing claims for educational malpractice. First, there is the lack of a satisfactory standard of care by which to evaluate an educator. Theories of education are not uniform, and "different but acceptable scientific methods of academic training [make] it unfeasible to formulate a standard by which to judge the conduct of those delivering the services." *** [Another] reason for denying this cause of action is the potential it presents for a flood of litigation against schools. As the district court noted, "education is a service rendered on an immensely greater scale than other professional services." The sheer number of claims that could arise if this cause of action were allowed might overburden schools. *** A final reason courts have cited for denying this cause of action is that it threatens to embroil the courts into overseeing the day-to-day operations of schools. This oversight might be particularly troubling in the university setting where it necessarily implicates considerations of academic freedom and autonomy.

We believe that the Illinois Supreme Court would find the experience of other jurisdictions persuasive and, consequently, that these policy considerations are compelling. Consequently, the Illinois Supreme Court would refuse to recognize the tort of educational malpractice. We therefore affirm the district court's dismissal of Mr. Ross' claim based on that theory.

2. "Negligent admission"

We believe that Illinois would reject this claim for "negligent admission" for many of the same policy reasons that counsel against recognizing a claim for educational malpractice. First, this cause of action would present difficult, if not insuperable, problems to a court attempting to define a workable duty of care. Mr. Ross suggests that the University has a duty to admit only students who are "reasonably qualified" and able to perform academically. However, determining who is a "reasonably qualified student" necessarily requires subjective assessments of such things as the nature and quality of the defendant institution and the intelligence and educability of the plaintiff. Such decisions are not open to ready determination in the judicial process. Second, such a cause of action might unduly interfere with a university's admissions decisions, to the detriment of students and society as a whole. As the district court noted, if universities and colleges faced tort liability for admitting an unprepared student, schools would be encouraged to admit only those students who were certain to succeed in the institution. The opportunities of marginal students to receive an education therefore would likely be lessened. Also, the academic practice of promoting diversity by admitting students from disadvantaged backgrounds might also be jeopardized.

* * * *

C. *The Contract Claims*

In counts two and three of his complaint, Mr. Ross alleges that Creighton breached an oral or a written contract that it had with him. When read as a totality, these allegations fairly allege that Creighton agreed, in exchange for Mr. Ross' promise to play on its basketball team, to allow him an opportunity to participate, in a meaningful way, in the academic program of the University despite his deficient academic background. The complaint further alleges, when read as a totality, that Creighton breached this contract and denied Mr. Ross any real opportunity to participate in and benefit from the University's academic program when it failed to perform five commitments made to Ross: (1) "to provide adequate and competent tutoring services," (2) "to require [Mr. Ross] to attend tutoring sessions," (3) to afford Mr. Ross "a reasonable opportunity to take full advantage of tutoring services," (4) to allow Mr. Ross to red-shirt, and (5) to provide funds to allow Mr. Ross to complete his college education.

It is held generally in the United States that the "basic legal relation between a student and a private university or college is contractual in nature. The catalogues, bulletins, circulars, and regulations of the institution made available to the matriculant become a part of the contract." As the district court correctly noted, Illinois recognizes that the relationship between a student and an educational institution is, in some of its aspects, contractual. It is quite clear, however, that Illinois would not recognize all aspects of a university-student relationship as subject to remedy through a contract action. ***

To state a claim for breach of contract, the plaintiff must do more than simply allege that the education was not good enough. Instead, he must point to an identifiable contractual promise that the defendant failed to honor. *** Ruling on this issue would not require an inquiry into the nuances of educational processes and theories, but rather an objective assessment of whether the institution made a good faith effort to perform on its promise.

We read Mr. Ross' complaint to allege more than a failure of the University to provide him with an education of a certain quality. Rather, he alleges that the University knew that he was not qualified academically to participate in its curriculum. Nevertheless, it made a specific promise that he would be able to participate in a meaningful way in that program because it would provide certain specific services to him. Finally, he alleges that the University breached its promise by reneging on its commitment to provide those services and, consequently, effectively cutting him off from *any* participation in and benefit from the University's academic program. To adjudicate such a claim, the court would not be required to determine whether Creighton had breached its contract with Mr. Ross by providing *deficient* academic services. Rather, its inquiry would be limited to whether the University had provided any real access to its academic curriculum at all.

Accordingly, we must disagree respectfully with our colleague in the district court as to whether the contract counts of the complaint can be dismissed at the pleadings stage. In our view, the allegations of the complaint are sufficient to warrant further proceedings. We emphasize, however, the narrow ground of our disagreement. We agree – indeed we emphasize – that courts should not "take on the job of supervising the relationship between colleges and student-athletes or creating in effect a new relationship between them." *** Nevertheless, we believe that the district court can adjudicate Mr. Ross' specific and narrow claim that he was barred from *any* participation in and benefit from the University's academic program without second-guessing the professional judgment of the University faculty on academic matters.

AFFIRMED in part, REVERSED in part and REMANDED.

1. Do university academic advisers have a duty to ensure that student-athletes take the correct number of credits to maintain eligibility? In a case involving extremely unique facts, the Supreme Court of South Carolina said "no" in *Hendricks v. Clemson*, 353 S.C. 449 (2003).

2. Consider the following quotation from the Minnesota District Court in deciding whether to order a basketball player into a degree program: "[The] university academic wing argues that if this Court orders the plaintiff into a degree program, its academic standards and integrity would be undermined. The plaintiff and his fellow athletes were never recruited on the basis of scholarship and it was never envisioned they would be on the Dean's List. Consequently we must view with some skepticism the defendant University's claim, regarding academic integrity. . . . It well may be true that a good academic program for the athlete is made virtually impossible by the demands of their sport at the college level. If this situation causes harm to the University, it is because they have fostered it and the institution rather than the individual should suffer the consequence." *Hall v. University of Minnesota*, 530 F. Supp. 104, 109 (D. Minn. 1982).

3. On January 10, 2005, the NCAA Division I Board of Directors created the new Academic Performance Program aimed at improving the overall academic experience of student athletes and their graduation rate. The program instituted the Academic Progress Rate (APR), which is based on individual academic performance and retention over a five-year period, and applies to all Division I men's and women's sports starting as of the 2005-2006 season. "If a team's APR falls below the minimum cut score of 925, which is roughly equivalent to a fifty percent graduation rate, the NCAA can cut scholarships by up to ten percent. When passing the requirement, the NCAA estimated "that 7.4% of all Division I sports teams, including 30.7% of football, 23.9% of baseball, and 20.1% of men's basketball teams" did not meet the APR standards. Walter Champion, *Fundamentals of Sports Law* § 12:3 (Supp. 2012-13).

4. Summarize Lynch's views regarding the relationship between amateurism, the pressure to win, and commercialism in collegiate athletics. Pay particular attention to the relationship between those things and academics.

5. What are the pros and cons of internal (schools, conferences, NCAA) versus external (courts, Congress) governance of intercollegiate athletics?

6. In his book, *The Carolina Way*, former University of North Carolina basketball coach Dean Smith made a number of suggestions for improving college athletics. Among his suggestions are the following:

1) Give each Division I men's and women's basketball player on scholarship and each Division I-A football scholarship athlete a $2,000 stipend.

2) Require all Division I basketball players to spend a year in residence at the college prior to becoming eligible. According to Coach Smith, "It would give the freshmen time to adjust to the academic demands of college life without the pressures, travel, and practice time involved in varsity basketball or football. Fewer classes would be missed."

3) "The NCAA should tell Division I schools that the lowest 1 percent of freshman admissions can't be recruited athletes. We would then help a small group of students who couldn't help us in athletics. That would also take care of the lame excuse presented by some coaches that just being on a college campus helps a young athlete, even if he or she has no chance to graduate. We all know that current NCAA admission standards requiring a certain SAT score, a certain grade average in certain core courses, and other requirements are not working."

Discuss each of these three suggestions, and explain what you consider to be the strengths and weaknesses of each.

7. For a critical view regarding these and similar issues, *see* Murray Sperber, Beer And Circus: How Big-Time College Sports is Crippling Undergraduate Education (2000).

ENGLISH V. NCAA
439 SO.2D 1218 (1983)
COURT OF APPEALS OF LOUISIANA, FOURTH CIRCUIT

PATRICK SCHOTT, CIRCUIT JUDGE

Plaintiff graduated from high school where he had been an outstanding quarterback in the spring of 1979 and entered Michigan State University in the fall on a football scholarship. Realizing that his prospects for playing at Michigan State were poor he enrolled at Allegheny Junior College in Pittsburgh, Pennsylvania, in the summer of 1980. At that time his family resided in Pittsburgh and his father, Wally English, was on the coaching staff of the University of Pittsburgh. Plaintiff attended Allegheny during the 1980-1981 school year, graduating in the spring, and enrolled at Iowa State University in the fall of 1981. He was on the football team there for the 1981 and 1982 seasons. Once again he recognized that his prospects for playing at Iowa State were poor so he decided to make another move. His family was now residing in New Orleans where his father had taken the position as head football coach at Tulane. In January of 1983 plaintiff enrolled at Delgado Junior College in New Orleans and graduated from there in the spring. In August, 1983, he enrolled at Tulane where he sought to play football.

[The NCAA Eligibility rule states that "a student who transfers to an NCAA member institution from a junior college after transferring from any four-year college, must complete one calendar year of residence at the NCAA member institution in order to be eligible to NCAA championships or post-season football games." The rule is designed to prohibit athletes from playing for two different major colleges in successive years. English seeks to prevent defendants, Tulane University and the NCAA from declaring him ineligible to play football for Tulane on the basis of the NCAA eligibility rule.]

* * *

In this court plaintiff contends that the trial court erred in denying him a preliminary injunction because 1) he was denied due process, 2) the NCAA's actions...were capricious, arbitrary, unfair, and discriminatory....

Plaintiff's due process argument is based on the theory that the NCAA did not adequately inform him of the rules regarding his eligibility. ****

[I]t is clear from the testimony of plaintiff's father, Coach English, that there was from the very beginning a question in plaintiff's mind about his eligibility notwithstanding the way he wanted to read the rule. He was plainly aware of the underlying and laudable policy of the NCAA to prevent a student from playing for two different colleges in successive years. *** [H]e had questions about NCAA legislation, and was obliged to contact the NCAA national office for answers. But he failed to avail himself of this opportunity. Instead, he embarked on a course which he knew was perilous and preferred to take a chance that somehow his interpretation might be accepted by the NCAA.

It is well to note here that plaintiff was determined to play for his father at Tulane if at all possible. His prospects at Iowa State, as at Michigan State previously, were poor and not at all conducive to his being considered for a professional football contract upon his graduation from college. He explained that his skills as a quarterback could be best developed under the tutelage of his father who was a pass oriented coach. Since this would be his last year of college ball it was important for him to make the most of it. Only his interpretation of the transfer rule would make all of this possible.

We find [the NCAA]'s interpretation of the rule to be absolutely correct. *** If one plays for a college one year he can't play for another college the next year. He must sit out for a year after playing for the first college. The rule does not and need not concern itself with the bizarre kind of a situation where one had played for yet a third college in the distant past. Reduced to its simplest terms a player may not jump from one college to another in successive years. ***

There is no support in the record for plaintiff's contention that the NCAA was arbitrary, capricious, unfair, or discriminatory in dealing with his case. Had he inquired of the NCAA as to his plans before he left Iowa State he would have been told that he could not play at another college in 1983. *** The record reflects that the NCAA, in adopting and implementing the transfer rule at issue here acted quite reasonably in its efforts to prevent players from jumping from one school to another in successive years. Plaintiff was not dealt with unfairly. He was the victim only of his own plans and his own hope for special treatment. ***

In the process of summarizing the evidence and analyzing plaintiff's arguments we have already demonstrated that there was no abuse of discretion in this case. As the trial judge pointed out in his reasons for judgment, the trial court "indulged" plaintiff with every opportunity to prove his case and he failed to convince the court that he was entitled to further injunctive relief. We conclude that plaintiff has failed to show an abuse of the trial court's discretion in dismissing plaintiff's application.

Accordingly, [t]he restraining order issued by this court on September 30, 1983, is recalled, vacated and set aside.

BARRY, JUSTICE, DISSENTING

This case involves a very unique and isolated situation involving a very narrow question of interpretation of one word in an NCAA Bylaw which may determine the eligibility for a student-athlete's last year of intercollegiate football competition.

Jon English, a Junior College transfer student to Tulane University, should be declared eligible to participate in intercollegiate football for the 1983 season because he has fulfilled all three requirements listed under the first exception to the general one-year residency rule as published in Bylaw 5-1-(k)-(1) of the *NCAA Manual for 1983-84*.

* * *

The NCAA virtually controls football in over 900 colleges. Its purpose is to regulate sports programs and maintain the integrity of amateur athletics. Member schools must adhere to rigid rules or suffer severe sanctions. Considering the NCAA's enormous control (and its laudable purposes), it must also bear some burden to account for its heavy hand options.

Along with the NCAA's privileges goes the duty to provide clear and accurate information when disseminating its many rules and regulations. Jon English's interpretation of Bylaw 5-1-(k)-(1) was reasonable....

The majority's opinion is a Monday morning quarterback's opinion of what should be, but wasn't; what was intended, but not expressed. *** Jon English relied on the NCAA bylaw and changed his position to his detriment. He was supported and encouraged in his belief by his more sophisticated superiors. Surely he has a right to protect his interests based on these extraordinary facts. That right should permit his eligibility under Bylaw 5-1-(k)-(1).

NOTES AND QUESTIONS

1. Recall the due process considerations discussed in Chapter 7. How does the court in *English* address Plaintiff's argument that the NCAA violated his due process rights?

2. Can individual conferences place increased residency requirements for students who transfer between schools within the conference? In *Tanaka v. University of Southern California,* 252 F.3d 1059 (9th Cir. 2001), the Ninth Circuit considered a Pac-10 transfer rule that required students who transferred between Pac-10 schools to fulfill a residency requirement of two academic years, rather than one. The court held that this rule did not directly harm the national market because it affected only Pac-10 schools. Students transferring to any other Conference had to follow only the NCAA's residency requirement.

3. In *Pugh v. Natl. Collegiate Athletic Assn.,* 115CV01747TWPDKL, 2016 WL 5394408 (S.D. Ind. Sept. 27, 2016), the court upheld an NCAA eligibility rule requiring a transfer football student athlete to sit out one year, reasoning that such a rule is presumptively procompetitive.

BLOOM V. NCAA
93 P.3D 621 (2004)
COLORADO COURT OF APPEALS, DIV. V

JOHN DAILEY, JUDGE

In this dispute concerning eligibility to play college football, plaintiff, Jeremy Bloom, appeals the trial court's order denying his request for a preliminary injunction against defendants, the National Collegiate Athletic Association (NCAA) and the University of Colorado (CU). We affirm.

I. Background

Bloom, a high school football and track star, was recruited to play football at CU. Before enrolling there, however, he competed in Olympic and professional World Cup skiing events, becoming the World Cup champion in freestyle moguls. During the Olympics, Bloom appeared on MTV, and thereafter was offered various paid entertainment opportunities, including a chance to host a show on Nickelodeon. Bloom also agreed to endorse commercially certain ski equipment, and he contracted to model clothing for Tommy Hilfiger.

Bloom became concerned that his endorsements and entertainment activities might interfere with his eligibility to compete in intercollegiate football. On Bloom's behalf, CU first requested waivers of NCAA rules restricting student-athlete endorsement and media activities and, then, a favorable interpretation of the NCAA rule restricting media activities.

The NCAA denied CU's requests, and Bloom discontinued his endorsement, modeling, and media activities to play football for CU during the 2002 fall season. However, Bloom instituted this action against the NCAA for declaratory and injunctive relief, asserting that his endorsement, modeling, and media activities were necessary to support his professional skiing career, something which the NCAA rules permitted.

In his complaint, Bloom alleged: (1) as a third-party beneficiary of the contract between the NCAA and its members, he was entitled to enforce NCAA bylaws permitting him to engage in and receive remuneration from a professional sport different from his amateur sport; (2) as applied to the facts of this case, the NCAA's restrictions on endorsements and media appearances were arbitrary and capricious; and (3) those restrictions constituted improper and unconscionable restraints of trade.

For these reasons, Bloom requested that the NCAA restrictions be declared inapplicable, and that the NCAA and CU be enjoined from applying them, to activities originating prior to his enrollment at CU or wholly unrelated to his prowess as a football player.

III. Claims on Appeal

Initially, we limit our consideration on appeal to Bloom's claims of breach of contract and arbitrary and capricious action by the NCAA. Although Bloom refers to his restraint of trade claim in a footnote in the opening brief, this reference is insufficient to warrant review of that claim.

* * *

A. Interpretation of NCAA Bylaws

* * * *

The interpretation of a contract and the determination whether it is ambiguous are questions of law subject to de novo review by this court.

Bloom relies on NCAA Bylaw 12.1.2, which states that "[a] professional athlete in one sport may represent a member institution in a different sport." He asserts that, because a professional is one who "gets paid" for a sport, a student-athlete is entitled to earn whatever income is customary for his or her professional sport, which, in the case of professional skiers, primarily comes from endorsements and paid media opportunities.

We recognize that, like many others involved in individual professional sports such as golf, tennis, and boxing, professional skiers obtain much of their income from sponsors. We note, however, that none of the NCAA's bylaws mentions, much less explicitly establishes, a right to receive "customary income" for a sport.

To the contrary, the NCAA bylaws prohibit every student-athlete from receiving money for advertisements and endorsements. In this regard, NCAA Bylaw 12.5.2.1 states:

"Subsequent to becoming a student-athlete, an individual shall not be eligible for participation in intercollegiate athletics if the individual: (a) Accepts any remuneration for or permits the use of his or her name or picture to advertise, recommend or promote directly the sale or use of a commercial product or service of any kind, or (b) Receives remuneration for endorsing a commercial product or service through the individual's use of such product or service.

Additionally, while NCAA Bylaw 12.5.1.3 permits a student-athlete to continue to receive remuneration for activity initiated prior to enrollment in which his or her name or picture is used, this remuneration is only allowed, if, as pertinent here, "the individual became involved in such activities for reasons independent of athletics ability; ... no reference is made in these activities to the individual's name or involvement in intercollegiate athletics; [and] ... the individual does not endorse the commercial product."

Further, NCAA Bylaw 12.4.1.1 prohibits a student-athlete from receiving "any remuneration for value or utility that the student-athlete may have for the employer because of the publicity, reputation, fame or personal following that he or she has obtained because of athletics ability."

Unlike other NCAA bylaws, the endorsements and media appearance bylaws do not contain any sport-specific qualifiers. [Citation Omitted]

In our view, when read together, the NCAA bylaws express a clear and unambiguous intent to prohibit student-athletes from engaging in endorsements and paid media appearances, without regard to: (1) when the opportunity for such activities originated; (2) whether the opportunity arose or exists for reasons unrelated to participation in an amateur sport; and (3) whether income derived from the opportunity is customary for any particular professional sport.

The clear import of the bylaws is that, although student-athletes have the right to be professional athletes, they do not have the right to simultaneously engage in endorsement or paid media activity and maintain their eligibility to participate in amateur competition. And we may not disregard the clear meaning of the bylaws simply because they may disproportionately affect those who participate in individual professional sports. Further, the record contains ample evidence supporting the trial court's conclusion that this interpretation is consistent with both the NCAA's and its member institutions' construction of the bylaws. An NCAA official testified that both the endorsement and media appearance provisions have been consistently applied and interpreted in a nonsport-specific manner. Indeed, another NCAA official related that association members had resisted efforts to change the endorsement rule to be sport-specific. ***

Thus, even if the bylaws were viewed as ambiguous, the record supports the trial court's conclusion that the bylaws would ultimately be interpreted in accordance with the NCAA's and its member institutions' construction of those bylaws.

B. Application of Bylaws to Bloom

Here, the trial court found that application of the endorsement and media appearance rules in Bloom's case was rationally related to the legitimate purpose of retaining the "clear line of demarcation between intercollegiate athletics and professional sports."

The trial court noted that salaries and bonuses are an acceptable means for attaining income from professional sports, but endorsement income is not acceptable if a student-athlete wishes to preserve amateur eligibility. According to NCAA officials: (1) endorsements invoke concerns about "the commercial exploitation of student-athletes and the promotion of commercial products"; and (2) it is not possible to distinguish the precise capacity in which endorsements are made. A CU official related that generally, the endorsement rule prevents students from becoming billboards for commercialism, and in Bloom's case, there would "be no way to tell whether he is receiving pay commensurate with his ... football ability or skiing ability."

* * *

Similar concerns underlie the NCAA's prohibition on paid entertainment activity. Paid entertainment activity may impinge upon the amateur ideal if the opportunity were obtained or advanced because of the student's athletic ability or prestige, even though that activity may further the education of student-athletes such as Bloom, a communications major. As the trial court noted, there are "various shades of gray within which such events could fall." And, as should be evident, the NCAA does not prohibit *unpaid* internships, externships, or other educational opportunities in the entertainment field.

In this case, Bloom presented evidence that some of his acting opportunities arose not as a result of his athletic ability but because of his good looks and on-camera presence. However, the record contains evidence that Bloom's agent and the Tommy Hilfiger company marketed Bloom as a talented multi-sport athlete, and a representative from a talent agency intimated that Bloom's reputation as an athlete would be advantageous in obtaining auditions for various entertainment opportunities. Further, the NCAA indicated, when asked to interpret its rules, that it was unable, due to insufficient information, to determine which of Bloom's requested media activities were, in fact, unrelated to his athletic ability or prestige.

Under these circumstances, we perceive no abuse of the trial court's discretion in failing to fault the NCAA for refusing to waive its rules, as requested by CU, to permit Bloom "to pursue any television and film opportunities while he is a student-athlete at CU."

* * *

Bloom has thus failed to demonstrate any inconsistency in application which would lead us to conclude that the NCAA was arbitrarily applying its rules.

* * *

The record thus supports the trial court's findings that the NCAA's administrative review process is reasonable in general and that it was reasonably applied in this case. As such, these findings, as well as those with respect to the NCAA's application of its bylaws, are not manifestly arbitrary, unreasonable, or unfair. For these reasons, we agree with the trial court that Bloom failed to demonstrate a reasonable probability of success on the merits.

* * *

Accordingly, the trial court's order is affirmed

1. Why did Bloom's endorsements make him ineligible to play college football, but being a professional athlete in skiing did not?

2. The court notes that certain athletes, such as professional golfers and skiers, receive a majority of their compensation from endorsements. Do you agree with the court's decision that endorsements from athletes in these sports still make a student ineligible to play a different sport?

3. Is it fair that the NCAA can profit off the likeliness and performance of student-athletes, but the student athletes cannot? Consider these figures:

    "Over 96% of the NCAA's revenues are generated from selling the games played by these students. In 1999, it signed a $6.3 billion contract with CBS to televise some of these performances. . . . In 2000, ABC agreed to pay the NCAA $400 million for the right to broadcast four performances a year of student-athletes in the Bowl Championship Series. Fox Sports has agreed to pay $220 million to broadcast football games in which student-athletes perform in the Big Twelve conference, of which CU is a member. In 2002, Coca-Cola agreed to pay the NCAA $500 million for the "right to advertise and promote its brands" in connection with championship performances. . . .

    The NCAA, its member institutions, and their coaches also generate money by entering into express endorsement contracts whereby the NCAA, its member institutions and their coaches receive direct cash payments from companies such as NIKE in exchange for requiring student-athletes to use, promote, advertise and endorse commercial products. These endorsements include wearing clothing and equipment bearing the manufacturer's logos during their amateur games and post-game celebrations."

    Brief of Appellant at 6-7, *Bloom v. NCAA,* 93 P.3d 621 (Colo. App. 2004) No. 02CA2302, 2003 WL 25478663 at 6-7.

4. *O'Bannon v. Nat'l Collegiate Athletic Ass'n,* 802 F.3d 1049, 1052, 1055 (9th Cir. 2015) is another case where student-athletes attempted to profit from their likeness and performance. Ed O'Bannon, a former UCLA basketball star, visited a friend's house in 2008 and learned from his friend's son that O'Bannon was depicted in a video game produced by Electronic Arts (EA). In what the court described as a "momentous case," O'Bannon, and a group of current and former college football and men's basketball players brought an antitrust class action against the NCAA. *O'Bannon v. Nat'l Collegiate Athletic Ass'n,* 802 F.3d 1049, 1052, 1055 (9th Cir. 2015). They alleged that NCAA rules prohibiting athletes from making money from their name, image and likeness (NIL) violated § 1 of the Sherman Act. *Id.* at 1049.

Overview of the District Court and Ninth Circuit's Decisions

After a bench trial, Judge Claudia Wilken of the United States District Court for the Northern District of California, entered judgment on August 8, 2014 for O'Bannon, stating that the NCAA rules on limiting the share of revenue to players from their names and images violated the Sherman Antitrust Act. The Ninth Circuit Court of Appeals affirmed in September 2015 and held that the NCAA's rules were more restrictive than necessary to achieve its goal of protecting amateurism in the college sports market. The court further noted that the Rule of Reason requires that the NCAA permit its schools to provide monetary stipends up to the cost of attendance to their student athletes. *O'Bannon v. National Collegiate Athletic Ass'n,* 802 F.3d 1049 (C.A.9 (Cal.), 2015). October 3, 2016, the U.S. Supreme Court denied certiorari.

Below is a more detailed account of the district court's and Ninth Circuit's decisions. Chapter 11 examines the doctrinal details of the right of publicity in greater depth and detail.

The District Court Decision

After a bench trial, the district court held the NCAA's no compensation rules were an unlawful restraint of trade – the first decision by any federal court to find that NCAA's amateurism rules violated antitrust laws. *Id.* at 1053. The district court identified two relevant markets affected by the NCAA's no compensation rules. "[A] college education market in which FBS [Football Bowl Series] and Division I basketball schools compete to recruit the best high school players by offering them unique bundles of goods and services that include not only scholarships but also coaching, athletic facilities and the opportunity to face high-quality athletic competition and, a group licensing market in which, but for the NCAA's compensation rules, college football and basketball athletes would be able to sell group licenses for the use of their NILs." *Id.* at 1056-57. The NCAA's no compensation rules potentially restrained trade in both markets. The district court then applied the Rule of Reason standard to determine the legality of the challenged rules. *Id.* Applying this standard, the district court balanced the procompetitive and anticompetitive effects of the NCAA's no compensation rules to determine whether they violate antitrust law. [*See* Chapter 6 *supra* for a discussion of antitrust law, including the Rule of Reason standard.]

The district court found that the NCAA's no compensation rules had an anticompetitive effect in the college education market because "were it not for these rules, schools would compete with each other by offering recruits compensation exceeding the cost of attendance, which would 'effectively lower the price that recruits must pay for the combination of educational and athletic opportunities.'" *Id.* at 1057. The district court described the NCAA's rules prohibiting compensation for student-athletes' NILs as a "price-fixing agreement [where] recruits pay for the bundles of service provided by colleges with their labor and their NILs, but the 'sellers' of these bundles – the colleges – collectively 'agree to value [NILs] at zero.'" *Id.* at 1057-58. "Under this theory, colleges and universities behave as a cartel – a group of sellers who have colluded to fix the price of their product." *Id.* at 1058. "The district court found in the alternative that the college education market can be thought of as a market in which student-athletes are sellers rather than buyers and the schools are the purchasers of athletic services." *Id.* at 1058. In this alternative view, the college education market is a "monopsony – [where] there is only one buyer (the NCAA schools, acting collectively) for a particular good or service (the labor and NIL rights for student-athletes), and the colleges' agreement not to pay anything to purchase the recruits' NILs causes harm to competition." *Id.*

In contrast to the college education market, the district court concluded that the NCAA's no compensation rules did not have an anticompetitive effect on any of the submarkets (e.g., the live game broadcast, the video game producer, and the archival footage submarkets) of the group licensing market. "[A]lthough these submarkets exist, there would be no competition in any of them if the challenged NCAA's rules were abolished, because live game broadcasters and video game producers would need to acquire every other NIL license available. [A] video game producer would want to acquire NIL rights for all of the teams it needed to include in the game. Given these requirements, the district court deemed it highly unlikely that groups of student-athletes would compete with each other to sell their NIL rights; on the contrary, they would have an incentive to cooperate to make sure that the package of NILs rights sold to buyers was as complete as possible." *Id.* at 1058.

The district court determined that the NCAA's no compensation rules serve two procompetitive purposes. First, it promotes the NCAA's "understanding of amateurism, which 'plays some role in preserving the popularity of the NCAA's product' and which in turn helps preserve consumer demand for college sports." *Id.* at 1059. Second, the no compensation restraint helps "integrate academics and athletics" by barring "student-athletes from being paid large sums of money not available to ordinary students, prevent[ing] the creation of a social 'wedge' between student-athletes and ordinary students. *Id.* The district court further stated that "even though the 'avoidance of such a "'wedge' is a legitimate procompetitive goal, it does not justify the 'sweeping prohibition' on paying student-athletes for the use of their NILs. *Id.* at 1060.

Having found two procompetitive effects of the NCAA's no compensation rules under the Rule of Reason standard, the district court moved to the third and final step of the standard. It considered whether there were alternatives that were 'substantially less restrictive' than a total ban on compensating student-athletes for use of their NILs." *Id.* at 1060. The court district held that the "plaintiffs had identified two legitimate less restrictive alternatives, (1) allowing schools to award stipends to student-athletes up to the full cost of attendance, thereby making up for any shortfall in their grants-in-aid, and (2) permitting schools to hold a portion of their licensing revenues in trust, to be distributed to student-athletes in equal shares after they leave college." *Id.* at 1060-61.

The district court entered a judgment for the plaintiffs on their antitrust claims. It permanently enjoined the NCAA from barring member schools from (1) compensating FBS football and Division I men's basketball players for the use of their NILs by awarding them grants-in-aid up to the full cost of attendance or (2) paying them up to $5,000 per year in deferred compensation for the use of their NILs, through trust funds distributable after they leave school. *Id.* at 1061.

The Ninth Circuit Court of Appeals Decision

The NCAA appealed and raised some preliminary legal arguments, including the idea that the NCAA's no compensation rules are rules of amateurism and therefore presumptively valid under *NCAA v. Board of Regents of the University of Oklahoma*, 468 U.S. 85 (1984). The NCAA also argued that the Sherman Act does not cover the NCAA's no compensation rules because the rule is not directed at commercial activity, a Sherman Act requirement. Finally, the NCAA argued that the plaintiffs did not suffer an antitrust injury.

The Ninth Circuit Court of Appeals rejected all of these preliminary arguments. The Ninth Circuit determined that the *Board of Regents* decision never declared the "NCCA's amateurism rules as categorically consistent with the Sherman Act." *Id.* at 1063. "Rather, [*Board of Regents*] held that, because many NCAA rules (among them, the amateurism rules) are part of the 'character and quality of the [NCAA's] product,' no NCAA rule should be invalidated without a Rule of Reason analysis." *Id.* The Ninth Circuit also disagreed with the NCAA's characterization that its no compensation rules are eligibility rules that do not regulate commercial activity. *Id.* at 1064-65. The circuit court held that commerce is a broad term and certainly "encompasses the transaction in which an athletic recruit exchanges his labor and NIL for a scholarship at a Division I school because it is undeniable that both parties to that exchange anticipate economic gain from it." *Id.* at 1065. The circuit court also held that the plaintiffs had shown they were injured in fact by the NCAA's rules because they "foreclosed the market for their NILs in video games. Absent the NCAA's compensation rules, video game makers would negotiate with student-athletes for the right to use their NILs." *Id.* at 1067.

After the rejecting the NCAA's preliminary arguments, the Ninth Circuit reviewed the plaintiffs' Section 1 claim on the merits. It concluded the "district court did not clearly err in finding that raising the grant-in-aid cap [to cover the cost of attendance] would be a substantially less restrictive alternative" than banning all compensation for student-athletes' NILs. *Id.* at 1053. However, the district court "clearly erred when it found that allowing students to be paid compensation for their NILs is virtually as effective as the NCAA's current amateur-status rule." *Id.* at 1074. The Ninth Circuit reversed the district court's ruling that allowed students to be paid compensation because "not paying student-athletes is *precisely what makes them amateurs*." *Id.* at 1076 (emphasis in the original). The court emphasized there is a major difference between "offering student-athletes education-related compensation and offering them cash sums untethered to educational expenses." *Id.* at 1078. "Once that line is crossed, we see no basis for returning to a rule of amateurism and no defined stopping point; we have little doubt that plaintiffs will continue to challenge the arbitrary limit imposed by the district court until they have captured the full value of their NILs. At that point, the NCCA will have surrendered its amateurism principles entirely and transitioned from its particular 'brand of football' to minor league status." *Id.* at 1078-79. The Ninth Circuit's decision was limited in its final holding: the district court was not permitted to require that the NCAA "allow its member schools to pay student-athletes up to $5,000 per year in deferred compensation," but was permitted to raise the grant-in-aid cap to cover the full cost of attendance. *Id.* at 1079.

Do you agree with Ninth Circuit's majority opinion that paying student-athletes up to $5,000 in deferred compensation would ultimately lead to the demise of the NCCA's principles of amateurism? Chief Judge Thomas wrote a separate opinion in *O'Bannon* concurring in part and dissenting part with the Ninth Circuit decision. He concluded "that the district court did not clearly err in ordering the NCAA to permit up to $5,000 in deferred compensation above the student-athletes' full cost of attendance. There was sufficient evidence in the record to support the award. The district court accepted the testimony of multiple experts that small amounts of compensation would not affect consumer demand [for NCAA games], and then used the lowest amount suggested by one of the NCAA's experts." *Id.* at 1079-81. Do you think $5,000 is too high or too low an amount for student-athletes' NILs and services?

Further Reading on the NCAA:

Michael Aiello, *Compensating the Student-Athlete,* 23 Sports Law. J. 157 (2016).

Ryan Appel, *Breaking Bad: An Examination of the NCAA's Investigation Practices over the Last Forty Years,* 22 U. Miami Bus. L. Rev. 83 (2014).

David J. Berri, *Paying NCAA Athletes,* 26 Marq. Sports L. Rev. 479 (2016).

Marc Bianchi, *Guardian of Amateurism or Legal Defiant? The Dichotomous Nature of NCAA Men's Ice Hockey Regulation,* 20 Seton Hall J. Sports & Ent. L. 165 (2010).

Victor Broccoli, *Policing the Digital Wild West: NCAA Recruiting Regulations in the Age of Facebook and Twitter,* 18 Sports Law. J. 43 (2011).

Burlette W. Carter, *Responding to the Perversion of in Loco Parentis: Using a Nonprofit Organization to Support Student Athletes,* 35 Ind. L. Rev. 851 (2001/2002).

Burlette W. Carter, *Student-Athlete Welfare in a Restructured NCAA,* 2 Va. J. Sports & L. 1 (2000).

John D. Colombo, *The NCAA, Tax Exemption, And College Athletics,* 2010 U. Ill. L. Rev. 109 (2010).

Kelly Charles Crabb, *The Amateurism Myth: A Case for A New Tradition,* 28 Stan. L. & Policy Rev. 181 (2017).

Robert N. Davis, *Athletic Reform: Missing the Bases in University Athletics,* 20 Cap. U.L. Rev. 597 (1991).

Timothy Davis, *A Model of Institutional Governance for Intercollegiate Athletics,* 1995 Wis. L. Rev 599 (1995).

Timothy Davis, *African American Student Athletes: Marginalizing the NCAA Regulatory Structure,* 6 Marq. Sports L.J. 199 (1996).

Timothy Davis, *An Absence of Good Faith: Defining A University's Educational Obligation to Student-Athletes,* 28 Hous. L. Rev. 743 (1991).

Timothy Davis, *Intercollegiate Athletics: Competing Models and Conflicting Realities,* 25 Rutgers L.J. 269 (1994).

Timothy Davis, *Intercollegiate Athletics in the Next Millennium,* 9 Marq. Sports L.J. 253 (1999).

Timothy Davis, *NCAA v. UNC: Challenging the NCAA's Jurisdiction,* 6 Ariz. St. Sports & Ent. L.J. 395, 395 (2017).

Timothy Davis & Christopher T. Hairston, PhD, *Majoring in Infractions: The Evolution of the National Collegiate Athletic Association's Enforcement Structure*, 92 Or. L. Rev. 979 (2014).

Marc Edelman, *The Future of Amateurism After Antitrust Scrutiny: Why A Win for the Plaintiffs in the NCAA Student-Athlete Name & Likeness Licensing Litigation Will Not Lead to the Demise of College Sports*, 92 Or. L. Rev. 1019 (2014).

Adam Epstein & Paul M. Anderson, *The Relationship Between A Collegiate Student-Athlete and the University: An Historical and Legal Perspective*, 26 Marq. Sports L. Rev. 287 (2016).

Virginia A. Fitt, *The NCAA's Lost Cause and the Legal Ease of Redefining Amateurism*, 59 Duke L.J. 555 (2009).

C. Peter Goplerud III, *Pay for Play for College Athletes: Now, More than Ever*, 38 S. Tex. L. Rev. 1081 (1997).

James Halt, *Andy Oliver Strikes Out the NCAA's "No-Agent" Rule for College Baseball*, 19 J. Legal Aspects Sport 185 (2009).

Michael T. Jones, *Real Accountability: The NCAA Can No Longer Evade Antitrust Liability Through Amateurism After O'bannon v. NCAA*, 56 B.C.L. Rev. E-Supplement 79, 79 (2015).

Anastasios Kaburakis, David A. Pierce, Olivia M. Fleming, Galen E. Clavio, Heather J. Lawrence, Dawn A. Dziuba, *NCAA Student-Athletes' Rights of Publicity, EA Sports, and the Video Game Industry*, 27 Ent. & Sports Law 1 (2009).

Richard Karcher, *Broadcast Rights, Unjust Enrichment, and The Student-Athlete*, 34 Cardozo L. Rev. 107 (2012).

Daniel E. Lazaroff, *An Antitrust Exemption for the NCAA: Sound Policy or Letting the Fox Loose in the Henhouse?*, 41 Pepp. L. Rev. 229 (2014).

T. Matthew Lockhart, *The NCAA Should Adopt a Uniform Student-Athlete Discipline Policy*, 16 UCLA Ent. L. Rev. 119 (2009).

Greg Lush, *Reclaiming Student Athletes' Rights to Their Names, Images, and Likenesses, Post O'Bannon v. NCAA: Analyzing NCAA Forms for Unconscionability*, 24 S. Cal. Interdisc. L. J. 767 (2015).

Alfred Dennis Mathewson, *Intercollegiate Athletics and the Assignment of Legal Rights*, 35 St. Louis U. L.J. 39 (1990).

Mary Grace Miller, *The NCAA and the Student-Athlete: Reform Is on the Horizon*, 46 U. Rich. L. Rev. 1141 (2012).

Michael J. Nichols, *Time For a Hail Mary? With Bleak Prospects of Being Aided By a College Version of the NFL's Rooney Rule, Should College Football Coaches Turn Their Attention to Title VII Litigation?* 8 Va. Sports & Enter. L.J. 147 (2008).

John Niemeyer, *The End of an Era: The Mounting Challenges to the NCAA's Model of Amateurism*, 42 Pepp. L. Rev. 883 (2015).

Jerry R. Parkinson, *Scoundrels: An Inside Look at the NCAA Infractions and Enforcement Processes*, 12 Wyo. L. Rev. 215 (2012).

M. Tae Phillips, *Un-Equal Protection: Preferential Admissions Treatment for Student Athletes*, 60 Ala. L. Rev. 751 (2009).

Brian L. Porto, *Neither Employees Nor Indentured Servants: A New Amateurism for A New Millennium in College Sports*, 26 Marq. Sports L. Rev. 301 (2016).

Brian L. Porto, *What Recruiters Don't Tell Athletes and Athletes Don't Think to Ask: A Critique of the NCAA's Nonacademic Eligibility Rules*, 13 Va. Sports & Ent. L.J. 240 (2014)

Josephine R. Potuto, *NCAA As State Actor Controversy: Much Ado About Nothing*, 23 Marq. Sports L. Rev. 1 (2012).

Nathaniel Richards, *The Judge, Jury, and Executioner: A Comparative Analysis of the NCAA Committee on Infractions Decisions*, 70 Ala. L. Rev. 1115, 1115 (2019).

Jason P. Rudderman, *Major Violations for the NCAA: How the NCAA Can Apply the Dodd-Frank Act to Reform Its Own Corporate Governance Scheme*, 23 Marq. Sports L. Rev. 103 (2012).

Ann Scales, *Student Gladiators and Sexual Assault: A New Analysis of Liability for Injuries Inflicted by College Athletes*, 15 Mich. J. Gender & L. 205 (2009).

Rodney K. Smith, *A Brief History of the NCAA Role in Regulating Intercollegiate Athletics*, 11 Marq. Sports L. Rev. 9 (2000).

Rodney K. Smith, *Little Ado About Something: Playing Games with the Reform of Big Time Intercollegiate Athletics*, 20 Cap. U. L. Rev. 567 (1991).

Anthony G. Weaver, Ph.D., *New Policies, New Structure, New Problems? Reviewing the NCAA's Autonomy Model*, 7 Elon L. Rev. 551 (2015).

John C. Weistart & Cym H. Lowell, Law of Sports, §§1.02-1.06 Regulation of Amateur Athletics (Bobbs-Merrill Company, Inc., 1979).

John C. Weistart & Cym H. Lowell, Law of Sports, §1.10 Regulation of Amateur Athletics (Bobbs-Merrill Company, Inc., 1979).

Maureen A. Weston, *NCAA Sanctions: Assigning Blame Where It Belongs*, 52 B.C. L. Rev. 551 (2011).

Stanton Wheeler, *Rethinking Amateurism and the NCAA*, 15 Stan. L. & Poly. Rev. 213 (2004).

Glen Wong, Warren Zola & Chris Deubert, *Going Pro in Sports: Providing Guidance to Student-Athletes in a Complicated Legal and Regulatory Environment*, 28 Cardozo Arts & Ent. L.J. 553 (2011).

Ray Yasser, *A Comprehensive Blueprint for the Reform of Intercollegiate Athletics*, 3 Marq. Sports L.J. 123 (1993).

Ray Yasser, *Are Scholarship Athletes at Big-Time Programs Really University Employees*, 9 Black L.J. 65 (1984).

Ray Yasser, *The Black Athletes Equal Protection Case Against the NCAA's New Academic Standard*, 19 Gonz. L. Rev. 83 (1983).

Sherry Young, *The NCAA Enforcement Program and Due Process, the Case for Internal Reform*, 43 Syracuse L. Rev. 747 (1992).

CHAPTER 10

AGENCY

This chapter examines a number of issues related to the representation of athletes, including the special and the unique fiduciary relationship between a sports agent and an athlete. Athletes may employ a variety of business intermediaries, such as accountants and lawyers, to help manage their business and personal matters. And many students enter a Sports Law class thinking that they would like to become sports agents. The actor Tom Cruise certainly made the life of a sports agent look appealing in the movie *Jerry McGuire*.

Stories about sports agencies and agents commonly appear in traditional print and electronic media, adding to the public's fascination with athletes and their representatives. For example, it was headline news in December 2013 when the large entertainment talent agency, William Morris Endeavor, increased its market share for negotiating endorsement, licensing and media-rights deals for athletes by acquiring IMG, the mega sports and media talent agency with 3,500 employees and offices in more than 30 countries. Attracting similar attention in 2013 was the New York Yankee, All-Star second baseman Robinson Cano's decision to fire super-agent Scott Boras and sign with popular recording artist, Jay-Z (Roc Nation Sports) and Creative Artists Agency. Cano ultimately signed a 10-year contract with the Seattle Mariners for $240 million – the third biggest contract in baseball history at that time.

Part A of this chapter introduces the multifaceted role of sports agents and explores some of their services and professional challenges. The *Argovitz* and *Brown* cases illustrate the type of conduct agents must vigilantly avoid in representing athletes. These materials underscore that, in addition to the glamour and prestige associated with sports agency, there is the potential for immoral and illegal activity that could lead to conflicts of interest and conflicts with a variety of authorities.

Part B begins by examining *Oliver v. NCAA* and the NCAA's bylaws governing the student-athlete and agent relationship. NCAA limitations on sports agent activities are important, in part, because NCAA Division I football, basketball and soccer serve as de facto minor leagues for those mega-industries. The NCAA argued in *Oliver* that its bylaws preserve a clear "line of demarcation between collegiate and professional sports." *Oliver* highlights the potentially serious consequences, such as the loss of collegiate athletic eligibility, that student-athletes face when they ignore NCAA rules and engage agents. *Oliver* also represents a rare adverse decision against the NCAA and its regulation of the relationship between student-athletes and their sports agents. More important, the trial court's finding in *Oliver* that the athlete was an intended third-party beneficiary of the contractual relationship between his institution, Oklahoma State University (OSU), and the NCAA, may offer student-athletes a roadmap to assert standing to challenge NCAA action in other contexts. The trial court concluded that both the NCAA and

OSU owed the intended third-party beneficiary, the student-athlete, a duty to act in good faith – not to be arbitrary or capricious.

The Sports Agent Responsibility & Trust Act (SPARTA), signed into law in September 2004, provides federal law and guidelines for sports agents and their dealings with amateur athletes. Part C contains key provisions of SPARTA, the first major federal statute on this topic. SPARTA prohibits an agent from giving a student athlete or anyone associated with a student athlete, for example, a family member, anything of value before the student athlete enters an agency agreement. Another provision requires agents to provide student athletes under the age of 18 with a "disclosure document" warning them that they may lose their eligibility to compete in their sport upon entering into an agency agreement. Both the student athlete and agent are required to notify the athletic director of the student's educational institution within 72 hours of entering into an agency contract. Part C also includes a portion of Chris Debuert's article, which outlines the current regulatory schemes for sports agents.

Part D concludes the chapter with an excerpt from Stacey Evans's article. It discusses the roles of agents, the need for agents, addresses some of the possible ethical issues facing agents, and also provides excellent practical advice for agents.

A. ROLE OF AGENTS

Historically, an agent's role primarily involved negotiating an athlete's performance contract with a team or a sponsor of an event, for example, a tennis tournament. Sports agents today are often expected to provide additional services, such as financial, tax and estate planning, public relations, travel assistance, and security, or find others who can provide such services. Large talent agencies, like IMG in sports or Creative Artists Agency in entertainment, offer clients "one-stop shopping" convenience where generally all of the talent's service needs are provided in-house, by the large agency. Individual agents and smaller agencies, like ICON Management, in Stow, Ohio (representing golfers and other talent) commonly assemble a team of outside advisers to assist in servicing some of an athlete's diverse needs. These advisers work closely with the agent. In this scenario, an agent functions like the head of an operations control room, managing the various advisers' efforts on behalf of the agent.

An agent's role in helping an athlete to succeed is multifaceted and demanding; it's a 24/7 job. The athlete's first telephone call or text message is often to his or her agent, whether in a large or small agency, for help with important and occasionally minor professional and personal needs. The agent-athlete relationship is very personal, built upon trust, support, and communication. Agents need to be accessible for their athlete-clients or risk losing them given the intense competition among agents for athletes.

The agency contract between the parties largely determines an agent's role for the athlete. It is important for an agent to know what kind of support the client-athlete needs or expects and the agency contract should articulate those needs. The scope of the contract may be broadly worded to include a number of functions and services, all of which entitle the agent to charge a commission for his services. Depending on the circumstances, an agent may provide one or more of the services below. Stacey Evans's article at the end of this chapter elaborates upon many of these.

1. *Negotiating a sports contract.* One of an agent's first responsibilities is to negotiate an employment contract between the athlete and the party (*e.g.*, sports franchise) purchasing his or her services. Agents must understand the athlete's sports industry and the financial status of the prospective purchaser in order to effectively negotiate favorable terms in the athlete's employment contract. An agent needs to build a case for the athlete's value, for example, by noting coaching and scouting recommendations, prior athletic accomplishments (e.g., scoring records and other honors) and physical evaluations (*e.g.*, agility, speed) and other skills demonstrated at a combine, pro-day, and/or tryout. The agent compares his client's talents and accomplishments with similar benchmarks for current and former athletes in the industry to gauge the client's fair market value. The agent's work will be influenced by overarching, collective bargaining agreements negotiated between player associations and team owners, such as in basketball and football. These agreements will guide the agent's work and require that certain league-wide minimum terms be part of the athlete's contract. For example, collective bargaining agreements determine the date of free agency, wearing of team athletic apparel, and the agent's rate of commission.

2. *Developing the athlete's commercial marketability.* Successful agents help their client-athletes obtain product and service endorsement deals to augment their player income. For example, tennis great, Andre Agassi, appeared in Cannon Camera television commercials in the 1980s. Many others come to mind: Bo Jackson (Nike); Tiger Woods (Buick, Nike, EA Sports, and others); Michael Jordan (Nike, Hanes); Marty Brodeur (Enterprise Rental Car); Richard Sherman (Campbell's Soup); Phil Mickelson (Enbrel). Lebron James earned $90 million dollars for his product endorsement deal with Nike. Some of these can be quite funny, such as Tiger Woods literally walking on water (EA Sports), and Boston Bruins' David Pasternak's Dunkin' Donuts commercial in which, after being sent to the penalty box, he: 1) laments that he needs to order a medium size rather than a large because he only has two minutes; 2) tells the referee to check his voice mail because he "missed some calls"; and, 3) explains to the NHL official in the box that the reason why the barrista knows his order is because he's "pretty much a regular here." Product endorsement or licensing deals are important to most athletes for both the money and the exposure. Although the mega endorsement deals attract widespread attention, it is difficult to find endorsement or licensing deals for non-star athletes even in local team markets. Agents might ask the athlete's team or event provider with a larger market presence for help in acquiring licensing deals when negotiating a player's team or event contract. Some licensing deals require athletes to use a particular sports product, for example, a golf club or tennis racket, during competition. An agent should negotiate an "escape clause" permitting the athlete to switch to a different product if it is negatively affecting the athlete's performance.

3. *Personal Management.* Some athletes need their agent to handle all of their business matters, ranging from scheduling appointments to handling all financial obligations (*e.g.*, collecting,

depositing and investing earnings, paying transportation and other expenses). The line between managing business and personal affairs is not always clear. For example an agent may help find a personal residence and then negotiate its purchase. Some athletes prefer their agents to play a greater role in managing their personal affairs (*e.g.,* paying for mortgages and medical insurance), freeing the athletes to focus on their sports careers. As fiduciaries, individual agents and small agencies are often responsible for assembling a team of experts and advisers to manage the athlete's long-term business and personal welfare, including the athlete's plans for a post-sports career.

4. *Financial planning.* Many athletes' careers last only a few years. For example, an NFL player's average career length is three and one-half seasons. Agents need to assist their athletes in developing a financial plan to provide for their long-term welfare. Agents often hire investment advisers and accountants to help with this function. The landscape of sports lore is replete with tales of athletes who earned large sums of money only to end up destitute. For example, one article reported that after two years of retirement, 78% of former NFL players were bankrupt or under financial stress and 60% of former NBA players were in a similar situation five years after retirement.

5. *Public relations.* An often overlooked but important agent function involves developing and marketing the athlete's public image. Agents may connect athletes to charitable and other public events and causes that not only provide intrinsic rewards for the athlete, but also may enhance the athlete's market value. Effective agents directly cultivate relationships with sports writers and other media personnel (*e.g.,* television interviews) to cover the athlete or hire public relations firms for the same purpose. These firms are especially important in helping to rehabilitate an athlete's image that may have suffered harm because of the athlete's questionable conduct.

DETROIT LIONS AND BILLY SIMS V. ARGOVITZ
580 F.SUPP.542 (1984)
UNITED STATES DISTRICT COURT, E.D. MICHIGAN, SOUTHERN DIVISION

DEMASCIO, DISTRICT JUDGE.

The plot for this Saturday afternoon serial began when Billy Sims, having signed a contract with the Houston Gamblers on July 1, 1983, signed a second contract with the Detroit Lions on December 16, 1983. On December 18, 1983, the Detroit Lions, Inc. (Lions) and Billy R. Sims filed a complaint...seeking a judicial determination that the July 1, 1983, contract between Sims and the Houston Gamblers, Inc. (Gamblers), is invalid because the defendant Jerry Argovitz (Argovitz) breached his fiduciary duty when negotiating the Gamblers' contract and because the contract was otherwise tainted by fraud and misrepresentation. ****

For the reasons that follow, we have concluded that Argovitz's breach of his fiduciary duty during negotiations for the Gamblers' contract was so pronounced, so egregious, that to deny recision would be unconscionable.

Sometime in February or March 1983, Argovitz told Sims that he had applied for a Houston franchise in the newly formed United States Football League (USFL). In May 1983, Sims attended a press conference in Houston at which Argovitz announced that his application for a franchise had been approved. The evidence persuades us that Sims did not know the extent of Argovitz's interest in the Gamblers. He did not know the amount of Argovitz's original investment, or that Argovitz was obligated for 29 percent of a $1.5 million letter of credit, or that Argovitz was the president of the Gamblers' Corporation at an annual salary of $275,000 and 5 percent the yearly cash flow. The defendants could not justifiably expect Sims to comprehend the ramifications of Argovitz's interest in the Gamblers or the manner in which that interest would create an untenable conflict of interest, a conflict that would inevitably breach Argovitz's fiduciary duty to Sims. Argovitz knew, or should have known, that he could not act as Sims' agent under any circumstances when dealing with the Gamblers. Even the USFL Constitution itself prohibits a holder of any interest in a member club from acting "as the contracting agent or representative for any player."

Pending the approval of his application for a USFL franchise in Houston, Argovitz continued his negotiations with the Lions on behalf of Sims. On April 5, 1983, Argovitz offered Sims's services to the Lions for $6 million over a four-year period. The offer included a demand for a $1 million interest-free loan to be repaid over 10 years, and for skill and injury, guarantees for three years. The Lions quickly responded with a counter offer on April 7, 1983, in the face amount of $1.5 million over a five-year period with additional incentives not relevant here. The negotiating process was working. The Lions were trying to determine what Argovitz really believed the market value for Sims really was. On May 3, 1983, with his Gamblers franchise assured, Argovitz significantly reduced his offer to the Lions. He now offered Sims to the Lions for $3 million over a four-year period, one-half of the amount of his April 5, 1983, offer. Argovitz's May 3rd offer included a demand for $50,000 to permit Sims to purchase an annuity. Argovitz also dropped his previous demand for skill guarantees. The May 10, 1983 offer submitted by the Lions brought the parties much closer.

On May 30, 1983, Argovitz asked for $3.5 million over a five-year period. This offer included an interest-free loan and injury protection insurance but made no demand for skill guarantees. The May 30 offer now requested $400,000 to allow Sims to purchase an annuity. On June 1, 1983, Argovitz and the Lions were only $500,000 apart. We find that the negotiations between the Lions and Argovitz were progressing normally, not laterally as Argovitz represented to Sims. The Lions were not "dragging their feet." Throughout the entire month of June 1983, Mr. Frederick Nash, the Lions' skilled negotiator and a fastidious lawyer, was involved in investigating the possibility of providing an attractive annuity for Sims and at the same time doing his best to avoid the granting of either skill or injury guarantees. The evidence establishes that on June 22, 1983, the Lions and Argovitz were very close to reaching an agreement on the value of Sims's services.

Apparently, in the midst of his negotiations with the Lions and with his Gamblers franchise in hand, Argovitz decided that he would seek an offer from the Gamblers. Mr. Bernard Lerner, one of Argovitz's partners in the Gamblers agreed to negotiate a contract with Sims. Since Lerner admitted that he had no knowledge whatsoever about football, we must infer that Argovitz at the very least told Lerner the amount of money required to sign Sims and further pressed upon Lerner the Gamblers' absolute need to obtain Sims' services. In the Gamblers' organization, only Argovitz knew the value of Sims' services and how critical it was for the Gamblers to obtain Sims. In Argovitz's words, Sims would make the Gamblers' franchise.

On June 29, 1983, at Lerner's behest, Sims and his wife went to Houston to negotiate with a team that was partially owned by his own agent. When Sims arrived in Houston, he believed that the Lions organization was not negotiating in good faith; that it was not really interested in his services. His ego was bruised and his emotional outlook toward the Lions was visible to [Gamblers' General manager, Gene] Burrough and Argovitz. Clearly, virtually all the information that Sims had up to that date came from Argovitz. Sims and the Gamblers did not discuss a future contract on the night of June 29th. The negotiations began on the morning of June 30, 1983, and ended that afternoon. At the morning meeting, Lerner offered Sims a $3.5 million five-year contract, which included three years of skill and injury guarantees. The offer included a $500,000 loan at an interest rate of 1 percent over prime. It was from this loan that Argovitz planned to receive the $100,000 balance of his fee for acting as an agent in negotiating a contract with his own team. Burrough testified that Sims would have accepted that offer on the spot because he was finally receiving the guarantee that he had been requesting from the Lions, guarantees that Argovitz dropped without too much quarrel. Argovitz and Burrough took Sims and his wife into another room to discuss the offer. Argovitz did tell Sims that he thought the Lions would match the Gamblers financial package and asked Sims whether he (Argovitz) should telephone the Lions. But, it is clear from the evidence that neither Sims nor Burrough believed that the Lions would match the offer. We find that Sims told Argovitz not to call the Lions for purely emotional reasons. As we have noted, Sims believed that the Lions' organization was not that interested in him and his pride was wounded. Burrough clearly admitted that he was aware of the emotional basis for Sims' decision not to have Argovitz phone the Lions, and we must conclude from the extremely close relationship between Argovitz and Sims that Argovitz knew it as well. When Sims went back to Lerner's office, he agreed to become a Gambler on the terms offered. At that moment, Argovitz irreparably breached his fiduciary duty. As agent for Sims he had the duty to telephone the Lions, receive its final offer, and present the terms of both offers to Sims. Then and only then could it be said that Sims made an intelligent and knowing decision to accept the Gamblers' offer.

During these negotiations at the Gamblers' office, Mr. Nash of the Lions telephoned Argovitz, but even though Argovitz was at his office, he declined to accept the telephone call. Argovitz tried to return Nash's call after Sims had accepted the Gamblers' offer, but it was after 5 p.m. and Nash had left for the July 4th weekend. When he declined to accept Mr. Nash's call, Argovitz's breach of his fiduciary duty became even more pronounced. Following Nash's example, Argovitz left for his weekend trip, leaving his principal to sign the contracts with the Gamblers the next day, July 1, 1983. ***

During the evening of June 30, 1983, Burrough struggled with the fact that they had not presented the Gamblers' offer to the Lions. He knew, as does the court, that Argovitz now had the wedge that he needed to bring finality to the Lions' negotiations. Burrough was acutely aware of the fact that Sims' actions were emotionally motivated and realized that the responsibility for Sims' future rested with him. We view with some disdain the fact that Argovitz had, in effect, delegated his entire fiduciary responsibility on the eve of his principal's most important career decision. On July 1, 1983, it was Lerner who gave lip service to Argovitz's conspicuous conflict of interest. It was Lerner, not Argovitz, who advised Sims that Argovitz's position with the Gamblers presented a conflict of interest and that Sims could, if he wished, obtain an attorney or another agent. Argovitz, upon whom Sims had relied for the past four years, was not even there. Burrough, conscious of Sims' emotional responses, never advised Sims to wait until he had talked with the Lions before making a final decision. Argovitz's conflict of interest and self dealing put him in the position where he would not even use the wedge he now had to negotiate with the Lions, a wedge that is the dream of every agent. Two expert witnesses testified that an agent should telephone a team that he has been negotiating with once he has an offer in hand. Mr. Woolf, plaintiff's expert, testified that an offer from another team is probably the most important factor in negotiations. *** The evidence here convinces us that Argovitz's negotiations with the Lions were ongoing and it had not made its final offer. Argovitz did not follow the common practice described by both expert witnesses. He did not do this because he knew that the Lions would not leave Sims without a contract and he further knew that if he made that type of call Sims would be lost to the Gamblers, a team he owned.

On November 12, 1983, when Sims was in Houston for the Lions game with the Houston Oilers, Argovitz asked Sims to come to his home and sign certain papers. He represented to Sims that certain papers of his contract had been mistakenly overlooked and now needed to be signed. Included among those papers he asked Sims to sign was a waiver of any claim that Sims might have against Argovitz for his blatant breach of his fiduciary duty brought on by his glaring conflict of interest. Sims did not receive independent advice with regard to the wisdom of signing such a waiver. Despite having sold his agency business in September, Argovitz did not even tell Sims' new agent of his intention to have Sims sign a waiver. Nevertheless, Sims, an unsophisticated young man, signed the waiver. This is another example of the questionable conduct on the part of Argovitz who still had business management obligations to Sims. In spite of his fiduciary relationship he had Sims sign a waiver without advising him to obtain independent counseling.

* * *

We are mindful that Sims was less than forthright when testifying before the court. However, we agree with plaintiff's counsel that the facts as presented through the testimony of other witnesses are so unappealing that we can disregard Sims' testimony entirely. We remain persuaded that on balance, Argovitz's breach of his fiduciary duty was so egregious that a court of equity cannot permit him to benefit by his own wrongful breach. We conclude that Argovitz's conduct in negotiating Sims' contract with the Gamblers rendered it invalid.

CONCLUSIONS OF LAW

* * * *

3. The relationship between a principal and agent is fiduciary in nature, and as such imposes a duty of loyalty, good faith, and fair and honest dealing on the agent. *Anderson v. Griffith,* 501 S.W.2d 695, 700 (Tex.Civ.App.1973).

4. A fiduciary relationship arises not only from a formal principal-agent relationship, but also from informal relationships of trust and confidence. *Thigpen v. Locke,* 363 S.W.2d 247, 253 (Tex.1962); *Adickes v. Andreoli,* 600 S.W.2d 939, 945-46 (Tex.Civ.App.1980).

5. In light of the express agency agreement, and the relationship between Sims and Argovitz, Argovitz clearly owed Sims the fiduciary duties of an agent at all times relevant to this lawsuit.

6. An agent's duty of loyalty requires that he not have a personal stake that conflicts with the principal's interest in a transaction in which he represents his principal. As stated in *Burleson v. Earnest,* 153 S.W.2d 869 (Tex.Civ.App.1941):

(T)he principal is entitled to the best efforts and unbiased judgment of his agent.... (T)he law denies the right of an agent to assume any relationship that is antagonistic to his duty to his principal, and it has many times been held that the agent cannot be both buyer and seller at the same time nor connect his own interests with property involved in his dealings as an agent for another. *Id.* at 874.

7. A fiduciary violates the prohibition against self-dealing not only by dealing with himself on his principal's behalf, but also by dealing on his principal's behalf with a third party in which he has an interest, such as a partnership in which he is a member. ****

8. Where an agent has an interest adverse to that of his principal in a transaction in which he purports to act on behalf of his principal, the transaction is voidable by the principal unless the agent disclosed all material facts within the agent's knowledge that might affect the principal's judgment. *Burleson v. Earnest,* 153 S.W.2d at 874-75.

9. The mere fact that the contract is fair to the principal does not deny the principal the right to rescind the contract when it was negotiated by an agent in violation of the prohibition against self-dealing. ****

10. Once it has been shown that an agent had an interest in a transaction involving his principal antagonistic to the principal's interest, fraud on the part of the agent is presumed. The burden of proof then rests upon the agent to show that his principal had full knowledge, not only of the fact that the agent was interested, but also of every material fact known to the agent which might affect the principal and that having such knowledge, the principal freely consented to the transaction.

11. It is not sufficient for the agent merely to inform the principal that he has an interest that conflicts with the principal's interest. Rather, he must inform the principal "of all facts that come to his knowledge that are or may be material or which might affect his principal's rights or interests or influence the action he takes." *Anderson v. Griffith,* 501 S.W.2d 695, 700 (Tex.Civ. App.1973).

12. Argovitz clearly had a personal interest in signing Sims with the Gamblers that was adverse to Sims' interest – he had an ownership interest in the Gamblers and thus would profit if the Gamblers were profitable, and would incur substantial personal liabilities should the Gamblers not be financially successful. Since this showing has been made, fraud on Argovitz's part is presumed, and the Gamblers' contract must be rescinded unless Argovitz has shown by a preponderance of the evidence that he informed Sims of every material fact that might have influenced Sims' decision whether or not to sign the Gamblers' contract.

* * * *

17. As a court sitting in equity, we conclude that recision is the appropriate remedy. We are dismayed by Argovitz's egregious conduct. The careless fashion in which Argovitz went about ascertaining the highest price for Sims' service convinces us of the wisdom of the maxim: no man can faithfully serve two masters whose interests are in conflict.

Judgment will be entered for the plaintiffs rescinding the Gamblers' contract with Sims.

NOTES & QUESTIONS

1. Is the court saying categorically that someone with an ownership interest in a professional team cannot legally also act as a player agent? Or is the court saying that someone with an ownership interest in a professional team may legally also act as a player agent, but if s/he does so, s/he has an obligation to make disclosures to his/her principal that are more open than those that Argovitz made to Sims?

2. Can you pinpoint a time at which Argovitz crossed the line and breached his fiduciary duty to Sims?

3. There probably are things that Sims should have done differently in an effort to avoid this type of situation with his agent. Give examples.

4. If you had been Argovitz's lawyer, what would you have advised him to do during his negotiations with the Lions?

5. The court cites numerous instances of Argovitz's wrongdoing. Make a list of them.

6. Does an attorney-sports agent carry the same professional responsibility requirements even when he is not engaged in the practice of law, only sports representation? The Arizona Supreme Court held, in *Matter of Dwight,* 117 Ariz. 407 (Ariz. 1997), that a lawyer is bound by the ethical requirements of the profession, and cannot defend his actions by contending that he was engaged in some other kind of professional activity.

7. For an interesting case involving an agent's fiduciary obligations to an athlete, *see Bias v. Advantage Int'l, Inc.,* 905 F.2d 1558 (D.C. Cir. 1990). The Boston Celtics chose the University of Maryland's Leonard K. Bias as the second pick in the 1986 NBA draft. Bias died of a cocaine overdose two months after signing a representation agreement with Lee Fentress of Advantage International, Inc. and two days after being drafted by the Celtics. Bias' estate sued Advantage and Fentress personally for breaching Fentress' fiduciary duty as Bias' agent by failing to obtain life insurance and to secure an endorsement deal with Reebok prior to Bias' death. The Court of Appeals affirmed the trial court's summary judgment decision for the defendants. The appellate court concluded that there were no genuine issues of material fact as to the insurability of Bias, a drug user, and there was no evidence that Fentress breached his duty to Bias by delaying the endorsement deal. Two days after the NBA draft was insufficient time to negotiate and sign an endorsement deal. *Bias* reminds agents nevertheless to obtain insurance as quickly as possible upon signing client-athletes, and to conclude endorsement deals expeditiously in an effort to avoid fiduciary litigation.

8. Given their fiduciary relationship, should agents counsel athletes about chronic traumatic encephalopathy (CTE), the degenerative disease linked to repeated blows to the head, when planning for their future? *See In re National Football League Players' Concussion Injury Litigation* Na 2:12-md-02323-AB (E.D. PA. Jan. 14, 2014)(expressing concerns about the fairness, reasonableness and adequacy of the parties' proposed $760 settlement over 20 years, Judge Anita B. Brody declined preliminary approval and class certification in this multidistrict litigation; and noting that more than 4,500 former NFL players claimed that the NFL and NFL Properties LLC breached their duties to the players by not protecting them from chronic risks associated with concussive and subconcinussive head injuries and concealing those risks). Of course we acknowledged this issue previously in the introduction to Chapter 4. Would your answer change if the athlete's parents were to contact you, the family lawyer, for advice about how to protect their child? Does the agent have any obligation to negotiate contract terms with a team limiting concussive contact (*e.g.,* fewer full contact practices), requiring certain equipment (*e.g.,* the latest protective headgear), and mandating regular medical testing? Should the agent's fiduciary duty to the client-athlete include obtaining baseline medical testing about athlete's brain activity to properly monitor the athlete's future medical welfare?

554 F.SUPP. 1206 (1983)

UNITED STATES DISTRICT COURT, S.D. INDIANA, INDIANAPOLIS DIVISION

STECKLER, DISTRICT JUDGE.

* * * *

The complaint in this diversity action seeks compensatory and punitive damages and the imposition of a trust on a fee Woolf allegedly received, all stemming from Woolf's alleged constructive fraud and breach of fiduciary duty in the negotiation of a contract for the 1974-75 hockey season for Brown who was a professional hockey player. Brown alleges that prior to the 1973-74 season he had engaged the services of Woolf, a well known sports attorney and agent, who represents many professional athletes, has authored a book, and has appeared in the media in connection with such representation, to negotiate a contract for him with the Pittsburgh Penguins of the National Hockey League. Brown had a professionally successful season that year under the contract Woolf negotiated for him and accordingly again engaged Woolf's services prior to the 1974-75 season. During the negotiations in July 1974, the Penguins offered Brown a two-year contract at $80,000.00 per year but Brown rejected the offer allegedly because Woolf asserted that he could obtain a better, long-term, no-cut contract with a deferred compensation feature with the Indianapolis Racers, which at the time was a new team in a new league. On July 31, 1974, Brown signed a five-year contract with the Racers. Thereafter, it is alleged the Racers began having financial difficulties. Brown avers that Woolf continued to represent [him] and negotiated two reductions in his compensation including the loss of a retirement fund at the same time Woolf was attempting to get his own fee payment from the Racers. Ultimately, the Racers' assets were seized and the organizers defaulted on their obligations to Brown. He avers that he received only $185,000.00 of the total $800,000.00 compensation under the Racer contract, but that Woolf received his full $40,000.00 fee (5% of the contract) from the Racers.

Brown alleges that Woolf made numerous material misrepresentations upon which he relied both during the negotiation of the Racer contract and at the time of the subsequent modifications. Brown further avers that Woolf breached his fiduciary duty to [him] by failing to conduct any investigation into the financial stability of the Racers, failing to investigate possible consequences of the deferred compensation package in the Racers' contract, failing to obtain guarantees or collateral, and by negotiating reductions in [his] compensation from the Racers while insisting on receiving all of his own. Brown theorizes that such conduct amounts to a prima facie case of constructive fraud for which he should receive compensatory and punitive damages and have a trust impressed on the $40,000.00 fee Woolf received from the Racers.

Woolf[]...attacks Brown's claim for punitive damages, contending that Brown has no evidence to support such an award and should not be allowed to rest on the allegations of his complaint. *** Woolf attacks several aspects of Brown's claims against him. He argues (1) that Brown cannot recover on a breach of contract theory because Robert G. Woolf, the individual, was acting merely as the agent and employee of Robert Woolf Associates, Inc. (RWA), (2) that Woolf's conduct could not amount to constructive fraud because (a) Brown alleges only negligent acts, (b) there is no evidence Woolf deceived Brown or violated a position of trust, (c) there is no showing of harm to the public interest, and (d) there is no evidence that Woolf obtained an unconscionable advantage at Brown's expense.

*** [T]he Court could find no Indiana case specifically discussing the availability of punitive damages in an action based upon the theory of constructive fraud. Cases from other jurisdictions reflect a division of authority. The Court concludes that Indiana courts would not adopt a per se rule prohibiting such damages in a constructive fraud action, but would rather consider the facts and circumstances of each case. If elements of recklessness, or oppressive conduct are demonstrated, punitive damages could be awarded. [Citations Omitted]

Indiana cases contain several formulizations of the tort of constructive fraud. Generally it is characterized as acts or a course of conduct from which an unconscionable advantage is or may be derived, or a breach of confidence coupled with an unjust enrichment which shocks the conscience, or a breach of duty, including mistake, duress or undue influence, which the law declares fraudulent because of a tendency to deceive, injure the public interest or violate the public or private confidence. [Citations Omitted] Another formulization found in the cases involves the making of a false statement, by the dominant party in a confidential or fiduciary relationship or by one who holds himself out as an expert, upon which the plaintiff reasonably relies to his detriment. The defendant need not know the statement is false nor make the false statement with fraudulent intent. *Coffey v. Wininger,* 156 Ind.App. 233, 296 N.E.2d 154 (1973); *Smart & Perry Ford Sales, Inc. v. Weaver,* 149 Ind.App. 693, 274 N.E.2d 718 (1971).

The Court believes that both formulizations are rife with questions of fact, *inter alia,* the existence or nonexistence of a confidential or fiduciary relationship, and the question of reliance on false representations, as well as questions of credibility.

[The court determined that there were factual questions that remained unanswered and therefore held that the case could not be resolved on a motion for summary judgment. Thus the case could move forward to trial.]

NOTES & QUESTIONS

1. Explain what the court means by the term "constructive fraud." What facts does Brown allege that arguably constitute constructive fraud?

2. Player unions regulate agents. *See Black v. National Football League Player Association (NFLPA),* 87 F. Supp. 2d. 1 (D.C. Dist. 2000)(collective bargaining agreement provides the union with the authority to license contract advisers who comply with NFPLA regulations); *Collins v. National Basketball Players Association,* 976 F.2d 740 (10th Cir. 1992) (unpublished opinion)(noting that NBPA agent regulation was established after 1986 to protect union members from agent abuses, and affirming the NBPA's right to refuse certification of an

agent who had "neglected his fiduciary duties as an investment agent and money manager" because he "could not be trusted to fulfill his duties as a negotiator.").

B. CONSEQUENCES TO STUDENT-ATHLETES

OLIVER V. NATIONAL COLLEGIATE ATHLETIC ASSOCIATION
155 OHIO MISC.2D 17, 920 N.E. 2D 203 (2009)
COURT OF COMMON PLEAS

TONE, JUDGE

***FACTS

The plaintiff [Andy Oliver] is currently in his junior year of college at Oklahoma State University ("OSU"). Since August 2006, the plaintiff has pitched for the baseball team at OSU.

The defendant, the National Collegiate Athletic Association ("NCAA"), is an unincorporated business association having its principal place of business in Marion County, Indiana; it has member institutions not only in Oklahoma but also in Ohio. OSU is a member institution of the defendant; the NCAA association regulates the student-athlete activities at OSU.

The plaintiff, in February 2006, retained the services of Robert M. Baratta, Tim Baratta, and Icon Sports Group, d.b.a. Icon Law Group, as his sports advisors and attorneys. In June of the same year, the Minnesota Twins of Major League Baseball drafted the plaintiff in the 17th round of the draft. At the end of the summer, the Minnesota Twins met with the plaintiff and his father at the Oliver family home in Vermilion before the plaintiff left for his freshman year of college. Tim Baratta also attended the meeting, at his own request, at the Oliver home. During the meeting the Minnesota Twins offered the plaintiff $390,000 to join their organization. After heeding the advice of his father, the plaintiff rejected the offer and chose to attend OSU in the fall on a full scholarship, for which he had already signed a letter of intent in the fall of 2005.

As a result of deciding to go to OSU and accepting amateur status, the plaintiff would not be eligible for the draft again until his junior year of college, in June 2009. The plaintiff played his freshman and sophomore years for OSU, and during that period he never received any invoices requesting payment for any services rendered by his advisors. In fact, the plaintiff avers that the advisors provided nothing of value to him.

In March 2008, plaintiff decided to terminate the Barattas and Icon Sports and retain the Boras Corporation. The plaintiff communicated his intention of termination to Robert Baratta. At that time, Robert Baratta attempted to reconnect with the plaintiff and his father, but to no avail. In April 2008, the plaintiff received a letter and an invoice from the Barattas for $113,750 for legal services. The invoice did not contain any detail of services rendered or time entries. The plaintiff took the invoice to the OSU baseball team coach, the OSU Athletic Compliance Office, and the Boras Corporation. Subsequently, the plaintiff retained attorney Michael Quiat to assist him with the matter. Quiat requested the time records supporting Baratta's invoice. In May, in response to the request, the Barattas sent a letter dated February 8, 2006, and a contract dated February 8, 2006, to Quiat. The letter listed six items of assistance rendered by them on behalf of the plaintiff. The plaintiff has argued that the contract is fictitious and the assistance stated in it was in fact never performed.

On May 19, 2008, the previous attorneys mailed, faxed, and e-mailed a letter to the defendant complaining about the plaintiff and reporting alleged violations by the plaintiff, i.e. the meeting at the Olivers' home that Tim Baratta had attended. As a result of the allegations, OSU and the defendant investigated the alleged violations in relationship to the plaintiff's amateur status. In May 2008, the plaintiff was indefinitely suspended from playing baseball and was informed by OSU staff that he had violated NCAA Bylaw 12.3.1 by (1) allowing his previous attorneys to contact the Minnesota Twins by telephone and (2) by allowing Tim Baratta to be present in his home when a representative from the Minnesota Twins tendered an offer to him.

On August 18, 2008, the plaintiff was reinstated as a result of a temporary restraining order issued by this court. However, in October 2008, OSU filed for reinstatement of the plaintiff with the NCAA even though the temporary restraining order had reinstated the plaintiff. Subsequently, in December 2008, the plaintiff was suspended for one year and charged a year of eligibility by the defendant. The penalty was subsequently reduced to 70 percent of the original suspension and no loss of eligibility for the plaintiff.

ARGUMENTS

The plaintiff requests that this court enter a declaratory judgment and injunctive relief enjoining the NCAA Bylaw 12.3.2.1 as unenforceable because the plaintiff retained legal counsel (the Barattas) to represent him and that legal counsel is subject to the exclusive regulation of the Ohio Supreme Court. Therefore, the defendant has no authority to promulgate a rule that would prevent a lawyer from competently representing his client. As such, the plaintiff maintains that NCAA Bylaw 12.3.2.1 is void because it is against the public policy of the state of Ohio.

Furthermore, the plaintiff argues that NCAA Bylaw 12.3.2.1 is arbitrary and capricious because it does not impact a player's amateur status but instead limits the player's ability to effectively negotiate a contract that the player or a player's parent could negotiate. In that regard, the plaintiff contends that he was the victim of unethical attorneys who, under the laws of the state of Ohio, had a duty to protect him, but instead the defendant punished him even though he bore no fault. Thus, according to the plaintiff, the defendant should vacate the findings that were the foundation of the plaintiff's suspension and reinstate him immediately with no further punishment.

Finally, the plaintiff requests that this court also enter a declaratory judgment and permanent injunction enjoining the defendant from enforcing NCAA Bylaw 19.7. The plaintiff argues that the bylaw interferes with the Ohio Constitution's delegation of all judicial power to the courts of this state and, consistent with that premise, exists solely to coerce or direct its agents and members to ignore court orders that are binding upon member institutions of the defendant.

***II. BREACH OF CONTRACT

Since the inception of this case, the defendant has argued that it has no contractual relationship with the plaintiff. What is obvious is that there is a contractual relationship between the defendant and its member institution, OSU. The defendant, as an unincorporated association consisting of public and private universities and colleges, adopts rules governing member institutions' recruiting, admissions, academic eligibility, and financial-aid standards for student athletes. The basic purpose of the NCAA is stated in Bylaw 1.3.1:

> The competitive athletics programs of member institutions are designed to be a vital part of the educational system. A basic purpose of this Association is to maintain intercollegiate athletics as an integral part of the educational program and the athlete as an integral part of the student body and, by so doing, retain a clear line of demarcation between intercollegiate athletics and professional sports.

The defendant has argued and this court agrees that there is no contract between the defendant and the plaintiff by way of the national letter of intent or the plaintiff's financial-aid package. However, an action for breach of contract by a third party can be brought when the parties to a contract intended to benefit the third party. The Ohio Supreme Court, in *Hill v. Sonitrol of Southwestern Ohio* addressed the difference between incidental and intended third-party beneficiaries when deciding whether a third party who lacks contractual privity is entitled to enforce the terms of the contract. The Ohio Supreme Court concluded that an intended third-party beneficiary has enforceable rights under the contract only when the contracting parties expressly intend that a third party should benefit from the contract. There must be evidence that the promisor assumed a duty to the third party. "The mere conferring of some benefit on the supposed beneficiary by the performance of a particular promise in a contract is insufficient; rather, the performance of that promise must also satisfy a duty owed by the promisee to the beneficiary."

It is unquestionable that the defendant and OSU's contractual agreement is created to confer a benefit on the student-athletes. The purpose of the NCAA (see Bylaws 1.2 and 1.3.1), and the obligation of member institutions (see Obligations of Member Institutions, Article 1.3.2), form a contract in which the defendant promises, among many things, to initiate, stimulate, and improve intercollegiate athletic programs for student athletes, see Article 1.2(a). OSU promises to enforce the defendant's legislation as it relates to its members and "protect and enhance the physical and educational well-being of student athletes." See Article 1.3.2 and 2.2. The constitution of the NCAA, the operating and the administrative bylaws (the NCAA Divisional Manual) represents the contract between the association and its member institutions whereby student-athletes remain amateurs in an intercollegiate sport, where they are "motivated primarily by education and by the physical, mental and social benefits to be derived." See Article 2.9. According to the principles of the agreement, "student participation in intercollegiate athletics is an avocation, and student-athletes should be protected from exploitation by professional and commercial enterprises." Id. Each entity binds itself to follow the directives of the contractual manual in order to promote an intercollegiate amateur athletic program for student-athletes.

As a rudimentary matter, to enforce rights as an intended third-party beneficiary, this court is satisfied that the plaintiff has established by way of the contractual agreements within the manual that there is an underlying enforceable contract and that there are duties owed by the promisee as well as the promisor to the plaintiff. The plaintiff argues that the defendant breached its duty of good faith and fair dealing to the plaintiff, thereby placing him in a tenuous position because his ignorance as to what was required became not only a menace but also an obstruction to the plaintiff's eligibility to compete as a student-athlete for OSU.

To the extent that the plaintiff's claim of arbitrary and capricious action asserts a violation of the duty of good faith and fair dealing that is implied in the contractual relationship between the NCAA and its members, his position as a third-party beneficiary of that contractual relationship affords him standing to pursue his claims. *** Ohio law now supports that good faith is part of a contract claim. Furthermore, the court in *Brown v. Otto C. Epp Mem. Hosp.* determined that "good faith is required of every contract," and this court is in agreement with that premise. Thus, this court holds that a party can be found to have breached its contract if it fails to act in good faith.

III. GOOD FAITH AND FAIR DEALING

*** [T]he defendant, and for that matter OSU, was required to deal honestly and reasonably with the plaintiff as a third-party beneficiary of its contractual relationship. Surely each party is entitled to the benefit of its bargain. With that stated, if this court determines that Bylaw 12.3.2.1 is void because it is against the public policy of Ohio or because it is arbitrary and capricious, and Bylaw 19.7 interferes with the delegation of judicial power to the courts of this state, then the defendant has not dealt with the plaintiff honestly or reasonably and the defendant has breached the contract.

The court continues this analysis by examining the plaintiff's argument that he retained lawyers to represent him and that those lawyers are subject to the exclusive regulation of the Ohio Supreme Court. Thus the defendant, according to the plaintiff, had no authority to promulgate Bylaw 12.3.2.1. The plaintiff asserts that the bylaw promulgated by the defendant prevented his lawyers from competently representing him. Therefore, the plaintiff argues, the bylaw is void because it is against public policy. Bylaw 12.3.2.1 states:

> A lawyer may not be present during discussions of a contract offer with a professional organization or have any direct contact (in person, by telephone or by mail) with a professional sports organization on behalf of the individual. A lawyer's presence during such discussions is considered representation by an agent.

In contrast, the defendant argues that Bylaw 12.3.2.1 helps to retain a clear line of demarcation between collegiate and professional sports that is a fundamental goal of the member institutions. Furthermore, according to the defendant, it preserves an amateur model of collegiate athletics, and the defendant contends that this court should not intervene since the bylaw is the will of the NCAA membership. *** Bylaw 12.3, entitled "Use of Agents," states the general principle that a student-athlete is ineligible to participate in intercollegiate sports if he or she agrees to be represented by an agent. Hence, the "no agent rule" is as follows:

> An individual shall be ineligible for participation in an intercollegiate sport if He or she ever agreed (orally or in writing) to be represented by an agent for The purpose of marketing his or her athletics ability or reputation in that sport. Further, an agency contract not specifically limited in writing to a sport or Particular sports shall be deemed applicable to all sports, and the individual shall Be ineligible to participate in any sport.

NCAA Bylaw 12.3.2.1.

However, the crux of this case falls under Bylaw 12.3.2, which carves out an exception to the no-agent rule by allowing a student-athlete to retain a lawyer (not even the defendant can circumvent an individual's right to counsel). Yet, the exception to the rule, which allows legal counsel for student-athletes, attempts to limit an attorney's role as to that representation and in effect, such as in the case here, puts the onus on the student-athlete. See NCAA Bylaw 12.3.2.1.

The status of the no-agent rule, as firmly pointed out in the direct testimony of Kevin Hennon, vice president of membership services, is a prohibition against agents, not lawyers. Therein lies the problem.

It is impossible to allow student-athletes to hire lawyers and attempt to control what that lawyer does for his client by Bylaws 12.3.2 or 12.3.2.1. These rules attempt to say to the student-athlete that he or she can consult with an attorney but that the attorney cannot negotiate a contract with a professional sport team. This surely does not retain a clear line of demarcation between amateurism and professionalism. The student-athlete will never know what his attorney is doing for him or her, and quite frankly, neither will the defendant. The evidence is very clear that this rule is impossible to enforce and as a result is being enforced selectively. Further, as in this case, it allows for exploitation of the student-athlete "by professional and commercial enterprises," in contravention of the positive intentions of the defendant.

Was Barratta's presence in that room a clear indication that the plaintiff, a teenager who admitted at trial that he was in no position to negotiate a professional contract and whose father testified to the same, was a professional? According to Bylaw 12.3.2.1, the no-agent rule, he was. As such the following issues must be resolved: Is the no-agent rule against the public policy of Ohio? Is it arbitrary? Is it capricious?

The plaintiff testified that he hired the Barattas in part because they were attorneys and they promised that they would protect his amateur status. From the testimony given at trial, the court is aware that the defendant permits student-athletes and their parents to negotiate contracts while in the presence of a sports representative but to have an attorney present in the room would in some way smear the line of demarcation between what is amateurism and what is professionalism. An attorney's duty, in Ohio, in Oklahoma, in all 50 states, is to represent his client competently.

For a student-athlete to be permitted to have an attorney and then to tell that student-athlete that his attorney cannot be present during the discussion of an offer from a professional organization is akin to a patient hiring a doctor, but the doctor is told by the hospital board and the insurance company that he cannot be present when the patient meets with a surgeon because the conference may improve his patient's decision-making power. Bylaw 12.3.2.1 is unreliable (capricious) and illogical (arbitrary) and indeed stifles what attorneys are trained and retained to do.

The process advanced by the NCAA hinders representation by legal counsel, creating an atmosphere fraught with ethical dilemmas and pitfalls that an attorney consulting a student-athlete must encounter. Will the attorney be able to advance what is best for the client or will a neutral party, the NCAA, tie his hands? What harm could possibly befall the student-athlete if such a rule were not found? What occurs if the parents of a student are attorneys or, for that matter, sport agents? What would have happened if Tim Baratta had been in the kitchen or outside or on the patio instead of in the same room as his client when the offer from the Minnesota Twins was made to the plaintiff?

This court appreciates that a fundamental goal of the member institutions and the defendant is to preserve the clear line of demarcation between amateurism and professionalism. However, to suggest that Bylaw 12.3.2.1 accomplishes that purpose by instructing a student-athlete that his attorney cannot do what he or she was hired to do is simply illogical. An example of a clear line of demarcation between amateurism and professionalism is indeed drawn within the bylaws and is done so in Bylaw 12.02.3:

> A professional athlete is one who receives any kind of payment, directly or indirectly, for athletics participation except as permitted by the governing legislation of the Association.

If the membership and the NCAA decide that Bylaw 12.02.3 does not accomplish that purpose, so be it. But no entity, other than that one designated by the state, can dictate to an attorney where, what, how, or when he should represent his client. With all due respect, surely that decision should not be determined by the NCAA and its member institutions, no matter what the defendant claims is the purpose of the rule. If the defendant intends to deal with this athlete or any athlete in good faith, the student-athlete should have the opportunity to have the tools present (in this case an attorney) that would allow him to make a wise decision without automatically being deemed a professional, especially when such contractual negotiations can be overwhelming even to those who are skilled in their implementation.

IV. ARBITRARY AND CAPRICIOUS

With that stated, the court now addresses the issue of whether Bylaw 19.7 is arbitrary and capricious. Bylaw 19.7 states:

> If a student athlete who is ineligible under the terms of the constitution, bylaws or other legislation of the Association is permitted to participate in intercollegiate competition contrary to such NCAA legislation but in accordance with the terms of a court restraining order or injunction operative against the institution attended by such student-athlete or against the Association, or both, and said injunction is voluntarily vacated, stayed or reversed or it is finally determined by the courts that injunctive relief is not or was not justified, the Board of Directors may take any one or more of the following actions against such institution in the interest of restitution and fairness to competing institutions: (a) through (e).

Following the above-mentioned paragraph, subsections (a) through (e) list penalties that impinge on institutions, student-athletes, or team records for following the dictates of a court order that may later be overturned by a higher court. The plaintiff would ask: "How could any entity punish an individual for accessing their right to Court?" The defendant argues that the member institutions agreed that it was improper to allow an institution to reap the benefits of playing a student-athlete who was finally adjudicated to be ineligible. Just because member institutions agree to a rule or bylaw does not mean that the bylaw is sacrosanct or that it is not arbitrary or capricious.

Bylaw 19.7 takes the rule of law as governed by the courts of this nation and gives it to an unincorporated business association. The bylaw is overreaching. For example, if a court grants a restraining order that permits a student-athlete the right to play, the institution will find itself in a real dilemma. Does the institution allow the student-athlete to play as directed by the court's ruling and, in so doing, face great harm should the decision be reversed on appeal? Alternatively, does the institution, in fear of Bylaw 19.7, decide that it is safer to disregard the court order and not allow the student-athlete to play, thereby finding itself in contempt of court? Such a bylaw is governed by no fixed standard except that which is self-serving for the defendant. To that extent, it is arbitrary and indeed a violation of the covenant of good faith and fair dealing implicit in its contract with the plaintiff, as the third-party beneficiary.

*** After this court has engaged in a balancing process that was designed to weigh the equities between the parties, the court determines by clear and convincing evidence that the plaintiff would suffer immediate and irreparable injury, loss, or damage if injunctive relief is not granted. If an injunction is not granted, the plaintiff would suffer loss of his college baseball experience, impairment or loss of his future professional baseball career, loss in being available for the upcoming draft because he is less likely to be seen, and ongoing damage to the plaintiff's reputation and baseball career.

In comparison, the defendant's witnesses stated that if relief were granted, it would be confusing as to which institutions would have to follow this court's ruling. Would it be Ohio members, Oklahoma members, all institutions? However, since this court has personam jurisdiction, this argument is not as persuasive as the plaintiff's, and the scales of justice have tilted in the plaintiff's favor.

Judgment accordingly.

NOTES & QUESTIONS

1. While *Oliver's* value as a precedent is limited because the judgment was vacated when the NCAA settled with the student-athlete for $750,000, the trial court's third-party intended beneficiary reasoning still provides a useful roadmap for future parties challenging NCAA regulation and for the courts deciding those cases. The NCCA has settled other problematical cases challenging its regulations. *See, e.g., White, et al. v. NCAA* No. CV 06-0999 VBF RGK (C.D. Calif. 2006)(denying a motion to dismiss a complaint by college football and basketball players alleging that the NCAA and its member institutions violated the Sherman Act by agreeing to limit the amount of athletics-based financial aid, and ultimately prompting the NCAA to settle the antitrust action with Class Members for 10 million dollars while offering another 218 million dollars to Division I NCAA institutions to aid student athletes' financial and academic needs).

2. In the next-to-last paragraph of the opinion, the court states that it "determines *by clear and convincing evidence* that..." Explain why you think that the court employed a "clear and convincing evidence" standard in order to grant Oliver injunctive relief. This intermediate standard of proof requires the plaintiff to offer more evidence than the usual "preponderance of evidence" standard (*i.e.,* requiring a showing of 51% on an evidentiary scale of 0 to 100) in civil cases but less evidence than the "beyond a reasonable doubt" standard (*i.e.,* significantly higher...perhaps approaching nearly 100 on a 0 to 100 scale) in criminal cases. What policy is served by requiring the intermediate standard?

3. The *Oliver* court finds that it is unquestionable that the NCAA and OSU's contractual relationship was created to confer a benefit on the athlete. Why?

4. Do you agree with the court's explanation for its finding that NCAA Bylaw 12.3.2.1 "is unreliable (capricious) and illogical (arbitrary)"? Is the court's analogy of a patient hiring a doctor who is told by the hospital board that she "cannot be present when the patient meets with a surgeon because the conference may improve her patient's decision-making power" a fair one?

5. Does the trial court give sufficient weight to the NCAA's argument that the "no agent rule" is necessary to preserve the line of demarcation between amateurism and professionalism?

Are there alternative ways to preserve this line besides precluding an athlete from having an agent-adviser to help negotiate or advise the athlete about a contract's terms?

6. The court cites the testimony of an NCAA vice president that the "no agent" rule "is a prohibition against agents and, not lawyers." Does this position give lawyers an unfair advantage in the competitive sport-agency field by saying that student-athletes can hire lawyers even though the NCAA does not allow attorneys to negotiate a contract with a professional team? The Securities and Exchange Commission and other governmental agencies increasingly regulate the practice of law before their bodies. Should the NCAA be similarly permitted to regulate what lawyers can do on behalf of their clients, student-athletes? The *Oliver* court emphasizes that no entity, including the NCAA, other than the Ohio Supreme Court can dictate to a lawyer "what, how, or when he should represent his client." Do you agree?

7. Explain why the Court finds NCAA Bylaw 19.7 arbitrary and capricious?

8. On June 10, 2010 the NCCA found that University of Southern California (USC) football star Reggie Bush, his mother and stepfather received impermissible benefits during 2004-05 in violation of NCAA Bylaws. Lloyd Lake and Michael Michaels, owners of a sports agency and marketing company, provided the benefits in return for Reggie promising to join the agency. The benefits included cash (*e.g.,* $10,000 for Bush's parents to purchase furniture and $5,000 for Reggie to purchase a new vehicle), merchandise (*e.g.,* a washer and dryer for the parents), housing (*e.g.,* a home for the parents who paid no rent), hotel lodging (*e.g.,* two-night vacation in Las Vegas and incidentals for Reggie Bush) and transportation (*e.g.,* airline tickets for Bush's family to see the 2005 Orange Bowl). USC, a "repeat offender," suffered serious consequences, including a public reprimand and censure, probation for four years, a postseason ban on playing in bowl games for 2010 and 2011, the loss of 30 football scholarships during 2011-14, and the vacatur of all wins in which Bush participated beginning in December 2004. *See Report of the Nat. Coll. Athletic Association Div. I Infractions Appeals Committee,* Report No. 323 (2011), *available at* www.ncaa.com/content/usc-public-report-o. When Bush signed with another agent, Lake ultimately sued Bush for breaching an oral contract to repay all monies lent to him. *Lake v. Griffin,* No. 37-2007-00078637_CU-BC-CTL., 2007 WL 3283192 (Cal Superior Oct. 30, 2007). The two settled for an undisclosed amount, spurring the NCAA investigation. *See* Maureen A. Weston, *NCAA Sanctions: Assigning Blame Where It Belongs,* 52 B.C.L. Rev. 551, (2011)(discussing the Bush case, in part, and arguing that the NCAA's current sanctioning process and penalties unfairly impact innocent players (*e.g.,* Bush's teammates who cannot participate in bowl games) and inadequately hold coaches accountable who generally keep their large earnings and move on to earn even greater sums (*e.g.,* citing news reports that Bush's USC coach, Peter Carrol, signed a five-year, $33 million Seattle Seahawks contract)). Bush returned the Heisman trophy after the NCAA vacated USC's 2005 season and declared him an ineligible athlete. The Heisman Trophy

Trust decided against having a 2005 Heisman Trophy winner after Bush's forfeited the title. *See* Jordan Moore, *Heisman Trust Statement on Reggie Bush,* Sept. 15, 2010, www.usctrojans. com/blog/2010/09/heisman-trust-statement-on-bush.html.

C. AGENT REGULATIONS

UNITED STATES PUBLIC LAWS
SPORTS AGENT RESPONSIBILITY AND TRUST ACT

An Act To designate certain conduct by sports agents relating to the signing of contracts with student athletes as unfair and deceptive acts or practices to be regulated by the Federal Trade Commission.

Be it enacted by the Senate and House of Representatives of the United States of America in Congress assembled,

15 USCA § 7801 NOTE

SECTION 1. SHORT TITLE.

This Act may be cited as the "Sports Agent Responsibility and Trust Act."

15 USCA § 7801

SEC. 2. DEFINITIONS.

As used in this Act, the following definitions apply:

(1) AGENCY CONTRACT.--The term "agency contract" means an oral or written agreement in which a student athlete authorizes a person to negotiate or solicit on behalf of the student athlete a professional sports contract or an endorsement contract.

(2) ATHLETE AGENT.--The term "athlete agent" means an individual who enters into an agency contract with a student athlete, or directly or indirectly recruits or solicits a student athlete to enter into an agency contract, and does not include a spouse, parent, sibling, grandparent, or guardian of such student athlete, any legal counsel for purposes other than that of representative agency, or an individual acting solely on behalf of a professional sports team or professional sports organization.

(3) ATHLETIC DIRECTOR.--The term "athletic director" means an individual responsible for administering the athletic program of an educational institution or, in the case that such program is administered separately, the athletic program for male students or the athletic program for female students, as appropriate.

(4) COMMISSION.--The term "Commission" means the Federal Trade Commission.

(5) ENDORSEMENT CONTRACT.--The term "endorsement contract" means an agreement under which a student athlete is employed or receives consideration for the use by the other party of that individual's person, name, image, or likeness in the promotion of any product, service, or event.

(6) INTERCOLLEGIATE SPORT.--The term "intercollegiate sport" means a sport played at the collegiate level for which eligibility requirements for participation by a student athlete are established by a national association for the promotion or regulation of college athletics.

(7) PROFESSIONAL SPORTS CONTRACT.--The term "professional sports contract" means an agreement under which an individual is employed, or agrees to render services, as a player on a professional sports team, with a professional sports organization, or as a professional athlete.

(8) STATE.--The term "State" includes a State of the United States, the District of Columbia, Puerto Rico, the United States Virgin Islands, or any territory or insular possession subject to the jurisdiction of the United States.

(9) STUDENT ATHLETE.--The term "student athlete" means an individual who engages in, is eligible to engage in, or may be eligible in the future to engage in, any intercollegiate sport. An individual who is permanently ineligible to participate in a particular intercollegiate sport is not a student athlete for purposes of that sport.

15 USCA § 7802

SEC. 3. REGULATION OF UNFAIR AND DECEPTIVE ACTS AND PRACTICES IN CONNECTION WITH THE CONTACT BETWEEN AN ATHLETE AGENT AND A STUDENT ATHLETE.

(a) CONDUCT PROHIBITED.--It is unlawful for an athlete agent to—

(1) directly or indirectly recruit or solicit a student athlete to enter into an agency contract, by-

(A) giving any false or misleading information or making a false promise or representation; or

(B) providing anything of value to a student athlete or anyone associated with the student athlete before the student athlete enters into an agency contract, including any consideration in the form of a loan, or acting in the capacity of a guarantor or co-guarantor for any debt;

(2) enter into an agency contract with a student athlete without providing the student athlete with the disclosure document described in subsection (b); or

(3) predate or postdate an agency contract.

(b) REQUIRED DISCLOSURE BY ATHLETE AGENTS TO STUDENT ATHLETES.—

(1) IN GENERAL.--In conjunction with the entering into of an agency contract, an athlete agent shall provide to the student athlete, or, if the student athlete is under the age of 18, to such student athlete's parent or legal guardian, a disclosure document that meets the requirements of this subsection. Such disclosure document is separate from and in addition to any disclosure which may be required under State law.

(2) SIGNATURE OF STUDENT ATHLETE.--The disclosure document must be signed by the student athlete, or, if the student athlete is under the age of 18, by such student athlete's parent or legal guardian, prior to entering into the agency contract.

(3) REQUIRED LANGUAGE.--The disclosure document must contain, in close proximity to the signature of the student athlete, or, if the student athlete is under the age of 18, the signature of such student athlete's parent or legal guardian, a conspicuous notice in boldface type stating: "Warning to Student Athlete: If you agree orally or in writing to be represented by an agent now or in the future you may lose your eligibility to compete as a student athlete in your sport. Within 72 hours after entering into this contract or before the next athletic event in which you

are eligible to participate, whichever occurs first, both you and the agent by whom you are agreeing to be represented must notify the athletic director of the educational institution at which you are enrolled, or other individual responsible for athletic programs at such educational institution, that you have entered into an agency contract."

15 USCA § 7803

SEC. 4. ENFORCEMENT.

(a) UNFAIR OR DECEPTIVE ACT OR PRACTICE.--A violation of this Act shall be treated as a violation of a rule defining an unfair or deceptive act or practice prescribed under section 18(a)(1)(B) of the Federal Trade Commission Act (15 U.S.C. 57a(a)(1)(B)).

(b) ACTIONS BY THE COMMISSION.--The Commission shall enforce this Act in the same manner, by the same means, and with the same jurisdiction, powers, and duties as though all applicable terms and provisions of the Federal Trade Commission Act (15 U.S.C. 41 et seq.) were incorporated into and made a part of this Act.

15 USCA § 7804

SEC. 5. ACTIONS BY STATES.

(a) IN GENERAL.—

(1) CIVIL ACTIONS.--In any case in which the attorney general of a State has reason to believe that an interest of the residents of that State has been or is threatened or adversely affected by the engagement of any athlete agent in a practice that violates section 3 of this Act, the State may bring a civil action on behalf of the residents of the State in a district court of the United States of appropriate jurisdiction to—

(A) enjoin that practice;

(B) enforce compliance with this Act; or

(C) obtain damage, restitution, or other compensation on behalf of residents of the State.

(2) NOTICE.—

(A) IN GENERAL.--Before filing an action under paragraph (1), the attorney general of the State involved shall provide to the Commission—

(i) written notice of that action; and

(ii) a copy of the complaint for that action.

(B) EXEMPTION.--Subparagraph (A) shall not apply with respect to the filing of an action by an attorney general of a State under this subsection, if the attorney general determines that it is not feasible to provide the notice described in that subparagraph before filing of the action. In such case, the attorney general of a State shall provide notice and a copy of the complaint to the Commission at the same time as the attorney general files the action.

(b) INTERVENTION.—

(1) IN GENERAL.--On receiving notice under subsection (a)(2), the Commission shall have the right to intervene in the action that is the subject of the notice.

(2) EFFECT OF INTERVENTION.--If the Commission intervenes in an action under subsection (a), it shall have the right—

(A) to be heard with respect to any matter that arises in that action; and

(B) to file a petition for appeal.

(C) CONSTRUCTION.--For purposes of bringing any civil action under subsection (a), nothing in this title shall be construed to prevent an attorney general of a State from exercising the powers conferred on the attorney general by the laws of that State to—

(1) conduct investigations;

(2) administer oaths or affirmations; or

(3) compel the attendance of witnesses or the production of documentary and other evidence.

(d) ACTIONS BY THE COMMISSION.--In any case in which an action is instituted by or on behalf of the Commission for a violation of section 3, no State may, during the pendency of that action, institute an action under subsection (a) against any defendant named in the complaint in that action.

(e) VENUE.--Any action brought under subsection (a) may be brought in the district court of the United States that meets applicable requirements relating to venue under section 1391 of title 28, United States Code.

(f) SERVICE OF PROCESS.--In an action brought under subsection (a), process may be served in any district in which the defendant—

(1) is an inhabitant; or

(2) may be found.

15 USCA § 7805

SEC. 6. PROTECTION OF EDUCATIONAL INSTITUTION.

(a) NOTICE REQUIRED.--Within 72 hours after entering into an agency contract or before the next athletic event in which the student athlete may participate, whichever occurs first, the athlete agent and the student athlete shall each inform the athletic director of the educational institution at which the student athlete is enrolled, or other individual responsible for athletic programs at such educational institution, that the student athlete has entered into an agency contract, and the athlete agent shall provide the athletic director with notice in writing of such a contract.

(b) CIVIL REMEDY.—

(1) IN GENERAL.--An educational institution has a right of action against an athlete agent for damages caused by a violation of this Act.

(2) DAMAGES.--Damages of an educational institution may include and are limited to actual losses and expenses incurred because, as a result of the conduct of the athlete agent, the educational institution was injured by a violation of this Act or was penalized, disqualified, or suspended from participation in athletics by a national association for the promotion and regulation of athletics, by an athletic conference, or by reasonable self-imposed disciplinary action taken to mitigate actions likely to be imposed by such an association or conference.

(3) COSTS AND ATTORNEYS FEES.--In an action taken under this section, the court may award to the prevailing party costs and reasonable attorneys fees.

(4) EFFECT ON OTHER RIGHTS, REMEDIES AND DEFENSES.--This section does not restrict the rights, remedies, or defenses of any person under law or equity.

15 USCA § 7806

SEC. 7. LIMITATION.

Nothing in this Act shall be construed to prohibit an individual from seeking any remedies available under existing Federal or State law or equity.

15 USCA § 7807

SEC. 8. SENSE OF CONGRESS.

It is the sense of Congress that States should enact the Uniform Athlete Agents Act of 2000 drafted by the National Conference of Commissioners on Uniform State Laws, to protect student athletes and the integrity of amateur sports from unscrupulous sports agents. In particular, it is the sense of Congress that States should enact the provisions relating to the registration of sports agents, the required form of contract, the right of the student athlete to cancel an agency contract, the disclosure requirements relating to record maintenance, reporting, renewal, notice, warning, and security, and the provisions for reciprocity among the States.

NOTES & QUESTIONS

1. What acts does SPARTA prohibit?

2. Identify the actions that SPARTA requires from agents.

3. What is the role of the State Attorneys General in the enforcement of SPARTA? What is the role of the FTC?

4. Explain the import of the warning required in the agency contract.

WHAT'S A "CLEAN" AGENT TO DO? THE CASE FOR A CAUSE OF ACTION AGAINST A PLAYER'S ASSOCIATION

CHRIS DEUBERT

18 VILL. SPORTS & ENT. L.J. 1 (2011)

*** Current Regulation Schemes

A. State Legislation

1. Uniform Athlete Agents Act ("UAAA")

As of March 2010, the Uniform Athlete Agents Act ("UAAA") has been adopted in thirty-nine states. The UAAA is, to each state that has passed it, the primary piece of legislation in the regulation and punishment of unscrupulous athlete-agents. In 1997, at the request of the NCAA and several major academic institutions, the National Conference of Commissioners on Uniform State Laws ("NCCUSL") agreed to draft a model law to be adopted by each state, which would regulate athlete-agents. The legislation was first presented in the fall of 2000 and was quickly passed in several states.

Section 2 of the UAAA, Definitions, defines "athlete agent" as "[a]n individual who enters into an agency contract with a student-athlete or, directly or indirectly, recruits or solicits a student-athlete to enter into an agency contract." Agents, however, have the important task of reviewing each state statute, which may define an athlete agent or student-athlete differently, and often more broadly, than the UAAA. Furthermore, one needs to recognize that under these broad definitions, nearly everyone attempting to create a professional relationship with an athlete may be considered an agent, including the largely unregulated and unknown population of agent "runners." The term "runner" generally describes someone employed by an agent, typically a young person, whose job is to become friendly with the student-athlete, providing the student-athlete with cash, meals, clothes or other gifts and ultimately steering the student-athlete towards the employing agent. Because runners operate in a shady world of independent contractual relationships, enforcement bodies face difficulties in tracking runners down and associating them and their illegal actions with specific agents.

Section 3 of the UAAA submits athlete agents to the jurisdiction of the state in which he or she is acting as an agent, and appoints the Secretary of State in that state as his or her agent for service of process in related civil actions. What constitutes "acting" in the state is a personal jurisdiction issue outside the scope of this article. Important to the regulation of agents is knowing who these agents are. Sections 4 through 9 require agents to register with the Secretary of State, set the fees and conditions of registration, and establish the right of the Secretary of State to deny, suspend, revoke or refuse to renew the agent's registration.

Section 10 controls the form and content of the representation contract that agents may sign with athletes, in particular student-athletes. Notably, this section provides that every contract must contain the following words as a "conspicuous notice in boldface type in capital letters stating:"

WARNING TO STUDENT-ATHLETE

IF YOU SIGN THIS CONTRACT:

(1) YOU MAY LOSE YOUR ELIGIBILITY TO COMPETE AS A STUDENT-ATHLETE IN YOUR SPORT;

(2) IF YOU HAVE AN ATHLETIC DIRECTOR, WITHIN 72 HOURS AFTER ENTERING INTO THIS CONTRACT, OR BEFORE THE NEXT SCHEDULED ATHLETIC EVENT IN WHICH YOU MAY PARTICIPATE, WHICHEVER OCCURS FIRST, BOTH YOU AND YOUR ATHLETE AGENT MUST NOTIFY YOUR ATHLETIC DIRECTOR; AND

(3) YOU MAY CANCEL THIS CONTRACT WITHIN 14 DAYS AFTER SIGNING IT. CANCELLATION OF THIS CONTRACT MAY NOT REINSTATE YOUR ELIGIBILITY.

Furthermore, Sections 11 and 12 require the agent to give notice to the educational institution within seventy-two hours and reiterates the athlete's right to cancel the contract. Section 14 lists Prohibited Acts, Section 15 provides for Criminal Penalties, and Section 16 provides for a civil remedy by the academic institution against an agent should the institution incur any damages as a result of the agent's actions.

The UAAA states that its primary purpose "is to protect student-athletes and educational institutions from athlete agents who engage in unsavory and, oftentimes, illegal practices."

Although the UAAA states that one of its purposes is to "provide a system that allows states to honor the registration of athlete agents from states with similar laws," there is no indication that the UAAA was passed with any direct intention to protect clean agents in their profession. Accordingly, if a state were to enact and effectively enforce the UAAA, clean agents would be protected. The UAAA boasts of its "strong penalties for violators" which would seem to effectuate the primary goal of the legislation.

On its face, the UAAA is the antidote for what ails the agency industry. In practice, the UAAA has been toothless and ineffective. Several, if not most of the sections of the UAAA are not complied with and not enforced. Most agents have been forced to register in each state where they are "doing business," and Section 14 (b)1 prohibits "initiat[ing] contact with a student-athlete unless registered under [the UAAA]." The regular practice of agents, however, includes recruitment of players in states where the agents are not registered and do not register unless and until they believe they are going to sign the player.

One reason agents do this is the failure of the only provision in the UAAA meant to help agents, whereby states would "honor" the registration of an agent in another state with similar legislation. Presently, only Alabama, Arizona, Oregon, Pennsylvania and South Dakota offer any kind of discount in registration for agents who have previously registered with another state. With annual or bi-annual registration fees generally costing a few hundred dollars in addition to expensive bonding requirements, states most likely see agent registration as an easy revenue source and an effective way to track and limit agents practicing in their respective states.

Reciprocal registration is not the only issue where the states are not sufficiently cooperating. The comment to Section 6 of the UAAA states that Secretaries of State ought to "exchange information about [the] denial, suspension, revocation or refusal to renew registration of athlete agents." The stated purpose of such an exchange would be to "reduce the expense of administering [the] act and provide for more effective enforcement." However, to date, there is no agreement among the states to share information about athlete agents.

Furthermore, pursuant to the UAAA, probably almost every agent-athlete contract is voidable by the player. Section 10(c) requires agents to give the conspicuous, boldface, capital letter statement copied above. Section 10(d) states that if this provision is not in the contract, the contract is then voidable by the student-athlete. As will be discussed in more detail below, each of the players' associations (PA's) in the Big Four (*i.e.,* Major League Baseball, National Football League, National Hockey League, and National Basketball Association) has regulations governing agent registration and conduct. These regulations also provide a required standard agreement to be used between the agent and the athlete. None of these standard agreements contain the language required by the UAAA, yet an agent in violation of this provision would probably argue that using the standard PA agreement is sufficient for satisfying the UAAA. While it is possible that agents execute side agreements with the players to comply with the UAAA, this is highly unlikely.

2. Other State Laws

California, Michigan and Ohio have not passed the UAAA but have otherwise passed state laws designed to regulate athlete agents. These laws provide varying degrees of regulation, by listing prohibited conduct, possible penalties and, in the cases of California and Ohio, requirements of registration. In addition, states are free to investigate and prosecute agents under criminal laws. The most realistic crimes an agent might be charged with are bribery, embezzlement, and criminal fraud. Criminal prosecutions of athlete-agents, however, have been rare.

Lastly, agents, like anyone else, are subject to potential liability under state common law and civil statutes. In this regard, agents potentially could be liable to a large number of claimants, including the athlete, a college, a business partner, the state or anyone else injured by the agent's conduct. For example, Section 16 of the UAAA provides for a right of action against an athlete agent by an educational institution. Additionally, Section 17 proposes to allow the Secretary of State to assess civil penalties against agents.

Despite all these criminal and civil remedies, a law is only as effective as its enforcement. Unfortunately, apparently neither the UAAA nor other state laws are being actively and effectively enforced. Consequently, athlete-agents have acted with relative impunity from state law.

B. Federal Legislation: Sports Agent Responsibility and Trust Act ("SPARTA")

In twenty-five years as the head coach of the [University of] Nebraska football team, Tom Osborne won three national championships and was widely regarded as a symbol of class in college football, even though his teams had their share of unsavory characters and were twice subjected to NCAA sanctions during his tenure. In 2000, three years after he retired from coaching, Osborne was elected as one of the U.S. House of Representatives from Nebraska. As a member of Congress, Osborne was instrumental in the passing of the Sports Agent Responsibility and Trust Act ("SPARTA") in 2004.

The heart of the act lists the unlawful activity covered..., including soliciting clients with misleading information, making false promises, providing anything of value as an inducement or neglecting to provide a required disclosure statement warning the student-athlete that he or she may forfeit eligibility. This statutory format is nearly identical to Section 10 of the UAAA described earlier. SPARTA deems any violation to be an "unfair or deceptive act or practice" within the jurisdiction of the Federal Trade Commission (FTC). In addition, SPARTA provides for civil causes of action by states and educational institutions against agents in the same manner as the UAAA.

Like the UAAA, SPARTA provides the legislative framework to end unethical and illegal behavior by agents. However, to date, the FTC has not brought an action against any agent and some members of its staff were generally unaware that the statute existed.

C. NCAA Rules and Bylaws

On the collegiate level there are two relevant sets of regulations: first, the NCAA Bylaws and second, the rules of each individual member institution. As a "voluntary organization through which the nation's colleges and universities govern their athletic programs," the NCAA has no jurisdiction over agents. The NCAA consists of over a thousand member institutions, all of which participate in the creation of NCAA rules and voluntarily submit to its authority. As a private organization not subject to the scrutiny of a state actor, the NCAA can only exercise plenary power over its member institutions, their employees and their student-athletes. Consequently, while the NCAA has extensive regulations concerning contact with agents, the NCAA can only enforce punishment against the member institution, its employees and student-athletes. One of the most common situations where regulation is involved is when a student-athlete loses eligibility for receiving a gift of some kind from an agent. If the student-athlete has already moved on to his professional career, however, the school often faces the penalties alone because the student is no longer within the "jurisdiction" of the NCAA.

The NCAA's enforcement of these bylaws has probably made discovering agent misconduct more difficult. Prior to the 2008 season, the NCAA suspended [University of] Oregon tackle Fenuki Tupou for one game after he received a meal and $100 from an agent. Tupou had met the agent for lunch to discuss future representation, as is customary among senior student-athletes. When the meal was over, the agent, Tim Norling of LMM Sports Management, allegedly paid for the meal and gave Tupou $100 in a handshake, despite Tupou's repeated refusals to take the money. Tupou told Oregon's director of compliance about the situation, who then reported the incident to the NCAA. While many would argue that the NCAA should commend Tupou for trying to do the right thing and reporting the incident in a timely fashion, the NCAA instead suspended Tupou. Apparently, the NCAA regards violations of its amateurism regulations as strict liability offenses despite the obviously chilling effect that such a suspension will have on players reporting violations in the future.

Although the NCAA has no direct jurisdiction over agents, as described earlier, the UAAA does empower educational institutions with certain regulatory powers and the ability to file civil suits. Many NCAA member institutions require each agent wishing to recruit a player at that school to also register with the school's athletic department or compliance office. The majority of agents, however, do not comply. Educational institutions have the best resources and incentives to enforce the UAAA. Schools know or can reasonably find out with which agents their athletes have signed, and then determine whether the agent has met the requirements of the school's athletic department and the UAAA, most notably Section 11, which requires notice to the educational institution within seventy-two hours of the agency contract.

NCAA Bylaws also permit member institutions to use Professional Sports Counseling Panels ("PSCPs") to aid student-athletes during the agent-hiring process. PSCPs generally consist of coaches, athletic department representatives and members of the school's faculty or administration. While registration with the school and the use of PSCPs is meant to protect the student-athlete and allow the school to closely monitor agent activity with its student-athletes, the PSCPs can also create conflicts of interest. PSCPs can be used as a way of excluding certain agents, pushing student-athletes towards other agents (such as those representing the school's coaches), and extracting additional (generally permissible) benefits from the agent on behalf of the student-athlete, such as training costs, stipends or favorable commission arrangements.

In addition, due to the increasing complexities of the agent selection process, some schools have begun hiring consulting services to handle the process. Such relationships inevitably come with more accusations of conflicts of interest and favoritism, as the consultants are hired by the school and might have the school's best interests in mind rather than the student-athlete's.

Although the NCAA often acts demonstrably and decisively in dealing with its own members, the NCAA has no authority over agents. Conversely, NCAA member institutions have some authority over athletes; however, enforcement is still relatively lacking. While NCAA member institutions and their compliance staffs work diligently to ensure that they will not face any NCAA sanctions, they are understandably less interested in what the student-athlete does once the athlete's eligibility has been exhausted, perhaps explaining their indifference to Section 11 of the UAAA.

D. Bar Association Ethics Rules

Approximately half of the NFLPA's certified agents have a law degree. Presumably most of them followed up their J.D. by becoming a licensed attorney in one of the 50 states. If admitted to a state's bar, those agents are subject to the ethics rules of each state's bar association in which the agent-attorney is licensed to practice.

The Model Rules of Professional Conduct ("MRPC") list a plethora of rules that could be implicated by some of the wrongful behavior of agents. For example, Rule 1.1 requires "competent" representation, Rule 1.7 governs conflicts of interest, Rule 1.15 strictly directs how a lawyer is to handle client money, and Rule 5.3 holds attorneys liable for the conduct of non-lawyer employees, such as "runners." In addition, Rule 7.1 prohibits false or misleading communications about a lawyer's services, Rule 7.2 prohibits a lawyer from giving anything of value to a person for recommending the lawyer's services, and Rule 7.3 limits a lawyer's ability to solicit clients.

Evidence of wrongful attorney-agent behavior is difficult to obtain or verify. Nevertheless, attorney-agents arguably have the most interest in seeing bar ethics rules enforced against their fellow attorney-agents. Rule 8.3 specifically requires attorneys to report a *known* violation of the MRPC. Although there is generally not a requirement to report *suspected* violations, agent-attorneys should report the unethical conduct of other agent-lawyers to their respective bar associations. Reliable evidence is difficult to find, but agent-attorneys who desire a clean industry must self-police the industry. Bar association reporting requirements are implemented irrespective of any arbitration procedure that a PA may use to settle disputes between agents, as will be discussed in more detail below.

Bar association ethics rules have no jurisdiction over agents who are not attorneys, thereby creating a regulatory disparity. To remedy this, some have argued that the business of being an athlete-agent should be considered the "practice of law," thereby requiring all agents to be attorneys. Complicating the matter even further, the MRPC does not define the practice of law. Instead the code only prohibits the "unauthorized practice of law." What constitutes the practice of law is left to the broad interpretations of state courts and state bar associations. Thus, the practice of law includes a variety of services, such as litigating cases in court, preparing documents to bring about various transactions, and advising clients on legal questions. When analyzing an agent's time, it is difficult to classify the bulk of it as the practice of law. Much of an agent's time is spent representing the athlete in his or her relationships with the team, league, media, sponsors or fans. Contract negotiation is not exclusively a legal skill and agents rarely do any substantive legal analysis.

E. Player Association (PA) Regulations

On a daily basis, the most important regulatory scheme with which agents must deal is the PA. Pursuant to §9(a) of the National Labor Relations Act ("NLRA"), the PAs, as the approved representative of the player-employees by the National Labor Relations Board ("NLRB"), are the exclusive representative of the player-employees for purposes of collective bargaining. As the representative of the players, a union's main role is to negotiate the terms and conditions of employment with the league in a collective bargaining agreement ("CBA"). As the exclusive representative of employees, unions can designate agents to represent employees in dealings with an individual employer, such as a team. Each of the CBAs between the "Big 4" leagues and its respective PA recognizes the PA's exclusive jurisdiction over player agents.

As restrictions on player movement diminished and free agency became a reality in the 1970s and beyond, the use of player agents proliferated. Player salaries increased along with player movement, attracting more people to the player representation industry, which necessitated regulation. In 1982, the NFLPA became the first PA to certify and regulate player agents with other leagues soon to follow. The NBPA has not updated their regulations since 1991, the MLBPA since 1997 and the NHLPA since 2008.

The NFLPA updates its regulations every few years, most recently in 2007. The NFL agent industry seems to be the most competitive. The competition arises for a variety of reasons, including the fact that there are almost 1,700 roster spots in the NFL, about the same as the MLB, the NBA and the NHL combined, and there are no established minor leagues, where an agent might have to support a player financially. In addition, the NFLPA has a stringent registration process, requiring an application fee of $1,650, a postgraduate degree and successful completion of a written examination covering the CBA and agent regulations.

The agent regulations of the respective PAs bear significant similarity to one another. In all of them, Section 3(B) outlines prohibited conduct, including providing anything of value as an inducement to obtain a client, providing materially false or misleading information to a prospective client, holding a financial interest in a team, engaging in any conflict of interest, and engaging in unlawful conduct, dishonesty, fraud or deceit. Only the NFLPA specifically prohibits borrowing money from a player or soliciting clients who already have agents. In addition, Section 5 of all the regulations requires any dispute between the agent and the PA or another agent to be arbitrated. Since 1994, the NFLPA has designated the same arbitrator, Roger Kaplan, for every arbitration hearing, calling into question the fairness of the arbitration process.

The PAs have the most direct interest, knowledge and resources necessary for proper regulation and enforcement of agent behavior. There are still however significant questions about the strength and consistency of the enforcement of the PAs. As discussed earlier, the states have a difficult administrative task in enforcing their athlete-agent laws, which is made even more difficult by the PAs failure to communicate with the states regarding agent activity. Perhaps the most abused rule is the provision prohibiting inducements. While offering student-athletes cash or other benefits before they are secured as clients is obviously in violation of the rules, agents customarily give players money after they have signed. The money may be called a "signing bonus" or a stipend or guaranteed marketing income, but the end result is the same, no matter how the money is classified, the act of giving the money is unethical.

In the 2008 NFL Draft, thirty players chosen in the first three rounds were college juniors. Agents were not allowed, however, to actively recruit them because of the so-called "Junior Rule" which prohibited agents from having any contact with players not yet eligible for the NFL Draft until January 15. In the NFL, a player is not eligible for the draft until three NFL seasons have elapsed since his high school graduation, generally after his junior year of college. The rule only ended up benefiting the agents who ignored the rule and reached oral agreements with juniors before the permissible date. Thus, the rule was amended after the 2008 season to permit agents to have contact with juniors at the latest of the student-athlete's final regular season game, bowl game or the first day in December.

In any case, the fact remains that many people interested in obtaining a financial benefit from association with a future NFL player can and do contact the student-athletes long before they declare for the draft. To combat this and other problems, the NFLPA began regulating and requiring the registration of Financial Advisers in 2002. This program has not been without issues, and now the perception is that the regulations only empower other non-agents and non-financial advisors who are not prohibited from gaining access to the student-athletes, such as marketing representatives.***

NOTES AND QUESTIONS

1. Many player unions have created a standard representative contract for athletes and agents, with the goal of protecting the athletes. For example, the National Football League Players Association (NFLPA) does not allow an agent to represent a player in contract negotiations unless "he/she is (1) currently certified as a Contract Advisor pursuant to these Regulations [NFLPA Regulations]; (2) signs a Standard Representation Agreement with the player; and (3) files a fully executed copy of the Standard Representation Agreement with the NFLPA. . . ." *NFLPA Regulations Governing Contract Advisors,* 153 (as amended through June 2012). *See* Article 48, Section 1, of the *Collective Bargaining Agreement between the NFL and the NFLA* (establishing the NFPLA's authority to promulgate the Contract Advisors Regulations). The collective bargaining agreements negotiated by player unions and team owners require teams to sign athletes to standard player agreements. Player unions also set an agent's commission rates. For example, a Contract Advisor's maximum fee for negotiating a player's contract with a team is capped at 3% of the player's annual compensation for each year covered by the contract. *Id.* at 11, Section 4. Compensation is defined as "only salaries, signing bonuses, reporting bonuses, roster bonuses, Practice Squad [PS] salary in excess of the minimum [PS salary], and any performance incentives earned by the player during the term of the

contract (including any option year) negotiated by the Contract Advisor." *Id.* at Section 4, B (3). Compensation does not include certain honor incentive bonuses (*e.g.,* ALL PRO, PRO BOWL, Rookie of the Year) that are collectively bargained for by the players and owners. *Id.*

2. What is the agent's general legal duty in performing his obligations under the standard representation agreement? In *Zinn v. Parrish,* 644 F.2d 360 (7th Cir. 1977), agent Zinn and athlete Parrish signed a professional management agreement whereby Zinn would negotiate contracts, provide advice on business and tax matters, seek endorsements for Parrish, and furnish off-season employment. Zinn did not assist Parrish with finding any substantial endorsements or off-season employment. The Court held that the Zinn's good faith effort to secure these opportunities, "constitute[d] full performance of [his agency] obligations." *Id.* at 366. What kinds of conduct by an agent reflect a "good faith" effort in performing his or her obligations?

3. To what damages are an agent entitled when an athlete breaches the standard representation agreement? Is the agent entitled to the commission he would have received had the athlete not breached the contract? In *Total Economic Athletic Management America Inc. v. Pickens,* 898 S.W.2d 98 (Mo. Ct. App. W.D. 1995), Bruce Pickens engaged Total Economic Athletic Management America to be his agent in negotiating his NFL player contract. However, before negotiations, he engaged another contract adviser who actually negotiated the player contract. To prove damages, the first agent attempted to use the contracts that the second agent secured for Pickens, asserting a right to their contingency agreement. The court held that "technically, the agent is only entitled to damages for the breach of contract, *i.e.,* the value of the promised performance reduced by any expenses saved. In addition, the agent is entitled to his commission only if he can show that, had he been permitted to continue performance, he would have been able to consummate the contracts upon which he claims commission." *Id.* at 108.

4. In June 2019, Duke University freshman sensation Zion Williamson, shortly before being selected #1 by the New Orleans Pelicans in the NBA draft, filed a lawsuit against Prime Sports Marketing, claiming that his agency agreement with Prime Sports violated the UAAA. Prime Sports then filed a countersuit against Williams, arguing that the Act did not apply to Williamson because he had made it clear that he was going pro when he signed the agency contract. *See e.g.,* https://www.forbes.com/sites/legalentertainment/2019/06/28/zion-williamsons-100-million-problem/#3347145e1fbf.

D. ETHICAL CONSIDERATIONS

SPORTS AGENTS: ETHICAL REPRESENTATIVES OR OVERLY AGGRESSIVE ADVERSARIES?

STACEY B. EVANS[1]

17 VILL. SPORTS & ENT. L.J. 91 (2010)

I. Introduction

A. Definition and Qualifications of a Sports Agent

Though sports agents can, and often do, perform almost every service for their clients, most "sports agent" definitions focus only on the bare-bones agent responsibilities. Degree Directory defines a sports agent as someone who "handles contract negotiations, public relations issues and finances, and he or she will often procure additional sources of income for the athlete (such as endorsements)." These definitions do not reflect the extent to which athletes often become dependent on their agents or that the agents become deeply entrenched in their clients' personal lives. For example, clients may look to their agents for guidance in personal business matters, such as investments and other financial decisions. Similarly, most definitions do not indicate the extensive skill base that agents must possess in order to effectively represent their clients. Knowing how to negotiate is perhaps the most important skill that a sports agent can possess. Negotiating a good employment contract directly affects an agent's salary, because an agent receives a commission that is usually based on between two and five percent of the contract, with additional percentage for any endorsement contracts.

Many sports agents have a legal background, enabling them competently to navigate complex contract provisions. It could be argued that attorney-agents receive valuable training in law school that non-attorney agents never learn, including ethical training. For this reason, many argue that an attorney-agent is more beneficial to a client than a non-attorney-agent.

Because attorneys typically receive training in contracts, negotiation, antitrust, and agency law, they possess a set of skills and education which allow them to help their clients obtain advantageous contracts. Moreover, an athlete can rest easy, knowing that an attorney-agent is held to a strict code of ethics and may face severe penalties if he or she is found to act unethically or illegally.

B. Public Opinion of Sports Agents and Sports Agents' Regulation

---

1 Stacey B. Evans is a 2008 graduate of the West Virginia University College of Law, and currently works as the U.S. Marketing Manager for Canada's #1-ranked law firm, Blake, Cassels & Graydon LLP. Prior to joining Blakes, Stacey was a Senior Legal Conference Director at the American Conference Institute.

2 See Melissa Steedle Bogad, *Maybe Jerry Maguire Should Have Stuck with Law School: How the Sports Agent Responsibility and Trust Act Implements Lawyer-Like Rules for Sports Agents*, 27 Cardozo L. Rev. 1889, 1893 (2006)(indicating that attorneys are subject to ethical codes and that violations can lead to sanctions).

The term "sports agent" often elicits images of sleazy, money hungry individuals.[3] Many people perceive agents as "serpents . . . poised to strike at the wealth professional athletes earn in such plenty."[4] Former Chicago Bears General Manager Jerry Vainisi even referred to agents as "parasites."[5] Additionally, many team owners and fans believe that player greed, encouraged by agents, is ruining professional sports. Efforts have been made to enact federal legislation to regulate sports agents, but such legislation is not binding on states. Each professional league and players' union is left to ensure that agents meet an ethical standard and that they act in a manner that is in the best interest of sports.

II. The Evolution of Sports Agents in Player Negotiations

A. History

Today's agents need to be creative when negotiating player bonuses, no-trade clauses, guaranteed contracts and multi-year deals. The career of an average professional athlete is relatively short, and they rely on agents to get the most money possible in order to ensure financial security for the future. In this atmosphere, agents must walk a fine line of being as hardnosed as possible, while still considering the best long-term strategy for their clients, and actually producing an ethically viable deal. In the short-term, working with teams concerned about the bottom line may prove difficult, but in the long run, this strategy will probably yield the best return for the players. Additionally, through negotiation methods like "Final Offer Arbitration," agents may negotiate for intangible and interest-based benefits such as single occupancy rooms during road trips, higher food allowances, and the use of private jets, which will reward the player for his hard work and skills without bleeding a league dry.

Because contemporary deals are often legally complex, there is an ever-increasing need for competent, reliable and trust-worthy sports agents. In the past athletes commonly negotiated their own contracts.[6] Those athletes did not possess the technical skills or knowledge to negotiate their own contracts effectively and could not hire others to help them. Athletes in every sport had to fight in order to win the right to negotiate contracts and obtain agent representation. Baseball players were among the first to use agents, and other sports leagues slowly caught onto the trend.

---

3 See Craig Neff, Den of Vipers, A Sports Scourge: Bad Agents, Sports Illustrated, Oct. 19, 1987, at 76, available at http://vault.sportsillustrated.cnn.com/vault/article/magazine/MAG1066585/1/index.htm (conveying generally negative reputation of agents).

4 Id. (describing sports agents according to popular perception).

5 See id. (stating Vainisi's opinion of agents).

6 See Kenneth L. Shropshire and Timothy Davis, The Business of Sports Agents 5 (University of Pennsylvania Press 2d ed. 2008) at 24 (proposing possible drawbacks to self-representation). Early examples of athletes negotiating for themselves include: Danny Ainge of the Boston Celtics, Alan Trammel of the Detroit Tigers, and Mike Singletary of the Chicago Bears. See id.

B. Specific Examples of Past Player-League Negotiations

Major League Baseball ("MLB") player and Hall of Fame inductee Ralph Kiner played during the 1940s and 1950s, when there were no agents or attorneys to assist players in negotiating contracts. Negotiations took place strictly between a player and his team's general manager. In that era, a player signed a baseball contract for life and not for a specified period of time. Because no-trade clauses did not yet exist, a player had three choices – agree to the contract, be traded, or not play baseball.

In 1952, Kiner challenged these norms by arriving to a MLB Executive Council meeting with his attorney. However, at the meeting, the Executive Council prohibited the attorney from becoming involved in the negotiation. Kiner responded by walking out of the room, and a lengthy bargaining impasse soon followed. This "take it or leave it" style of negotiating created a lack of player autonomy, and eventually in 1966, baseball players formed the MLB Players' Association ("MLBPA") in order to protect the rights to their careers. In 1970, the MLBPA negotiated for its players to the right to select the agents who could represent them during their individual contract negotiations.

Other leagues gradually followed, as Baseball was not the only sport in which professional players needed agents. One example of this is Billy Cannon, an All-American football player at Louisiana State University in the late 1950s.[7] Cannon entered the 1960 NFL draft and was drafted by the Los Angeles Rams. After Cannon signed three standard player contracts with the Rams, a representative from the Houston Oilers, a team in the rival American Football League ("AFL"), contacted him about playing for their team. Following a meeting with the Oilers' management, Cannon sent a letter to the Rams stating he no longer wished to remain a Ram and returned the money he had been given. The Rams sought an injunction to prevent Cannon from playing in the AFL. The Court allowed Cannon to breach his contract, stating that because he was "without counsel or advice and the whole transaction . . . was completed in less than 48 hours," the actions of Cannon and the Rams did not create a binding contract. The Southern District of California found that "amateur athletes need agent representation in order to protect their interests and match the negotiating skill of a general manager or member of a professional team."

Historically, coaches and sports leagues have been wary of working with sports agents, perhaps because sports agents empower their players, helping them get more money and benefits than the leagues would like to give. For example, Jim Ringo, a 1960s all-pro center Green Bay Packers needed to negotiate a new contract early in his career. Ringo brought an agent with him to a 1963 meeting with legendary Packer's coach Vince Lombardi. Coach Lombardi left the room and phoned the Philadelphia Eagles to make a trade. At the time, Lombardi probably refused to negotiate with the agent, because agents had a bad reputation and were not widely utilized in the league.

Today agents are an ordinary and essential part of any professional athlete's life. Nevertheless, there exists a potential for agents to earn large commissions at the expense of their clients and

---

7   *See L.A. Rams Football Club v. Cannon*, 185 F. Supp. 717, 719 (S.D. Cal. 1960)(providing background information about Cannon).

against the interest of the player's team. Therefore, sound training for agents in collaborative negotiations and the application of a code of strict ethical regulations (which will force agents to work more with sports leagues instead of against them) is necessary.

C. The Expanding Role of Sports Agents and Their Questionable Ethical Practices

1. Sports Agent Training and Responsibilities

Competition among sports agents has created an intense pressure to successfully negotiate contracts for big-name athletes. Although, the original function of sports agents was to negotiate contracts for players, the role of the agent has greatly expanded. Many agents now serve as financial managers, public relations specialists, investment as well as tax experts, and legal counsel, all of which require agents to perform specific functions.

Among the services that sports agents provide are the following: (1) Determining the value of a player's services; (2) Negotiation of the player's contract with the club, including salary, incentives, bonuses, guarantees, no-trade clauses, and length of contract; (3) Soliciting and arranging product endorsements, speaking engagements, and other uses of the player's name and image for commercial purposes; (4) Promoting the athlete's career through public relations, media coverage, and charitable activities; (5) Providing financial management services; (6) Resolving conflicts that arise concerning areas such as enforcement of employment contracts, and behavioral problems such as substance abuse; (7) Representing players in salary or grievance arbitration matters; (8) Arranging for movement of the player in the labor market; and, (9) Counseling a player about his post-career years.[8]

Given these expanded roles, legal training can be a distinct asset for an agent. In addition to learning attention to detail, legal training may benefit athletes with "property sales and purchases, investment oversight, formulation of trust, wills, and LLCs, prenuptials, and other needs that high-income earners may have."[9] The non-attorney-agent may not possess the same skill set to help safeguard an athlete's assets. The media has reported stories of athletes who made millions of dollars and squandered the money before the end of their careers. These athletes typically did not have the assistance of a trained professional to help them make better financial and life choices.

Another significant problem with non-attorney agents is that, other than passing a licensing test, sports agents licensing requires little to no requirements or background checks. This problem, in turn, creates the problem of inability to seek redress against negligent non-attorney agents. The process of licensing agents does not provide training sessions or specific ethical instructions. Unlike state bar associations that conduct rigorous background and character

---

1   8   Paul D. Staudohar, *So You Want to Be a Sports Agent*, 57 Lab. L.J. 4, 251 (2006) available at *http://www.allbusiness.com/human-resources/employee-benefits-benefits/4063876-1.html.* ("However, a single person rarely provides all of the functions. It is not uncommon for the agency function to be bifurcated into a single agent handling all aspects of negotiations on behalf of players ... while another agent or firm handles financial management and planning tasks.").

2   9   Jack Bechta, Two Paths to Becoming an Agent, Nat'l Football Post, June 30, 2009, available at http://www.nationalfootballpost.com/Two-paths-to-becoming-an-agent.html.

checks on each lawyer before admitting them, a players' association may not take the time or use the resources to conduct a comprehensive investigation. Similarly, agent licensing does not necessarily include any assessment of skill level or character. Conversely, attorneys have strict codes of professional conduct.

2. The Unethical Side of Sports Agenting

Ethics play a large part in the agent industry. Unfortunately, for clients with "non-attorney" agents, there are no mandated ethical codes of conduct. Furthermore, there is dispute among attorney-agents as to whether they should be held to the Model Rules of Professional Responsibility when their non-attorney agent counterparts are not. This view, however, has not been shared by some courts, which have held that "[a]s long as a lawyer is engaged in the practice of law, he is bound by the ethical requirements of that profession, and he may not defend his actions by contending that he was engaged in some other kind of professional activity."[10] This standard may place attorney-agents at a marketplace disadvantage to their "non-attorney-agent counterparts" who are not held to such ethical rules.

The amount of money typically made by professional athletes has caused several agents to go to unscrupulous measures to make the most money possible.[11] In some instances, agents are not interested in the best possible playing scenario for their client, but instead, how they personally can make the most money. Depending on the collective bargaining agreement of the league, agents stand to make anywhere from two to five percent commission on a player's negotiated contract. For example, Scott Boras could have made $14 million on the 2008 deal he negotiated for the Yankees' Alex Rodriguez.

Besides the general perils of negotiation and agent-league relations, collective bargaining agreements present another potential contractual hindrance for players and agents. In a typical collective bargaining agreement, an individual player gives up the freedom to contract for him or herself "for the good of the group." Salary terms and other conditions of employment bind all members of the collective bargaining unit under the terms of one contract. Therefore, an existing collective bargaining agreement constrains the ability of an agent to negotiate for an individual player, and thus, can create tensions between one player and the rest of the team, since additional money given to one player takes money away from his teammates. An example of one such constraint is the NFL's rookie pool. In the NFL rookie pool, the NFL establishes an amount of money that may be used for first-year players. In this rookie pool, while agents are helpful in negotiating roster or signing bonuses, the collective bargaining agreement uses a de facto slotted pay scale. This scale "involves paying draft choices the same amount of money received by the player drafted in the same position or slot in the previous draft, plus a percentage

---

10   In re Dwight, 573 P.2d 481, 484 (Ariz. 1977).

11   See Bryan Couch, *How Agent Competition and Corruption Affects Sports and the Athlete-Agent Relationship and What Can Be Done to Control It*, 10 SETON HALL J. SPORT L. 111, 118 (2000)("The only concern was the almighty dollar, both for the player and the agent, which turns athletics into a business full of overpaid egomaniacs more concerned with the best contract or endorsement deal than with the game itself."). Because of limits on the amount of an agent's commission, some agents resort to lies and exaggeration in order to steal clients from other agents. See id. at 119-20.

raise to reflect inflation."[12] An agent who claims that he or she can get an NFL draftee the most amount of money is not being entirely truthful with the client, because the funds are coming from a finite pool that is largely predetermined based on draft number; perhaps the agent could negotiate for a contract that offered more than the team originally intended, but each team still has a salary cap. These situations can become tense, as agents try to wrestle more money away from the league and the team. Additionally, agents in these situations may resort to adversarial or deceptive tactics to try get as much money as possible in the short-term for their clients and also to make the client think that all money and benefits received were solely because of his negotiating. Agents need to be held accountable for all unethical practices that arise in these situations, and perhaps the best way to hold agents accountable would be by developing an industry-wide sports agent's ethical code.

3. How Necessary Is a Sports Agent?

Players are constantly expecting more from their agents, but many do not realize that a contract has very little to do with the agent's negotiating talents. It is the player's success on the field, court, or ice, rather, that leads to a more lucrative contract. The market for an athlete in a sports league is largely a result of team needs and how a team views the free-agent market-place. However, agents sometimes misread the marketplace, at great costs to their clients. For example, baseball player Manny Ramirez overestimated the demand for his skills and damaged his prospects as a result. In 2008, he turned down several lucrative short-term offers based on the advice of his agent Scott Boras, who was convinced that Manny could get a four-or-five year contract. As of February 2009, with Manny unsigned, it became clear that he would not receive the massive contract he initially sought. Subsequently in March 2009, Ramirez signed a two-year, $45 million contract with the Los Angeles Dodgers, including a whopping $25 million of deferred monies.

Though, it is important to note that while an athlete's skills are the most important factor in the athlete's contractual power, athletes still need advice on the legal matters involved in creating those contracts. As NBA superstar LeBron James discovered, agents need to be available to athletes to make sure the athletes' contracts and finances are protected and soundly invested. In 2005, LeBron James shocked the league when he fired his agent and hired three friends to take over management duties. As one of the most popular, lucrative, and visible athletes in the world, NBA management was worried about how three highly inexperienced young men would manage James's career. James, however, soon realized the need for an attorney-agent. In addition to the team of legal, financial, and public relations professionals associated with LeBron's

---

1   12   Id. ESPN analyst Len Pasquarelli described the pool as follows:

The rookie pool is essentially a cap within a cap. It represents the maximum amount that each franchise can spend, in terms of total cap dollars, on its first-year players. A team's rookie allocation pool is part of, not in addition to, the league's overall spending limit of about $127 million per franchise. The formula for arriving at each team's rookie pool is viewed as somewhat Byzantine by even the most astute number-crunchers in the NFL. It is basically a function of how many overall choices each club makes and where those picks are slotted in each round. Len Pasquarelli, Lions Lead in Rookie Allocation Money, ESPN.com, http:// sports.espn.go.com/nfl/news/story?id=4111513 (last visited Oct. 31, 2009).

friend-run marketing empire, he has now retained the services of Leon Rose, a well-known attorney-agent. When hundreds of millions of dollars are on the line, a professional athlete's affairs cannot be left to inexperience, chance, and friendship.

Even though a player's skill is his best selling point, agents are still necessary to ensure that the player is protected, compensated and remains in the sport as long as possible. Though agents often overestimate and overstate their power in contract negotiation to their clients, they still have value and are necessary to athletes to explain legal, contractual, financial and other concepts.

III. Current Agent Regulations

In 1983, as a result of National Football League Players Association ("NFLPA") action, the NFL became the first professional sports league to regulate agents. Under the agreement, teams can only negotiate a player's contract with certified agents.[13] Any Individual seeking certification as an NFL contract adviser must take a test and fulfill other essential requirements.[14] The test has questions based on the collective bargaining agreement, the salary cap and the free agency system. Potential agents who fail this exam may be suspended or decertified by the NFL Players Association.

In addition to the NFL, some states have agent regulation acts aimed at protecting student-athletes. Many rookie athletes are too trusting and vulnerable when negotiating their first contract with an agent. One problem is that if an agent is not an attorney, a player cannot bring suit against the agent for malpractice. Although, a players' union may require an agent to carry professional liability insurance, the NFL Players' Association is the only player's union to require an agent to carry malpractice insurance. The National Collegiate Athletic Association's ("NCAA") guidelines specify that a student-athlete may receive advice from an attorney regarding a proposed professional contract, but that attorney may not represent the athlete in negotiation.

A. Issues Involving Conflicts of Interest

1. Agents Representing Multiple Clients

A conflict of interest occurs when a duty owed to one party is "compromised by a separate interest or agreement with a third party."[15] Conflicts of interest may arise if an agent represents

---

13   See NFL Players Association, NFLPA Regulations Governing Contract Advisors, at 7-9, available at *http://www.nflplayers.com/user/template.aspx?fmid=181&lmid=233&pid=0&type=l* (follow "download a PDF version of the regulations" hyperlink)(establishing rules governing negotiations between teams and agents).

14   See *id.* at 10-14 (providing requirements for becoming NFL agent). Individuals wishing to be certified as NFL agents must now have a master's degree. Id. Other certification requirements include: a $1,650.00 application fee, passing the NFLPA test, attendance at a two (2) day seminar in Washington, DC, and successful completion of a written, proctored examination. Id. Following successfully passing the exam, the agent must obtain professional liability insurance from an approved carrier. Id.; see also The Sports Law Professor, The Problem with NFL Player Agents, *http:// thesportslawprofessor.blogspot.com/2007/10/problem-with-nfl-player-agents.html* (last visited Oct. 31, 2009) (exemplifying that moving toward greater education is one way NFL tries to protect its players).

15   Shropshire & Davis, supra note 6, at 79.

multiple players who play the same position, or play for the same team, and both are trying to negotiate contracts. In 1996, attorney-agent David Falk faced this problem when he represented top basketball player Juwan Howard and tried to negotiate a deal with the NBA's Miami Heat. When the deal fell through, Falk secured a contract for Howard with the Washington Bullets. In doing so, Falk arguably neglected one of his average players, Rex Chapman, who wanted to re-sign with the Miami Heat and was unable to do so. If an agent secures a more lucrative contract for one player, it may cause a rift in his or her relationship with another player, or may slight the average player in favor of the superstar client.

In the case of rookie NFL players, an agent may try to negotiate two or more contracts from a finite pool of money, because when one player takes up more salary cap room, less money is available for the other player. Such an example occurred in 2006 when quarterback Jay Cutler entered the NFL draft from Vanderbilt University. He hired James "Bus" Cook, a licensed attorney, to represent him. Cutler and his family told Cook that they did not want Cook to represent another top quarterback, a reasonable request for a player desiring his agent to look out for his best interests. Despite the request, Cook signed University of Texas quarterback Vince Young to a client representation agreement. The Tennessee Titans drafted Young third overall, while the Denver Broncos drafted Cutler eleventh overall. It is unclear how Cook could effectively represent both players, as they were vying to be drafted from the same pool of teams.

There are many situations in which an agent cannot adequately represent two clients, because the interests of the clients are directly adverse. In these situations, the clients would benefit from an ethical rule similar to the attorney ethical conflict rule that forbids an agent to act in these situations. Such a rule should be created to best protect professional athletes.

2. The Importance of Trust In Agent-Client Relationships

The relationship between athlete and agent is based on trust. Most athletes spend a great deal of time evaluating representatives in attempting choose the right one. Unfortunately, sometimes vetting is not enough and athletes often find themselves misguided, misled and defrauded.

Picking the wrong agent can adversely affect the rest of an athlete's life, wasting the athlete's life's work and earnings and threatening his family's welfare. For example, one agent named Richard Sorkin, who could not properly manage his clients' affairs, damaged their careers and finances. Sorkin was a sportswriter turned non-attorney agent who represented more than fifty NHL and NBA players in the 1970s. Sorkin "squandered an estimated $1.2 million of his clients' money, much of it on his own gambling and stock market ventures." In 1978, Sorkin pleaded guilty to seven counts of grand larceny and was sentenced to three years in prison. Sorkin is not alone, as he is just one among a number of agents who have utilized a position of trust with their clients in order to bilk millions of dollars from them.

In other cases, conflicts with agents result in lawsuits, as was the case with late Hall of Fame NFL player, Reggie White, who spent eight years as a defensive end for the Philadelphia Eagles. During his time with the Eagles, non-attorney agent Patrick Forte represented White. While Forte was negotiating a new contract between White and the Eagles, he was also negotiating on his own behalf to become an assistant to Eagles' president, Harry Gamble. White filed suit in U.S. District Court seeking $1.5 million from Forte. White alleged Forte neglected to tell him about an option year on his contract.[16] White charged that Forte "pursued his [Forte's] employment with the Eagles at the same time that he was ostensibly representing the best interests of White." The suit was later dropped after White was able to come to a contract agreement with the Eagles, but his relationship with the team was irreparably cracked. In 1993, this fissure came to a head when White left the Eagles as a free agent to join the Green Bay Packers.

William "Tank" Black is another example of a non-attorney sports agent who allowed greed and unethical behavior to interfere with the job he was hired to perform. Black was certified as a player-agent with both the NFL and NBA. Yet, he misappropriated more than $14 million from his clients. Black was convicted in Florida of fraud, conspiracy, and obstruction of justice charges, for which he spent five years in prison. One of Black's clients, Fred Taylor, was drafted ninth by the Jacksonville Jaguars in the 1998 NFL Draft. Taylor selected Black because of his ability to work with people and foster personal relationships. At Black's trial, Taylor, who had been swindled out of his $5 million signing bonus, sat on the witness stand crying, "I agreed with everything he said . . . I trusted him with my life, with my daughter's life." Black abused the position of trust and confidence that he enjoyed with his clients and acted as an unregistered investment adviser and unregistered broker-dealer, in violation of regulations promulgated by the Securities and Exchange Commission.

If consistent professional rules of conduct were in place for sports agents, there would be established ethical standards to which every player representative would be held. With sports being a multi-billion dollar industry, agents must be held accountable in order to protect athletes' best interests. Bad business advice may leave an athlete unprepared to wisely invest the money he or she has earned during his or her playing days, money that in many cases must last for the duration of the athlete's life. Several states have passed legislation to require agent registration.[17] Enforcement by states, however, has been "uneven and unpredictable." Agent regulation continues to be a business and legal battleground.

V. Recommendations

The sports agent industry is largely "devoid of systematically enforceable regulations, which truly dictate minimum levels of professional expertise or accountability."[18] Sports leagues should enact a uniform regulation system, such as the American Bar Association Model Rules

---

16 See *id.* (noting allegations involved in player's lawsuit against agent).

17 See Doyice Cotton and John T. Wolohan, Law For Recreation and Sport Managers 657 (Kendall Hunt Publ'g Co. 2003) (listing regulations imposed by states). A number of states now regulate the activities of sports agent. Id. A problem arises; however, because most state regulations are vague and vary considerably from state to state. Id. This lack of uniformity has limited the number of sports agents who actually register in each state. Id. An agent who intends to do business in a large number of states may find himself trying to comply with 30 different sets of registration requirements and regulatory schemes. Id.

18 Marc J. Kessler, Who Can Best Represent Professional Athletes: Lawyer vs. Non-Lawyer, Columbus Bar Ass'n J. (2005), available at http:// www.peoplesbar.org/legalresources/ Articles/AthleteRepresentation.pdf.

of Professional Conduct ("Model Rules").[19] With no strict guidelines, the leagues essentially give sports agents unrestricted power in the way they operate. Leagues could also benefit by enacting a continuing education program to ensure that agents are current with regard to the laws and practices of each league. Players would be well advised to understand the difference between attorney and non-attorney representatives. The NFL now requires a graduate degree before an individual will be certified as a player agent. This added emphasis on education should serve as a wake-up call to professional athletes. Attorneys have the educational background to have a better understanding of contracts, labor laws and tax ramifications. An attorney-agent is bound by the Model Rules, and failure to comply with this code of ethics may result in disciplinary action. Attorney agents offer substantial, significant, and meaningful advantages for athletes that non-attorney agents simply cannot.

In the growing era of "show me the money," it would be wise for athletes to hire an attorney to help them maximize their potential earnings. However, this attorney cannot be just any attorney. He must be a well educated, well trained and ethical, and most importantly, he must seek to promote his client and not himself. As the late attorney-agent Mark McCormack – founder of IMG and the representative for Jack Nicklaus, Gary Player, Greg Norman, and Annika Sorenstam, among many others – once said: "The client is the story, not the agent . . . . We make money by helping the client make money. The second you become more important than the client you represent is the moment you need to get out of this business."[20]

NOTES & QUESTIONS

1. In addition to the special considerations regarding the capacity to contract, there are other legal problems associated with representing minor athletes (typically figure skaters and gymnasts). For example what problems do you think that you might encounter in arranging production of a television commercial? Do you suppose, for example, that there are state child labor laws that affect the hours that a minor can work on the set? Do you suppose that there are state laws regarding providing tutoring in the event that the minor has to miss school for training or taping commercial advertisements?

2. Do non-attorney agents commit the unauthorized practice of law when they negotiate and advise clients on the legal effects of contracts? See David S. Caudill, *Sports and Entertainment Agents and Agent-Attorneys: Discourses and Conventions Concerning Crossing Jurisdictional and Professional Boarders,* 43 Akron L. Rev. 697 (2010)(arguing that negotiating contracts on behalf of clients and advising them about their legality constitutes the unauthorized practice of law, although most courts reject this argument).

---

19 See Model Rules of Professional Conduct (2009), http:// www.abanet.org/cpr/mrpc/mrpc_toc.html (listing Model Rules); see also Kessler, supra note 18 (contrasting attorney-agents, who are held to profession's ethical standards, with non-attorney-agents, who are not).

20 Betsy Nagelson McCormack & Steve Eubanks, Golf's Ultimate CEO: Mark McCormack was the World's First Super-Agent, and His Methods Stand Up Today, Golf Digest, Oct. 2006, at 35 (explaining role of agents).

Further Reading on Agency:

An Inside Look at the World of Agents: Past, Present, and Future: Panels 1 & 3., 21 Jeffrey S. Moorad Sports L.J. 259 (2014).

Walter T. Champion, *Attorneys Qua Sports Agents: An Ethical Conundrum,* 7 Marq. Sports L.J. 349 (1997).

Phillip Closius, *Hell Hath No Fury Like a Fan Scorned: State Regulation of Sports Agents,* 30 U. Tol. L. Rev. 511 (1999).

Robert N. Davis, *Exploring the Contours of Agent Regulation: The Uniform Athlete Agents Act,* 8 Vill. Sports & Ent. L.J. 1 (2001).

Marc Edelman, *Disarming the Trojan Horse of the Uaaa and Sparta: How America Should Reform Its Sports Agent Laws to Conform with True Agency Principles,* 4 Harv. J. Sports & Ent. L. 145 (2013).

Chris J. Evanoff, *Show Me the Money: How the ABA Model Rules of Professional Conduct Can Deter NCAA Rules Violations Involving Sports Agents & College Athletes,* 8 DePaul J. Sports L. & Contemp. Probs. 63 (2011).

W. Jack Grosse, *The Regulation, Control, and Protection of Athlete Agents,* 19 N. Ky. L. Rev. 49 (1991).

James Halt, *Andy Oliver Strikes Out the NCAA's "No-Agent" Rule for College Baseball,* 19 J. Legal Aspects Sport 185 (2009).

Darren A. Heitner & Bryan Saul, *Jay Z Has 99 Problems, and Being A Sports Agent May Be One,* 24 Marq. Sports L. Rev. 59 (2013).

James Masteralexis et. al., *Enough Is Enough: The Case for Federal Regulation of Sport Agents,* 20 Jeffrey S. Moorad Sports L.J. 69 (2013).

Jeffrey C. Meehan, *Harvard or Hardball? An Examination of Ethical Issues Faced by Lawyer-Agents,* 21 Sports Law. J. 45 (2014).

Matthew Mills, T*here Is No Need to Reinvent the Wheel: The Tools to Prevent Agent-Related NCAA Violations May Already Be in Our Hands,* 22 Seton Hall J. Sports & Ent. L. 345 (2012).

Jerry R. Parkinson, *Oliver with A Twist: The NCAA's No-Agent Rules Applied to Non-Lawyer Representatives of Baseball Student-Athletes,* 41 J.C. & U.L. 257 (2015).

Zach Schreiber, *Leveling the Playing Field for Sports Agents: How the Two-Hat Theory and the Model Rules of Professional Conduct Collide,* 19 Tex. Rev. Ent. & Sports L. 13 (2018).

Jan Stiglitz, *NCAA Based Agent Regulation, Who are We Protecting,* 67 N.D. L. Rev. 215 (1991).

Ross Viltz, Chad Seifried, Jeremy Foreman, *An Analysis of Sports Agent Regulation in Intercollegiate Athletics: A Call for Cooperation,* 24 J. Leg. Aspects Sport 62 (2014).

John C. Weistart & Cym H. Lowell, Law of Sports, § 3.17-3.19 (Bobbs-Merrill Company, Inc., 1979.

CHAPTER 11
INTELLECTUAL PROPERTY

A significant number of legal concerns in today's sports marketplace relate to intellectual property. Broadcast rights and copyrights for sporting events form the bases for multimillion dollar industries. The growth of sports-exclusive television such as ESPN has been phenomenal (*i.e.,* ESPN 2, ESPN-News, ESPNU, TSN, the NHL Network, *etc.*). The cases in this chapter introduce several key concepts and questions about copyright, misappropriation, trademark law, and the right of publicity. *Pittsburgh Athletic* and *Motorola* introduce the fundamental rules regarding Copyright and Misappropriation. *Monster Communications* expands our understanding of Copyright Law and sheds light on one of the most intriguing aspects of copyright, fair use.

The *Adidas* case[1] introduces trademark principles. Trademark law affects sports in diverse ways. Athletic equipment companies use trademarks for their products and franchises use them for their teams. For example, trademark rights questions frequently arise in situations where franchises relocate and change their names with increasing regularity (*e.g.,* the transformation of the Montreal Expos to the Washington Nationals). And trademark law can pose serious ethical concerns, for example in situations involving Native American team names such as the Washington Redskins and Chicago Blackhawks.[2]

O'Brien offers an historical perspective on the important right of publicity. And *Abdul-Jabbar* exemplifies a more modern application of the principles first developed in the *O'Brien*

---

1 The authors have liberally edited this case. In fact, this case has been edited so extensively that we have departed from what has been our normal and customary practice throughout most of this casebook, and have largely omitted the use of asterices and elipses to denote omitted words, sentences, and paragraphs.

2 For decades public debate and legal battles have focused on sports teams' use of Native American nicknames and mascots. The most prominent of these battles centered on the Washington Redskins. Among others, the Cleveland Indians' mascot, Chief Wahoo, has also engendered controversy. The legal battle hinged primarily on the federal trademark statute, the Lanham Act, which prohibited registration of disparaging trademarks. On June 19, 2017, the United States Supreme Court rendered its decision in *Matal v. Tam.* 137 S.Ct. 1744 (2017). Writing for the Court, Justice Alito held that the "may disparage" provision of § 2(a) of the Lanham Act (disparagement clause) is unconstitutional because it violates the Free Speech clause of the First Amendment. Id. at 1751. Two years prior, the Eastern District of Virginia had upheld the Trademark Trial and Appeal Board's decision to cancel the Redskins trademarks. *Pro-Football, Inc. v. Blackhorse,* 112 F. Supp. 3d 439 (E.D. Va. 2015). Pro-Football, Inc., appealed the case to the Fourth Circuit in October 2015, and then, after the Supreme Court granted certiorari for *Tam,* Pro-Football filed a special request to join that appeal. The Supreme Court denied Pro-Football, Inc.'s petition on October 3, 2016, and on October 19, 2016, the Fourth Circuit agreed to postpone *Blackhorse* until after the Supreme Court's decision in Tam. Shortly after the Supreme Court's decision in *Tam,* the Fourth Circuit reversed and vacated the District Court's Blackhorse decision. Professor VerSteeg has written two articles discussing and exploring many of the issues related to these matters. RussVerSteeg, *Blackhawk Down or Blackhorse Down? The Lanham Act's Prohibition of Trademarks that "May Disparage" & the First Amendment,* 68 Okla. L. Rev. 677 (2016) and Russ VerSteeg, *Historical Perspectives & Reflections on Matal v. Tam and the Future of Offensive Trademarks,* 25 J. INTELLECTUAL PROPERTY 109 (2017). Meanwhile, the Cleveland Indians retired the use of Chief Wahoo on their uniforms after the 2018 season. *See e.g., http://www.espn.com/mlb/story/_/id/22255143/cleveland-indians-removing-chief-wahoo-logo-uniforms.*

dissent, and presents a fairly matter-of-fact summary of the current status of the law. The note about *C.B.C. Distribution and Marketing* summarizes a number of intellectual property and right of publicity issues as they relate to online fantasy league games.

A. MISAPPROPRIATION & COPYRIGHT

PITTSBURGH ATHLETIC CO. V. KQV BROADCASTING
24 F.SUPP. 490 (1938)
DISTRICT COURT, W.D. PENNSYLVANIA

SCHOONMAKER, DISTRICT JUDGE.

This is an action in equity in which plaintiffs ask for a preliminary injunction to restrain defendant from broadcasting play-by-play reports and descriptions of baseball games played by the "'Pirates," a professional baseball team owned by Pittsburgh Athletic Company, both at its home baseball park in Pittsburgh, known as "Forbes Field," and at baseball parks in other cities.

* * *

Defendant disclaimed any intention to broadcast the news of any games played by the "Pirates" in cities other than Pittsburgh during the current season; and by affidavit filed in this case stated that no news had been broadcast by it of such "away" games since May 26, 1938. For that reason there appears to be no such danger of imminent injury to the rights of the plaintiffs as to justify a preliminary injunction, so far as concern any games played by the "Pirates" in cities other than Pittsburgh.

As to the games played, and to be played at Forbes Field in Pittsburgh, defendant admits it has broadcast play-by-play news of the Pittsburgh games, and asserts its intention to continue so to do, averring it secures the news thus broadcast and to be broadcast by it in the future from observers whom it has stationed at vantage points outside Forbes Field who can see over the enclosure of that field and observe the plays as they are made. It asserts it has a legal right to continue this practice.

The essential facts are not in dispute. The question at issue is primarily a question of law. Is the defendant within its legal rights in the practices thus pursued by it? The essential facts of the case may be briefly summarized as follows:

The plaintiff Pittsburgh Athletic Company owns a professional baseball team known as the "Pirates," and is a member of an association known as the "National League." With the several teams of the members of the League, the "Pirates" play baseball both at its home field and at the home fields of the other members of the League in various cities. The home games are played at a baseball park known as "Forbes Field" which is enclosed by high fences and structures so that the public are admitted only to the Park to witness the games at Forbes Field by the payment of an admission ticket, which provides that the holder of the admission ticket agrees not to give out any news of the game while it is in progress.

The Pittsburgh Athletic Company has granted by written contract, for a valuable consideration, to General Mills, Inc., the exclusive right to broadcast, play-by-play, descriptions or accounts of the games played by the "Pirates" at this and other fields. The National Broadcasting Company, also for a valuable consideration, has contracted with General Mills, Inc., to broadcast by radio over stations KDKA and WWSW, play-by-play descriptions of these games. The Socony-Vacuum Oil Company has purchased for a valuable consideration a half interest in the contract of the General Mills, Inc.

The defendant operates at Pittsburgh, a radio broadcasting station known as KQV, from which it has in the past broadcast by radio play-by-play descriptions of the games played by the "Pirates" at Pittsburgh, and asserts its intention to continue in so doing. The defendant secures the information which it broadcasts from its own paid observers whom it stations at vantage points outside Forbes Field on premises leased by defendant. These vantage points are so located that the defendant's observers can see over the enclosures the games as they are played in Forbes Field.

On this state of facts, we are of the opinion that the plaintiffs have presented a case which entitles them under the law to a preliminary injunction.

It is perfectly clear that the exclusive right to broadcast play-by-play descriptions of the games played by the "Pirates" at their home field rests in the plaintiffs, General Mills, Inc., and the Socony-Vacuum Oil Company under the contract with the Pittsburgh Athletic Company. That is a property right of the plaintiffs with which defendant is interfering when it broadcasts the play-by-play description of the ball games obtained by the observers on the outside of the enclosure.

The plaintiffs and the defendant are using baseball news as material for profit. The Athletic Company has, at great expense, acquired and maintains a baseball park, pays the players who participate in the game, and have, as we view it, a legitimate right to capitalize on the news value of their games by selling exclusive broadcasting rights to companies which value them as affording advertising mediums for their merchandise. This right the defendant interferes with when it uses its broadcasting facilities for giving out the identical news obtained by its paid observers stationed at points outside Forbes Field for the purpose of securing information which it cannot otherwise acquire. This, in our judgment, amounts to unfair competition, and is a violation of the property rights of the plaintiffs. For it is our opinion that the Pittsburgh Athletic Company, by reason of its creation of the game, its control of the park, and its restriction of the dissemination of news therefrom, has a property right in such news, and the right to control the use thereof for a reasonable time following the games.

* * *

On the unfair competition feature of the case, we rest our opinion on the case of *International News Service v. Associated Press,* 248 U.S. 215, 39 S.Ct. 68, 63 L.Ed. 211, 2 A.L.R. 293. In that case the court enjoined the International News Service from copying news from bulletin boards and early editions of Associated Press newspapers, and selling such news so long as it had commercial value to the Associated Press. The Supreme Court said:

> * * * Regarding the news, therefore, as but the material out of which both parties are seeking to make profits at the same time and in the same field, we hardly can fail to recognize that for this purpose, and as between them, it must be regarded as quasi property, irrespective of the rights of either as against the public.

> In order to sustain the jurisdiction of equity over the controversy, we need not affirm any general and absolute property in the news as such. The rule that a court of equity concerns itself only in the protection of property rights treats any civil right of a pecuniary nature as a property right...and the right to acquire property by honest labor or the conduct of a lawful business is as much entitled to protection as the right to guard property already acquired. * * *

And again at pages 239, 240, 39 S.Ct. at page 72:

> * * * The right of the purchaser of a single newspaper to spread knowledge of its contents gratuitously, for any legitimate purpose not unreasonably interfering with the complainant's right to make merchandise of it, may be admitted; but to transmit that news for commercial use, in competition with complainant – which is what defendant has done and seeks to justify – is a very different matter. * * *

Defendant contends it is not unfairly competing...because it obtains no compensation from a sponsor or otherwise from its baseball broadcasts. It concedes, however, that KQV seeks by its broadcast of news of baseball games to cultivate the good will of the public for its radio station. The fact that no revenue is obtained directly from the broadcast is not controlling, as these broadcasts are undoubtedly designed to aid in obtaining advertising business. [Citations Omitted]

Defendant seeks to justify its action on the ground that the information it receives from its observers stationed on its own property, without trespassing on plaintiffs' property, may be lawfully broadcast by it. We cannot follow defendant's counsel in this contention for the reasons above stated. The cases cited by them we have carefully studied and are unable to accept as authority. In the Australian case, *Victoria Park Racing, etc., v. Taylor,* 37 New South Wales 322, where the information broadcast was obtained from a tower adjoining a race track, the court refused an injunction, because there was neither a trespass on plaintiff's race track, or a nuisance created by defendant.

The doctrine of unfair competition is not recognized under the English Common Law. Therefore this decision is not an authority.

In the case of *Sports and General Press Agency v. Our Dogs Publishing Company*, (1916) 2 K.B. 880, which involved the taking of photographs from a point outside the dog-shows grounds, is likewise a case for the application of English law. The question of unfair competition was not considered at all, and could not be recognized under the English law.

* * *

CONCLUSIONS OF LAW.

1. This Court has jurisdiction of this cause by reason of diversity of citizenship and the amount in controversy.

2. The right, title and interest in and to the baseball games played within the parks of members of the National League, including Pittsburgh, including the property right in, and the sole right of, disseminating or publishing or selling, or licensing the right to disseminate, news, reports, descriptions, or accounts of games played in such parks, during the playing thereof, is vested exclusively in such members.

3. The actions and threatened actions of the defendant constitute a direct and irreparable interference with, and an appropriation of, the plaintiffs' normal and legitimate business; and said action is calculated to, and does, result in the unjust enrichment of the defendant at the expense of the plaintiffs and each of them.

4. The defendant's unauthorized broadcasts of information concerning games played by the Pittsburgh team constitute unfair competition with the plaintiffs and each of them.

5. The defendant wrongfully deprives the plaintiffs and each of them of the just benefits of their labors and expenditures in respect of the baseball games and the public dissemination of news thereof as alleged in the complaint....

****

8. The plaintiffs have no adequate remedy at law.

9. The plaintiffs are entitled to and are hereby granted a preliminary injunction.

NOTES & QUESTIONS

1. According to the court, "It is perfectly clear that the exclusive right to broadcast play-by-play descriptions of the games played by the 'Pirates' at their home field rests in the plaintiffs, General Mills, Inc., and the Socony-Vacuum Oil Company under the contract with the Pittsburgh Athletic Company." Why is that so perfectly clear? A play-by-play account is essentially a description of raw data – merely facts, *i.e.*, who's on first, how many out, balls, strikes, *etc.* Facts are news, and news is generally deemed to be in the public domain.

2. The *NBA v. Motorola* case that follows explains the *International News Service* case in greater depth.

THE NATIONAL BASKETBALL ASSOCIATION V. MOTOROLA, INC.

105 F.3D. 841 (1997)

UNITED STATES COURT OF APPEALS, SECOND CIRCUIT

WINTER, CIRCUIT JUDGE:

Motorola, Inc. and Sports Team Analysis and Tracking Systems ("STATS") appeal from a permanent injunction entered by Judge [Loretta] Preska. The injunction concerns a handheld pager sold by Motorola and marketed under the name "SportsTrax," which displays updated information of professional basketball games in progress. The injunction prohibits appellants, absent authorization from the National Basketball Association and NBA Properties, Inc. (collectively the "NBA"), from transmitting scores or other data about NBA games in progress via the pagers, STATS's site on America On-Line's computer dial-up service, or "any equivalent means."

The crux of the dispute concerns the extent to which a state law "hot-news" misappropriation claim based on *International News Service v. Associated Press,* 248 U.S. 215, 39 S.Ct. 68, 63 L.Ed. 211 (1918) ("INS "), survives preemption by the federal Copyright Act and whether the NBA's claim fits within the surviving INS-type claims. We hold that a narrow "hot-news" exception does survive preemption. However, we also hold that appellants' transmission of "real-time" NBA game scores and information tabulated from television and radio broadcasts of games in progress does not constitute a misappropriation of "hot news" that is the property of the NBA.

*   *   *

I. BACKGROUND

The facts are largely undisputed. Motorola manufactures and markets the SportsTrax paging device while STATS supplies the game information that is transmitted to the pagers. The product became available to the public in January 1996, at a retail price of about $200. SportsTrax's pager has an inch-and-a-half by inch-and-a-half screen and operates in four basic modes: "current," "statistics," "final scores" and "demonstration." It is the "current" mode that gives rise to the present dispute.[3] In that mode, SportsTrax displays the following information on NBA games in progress: (i) the teams playing; (ii) score changes; (iii) the team in possession of the ball; (iv)

---

3 The other three SportsTrax modes involve information that is far less contemporaneous than that provided in the "current" mode. In the "statistics" mode, the SportsTrax pager displays a variety of player and team statistics, such as field goal shooting percentages and top scorers. However, these are calculated only at half-time and when the game is over. In the "final scores" mode, the unit displays final scores from the previous day's games. In the "demonstration" mode, the unit merely simulates information shown during a hypothetical NBA game. The core issue in the instant matter is the dissemination of continuously-updated real-time NBA information in the "current" mode. Because we conclude that the dissemination of such real-time information is lawful, the other modes need no further description or discussion.

whether the team is in the free throw bonus; (v) the quarter of the game; and (vi) time remaining in the quarter. The information is updated every two to three minutes, with more frequent updates near the end of the first half and the end of the game. There is a lag of approximately two or three minutes between events in the game itself and when the information appears on the pager screen.

SportsTrax operation relies on a "data feed" supplied by STATS reporters who watch the games on television or listen to them on the radio. The reporters key into a personal computer changes in the score and other information such as successful and missed shots, fouls, and clock updates. The information is relayed by modem to STATS's host computer, which compiles, analyzes, and formats the data for retransmission. The information is then sent to a common carrier, which then sends it via satellite to various local FM radio networks that in turn emit the signal received by the individual SportsTrax pagers.

* * *

II. THE STATE LAW MISAPPROPRIATION CLAIM

A. Summary of Ruling

*** The issues before us are ones that have arisen in various forms over the course of this century as technology has steadily increased the speed and quantity of information transmission. Today, individuals at home, at work, or elsewhere, can use a computer, pager, or other device to obtain highly selective kinds of information virtually at will. *International News Service v. Associated Press,* 248 U.S. 215, 39 S.Ct. 68, 63 L.Ed. 211 (1918) ("INS") was one of the first cases to address the issues raised by these technological advances, although the technology involved in that case was primitive by contemporary standards. INS involved two wire services, the Associated Press ("AP") and International News Service ("INS"), that transmitted news stories by wire to member newspapers. Id. INS would lift factual stories from AP bulletins and send them by wire to INS papers. Id. at 231, 39 S.Ct. at 69-70. INS would also take factual stories from east coast AP papers and wire them to INS papers on the west coast that had yet to publish because of time differentials. Id. at 238, 39 S.Ct. at 72. The Supreme Court held that INS's conduct was a common-law misappropriation of AP's property. Id. at 242, 39 S.Ct. at 73-74.

With the advance of technology, radio stations began "live" broadcasts of events such as baseball games and operas, and various entrepreneurs began to use the transmissions of others in one way or another for their own profit. In response, New York courts created a body of misappropriation law, loosely based on INS, that sought to apply ethical standards to the use by one party of another's transmissions of events.

Federal copyright law played little active role in this area until 1976. Before then, it appears to have been the general understanding – there being no caselaw of consequence – that live events such as baseball games were not copyrightable. Moreover, doubt existed even as to whether a recorded broadcast or videotape of such an event was copyrightable. In 1976, however, Congress passed legislation expressly affording copyright protection to simultaneously-recorded broadcasts of live performances such as sports events. See 17 U.S.C. § 101. Such protection was not extended to the underlying events.

The 1976 amendments also contained provisions preempting state law claims that enforced rights "equivalent" to exclusive copyright protections when the work to which the state claim was being applied fell within the area of copyright protection. See 17 U.S.C. § 301. Based on legislative history of the 1976 amendments, it is generally agreed that a "hot-news" INS-like claim survives preemption. H.R. No. 94-1476 at 132 (1976), reprinted in 1976 U.S.C.C.A.N. 5659, 5748. However, much of New York misappropriation law after INS goes well beyond "hot-news" claims and is preempted.

We hold that the surviving "hot-news" INS-like claim is limited to cases where: (i) a plaintiff generates or gathers information at a cost; (ii) the information is time-sensitive; (iii) a defendant's use of the information constitutes free riding on the plaintiff's efforts; (iv) the defendant is in direct competition with a product or service offered by the plaintiffs; and (v) the ability of other parties to free-ride on the efforts of the plaintiff or others would so reduce the incentive to produce the product or service that its existence or quality would be substantially threatened. We conclude that SportsTrax does not meet that test.

B. Copyrights in Events or Broadcasts of Events

The NBA asserted copyright infringement claims with regard both to the underlying games and to their broadcasts. The district court dismissed these claims, and the NBA does not appeal from their dismissal. Nevertheless, discussion of the infringement claims is necessary to provide the framework for analyzing the viability of the NBA's state law misappropriation claim in light of the Copyright Act's preemptive effect.

1. Infringement of a Copyright in the Underlying Games

In our view, the underlying basketball games do not fall within the subject matter of federal copyright protection because they do not constitute "original works of authorship" under 17 U.S.C. § 102(a). Section 102(a) lists eight categories of "works of authorship" covered by the act, including such categories as "literary works," "musical works," and "dramatic works." The list does not include athletic events, and, although the list is concededly non-exclusive, such events are neither similar nor analogous to any of the listed categories.

The text of Section 102(a) reads:

> § 102. Subject matter of copyright: In general
> (a) Copyright protection subsists, in accordance with this title, in original works of author-ship fixed in any tangible medium of expression, now known or later developed, from which they can be perceived, reproduced, or otherwise communicated, either directly or with the aid of a machine or device. Works of authorship include the following categories:
> (1) literary works;
> (2) musical works, including any accompanying words;
> (3) dramatic works, including any accompanying music;

(4) pantomimes and choreographic works;

(6) motion pictures and other audiovisual works;

(7) sound recordings; and

(8) architectural works.

Sports events are not "authored" in any common sense of the word. There is, of course, at least at the professional level, considerable preparation for a game. However, the preparation is as much an expression of hope or faith as a determination of what will actually happen. Unlike movies, plays, television programs, or operas, athletic events are competitive and have no underlying script. Preparation may even cause mistakes to succeed, like the broken play in football that gains yardage because the opposition could not expect it. Athletic events may also result in wholly unanticipated occurrences, the most notable recent event being in a championship baseball game in which interference with a fly ball caused an umpire to signal erroneously a home run.

What "authorship" there is in a sports event, moreover, must be open to copying by competitors if fans are to be attracted. If the inventor of the T-formation in football had been able to copyright it, the sport might have come to an end instead of prospering. Even where athletic preparation most resembles authorship – figure skating, gymnastics, and, some would uncharitably say, professional wrestling – a performer who conceives and executes a particularly graceful and difficult – or, in the case of wrestling, seemingly painful – acrobatic feat cannot copyright it without impairing the underlying competition in the future. A claim of being the only athlete to perform a feat doesn't mean much if no one else is allowed to try.

For many of these reasons, *Nimmer on Copyright* concludes that the "[f]ar more reasonable" position is that athletic events are not copyrightable. 1 M. Nimmer & D. Nimmer, Nimmer on Copyright § 2.09[F] at 2-170.1 (1996). Nimmer notes that, among other problems, the number of joint copyright owners would arguably include the league, the teams, the athletes, umpires, stadium workers and even fans, who all contribute to the "work."

* * *

2. Infringement of a Copyright in the Broadcasts of NBA Games

> As noted, recorded broadcasts of NBA games – as opposed to the games themselves – are now entitled to copyright protection. The Copyright Act was amended in 1976 specifically to insure that simultaneously-recorded transmissions of live performances and sporting events would meet the Act's requirement that the original work of authorship be "fixed in any tangible medium of expression." 17 U.S.C. § 102(a). ***

The House Report also makes clear that it is *the broadcast, not the underlying game,* that is the subject of copyright protection [emphasis added]. In explaining how game broadcasts meet the Act's requirement that the subject matter be an "original work[ ] of authorship," 17 U.S.C. § 102(a), the House Report stated:

> When a football game is being covered by four television cameras, with a director guiding the activities of the four cameramen and choosing which of their electronic images are sent out to the public and in what order, there is little doubt that what the cameramen and the director are doing constitutes "authorship." H.R. No. 94-1476 at 52, *reprinted in* 1976 U.S.C.C.A.N. at 5665.

Although the broadcasts are protected under copyright law, the district court correctly held that Motorola and STATS did not infringe NBA's copyright because they reproduced only facts from the broadcasts, not the expression or description of the game that constitutes the broadcast. The "fact/expression dichotomy" is a bedrock principle of copyright law that "limits severely the scope of protection in fact-based works." *Feist Publications, Inc. v. Rural Tel. Service Co.,* 499 U.S. 340, 350, 111 S.Ct. 1282, 1290, 113 L.Ed.2d 358 (1991). "'No author may copyright facts or ideas. The copyright is limited to those aspects of the work – termed 'expression' – that display the stamp of the author's originality.'" *Id.* (quoting *Harper & Row, Publishers, Inc. v. Nation Enter.,* 471 U.S. 539, 547, 105 S.Ct. 2218, 2224, 85 L.Ed.2d 588 (1985)).

We agree with the district court that the "[d]efendants provide purely factual information which any patron of an NBA game could acquire from the arena without any involvement from the director, cameramen, or others who contribute to the originality of a broadcast." 939 F.Supp. at 1094. Because the SportsTrax device and AOL site reproduce only factual information culled from the broadcasts and none of the copyrightable expression of the games, appellants did not infringe the copyright of the broadcasts.

C. *The State-Law Misappropriation Claim*

* * *

1. *Preemption Under the Copyright Act*
a) Summary

When Congress amended the Copyright Act in 1976, it provided for the preemption of state law claims that are interrelated with copyright claims in certain ways. Under 17 U.S.C. § 301, a state law claim is preempted when: (i) the state law claim seeks to vindicate "legal or equitable rights that are equivalent" to one of the bundle of exclusive rights already protected by copyright law under 17 U.S.C. § 106 – styled the "general scope requirement;" and (ii) the particular work to which the state law claim is being applied falls within the type of works protected by the Copyright Act under Sections 102 and 103 – styled the "subject matter requirement."

* * *

[The Court's extensive discussion of "Partial Preemption" has been omitted].

Our conclusion...is that only a narrow "hot-news" misappropriation claim survives preemption for actions concerning material within the realm of copyright. ***

In our view, the elements central to an *INS* claim are: (i) the plaintiff generates or collects information at some cost or expense, [Case Citations Omitted]; (ii) the value of the information is highly time-sensitive, [Case Citations Omitted]; Restatement (Third) Unfair Competition, § 38 cmt. c.; (iii) the defendant's use of the information constitutes free-riding on the plaintiff's costly efforts to generate or collect it, [Case Citations Omitted]; Restatement § 38 at cmt. c.; McCarthy, § 10:73 at 10-139; (iv) the defendant's use of the information is in direct competition with a product or service offered by the plaintiff, [Case Citations Omitted]; (v) the ability of other parties to free-ride on the efforts of the plaintiff would so reduce the incentive to produce the product or service that its existence or quality would be substantially threatened, [Case Citation Omitted]; Restatement, § 38 at cmt. c.; INS, 248 U.S. at 241, 39 S.Ct. at 73 ("[INS's conduct] would render [AP's] publication profitless, or so little profitable as in effect to cut off the service by rendering the cost prohibitive in comparison with the return.").

INS is not about ethics; it is about the protection of property rights in time-sensitive information so that the information will be made available to the public by profit seeking entrepreneurs. If services like AP were not assured of property rights in the news they pay to collect, they would cease to collect it. The ability of their competitors to appropriate their product at only nominal cost and thereby to disseminate a competing product at a lower price would destroy the incentive to collect news in the first place. The newspaper-reading public would suffer because no one would have an incentive to collect "hot news."

We therefore find the extra elements – those in addition to the elements of copyright infringement – that allow a "hotnews" claim to survive preemption are: (i) the time-sensitive value of factual information, (ii) the free-riding by a defendant, and (iii) the threat to the very existence of the product or service provided by the plaintiff.

2. The Legality of SportsTrax

We conclude that Motorola and STATS have not engaged in unlawful misappropriation under the "hot-news" test set out above. To be sure, some of the elements of a "hot-news" INS claim are met. The information transmitted to SportsTrax is not precisely contemporaneous, but it is nevertheless time-sensitive. Also, the NBA does provide, or will shortly do so, information like that available through SportsTrax. It now offers a service called "Gamestats" that provides official play-by-play game sheets and half-time and final box scores within each arena. It also provides such information to the media in each arena. In the future, the NBA plans to enhance Gamestats so that it will be networked between the various arenas and will support a pager product analogous to SportsTrax. SportsTrax will of course directly compete with an enhanced Gamestats.

However, there are critical elements missing in the NBA's attempt to assert a "hot-news" INS-type claim. As framed by the NBA, their claim compresses and confuses three different informational products. The first product is generating the information by playing the games;

the second product is transmitting live, full descriptions of those games; and the third product is collecting and retransmitting strictly factual information about the gamesThe first and second products are the NBA's primary business: producing basketball games for live attendance and licensing copyrighted broadcasts of those games. The collection and retransmission of strictly factual material about the games is a different product: *e.g.*, box-scores in newspapers, summaries of statistics on television sports news, and real-time facts to be transmitted to pagers. In our view, the NBA has failed to show any competitive effect whatsoever from SportsTrax on the first and second products and a lack of any free-riding by SportsTrax on the third.

With regard to the NBA's primary products – producing basketball games with live attendance and licensing copyrighted broadcasts of those games – there is no evidence that anyone regards SportsTrax or the AOL site as a substitute for attending NBA games or watching them on television. In fact, Motorola markets SportsTrax as being designed "for those times when you cannot be at the arena, watch the game on TV, or listen to the radio ..."

The NBA argues that the pager market is also relevant to a "hot-news" INS-type claim and that SportsTrax's future competition with Gamestats satisfies any missing element. We agree that there is a separate market for the real-time transmission of factual information to pagers or similar devices, such as STATS's AOL site. However, we disagree that SportsTrax is in any sense free-riding off Gamestats.

An indispensable element of an INS "hot-news" claim is free riding by a defendant on a plaintiff's product, enabling the defendant to produce a directly competitive product for less money because it has lower costs. SportsTrax is not such a product. The use of pagers to transmit real-time information about NBA games requires: (i) the collecting of facts about the games; (ii) the transmission of these facts on a network; (iii) the assembling of them by the particular service; and (iv) the transmission of them to pagers or an on-line computer site. Appellants are in no way free-riding on Gamestats. Motorola and STATS expend their own resources to collect purely factual information generated in NBA games to transmit to SportsTrax pagers. They have their own network and assemble and transmit data themselves.

To be sure, if appellants in the future were to collect facts from an enhanced Gamestats pager to retransmit them to SportsTrax pagers, that would constitute free-riding and might well cause Gamestats to be unprofitable because it had to bear costs to collect facts that SportsTrax did not. If the appropriation of facts from one pager to another pager service were allowed, transmission of current information on NBA games to pagers or similar devices would be substantially deterred because any potential transmitter would know that the first entrant would quickly encounter a lower cost competitor free-riding on the originator's transmissions.

However, that is not the case in the instant matter. SportsTrax and Gamestats are each bearing their own costs of collecting factual information on NBA games, and, if one produces a product that is cheaper or otherwise superior to the other, that producer will prevail in the marketplace. This is obviously not the situation against which INS was intended to prevent: the potential lack of any such product or service because of the anticipation of free-riding.

* * *

IV. CONCLUSION

We vacate the injunction entered by the district court and order that the NBA's claim for misappropriation be dismissed. ***

NOTES & QUESTIONS

1. Isn't this case merely a modern version of *Pittsburgh Athletic?* Observers relay factual information about the course of an athletic contest to the public. Does the holding of this case conflict with *Pittsburgh Athletic?* Or is there a rational way to distinguish these cases? Explain.

2. Explain what the court means when it says, quoting Professor Nimmer, that "athletic events are not copyrightable." If that is true, then why do broadcasts of all sporting events claim to be copyrighted?

3. If the facts of sports broadcasts are not copyrightable, then what is the subject of copyright protection about sporting events?

4. The court denies that SportsTrax is free-riding. Do you think that KQV was free-riding in *Pittsburgh Athletic?* Explain.

MONSTER COMMUNICATIONS, INC., V. TURNER BROADCASTING SYSTEM, INC.
935 F.SUPP. 490 (1996)
UNITED STATES DISTRICT COURT, S.D. NEW YORK

KAPLAN, DISTRICT JUDGE.

For two decades, Muhammed Ali, born Cassius Clay, was the dominant public figure in the world of boxing as an Olympic gold medalist, professional contender, and heavyweight champion of the world three times. He was also an arresting personality and a controversial figure whose flamboyance, adherence to the Nation of Islam, conviction for draft evasion despite a claim of conscientious objector status, and ultimate vindication on the draft charge by a unanimous Supreme Court [1] frequently made him a focus of public attention. It therefore is far from surprising that his life has become a subject of intense interest to film makers, the circumstances that gives rise to this case.

Plaintiff Monster Communications, Inc. ("Monster"), made and owns an 84 minute motion picture called "When We Were Kings" ("Kings") which is scheduled for world theatrical release

---

1 *Clay v. United States*, 403 U.S. 698, 91 S.Ct. 2068, 29 L.Ed.2d 810 (1971).

in October 1996. The film is an account of the 1974 heavyweight title fight between Ali and George Foreman that was held in Zaire and referred to by Ali and others as the "rumble in the jungle." It is a serious film, and it recently won a grand jury award at the Sundance Film Festival. Monster believes that "Kings" has a substantial chance of achieving great commercial and critical success.

The cloud on the horizon, from Monster's point of view, is a documentary called "Ali – The Whole Story" ("Story"), which is scheduled to premiere on Turner Network Television on Tuesday, September 3, 1996. Monster claims that Story infringes its copyright in film footage contained in Kings because Story contains a number of film clips, aggregating approximately between 41 seconds and two minutes, that appear in Kings and allegedly are owned by Monster. ***

At the commencement of this action, plaintiff claimed that there were twenty film clips in Story totaling two to three minutes in length that appear also in Kings. During the hearing on September 1, plaintiff indicated that it would not press this motion, although reserving its rights to seek other relief, with respect to three of the twenty clips.[2] Turner edited three of the allegedly infringing clips out of Story before the hearing. It contends that four of the remaining fourteen allegedly infringing clips, which aggregate 16 seconds in Story, are not the same as plaintiff's footage in Kings and must have been taken by another photographer.[3] It concedes that nine of the clips appear both in Kings and Story and that their aggregate duration in Story is 41 seconds. In consequence, it is clear for purposes of this motion that the Turner film contains between nine and fourteen clips that appear also in Kings and which aggregate a minimum of 41 seconds and perhaps as much as two minutes, although it seems likely that the aggregate duration is more like one minute.

* * *

Section 107 of the Copyright Act, 17 U.S.C. § 107, codifies the defense of fair use. One may use and reproduce a copyrighted work "for purposes such as criticism, comment, news reporting, teaching ..., scholarship, or research" provided the use is a fair one. The factors to be considered in determining the fairness of the use include "(1) the purpose and character of the use, including whether such use is of a commercial nature or is for nonprofit educational purposes; (2) the nature of the copyrighted work; (3) the amount and substantiality of the portion used in relation to the copyrighted work as a whole; and (4) the effect of the use upon the potential market for or value of the copyrighted work." *Id.*

---

2 The three clips in question do not appear in Kings, but appear in other footage in which plaintiff claims copyright. Plaintiff did not press the motion as to these clips because it was unable to produce, on the expedited schedule on which the motion was heard, a certificate of registration of copyright covering those clips.

3 The Court viewed the four disputed clips at the hearing. The limitations of the format in and the equipment by which they were presented did not permit, in the available time, a determination as to whether these four clips are identical to footage that appears in Kings. Turner contends also that one of the clips plaintiff says appears in Story in fact is not there. As the clip is extremely short, a determination would have required a more detailed examination of Story than time permitted. As will appear, the uncertainties as to the disputed clips are not material to disposition of the motion.

The allegedly infringing work, Story, is a biography. While it is commercial in nature, it "undeniably constitutes a combination of comment, criticism, scholarship and research, all of which enjoy favored status under § 107." *Arica Institute, Inc. v. Palmer*, 761 F.Supp. 1056, 1067 (S.D.N.Y.1991), *aff'd*, 970 F.2d 1067 (2d Cir.1992). As Turner argues, there can be little doubt that Ali is a figure of legitimate public concern and that his television biography is a subject of public interest. Hence, the first of the fair use factors cuts in favor of Turner although, as the Nimmers point out, it does not "necessitate a finding of fair use." 3 MELVILLE B. NIMMER & DAVID NIMMER, NIMMER ON COPYRIGHT ("NIMMER") § 13.05[A][1][*a*], at 13- 161 to 162 (1995); *see also New Era Publications International, ApS v. Henry Holt & Co., Inc.*, 873 F.2d 576, 583 (2d Cir.1989), *cert. denied*, 493 U.S. 1094, 110 S.Ct. 1168, 107 L.Ed.2d 1071 (1990); *Rosemont Enterprises, Inc. v. Random House, Inc.*, 366 F.2d 303, 307 (2d Cir.1966), *cert. denied*, 385 U.S. 1009, 87 S.Ct. 714, 17 L.Ed.2d 546 (1967).

The second of the factors, the nature of the copyrighted work, focuses on the degree of creativity of the copyrighted work. "[T]he more creative the primary work, the more protection it should be accorded from copying." *Amsinck v. Columbia Pictures Industries, Inc.*, 862 F.Supp. 1044, 1050 (S.D.N.Y.1994). *Accord*, 3 NIMMER § 13.05[A][2][*a*], at 13-174 to 175. Here there is no doubt in the Court's mind that plaintiff's film, Kings, is a creative and notable work. But defendants are not alleged to be infringing Kings. Rather, the claim is that Story uses certain film clips – photographic images – of actual historical events that appear also in Kings.[4]

Anyone who has seen any of the great pieces of photojournalism – for example, Alfred Eisenstadt's classic image of a thrilled sailor exuberantly kissing a woman in Times Square on V-J Day and the stirring photograph of U.S. Marines raising the American flag atop Mount Surabachi on Iwo Jima – or, perhaps in some eyes, more artistic, but nevertheless representational, photography – such as Ansel Adams' work and the portraits of Yousuf Karsh – must acknowledge that photographic images of actual people, places and events may be as creative and deserving of protection as purely fanciful creations. Nevertheless, history has its demands. There is a public interest in receiving information concerning the world in which we live. The more newsworthy the person or event depicted, the greater the concern that too narrow a view of the fair use defense will deprive the public of significant information. Moreover, only a finite number of photographers capture images of a given historical event. Hence, without denying for a moment the creativity inherent in the film clips of actual events relating to the Zaire fight, the degree of protection that properly may be afforded to them must take into account that too narrow a view of the fair use defense could materially undermine the ability of other Ali biographers to tell, in motion picture or perhaps still photographic form, an important part of his story. *See, e.g., Rosemont Enterprises, Inc.*, 366 F.2d at 307. This of course is not to say that

---

4 The footage is not of the fight itself. It includes shots of Ali and Foreman training, arriving in Zaire, of Ali walking with his wife, and other such events.

historical film footage loses all copyright protection,[5] only that its character as historical film footage may strengthen somewhat the hand of a fair use defendant as compared with an alleged infringer of a fanciful work or a work presented in a medium that offers a greater variety of forms of expression.

Here, the footage in question, although historical, does not remotely approach the Second Circuit's paradigmatic example of an image the informational content of which would weigh heaviest in favor of an alleged infringer, the Zapruder film of the Kennedy assassination. *See Roy Export Co. Establishment of Vaduz, Liechtenstein v. Columbia Broadcasting System, Inc.*, 672 F.2d 1095 at 1099. Moreover, having viewed both films, the Court finds that Story would not have been diminished in any material way had it not included the allegedly infringing footage. On the other hand, the level of creativity inherent in this footage, as distinguished from the use made of the footage in Kings, appears not to be especially substantial. All things considered, the second of the fair use factors is essentially neutral.

The third of the fair use factors is the amount and substantiality of the portion used, a factor that cuts very heavily in favor of Turner for several reasons.

The first is that Kings is 84 minutes in length; Story is 94. The allegedly infringing portions of Story consist of nine to fourteen film clips aggregating a minimum of 41 seconds and a maximum of one to two minutes, which is 0.7 to 2.1 percent of the film. A number of the allegedly infringing clips are less than three seconds long. From any quantitative standpoint, the allegedly infringing use is small.

Second, the allegedly infringing footage is by no means the focus of Story. Indeed, the two movies are quite different. Kings is devoted almost entirely to the Zaire fight. It touches only fleetingly on the rest of Ali's life and career. It focuses heavily on the fact that the Zaire fight involved two African-American fighters traveling to fight in Africa, the continent of their ancestors' origin, and the impact of that experience on them and on Zaire. Story, on the other hand, is a biography of Ali from childhood to the present. It is, as its title promises, "Muhammed Ali – The Whole Story." The segment concerning the Zaire fight occupies approximately nine of its 94 minutes. It is a very different work.

Third, the Court viewed both movies within a short span of hours, Kings first and then Story, for the purpose of attempting to detect in Story, without prompting, whether and to what extent it employed footage used in Kings. Although there were a couple of occasions on which such uses were apparent, they were far fewer than the seventeen that plaintiff claims exist. That of course is not to say that the parties are mistaken. Rather, the conclusion that flows is that the allegedly infringing uses are not particularly noticeable even if one is looking for them.

---

5 While the Second Circuit has "acknowledged in passing the conceivable occurrence of some 'rare,' 'almost unique' circumstance, such as those surrounding the Zapruder film [of President Kennedy's assassination], in which 'it is at least arguable that the informational value of [the] film cannot be separated from the photographer's expression, ... thereby indicating that both should be in the public domain,' *Iowa State University Research Foundation, Inc. v. American Broadcasting Cos., Inc.*, 621 F.2d 57, 61 n. 6 (2d Cir.1980), [it has] also stated the general rule that '[c]onflicts between interests protected by the first amendment and the copyright laws thus far have been resolved by application of the fair use doctrine,' *Wainwright Securities, Inc. v. Wall Street Transcript Corp.*, [558 F.2d 91,] 95 [2d Cir.1977]." *Roy Export Co. Establishment of Vaduz, Liechtenstein v. Columbia Broadcasting System, Inc.*, 672 F.2d 1095, 1100 (2d Cir.), cert. denied, 459 U.S. 826, 103 S.Ct. 60, 74 L.Ed.2d 63 (1982).

For all of these reasons, the Court finds that the "amount and substantiality" factor strongly favors the defendants. *Harper & Row Publishers, Inc. v. Nation Enterprises,* 471 U.S. 539, 105 S.Ct. 2218, 85 L.Ed.2d 588 (1985), is not to the contrary. While the Supreme Court there concluded that the use of only 300 of 200,000 words of the memoirs of former President Ford was a substantial appropriation, it did so on the basis of the trial court's finding that the alleged infringer "took what was essentially the heart of the book." *Id.* at 564-65, 105 S.Ct. at 2233 (quoting 557 F.Supp. 1067, 1072 (S.D.N.Y.1983)). The material at issue here has no remotely comparable significance in Kings.

The final fair use factor, the effect of the infringing use on the market for the original copyrighted work, is the most important. *Harper & Row Publishers, Inc.,* 471 U.S. at 566, 105 S.Ct. at 2233. In considering it, however, it is critical to bear in mind that the only effect of which plaintiff properly may complain is that caused by the alleged infringement. [Citations Omitted] In other words, the issue here is not whether the wide dissemination of Turner's television biography of Ali only weeks before the theatrical release of Monster's film will undercut the market for Kings. It is whether the use in Turner's film of up to fourteen clips of historical footage, aggregating between 41 seconds and two minutes, will undercut the market for Kings. Having viewed both movies, the Court concludes that the segments in Story are unlikely to have any such effect. The uses in Story are too few, too short, and too small in relation to the whole. If the broadcast of Story impacts Kings' reception, it almost surely will be as a result of their common subject, not their minute or so of common footage. As the *New Era* court wrote in a case involving two written biographies of L. Ron Hubbard:

"[T]here may be purchasers who are sufficiently interested in Hubbard to purchase one book about him but not two. [Defendant's book] may have an adverse impact on the marketability of Hubbard's [autobiography] with those purchasers simply by exhausting their interest. *That is not within the concern of the copyright statute.*" *Id.* at 1523 (emphasis supplied).

*   *   *   *

*** The balance of the statutory fair use factors appear to cut heavily in favor of the defendants. Accordingly, the Court concludes that...the defendants are likely to establish that their use is a fair one within the meaning of the Copyright Act.

*   *   *   *

NOTES & QUESTIONS

1. Explain how each § 107 fair use factor either favors or disfavors a finding of fair use. What is the relevance of each factor to the issue of whether a use should be considered "fair"?

B. TRADEMARKS

ADIDAS-AMERICA, INC. V. PAYLESS SHOESOURCE, INC.
546 F.SUPP.2D 1029 (D. OR. 2008)
KING, JUDGE.

I. The Parties and Their Products

Adidas manufactures and sells athletic and casual footwear. As early as 1952, Adidas began placing three parallel bands on athletic shoes, and in 1994, Adidas registered the first of several variations of Three-Stripe trademark with the U.S. Patent and Trademark Office. The 1994 Three-Stripe mark consists of three parallel and equidistant double-serrated stripes of contrasting color on the side of the shoe running diagonally from the mid-sole forward to the shoelaces. In 1999, Adidas registered a slight variation of the Three-Stripe mark, which consists of three parallel and equidistant straight-edged stripes of contrasting color running diagonally from the mid-sole forward to the laces on the side of the shoe.

Adidas has used and promoted the Three-Stripe Mark since 1952, and promotes itself as "The Brand With Three Stripes." Adidas has used the mark in connection with its frequent sponsorship of professional sports events and organizations, such as the World Cup soccer tournament, the Boston Marathon, the New York Yankees, University of Notre Dame, the University of California at Los Angeles, the University of Nebraska, and the University of Tennessee. Adidas also sponsors numerous professional athletes who wear apparel bearing the Three-Stripe mark. Since introducing the Three-Stripe mark, Adidas has spent millions of dollars promoting the mark and products bearing the mark. In recent years, Adidas' annual sales of products bearing the Three-Stripe mark have totaled in the billions of dollars globally, and in the hundreds of millions of dollars within the United States.

Adidas also claims protected rights in a Superstar Trade Dress. Adidas first introduced the Superstar Trade Dress in 1969 and its principle features have not changed since that time. It consists of: (1) three parallel stripes (*i.e.,* the Three-Stripe Mark) on the side of the shoe parallel to equidistant small holes; (2) a rubber "shell toe"; (3) a particularly flat sole; and (4) a colored portion on the outer back heel that identifies the shoes as Adidas' brand.

Adidas has used and promoted the Superstar Trade Dress since its introduction in 1969. The general public, professional and amateur athletes, hip-hop music artists, and the media commonly associate the Superstar Trade Dress with Adidas. The Superstar was widely used by professional basketball players in the 1970s. In the late 1980s, the Adidas "shell toe" reemerged as a fashion shoe, made popular by hip-hop music artists such as the Beastie Boys and RunDMC. Since 1999, sales of Superstar shoes have exceeded $711 million, with more than 5 million pair sold in the United States in 2001.

Payless is one of the nation's largest retailers of discount casual and athletic footwear. Payless operates approximately 4,500 stores in 49 states, and sells more than 200 million pairs of shoes annually. Since at least 1994, Payless has marketed and sold athletic shoes bearing parallel stripes. Though Payless no longer sells footwear bearing three parallel stripes, Payless does sell several models of athletic footwear that bear two or four parallel straight-edged stripes, running diagonally from the mid-sole forward to the laces. Payless does use stripe designs on shoes not to signify source, but as mere decoration or ornamentation.

Payless also sells shoes that have a rubber "shell toe," a flat sole, and a colored portion on the outer back heel. Instead of using three stripes, however, Payless' "shell toe" shoe bears four parallel straight-edge stripes on the side of the shoe, parallel to equidistant small holes. Payless acknowledges that it uses Adidas' shoes as "inspirations" for its stripe-shoe designs.

None of Payless' allegedly infringing shoes bear three stripes. Rather, they all bear either two or four parallel stripes running diagonally from the mid-sole to the laces. Payless shoes are sold almost exclusively at Payless retail stores, and Adidas shoes are not available at Payless retail stores. Although the parties dispute whether they compete for the same consumers, Adidas and Payless do advertise their respective products through at least some of the same media channels.

II. Legal Standards

To prevail on a trademark or trade dress infringement claim under the Lanham Act, a plaintiff must prove that the alleged infringer used the plaintiff's validly registered trademark or trade dress "in commerce," and that the use is "likely to cause confusion, or to cause mistake, or to deceive consumers," as to the source of the product. *Reno Air Racing Ass'n, Inc. v. McCord,* 452 F.3d 1126, 1134 (9th Cir.2006). In the Ninth Circuit, neither an intent to confuse, nor actual confusion are required elements of a trademark infringement claim. *Coca-Cola Co. v. Overland, Inc.,* 692 F.2d 1250, 1256 n. 16 (9th Cir.1982). Instead, the central inquiry is whether a "reasonably prudent customer in the marketplace is likely to be confused as to the origin of the good or service bearing one of the marks," because of the similarities between the two marks. *Dreamwerks Prod. Group, Inc. v. SKG Studio,* 142 F.3d 1127, 1129 (9th Cir.1998). Likelihood of confusion is considered by examining the "total effect of the defendant's product and package on the eye and mind of an ordinary purchaser." *First Brands Corp. v. Fred Meyer, Inc.,* 809 F.2d 1378, 1383-84 (9th Cir.1987).

In the Ninth Circuit, courts examine the following eight factors in evaluating the likelihood of confusion: (1) the similarity of the marks; (2) the relatedness of the parties' goods; (3) the similarity of trade or marketing channels; (4) the strength of the plaintiff's marks; (5) defendant's intent; (6) evidence of actual confusion; (7) the degree of care exercised by the average purchaser; and (8) the likelihood of expansion into other markets. *AMF Inc. v. Sleekcraft Boats,* 599 F.2d 341, 348-49 (9th Cir.1979). The eight-factor *Sleekcraft* test is not a rigid one, however, and "[o]ther variables may come into play depending on the particular facts presented." *Sleekcraft,* 599 F.2d at 348 n. 11; *see also Entrepreneur Media, Inc. v. Smith,* 279 F.3d 1135, 1141 (9th Cir.2002) (Likelihood of confusion is not determined by mechanically counting the number of factors that weigh in favor of each party, or by giving the same weight to a particular factor in each case).

III. Analysis of the Sleekcraft Factors

a. Similarity of the Marks

"[T]he greater the similarity between the two marks at issue, the greater the likelihood of confusion." [Citation Omitted] In the similarity analysis: "(1) Marks should be considered in their entirety and as they appear in the marketplace; (2) Similarity is best adjudged by appearance, sound, and meaning; and (3) Similarities weigh more heavily than differences." *Entrepreneur Media,* 279 F.3d at 1144. "[S]imilarity of design is determined by considering the overall impression created by the mark as a whole rather than simply comparing individual features." *Exxon Corp. v. Texas Motor Exch., Inc.,* 628 F.2d 500, 505 (5th Cir.1980).

Here, the similarities between Payless' stripe designs and Adidas' Three-Stripe Mark are unmistakable. Like Adidas' Three-Stripe Mark, Payless' stripes contrast with the background color of the shoe, and run parallel, at the same angle, from the mid-sole of the shoe diagonally forward to the laces. "Considered in their entirety and as they appear in the marketplace," the stripe designs on Payless' athletic and casual shoes are similar to Adidas' Three-Stripe Mark. *Official Airline Guides, Inc. v. Goss,* 6 F.3d 1385, 1392 (9th Cir.1993).

With respect to Payless' allegedly infringing imitation of Adidas' Superstar Trade Dress, the similarities are even more striking. Like the Adidas' Superstar, Payless' shoe prominently displays parallel, equidistant stripes, running parallel to small equidistant holes on the sides of the shoes. Both versions of the Superstar have a rubber "shell toe" design, a particularly flat sole, and a similarly shaped heel patch. Notably, Payless' rubber "shell toe" designs-the overall shape, raised lines fanning out (like a sea shell), even the tiny "x's" embossed between the ridges of the toe-are almost indistinguishable from the Adidas' "shell toe."

Payless' argument is that because "two or four stripes do not equal three stripes," there can be no actionable similarity between its use of two and four stripe designs and Adidas' Three-Stripe Mark. I disagree.

Payless cannot avoid liability for infringement merely by adding (or subtracting) an identical, parallel stripe to Adidas' Three-Stripe Mark. "[W]hat is critical is the *overall* appearance of the mark as used in the marketplace, not a deconstructionist view of the different components of the marks." *Playmakers, LLC v. ESPN, Inc.,* 297 F.Supp.2d 1277, 1283 (W.D.Wash.2003), *aff'd,* 376 F.3d 894 (9th Cir.2004) (emphasis in original). As one court aptly noted, "few would be stupid enough to make exact copies of another's mark or symbol. It has been well said that the most successful form of copying is to employ enough points of similarity to confuse the public with enough points of difference to confuse the courts." *Baker v. Master Printers Union,* 34 F.Supp. 808, 811 (D.N.J.1940). Here, although there may be minor differences between Payless' use of stripes and Adidas' Three-Stripe mark, "the *overall impression* created by the marks is essentially the same, [and thus] it is very probable that the marks are confusingly similar." 4 J. Thomas McCarthy, *McCarthy on Trademarks and Unfair Competition* § 24:22 (4th ed.2007) (emphasis added).

Although three stripes obviously do not equal four stripes, the issue is not simply the number of stripes. Instead, the issue is whether the total effect of the allegedly infringing design is likely to cause confusion in the minds of an ordinary purchaser. While there can be no debate that defendants' four stripe mark has one stripe more than Adidas' Three Stripe Mark, so too there can be no debate that many of the other features of the stripes displayed on defendants' [shoes] are strikingly similar – if not identical – to the features of the Three Stripe Mark displayed on some models.... The stripes are equal in size, are placed equidistant at a similar or identical angle, are in substantially the same location between the sole and the reinforced area which supports the shoelace holes (with the necessary adjustment to accommodate four rather than three stripes), are displayed in colors which contrast with the background color of the shoes, and have serrated edges. Thus, this court cannot simply count the number of stripes and determine as a matter of law that four stripes are not confusingly similar to three stripes.

Given...the clear similarities between the parties' respective stripe designs, I conclude that, as a matter of law, there is an actionable similarity between Payless' use of two or four stripes and the Three-Stripe Mark.

b. Relatedness or Proximity of the Parties' Goods

"Related goods are generally more likely than unrelated goods to confuse the public as to the producers of the goods." *Brookfield Communications, Inc. v. West Coast Entertainment Corp.,* 174 F.3d 1036, at 1055 (9th Cir. 1999). Related goods are those "which would be reasonably thought by the buying public to come from the same source if sold under the same mark." *Id.* at 348 n. 10. [Citation Omitted]

Here, the parties' products are essentially identical in use and function. Both parties sell athletic and casual footwear. Aside from arguable differences in quality, the parties' products are "reasonably interchangeable by buyers for the same purposes," and thus competitive. *McCarthy* § 24.23. Where goods are directly competitive, "the degree of similarity of the marks needed to cause likely confusion is less than in the case of dissimilar goods...." *Id.* § 24.22. Given the substantial similarity of the marks at issue, I find that this *Sleekcraft* factor weighs heavily in favor of finding a likelihood of confusion.

c. Similarity of Trade or Marketing Channels

A consideration of how and to whom the respective goods of the parties are sold is relevant to the issue of likelihood of confusion. *McCarthy* § 24:51. "Convergent marketing channels increase the likelihood of confusion." *Sleekcraft,* 599 F.2d at 353. In addition, when the "general class" of purchasers of the parties' respective products is the same, confusion is more likely. *Id.* On the other hand, significant differences in the price of the products, or the type of stores (*e.g.,* discount or specialty) at which the respective products are sold may decrease the likelihood of confusion. *L.A. Gear, Inc. v. Thom McAn Shoe Co.,* 988 F.2d 1117, 1134 (Fed.Cir.1993).

Although Adidas' and Payless' shoes are generally sold through different retail outlets and at different prices, Adidas has submitted evidence that the parties' marketing channels are similar, and that the parties compete for at least some of the same customers. In fact, Payless' counsel conceded that the parties' markets "certainly overlap." Knops Dep. 103:14-104:1. Adidas and Payless place advertisements for their respective products in the same magazines, and on the same Internet websites. Further, at least some of the Payless shoes at issue were actually sold in stores where Adidas' shoes were also sold. Though not identical, there is evidence the parties' marketing channels partially overlap.

Given the similarity of the parties' respective products and Adidas' credible evidence of the overlap of marketing channels, I find this factor favors Adidas.

d. Strength of the Mark

The scope of protection afforded a trademark "depends upon the strength of the mark, with stronger marks receiving greater protection than weak ones." *Entrepreneur Media,* 279 F.3d at 1141. The strength of the trademark is evaluated in terms of its conceptual strength and commercial strength. *GoTo.com Inc. v. The Walt Disney Corp.,* 202 F.3d, 1199 at 1207 (9th Cir. 2000).

With respect to conceptual strength, marks are generally classified by their placement on a continuum of increasing distinctiveness: generic, descriptive, suggestive, and fanciful or arbitrary. *E. & J. Gallo Winery v. Spider Webs Ltd.,* 967 F.2d, 1280 at 1291 (9th Cir. 1992). Suggestive, fanciful, and arbitrary marks are deemed inherently distinctive and entitled to the most protection because their intrinsic nature serves to identify a particular source of a product. *Two Pesos, Inc. v. Taco Cabana, Inc.,* 505 U.S. 763, 768, 112 S.Ct. 2753, 120 L.Ed.2d 615 (1992). A fanciful mark is "a coined word or phrase, such as Kodak, invented solely to function as a trademark." *Official Airline Guides, Inc. v. Goss,* 6 F.3d 1385, 1390 (9th Cir.1993). An arbitrary mark is a common word that is "non-descriptive of any quality of the goods or services." *Id.* "A suggestive mark is one for which a consumer must use imagination or any type of multistage reasoning to understand the mark's significance, ... the mark does not describe the product's features but suggests them." *Entrepreneur Media,* 279 F.3d at 1142. [Citation Omitted] In contrast, "generic" marks-or, names that refer to an entire class of products-are the weakest and receive no trademark protection. *Id.* A "descriptive" (*e.g.,* one that describes the quality or features of a product) mark may be entitled to protection only if it has acquired distinctiveness through secondary meaning. *Two Pesos,* 505 U.S. at 769, 112 S.Ct. 2753. Secondary meaning is the consumer's association of the mark with a particular source. *E. & J. Gallo,* 967 F.2d at 1291. In other words, to be entitled to trademark protection, the owner of a merely descriptive trademark must show that buyers identify that mark with a single commercial source. *McCarthy* § 15:1.

[T]his court found in a related case that the Adidas Three-Stripe Mark was "arbitrary because three stripes do not define, describe or suggest the various products that bear them." *Adidas v. Target,* No. 01-1582-RE, slip op. at 13 (D.Or. Jan. 29, 2003). Though the spectrum of distinctiveness does not easily translate into the world of shapes and images, *McCarthy* §§ 8:13, 11:2, I agree with this court's previous conclusion that the Three-Stripe Mark is strong and entitled to protection.

Even if the Three-Stripe Mark is not inherently distinctive, a fact-finder could reasonably conclude that Adidas' Three-Stripe Mark and Superstar Trade Dress have acquired distinctiveness through secondary meaning. Adidas owns a valid and incontestable registration for the Three-Stripe Mark, which serves as conclusive proof that the mark has secondary meaning. *Entrepreneur Media,* 279 F.3d at 1142 n. 3. Adidas has also submitted evidence that it has expended hundreds of millions of dollars in promoting the sale of its goods bearing both the Three-Stripe

Mark and Superstar Trade Dress. Adidas' substantial advertising and promotional efforts are significant evidence of the strength of its mark.

Given the previous court findings on this issue and the significant evidence that Adidas' Three-Stripe Mark and Superstar Trade Dress have acquired secondary meaning, this factor weighs in favor of Adidas.

e. Defendant's Intent

Though a showing of "intent to confuse consumers is not required for a finding of trademark infringement," *Brookfield,* 174 F.3d at 1059, Adidas has submitted sufficient evidence of Payless' intent to imitate the Three-Stripe Mark to create a genuine issue of material fact as to likelihood of confusion. *See Academy of Motion Picture Arts & Scis. v. Creative House,* 944 F.2d 1446, at 1456 (9th Cir. 1991)("When one party knowingly adopts a mark similar to another's, reviewing courts presume that the defendant will accomplish its purpose, and that the public will be deceived.").

Here, there is no dispute that Payless was aware of the Three-Stripe Mark when it began selling the accused footwear. In addition, there is substantial circumstantial and direct evidence that Payless intentionally copied Adidas' mark. For example, Payless' employees repeatedly referred to their shoes by the name of the corresponding Adidas model (such as the Country Ripple or Samoa), or simply as "Adidas" shoes. Payless buyers also acknowledge "knocking off" or "interpreting" Adidas styles.

Given the substantial similarity of the parties' respective products, the evidence of Payless' knowing imitation of Adidas' mark raises substantial issues of material fact as to Payless' intent. This factor weighs against granting summary judgment in Payless' favor on the issue of infringement.

f. Actual Confusion

As an initial matter, Adidas acknowledges that there is no likelihood of consumer confusion at the point-of-sale. Rather, Adidas' infringement claims are based on the likelihood of initial-interest and post-sale confusion. Payless argues that both of those theories fail in this context. I disagree.

"The Ninth Circuit has explicitly recognized that the use of another's trademark in a manner calculated 'to capture initial consumer attention, even though no actual sale is finally completed as a result of the confusion, may still be an infringement.'" *Adidas v. Target,* 228 F.Supp.2d at 1211 (quoting *Dr. Seuss, L.P. v. Penguin Books USA, Inc.,* 109 F.3d 1394, at 1405)(9th Cir. 1997). Similarly, "the law in the Ninth Circuit is clear that 'post-purchase confusion,' *i.e.,* confusion on the part of someone other than the purchaser who, for example, simply sees the item after its has been purchased can establish the required likelihood of confusion under the Lanham Act." *Karl Storz Endoscopy, Inc. v. Surgical Technologies, Inc.,* 285 F.3d 848, at 854 (9th Cir. 2001).

Moreover, this court has specifically endorsed the use of both initial-interest and post-sale confusion in *factually identical* cases involving two-and four-stripe footwear that allegedly infringed Adidas' Three-Stripe Mark. *Adidas v. Target,* 228 F.Supp.2d at 1211; *ACI v. Adidas,* 359 F.Supp.2d at 921. I agree with the rationale and conclusions in those cases. Initial-interest and post-sale confusion are well established forms of confusion in this context, and Adidas' failure to allege point-of-sale confusion is of no consequence.

Furthermore, Adidas has submitted evidence that Payless' stripe designs negatively impact consumer perceptions of the Adidas brand as a source of quality footwear. Indeed, consumers who view Payless' shoes in the post-sale context "may attribute any perceived inferior quality of Payless shoes to [Adidas]." *Payless v. Reebok*, 998 F.2d at 989. Here, there is evidence that Payless shoes are actually inferior to Adidas' shoes in quality. Perhaps more importantly, there is evidence that consumers actually perceive Payless' shoes to be of inferior quality. Indeed, Payless is aware of the perception among consumers that its shoes are low quality. This is credible evidence of harm to Adidas because "[o]ne of the most valuable and important protections afforded by the Lanham Act is the right to control the quality of the goods manufactured and sold under the holder's trademark." *El Greco Leather Prods. Co., Inc. v. Shoe World, Inc.*, 806 F.2d 392, 395 (2d Cir.1986). Finally, there is evidence that Payless' shoes are likely to have a negative effect on Adidas' customer loyalty. In sum, Adidas has submitted sufficient evidence of actual harm to create a genuine issue of material fact as to initial-interest and post-sale confusion.

Given Adidas' showing of actual consumer confusion, and the evidence of harm to Adidas resulting from initial-interest and post-sale confusion, I find there are significant issues of material fact as to actual confusion. Accordingly, this factor weighs against granting Payless summary judgment on the issue of infringement.

g. Degree of Care Exercised by the Average Purchaser

"In assessing the likelihood of confusion to the public, the standard used by the courts is the typical buyer exercising ordinary caution." *Sleekcraft*, 599 F.2d at 353. Where goods are expensive, or purchased after careful consideration, it is less likely that a reasonably prudent buyer would be confused as to the source of the goods. *Sleekcraft*, 599 F.2d at 353 ("[W]hen the goods are expensive the buyer can be expected to exercise greater care in his purchases; again, though, confusion may still be likely."); *McCarthy* § 23:96 ("The reasonably prudent buyer is assumed to take more care in purchasing 'expensive' items which he buys infrequently, than in buying everyday, relatively inexpensive items.").

Courts have found that purchasers of "relatively inexpensive athletic and sportswear" are "not likely to exercise a great deal of care in distinguishing between trademarks when purchasing the goods." *M'Otto Enters., Inc. v. Redsand, Inc.*, 831 F.Supp. 1491, 1502 (W.D.Wash.1993). Moreover, Payless' counsel acknowledges that Payless' consumers are "not particularly sophisticated." Knops Dep. at 104:6-16. Relatively unsophisticated value-conscious customers are more likely to be attracted to, and confused by imitations of Adidas' Three-Stripe Mark. This factor tips in favor of Adidas.

h. Likelihood of Expansion into Other Markets

The parties agree that this factor is not relevant in this case.

IV. Conclusion

Having considered the *Sleekcraft* factors, I find Adidas has produced substantial evidence of the likelihood of confusion between the Three-Stripe Mark and Payless' use of two or four stripes on footwear. There are significant issues of material fact as to several of the *Sleekcraft* confusion factors. Many of these issues will turn on questions of credibility and intent. As such, Payless' motion for summary judgment on Adidas' infringement claims is denied.

NOTES & QUESTIONS

1. The court quotes *Entrepreneur Media, Inc. v. Smith,* 279 F.3d 1135, 1141 (9th Cir.2002) for the proposition that "Likelihood of confusion is not determined by mechanically counting the number of factors that weigh in favor of each party, or by giving the same weight to a particular factor in each case." Explain the meaning and significance of this statement.

2. Explain what the court means when it says that "marks are generally classified by their placement on a continuum of increasing distinctiveness: generic, descriptive, suggestive, and fanciful or arbitrary."

3. In *Harlem Wizards Entertainment Basketball v. NBA Properties, Inc.,* 952 F.Supp. 1084 (1997) The United States District Court, District of New Jersey determined:

   > that plaintiff's mark is suggestive rather than, as plaintiff asserts, arbitrary or fanciful. The term WIZARDS does not describe accurately plaintiff's services because regardless how talented plaintiff's team members may be, they do not perform magic or even magically. Rather, the mark WIZARDS is accurately defined as suggestive because it asks the consumer to fantasize, to use his or her imagination to connect the idea of magic and the supernatural with show basketball.

   The court's evaluation of the mark "Wizards" as it relates to basketball is certainly a subtle, clever, and accurate assessment.

4. Why does a court need to analyze 8 *Sleekcraft* factors in order to assess "likelihood of confusion"? Why can't the court simply compare the plaintiff's mark with the defendant's and assess whether the two marks are substantially similar?

5. *Denimafia Inc. v. New Balance Athletic Shoe, Inc.,* 12 CIV. 4112 AJP, 2014 WL 814532 (S.D.N.Y. Mar. 3, 2014). After the analyzing the likelihood of confusion factors relating to New Balance's use of a mark that was allegedly similar to Denimafia's mark, the court granted New Balance's motion for summary judgment, holding that Denimafia was unlikely to prove likelihood of confusion.

6. *NBA Properties, Inc. v. Yan Zhou.*, No. 16-cv-11117, 2017 WL 4074020 (N.D. Ill. Sept. 14, 2017). Upon showing of likelihood of consumer confusion, court granted summary judgment for permanent injunction, statutory damages, and attorneys' fees to NBA Properties, MLB Advance Media, and NHL Enterprises against online sellers of merchandise for infringement of numerous registered trademarks.

C. RIGHT OF PUBLICITY

O'BRIEN V. PABST SALES CO.
124 F. 2D. 167 (1942)
CIRCUIT COURT OF APPEALS, FIFTH CIRCUIT

HUTCHESON, CIRCUIT JUDGE.

Plaintiff [Davey O'Brien], in physique as in prowess as a hurler, a modern David, is a famous football player. Defendant, in bulk, if not in brass and vulnerability, a modern Goliath, is a distributor of Pabst beer. Plaintiff, among other honors received during the year 1938, was picked by Grantland Rice on his Collier's All American Football Team. Defendant, as a part of its advertising publicity for 1939, following its custom of getting out football schedule calendars, placed an order with the Inland Lithographing Company, to prepare for and furnish to it, 35,000 Pabst 1939 football calendars. The calendars were to carry complete schedules of all major college games; professional schedules; and pictures of Grantland Rice's 1938 All American Football Team, the Inland Company to furnish photographs and necessary releases.

At the top of the calendar, as thus printed and circulated, were the words 'Pabst Blue Ribbon.' Directly underneath were the words 'Football Calendar, 1939'; to the left of these words was a photograph of O'Brien in football uniform characteristically poised for the throw; to the right of them was a glass having on it the words 'Pabst Breweries, Blue Ribbon Export Beer'; and to the right of the glass still, a bottle of beer, having on it 'Pabst Blue Ribbon Beer.' Directly below these was the intercollegiate football schedule for 1939, and in the center of the calendar were pictures, including that of O'Brien, of Grantland Rice's All American Football Team for 1938. Near the bottom was the schedule of the national football league and on the very bottom margin, were the words 'Pabst Famous Blue Ribbon Beer.'

Claiming that this use of his photograph as part of defendant's advertising was an invasion of his right of privacy and that he had been damaged thereby, plaintiff brought this suit.

The defenses were three. The first was that if the mere use of one's picture in truthful and respectable advertising would be an actionable invasion of privacy in the case of a private person, the use here was not, as to plaintiff, such an invasion, for as a result of his activities and prowess in football, his chosen field, and their nationwide and deliberate publicizing with his consent and in his interest, he was no longer, as to them, a private but a public person, and as to their additional publication he had no right of privacy. The second defense was that plaintiff, in his own interest and that of Texas Christian University, had posed for and had authorized the publicity department of T.C.U. to distribute his picture and biographical data to newspapers, magazines, sports journals and the public generally, and that the particular picture whose use is complained of had been in due course obtained from and payment for it had been made to the T.C.U. publicity department. Third, no injury to appellant's person, property or reputation had been or could be shown and there was therefore no basis for a recovery. The testimony fully supported these defenses. It showed that plaintiff, then 23 years old, had been playing football for 14 years, four years of that time with Texas Christian University, and two with the Philadelphia Eagles, a professional football team. During that period he had received many and distinguished trophies and honors as an outstanding player of the game. He had in fact been the recipient of practically every worthwhile football trophy and recognition, being picked by Grantland Rice on his Collier's All American Football Team, and by Liberty on their All Players All American Team, and many other so-called All American Football Teams. Plaintiff testified that he had not given permission to use his picture, indeed had not known of the calendar until some time after its publication and circulation; that he was a member of the Allied Youth of America, the main theme of which was the doing away with alcohol among young people; that he had had opportunities to sell his endorsement for beer and alcoholic beverages and had refused it; and that he was greatly embarrassed and humiliated when he saw the calendar and realized that his face and name was associated with publicity for the sale of beer. But he did not, nor did anyone for him, testify to a single fact which would show that he had suffered pecuniary damage in any amount. In addition, on cross-examination he testified; that he had repeatedly posed for photographs for use in publicizing himself and the T.C.U. football team; that Mr. [J. Willard] Ridings, director of publicity and news service of T.C.U., without obtaining particular, but with his general, approval and consent, had furnished numberless photographs to various people, periodicals and magazines; and that the pictures of those composing Grantland Rice's All American Football Team which appeared on the calendar including his own picture, were first publicized in Collier's magazine, a magazine of widest circulation.

On defendants' part, it was shown that following the instructions given by the defendant, the calendar company had written to the T.C.U. Director of publicity for, and obtained from him, the photograph for use in the calendar, paying him $1 therefor, and that the photograph had been used in the belief that the necessary consent to do so had been obtained. The proof that plaintiff had posed for many football pictures for the publicity department of T.C.U. for the purpose of having them widely circulated over the United States was overwhelming and uncontradicted. Mr. Riding, director of publicity, testified that Davey O'Brien was perhaps the most publicized football player of the year 1938-39; that it was the function of his office to permit and increase the publicity of football players; that his office had furnished some 800 photographs of plaintiff to sports editors, magazines, etc.; that if anybody made a request for a picture of O'Brien he would ordinarily grant the request without asking what they were going to do with it; that the picture in the upper left hand corner of the calendar is a very popular picture of O'Brien and perhaps his most famous pose, and that the publicity department had general authority to furnish plaintiff's pictures for publicity purposes but had never knowingly furnished any for use in commercial advertising except with O'Brien's consent and approval.

At the conclusion of this evidence, it being apparent that the picture had been obtained from one having real or apparent authority to furnish it, that no right of privacy of O'Brien's had been violated by the mere publishing of his picture and that if any actionable wrong had been done him, it must be found in the fact that the publication impliedly declared that O'Brien was endorsing or recommending the use of Pabst beer, plaintiff's contention centered around this point.

The District Judge agreed with defendant that no case had been made out. He was of the opinion: that considered from the standpoint merely of an invasion of plaintiff's right of privacy, no case was made out, because plaintiff was an outstanding national football figure and had completely publicized his name and his pictures. He was of the opinion too, that considered from the point of view that the calendar damaged him because it falsely, though only impliedly, represented that plaintiff was a user of or was commending the use of, Pabst beer, no case was made out because nothing in the calendar or football schedule could be reasonably so construed; every fact in it was truthfully stated and there was no representation or suggestion of any kind that O'Brien or any of the other football celebrities whose pictures it showed were beer drinkers or were recommending its drinking to others; the business of making and selling beer is a legitimate and eminently respectable business and people of all walks and views in life, without injury to or reflection upon themselves, drink it, and that any association of O'Brien's picture with a glass of beer could not possibly disgrace or reflect upon or cause him damage. He directed a verdict for defendant.

*** We think it perfectly plain that the District Judge was right both in the view he took that nothing in the publication violated plaintiff's right of privacy and that nothing in it could be legitimately or reasonably construed as falsely stating that he used, endorsed, or recommended the use of Pabst's beer.

Assuming then, what is by no means clear, that an action for right of privacy would lie in Texas at the suit of a private person we think it clear that the action fails; because plaintiff is not such a person and the publicity he got was only that which he had been constantly seeking and receiving; and because the use of the photograph was by permission, and there were no statements or representations made in connection with it, which were or could be either false, erroneous or damaging to plaintiff. ***

HOLMES, CIRCUIT JUDGE (DISSENTING).

There is no Texas statute or decision directly in point, but I think, under the Texas common law, the appellant is entitled to recover the reasonable value of the use in trade and commerce of his picture for advertisement purposes, to the extent that such use was appropriated by appellee.

* * *

The right of privacy is distinct from the right to use one's name or picture for purposes of commercial advertisement. The latter is a property right that belongs to every one; it may have much or little, or only a nominal, value; but it is a personal right, which may not be violated with impunity.

*   *   *

No one can doubt that commercial advertisers customarily pay for the right to use the name and likeness of a person who has become famous. The evidence in this case shows that appellant refused an offer by a New York beer company of $400 for an endorsement of its beer, and the appellee apparently recognized that it was necessary to obtain the consent of the various football players, because it required that releases be obtained from them. This admittedly was not done. The fact that appellant made this stipulation with the publishers of the calendars may save it from the infliction of punitive damages, but cannot relieve it from the payment of actual damages measured by the value of the unauthorized use of appellant's picture.

*   *   *

The decision of the majority leaves the appellant without remedy for any non-libellous use made of his picture by advertisers of beer, wine, whiskey, patent medicines, or other non-contraband goods, wares, and merchandise. It also places every other famous stage, screen, and athletic star in the same situation. If one is popular and permits publicity to be given to one's talent and accomplishment in any art or sport, commercial advertisers may seize upon such popularity to increase their sales of any lawful article without compensation of any kind for such commercial use of one's name and fame. This is contrary to usage and custom among advertisers in the marts of trade. They are undoubtedly in the habit of buying the right to use one's name or picture to create demand and good will for their merchandise.[1] It is the peculiar excellence of the common law that, by general usage, it is shaped and molded into new and useful forms.

*   *   *

---

[1] Illustrative of the value of the use of one's picture for advertising purposes, Gene Tunney says: 'While I was training for my second fight with Jack Dempsey I was offered $15,000 to endorse a certain brand of cigarettes. I didn't want to be rude, so, in declining, I merely said I didn't smoke. Next day, the advertising man came back with another offer: $12,000 if I would let my picture be used with the statement that 'Stinkies must be good, because all my friends smoke them.'(This offer was also refused.) Reader's Digest for December, 1941, page 23.

ABDUL-JABBAR V. GENERAL MOTORS CORPORATION

85 F.3D. 407 (1996)

UNITED STATES COURT OF APPEALS, NINTH CIRCUIT

not birth names

T.G. NELSON, CIRCUIT JUDGE:

Former basketball star Kareem Abdul-Jabbar appeals the district court's summary judgment in favor of General Motors Corporation ("GMC") and its advertising agency, Leo Burnett Co., in his action alleging violations of the Lanham Act, 15 U.S.C. § 1125(a), and California's statutory and common law right of publicity. Abdul-Jabbar argues that GMC violated his trademark and publicity rights by using his former name, Lew Alcindor, without his consent, in a television commercial aired during the 1993 NCAA men's basketball tournament. The district court based its judgment on all causes of action largely on its findings that Abdul-Jabbar had abandoned the name "Lew Alcindor," and that GMC's use of the name could not be construed as an endorsement of its product by Abdul-Jabbar. Having jurisdiction pursuant to 28 U.S.C. § 1291, we reverse and remand for trial.

FACTS AND PROCEDURAL HISTORY

This dispute concerns a GMC television commercial aired during the 1993 NCAA men's basketball tournament. The record includes a videotape of the spot, which plays as follows: A disembodied voice asks, "How 'bout some trivia?" This question is followed by the appearance of a screen bearing the printed words, "You're Talking to the Champ." The voice then asks, "Who holds the record for being voted the most outstanding player of this tournament?" In the screen appear the printed words, "Lew Alcindor, UCLA, '67, '68, '69." Next, the voice asks, "Has any car made the 'Consumer Digest's Best Buy' list more than once? [and responds:] The Oldsmobile Eighty-Eight has." A seven-second film clip of the automobile, with its price, follows. During the clip, the voice says, "In fact, it's made that list three years in a row. And now you can get this Eighty-Eight special edition for just $18,995." At the end of the clip, a message appears in print on the screen: "A Definite First Round Pick," accompanied by the voice saying, "it's your money." A final printed message appears: "Demand Better, 88 by Oldsmobile."

The following facts are undisputed. Kareem Abdul-Jabbar was named Ferdinand Lewis ("Lew") Alcindor at birth, and played basketball under that name throughout his college career and into his early years in the National Basketball Association ("NBA"). While in college, he converted to Islam and began to use the Muslim name "Kareem Abdul-Jabbar" among friends. Several years later, in 1971, he opted to record the name "Kareem Abdul-Jabbar" under an Illinois name recordation statute, and thereafter played basketball and endorsed products under that name. He has not used the name "Lew Alcindor" for commercial purposes in over ten years.

GMC did not obtain Abdul-Jabbar's consent, nor did it pay him, to use his former name in the commercial described above. When Abdul-Jabbar complained to GMC about the commercial, the company promptly withdrew the ad. The ad aired about five or six times in March 1993 prior to its withdrawal. The parties dispute whether Abdul-Jabbar abandoned the name Lew

Alcindor and whether the ad could be construed as an endorsement by Abdul-Jabbar of the 88 Oldsmobile.

Abdul-Jabbar brought suit in federal district court in May 1993, alleging claims under the Lanham Act and California's statutory and common law rights of publicity. The district court held a hearing on March 14, 1994. During the hearing, incorporated by reference into the order of summary judgment, the district court announced its "tentative finding that plaintiff has abandoned the name Lew Alcindor, and has abandoned the right to protect that name, and the right to assert any other rights that flow from his having had that name at one time in the past." This finding forms the basis for the district court's decision to grant summary judgment in favor of GMC on both the Lanham Act and the state law causes of action. Abdul-Jabbar timely appealed.

ANALYSIS

* * * *

I.

The Lanham Act

"[A]n express purpose of the Lanham Act is to protect commercial parties against unfair competition." *Waits v. Frito-Lay, Inc.,* 978 F.2d 1093, 1108 (9th Cir.1992). In *Waits,* we held as a matter of first impression that false endorsement claims are properly cognizable under section 43(a), 15 U.S.C. § 1125(a), of the Lanham Act. Id. at 1107. "Section 43(a) [as amended in 1988] ... expressly prohibits, inter alia, the use of any symbol or device which is likely to deceive consumers as to the association, sponsorship, or approval of goods or services by another person." Id.

Abdul-Jabbar contends that GMC's unauthorized use of his birth name, Lew Alcindor, was likely to confuse consumers as to his endorsement of the Olds 88, and thus violates the Lanham Act.

GMC offers two defenses in response to this claim: 1) Abdul-Jabbar lost his rights to the name Lew Alcindor when he "abandoned" it; and 2) GMC's use of the name Lew Alcindor was a nominative fair use which is not subject to the protection of the Lanham Act. The district court held both defenses applicable.

a) Abandonment under the Lanham Act

*** Title 15 U.S.C. § 1127 (1992) provides in pertinent part:

A mark shall be deemed to be "abandoned" when either of the following occurs:

> (1) When its use has been discontinued with intent not to resume such use. Intent not to resume may be inferred from circumstances. Nonuse for two consecutive years shall be prima facie evidence of abandonment.[2] "Use" of a mark means the bona fide use of that mark made in the ordinary course of trade, and not merely to reserve a right in a mark.

---

2   Editors' note: The statute has been amended to three years now instead of two.

*** While the Lanham Act has been applied to cases alleging appropriation of a celebrity's identity, the abandonment defense has never to our knowledge been applied to a person's name or identity. We decline to stretch the federal law of trademark to encompass such a defense. One's birth name is an integral part of one's identity; it is not bestowed for commercial purposes, nor is it "kept alive" through commercial use. A proper name thus cannot be deemed "abandoned" throughout its possessor's life, despite his failure to use it, or continue to use it, commercially.

In other words, an individual's given name, unlike a trademark, has a life and a significance quite apart from the commercial realm. Use or nonuse of the name for commercial purposes does not dispel that significance. An individual's decision to use a name other than the birth name – whether the decision rests on religious, marital, or other personal considerations – does not therefore imply intent to set aside the birth name, or the identity associated with that name.

While the issue of whether GMC's use of the name Lew Alcindor constituted an endorsement of its product is far from clear, we hold that GMC cannot rely on abandonment as a defense to Abdul-Jabbar's Lanham Act claim.

b) *Lanham Act "fair use" doctrine*

The district court cited the "fair use" defense, 15 U.S.C. § 1115(b)(4), as an alternative ground for dismissal of plaintiff's Lanham Act claim. We discussed this defense in *New Kids on the Block v. News America Publishing, Inc.* 971 F.2d 302 (9th Cir. 1992), where we held that the use by two newspapers of the "New Kids" name to conduct phone-in polls measuring the group's popularity was a nominative or non-trademark "fair use" of the name not subject to protection under the Lanham Act. 971 F.2d at 306-09.

"[T]rademark law recognizes a defense where the mark is used only 'to describe the goods or services of [a] party, or their geographic origin.'" *Id.* at 306; (quoting 15 U.S.C. § 1115(b)(4)). We cited the example of a Volkswagen repair shop which used the name "Volkswagen" in the sign advertising its business. *Volkswagenwerk Aktiengesellschaft v. Church*, 411 F.2d 350, 352 (9th Cir.1969). There, we had recognized that it "'would be difficult, if not impossible, ... to avoid altogether the use of the word "Volkswagen" or its abbreviation "VW" ... [to] signify appellant's cars.' ... Therefore, his use of the Volkswagen trademark was not an infringing use." *Id.* at 307 (quoting *Volkswagenwerk Aktiengesellschaft v. Church*, 411 F.2d 350, 352 (9th Cir.1969)).

We explained that "[c]ases like these are best understood as involving a non-trademark use of a mark – a use to which the infringement laws simply do not apply." *Id.*

*** [W]e held that in such cases, a commercial user is nevertheless entitled to the nominative fair use defense if it meets three requirements:

> First, the product or service in question must be one not readily identifiable without use of the trademark; second, only so much of the mark or marks may be used as is reasonably necessary to identify the product or service; and third, the user must do nothing that would, in conjunction with the mark, suggest sponsorship or endorsement by the trademark holder. *Id.* (footnotes omitted).

Because 1) the New Kids rock band could not be referenced without using its name; and 2) the newspapers used the name only to the extent necessary to identify them; and 3) nothing in the newspaper announcements implied sponsorship or endorsement by the New Kids, we held that the papers were entitled to the nominative fair use defense. *Id.* at 308-10.

The district court here found that GMC met the three *New Kids* requirements as a matter of law. We conclude, however, that there was a genuine issue of fact as to the third requirement, implied endorsement or sponsorship. Like the newspapers in *New Kids*, General Motors could not refer to plaintiff without using his name, and it used no more than was necessary to refer to him. Also, analogously to the newspapers in *New Kids* asking their readers which New Kid was the best, sexiest, etc., the defendant was selling something, newspapers or cars, different from the product the plaintiff was selling, and their products could not be confused.

The distinction between this case and *New Kids* is that use of celebrity endorsements in television commercials is so well established by commercial custom that a jury might find an implied endorsement in General Motors' use of the celebrity's name in a commercial, which would not inhere in a newspaper poll. Newspapers and magazines commonly use celebrities' names and photographs without making endorsement contracts, so the public does not infer an endorsement agreement from the use. Many people may assume that when a celebrity's name is used in a television commercial, the celebrity endorses the product advertised. Likelihood of confusion as to endorsement is therefore a question for the jury. *White v. Samsung Elec. Am., Inc.*, 971 F.2d 1395, 1400-01 (9th Cir.1992)(holding that use of a robot dressed and posed like Vanna White next to a "Wheel of Fortune" set raised sufficient question of fact as to endorsement under the Lanham Act to preclude summary judgment), *cert. denied,* 508 U.S. 951, 113 S.Ct. 2443, 124 L.Ed.2d 660 (1993).

* * *

II.

State law claims: Common Law and Statutory Rights of Privacy

"California has long recognized a common law right of privacy ... [which includes protection against] appropriation, for the defendant's advantage, of the plaintiff's name or likeness." *Eastwood v. Superior Court for Los Angeles County,* 149 Cal.App.3d 409, 198 Cal.Rptr. 342, 346 (1983). [Citations Omitted] The right to be protected against such appropriations is also referred to as the "right of publicity." Id., 198 Cal.Rptr. at 347. ***

As set out in *Eastwood*, a common law cause of action for appropriation of name or likeness may be pleaded by alleging "(1) the defendant's use of plaintiff's identity; (2) the appropriation of plaintiff's name or likeness to defendant's advantage, commercially or otherwise; (3) lack of consent; and (4) resulting injury." 198 Cal.Rptr. at 347.

* * * *

California's common law cause of action is complemented legislatively by Civil Code section 3344. As the *Eastwood* court explained, the statute is best understood as "complementing," rather than enacting, the common law cause of action, because the two are not identical. 198 Cal.Rptr. at 346. Section 3344(a) provides in pertinent part:

> Any person who knowingly uses another's name, voice, signature, photograph, or likeness, in any manner, on or in products, merchandise, or goods, or for purposes of advertising or selling, or soliciting purchases of, products, merchandise, goods or services, without such person's prior consent ... shall be liable for any damages sustained by the person ... injured as a result thereof. Cal. Civil Code § 3344(a) (1971).

* * *

We have construed the statute's protection of "name, voice, signature, photograph, or likeness," more narrowly than the common law's protection of "identity." See, *e.g., White,* 971 F.2d at 1397 (holding plaintiff stated a cause of action under common law but not under section 3344 where likeness in question was robot impersonating celebrity); *Midler v. Ford Motor Co.,* 849 F.2d 460, 463 (9th Cir.1988)(holding common law but not statutory cause of action applicable to appropriation of singer's voice by voice-impersonator).

* * *

We have frequently held that California's common law right of publicity protects celebrities from appropriations of their identity not strictly definable as "name or picture." *Motschenbacher v. R.J. Reynolds Tobacco Co.,* 498 F.2d 821, 827 (9th Cir.1974)(use of famous race car driver's well-known race car in televised cigarette ad sufficed to constitute an appropriation of his identity); *Midler,* 849 F.2d at 463 (use of sound-alike voice in radio ad supported a cause of action under California's common law right of publicity, though not under section 3344); *Waits,* 978 F.2d at 1098 (same); *White,* 971 F.2d at 1397-99 (use of robot dressed and posed like Vanna White next to a "Wheel of Fortune" set sufficiently identified her to state a cause of action under California common, but not statutory, law).

* * * *

We hold that Abdul-Jabbar has alleged sufficient facts to state a claim under both California common law and section 3344. The statute's reference to "name or likeness," is not limited to present or current use. To the extent GMC's use of the plaintiff's birth name attracted television viewers' attention, GMC gained a commercial advantage. *See Eastwood,* 198 Cal.Rptr. at 349 ("The first step toward selling a product or service is to attract the consumers' attention.").***

*** Abdul-Jabbar alleges, and submits evidence to show, that he was injured economically because the ad will make it difficult for him to endorse other automobiles, and emotionally because people may be led to believe he has abandoned his current name and assume he has renounced his religion. These allegations suffice to support his action. Injury to a plaintiff's right of publicity is not limited to present or future economic loss, but "may induce humiliation, embarrassment, and mental distress." [Case Citation Omitted] ***

For the reasons set out above, we reverse.

NOTES & QUESTIONS

1. How would you describe the difference of opinion between the *Pabst* majority and the dissent of Judge Holmes?

2. Should an athlete have a right of publicity in a nickname, such as "Big Papi," "Rocket," "Noodles," "Gator," "Scooter," "Catfish," etc.? If so why? If not, why not?

3. The *Abdul-Jabbar* court treats a birth name as something that cannot be abandoned. Explain the rationale for the court's conclusion on this issue.

4. Explain what the "fair use" defense in right of publicity cases entails. How does the *Abdul-Jabbar* court draw the line between a use that is fair and one that is not?

5. What types of things – other than merely a person's name or visual image – might come within the scope of his/her right of publicity?

6. Recent cases continue to eplore the nuances of an athlete's right to publicity in the age of digital media. For example: 1) *Brown v. Elec. Arts, Inc.,* 724 F.3d 1235 (9th Cir. 2013). Although EA Sports did use famous NFL running back's likeness in its video game, plaintiff failed to plead that the video game company's conduct was misleading regarding Brown's involvement with the game). 2) *Jordan v. Dominick's Finer* Foods, 115 F. Supp. 3d 950 (N.D. Ill. 2015). Without permission defendant supermarket used Michael Jordan's persona in advertisements. The Court ruled that damages may be proved by the fair market value of licensing an athlete's persona at the time of the misappropriation. 3) And a case that is strangely reminiscent of *O'Brien* in some respects is *Lightbourne v. Printroom Inc.,* 122 F. Supp. 3d 942 (C.D. Cal. 2015). Upholding validity of University of Texas at El Paso football player's consent given when he signed a Student-Athlete Image Authorization form; thus player could not recover against company that licensed his image from UTEP.

NOTE: C.B.C. DISTRIBUTION AND MARKETING V. MAJOR LEAGUE BASEBALL ADVANCED MEDIA[1]

Fantasy sports leagues have expanded and grown significantly during the past twenty years, especially in the wake of improved computer technology. Numerous websites now offer fantasy games for many professional sports. For example, NBA.com, CBS, and Yahoo are among the most popular. Fantasy basketball games allow the public to play an interesting "mind game." Typically, members of the public pay a fee to a fantasy game provider in order to participate. These fantasy game players "draft," or select NBA players for their fantasy rosters at the beginning of a season. Then, as the basketball players play games during the course of the season, they accumulate statistics in categories such as points, rebounds, assists, blocks, three point field goals, and free throws. Some fantasy basketball leagues use as few as three statistical categories while others use over ten. Fantasy game providers then use computers to calculate and compile the player statistics as a means by which to assign numerical rankings for the fantasy game players. Throughout the season, fantasy game players may at times, depending on the sophistication of the fantasy game, trade players and make other roster changes. As the season progresses, fantasy game players can follow their fantasy teams and keep track of their own progress. At the end of the season, fantasy game players can assess their own performances in the final rankings, and evaluate their own "managerial" skills.[2]

Needless to say, the right to use, copy, and disseminate player statistics is essential in order to operate a fantasy sports league. *C.B.C. Distribution and Marketing v. Major League Advanced Media* is an important case because it reconsiders the issues relating to sports data and statistics in the context of computer fantasy baseball.[3] Traditionally, sports data and statistics have been considered non-copyrightable as facts. Sports data and statistics are analogous to the "news" at issue in the *INS* case. In many respects, the *CBC* case is far easier than *NBA v. Motorola*, because, unlike the transmission of facts in *NBA v Motorola,* CBC's transmission of facts occurred with

---

1 C.B.C. Distrib. & Mktg., Inc. v. Major League Baseball Advanced Media, L.P., 505 F.3d 818 (8th Cir. 2007) [hereinafter CBC]. This note is an edited small portion of a chapter that Professor VerSteeg wrote for LEGAL ISSUES IN PROFESSIONAL BASKETBALL (2011): "Law, Technology, and Professional Basketball."

2 C.B.C. Distrib. & Mktg., Inc. v. Major League Baseball Advance Media, L.P., 443 F. Supp. 2d 1077, 1080 (E.D. Mo. 2006)("[T]he business of fantasy sports games is a multimillion dollar industry in the United States.")

In addition to fantasy sports games, CBC's website provides up-to-date information on each player to assist game participants in selecting players for and trading players on their fantasy teams. This information includes information which is typically found in box scores in newspapers such as players' batting averages, at bats, hits, runs, doubles, triples, home runs, etc.

Id. (footnote omitted); see also Adam L. Sheps, Note, *Swinging for the Fences: The Fallacy in Assigning Ownership to Sports Statistics and its Effect on Fantasy Sports,* 38 Conn. L. Rev. 1113, 1114 (2006)("Publicly available statistics relating to players and teams are tracked and posted to establish which team is winning the league, as well as to aid owners in choosing whom to play, trade, or release. Essentially, it is a game governed by player statistics.").

3 CBC, *supra.*

[D]etermining whether there is a protectable intellectual property interest in an athlete's performance statistics is central to assessing the legal status of fantasy sports providers or anyone who utilizes sports statistics for their product. The answer to this question can be found after analyzing whether the doctrines of copyright law, misappropriation, or the right of publicity protection extend to athletes' performance statistics.

Sheps, *supra*, at 1115.

a significant lapse of time from the occurrence of events on the field of play to transmission by CBC and then to reception by the public.[4] Professor Mitten has argued that economic policy recommends that consumers ought to have free access to the information generated when a game is played. He argues that there is a positive economic advantage: "Allowing free access to game scores, real-time game accounts, and player statistics will stimulate the development of new collateral products desired by consumers, without discouraging the production of 'officially licensed or authorized' products by sports leagues and athletes or their licensees."[5]

In order to operate a fantasy baseball game, CBC needed to possess the right to copy and display statistics associated with Major League Baseball Players.[6] For a number of years, CBC had been under contract with the Major League Baseball Players Association (MLBPA) to pay the MLBPA 9% of its royalties in exchange for the right to use the MLBPA players' names and statistics. Then when its contract with CBC expired, the MLBPA negotiated a new contract with Advanced Media, a different computer fantasy game provider.[7] That prompted CBC to pursue litigation as a means to secure the right to use those statistics. CBC argued that the players' statistics were in the pubic domain and freely available for them to use without paying a license fee to the MLBPA.[8]

Advanced Media, the union's licensee, presented two principal legal theories against CBC. First, it argued that CBC's use of players' names constituted an infringement of the players' right of publicity. Second, it argued that CBC's use of statistics infringed the players' rights to that data. The United States District Court for the Eastern District of Missouri held that the players did not have a right of publicity associated with their names and statistics, and that even if they did, First Amendment protections would still allow CBC to use them:

> [T]he court finds that the undisputed facts establish that the players do not have a right of publicity in their names and playing records as used in CBC's fantasy games and that CBC has not violated the players' claimed right of publicity. The court further

---

4 CBC, *supra*, at 820 ("Its fantasy baseball products incorporate the names along with performance and biographical data of actual major league baseball players.").

5 Mitten, *supra*, at 569, 574.

6 CBC, *supra*, at 820 (CBC wanted "to establish its right to use, without license, the names of and information about major league baseball players in connection with its fantasy baseball products.").

Services like C.B.C. have created sophisticated software programs and easy web interfaces to track such things as performance statistics, player drafts, trades, and the like. In exchange for these sophisticated services, participants in fantasy leagues pay a franchise or original fee to join a specific fantasy league (or are assigned one if they do not choose a specific league), and, depending on the service provider, may also pay a fee per transaction.

Williams, *supra*, at 694-95.

7 Advanced Media, which was granted the exclusive right to use baseball players' names and performance information for exploitation through all interactive media, is the Internet and interactive media arm of Major League Baseball.

8 Sheps, *supra*, at 1114 ("Before this agreement, C.B.C Distribution and Marketing, Inc. (CDM), a fantasy sports provider, had been paying the MLBPLA nine percent of gross royalties to use players' statistics within their fantasy sports leagues.").

finds, alternatively, that even if the players have a claimed right of publicity, the First Amendment takes precedence over such a right.[9]

In addition, the district court emphatically recognized that the players' statistics were not copyrightable and were in the public domain: "[T]he statistical information about Major League baseball players, including their hits, runs, doubles, etc., which CBC disseminates, represents historical facts about baseball players."[10]

In many respects the easiest question in the *CBC* case was whether the baseball players' statistics were protected by copyright. To be sure, the facts themselves as well as the compilations of them, in either ascending or descending numerical order, are not copyrightable.[11]

The Court of Appeals for the Eighth Circuit, on the other hand, took the position that CBC did use the players' names in a way that constituted a violation of the players' rights of publicity. According to the court:

Because we think that it is clear that CBC uses baseball players' identities in its fantasy baseball products for purposes of profit, we believe that their identities are being used for commercial advantage and that the players therefore offered sufficient evidence to make out a cause of action for violation of their rights of publicity under Missouri law.[12]

The distinction between using a professional athlete's name for a commercial purpose versus using it for descriptive purposes or to convey functional information is critical. It is only when it is used in an advertising or endorsement manner that it is actionable under a theory of right of publicity.[13] Realistically speaking, if a state right of publicity were to encompass a player's name

---

9   C.B.C Distribution & Marketing, Inc. v. Major League Baseball Advanced Media, 443 F. Supp. 2d 1077, 1107 (E.D. Mo. 2006).

10   *Id.* at 1093.

Further, CBC's games disseminate statistical information about baseball players; this statistical information is historical fact...[T]he players' records which CBC provides are available to the public at large by watching games and are disseminated to the public in newspapers and by statistics providers; CBC uses players' names to convey information, the players' records, which information is already in the public domain.

Id. at 1093-1095.

11   Sheps, *supra*, at 1119.

[P]rofessional leagues cannot claim that the manner in which they compile statistics is so unique as to warrant copyright protection. Updating the information and breaking it down into statistical categories is analogous to an alphabetical phone book. It is clearly the most logical and useful manner in which to utilize the information.

Id.

12   CBC, *supra*, at 822-23. The right of publicity, a body of state law, prohibits the use of a person's name, likeness, or other indicia of identity ("persona") for commercial purposes without his consent. *See* RESTATEMENT (THIRD) OF UNFAIR COMPETITION § 46 (1995)(appropriation of the commercial value of a person's identity: the right of publicity).

13   Mitten, *supra*, at 578.

Like an unauthorized biography of a famous professional athlete, questions about his sports records in a Trivial Pursuit or Jeopardy game, or a board game incorporating his playing statistics, a fantasy sports league is based on facts in the public domain and uses his name only for descriptive purposes. . . . However, by holding that this conduct violated the players' publicity rights, [the court] failed to recognize that public domain baseball statistics in the form of a fantasy league game--not player identities or personas--is the collateral product offered to the public.

Id. at 575; *see also* Kareem Abdul-Jabbar v. General Motors Corp., 83 F.3d 407 (9th Cir. 1996).

and associated statistical data in a manner contemplated in the *CBC* case, it would limit the use of public domain information, injure the market for collateral products, and force the public to pay more for using public domain information.[14]

Nevertheless, even though the court ruled that CBC had infringed the players' right of publicity, the Eight Circuit managed to find a way to shield the CBC from liability. The court of appeals, in a manner similar to the district court, also recognized that there was an inherent contradiction or conflict between the players' publicity rights and CBC's First Amendment rights. Citing *Zacchini v. Scripps-Howard Broadcasting*,[15] the court noted, "The Supreme Court has directed that state law rights of publicity must be balanced against first amendment considerations... and here we conclude that the former must give way to the latter. First, the information used in CBC's fantasy baseball games is all readily available in the public domain, and it would be strange law that a person would not have a first amendment right to use information that is available to everyone."[16]

Although the court held that the fantasy game provider's First Amendment rights "trumped" the players' publicity rights, nevertheless, it is questionable whether the use of players' names in this manner actually constitutes a publicity rights infringement. The Eighth Circuit's holding that Major League players have a right of publicity that is infringed by the publication of their names in association with statistics by fantasy game providers has been criticized and is certainly worth a second look.[17]

NOTES & QUESTIONS

1. For a recent case that raises similar issues, *see Daniels v. FanDuel, Inc.* No. 1:16-cv-01230-TWP-DKL, 2017 WL 4340329 (S.D. Ind. Sept. 29, 2017). Court determined that the Indiana right of publicity statute's exceptions relating to public interest and newsworthiness

---

14 Mitten, *supra*, at 579.

> Extending the right of publicity to require C.B.C. to pay a licensing fee would create an exclusive property right that precludes, or severely limits, the commercial use of public domain information, reduces the availability of collateral products, and/or increases the costs to consumers. Such a broad state-created "right of publicity on steroids," is legally and economically unjustified.

> *Id.*

15 433 U.S. 562 (1977).

16 CBC, *supra*, at 823.

17 *See* Sheps, *supra*, at 1145:

> There is a difference between presenting another's name or identity in the context of selling a product versus in the context of news reporting. Therefore, no misrepresentation is occurring when statistics are reported and utilized. No individual who reads an athlete or any celebrity's name either in written media or on the Internet automatically assumes that person sanctioned that publication; to argue otherwise would be like saying every person who appeared in this morning's newspaper was openly endorsing that newspaper. Similarly, when one reads the box scores from the last game or the current league standings in the paper, there is no assumption that every player or every team has either granted permission to be associated with the paper or that the newspaper is attempting to trick its readers into thinking their favorite team has given its stamp of approval to the paper.

shielded defendant (*i.e.,* a gambling website) from college football players' claims relating to defendant's use of their names.

Further Reading on Intellectual Property:

Howard Brill, *The Name of the Departed Team: Who Can Use It,* 15 Whittier L. Rev. 1003 (1994).

Timothy J. Bucher, *Game on: Sports-Related Games and the Contentious Interplay Between the Right of Publicity and the First Amendment,* 14 Tex. Rev. Ent. & Sports L. 1 (2012).

Dan L. Burk, *Owning E-Sports: Proprietary Rights in Professional Computer Gaming,* 161 U. Pa. L. Rev. 1535 (2013).

Walter Champion, Jr., *Baseball Cards Now Big Business: The Fleer Case,* 81 Pa. L. J. Rep. 1 (Oct. 5, 1981).

Mark Conrad, *Matal v. Tam-A Victory for the Slants, A Touchdown for the Redskins, but an Ambiguous Journey for the First Amendment and Trademark Law,* 36 Cardozo Arts & Ent. L.J. 83 (2018).

Marc Edelman, *A Short Treatise on Fantasy Sports and the Law: How America Regulates Its New National Pastime,* 3 Harv. J. Sports & Ent. L. 1 (2012).

Marc Edelman, *From Meerkat to Periscope: Does Intellectual Property Law Prohibit the Live Streaming of Commercial Sporting Events?,* 39 Colum. J.L. & Arts 469 (2016).

William K. Ford & Raizel Liebler, *Games Are Not Coffee Mugs: Games and the Right of Publicity,* 29 Santa Clara Computer & High Tech. L.J. 1 (2013).

Christian Frodl, *Commercialisation of Sports Data: Rights of Event Owners over Information and Statistics Generated About Their Sports Events,* 26 Marq. Sports L. Rev. 55 (2015).

Giuliana R. Garcia, *He Shoots, He Scores...and Receives Copyright Protection? How the Current State of Intellectual Property Law Fumbles with Sports,* 2011 Den. U. Sports & Ent. L.J. 81 (2011).

Michael Gerton, *Kids' Play: Examining the Impact of the CBC Distribution Decision on College Fantasy Sports,* 11 Tex. Rev. Ent. & Sports L. 153 (2009).

Roger M. Groves, *"Can I Profit from My Own Name and Likeness As A College Athlete?" the Predictive Legal Analytics of A College Player's Publicity Rights vs. First Amendment Rights of Others,* 48 Ind. L. Rev. 369 (2015).

Lara Grow & Nathaniel Grow, *Protecting Big Data in the Big Leagues: Trade Secrets in Professional Sports,* 74 Wash. & Lee L. Rev. 1567 (2017).

Marie Hopkins, *Live Sports Virtual Reality Broadcasts: Copyright and Other Protections,* 16 Duke L. & Tech. Rev. 141 (2018).

Shigenori Matsui, *Does It Have to Be A Copyright Infringement?: Live Game Streaming and Copyright,* 24 Tex. Intell. Prop. L.J. 215 (2016).

Michelle R. Hull, *Sports Leagues' New Social Media Policies: Enforcement Under Copyright Law and State Law,* 34 Colum. J.L. & Arts 457 (2011).

Michael Huntowski, *Blades of Steal? The Fight for Control of Sports Clubs' Websites and Media Rights in Madison Square Garden L.P. v. National Hockey League,* 16 Vill. Sports & Ent. L.J. 123 (2009).

J. Gordon Hylton, *The Over-Protection of Intellectual Property Rights in Sport in the United States and Elsewhere*, 21 J. Legal Aspects Sport 43 (2011).

J. Gordon Hylton, *Baseball Cards and the Birth of the Right of Publicity: The Curious Case of Haelan Laboratories v. Topps*, 12 Marq. Sports L. Rev. 273 (2001).

Eric E. Johnson, *The NFL, Intellectual Property, and the Conquest of Sports Media*, 86 N.D. L. Rev. 759 (2010).

Anastasios Kaburakis, David A. Pierce, Olivia M. Fleming, Galen E. Clavio, Heather J. Lawrence, Dawn A. Dziuba, *NCAA Student-Athletes' Rights of Publicity, EA Sports, and the Video Game Industry*, 27 Ent. & Sports Law 1 (2009).

Shigenori Matsui, *Does It Have to Be A Copyright Infringement?: Live Game Streaming and Copyright*, 24 Tex. Intell. Prop. L.J. 215 (2016).

Stephen McKelvey et. al., *The Air Jordan Rules: Image Advertising Adds New Dimension to Right of Publicity-First Amendment Tension*, 26 Fordham Intell. Prop. Media & Ent. L.J. 945 (2016).

Michael J. Mellis, *Internet Piracy of Live Sports Telecasts*, 8 Marq. Sports L. Rev. 259 (2008).

Ashley Messenger, *Rethinking the Right of Publicity in the Context of Social Media*, 24 Widener L. Rev. 259 (2018).

Robert C. O'Brien, Bela G. Lugosi, *Update to the Commercial Value of Rights of Publicity: A Picture is Worth a Thousand Words ... or Sometimes a Million Dollars*, 27 Ent. & Sports Law 2 (2009).

Jennifer E. Rothman, *E-Sports As A Prism for the Role of Evolving Technology in Intellectual Property*, 161 U. PA. L. Rev. Online 317 (2013).

Gary R. Roberts, *The Legality of the Exclusive Collective Sale of Intellectual Property Rights by Sports Leagues*, 3 VA. J. Sports & L. 52 (2001).

Gary R. Roberts, *The Scope of the Exclusive Right to Control Dissemination for Real-Time Sports Event Information*, 15 Stan. L. & Poly. Rev. 167 (2004).

Andrew T. Warren, *Gif Gaffe: How Big Sports Ignored Lenz and Used the Dmca to Chill Free Speech on Twitter*, 27 Fordham Intell. Prop. Media & Ent. L.J. 103 (2016).

Risa J. Weaver, *Online Fantasy Sports Litigation and the Need for a Federal Right of Publicity Statute*, 2010 Duke L. & Tech. Rev. 2 (2010).

John C. Weistart & Cym H. Lowell, Law of Sports, § 8.17 Defamation and Invasion of Privacy (Bobbs-Merrill Company, Inc., 1979).

Jack F. Williams, *Who Owns the Back of a Baseball Card?*, 23 Cardozo L. Rev. 1705 (2002).

Darryl C. Wilson, *The Pay Cable TV Sports Broadcasting Nexus*, 8 Comm. & L. 43 (1986).

INDEX

A

Amateur, 2, 5-13, 24, 26-29, 34, 48, 51, 56, 95, 119, 132, 179, 203, 208-209, 218, 222, 252-253, 259-260, 263-264, 273, 278, 295, 326, 341, 344, 351-353, 360-364, 368-369, 376, 379, 381-392, 403-410, 416, 420, 427, 453

Amateur Athletic Union (AAU), 7, 12

Amateur Softball Association (ASA), 119

Amateur Sports Act of 1978, 2, 5-6, 11-13, 24-29, 273

Ambulance, 105-107

America On-Line, 441

American Association of Cheerleading Coaches and Administrators (AACCA), 84

American Arbitration Association (AAA), 30, 43

American Football League (AFL), 136, 141, 208-209, 259, 262, 427

American Society for Testing [and] Materials (ASTM), 87

Americans with Disabilities Act of 1990 (ADA), xxii, 302, 326-332, 344-349, 350-351

Amphetamine(s) (see also Drugs, Banned Substances), 11, 293

Anderson, (Gettysburg College Lacrosse Coach), 105-106

Ankiel, Rick, 35

Antitrust, xxi, 154, 208-265, 352, 358, 360, 362-364, 384-389

Arbitration, 1, 13-14, 18, 21, 24-31, 43, 46-47, 177, 179, 181, 184-185, 206-207, 246, 278, 421-422, 426, 428

Archery, 325

Argovitz, Jerry, 391, 394-399

Arizona State University, 296

Armstrong, Lance, 46

Assault, 49, 284, 290

Assign, Assignee, Assignment, Assignor, 58, 60, 81, 91, 102, 105, 123, 126, 156, 158, 163-165, 169, 176, 178, 182, 197, 201, 204, 220, 272, 275, 289, 307, 320, 367, 373, 389-390, 411, 471-472

Associated Press, 33, 439, 441-442

Assumption of Risk (see also Primary Implied Assumption of Risk), 51, 53, 55, 62-66, 75, 79-86, 94-95, 104, 117, 122, 125-126, 128, 132

Asthma, 15-16

Athletic(s) Director, Director of Athletics, 150, 152, 226, 284, 291, 334, 364-365, 392, 412, 414-415, 417

Attention Deficit Disorder (ADD), 330

Attorney(s) General, 210, 275, 414-16

Author, Authorship, xxi, xxiii, xxvi, 75, 274, 352, 436, 443, 445

Automobile (see also Car(s)), 58-59, 112, 179, 290, 366, 465, 470,

Avatar, 295, 298-300

B

Backstop, 118

C

Doctor(s), Dr. (see also Physician(s)), 16-17, 25, 31, 64, 83-85, 113, 115, 125, 132, 176, 251, 289, 333-338, 408, 410, 458

Donicke, Dr. Manfred, 31

Donolli, Joseph, 105-106, 108, 110

Doping (see also Blood), 14-26, 28-29, 41-48,

Douglas, Justice (William O.), 258, 261

Draft (Player), 136, 139, 142, 144, 208, 222, 226, 234, 243, 247-250, 259-260, 263-264, 363, 400, 403, 409, 416, 423-424, 427, 429-430, 432-433, 471-472

Drug(s) (see also Banned Substances, Performance Enhancing Drugs, Doping), xxi, 1-48, 106, 167, 176-177, 185-186, 266, 278-279, 283-284, 288-290, 292-294, 333, 400

Drug Test(ing), 14, 17, 19, 24

Drunk (see also Alcohol), xxvii, 290

Due Process (see also Fifth Amendment), 8-9, 265-267, 273-274, 277-278, 280-281, 283, 285-287, 328, 357, 360, 378-379, 390

Duke University, xxv, 225, 312-315, 424,

Dunkin' Donuts, 393

Duress, 123, 402

Duty (legal), 11, 13, 28-29, 47, 49-56, 58, 60-64, 75-77, 79-80, 82, 84, 88-89, 95, 98, 103-104, 107-113, 115-121, 123, 131, 291, 373-376, 379, 392, 394-402, 404-406, 408, 424, 431

Breach of..., 11, 49-52, 56, 61, 75-76, 80, 104, 107, 110-112, 120-121, 394-402, 406

Limited Duty, 60-62

E

Economic(s), Economist(s), Economy, Economically, 4, 95-97, 111, 134, 186, 207, 209, 218, 227, 229, 231-233, 242, 245, 250-253, 286, 323, 357-363, 369-371, 424, 470, 472, 474

Edgecombe Speedway, 57, 59

Edmonton Oilers, 246

Eisenstadt, Alfred, 450

Electronic(s), Electronically (see also Technology, Science), 17, 33, 61, 205, 308, 391, 445

Electronic Arts, Inc. (EA Sports), 384

Eligibility, 12, 17-19, 22, 25-29, 36, 41, 211-212, 214-218, 222-223, 226, 228, 264, 268, 273-274, 279, 281, 301-302, 306, 327-328, 330-332, 334, 338-343, 362, 364, 366-367, 370, 376, 378-380, 382, 387, 390-392, 404-406, 413, 417, 419-421

Eliot, President (Charles William), 353

Emergency, 4, 103, 105-106, 108, 110-111, 113, 167, 193, 283, 335

EMT's (Emergency Medical Technicians, 113

Employee(s), 37, 39, 74-75, 104, 107-108, 124, 126, 131, 147, 186, 198, 200, 204, 211, 235-237, 239, 243, 246, 249-253, 263, 265, 268, 272, 282, 292, 301, 373, 390-391, 402, 420-422, 428, 458

Employer(s), 72, 74, 102, 186, 211, 237, 243, 248-253, 292, 327, 336, 382, 422

Enbrel, 393

F

G

H

I

J

K

M

N

O

Osborne, Tom, 419
Owens, R. C., 235

P

Pabst Beer, Pabst Blue Ribbon, 461-464, 470
Page, Alan, 242
Palmeiro, Rafael, 35
Pan American Games, 7, 10
Parent(s)(In Loco Parentis)(see also Guardian), 86, 101, 103-104, 114-115, 117, 128, 130-132, 134, 195, 200, 232-233, 266, 269, 278, 288-289, 311, 338, 240, 388, 400, 404, 407-408, 411-413
Parker, Judge Barrington Daniels, 30
Parody, 298
Pasquarelli, Len, 430
Pasternak, David, 393
Patera, Coach (Jack), 251
Payless Shoesource, Inc., 453-460
Pennsylvania Interscholastic Athletic Association (PIAA), 276, 343
Pepsico, 210
Performance Enhancing Drugs (see also Drugs, Banned Substances, Doping), 1, 11, 34-36, 38-41, 45-46, 48, 279
Pell, Lauren M., 66, 91-94, 118
Pelletier, David, 32
Penland, Thomas M. Jr., 123
Persona, 470, 473
Personal Injury, xxvii, 52, 99, 100-101, 123-125, 132, 163
Pettitte, Andy, 35
Phelps, Michael, 211
Philadelphia 76ers, 247-248
Philadelphia Eagles, 427, 432, 462
Philadelphia Phillies, 254, 258
Photograph(s), Photography, Photographer(s) (see also Picture(s)), xi, 161, 179, 188, 191, 299-300, 308-309, 440, 449-451, 460, 462-463, 468-469
Physical Education, 117-118, 219, 224, 350, 367
Physical Exam, 291
Physician(s) (see also Doctor(s)), 35, 107, 115, 133, 155, 163, 168, 175-178, 185, 334-335, 337-338
Pickens, Bruce, 424
Pickford, Kaylan, 71
Pickford, Steven, 71
Picture(s) (see also Photograph(s), 25, 161-162, 179-180, 295, 297, 312, 381-382, 444, 448, 450, 458, 461-464, 469, 476

Q

R

Twain, Mark, 348

U

Unsportsmanlike Conduct, 119-121, , 185, 301

V

W

Y

Z